Futures Markets
Volume II

The International Library of Critical Writings in Financial Economics
Series Editor: Richard Roll

Allstate Professor of Economics
The Anderson School at UCLA, US

This major series presents by field outstanding selections of the most important articles across the entire spectrum of financial economics – one of the fastest growing areas in business schools and economics departments. Each collection has been prepared by a leading specialist who has written an authoritative introduction to the literature.

1. The Theory of Corporate Finance (Volumes I and II)
   Michael J. Brennan

2. Futures Markets (Volumes I, II and III)
   A.G. Malliaris

Future titles will include:

Market Efficiency: Stock Market Behaviour in Theory and Practice
Andrew W. Lo

The Debt Market
Stephen A. Ross

Empirical Corporate Finance
Michael J. Brennan

Options Markets

Financial Markets

International Securities

Continuous Time Finance

Futures Markets
Volume II

Edited by

A.G. Malliaris

Walter F. Mullady Sr. Professor of Business Administration
Department of Economics
Loyola University Chicago, US

THE INTERNATIONAL LIBRARY OF CRITICAL WRITINGS IN FINANCIAL ECONOMICS

An Elgar Reference Collection
Cheltenham, UK • Brookfield, US

© A.G. Malliaris 1997. For copyright of individual articles please refer to the Acknowledgements.

All rights reserved. No part of this publication may be reproduced, stored in a retrieval system, or transmitted in any form or by any means, electronic, mechanical, photocopying, recording, or otherwise without the prior permission of the publisher.

Published by
Edward Elgar Publishing Limited
8 Lansdown Place
Cheltenham
Glos GL50 2HU
UK

Edward Elgar Publishing Company
Old Post Road
Brookfield
Vermont 05036
US

A catalogue record for this book is available from the British Library.

Library of Congress Cataloging in Publication Data
Futures markets / editor, A.G. Malliaris.
    p. cm. — (International library of critical writings in
financial economics ; 2)
   Includes bibliographical references and index.
   Contents: v. 1. Institutions, volatility, and speculation — v.
2. Pricing, efficiency, chaos, and hedging — v. 3. Financial
futures.
   ISBN 1-85898-070-4
   1. Futures market. 2. Financial futures. I. Malliaris, A. G.
II. Series.
HG6024.A3F878 1996
332.64'5—dc20

96-24637
CIP

ISBN 1 85898 070 4 (3 volume set)

Printed in Great Britain by Galliard (Printers) Ltd, Great Yarmouth

Contents

Acknowledgements	vii
Foreword by Richard Roll	ix
Introduction by the editor: 'Futures Markets: How Do Prices Behave?'	xi

PART I PRICING

1. Anne E. Peck (1976), 'Futures Markets, Supply Response, and Price Stability', *Quarterly Journal of Economics*, XC, 407–23   3
2. Kenneth D. Garbade and William L. Silber (1983), 'Price Movements and Price Discovery in Futures and Cash Markets', *Review of Economics and Statistics*, LXV, 289–97   20
3. Kenneth R. French (1983), 'A Comparison of Futures and Forward Prices', *Journal of Financial Economics*, **12**, 311–42   29
4. Eugene F. Fama and Kenneth R. French (1987), 'Commodity Futures Prices: Some Evidence on Forecast Power, Premiums, and the Theory of Storage', *Journal of Business*, **60** (1), 55–73   61
5. Jerome L. Stein (1992), 'Cobwebs, Rational Expectations and Futures Markets', *Review of Economics and Statistics*, LXXIV, 127–34   80

PART II EFFICIENCY

6. Raymond M. Leuthold (1972), 'Random Walk and Price Trends: The Live Cattle Futures Market', *Journal of Finance*, **XXVII** (3), June, 879–89   91
7. Charles C. Cox (1976), 'Futures Trading and Market Information', *Journal of Political Economy*, **84** (6), 1215–37   103
8. Salih N. Neftci and Andrew J. Policano (1984), 'Can Chartists Outperform the Market? Market Efficiency Tests for "Technical Analysis"', *Journal of Futures Markets*, **4** (4), 465–78   126
9. David H. Goldenberg (1989), 'Memory and Equilibrium Futures Prices', *Journal of Futures Markets*, **9** (3), 199–213   140
10. Christopher K. Ma, William H. Dare and Darla R. Donaldson (1990), 'Testing Rationality in Futures Markets', *Journal of Futures Markets*, **10** (2), 137–52   155

PART III PRICE DISTRIBUTIONS

11. Benoit Mandelbrot (1963), 'The Variation of Certain Speculative Prices', *Journal of Business*, **XXXVI** (4), October, 394–419   173

	12.	Joyce A. Hall, B. Wade Brorsen and Scott H. Irwin (1989), 'The Distribution of Futures Prices: A Test of the Stable Paretian and Mixture of Normals Hypotheses', *Journal of Financial and Quantitative Analysis*, **24** (1), March, 105–16	199
	13.	Donald W. Gribbin, Randy W. Harris and Hon-Shiang Lau (1992), 'Futures Prices Are Not Stable-Paretian Distributed', *Journal of Futures Markets*, **12** (4), 475–87	211
PART IV	CHAOS		
	14.	Steven C. Blank (1991), '"Chaos" in Futures Markets? A Nonlinear Dynamical Analysis', *Journal of Futures Markets*, **11** (6), 711–28	227
PART V	**THEORIES OF HEDGING**		
	15.	Louis H. Ederington (1979), 'The Hedging Performance of the New Futures Markets', *Journal of Finance*, **XXXIV** (1), March, 157–70	247
	16.	Jacques Rolfo (1980), 'Optimal Hedging under Price and Quantity Uncertainty: The Case of a Cocoa Producer', *Journal of Political Economy*, **88** (1), 100–116	261
	17.	Robert J. Myers (1991), 'Estimating Time-Varying Optimal Hedge Ratios on Futures Markets', *Journal of Futures Markets*, **11** (1), 39–53	278
PART VI	**PORTFOLIO SELECTION WITH FUTURES**		
	18.	Michael Adler and Jerome Detemple (1988), 'Hedging with Futures in an Intertemporal Portfolio Context', *Journal of Futures Markets*, **8** (3), 249–69	295
	19.	John F. Marshall and Anthony F. Herbst (1992), 'A Multiperiod Model for the Selection of a Futures Portfolio', *Journal of Futures Markets*, **12** (4), 411–28	316
PART VII	**VARIOUS MARKETS**		
	20.	Richard Roll (1984), 'Orange Juice and Weather', *American Economic Review*, **74** (5), 861–80	337
	21.	Eugene F. Fama and Kenneth R. French (1988), 'Business Cycles and the Behavior of Metals Prices', *Journal of Finance*, **XLIII** (5), December, 1075–93	357
	22.	Stanley C. Stevens (1991), 'Evidence for a Weather Persistence Effect on the Corn, Wheat, and Soybean Growing Season Price Dynamics', *Journal of Futures Markets*, **11** (1), 81–8	376
	23.	Antonios Antoniou and Andrew J. Foster (1992), 'The Effect of Futures Trading on Spot Price Volatility: Evidence for Brent Crude Oil Using GARCH', *Journal of Business Finance & Accounting*, **19** (4), June, 473–84	384

Name Index   397

Acknowledgements

The editor and publishers wish to thank the authors and the following publishers who have kindly given permission for the use of copyright material.

American Economic Association for article: Richard Roll (1984), 'Orange Juice and Weather', *American Economic Review*, **74** (5), 861–80.

American Finance Association for articles: Raymond M. Leuthold (1972), 'Random Walk and Price Trends: The Live Cattle Futures Market', *Journal of Finance*, **XXVII** (3), June, 879–89; Louis H. Ederington (1979), 'The Hedging Performance of the New Futures Markets', *Journal of Finance*, **XXXIV** (1), March, 157–70; Eugene F. Fama and Kenneth R. French (1988), 'Business Cycles and the Behavior of Metals Prices', *Journal of Finance*, **XLIII** (5), December, 1075–93.

Blackwell Publishers Ltd for article: Antonios Antoniou and Andrew J. Foster (1992), 'The Effect of Futures Trading on Spot Price Volatility: Evidence for Brent Crude Oil Using GARCH', *Journal of Business Finance & Accounting*, **19** (4), June, 473–84.

Elsevier Science B.V. for articles: Kenneth D. Garbade and William L. Silber (1983), 'Price Movements and Price Discovery in Futures and Cash Markets', *Review of Economics and Statistics*, **LXV**, 289–97; Jerome L. Stein (1992), 'Cobwebs, Rational Expectations and Futures Markets', *Review of Economics and Statistics*, **LXXIV**, 127–34.

Elsevier Science S.A. for article: Kenneth R. French (1983), 'A Comparison of Futures and Forward Prices', *Journal of Financial Economics*, **12**, 311–42.

Journal of Financial and Quantitative Analysis for article: Joyce A. Hall, B. Wade Brorsen and Scott H. Irwin (1989), 'The Distribution of Futures Prices: A Test of the Stable Paretian and Mixture of Normals Hypotheses', *Journal of Financial and Quantitative Analysis*, **24** (1), March, 105–16.

MIT Press Journals for article: Anne E. Peck (1976), 'Futures Markets, Supply Response, and Price Stability', *Quarterly Journal of Economics*, **XC**, 407–23.

University of Chicago Press for articles: Benoit Mandelbrot (1963), 'The Variation of Certain Speculative Prices', *Journal of Business*, **XXXVI** (4), October, 394–419; Charles C. Cox (1976), 'Futures Trading and Market Information', *Journal of Political Economy*, **84** (6), 1215–37; Jacques Rolfo (1980), 'Optimal Hedging under Price and Quantity Uncertainty: The Case of a Cocoa Producer', *Journal of Political Economy*, **88** (1), 100–116;

Eugene F. Fama and Kenneth R. French (1987), 'Commodity Futures Prices: Some Evidence on Forecast Power, Premiums, and the Theory of Storage', *Journal of Business*, **60** (1), 55–73.

John Wiley & Sons, Inc. for articles: Salih N. Neftci and Andrew J. Policano (1984), 'Can Chartists Outperform the Market? Market Efficiency Tests for "Technical Analysis"', *Journal of Futures Markets*, **4** (4), 465–78; Michael Adler and Jerome Detemple (1988), 'Hedging with Futures in an Intertemporal Portfolio Context', *Journal of Futures Markets*, **8** (3), 249–69; David H. Goldenberg (1989), 'Memory and Equilibrium Futures Prices', *Journal of Futures Markets*, **9** (3), 199–213; Christopher K. Ma, William H. Dare and Darla R. Donaldson (1990), 'Testing Rationality in Futures Markets', *Journal of Futures Markets*, **10** (2), 137–52; Robert J. Myers (1991), 'Estimating Time-Varying Optimal Hedge Ratios on Futures Markets', *Journal of Futures Markets*, **11** (1), 39–53; Stanley C. Stevens (1991), 'Evidence for a Weather Persistence Effect on the Corn, Wheat, and Soybean Growing Season Price Dynamics', *Journal of Futures Markets*, **11** (1), 81–8; Steven C. Blank (1991), '"Chaos" in Futures Markets? A Nonlinear Dynamical Analysis', *Journal of Futures Markets*, **11** (6), 711–28; John F. Marshall and Anthony F. Herbst (1992), 'A Multiperiod Model for the Selection of a Futures Portfolio', *Journal of Futures Markets*, **12** (4), 411–28; Donald W. Gribbin, Randy W. Harris and Hon-Shiang Lau (1992), 'Futures Prices Are Not Stable-Paretian Distributed', *Journal of Futures Markets*, **12** (4), 475–87.

Every effort has been made to trace all the copyright holders but if any have been inadvertently overlooked the publishers will be pleased to make the necessary arrangement at the first opportunity.

In addition the publishers wish to thank the Library of the London School of Economics and Political Science and the Marshall Library of Economics, Cambridge University, for their assistance in obtaining these articles.

Foreword

Richard Roll

Professor Malliaris introduces his collection of articles on Futures by noting their rarity. Among the very large number of commodites traded in cash markets only a few enjoy the accompaniment of organized futures trading. Yet futures prices evoke interest out of all proportion to their scarcity. The financial media devote extraordinary attention to reporting them and commenting upon their significance. It is unusual to hear a financial report about the cash price of a commodity, say dishwashing detergent, but futures prices are summarized daily in all media and are even available by the minute from sources such as the Internet.

Apparently then, futures represent a barometer of the economy particularly sensitive to the general mood of its participants. By observing futures markets, we derive an impression of what is happening in the collective mind of *Homo economicus*. We may not really care very much about the price of copper or frozen concentrated orange juice, but we are fascinated if they suddenly jump in price or if their trading volume changes unexpectedly and dramatically.

Scholarly research about futures markets is extensive and sophisticated. Thinking about futures has been a popular occupation now for several generations of economists; many of their most interesting conclusions are divulged in the papers in these three volumes. Volumes I and II cover the general nature of futures markets while Volume III is devoted to the particularly important subject of financial futures.

In *Volume I* Professor Malliaris has assembled papers that investigate fundamental questions: Why do futures markets exist? What are their common institutional features? What are the motives of futures traders? Does the existence of futures trading induce changes in the characteristics of the associated cash market?

In his introductory essay to this volume, Professor Malliaris provides a particularly cogent analysis of speculation and hedging, topics that are hard to define precisely but are nonetheless the foci of attention of many scholars. Financial journalists tend to regard futures markets as just legal casinos populated by greedy gamblers. Yet most economists have recognized that futures markets serve an invaluable social purpose: they provide a cost-effective method for sharing risk. This social role is, of course, of the greatest importance when the cash price of a commodity is highly volatile. In volatile circumstances, production, distribution and consumption can be risky for all parties, particularly when there is a lengthy planning cycle such as with agricultural commodities. Futures markets provide the wherewithal to hedge such risks by allocating them among a broader number of individuals.

It is interesting to note that despite the fears of journalists, regulators, and legislators, no one has ever found any evidence that futures markets cause harm or increase volatility in cash markets. Instead, the general tenor of the scholarly research reflects the very positive social benefits of futures markets.

In *Volume II* Malliaris summarizes the mainly empirical research describing the reality of futures prices, their efficiency in reflecting information, their intertemporal movements and their effectiveness in hedging.

A basic concept in financial theory, efficiency, deals with the information encapsulated in a market price. When applied to futures, testing for efficiency involves ascertaining whether prices properly reflect what is knowable about subsequent cash prices and whether futures prices themselves fluctuate appropriately. Changes in futures prices should not be very predictable; this would imply that the predictability itself had not been efficiently evaluated by futures traders. Most empirical papers find that organized futures markets are indeed relatively efficient.

In contrast to market efficiency, there is little theoretical guidance about why futures price changes should conform to any particular probability distribution. Empirically, futures price changes have 'thick tails', a high frequency of large observations, either positive or negative, relative to the ubiquitous normal, or Gaussian, distribution. There is some controversy over the underlying causes of this empirical phenomenon, but whatever the cause, it has material consequences for traders and for modelling, hedging and valuation.

In his introductory essay to Volume II, Professor Malliaris devotes considerable attention to the question of probability distributions, including a detailed analysis of a relatively new idea, that futures markets can be modelled as chaotic processes. The motivation for this emphasis derives from the importance of the question for hedging effectiveness. This goes to the very *raison d'être* of futures markets: risk sharing. Risk sharing will be most effective if hedging provides a definitive method for removing the intertemporal volatility of a cash position.

Volume III contains significant scholarly writings about *financial* futures, surely one of the most important new product innovations of the past several decades over *all* markets. For anyone in daily contact with financial markets, it is indeed hard now to imagine the world without financial futures, yet they hardly existed before the mid-1970s. Significantly, the earliest paper in this volume was originally published in 1981, only fifteen years ago.

As with any futures market, sharing the risk of a volatile commodity remains the most important characteristic. Equities, interest rates, and foreign exchange rates are nothing if they are not volatile; so stock index futures, bond futures and foreign exchange futures are among the most heavily-traded of all futures contracts. Today, they provide a means of hedging unavailable to an earlier generation of investors, fund managers, corporations and governments.

True, financial futures have created anxiety among certain segments of the uninformed public; politicians have exploited this anxiety in their usual manner, especially after some publicity-worthy trading debacle. The positive benefits of financial futures do not sell newspapers nor draw large television audiences, but they far outweigh the losses of the occasional unlucky young trader. We must remember that futures trading losses are not losses to society in aggregate; for every loser there is a winner. This is the essence of risk sharing.

This volume ought to be required reading for financial journalists and politicians because it removes the mystery of financial futures and amasses the evidence of their benefits. Perhaps it is too much to hope that the average anxiety-ridden citizen read through this volume, but such a reading would be an antidote, physically safer than valium or prozac!

Introduction: Futures Markets: How Do Prices Behave?

A.G. Malliaris

---

1. Introduction

The fundamental role of every market is the formation of prices. In futures markets, such price formation receives even greater importance because risk transference and price discovery, as the two major contributions of these markets, both depend on the process of price formation.

It is the purpose of this Introduction to analyse the behaviour of prices in futures markets. More specifically we offer a discussion on three interrelated questions:

1. How are futures prices formed?
2. Do futures prices follow a random walk?
3. What is the distribution of future prices?

2. Pricing

Consider a representative futures market such as the futures market for gold. At the most elementary level, the answer to the question of how futures prices are formed is by supply and demand. But what are supply and demand in the context of a futures market?

Recall that trading in a futures market involves the buying and selling of well designed contracts. Therefore, supply and demand refer to schedules of prices and corresponding quantities supplied and demanded for a specific contract of 100 oz of gold of certain purity for delivery on a specific date. Buyers of this contract express their demand as a schedule of futures prices with corresponding quantities demanded for this contract while sellers express their supply, again as a schedule of futures prices with corresponding quantities offered for the same contract.

Given the special nature of futures markets with hedgers, speculators, and market makers being the main participants, we can aggregate among all hedgers and speculators, some of whom may be sellers while others are buyers and assume that hedgers are in the aggregate net sellers while speculators are net buyers. This is not an unrealistic assumption because hedging usually involves insuring an asset with a short futures position. Large commercial hedgers are usually short futures. To account for the possibility that hedgers may also be long futures, we aggregate all hedging positions and simply assume that the overall net position of hedgers is short, that is, volume of short positions by hedgers is larger than the volume of long positions. For a proper functioning of a futures market and formation of prices, this net short position must be met at equilibrium with a net long position initiated by speculators and market makers.

3. An Illustration

Suppose that the daily demand by speculators for the December gold futures contract is given by

$$P_s = 410 - 0.003\ Q_s \tag{3.1}$$

where P_s and Q_s denote futures price and quantity of futures contracts traded by speculators.

Unlike the ordinary demand schedule of microeconomics where the intercept does not have any particular meaning other than describing the price at which no quantity is demanded, the number 410 in equation (3.1) reflects an expectation of speculators. Note that equation (3.1) describes the buying behaviour of speculators when the expected future spot price is below $410. If speculators have homogeneous expectations that the expected future spot price at the expiration of the December futures contract will be $410, then they will be buyers at lower December futures prices because buying low and selling at a higher expected price offers an expected gain. If on the other hand, speculators have the same expectation about $410 but the December futures contract trades at higher prices, these speculators will become net sellers of the December futures. This is why equation (3.1) is graphed to illustrate that speculators can be either long or short depending on their expectations.

Consider next the supply offered by hedgers given by

$$P_h = 260 + 0.002\ Q_h \tag{3.2}$$

where P_h and Q_h denote price and quantity of the supply schedule of hedgers. Notice that hedgers are net sellers only when the futures price is above $260. Below $260, hedgers reverse their position by becoming net buyers. For example, hedgers may believe that at expected future spot price below $260, commercial producers will not cover their marginal cost and thus gold futures contracts selling below $260 must be a buying opportunity.

Combining equations (3.1) and (3.2) we can solve for the equilibrium December futures price of $320 and equilibrium quantity of December futures contracts of 30 000. Graph 3.1 describes the analysis presented.

Next, suppose that speculators receive new information and revise their homogeneous expectations of the expected future spot price to $415. Their increased demand now is

$$P_s = 415 - 0.003\ Q_s \tag{3.3}$$

which with the unchanged supply of equation (3.2) yields a new December futures price of $322, and a new equilibrium quantity of December futures contracts of 31 000. Thus, the increased expectations of speculators are incorporated into the December futures price.

This simple analysis has identified the critical factors in the formation of futures prices, that is the behaviour of hedgers and speculators and their expectations. As information

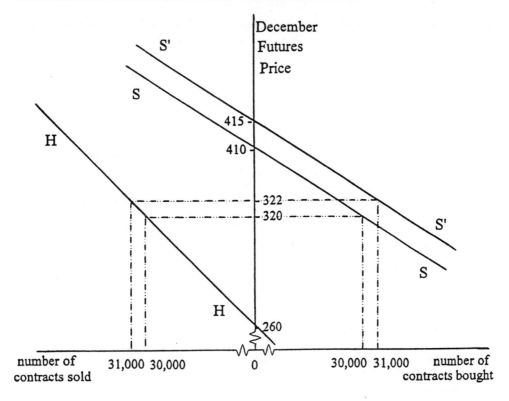

Graph 3.1

flows into the market and as this information is used to revise the demand and supply schedules, futures prices incorporate the arrival of such information. Unlike non futures markets where buyers and sellers seldom reverse their roles, in futures markets participants reverse their positions continuously.

4. Pricing Models

The introductory analysis and numerical example of the last two sections incorporate two important elements of most pricing models, the risk transference and price discovery functions of futures markets.

The risk transference function refers to hedgers using futures contracts to minimize their risk exposure from price fluctuations of their production output or inventory. This behaviour is expressed as a supply function assuming that hedgers are in the aggregate net short sellers. The *risk transference* function is accomplished when speculators and market makers, at appropriate futures prices, buy futures contracts from hedgers. Such a transaction shifts the price risk from hedgers to speculators and establishes the risk transference role of futures markets.

The price discovery function of futures markets means that the formation of futures prices impacts the pricing in cash markets. Of course, cash prices also influence futures prices with such simultaneous price dynamics being determined by an arbitrage process. However, the influence of cash prices on futures prices is not surprising because futures are derivative markets whose existence depends on cash markets. What economists wish to emphasize by the price discovery property is that futures markets are certainly influenced by cash markets but more importantly they also influence cash markets. Furthermore these price dynamics involve not only cash and futures prices, that is the basis, but also current futures prices and expected future spot prices at the expiration of a given contract.

The interdependence between cash and futures markets is captured in the numerical illustration by the intercepts of equations (3.1) and (3.2) because such numbers denote the aggregate homogeneous expectations of speculators and hedgers about the expected future spot price. The expectations about cash prices at a future date when the futures contract will expire, influence currently formed futures prices.

What needs to be emphasized is that the December futures price of $320 also offers valuable information to the cash market traders who, by using it in their trading, will cause the cash price to be impacted by the futures one. Futures traders' expectations about future spot prices corresponding to the expiration data of the futures contract will, along with other variables such as the elasticity of the demand and supply schedules in equations (3.1) and (3.2), determine futures prices. Expectations about future spot prices via futures trading translate into actual futures prices.

The ideas presented above have been formalized in numerous pricing models. Conceptually there are two broad categories of pricing models. The first group has its origin in the theory of storage of Kaldor (1939), Working (1948), Brennan (1958), Telser (1958) and others. According to the theory of storage, the difference between the contemporaneous spot and futures prices, that is the basis, for storable commodities can be explained in terms of interest and warehousing costs and a convenience yield on inventory. Let $F(t,T)$ and $S(t)$ denote futures price at time t with settlement or expiration at T and the spot price at time t, respectively. The theory of storage proposes the relationship

$$F(t,T) = S(t) [1 + R(t,T)] + W(t,T) - C(t,T) \qquad (4.1)$$

where $S(t) R(t,T)$ is the interest foregone, $W(t,T)$ is storage and insurance cost and $C(t,T)$ is the marginal convenience yield from an additional unit of inventory. Observe that the convenience yield arises because holding physical inventory could offer value when such inventory is needed to meet unexpected demand.

In contrast to the theory of storage, Cootner (1960), Dusak (1973) and others have proposed that the futures price can be expressed as

$$F(t,T) = S(t) + E_t[P(t,T)] + E_t[S(T) - S(t)] \qquad (4.2)$$

In equation (4.2), the futures price is the sum of the spot price plus two additional terms. The term $E_t[P(t,T)]$ denotes an expected risk premium and $E_t[S(T) - S(t)]$ denotes an expectation or forecast of the spot price change between t and the expiration T.

In Chapter 4 Fama and French discuss these two models in some detail and empirically test them for 21 agricultural, wood and animal products and metals. Their sample data range from early 1966 to mid-1984. Detailed statistical testing offers evidence in support of equation (4.1). For the second model in equation (4.2), the authors find evidence of forecast power for 10 out of 21 commodities and time-varying expected risk premiums for only five commodities.

In Chapter 2 Garbade and Silber develop a model that describes the interrelationship between futures and spot prices. Under certain assumptions such as no taxes or transaction costs, no limitations on borrowing, no warehouse fees and no spoilage, no limitations on short sales and a term structure of interest rates that is flat, they derive an equation similar to (4.2) with the futures price being equal to the spot prices plus a premium. They then argue that such an equation would hold provided that the supply of arbitrage services was infinitely elastic. This means that if the equality between the futures price and cash price plus the premium or more generally the equalities in equations (4.1) or (4.2) are violated, then a market participant can earn a riskless profit by following an appropriate strategy. The very large response by market participants to benefit from such a riskless arbitrage when the equality in the pricing model is violated, is defined as an infinitely elastic supply of arbitrage.

For reasons such as transaction costs, taxes and possible non-availability of large credit, the response of traders to pricing violations is not infinitely elastic. Put differently, it is possible to observe significant deviations from pricing relationship of the type in equations (4.1) or (4.2). Garbade and Silber show that at one extreme, when there is no arbitrage, the spot and futures prices will follow uncoupled random walks which means that there will be no tendency for prices in the futures and cash markets to converge. In this extreme case, the risk transfer and price discovery functions of futures markets are eliminated.

At the other extreme, when arbitrage activities are highly elastic so that even the most minor price violation is immediately restored, the prices in futures and cash markets will follow identical random walks and there will be no meaningful economic distinction between them. For the intermediate cases, prices will follow an intertwined random walk. Empirical analysis by Garbade and Silber for seven commodities shows that all of the markets are well integrated over a period of one or two months but that there is considerable slippage between cash and futures markets over shorter periods, especially for grains. The gold and silver markets however are highly integrated even over one day.

At a more advanced level, Peck (Chapter 1) and more recently Stein (Chapter 5) offer pricing models for futures markets which extend the supply and demand relationships for hedgers and speculators by incorporating rational expectations. As a consequence of these models, the stabilizing role of the futures markets on cash markets can be clearly demonstrated. One way to show the stabilizing role of the futures market is to first develop supply and demand dynamics for the cash market that generate cobweb cycles. In the absence of a futures market, cobweb cycles occur because market participants have no alternative but to form their expectations from past price behaviour. However, in the presence of an active futures market, producers use the futures prices rather than lagged spot prices to make their decisions, thus creating convergent fluctuations that stabilize the cash market. A detailed proof is presented in the chapters by both Peck and Stein.

5. Futures and Forwards Prices

The analysis presented and models discussed have exclusively emphasized the formation of futures prices. Contrary to popular opinion, forward prices are not always equal to futures prices. Often differences exist. French gives a comprehensive comparison of both the theoretical reasons and empirical evidence on this issue in Chapter 3.

To motivate the pricing of a forward contract, which almost always involves physical delivery, consider the simple two period case. Let t denote today and $t + 1$, $t + 2$ denote the subsequent two periods. The contract will be executed on period $t + 2$. Denote by V_{ij} the price of the asset when economy is at state i at $t + 1$ and at state j at $t + 2$. Assume that both $i = 1,2$ and $j = 1,2$. In other words, we assume that the economy experiences two states in each period. Allowing more states is straightforward.

There are two relevant economic variables: V_{ij}, the price of the asset, and r_{ij}, interest rates. Schematically, use the following decision diagram:

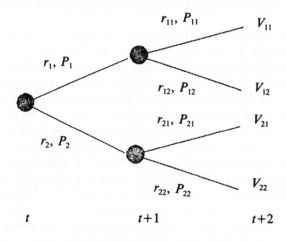

Figure 5.1

Figure 5.1 illustrates that moving from period t, now, to period $t + 1$, tomorrow, the economy's interest rates will go either to r_1, with probability P_1 or to r_2 with probability $P_2 = 1 - P_1$. From period $t + 1$ to $t + 2$, interest rates will go to r_{11} or r_{12}, provided they were at r_1 at $t + 1$ (with probabilities P_{11} and P_{12} respectively) or to r_{21} or r_{22} (with probabilities P_{21} and P_{22} respectively) provided they were at r_2 at $t + 1$. The V_{ij} denote expectations about the price of asset at time j provided that state i of the economy materialized at time $t + 1$.

Since no money changes hands at time t, both the buyer and the seller of a forward contract are willing to transact if the present values of the expected price V_{ij} and the forward price, denoted $G(t)$ are equal. Note that although $G(t)$, the forward price, is agreed upon today (at time t) it is paid at time $t + 2$; this explains why we consider present values. Such present values are given by

$$G(t) \left[\frac{P_1 P_{11}}{(1+r_1)(1+r_{11})} + \frac{P_1 P_{12}}{(1+r_1)(1+r_{12})} + \frac{P_2 P_{21}}{(1+r_2)(1+r_{21})} + \frac{P_2 P_{22}}{(1+r_2)(1+r_{22})} \right]$$

$$= \frac{V_{11} P_1 P_{11}}{(1+r_1)(1+r_{11})} + \frac{V_{12} P_1 P_{12}}{(1+r_1)(1+r_{12})} + \frac{V_{21} P_2 P_{21}}{(1+r_2)(1+r_{21})} + \frac{V_{22} P_2 P_{22}}{(1+r_2)(1+r_{22})}. \quad (5.1)$$

From (5.1) we can immediately solve for the forward price $G(t)$ given below

$$G(t) = \frac{\dfrac{V_{11} P_1 P_{11}}{(1+r_1)(1+r_{11})} + \dfrac{V_{12} P_1 P_{12}}{(1+r_1)(1+r_{12})} + \dfrac{V_{21} P_2 P_{21}}{(1+r_2)(1+r_{21})} + \dfrac{V_{22} P_2 P_{22}}{(1+r_2)(1+r_{22})}}{\dfrac{P_1 P_{11}}{(1+r_1)(1+r_{11})} + \dfrac{P_1 P_{12}}{(1+r_1)(1+r_{12})} + \dfrac{P_2 P_{21}}{(1+r_2)(1+r_{21})} + \dfrac{P_2 P_{22}}{(1+r_2)(1+r_{22})}} \quad (5.2)$$

Having obtained the forward price for the simplified two state, two period case we next present the futures price.

Let $F(t)$ denote the futures price agreed upon today to be executed at period $t + 2$. What makes the computation of the futures price interesting is the *daily settlement* procedure. According to this procedure, administered by the Clearing House of futures exchanges, the futures contract, both for the buyer and the seller, is priced to market daily. Thus, if the futures price at $t + 1$ is F_i with $i = 1,2$ denoting the state of the economy, then unless $F_i = F(t)$, the party in whose favour the price moved by $F_i - F(t)$ must immediately be paid this amount by the losing party. Recall that such a settlement does not occur in a forward market. The economic justification of daily settlement is explained by the desire of organized exchanges to reduce risk by allocating potential price changes across the life of the futures contract in lieu of a one time settlement at the maturity of the contract.

Using the same decision theoretic diagram as Figure 5.1, note that daily settlement means that the F_i, $i = 1,2$ must be adjusted by the amount

$$F_i - F(t) \quad (5.3)$$

which, if appropriately discounted should be a fair game with zero present value. In symbols,

$$\sum_i \frac{[F_i - F(t)] P_i}{1+r_i} = 0 \quad (5.4)$$

which yields that

$$F(t) = \frac{\dfrac{F_1 P_1}{(1+r_1)} + \dfrac{F_2 P_2}{(1+r_2)}}{\dfrac{P_1}{(1+r_1)} + \dfrac{P_2}{(1+r_2)}}. \quad (5.5)$$

So far, it appears that $F(t)$ in equation (5.5) resembles (5.2). However, note that F_1 and F_2 in (5.5) are each discounted values of asset prices expected to prevail at $t + 2$. For $i = 1,2$, observe that

$$F_i = \frac{\dfrac{V_{i1}P_{i1}}{1+r_{i1}} + \dfrac{V_{i2}P_{i2}}{1+r_{i2}}}{\dfrac{P_{i1}}{1+r_{i1}} + \dfrac{P_{i2}}{1+r_{i2}}}. \tag{5.6}$$

Put F_i, $i = 1,2$ of equation (5.6) in equation (5.5) and perform the necessary algebra to conclude that

$$F(t) = \frac{\dfrac{V_{11}P_1P_{11}}{(1+r_1)(1+r_{11})} + \dfrac{V_{12}P_1P_{12}}{(1+r_1)(1+r_{12})} + \dfrac{V_{21}P_2P_{21}}{(1+r_2)(1+r_{21})} + \dfrac{V_{22}P_2P_{22}}{(1+r_2)(1+r_{22})}}{\left[\dfrac{P_1}{1+r_1} + \dfrac{P_2}{1+r_2}\right]\left[\dfrac{P_1P_{11}}{1+r_{11}} + \dfrac{P_1P_{12}}{1+r_{12}} + \dfrac{P_2P_{21}}{1+r_{21}} + \dfrac{P_2P_{22}}{1+r_{22}}\right]} \tag{5.7}$$

A simple comparison of equations (5.2) and (5.7) shows that both expressions have the same numerator. Therefore differences or similarities between $G(t)$ and $F(t)$ depend on the denominator. Fisher Black (1976) showed that when interest rates are nonstochastic, that is constant, then $G(t) = F(t)$. This is trivial to see from the explicit expression in equations (5.2) and (5.7). In general however, forward prices $G(t)$, need not be equal to futures prices $F(t)$.

6. Efficiency

The random walk behaviour of futures prices was initially suggested by Working (1934) who also developed a theory of anticipatory prices in Working (1958). The exhaustive literature on the random walk behaviour of asset prices is known as *market efficiency*. Despite the existence of several puzzling and conflicting results, in general, and in futures markets in particular, the theory of efficient markets remains a central pillar of modern financial economics.

Paul Samuelson (1965) developed the efficient market hypothesis to rationalize the random walk behaviour, whereby the current price fully reflects all relevant information. Since the flow of such information between now and the next period cannot be anticipated, efficient market price changes are serially uncorrelated. In other words, the randomness in price changes is caused by the random flow of unanticipated information.

During the past twenty years, the theory of market efficiency has been refined analytically, mathematically and statistically. The concept of information has been made more precise. The notion of random walk was generalized to martingales and Itô processes and numerous sophisticated statistical tests were employed to test the theory. Grossman and Stiglitz (1980) have addressed several important analytical issues of the theory of efficient markets. They argue that the notion of market efficiency is inconsistent with the reality of costly arbitrage. They develop a simple model with a constant absolute risk-aversion utility function and show that costless information is both necessary and sufficient for prices to fully reflect all available information. Efficient markets theorists realize that costless information is a sufficient condition for market efficiency. However, they are not always clear that it is also a necessary condition.

It is not surprising to find that along with numerous studies confirming market efficiency, there are many studies rejecting it. Two important surveys by Fama (1970) and (1991) review several aspects of the market efficiency debate. These apply to asset prices in general rather than to futures prices more specifically.

Among the numerous papers that studied the appropriateness of random walk or the martingale model on futures markets, we mention selectively the following: Firstly, the Treasury-Bill, Treasury-Bond and gold futures markets were investigated by Chance (1985), Klemkosky and Lasser (1985), Cole, Impson and Reichenstein (1991), and MacDonald and Hein (1993); secondly, the Agricultural Commodities and Live Cattle markets were investigated by Leuthold (Chapter 6), Bigman, Goldfarb and Schechtman (1983), Canarella and Pollard (1985), Maberly (1985), Bird (1985), Elam and Dixon (1988) and Johnson, Zulauf, Irwin and Gerlow (1991); thirdly, the metal futures market was investigated by Gross (1988) and Chowdhury (1991); fourthly, the foreign currency markets were investigated by Glassman (1987), Ogden and Tucker (1987), Harpaz, Krull and Yagil (1990), and Lai and Lai (1991).

Evaluating the above studies one observes that many writers hold positive opinions on market efficiency. Chance (1985) believes that the Treasury-Bond futures market correctly anticipates the information contained in the announcement of the rate of change of the Consumer Price Index. MacDonald and Hein (1993) comment that the Treasury-Bill futures market may not be as inefficient as once presumed in terms of weak form efficiency, though this market does not provide optimal forecasts. Maberly (1985) demonstrates that in the grain futures markets, the inference that the market is inefficient for more distant futures contracts is due to the bias that results from using inappropriate statistical estimation methods. Elam and Dixon (1988) attack the inefficiency grain market argument using several Monte-Carlo experiments to demonstrate that very often the F-test tends to wrongly reject the true model. The research of Canarella and Pollard (1985) suggests that the efficient market hypothesis cannot be rejected for corn, wheat, soybeans and soybean oil. Gross (1988) claims that the hypothesis of efficient copper and aluminium markets cannot be rejected on the evidence of semi-strong efficiency tests. Saunders and Mahajan (1988) show that stock index futures pricing is efficient.

However, numerous investigators have identified evidence of market inefficiency. Leuthold concludes in Chapter 6 that his results cast serious doubt that cattle futures prices behave randomly. Bird (1985) discovers that for coffee and sugar the efficient market hypothesis is invalid and for cocoa there is also some evidence of inefficiency, but of limited economic significance. Harpaz, Krull and Yagil (1990) perform tests for efficiency of the US Dollar Index futures contracts during the period 1985–8, which result in their rejection of the null hypothesis that this futures market is efficient during the period. By using methods of cointegration for the five major forward currency markets, Lai and Lai (1991) offer evidence not favourable to the joint hypothesis of market efficiency and no-risk premium. In Chapter 9 Goldenberg argues that the theory of market efficiency implies that futures prices have no memory. Yet his results show that intraday transaction prices of the S&P 500 Index futures contracts have memory. The empirical results presented in Chowdhury (1991) indicate the rejection of the efficient market hypothesis for four nonferrous metals – copper, lead, tin and zinc – traded on the London Metal Exchange. In Chapter 10 Ma, Dare and Donaldson challenge the market efficiency hypothesis by confirming the presence of overreaction in several futures markets. They find that agricultural futures tend to overreact to significant events, whereas financial futures prices tend to underreact to significant events.

Finally, many authors have considered the appropriateness of the efficient market hypothesis for specific futures contracts in specific time periods. Bigman, Goldfarb and Schechtman (1983) believe that the market can be generally characterized as efficient for the futures contracts on wheat, soybeans and corn, six weeks before delivery or less. For longer-term futures contracts, their tests reject the market efficiency hypothesis. Johnson, Zulauf, Irwin and Gerlow (1991) use a combination of profit margin trading rules to test the market efficiency of the soybean complex. Their findings suggest that while nearby soybean complex futures price spreads are efficient, distant soybean complex futures price spreads are not efficient. The results of Klemkosky and Lesser's (1985) Treasury-Bond market efficiency tests do not agree totally with the conclusions drawn from earlier studies. Glassman (1987) reports evidence of joint multimarket inefficiency in foreign currency futures markets during some of the 38 contract periods studied. Much of the inefficiency appeared to be short term in duration (one week or less). Cole, Impson and Reichenstein (1991) conclude that the Treasury-Bill futures rates provide rational one- and two-quarters-ahead forecasts of futures spot rate, which are the forecast horizons that seem to be of most interest to the public. However, they believe the rationality of four-quarters-ahead futures forecasts should be rejected. Neftci and Policano (Chapter 8) investigate the effectiveness of technical analysis by examining the performance of two strategies: trendline and moving averages. Using daily observations for gold and Treasury Bills for about five years, they conclude that the moving average method has some predictive power while the results are mixed for the trendline approach.

Although the papers cited thus far investigate the market efficiency of futures trading, Cox (Chapter 7) investigates the effect of organized futures trading on the efficiency in spot markets. Cox develops a theoretical model and tests it for six different commodities. He shows that futures trading increases market information and contributes to market efficiency of the spot market. Cox confirms the value of the price discovery function of futures markets by demonstrating that a spot market becomes more efficient when there is futures trading.

7. Price Distributions

The actual distribution of spot or futures price changes or returns is an issue of great importance. In an efficient market such returns are often postulated to be normally distributed. The theoretical foundations underlying such assumptions are not always clear. Most often, these assumptions are motivated by the methodology of statistical inference.

It was Bachelier (1900) who first constructed a random walk model for security and commodity prices. Bachelier assumed that successive price differences $P(t + dt) - P(t)$ are independent and normally distributed random variables with mean μdt and variance $\sigma^2 dt$, that is

$$P(t + dt) - P(t) \sim N(\mu dt, \sigma^2 dt). \qquad (7.1)$$

Later on, as a result of the empirical work of Osborne (1959), such normal distributions were replaced by the notion that asset returns are independent and log-normally distributed that is

$$\ln [P(t + dt)/P(t)] \sim N(\mu dt, \sigma dt). \qquad (7.2)$$

This idea had a phenomenal impact on financial theory by introducing processes to describe the behaviour of security and futures prices. The Black-Scholes option pricing model is one of the most celebrated results of this tradition.

In a seminal paper, Mandelbrot (Chapter 11) proposed a radically new approach to the modelling of price variation. He replaced the normal distribution by another family of probability laws, referred to as *stable-Paretian*.

From the papers by Osborne (1959) and Mandlebrot followed Fama and Roll (1968, 1971) and numerous other papers. These are carefully reviewed in Akgiray and Booth (1988) with emphasis on stock returns. Although most papers reject the normal distribution hypothesis in favour of the stable-Paretian, studies exist that further reject the stable-Paretian, but not in favour of normality.

Earlier, Stevenson and Bear (1970) and Dusak (1973) offered evidence in support of the stable-Paretian distribution. More recently, Helms and Martell (1985), using data for commodities traded on the Chicago Board of Trade, conclude that returns of futures prices, although they are not normally distributed, are closer to normal than to other members of the family of Pareto distributions. Contrary to their results, Cornew, Town and Crowson (1984) claim that the stable-Paretian distribution offers a bitter fit for futures returns of several contracts than the normal distribution. Similarly, So (1987) confirms that currency futures and spot returns are stable-Paretian while Hall, Brorsen and Irwin (Chapter 12) and Hudson, Leuthold and Sarassoro (1987) claim that futures returns are not stable-Paretian. Finally, Gribbin, Harris and Lau (Chapter 13) use a newly developed statistical methodology to conclude that futures prices are not stable-Paretian distributed.

8. Chaos

The various empirical studies that have rejected the theory of market efficiency have also encouraged financial economists to seek alternative explanations for the time series behaviour of asset returns. This literature is known as the *chaotic dynamics* approach to asset returns. Several studies, such as Blank (Chapter 14) and Decoster, Labys and Mitchell (1992), have offered evidence that futures prices appear to follow low dimensional chaotic dynamics. Below, some essential aspects of this new methodology are described.

The logical way to proceed in the analysis of chaotic dynamics is to give a precise definition. The definition given is purely mathematical and can be found in several books such as Devaney (1986). First, it is necessary to explain a few terms.

Consider a real-valued function $f: R \to R$. We are interested in the time series generated by this function starting from some arbitrary $x_0 \in R$. Denote by $f^2 \equiv f[f(x)] \equiv f \circ f(x)$ where

o means composition and in general let $f^n = fofo \ldots of(x)$ mean n compositions. The time series takes the values

$$x_o, f(x_o), f^2(x_o), \ldots, f^n(x_o), \ldots, \tag{8.1}$$

for $t = 0, 1, 2, \ldots, n$. For equation (8.1) to describe a chaotic function it must satisfy three requirements.

First it must sample infinitely many values. To make this idea precise we say that $f: R \rightarrow R$ is *topologically transitive* if for any pair of open sets U and V in the real line R there is an integer $k > 0$ such that $f^k(U) \cap V \neq \phi$.

The second requirement is sensitive dependence on initial conditions. We say that the function $f: R \rightarrow R$ has *sensitive dependence* on initial conditions if there exists a $\delta > 0$ such that for any $x \in R$ and any neighbourhood N of x, there is a $y \in N$ and an integer $n > 0$ such that

$$|f^n(x) - f^n(y)| > \delta. \tag{8.2}$$

This condition says that there are time series that start very close to each other but diverge exponentially fast from each other.

The third requirement involves a property of the periodic points of the function f, namely that these periodic points are dense in R. We say that a point $x \in R$ is *periodic* if for $n > 0$, $f^n(x) = x$. The least positive integer n for which $f^n(x) = x$ is called the *prime period* of x.

We can summarize our analysis by giving the definition of a chaotic function. We say that a function $f: R \rightarrow R$ is *chaotic* if it satisfies three conditions:

1. f is topologically transitive.
2. f has sensitive dependence on initial conditions.
3. f has periodic points that are dense in the real numbers.

Observe that this is a precise mathematical definition which is not motivated by stock market price behaviour. Yet, each condition can be given a financial interpretation. The first condition requires the time series dynamics to be rich in the sense that it takes infinitely many different values. This condition makes a chaotic map similar to random walk because each value is different from all the previous ones. Of course, in random walk this happens because we are sampling from an infinite population. On the other hand, in chaotic dynamics we do not have sampling; instead we have a nonlinear equation that generates many different values. Note that for both the random walk and for the chaotic dynamics, it is possible for certain values to occur more than once in the time series. What we are emphasizing is that such a repetition is very unlikely. The first condition of topological transitivity requires the time series to be rich in the sense that it takes infinitely many different values. Intuitively, such a map can move under iteration, that is through time, from one arbitrarily small neighbourhood to any other. Since the space cannot be decomposed into two disjoint open sets which are invariant under the map (by definition) the points not only can wander anywhere (since they cannot be blocked) but actually will wander everywhere.

The second condition casts serious difficulties on forecasting. Although a chaotic map is deterministic and knowing today's value immediately allows one to compute tomorrow's price, the same exact equation can generate very dissimilar time series if we are uncertain about when the series got started and at what initial value x_o. To contrast with a random walk, recall that the past and future values are independent because we are sampling from an infinite population of values. The inability to forecast is due precisely to this statistical independence. In a chaotic function, however, we know exactly the relationship between the past and the future but we are unable to predict because we cannot be sure as to when we started and with what value.

The third condition gives a chaotic function structure. It essentially requires that the chaotic function exhibit important regularities. However, these regularities are hidden in the sense that no researcher could explore the infinite number of patterns of the periodic points and their limits. In an analogous manner, the random walk can be said to have some structure given to it by the properties of the distribution that characterizes the population. Again, no researcher could explore the infinite sample paths that a random walk process can generate. This analogy between the structure of a chaotic function and a random walk should not be understood as meaning that both have exactly the same structure. Although we do not know how to compare correctly the structure of a chaotic function to that of a random walk, a chaotic map involves infinite nonlinear iterations functions and, therefore, its structure could be viewed as being more complex compared to the structure of a random walk. More technically, one can argue that in chaotic dynamics because the set of periodic points is dense in R, for any point in R, there exists a sequence of periodic points which converges to this point. Thus, it appears intuitively that a structure exists because of the mere existence of the periodic points which clustered around each point in the domain. Therefore, due to the fact that periodic points are dense, each point in the domain can be identified by a sequence of periodic points, which converges to it. However, in the random walk case, each point is identified by its probability of occurrence which is described by the normal density function.

The mathematical result that makes chaotic dynamics very interesting is the existence of *strange attractors*. In studying various chaotic maps, mathematicians discovered that as time increases, despite the turbulent behaviour of such maps that appears random, the time series values indeed converge to a set. Furthermore, the set which, of course, depends on the specific map is not one of the standard sets of stability theory such as a point, a circle, or a torus. Because the attractors of chaotic maps are not as the regular attractors of ordinary differential equations, they were named *strange*.

A precise mathematical definition of a strange attractor is given in Guckenheimer and Holmes (1983) along with several beautiful illustrations. A simple definition of a *strange attractor* of a chaotic dynamical system is a compact set, denoted S, such that almost all initial conditions in the neighbourhood of S converge to S. The neighbourhood of S from where almost all initial conditions yield time series that converge to S is called the *basin of the strange attractor*.

The existence of a strange attractor implies that the randomness of chaotic dynamics has significant hidden structure. In contrast, the random walk behaviour of a time series describes uncertainty in a more extreme way than chaotic dynamics because a random walk series does not converge to a strange attractor but instead wanders forever. Naturally, the important empirical question is: Given a time series of futures prices, how can we distinguish whether it is generated by a random walk or a chaotic process?

There are several techniques that can be used. Brock and Malliaris (1989) give a brief description of these methods while Brock, Hsieh and LeBaron (1991) discuss them in detail. Here we plan to describe only one of the most fundamental techniques called the correlation dimension because it is used widely in the futures literature. This method was developed by Grassberger and Procaccia (1983).

Suppose that we are given a time series of price changes $\{dP(t) : t = 0, 1, 2, ...T\}$. Suppose that T is large enough so that a strange attractor has begun to take shape. Use this time series to create pairs, that is $dP^2(t) \equiv \{[dP(t), dP(t+1)] : t = 0, 1, 2, ... T\}$ and then triplets and finally M-histories, that is $dP^M(t) \equiv \{[dP(t), ... dP(t+M-1)] : t = 0, 1, 2, ... T\}$. In other words we convert the original time series of singletons into vectors of dimension 2, 3, ... M. In generating these vectors we allow for overlapping entries. For example if $M = 3$ we have a set of the form $\{[dP(0), dP(1), dP(2)], [dP(1), dP(2), dP(3)], ... [dP(T-2), dP(T-1), dP(T)]\}$. Such a set will have $(T+1) - (M-1)$ vectors. Mathematically, the process of creating vectors of various dimension from the original series is called an *embedding*.

Suppose that for a given embedding dimension, say M, we wish to measure if these M-vectors fill the entire M-space or only a fraction. For a given $\epsilon > 0$ define the *correlation integral*, denoted by

$$C^M(\epsilon) = \frac{\text{the number of pairs } (s, t) \text{ whose distance } \| dP^M(s) - dP^M(t) \| < \epsilon}{T^2_M} \quad (8.3)$$

$$= \frac{\text{the number of } (s, t), 1 \leq t, s \leq T, \| dP^M(s) - dP^M(t) \| < \epsilon,}{T^2_M}$$

where $T_M = (T+1) - (M-1)$, and as before

$$dP^M(t) = [dP(t), dP(t+1), ..., dP(t+M-1)].$$

Observe that $\| \cdot \|$ in (8.3) denotes vector norm. Using the correlation integral we can define the *correlation dimension* for an embedding dimension M as

$$D^M = \lim_{\substack{\epsilon \to 0 \\ T \to \infty}} \frac{\ln C^M(\epsilon)}{\ln \epsilon}. \quad (8.4)$$

In (8.4) ln denotes natural logarithm. Finally, the correlation dimension D is given by

$$D = \lim_{M \to \infty} D^M. \quad (8.5)$$

Technical accuracy requires that D^M in equation (8.4) is a double limit, first in terms of $T \to \infty$ and then in terms of $\epsilon \to 0$. However, in practice T is usually given and it is impossible to increase it to infinity. Thus the limit $T \to \infty$ is meaningless in practice and moreover M is practically bounded by T. Therefore, we only consider the limit $\epsilon \to 0$ in (8.4).

Blank (Chapter 14) discusses in detail the empirical aspects of the methodology of chaos and offers several calculations for soybeans and the S&P 500 futures contracts. His correlation dimension estimates are low and interpreted along with other techniques offer evidence that soybeans and the S&P 500 futures contracts have a chaotic nonlinear generating process.

9. Hedging

Suppose that a gold mining firm has a weekly output of 10 000 oz of gold. Because the recent trend of spot gold pricing has been a gradually declining one, the gold producer decides to hedge his total weekly production in the futures market by selling 100 December futures contracts at $386.20. Table 9.1 summarizes the cash and futures position today and a week later.

Table 9.1.

Cash Position	Futures Position
Today: Anticipate output of 10 000 oz in one week which if available today could be sold for $383.10 an ounce.	*Today*: Sell 100 December futures contracts of 100 oz each for $386.20
A Week Later: Output is produced and 10 000 oz are sold in the cash market for $378.00 an ounce.	*A Week Later*: Buy 100 December futures contracts of 100 oz each for $381.10
Foregone cash receipts = 10 000*5.10 = **$51 000**	*Profits from futures* = 100*100*5.10 = **$51 000**

Notice that in the illustration of Table 9.1 the reduced cash receipts due to the drop in price from $383.10 today to $378.00 a week later are recovered exactly by the profits from the futures transactions. The two amounts of $51 000 are exactly equal because the difference between futures and cash prices today, called *basis*, is equal to (386.20 − 383.10 = 3.10) and is the same a week later, that is (381.10 − 378 = 3.10).

Motivated by this illustration we can now discuss two theories of hedging: the traditional and portfolio approaches. Let P_s^1, P_f^1 denote spot and futures prices today and P_s^2, P_f^2 be the corresponding prices next period. The units of the asset to be hedged are written as X_s.

First consider the unhedged position given by

$$U = X_s [P_s^2 - P_s^1] \qquad (9.1)$$

which simply describes the profit or loss from the spot price change between two periods. Assuming that prices, both cash and futures, follow random walks or more generally martingales with mean zero and variances σ_s^2 and σ_f^2 respectively, the expectation and the risk of the unhedged position are

$$E(U) = E\{X_s[P_s^2 - P_s^1]\} = X_s E[P_s^2 - P_s^1] = X_s[E(P_s^2) - P_s^1] = 0 \quad (9.2)$$

$$\text{Var}(U) = X_s^2 \, \sigma_s^2 > 0. \quad (9.3)$$

Equation (9.2) says that because prices from one period to the next are as likely to increase as they are to decrease, the average gain or loss of an unhedged position is zero. However, the unhedged position remains risky because the variance of price changes is positive.

Next, consider the hedged position, H, assuming that the basis does not change as in the illustration of Table 9.1

$$H = X_s\,[P_s^2 - P_s^1] - X_f[P_f^2 - P_f^1]. \quad (9.4)$$

In (9.4), let $X_s = X_f$ with futures position being the opposite of the cash. Taking the expectation and computing the risk of (9.4) write

$$E(H) = X_s[E(P_s^2) - P_s^1] - X_f[E(P_f^2) - P_f^1] = 0 \quad (9.5)$$

$$\text{Var}(H) = X_s^2 \, \sigma_b^2 = 0. \quad (9.6)$$

Note again that the expectation of the hedged position described in (9.5) is equal to zero, as in (9.2), for the same reason, namely, the martingale behaviour of cash and futures prices. But unlike (9.3) which expresses the positive risk of the unhedged position, (9.6) shows that the risk of the hedged position is nonexistent because $\sigma_b^2 = 0$. This means that the variance of the basis is zero which follows from the assumption that the basis is constant. Thus the traditional hedging approach described in (9.5) and (9.6) is preferred to the unhedged position in (9.2) and (9.3) because it eliminates risk. What causes risk to be totally eliminated is the assumption that the basis remains constant.

In an influential paper, Ederington (Chapter 15) analyses the general case of hedging when the basis does not remain constant. Using the general methodology of portfolio theory, Ederington formulates the hedging decision as follows: let R denote the return on a portfolio that includes both a spot asset of a quantity X_s and a futures asset of a quantity X_f. The quantities X_s and X_f need not be equal. Let

$$R = X_s[P_s^2 - P_s^1] - X_f[P_f^2 - P_f^1] \quad (9.7)$$

denote the return from the cash and futures position. Usually the futures position is the opposite in sign to that of the cash but in (9.7) there is no such restriction. Taking the expectation of (9.7) and using the martingale property of price behaviour, we obtain

$$E(R) = X_s\,E[P_s^2 - P_s^1] - X_f\,E[P_f^2 - P_f^1] = 0. \quad (9.8)$$

The risk associated with (9.7) is given by

$$\text{Var}(R) = X_s^2 \, \sigma_s^2 + X_f^2 \, \sigma_f^2 + 2X_s X_f \, \sigma_{sf} \quad (9.9)$$

where σ_s^2, σ_f^2 and σ_{sf} denote the variance of differences in the spot price, futures price and covariance between spot and futures prices, respectively.

Let $b = [-X_f/X_s]$ denote the proportion of the spot quantity that is hedged. Using b, equation (9.9) can be rewritten as

$$\text{Var}(R) = X_s^2 [\sigma_s^2 + b^2\sigma_f^2 - 2b\sigma_{sf}]. \tag{9.10}$$

The objective is to minimize the risk in (9.10) by optimally choosing the hedge ratio b, that is

$$\partial \text{Var}(R)/\partial b = X_s^2 [2 b\sigma_f^2 - 2\sigma_{sf}] = 0, \tag{9.11}$$

which yields

$$b = \sigma_{sf}/\sigma_f^2. \tag{9.12}$$

The result in (9.12) says that if the investor wishes to reduce the risk due to price fluctuations, she may choose the optimal hedge ratio in (9.12) computed as the covariance of spot and futures price differences over the variance of futures price differences. In practice (9.12) is also computed using ordinary least squares with spot price differences being the dependent variable and futures price differences being the independent variable. For more sophisticated methodologies of hedge ratio estimation see Myers (Chapter 17). Adler and Detemple (Chapter 18) and Marshall and Herbst (Chapter 19) also generalize the hedging decision in the context of portfolio selection. We conclude this section with an illustration.

Consider the following weekly spot and settlement futures prices of crude oil.

Spot price in Dollars per barrel	December *Futures* Price in Dollars per barrel Traded at NYM; Contract size 1000 per barrel
17.00	18.00
19.80	20.00
17.70	18.50
16.30	17.50
20.50	20.50
22.95	22.25
25.96	24.40
24.49	23.35
30.09	27.35
25.89	24.35

Suppose that an oil refinery buys 50 000 barrels of crude oil at $25.89 and to cover itself from the risk of a price drop in crude oil it immediately places a short hedge by selling futures contracts at $24.35 each. One week later the oil refinery sells the 50 000 barrels of crude oil at a spot price of $20.99 and closes its hedge by buying futures contracts at a price of $20.85.

There are two ways to compute the optimal hedge ratio b:

(a) by using σ_{sf}/σ_f^2.
(b) by using the regression analysis:

$$b = \frac{N \cdot \sum_{i=1}^{n}(F_i S_i) - (\sum_{i=1}^{n} F_i)(\sum_{i=1}^{n} S_i)}{N \cdot \sum_{i=1}^{n} F_i^2 - (\sum_{i=1}^{n} F_i)^2}.$$

i	Spot	Futures	S_i	F_i	S_i*F_i	F_i^2	$(S_i-\mu_s)$	$(F_i-\mu_f)$	$(F_i-\mu_f)^2$	$(S_i-\mu_s)(F_i-\mu_f)$
0	17	18								
1	19.8	20	2.8	2	5.6	4	1.812222	1.294444	1.675586	2.345821
2	17.7	18.5	−2.1	−1.5	3.15	2.25	−3.08778	−2.20556	4.864475	6.810265
3	16.3	17.5	−1.4	−1	1.4	1	−2.38778	−1.70556	2.90892	4.072488
4	20.5	20.5	4.2	3	12.6	9	3.212222	2.294444	5.264475	7.370265
5	22.95	22.25	2.45	1.75	4.2875	3.0625	1.462222	1.044444	1.090864	1.52721
6	25.96	24.4	3.01	2.15	6.4715	4.6225	2.022222	1.444444	2.08642	2.920988
7	24.49	23.35	−1.47	−1.05	1.5435	1.1025	−2.45778	−1.75556	3.081975	4.314765
8	30.09	27.35	5.6	4	22.4	16	4.612222	3.294444	10.85336	15.19471
9	25.89	24.35	−4.2	−3	12.6	9	−5.18778	−3.70556	13.73114	19.2236
Sum			8.89	6.35	70.0525	50.0375			45.55722	63.78011
Average			0.987778	0.705556						

Using the data in the above worksheet, the first method yields:

$$\sigma_f^2 = \frac{\sum_{i=1}^{n}(F_i - \mu_f)^2}{N}, \quad \sigma_{sf} = \frac{\sum_{i=1}^{n}[(F_i-\mu_f)(S_i-\mu_s)]}{N}, \quad b = \frac{\sigma_{sf}}{\sigma_f^2} = \frac{263.78011}{45.55722} = 1.4$$

The second method yields:

$$b = \frac{N*\sum_{i=1}^{n}(F_i S_i) - (\sum_{i=1}^{n} F_i)(\sum_{i=1}^{n} S_i)}{N*\sum_{i=1}^{n} F_i^2 - (\sum_{i=1}^{n} F_i)^2} = \frac{9*70.0525 - 6.35*8.89}{9*50.0375 - 6.35^2} = 1.4.$$

The results of the traditional and optimal hedge are summarized in Tables 9.2 and 9.3.

Table 9.2 *Using the traditional hedge*

Cash Position	Futures Position
Today: Buy 50 000 barrels of crude oil at $25.89	*Today:* Sell 50 December futures contracts of 1000 barrels each at $24.35
A Week Later: The 50 000 barrels of crude oil are sold at $20.99.	*A Week Later:* Buy 50 December futures contracts of 1000 barrels each at $20.85.
Loss = 50 000*4.90 = **$245 000**	Profits from futures = 50*1000*3.50 = **$175 000**

Table 9.3   *Using the optimal hedge*

Cash Position	Futures Position
Today: Buy 50 000 barrels of crude oil at $25.89.	Today: Sell 1.4*50 = 70 December futures contracts of 1000 barrels each at $24.35.
A Week Later: The 50 000 barrels of crude oil are sold at $20.99. Loss = 50 000*4.90 = **$245 000**	A Week Later: Buy 70 December futures contracts of 1000 barrels each at $20.85. Profits from futures = 70*1000*3.50 = **$245 000**

10. Conclusions

This chapter has asked the key question of how futures prices behave and has provided an extensive analysis. The behaviour of futures prices is determined in highly liquid futures markets where speculators, hedgers, arbitrageurs, market makers and other traders buy and sell well designed contracts via an open outcry continuous auction. This price formation is both affected by and also influences the underlying cash market and offers the valuable functions of price discovery and risk transference.

The behaviour of futures prices and their interrelationship with the underlying spot market have been conceptually presented in two broad categories of pricing models. The first category emphasizes the theory of storage which explains the difference between the contemporaneous spot and futures prices for storable commodities in terms of interest and warehousing costs and convenience yield on inventory. The second category expresses the futures price as the sum of the spot price plus two additional terms: an expected risk premium and a forecast of the spot price between now and the expiration of the futures contract.

Related to price behaviour is the central question of whether futures prices follow random walks. Actually some of the early work by Working (1934) described the random walk behaviour of futures prices long before such behaviour was considered for cash assets. The statistical behaviour of random walk and the financial theory of market efficiency are discussed. Several studies, which investigate the appropriate applications of these theories are examined. The recent methodology of chaos is also presented.

Because futures prices vary in relation to cash prices and natural variations in cash prices create risk, the hedging activity emerges. Hedging occurs whenever an asset may decrease in value or an obligation may increase. This essay offers a detailed analysis of hedging both for the simple case when the basis is constant and the more general case when the basis fluctuates.

Thus far, the price behaviour, market efficiency and hedging involved all futures markets. However, each of the existing numerous futures markets offers remarkable insights into the functioning and special characteristics of such specific markets. A valuable selection of individual markets is found in Roll (Chapter 20), Fama and French (Chapter 21), Stevens (Chapter 22) and Antoniou and Foster (Chapter 23).

Acknowledgements

I wish to thank the publishers Edward and Sandy Elgar and the general editor Professor Richard Roll for the invitations to be the volume editor of the *Futures Markets*. Their support, suggestions and encouragement were very effective in helping me do my work joyfully and with no major delays.

Having taught a graduate course in Futures Markets every year during the past decade, my first step was to consult my various Reading Lists and select about two dozen of the most influential articles in the field. Very soon, it became obvious to me that two dozen articles, independent of their individual greatness, could not offer a reader the full flavour of the rich past of the field nor an adequate taste of its current feverish research activities. So the project expanded from one to three volumes. What constrained me to stop with three was the realization that increasing the number of articles further would naturally reduce the impact of the truly great contributions.

After I organized the papers selected into three volumes under topics reflecting the entire scope of the area, I sought the advice of some of the leaders in the field. I mailed my tentative list of the articles, organized by topics in three volumes, to 15 colleagues asking them to tell me what selections they liked, the ones they thought were marginal and ought to be removed and more importantly what special gems had I overlooked.

The response was phenomenal. As I am writing this piece I have spread all over my office floor the individuals files with the detailed responses. I have taken every suggestion very seriously. Some articles have been eliminated, others added and on a couple of occasions new sections were introduced. Thus, although I assume full responsibility of the final product, the reader must know that every effort has been made to offer him and her the most representative collection.

Because the help that I have received is enormous, so is my intellectual debt to these very special colleagues. I acknowledge with much gratitude the help, suggestions, remarks, comments, agreements and gentle disagreements of the following persons listed alphabetically:

Peter Alonzi   (Chicago Board of Trade)
Tony Antoniou   (Brunel University)
George Constantinides   (University of Chicago)
Rafaella Cremonesi   (University of Brescia, Italy)
Frank Edwards   (Colombia University)
Ian Garrett   (Brunel University)
Anthony Herbst   (Editor of the *Journal of Financial Engineering*)
Scott Irwin   (The Ohio State University)
Robert Kolb   (University of Miami)
James Moser   (Federal Reserve Bank of Chicago)
Mark Powers   (Editor of *The Journal of Futures Markets*)
Jerome Stein   (Brown University)
William Tomek   (Cornell University)
Kay Torshen   (Torshen Financial, Inc.)
Jorge Urrutia   (Loyola University Chicago)
Robert Whaley   (Duke University)

The next important group I wish to thank are the authors of the papers selected. They are the ones who produced these important contributions which have shaped the field. Without these pieces of valuable scholarship there would be no need for our three volumes.

Finally, I conclude by thanking my research assistants Larry Yu and Alice Djung for their detailed and careful work, my colleagues at Loyola's Business School for their support, my family for their great encouragement and you, the reader for your interest in this work.

References

Akgiray, V. and Booth, G. (1988), 'The Stable Law Model of Stock Returns', *Journal of Business & Economic Statistics*, **6**, 51–7.

Bachelier, L. (1900), 'Théorie de la Spéculation', *Annales de l'Ecole Normale Superieure*, Ser. 3, **XVII**, 21–86.

Bigman, D., Goldfarb, D. and Schechtman, E. (1983), 'Futures Market Efficiency and the Time Content of the Information Sets', *Journal of Futures Markets*, **3**, 321–34.

Bird, P.J.W.N. (1985), 'Dependency and Efficiency in the London Terminal Markets', *Journal of Futures Markets*, **5**, 433–46.

Black, F. (1976), 'The Pricing of Commodity Contracts', *Journal of Financial Economics*, **3**, 167–79.

Brennan, L. (1958), 'The Supply of Storage', *American Economic Review*, **48**, 50–72.

Brock, W., Hsieh, D. and LeBaron, B. (1991), *Nonlinear Dynamics, Chaos and Instability: Statistical Theory and Economic Evidence*, Cambridge, Massachusetts: The MIT Press.

Brock, W. and Malliaris, A.G. (1989), *Differential Equations, Stability and Chaos in Dynamic Economics*, Advanced Textbooks in Economics, Amsterdam: North-Holland Publishing Company.

Canarella, G. and Pollard, S.K. (1985), 'Efficiency of Commodity Futures: A Vector Autoregression Analysis', *Journal of Futures Markets*, **5**, 57–76.

Chance, D.M. (1985), 'A Semi-Strong Form Test of the Efficiency of Treasury Bond Futures Market', *Journal of Futures Markets*, **5**, 385–405.

Chowdhury, A.R. (1991), 'Futures Market Efficiency: Evidence from Cointegration Tests', *Journal of Futures Markets*, **11**, 577–89.

Cole, C.S., Impson, M. and Reichenstein, W. (1991), 'Do Treasury Bill Futures Rates Satisfy Rational Expectation Properties?', *Journal of Futures Markets*, **11**, 591–601.

Cootner, P.H. (1960), 'Returns to Speculators: Telser vs. Keynes', *Journal of Political Economy*, **68**, 396–404.

Cornew, R., Town, D. and Crowson, L. (1984), 'Stable Distribution, Futures Prices, and the Measurement of Trading Performance', *Journal of Futures Markets*, **4**, 531–57.

Decoster, G.P., Labys, W.C. and Mitchell, D.W. (1992), 'Evidence of Chaos in Commodity Futures Prices', *Journal of Futures Markets*, **12**, 291–305.

Devaney, R. (1986), *An Introduction to Chaotic Dynamical Systems*, Menlo Park, California: Benjamin/Cummings Publishing.

Dusak, K. (1973), 'Futures Trading and Investor Returns: An Investigation of Commodity Market Risk Premiums', *Journal of Political Economy*, **81**, 1387–405.

Elam, E. and Dixon, B.L. (1988), 'Examining the Validity of a Test of Futures Market Efficiency', *Journal of Futures Markets*, **8**, 365–72.

Fama, E.F. (1970), 'Efficient Capital Markets: Review of Theory and Empirical Work', *Journal of Finance*, **25**, 383–417.

Fama, E.F. (1991), 'Efficient Capital Markets: II', *Journal of Finance*, **70**, 1575–617.

Fama, E.F. and Roll, R. (1968), 'Some Properties of Symmetric Stable Distributions', *Journal of The American Statistical Association*, **63**, 817–36.

Fama, E.F. and Roll, R. (1971), 'Parameter Estimates for Symmetric Stable Distributions', *Journal of The American Statistical Association*, **66**, 331–8.

Fama, E.F. and French, K.R. (1988), 'Business Cycles and the Behavior of Metals Prices', *Journal of Finance*, **43**, 1075–93.
Glassman, D. (1987), 'The Efficiency of Foreign Exchange Futures Markets in Turbulent and Non-Turbulent Periods', *Journal of Futures Markets*, **7**, 245–67.
Grassberger, P. and Procaccia, I. (1983), 'Measuring the Strangeness of Strange Attractors', *Physics*, **9-D**, 189–208.
Gribbin, D.W., Harris, R.W. and Lau, H.S. (1992), 'Futures Prices Are Not Stable-Paretian Distributed', *Journal of Futures Markets*, **12**, 475–87.
Gross, M. (1988), 'A Semi-Strong Test of the Efficiency of the Aluminum and Copper Markets at the LME', *Journal of Futures Markets*, **8**, 67–77.
Grossman, S.J. and Stiglitz, J.E. (1980), 'On the Impossibility of Informationally Efficient Markets', *American Economic Review*, **70**, 393–408.
Guckenheimer, J. and Holmes, P. (1983), *Non linear Oscillations, Dynamical Systems and Bifurcations of Vector Fields*, New York: Springer-Verlag.
Harpaz, G., Krull, S. and Yagil, J. (1990), 'The Efficiency of the U.S. Dollar Index Futures Market', *Journal of Futures Markets*, **10**, 469–79.
Helms, B.P. and Martell, T.F. (1985), 'An Examination of the Distribution of Futures Price Changes', *Journal of Futures Markets*, **5**, 259–72.
Hudson, M., Leuthold, R. and Sarassoro, G. (1987), 'Commodity Futures Prices Changes: Recent Evidence for Wheat, Soybeans, and Live Cattle', *Journal of Futures Markets*, **7**, 287–301.
Johnson, R.L., Zulauf, C.R., Irwin, S.H. and Gerlow, M.E. (1991), 'The Soybean Complex Spread: An Examination of Market Efficiency From the Viewpoint of a Production Process', *Journal of Futures Markets*, **11**, 25–37.
Kaldor, N. (1939), 'Speculation and Economic Stability', *Review of Economic Studies*, **7**, 1–27.
Klemkosky, R.C. and Lasser, D.J. (1985), 'An Efficiency Analysis of the T-Bond Futures Market', *Journal of Futures Markets*, **5**, 607–20.
Lai, K.S. and Lai, M. (1991), 'A Cointegration Test for Market Efficiency', *Journal of Futures Markets*, **11**, 567–75.
Maberly, E.D. (1985), 'Testing Futures Market Efficiency: A Restatement', *Journal of Futures Markets*, **5**, 425–32.
MacDonald, S.S. and Hein, S.E. (1993), 'An Empirical Evaluation of Treasury Bill Futures Market Efficiency: Evidence From Forecast Efficiency Tests', *Journal of Futures Markets*, **13**, 199–211.
Ogden, J.P. and Tucker, A. (1987), 'Empirical Tests of the Efficiency of the Currency Futures Options Market', *Journal of Futures Markets*, **7**, 695–703.
Osborne, M.F.M. (1959), 'Brownian Motion in the Stock Market', *Operations Research*, **7**, 145–73.
Samuelson, P. (1965), 'Proof that Property Anticipated Prices Fluctuate Randomly', *Industrial Management Review*, **6**, 41–9.
Saunders, E.M. and Mahajan, A. (1988), 'An Empirical Examination of Composite Stock Index Futures Pricing', *Journal of Futures Markets*, **8**, 210–28.
So, J. (1987), 'The Sub-Gaussian Distribution of Currency Futures: Stable Paretian or Non-stationary?', *Review of Economics and Statistics*, **69**, 100–107.
Stevenson, R.A. and Bear, R.M. (1970), 'Commodity Futures: Trends or Random Walks?', *Journal of Finance*, **25**, 65–81.
Telser, L.G. (1958), 'Futures Trading and the Storage of Cotton and Wheat', *Journal of Political Economy*, **66**, 233–55.
Working, H. (1934), 'A Random-Difference Series for Use in the Analysis for Time Series', *Journal of The American Statistical Association*, **29**, 11–24.
Working, H. (1948), 'Theory of the Inverse Carrying Charge in Futures Markets', *Journal of Farm Economics*, **30**, 1–28.
Working, H. (1958), 'A Theory of Anticipatory Prices', *American Economic Review*, **48**, 188–99.

Part I
Pricing

Part 1
Pricing

[1]

FUTURES MARKETS, SUPPLY RESPONSE, AND PRICE STABILITY*

ANNE E. PECK

The forward-pricing mechanism in an annual context, 408.—Price behavior under the adaptive expectations assumption, 412.—Price behavior with the futures market included, 414.—Price behavior for a nonstorable commodity with a futures market, 419.—Conclusions and implications, 422.

Models of the determination of agricultural prices have become increasingly complex. Each successive model attempted to correct the deficiencies of the previous formulation, noting either contradictions between observed and predicted price behavior or seeming irrationalities in the assumptions themselves. The progression of models includes the classic cobweb model, the adaptive expectations formulation, the rational expectations approach, and finally the harmonic motion model.[1] The element of commonality among these models is their assumption that the producer, for lack of an alternative, must make his basic production decision from an evaluation of past price behavior.

The present paper begins from the observation that an alternative does exist. Futures markets have long played an important role in the determination of prices for many agricultural commodities. Interest in these markets, however, has tended to focus upon their contributions in facilitating storage decisions. This focus no doubt reflects the historical importance of futures markets for the grains, where large inventories are continuously carried. The relatively recent proliferation of futures trading in a variety of commodities, both agricultural and nonagricultural, has renewed interest in the forward-pricing role also performed by these markets.[2] Futures markets, with

---

*Journal Paper No. 6144, Purdue Agricultural Experiment Station. Research reported in the paper was carried out under Project 1806 of the Purdue Agricultural Experiment Station. Much of the original analysis presented here was done while the author was a graduate student at the Food Research Institute, Stanford University.

1. The adaptive expectations and cobweb models are compared in M. Nerlove, "Adaptive Expectations and Cobweb Phenomena," this *Journal*, LXXII (May 1958), 227–40. Larson compares the cobweb model with a harmonic model in "The Quiddity of the Cobweb Theorem," *Food Research Institute Studies*, VII (1967), 165–75. Finally, the rational expectations approach is described in J. F. Muth, "Rational Expectations and the Theory of Price Movements," *Econometrica*, XXIX (July 1961), 315–35.

2. W. G. Tomek and R. W. Gray ("Temporal Relationships Among Prices on Commodity Futures Markets: Their Allocative and Stabilizing Roles," *American Journal of Agricultural Economics*, LII (Aug. 1970), 372–80; and R. W. Gray and W. G. Tomek, "Temporal Relationships Among Futures Prices: Reply," *American Journal of Agricultural Economics*, LIII (May 1971), 362–66) contrasted the performance of the Maine potato futures market with that of corn and soybean futures markets. More recently, T. A. Kofi ("A Framework for Comparing the Efficiency of Futures Markets,"

© 1976 by the President and Fellows of Harvard College. Published by John Wiley & Sons, Inc.

simultaneous trading in successive maturities, provide forward prices that could be used by a producer in formulating his production decisions.

One contract, the first in the new crop year, is of particular concern. Generally, this new crop future is traded well in advance of the time that the production decision must be made. In the corn market, for instance, the first new crop future is the December contract, and its trading typically begins ten to twelve months earlier. In recent years there has been a tendency for trading to begin even earlier. These lead times mean that a new crop price is available to corn producers well before the actual planting occurs in late April and May. Unlike a price forecast or expectation, this is a forward price that is a market price. Neglecting individual delivery problems, the producer could sell his expected output at that price.[3]

The intent of this paper is to examine the effects this forward price might have on the stability of commodity prices. The first section develops the framework whereby the futures mechanism can be included in the more traditional commodity models. The focus is on long-run stability; the potential effects of futures markets on intrayear price stability are not considered. The analysis then proceeds to consider the effects of this system on long-run price stability. The next section considers an adaptation of the model, which reflects the characteristics of a nonstorable commodity. Finally, implications of this analysis are considered.

THE FORWARD-PRICING MECHANISM IN AN ANNUAL CONTEXT

In order to provide comparisons of expected price behavior among commodity markets with and without a futures market, a model must be conceived that captures the futures market mechanism in an annual framework. Basically, the desire is to replace the behavioral assumptions of the more traditional models, which describe

---

American Journal of Agricultural Economics, LV (Nov. 1973), 854–94) has provided evidence for a variety of commodities. R. L. Leuthold ("The Price Performance on the Futures Market of a Nonstorable Commodity: Live Beef Cattle," *American Journal of Agricultural Economics*, LVI (May 1974), 271–79) has compared the forecasting performance of cash and futures prices for live cattle.

3. Calculating the expected output is no small matter. Further, if the decisions are cast as a portfolio problem, it is likely that there will be high correlation between the output and price-level forecasting errors. See, for instance, R. McKinnon's analysis, "Futures Markets, Buffer Stocks, and Income Stability for Primary Producers," *Journal of Political Economy*, LXXV (Dec. 1967), 844–61. This does not, however, change the basic difference noted here between a price forecast and a market-determined, forward price.

FUTURES, SUPPLY, AND PRICE STABILITY

how price expectations are formed, with a relationship describing the formation of a futures price. The futures contract of particular concern is the one that represents the new crop maturity. If this relationship can be formalized, then the comparisons are straightforward. Previous analyses that have captured the simultaneities of cash and futures price determination have been generally short-run in nature.[4] For any particular commodity a number of futures contracts are traded simultaneously, calling for deliveries at two- or three-month intervals. Any one contract is traded for about a year. Further, analyses of futures markets focus naturally on intertemporal price relationships, emphasizing the important role these markets perform in allocating inventories within a crop year. Changing this focus, to investigate the interyear effects of futures trading, is not intended to belie the importance of these analyses. The approach used here draws heavily from previous work, especially the theoretical analyses, in attempting to model the complete system.

Futures prices are determined directly by hedger and speculator demand for and supply of futures contracts. Hedgers are individuals (firms) that deal with the actual commodity, as well as with future contracts. Speculators, on the other hand, have no direct connection to the cash commodity; the sole source of their profits is in futures price changes. Both hedgers and speculators may be either long or short in the futures market. Market equilibrium, represented in the futures price, is the balance of hedger and speculator demand. Recent applications of the portfolio theory to these demands provide a way to formalize this situation.[5]

Consider a contract with delivery in month m. Let i represent the current month, $m-i$ months prior to expiration. Define H_i^m as net hedging in month i in the contract maturing in month m and SP_i^m as

---

[4]. The relationship among futures prices of different maturities was first elucidated by H. Working, "A Theory of Anticipatory Prices," *American Economic Review*, XLVIII (May 1958), 188–99; and "The Theory of the Price of Storage," *American Economic Review*, XXXIX (Dec. 1949). Theoretical models of the simultaneous determination of cash and futures prices include those of L. L. Johnson, "The Theory of Hedging and Speculation in Commodity Futures," *Review of Economic Studies*, XXVI–XXVII (1958–60), 139–151; J. L. Stein "The Simultaneous Determination of Spot and Futures Prices," *American Economic Review*, LI (Dec. 1961), 1012–25; and D. J. S. Rutledge, "Hedgers' Demand for Futures Contracts: A Theoretical Framework with Applications to the United States Soybean Complex," *Food Research Institute Studies*, XI (1972), 237–56. F. L. Vannerson, ("An Econometric Analysis of the Postwar U.S. Wheat Market," Ph.D. thesis, Princeton Universtity, 1969); (and to a certain extent F. H. Weymar (*The Dynamics of the World Cocoa Market;* Cambridge, Massachusetts: Massachusetts Institute of Technology Press, 1968) have attempted to include these simultaneities in empirical models.

[5]. A more detailed discussion of the various motivations leading to a hedged position is available in Rutledge, *op. cit.* The application of the portfolio theory to this problem is taken largely from his work.

net speculation in contract m in month i. Using net positions here merely simplifies the analysis; more generally, one would probably want to consider long and short hedging and speculation separately. Applying the portfolio theory to individual hedger and speculator demands and aggregating results in the following equations:

$$H_i^m = \psi_1(\Delta^* P_i; \Delta^* B_i; V_i)$$

$$SP_i^m = \psi_2(\Delta^* P_i^m; v_i)$$

$$H_i^m = SP_i^m,$$

where $\Delta^* P_i$, $\Delta^* B_i$, and $\Delta^* P_i^m$ are expected changes in the cash, the basis, and the futures prices, respectively; V_i and v_i are the appropriate variance-covariance matrices for hedgers' and speculators' portfolios.

Hedgers' demand for futures contracts depends upon expectations about both the cash price and the difference between futures and cash prices, the basis. This duality recognizes their direct connection to the cash market. Speculators, on the other hand, must depend only on their futures positions for their profits. Hence, only expected futures price changes enter this demand equation. In the remainder of this paper the variance-covariance terms of these relationships will be ignored. By assumption, these are exogenous to the price formation process, being subjective probability distributions. In an empirical application of this approach, they would serve to help identify statistically these relationships; they would likely add nothing to the dynamics of the complete system.

This three-equation system cannot be viewed in isolation. In the complete system, the price variables as well as their expectations must be viewed as endogenously determined. That is, these relationships are only a part of a more general cash and futures market system. The general model would include equations specifying demand for direct consumption or export of the cash commodity, demand for storage of the commodity, perhaps a supply relationship, and a market-clearing quantity relationship. Additionally, the basic price identity is needed, which states that the basis is the futures minus the cash price. However, the concern here is in an annual model; the analysis proceeds to consider how the above formulation of hedger and speculator behavior may be recast into an annual model.

The third equation above, stating that net hedging in a contract must equal net speculation in that contract, is a clearing assumption for the futures market. It holds by definition, since an individual cannot enter the market either long or short unless someone else is

FUTURES, SUPPLY, AND PRICE STABILITY

willing to take the offsetting position. Substituting the specified hedger and speculator demand equations into this relationship, we may view the set of equations as implicitly determining the futures price:

$$P_i^m = \psi(\Delta^* P_i; {^*P_i^m}; \Delta^* B_i^m).$$

The current price of the commodity for delivery in month m (P_i^m) is a function of expected cash and basis price changes and the expected futures price. The interest in this paper centers on price relationships between crop years. Therefore, m, the delivery month, is explicitly the first new crop contract. In the corn market, m would be December; in the soybean market, m would be November. The current month (i), on the other hand, must be before planting occurs for that harvest. It must be in the prior crop year. Thus, translating this relationship to an annual model, we see that the current period (i) is the current crop year, while m is the next crop year.

To specify the nature of the expectation variables in the preceding equation, cash and futures prices are assumed to be equal in the delivery period. This implies first that the expected values of the cash and futures prices are equal. Therefore, both can be seen to be functions of the expected supply in the new crop year relative to expected demand. Second, if the cash and the futures price are equal in the delivery period, then the expected basis change is simply the current basis.[6] The current basis is primarily a function of the size of the inventory to be carried between years. Admittedly, other expectational variables are likely to be important in both these relationships; not all the participants in the futures market will use these variables. The argument here, however, is that the aggregate of their expectations may be represented by these variables. Additionally, even though other exogenous variables may be important, they will not affect the internal dynamics of the complete system. The resulting implicit equation describing the determination of the new crop futures price is

$$P_t^{t+1} = \Phi(I_t, S_{t+1}, D_{t+1}),$$

where P_t^{t+1} is the new crop futures price quoted in the current crop year, I_t is the carryout of the current crop year, S_{t+1} is the supply

---

6. That is, with equal cash and futures prices at delivery, the basis is zero. Therefore the basis change, the current basis minus the expected basis, is the current basis. H. Working ("Hedging Reconsidered," *Journal of Farm Economics*, XXXV (Nov. 1953), 544–61) presents some empirical evidence on the reliability of this relationship.

expected in the new crop year, and D_{t+1} is the expected demand for that new crop.

This final equation represents the determination of the new crop futures price, translated into an annual framework. It was derived in a consistent fashion from consideration of hedger and speculator demand for futures contracts and the variables that determine those demands. It remains, however, only a representation of the processes involved. With this derivation the long-run effects of forward-oriented production responses can be considered.

Price Behavior Under the Adaptive Expectations Assumption

In the absence of a futures market, the producer has no alternative but to form an expected price for the crop he is about to plant. Nerlove's model of the adaptive expectations process is assumed to represent this process.[7] The model used there did not contain inventories, and hence, total production in any year was consumed in that year. To provide comparisons with a futures model, the behavior of the Nerlove model must be derived when inventories are present.

Assuming linear relationships among the variables and defining all variables in deviation form, we see that the basic model will contain five equations:

$$D_t = \alpha_1 P_t \quad \text{(Demand)}$$

$$S_t = \beta_1 P^*_{t-1} \quad \text{(Supply)}$$

$$P^*_t - P_t = \gamma_1 I_t \quad \text{(Supply of storage)}$$

$$I_t = I_{t-1} + S_t - D_t \quad \text{(Market-clearing)}$$

$$P^*_t - P^*_{t-1} = \beta(P_t - P^*_{t-1}) \quad \text{(Adaptive expectations),}$$

where D_t is consumption, S_t is supply, I_t is carryout, and P_t is price, all in year t. P^*_t is the price expected to exist in year $t+1$, the expectation being held in year t. The demand and supply equations are familiar. The third equation, the supply of storage equation, states that the size of the carryout determines the expected price difference between crop years. The larger the carryout, the greater the expected

---

7. Nerlove, *op. cit.* As noted in the introduction, several alternative hypotheses are possible. The adaptive expectations model is taken to be the most general, however. The pure cobweb is a special case, the rational expectation approach results in a similar price equation, and the harmonic motion model collapses to a cobweb model when an annual crop is considered.

price change. This relationship is generally assumed to be a nonlinear one. However, Working has shown that it can be closely approximated by two line segments, a positively sloped segment over relatively small levels of carryout and a horizontal segment at full carrying charges.[8] The derivations here assume that carryover will remain in the range where the positively sloped segment of the supply of storage curve applies. The fourth equation is the appropriate market-clearing identity. Finally, the adaptive expectation assumption describes how price expectations are formed.

In the absence of a futures market, stockholders and producers have no alternative but to form their expectations from past price behavior. Solving this system of five equations for price gives a second-order, homogeneous difference equation:

$$P_t = \left[\frac{\gamma_1\beta(\beta_1 - \alpha_1) - (1-\beta)}{\alpha_1\gamma_1 - (1-\beta)} + 1\right] P_{t-1} + \left[\frac{1-\beta}{\alpha_1\gamma_1 - (1-\beta)}\right] P_{t-2}.$$

The stability of the price series described by this relationship depends upon the roots of the appropriate characteristic equation.[9] If the roots are complex, then the general solution of this equation is

$$P_t = \left[\frac{-(1-\beta)}{\alpha_1\gamma_1 - (1-\beta)}\right]^t (A_1 \cos\theta t + A_2 \sin\theta t),$$

where A_1 and A_2 are constants that depend upon unspecified initial conditions and θ is a function of the various parameters. With a negatively sloped demand curve ($\alpha_1 < 0$) and a positively sloped supply of storage curve ($\gamma_1 > 0$), the implied price fluctuations would always converge.

Thus, the important condition on the parameters is whether or not they provide complex roots to the characteristic equation.[10] Because of the large number of parameters involved, the formal condition does not have any intuitive appeal. However, by assigning arbitrary, reasonable values to some of the parameters, values of the basic supply and demand parameters, which provide stability, can be considered. From Nerlove's work, a reasonable value of β would be 0.5. From Working's approximation of the supply of storage curve,

---

8. Working, op. cit. (1953).
9. R. G. D. Allen (*Mathematical Economics*, Second Edition; London: MacMillan and Co., Ltd., 1959) provides a concise discussion of the analytics of difference equations.
10. The roots of the characteristic equation will be complex if the following condition holds:

$$[[\gamma_1\beta(\beta_1 - \alpha_1) - 2(1-\beta) + \alpha_1\gamma_1]^2 + 4(1-\beta)(\alpha_1\gamma_1 - (1-\beta))] < 0.$$

In this case, the solution equation in the text is appropriate.

a reasonable value of γ_1 would be 0.8.[11] Figure I shows the combinations of values of the supply and demand parameters that provide a convergent, stable price series with these assumed values. It also reveals changes in this set as the preassigned parameters are varied. The set appears relatively sensitive to the value of β that is used, and insensitive to the choice of the parameter γ_1.

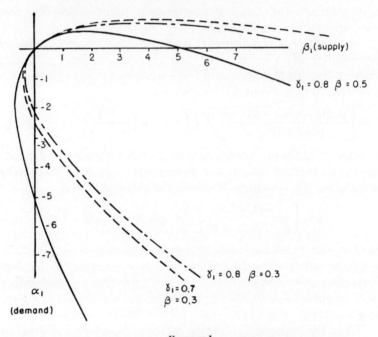

FIGURE I
Convex sets of demand and supply parameters for which long-run price fluctuations are stable, using Nerlove's adaptive expectations model with an inventory adjustment mechanism.

Price Behavior with the Futures Market Included

In the presence of an active futures market, stockholders are generally assumed to base their inventory decisions upon the cash price relative to the futures price. Thus, the first case considered here uses the futures price in the supply of storage relationship, while assuming that producers continue to formulate their expectations in

11. Nerlove, op. cit., p. 237; and Working, op. cit. (1953), p. 556. Note that with a linear model the units of measurement are important. Here, inventories, were measured in ten million bushel units and prices are in cents.

the Nerlovian fashion. A sixth equation is required, that representing the determination of the futures price. Specifically,

$$P_t^{t+1} = \delta_1 I_t + \delta_2 S_{t+1} \text{ (futures price)},$$

where P_t^{t+1} is the price of the futures contract in period t that calls for delivery in period $t + 1$.[12] Additionally, the supply of storage equation must be changed to indicate that the expected price there is now the new crop futures price (P_t^{t+1}). The adaptive expectations assumption is still needed, since producers are not using the futures price.

Solving this system of six equations for price gives

$$P_t = \left[\frac{\beta(\gamma_1 - \delta_1)(\beta_1 - \alpha_1) - (1 - \beta)}{\alpha_1(\gamma_1 - \delta_1) - (1 - \delta_2\beta_1\beta)} + 1 \right] P_{t-1}$$

$$+ \left[\frac{1 - \beta}{\alpha_1(\gamma_1 - \delta_1) - (1 - \delta_2\beta_1\beta)} \right] P_{t-2}.$$

Assuming that the roots of its characteristics equation are complex, we see that the solution to this price equation is[13]

$$P_t = \left[\frac{-(1 - \beta)}{\alpha_1(\gamma_1 - \delta_1) - (1 - \delta_2\beta_1\beta)} \right]^t (A_1 \cos \theta t + A_2 \sin \theta t),$$

where again A_1 and A_2 are constants that depend upon the unspecified initial conditions and θ is a function of all the parameters. Comparison of this equation describing price behavior with that found earlier reveals that these price cycles are more stable. All else equal, they will dampen more rapidly to zero as long as δ_1 and δ_2, the parameters of the futures price equation, are negative.

Thus, the presence of a futures market with rather general assumptions about the parameters of the futures price equation, has been shown to stabilize prices in the long run. A question remains as to whether the set of supply and demand parameters, which guarantee stable fluctuations, has been increased or reduced. That is, it may be possible to find demand and supply slopes that provide for stable solutions in the first case but that create an unstable price in this situation. All that has been shown so far is that if a pair of α_1 and β_1

---

12. Note that the expected consumption variable has been omitted. Its exclusion here does not materially change the comparative results, and it does simplify the calculations. An equivalent assumption is that expected consumption always equals its long-run average (i.e., the deviation from the mean value is zero).

13. The roots are complex if the following condition holds:

$$[[\beta(\gamma_1 - \delta_1)(\beta_1 - \alpha_1) - (1 - \beta) + \alpha_1(\gamma_1 - \delta_1) - (1 - \delta_2\beta_1\beta)]^2$$
$$+ 4(1 - \beta)(\alpha_1(\gamma_1 - \delta_1) - (1 - \delta_2\beta_1\beta))] < 0.$$

parameters are common to both solution sets, then prices will be more stable in the latter case. However, a comparison of the required stable solution sets will be put off until the final case has been considered. Then, all three may be considered together.

The situation remaining to be considered is the one that was originally set as the goal. What can be said about long-run price stability if producers are assumed to base their production decisions on the new crop futures price? The basic model is once again five equations. The Nerlovian adaptive expectations equation is dropped. The supply relationship must be altered; the expected price (P_{t-1}^*) is now the price of the futures contract maturing in the current period as quoted in the previous year (P_{t-1}^t). Stockholders continue to base their inventory decision on the difference between the cash and the futures price.

Solving this system of five equations for price gives the following first-order difference equation:

$$P_t = -\left[\frac{1 - \delta_2\beta_1 + \delta_1\beta_1}{\alpha_1(\gamma_1(1 - \delta_2\beta_1) - \delta_1) - (1 - \delta_2\beta_1)}\right] P_{t-1}.$$

The solution of this difference equation is simply

$$P_t = A_1 \left[\frac{1 - \delta_2\beta_1 + \delta_1\beta_1}{\alpha_1(\gamma_1(1 - \delta_2\beta_1) - \delta_1)(1 - \delta_2\beta_1)}\right]^t.$$

The price fluctuations described by this relationship are stable as long as the term in the brackets is less than one in absolute value. Unfortunately, direct comparison with the two previous results is impossible.

However, the range of supply and demand slopes that provide for stable solutions can be considered. Earlier, it was argued that reasonable values for the adaptive expectations parameter β and the supply of storage parameter γ_1 were 0.5 and 0.8, respectively. If the futures price equation coefficients, δ_1 and δ_2, can be specified, the range of α_1 and β_1 can be considered. The two coefficients, δ_1 and δ_2, describe the reaction of the futures price to changes in the carryout and in the new crop supplies. Most likely they are negative. Further, they are likely to be approximately equal as there is no a priori reason to expect changes in the carryout to have a different effect on price than changes in production. Figures II, III, and IV compare the stable ranges of the supply and demand parameters of the different models for three different values of the δ_1 and δ_2 coefficients.

In all three figures the solid line depicts the Nerlovian model, the first case considered here. It is the same in all three figures, since β

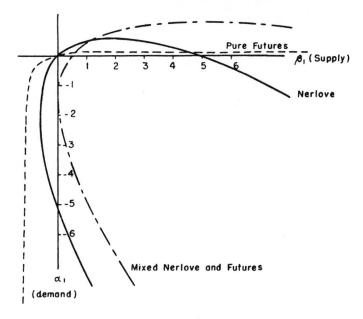

FIGURE II
Convex sets of supply and demand parameters for which long-run prices will be stable when $\gamma_1 = 0.8$, $\beta = 0.5$, and $\delta_1 = \delta_2 = -0.1$.

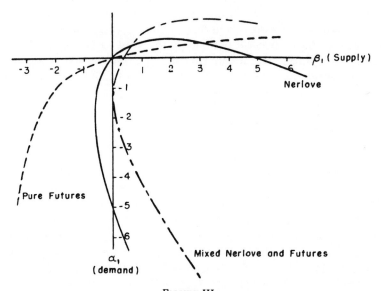

FIGURE III
Convex sets of supply and demand parameters for which long-run prices will be stable when $\gamma_1 = 0.8$, $\beta = 0.5$, and $\delta_1 = \delta_2 = -0.3$.

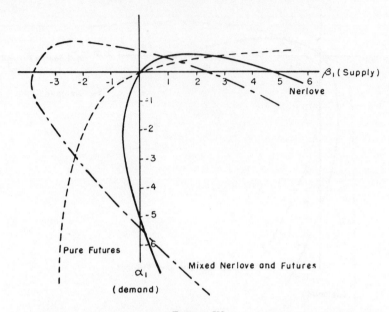

FIGURE IV
Convex sets of supply and demand parameters for which long-run prices will be stable when $\gamma_1 = 0.8$, $\beta = 0.5$, and $\delta_1 = \delta_2 = -0.5$.

and δ_1 are fixed. With no futures price equation in that model, changes in the two parameters, δ_1 and δ_2, have no effect on that set of stable solutions. The convex set defined by the solid curve is the set of demand and supply parameters that provide the complex roots to the fundamental, second-order difference equation. Thus, long-run price behavior is described by the relationship noted earlier where the fluctuations were shown to be convergent.

The broken line, long and short dashes, defines the set of demand and supply parameters that provide stability given the mixed, adaptive expectations and futures market model (the second case). In discussing this solution, an increase in stability was noted relative to the first model. For values of the demand and supply parameters that were contained in both solution sets, the price fluctuations described in the second model were found to converge more rapidly. Introducing a futures equation and allowing inventory decisions to be guided by this price increased long-run price stability. Note, however, that the set of stable supply and demand parameters required in this case does not include all the parameters of the simple adaptive expectations model. Thus, in this sense, price stability has not been increased.

FUTURES, SUPPLY, AND PRICE STABILITY

The solution set for this second model appears to be moderately sensitive to the selected values of the coefficients for the futures price equation. Comparing the three figures, we see that this set appears to change the most. However, it generally includes a large portion of the set of negative demand and positive supply coefficients. Further, it does contain a large portion of the set of coefficients found to produce stability in the first model. If the demand and supply parameters created stable price fluctuations in the absence of a futures market, introducing the futures market will most likely dampen these fluctuations.

The third situation developed above considered the implications of producer use of the futures price in their production decision. In the three figures here the convex set described by the dashed line represents the values of the supply and demand parameters that produce stability under this assumption. For all three specifications of the futures equation coefficients, all negative demand and positive supply coefficients provide stable solutions. In this sense, then, the presence of the futures market has increased stability relative to the alternatives considered here. This result is hardly surprising, but it is reassuring. With producers and stockholders responding to an endogenously determined forward price, one would expect that price would be more stable in the long-run sense. The forward price, determined in the market, provides instantaneous feedback to these decision makers about the effects of their decisions.

Interestingly, these results do not depend upon active producer participation in the futures market. They need not be active hedgers or speculators. All that is required is their use of the price generated in the futures market in their production decisions, and the realization by other market participants that this price is used in this fashion. Producer use of this price will be reflected in the expectations variables of the actual participants. It should be noted that it would be possible to specify speculator or hedger behavior that would change these results. Coefficients of the futures price equation, δ_1 and δ_2, could be found such that reasonable values of the demand and supply slopes produce divergent price fluctuations. These values are not likely in practice, however, because of the close connections between the cash and the futures prices.

PRICE BEHAVIOR FOR A NONSTORABLE COMMODITY WITH A FUTURES MARKET

Thus far, the analysis has focused entirely upon alternative models of a commodity that is continuously inventoried. In part, this reflects the importance of these commodities in the historical development of futures trading. It also reflects, however, the state of our understanding of price relationships in these markets. Nearly all the received theory of futures markets and futures price behavior deals with these kinds of markets. Active futures trading in commodities with different characteristics is a relatively recent phenomenon. Live cattle and live hogs, while not storable in their finished form, are storable in the feedlot, to a certain extent. Fresh eggs are not storable; yet, production inventories exist in the laying flocks. Potatoes are storable for a period after harvest, but are not storable between crop years. The spectrum of storability characteristics of the commodities now traded in futures markets is nearly continuous.

The relative importance of the inventory-allocation and the forward-pricing role performed by futures markets is likely to be different as these characteristics change. In order to provide some understanding of potential effects of futures trading for some of these commodities, an adaptation of the preceding model is developed below to consider a nonstorable commodity. A completely nonstorable commodity probably represents the opposite end of the spectrum from the inventoried ones. Investigation of the properties of a model with these characteristics should provide insight into the price behavior of commodities with characteristics between the extremes considered here.

Again, the point of reference is Nerlove's adaptive expectations model, in this case without inventories. The equilibrium price path is well-known and described by[14]

$$P_t = A_1 \left[\frac{\beta(\beta_1 - \alpha_1)}{\alpha_1} + 1 \right]^t.$$

To consider the effect of futures trading, a representative futures price equation must be derived and appended to the model implicit in the above equation. Following the development of an earlier section, we see that this requires formulating hedger and speculator demand functions for futures contracts. In the absence of stocks to be carried between periods, arbitrage between cash and futures prices cannot exist in the traditional sense. Further, assuming that cash and futures prices converge in the delivery month (here, the new-crop year), we see that the expected cash and futures prices are equal. Thus, both hedger and speculator demands are functions of futures price expectations only. Again, the variance-covariance matrix, required in

---

14. Nerlove, *op. cit*. The model is four equations: demand; supply; market clearing; and the adaptive expectations assumption.

FUTURES, SUPPLY, AND PRICE STABILITY

the formal portfolio model, is ignored in these formulations because of its dependence on exogenous or predetermined variables. Following the arguments of the first section, we see that this leads to the following equation that explicitly determines the current year's quote of the new crop future for a commodity without continuously held inventories:

$$P_t^{t+1} = \delta_1 S_{t+1}.$$

The current year's futures price for the commodity deliverable in the next year is a function of the size of the new-crop harvest. Linearity has been assumed, variables are in deviation form, and the expected consumption variable has been omitted in this equation, all for computational convenience.

The complete model is four equations: a demand equation; a supply equation specifying that producers use the new crop futures price in their production decisions; the market-clearing identity; and, the above futures price equation that replaces the adaptive expectations assumption. Solving this system of four equations for price gives the following interesting result:

$$P_t = 0.$$

Since variables are in deviation form, the current price is the long-run average price. Assuming the producers use the new crop futures price in their production decision, absolute price stability results. Additionally, all the other variables in the system are at their long-run equilibrium values.

Obviously, the result here is extreme. All producers must be using the futures price. Changes due to random yield fluctuations or systematic shifts in either the demand or the supply equation have been ignored. Thus, absolute stability is improbable in practice. However, recent evidence from the Maine potato market suggests that the implications derived here are substantially correct.[15] The preplanting quote of the new crop future (here, P_t^{t+1}) was found to be virtually constant from year to year at the long-run equilibrium price. A cobweb-type pattern did remain, however, in the actual harvest quantities and prices. This could reflect only partial use of the futures price by producers, with some still basing their price expectations on past prices. Interestingly, however, estimated supply response relationships for Maine producers suggested that Maine production had in fact stabilized relative to the prefutures market period. Cobweb-type

---

15. See R. W. Gray, "The Futures Market for Maine Potatoes: An Appraisal," *Food Research Institute Studies*, XI (1972), 313–41; and, Tomek and Gray, *op. cit.*

patterns remained for producing groups from other regions, which, through competition, imply cobweb-type prices for Maine potatoes.

Conclusions and Implications

The price effects determined above emphasize the dual role that a futures market can perform. In facilitating the storage decision, the market dampened price fluctuations. Producer use of the futures price in production decisions created convergent fluctuations for virtually any reasonable combination of demand and supply parameters. This was the effect of a forward-pricing role, providing an immediate feedback to producers about the implications of their decisions. When only the forward-pricing role was of interest because there were no inventories, cash price stabilization was complete.

Recently, interest has again emerged in questions of price stability in the "free" market setting and of the benefits of some kind of government storage scheme. The results presented here should not be interpreted as obviating the need for studies of these questions. That prices are more stable with futures trading than without that trading, at least in the long run, does not say that they are sufficiently stable enough from society's point of view, given the nature of recent "exogenous" shocks. It does suggest, however, that changes must be made in traditional approaches to evaluating this problem. Models must include the presence of substantial, between-year inventories that are carried even in the absence of government controls. These stocks fluctuate from year to year; their determination must be endogenous in these models. Further, some consideration must be given to behavior in the presence of futures trading. Futures markets exist for most of the major agricultural commodities; to ignore their presence in analyzing these markets is to present a partial analysis, at best.

The analysis above also raises interesting questions as to actual producer use of futures markets and prices in their decision processes. The analysis did not depend upon producers actually having participated in futures markets, as, for instance, hedgers. All that was required was that the actual participants knew what criteria producers were using. Do producers use futures prices (or the local market equivalent) in their production decisions? An analysis of the appropriate behavioral assumption is clearly needed.

Finally, the derived effects of futures trading were seen to depend upon the underlying characteristics of the commodity being considered. Recent empirical analyses of the forward-pricing performance of different futures markets emphasize these differences. Pricing performance should not be isolated from commodity characteristics; all markets are not expected to perform in the same manner. The relative importance of storage will measurably affect the kind of results that can be expected.

PURDUE UNIVERSITY

[2]
PRICE MOVEMENTS AND PRICE DISCOVERY IN FUTURES AND CASH MARKETS

Kenneth D. Garbade and William L. Silber*

I. Introduction

RISK transfer and price discovery are two of the major contributions of futures markets to the organization of economic activity (Working (1962), Evans (1978, p. 80), and Silber (1981)). Risk transfer refers to hedgers using futures contracts to shift price risk to others. Price discovery refers to the use of futures prices for pricing cash market transactions (Working (1948), Wiese (1978, p. 87), and Lake (1978, p. 161)). The significance of both contributions depends upon a close relationship between the prices of futures contracts and cash commodities.

This paper examines the characteristics of price movements in cash (or spot) markets and futures markets for storable commodities. Section II presents an analytical model of simultaneous price dynamics which suggests that, over short intervals of time, the correlation of price changes is a function of the elasticity of arbitrage between the physical commodity and its counterpart futures contract. Greater elasticity fosters more highly correlated price changes, and thereby facilitates the risk transfer function. The elasticity of supply of arbitrage services is constrained by, among other things, storage and transaction costs. Thus, futures contracts will not, in general, provide perfect risk transfer facilities over short time horizons.

The essence of the price discovery function of futures markets hinges on whether new information is reflected first in changed futures prices or in changed cash prices (Hoffman (1932, pp. 258-259)). The model in section II provides a framework for analyzing whether one market is dominant in terms of information flows and price discovery. In section III we develop a model based on section II which is appropriate for estimating the lead-lag relationship between cash prices and futures prices.

Section IV presents empirical estimates of the parameters of the model for seven different storable commodities: wheat, corn, oats, frozen orange juice concentrates, copper, gold, and silver. The cost of arbitrage between cash and futures differs across these commodities. For this reason we are not surprised to find inter-commodity differences in the correlation of short-run price changes and in the substitutability of futures contracts for cash market positions. With respect to the price discovery function of futures markets, we find that while futures markets dominate cash markets, cash prices do not merely echo futures prices; there are reverse information flows from cash markets to futures markets as well.

II. A Model of Simultaneous Price Dynamics

This section sets forth a model of concurrent price changes in a cash market and a futures market, and uses that model to examine: (1) the effect of arbitrage on the correlation of price changes in the two markets; and (2) the notion of price discovery. We first present an equilibrium price relationship assuming an infinite elasticity of supply of arbitrage services, and then extend that relationship to the case of a finite elasticity of supply.

A. Equilibrium Prices with Infinitely Elastic Arbitrage

Let C_k be the natural logarithm of the cash market price of a storable commodity in period k, and let F_k be the natural logarithm of the contemporaneous price on a futures contract for that commodity for settlement after a time interval τ_k. (All prices are expressed in natural logarithms.) If the following "perfect market" assumptions hold: (1) no taxes or transaction costs; (2) no limitations on borrowing; (3) no costs (other than financing) to storing a long cash market position, e.g., no

---

Received for publication December 15, 1981. Revision accepted for publication July 29, 1982.
* New York University.
This paper was supported by NSF Grant No. SES-8103156 and by grants from J. Aron & Co. and Bankers Trust Co. Deborah Black provided excellent assistance, and Mary Jaffier typed the drafts with her usual speed and accuracy.

warehouse fees and no spoilage; (4) no limitations on short sales of the commodity in the cash market, and no restrictions on use of the proceeds of any short sales; and if the following two additional assumptions hold: (5) the term structure of interest rates is flat and stationary at a continuously compounded yield of r per unit time; and (6) the cash market value of the commodity follows a Gaussian diffusion process; then we can show (the derivation is available on request) that the cash and futures markets will be in partial equilibrium if

$$F_k = C_k + r \cdot \tau_k. \qquad (1)$$

This equation says that the futures price will equal the cash price plus a premium which reflects the deferred payment on a futures contract. It does not say that expectations of future cash prices have no effect on futures prices, but that such expectations affect the current cash price as well as the futures price. (For a similar result on forward foreign exchange rates, see Frenkel and Levich (1975), McCallum (1977), McCormick (1979) and Phaup (1981).)

The assumptions which lead to equation (1) imply that the supply of arbitrage services will be infinitely elastic whenever that equation is violated. For example, if $F_k < C_k + r \cdot \tau_k$, a market participant can earn a riskless profit by purchasing futures contracts, short selling the cash commodity, and investing the proceeds of the short sale in debt securities. This hedged position is held until the equality of equation (1) is reestablished. (The equality will surely reappear on the settlement date of the futures contract, but may appear sooner.)

B. Equilibrium Prices When the Elasticity of Supply of Arbitrage Services Is Finite

A number of the assumptions underlying the derivation of equation (1) are likely to be modified in the real world. For example, transaction costs and storage costs for a cash commodity are substantial for most commodities traded in futures markets.[1] This suggests that there can be significant deviations from the relationship between cash and futures prices described by equation (1).[2] Our analysis focuses on such deviations.

As a starting point, we use equation (1) to derive from an observed futures price, F_k, a "cash equivalent price" F'_k defined as $F'_k = F_k - r \cdot \tau_k$. The value F'_k is the cash price which would prevail in period k if all the assumptions which led to equation (1) were justified. We are interested in the dynamics of C_k and F'_k, or in the dynamics of cash prices and futures prices net of their financing component.

To describe the interaction between cash and futures prices we must first specify the behavior of agents in the marketplace. Suppose there are N_c participants who deal only in the cash market, N_f participants who deal only in the futures market, and an unspecified number of arbitrageurs who deal in both markets.[3] The demand schedule of the ith participant in the cash market in period k is

$$E_{i,k} - A \cdot (C_k - r_{i,k}) \qquad A > 0,$$
$$i = 1, \ldots, N_c \qquad (2)$$

where $E_{i,k}$ is the commodity endowment of the ith participant immediately prior to period k; $r_{i,k}$ is the reservation price at which that participant is willing to hold the endowment $E_{i,k}$; and C_k is the cash market price. The elasticity of demand, denoted A, is assumed the same for all participants.

The aggregate cash market demand schedule of arbitrageurs in period k is

$$H \cdot (F'_k - C_k) \qquad H > 0. \qquad (3)$$

Under the assumptions in section II.A there are no costs to arbitrage other than financing costs, so the elasticity of cash market demand by arbitrageurs, denoted H, would be infinite when $F'_k \ne C_k$. In more realistic cases we expect that H will be finite, because the arbitrage transactions of buying in the cash market and selling the futures contract or vice versa are not riskless. As pointed out by Working (1953), Hoffman (1932, pp. 257–258) and Houthakker (1968), the spread between cash and futures prices (called the basis) can change as a

---

[1] Storage "costs" may be negative if there is a convenience yield to having the physical commodity available for merchandising. See Working (1949), Brennan (1958), and Weymar (1966).

[2] The interest rate parity theorem may fail for some of the same reasons. See Prachowny (1970), Stoll (1972), Aliber (1973), Frenkel and Levich (1975), Allen (1977), and Dooley and Isard (1980).

[3] We do not examine here the determinants of N_c or N_f or the elasticity of supply of arbitrage services. A more complete and complex model would explain the size of the cash and futures markets and the elasticity of arbitrage. See Silber (1981) for the significance of size and liquidity in futures markets.

result of heterogeneity in the grade and location of the cheapest deliverable commodity, constraints on warehouse space, and the short-run availability of arbitrage capital. Thus, cash-futures arbitrage is often referred to as basis speculation and is best represented as a type of "risk arbitrage." The elasticity of supply of arbitrage services in equation (3) is, therefore, likely to be finite.

In order to derive the implications of less than infinitely elastic arbitrage, we first solve for clearing prices in the cash and futures markets. From equations (2) and (3), the cash market will clear at the value of C_k which solves the supply/demand equation:

$$\sum_{i=1}^{N_c} E_{i,k} = \sum_{i=1}^{N_c} \{E_{i,k} - A \cdot (C_k - r_{i,k})\} + H \cdot (F'_k - C_k). \quad (4)$$

A similar analysis of the futures market shows that it will clear at the value of F'_k which solves the supply/demand equation:

$$\sum_{j=1}^{N_f} E_{j,k} = \sum_{j=1}^{N_f} \{E_{j,k} - A \cdot (F'_k - r_{j,k})\} - H \cdot (F'_k - C_k). \quad (5)$$

Equations (4) and (5) can be solved for C_k and F'_k as a function of the mean reservation price of cash market participants ($r_k^c = N_c^{-1} \sum_{i=1}^{N_c} r_{i,k}$) and the mean reservation price of futures markets participants ($r_k^f = N_f^{-1} \sum_{j=1}^{N_f} r_{j,k}$):

$$C_k = \frac{\{1 + H/(N_f \cdot A)\} \cdot r_k^c + \{H/(N_c \cdot A)\} \cdot r_k^f}{\{1 + H/(N_f \cdot A) + H/(N_c \cdot A)\}} \quad (6a)$$

$$F'_k = \frac{\{H/(N_f \cdot A)\} \cdot r_k^c + \{1 + H/(N_c \cdot A)\} \cdot r_k^f}{\{1 + H/(N_f \cdot A) + H/(N_c \cdot A)\}}. \quad (6b)$$

Note that if there is no arbitrage ($H = 0$), then $C_k = r_k^c$ and $F'_k = r_k^f$, i.e., each market will clear at the mean reservation price of its "own" participants. If the supply of arbitrage services is infinitely elastic ($H = \infty$), then $C_k = F'_k = (N_c \cdot r_k^c + N_f \cdot r_k^f)/(N_c + N_f)$, so that both markets will clear at the global mean reservation price. The equality of C_k and F'_k when $H = \infty$ shows that the model of equation (6) converges to equation (1) when the elasticity of supply of arbitrage services is infinite.

To derive dynamic price relationships, the model of equation (6) must be supplemented with a description of the evolution of reservation prices. We begin by noting that immediately after the market clearing in period $k - 1$, the ith cash market participant was willing to hold amount $E_{i,k}$ at price C_{k-1}. This implies that C_{k-1} was his reservation price after that clearing. We assume this reservation price changes to $r_{i,k}$ according to the equation:

$$r_{i,k} = C_{k-1} + v_k + w_{i,k} \quad i = 1, \ldots, N_c \quad (7)$$
$$v_k \sim N(0, T\nu^2), w_{i,k} \sim N(0, T\omega^2)$$
$$\text{cov}[v_k, w_{i,k}] = 0 \quad \text{for all } i,$$
$$\text{cov}[w_{i,k}, w_{e,k}] = 0 \quad \text{for all } i \neq e.$$

The price change $r_{i,k} - C_{k-1}$ reflects the arrival of new information between period $k - 1$ and period k which changes the price at which the ith participant is willing to hold the quantity $E_{i,k}$ of the commodity. The price change has a component common to all participants (v_k), and a component idiosyncratic to the ith participant ($w_{i,k}$). T is the chronological time between market clearings. ν^2 is the variance per unit time of the common component, and ω^2 is the variance per unit time of the idiosyncratic component.[4] A similar equation describes the evolution of the reservation price of a participant in the futures market:

$$r_{j,k} = F'_{k-1} + v_k + w_{j,k} \quad j = 1, \ldots, N_f. \quad (8)$$

The common components in equations (7) and (8) are identical for simplicity.

Equations (7) and (8) imply that the mean reservation price in each market in period k will be

$$r_k^c = C_{k-1} + v_k + w_k^c \quad (9a)$$
$$r_k^f = F'_{k-1} + v_k + w_k^f \quad (9b)$$
$$v_k \sim N(0, T\nu^2), \quad w_k^c \sim N(0, T\omega^2/N_c),$$
$$w_k^f \sim N(0, T\omega^2/N_f).$$

Substituting these expressions for r_k^c and r_k^f into equation (6) yields our model of simultaneous

---

[4] Equivalently, we could have assumed $r_{i,k} = C_{k-1} + q_{i,k}$ with $q_{i,k} \sim N(0, T\eta^2)$ and corr $[q_{i,k}, q_{j,k}] = \rho$; where $\eta^2 = \nu^2 + \omega^2$ and $\rho = \nu^2/(\nu^2 + \omega^2)$. This alternative model specifies directly that the new information which becomes available to one participant is correlated with the new information which becomes available to another participant. The correlation coefficient ρ measures the commonality of the new information between any two participants.

price dynamics:

$$\begin{bmatrix} C_k \\ F'_k \end{bmatrix} = \begin{bmatrix} 1-a & a \\ b & 1-b \end{bmatrix} \begin{bmatrix} C_{k-1} \\ F'_{k-1} \end{bmatrix} + \begin{bmatrix} u_k^c \\ u_k^f \end{bmatrix} \quad (10)$$

where

$$a = \frac{H/(N_c \cdot A)}{\langle 1 + H/(N_c \cdot A) + H/(N_f \cdot A) \rangle}$$

$$b = \frac{H/(N_f \cdot A)}{\langle 1 + H/(N_c \cdot A) + H/(N_f \cdot A) \rangle}$$

$$\text{var}[u_k^c] = T\nu^2 + T\omega^2[(1-a)^2/N_c + a^2/N_f]$$

$$\text{var}[u_k^f] = T\nu^2 + T\omega^2[b^2/N_c + (1-b)^2/N_f]$$

$$\text{cov}[u_k^c, u_k^f] = T\nu^2 + T\omega^2[b(1-a)/N_c + a(1-b)/N_f].$$

The model of equation (10) forms the basis of our empirical estimates. Thus, it will be useful to elaborate on the relationship between C_k and F'_k implied by the equation.

C. Implications of the Model

Equation (10) is a bi-variate random walk whose character depends on the elasticity of supply of arbitrage services, H. At one extreme, if there is no arbitrage (because, for example, the deliverable cash commodity cannot be easily located and stored), the spot and futures prices will follow uncoupled random walks. That is, if $H = 0$, then $a = b = 0$ in equation (10) and there will be no tendency for prices in the two markets to come together. The absence of price convergence holds even on the settlement date of the futures contract, because, in our model, the only linkage between the two markets is arbitrage.[5] Thus, in the extreme case where $H = 0$ the futures contract will be a poor substitute for a cash market position, and prices in one market will have no implications for prices in the other market. This eliminates both

[5] A more general model might specify that markets are also linked by participants liquidating a position in one market and acquiring a comparable position (at a better price) in another market, or by participants choosing to acquire or liquidate a position in the market which has the most favorable price. These search activities will, like arbitrage, tend to force prices together. Compare, e.g., Deardorff (1979) with Frenkel and Levich (1975). We choose to represent all three activities as "arbitrage."

the risk transfer and price discovery functions of futures markets.

At the other extreme, suppose the supply of arbitrage services is highly elastic. As H grows large, the model of equation (10) converges to

$$\begin{bmatrix} C_k \\ F'_k \end{bmatrix} = \begin{bmatrix} 1-\theta & \theta \\ 1-\theta & \theta \end{bmatrix} \begin{bmatrix} C_{k-1} \\ F'_{k-1} \end{bmatrix} + \begin{bmatrix} u_k^c \\ u_k^f \end{bmatrix} \quad (11)$$

$$\theta = N_f/(N_c + N_f)$$

$$\text{var}(u_k^c) = \text{var}(u_k^f) = \text{cov}(u_k^c, u_k^f)$$
$$= T\nu^2 + T\omega^2/(N_c + N_f).$$

In this case, C_k and F'_k will be identical and follow a common random walk. The futures contract will be a perfect substitute for a cash market position, and prices will be "discovered" in both markets simultaneously. In fact, there will be no meaningful distinction between the two markets.

For intermediate cases ($0 < H < \infty$), prices in the two markets will follow an intertwined random walk.[6] Greater elasticity of supply of arbitrage services (larger H) will have two results. First, unexpected changes in cash and futures prices will be more correlated, i.e., $\partial \text{cov}[u_k^c, u_k^f]/\partial H > 0$, so that prices in the two markets will be less likely to move apart. Second, any price separation which does occur will be eliminated more rapidly, i.e., $\partial \exp[\|F'_k - C_k\|F'_{k-1} - C_{k-1}\|]/\partial H < 0$. Both consequences will provide for a more stable "basis" over time, will enhance the substitutability of futures for cash positions, and will improve the risk transfer function of futures markets. Or, looked at another way, to the extent that lower storage and transaction costs and greater homogeneity of the underlying cash commodity encourage arbitrage activities, the linkages between the two markets will be enhanced, thereby improving the risk transfer functions of futures markets.

The notion of price discovery can also be characterized in cases where $0 < H < \infty$. If $0 \leq b < a$ in equation (10), the futures market "dominates" the cash market (see Garbade and Silber (1979)). In particular, any difference between F'_{k-1}

[6] More specifically, the weighted average price $(b \cdot C_k + a \cdot F'_k)/(a + b)$ will follow a random walk with zero drift and variance $T\nu^2 + T\omega^2/(N_c + N_f)$, and the price difference $F'_k - C_k$ will follow a stable first-order Markov process with a single-period persistence coefficient of $1 - a - b$ and with a disturbance term which is uncorrelated with the disturbance term on the weighted average price. The weighted average price and the price difference are the eigenstates of equation (10).

and C_{k-1} will be narrowed by a movement of C_k towards F'_{k-1} which exceeds the movement of F'_k towards C_{k-1}. In other words, cash prices will move further towards futures prices than futures prices will move towards cash prices. The converse holds if $0 \leq a < b$ in equation (10), i.e., the cash market would dominate the futures market.

We use the ratio $a/(a + b)$ to measure the importance of the futures market relative to the cash market in the price discovery process. From the definition of a and b following equation (10) we have $a/(a + b) = N_f/(N_c + N_f)$, so that, in our model, price discovery is a function of the size of a market.

D. A Multi-period Model

To use the model of equation (10) for empirical estimation it is necessary to specify a multi-period version of the model. This allows us to relate C_k and F'_k to C_{k-n} and F'_{k-n} where n is greater than 1. When $0 < H < \infty$ the multi-period model is

$$\begin{bmatrix} C_k \\ F'_k \end{bmatrix} = \begin{bmatrix} (b + a(1 - a - b)^n)/(a + b) & (a - a(1 - a - b)^n)/(a + b) \\ (b - b(1 - a - b)^n)/(a + b) & (a + b(1 - a - b)^n)/(a + b) \end{bmatrix} \begin{bmatrix} C_{k-n} \\ F'_{k-n} \end{bmatrix} + \begin{bmatrix} \tilde{u}^c_k \\ \tilde{u}^f_k \end{bmatrix}. \quad (12)$$

This form of our model is important because we use once-a-day observations from markets which trade (clear) continuously.

It should be noted that as n grows large the model of equation (12) will converge to the model of equation (11), with Tn replacing T in equation (11).[7] This result shows that even if the supply of arbitrage services is relatively inelastic from clearing to clearing, over longer intervals the markets will appear more perfectly integrated. This occurs because discrepancies between cash and futures prices encourage continued arbitrage over time, thereby putting sustained pressure on the spread between C_k and F'_k. Thus, over longer time horizons, futures markets will offer risk transfer opportunities that might be absent over shorter periods. In other words, the substitutability of futures contracts for cash market positions will improve as a direct function of the horizon over which substitution is contemplated.

III. Implementing the Model

The preceding section developed a model for evaluating the relationship between cash prices and futures prices over time intervals which include multiple market clearings. While the notion of price correlation underlies both the risk transfer and price discovery functions of futures markets, the structure of equation (12) permits a more complete examination of the questions of whether a futures contract is a good substitute for a cash market position, and whether price changes appear first in the futures market or in the cash market.

The issue of price discovery can be examined with a model of daily price behavior derived from equation (12). Let C_t be the logarithm of the cash price on day t and let F'_t be the logarithm of the discounted futures price on the same day. If there are m periods between daily observations (we do not need to know m), equation (12) becomes

$$\begin{bmatrix} C_t \\ F'_t \end{bmatrix} = \begin{bmatrix} \alpha_c \\ \alpha_f \end{bmatrix} + \begin{bmatrix} 1 - \beta_c & \beta_c \\ \beta_f & 1 - \beta_f \end{bmatrix} \begin{bmatrix} C_{t-1} \\ F'_{t-1} \end{bmatrix} + \begin{bmatrix} e^c_t \\ e^f_t \end{bmatrix} \quad (13)$$

where $\beta_c = (a - a(1 - a - b)^m)/(a + b)$ and $\beta_f = (b - b(1 - a - b)^m)/(a + b)$. Note that $\beta_c \geq 0$ and $\beta_f \geq 0$. The constant terms, α_c and α_f, have been added to equation (13) to reflect any secular price trends in our data and any persistent differences between cash prices and futures prices attributable to different quotation conventions.[8]

The identification of the coefficients β_c and β_f implies that $\beta_c/(\beta_c + \beta_f) = a/(a + b)$. If this ratio is unity (so that $\beta_f = 0$), convergence of cash and futures prices occurs because cash prices always move towards futures prices. This is an extreme case where the cash market is a "pure

---

[7] For example, the (1, 1) element in the matrix in equation (12) converges to $b/(a + b)$ as n grows large. From the definition of a and b in equation (10), we have $b/(a + b) = (1/N_f)/((1/N_c) + (1/N_f)) = N_c/(N_f + N_c) = 1 - \theta$, where $1 - \theta$ is the (1, 1) element of the matrix in equation (11).

[8] For example, grain futures are settled with grain in a warehouse, while cash grain prices are for grain "on track," i.e., grain in a hopper car.

satellite" of the futures market. If $\beta_c/(\beta_c + \beta_f) = 0$ (so that $\beta_c = 0$), then futures prices always adjust towards cash prices and the futures market is a pure satellite. Intermediate values between zero and one imply mutual adjustments and feedback effects from one market to the other.

To examine the risk transfer (or hedging) functions of futures markets, we solve equation (13) for $F'_t - C_t$ as a function of $F'_{t-1} - C_{t-1}$, producing:

$$F'_t - C_t = \alpha + \delta(F'_{t-1} - C_{t-1}) + e_t \quad (14)$$

where $\alpha = \alpha_f - \alpha_c$, $\delta = 1 - \beta_f - \beta_c$, and $e_t = e_t^f - e_t^c$.

The identification of δ implies that $\delta = (1 - a - b)^m$. Moreover, $\partial \delta/\partial H < 0$, because $\partial a/\partial H > 0$ and $\partial b/\partial H > 0$. Thus, δ is an inverse measure of the elasticity of supply of arbitrage services. As we noted in section II.B, greater elasticity enhances the substitutability of futures contracts for cash market positions, and hence improves the risk transfer function of futures markets. In the context of equation (14), δ measures the rate of convergence of cash and futures prices over daily intervals. If δ is small, prices will converge quickly because only a small fraction of the price difference on day $t-1$ will persist to day t.

To summarize, we have derived and interpreted two parameters which can be estimated from observed prices. The parameter δ measures (the inverse of) the elasticity of supply of arbitrage services. The parameter $\beta_c/(\beta_c + \beta_f)$ measures the relative dominance of the futures market compared to the cash market in the price discovery process. Note that neither of these parameters could be obtained from a simple analysis of correlations of price changes. We turn now to examine our empirical results.

IV. Empirical Results

The data used to estimate the models of equations (13) and (14) are described in table 1. Several comments about that data are important. A futures contract trading in its settlement month may, at the option of the seller, be liquidated at any time by physical delivery, so the cash equivalent price is then identical to the settlement price of that contract. The cash equivalent price of a contract trading for deferred delivery was computed as

$$\ln[\text{cash equivalent price}] = \ln[\text{settlement price}] \\ - \ln[1 + R \cdot \tau/360]$$

where τ is the number of days to the first delivery date of the underlying commodity, and where R is (a) the 90-day CD rate if $\tau \leq 90$; (b) the 180-day CD rate if $\tau \geq 180$; and (c) an interpolated average of the 90-day and 180-day CD rates if $90 < \tau < 180$.

TABLE 1.—DESCRIPTION OF DATA

Commodity	Cash	Futures
Wheat	no. 2 soft red wheat "on track" in Chicago	closing prices on the Chicago Board of Trade[a]
Corn	no. 2 yellow corn "on track" in Chicago	closing prices on the Chicago Board of Trade[a]
Oats	no. 2 milling oats "on track" in Minneapolis[b]	closing prices on the Chicago Board of Trade[a]
Orange Juice	transactions for delivery in two days on the New York Cotton Exchange	closing prices on the New York Cotton Exchange
Copper	no. 2 scrap wire	closing prices on the Commodity Exchange (Comex)
Gold	afternoon London fixing	opening prices on the Commodity Exchange (Comex)[c]
Silver	noon-time Handy and Harman base price	opening prices on the Commodity Exchange (Comex)[d]

[a] Current crop only.
[b] Although Minneapolis is not the delivery point for the Chicago Board of Trade oats contract, it is the location of the active cash market in oats.
[c] Active contracts only (February, April, June, August, October, and December).
[d] Active contracts only (January, March, May, July, September, and December).

TABLE 2.—CROSS-SECTIONAL AVERAGE VALUES OF ESTIMATED
PARAMETERS, CASH PRICES VS. FUTURES PRICES[a]

Commodity	$\hat{\beta}_c/(\hat{\beta}_c + \hat{\beta}_f)$[b,c]	$\hat{\delta}$
Wheat	.85	.97
Corn	.76	.96
Oats	.54	.96
Orange Juice	.75	.84
Copper	.54	.92

[a] Averaged over contracts with futurities of from 0 to 9 months.
[b] Negative estimates of β_c or β_f set to zero before averaging since there is no theoretical reason to expect negative values (see text following equation (13)). None were statistically significantly less than zero. The sum of β_c and β_f was significantly greater than zero in 37 out of 50 cases, implying that cash and futures prices are not independent and that they do converge.
[c] A test of the null hypothesis that $\beta_c = \beta_f$, against the alternative hypothesis that $\beta_c > \beta_f$, i.e., that the futures market dominates the cash market, led to rejecting the null hypothesis at the 1% confidence level for wheat, corn, and orange juice. The null hypothesis could not be rejected for oats and copper even at the 10% confidence level.

All of our results are based on data from *chronologically consecutive* trading days, e.g., Friday to Monday price changes were excluded. We also excluded observations of futures prices that were constrained by limits and which therefore did not represent market-clearing prices. Because the focus of our model is on storage (rather than production) arbitrage, we confined our analysis of the grains to contracts settling in the current crop year.[9]

The analytical results derived in section II assumed there was a cash price and a single futures price. In fact, however, for any commodity there are a series of futures prices associated with different delivery months. We estimated the parameters of equations (13) and (14) for futures contracts with delivery months ranging from the current month to nine months in the future. These detailed results are available on request. Our main interest is with the overall relationship between cash and futures markets. Table 2 presents the cross-sectional average estimated values of the two parameters crucial to our analysis: $\beta_c/(\beta_c + \beta_f)$, showing the relative contribution of the futures market to the price discovery process; and δ, measuring the rate of convergence of cash and futures prices.

The short-run elasticity of supply of arbitrage services in the grains does not appear to be very high. The average values of $\hat{\delta}$ for wheat, corn, and oats imply that more than 95% of the price difference $F'_{t-1} - C_{t-1}$, on day $t - 1$ persists to day t. On the other hand, the average value of $\hat{\delta}$ is

[9] The first futures contract in a new crop year is the July contract for wheat and oats, and the December contract for corn.

0.92 for copper and 0.84 for frozen orange juice, implying higher short-run elasticities.

While these results seem to suggest a substantial degree of risk exposure to hedgers in grain futures, there are two points that mitigate such a conclusion. First, the estimates for δ measure elasticities over one day. The elasticities (and market integration) will grow over longer horizons. Thus, while unusual price discrepancies between cash and futures may persist on a day-to-day basis, a hedger concerned with co-movement over a one-month or two-month interval need not be concerned. Second, the values of $\hat{\delta}$ in table 2 are averages over contracts with different futurities. An examination of the values of $\hat{\delta}$ for the individual months (available on request) reveals that the implied short-run elasticities are higher for near-term contracts than for more distant contracts. This is reasonable because the costs of arbitraging the latter contracts against the cash market are greater than the costs of arbitraging the former contracts.

Table 2 supports the casual observation of many market participants that the futures markets in wheat and corn play a crucial role in the price discovery process. More than 75% of the pricing of those grains appears to occur in the futures markets. A similar result holds for orange juice. This suggests that the futures markets for those commodities dominate their respective cash markets. On the other hand, the pricing of oats and copper is split approximately evenly between the cash and futures markets.

The lesser importance of the futures market for oats compared to the futures markets for wheat and corn emphasizes the importance of market size and liquidity to the price discovery role of futures markets. Corn and wheat futures are large and very liquid contracts, but there is significantly less trading and liquidity in oat futures.

Before turning to the results for gold and silver it is necessary to discuss the effect of the timing of price observations used in our regressions. If a cash market price is collected later in the day than a futures price, the coefficient β_c in equation (13) will be biased downwards towards zero, because C_{t-1} provides "fresher" information than F_{t-1} for predicting C_t. Similarly, the coefficient β_f will be biased upwards towards unity. These biases imply that the cash market will appear more important for price discovery than is, in fact, the case. Conversely, if a futures price is collected later in the day than a cash price, the futures market will appear more important for price discovery than is really the case.

Cash market prices in our sample set were obtained as follows. The prices for the grains are collected by the U.S. Department of Agriculture shortly after the close of futures trading. The cash market price in orange juice is reported by the New York Cotton Exchange and reflects trading immediately before the close of futures trading. The cash prices in copper are collected by the *Wall Street Journal* throughout the day.

These data sources imply that our results are biased towards showing a somewhat smaller significance in the price discovery process for grain futures than may actually be the case. Since grain futures are dominant according to table 2, the bias does not affect our conclusion. Our results may also overstate slightly the significance of the futures markets for the discovery of prices for copper and orange juice, although the problem is not likely to be large for orange juice since the time delay is on the order of only fifteen minutes.

With this background, we can turn to our results for gold and silver. Our cash market price for gold was the afternoon London fixing price, which is determined slightly after 10 A.M. New York time. When we compared Comex opening prices with the cash market price of gold, the cash market appeared to be the locus of price discovery, i.e., $\hat{\beta}_c/(\hat{\beta}_c + \hat{\beta}_f)$ was near zero. The reverse held true when we compared Comex closing prices with the cash market price. A similar result was found in the case of silver, where the cash market price is the 12 o'clock base price quoted by the bullion dealer, Handy and Harman. These results suggest that the cash and futures markets for gold and silver are exceedingly well integrated. In the case of gold, even a 30 minute delay in the observation of the cash price relative to the opening futures price is enough to make the cash market appear completely dominant.

Although our data do not permit a reliable analysis of cash versus futures trading in gold and silver, we can compare trading for the spot contract (current month) versus deferred contracts in those two metals. (In general, futures market participants with long positions in spot gold and silver contracts receive delivery of the physical commodity within two days.) Table 3 reports the results of that comparison.

TABLE 3.—CROSS-SECTIONAL AVERAGE VALUES OF ESTIMATED PARAMETERS, SPOT CONTRACT PRICES VS. DEFERRED CONTRACT PRICES[a]

Commodity	$\hat{\beta}_c/(\hat{\beta}_c + \hat{\beta}_f)$[b,c]	$\hat{\delta}$
Gold	.86	.59
Silver	.67	.56

[a] Averaged over contracts with futurities of from 1 to 9 months.
[b] Negative estimates of β_c or β_f set to zero before averaging. None were statistically significantly less than zero. In all 13 cases the sum of β_c and β_f was statistically significantly greater than zero, implying that spot and futures prices are not independent and that they do converge.
[c] The null hypothesis that $\beta_c = \beta_f$ can be rejected at the 1% confidence level in favor of the alternative hypothesis that $\beta_c > \beta_f$ for both gold and silver.

The elasticities of supply of arbitrage services in the gold and silver markets are much higher than the elasticities of supply of arbitrage services for the commodities shown in table 2, i.e., the average values of $\hat{\delta}$ are all below 0.6 in table 3 and are all above 0.8 in table 2. These results follow from a number of differences between gold and silver and the other commodities. First, the transaction and storage costs in precious metals are relatively cheap compared to transaction and storage costs in, for example, the grains. In addition, precious metals can be more easily sold short in the cash market (there exist markets in New York for the borrowing of gold and silver for delivery against short sales). Finally, there is much less heterogeneity in the varieties of gold and silver that can be delivered in satisfaction of a short futures position compared with the deliverable varieties of corn or wheat. In other words, the pure financing model of futures prices shown in equation (1) is much more appropriate for the precious metals. Thus, the estimated results for gold and silver more nearly reflect the unconstrained arbitrage model that underlies equation (1), while the empirical results for the grains reflect constrained arbitrage.

As far as price discovery is concerned, table 3 shows that the spot contract in gold is largely a satellite of deferred futures, while for silver the pricing process is more evenly divided between spot and deferred contracts.

V. Concluding Remarks

We have specified and estimated a model which describes the interrelationship between cash market prices and futures prices of storable commodities. Our theoretical results suggest that the degree of market integration over short horizons is a function of the elasticity of supply of arbitrage services. Empirical results are reported for seven commodities. While all of the markets are well integrated over a month or two, there is considerable slippage between cash and futures markets over shorter time intervals, especially for the grains—corn, wheat and oats. The gold and silver markets, however, are highly integrated even over one day.

These results on market integration and co-movement in prices are important for the usefulness of futures markets to hedgers. The empirical work indicates that there is nontrivial risk exposure to hedgers over short time intervals (e.g., a week) in the futures markets for grains and, to a lesser extent, copper and orange juice.

The second component of our analysis focused on the role of futures markets in providing price information. This price discovery function of futures markets hinges on whether price changes in futures markets lead price changes in cash markets more often than the reverse. We find that, in general, futures markets dominate cash markets. The evidence suggests that the cash markets in wheat, corn, and orange juice are largely satellites of the futures markets for those commodities, with about 75% of new information incorporated first in futures prices and then flowing to cash prices. This also seems to be the case with gold, although data-limitations prevent a conclusive statement. The pricing of silver and especially oats and copper are more evenly divided between the cash and futures markets.

REFERENCES

Aliber, Robert, "The Interest Rate Parity Theorem: A Reinterpretation," *Journal of Political Economy* 81 (Nov./Dec. 1973).

Allen, William, "A Note on Uncertainty, Transactions Costs and Interest Parity," *Journal of Monetary Economics* 3 (July 1977).

Brennan, Michael, "The Supply of Storage," *American Economic Review* 48 (Mar. 1958).

Deardorff, Alan, "One-Way Arbitrage and Its Implications for the Foreign Exchange Markets," *Journal of Political Economy* 87 (Apr. 1979).

Dooley, Michael, and Peter Isard, "Capital Controls, Political Risk, and Deviations from Interest Rate Parity," *Journal of Political Economy* 88 (Apr. 1980).

Evans, E. B., "Country Elevator Use of the Market," in A. Peck (ed.), *Views from the Trade* (Chicago: Board of Trade of the City of Chicago, 1978).

Frenkel, Jacob, and Richard Levich, "Covered Interest Arbitrage: Unexploited Profits?," *Journal of Political Economy* 83 (Apr. 1975).

Garbade, Kenneth, and William Silber, "Dominant and Satellite Markets: A Study of Dually-Traded Securities," this REVIEW 61 (Aug. 1979).

Hoffman, G. Wright, *Future Trading Upon Organized Commodity Markets in the United States* (Philadelphia: University of Pennsylvania, 1932).

Houthakker, Hendrik, "Normal Backwardation," in J. N. Wolfe (ed.), *Value, Capital, and Growth* (Edinburgh: University of Edinburgh, 1968).

Lake, Fred, "The Miller's Use of the Commodity Exchange," in A. Peck (ed.), *Views from the Trade* (Chicago: Board of Trade of the City of Chicago, 1978).

McCallum, B. T., "The Role of Speculation in the Canadian Forward Exchange Market: Some Estimates Assuming Rational Expectations," this REVIEW 59 (May 1977).

McCormick, Frank, "Covered Interest Arbitrage: Unexploited Profits? Comment," *Journal of Political Economy* 87 (Apr. 1979).

Phaup, E. Dwight, "A Reinterpretation of the Modern Theory of Forward Exchange Rates," *Journal of Money, Credit, and Banking* 13 (Nov. 1981).

Prachowny, Martin, "A Note on Interest Parity and the Supply of Arbitrage Funds," *Journal of Political Economy* 78 (May/June 1970).

Silber, William, "Innovation, Competition, and New Contract Design in Futures Markets," *Journal of Futures Markets* 2 (Summer 1981).

Stoll, Hans, "Causes of Deviation from Interest Rate Parity," *Journal of Money, Credit, and Banking* 4 (Feb. 1972).

Weymar, F. Helmut, "The Supply of Storage Revisited," *American Economic Review* 56 (Dec. 1966).

Wiese, Virgil, "Use of Commodity Exchanges by Local Grain Marketing Organizations," in A. Peck (ed.), *Views from the Trade* (Chicago: Board of Trade of the City of Chicago, 1978).

Working, Holbrook, "Theory of the Inverse Carrying Charge in Futures Markets," *Journal of Farm Economics* 30 (Feb. 1948).

———, "The Theory of Price of Storage," *American Economic Review* 39 (Dec. 1949).

———, "Futures Trading and Hedging," *American Economic Review* 43 (June 1953).

———, "New Concepts Concerning Futures Markets and Prices," *American Economic Review* 52 (June 1962).

Journal of Financial Economics 12 (1983) 311–342. North-Holland

A COMPARISON OF FUTURES AND FORWARD PRICES*

Kenneth R. FRENCH

University of Chicago, Chicago, IL 60637, USA

Received September 1982, final version received May 1983

This paper uses the pricing models of Cox, Ingersoll and Ross (1981), Richard and Sundaresan (1981), and French (1982) to examine the relation between futures and forward prices for copper and silver. There are significant differences between these prices. The average differences are generally consistent with the predictions of the futures and forward price models. However, these models are not helpful in describing intra-sample variations in the futures-forward price differences. This failure is apparently caused by measurement errors in both the price differences and in the explanatory variables.

1. Introduction

Futures and forward contracts are very similar; both contracts represent an agreement to trade an asset at a specific time in the future. Because of this similarity, these contracts are often treated as though they are identical. However, futures and forward contracts are not identical; the daily gain or loss from holding a futures contract is transferred between the traders at the end of each day, while the profits or losses from holding a forward contract accumulate until the contract matures. A number of recent papers have examined the theoretical implications of this difference for the relation between futures and forward prices. For example, Margrabe (1976), Cox, Ingersoll and Ross (1977), and Jarrow and Oldfield (1981) demonstrate that these prices will not be equal unless interest rates are non-stochastic. Cox, Ingersoll and Ross (1981), Richard and Sundaresan (1981), and French (1982) build models of futures and forward prices which allow them to make more specific predictions about the relation between these prices. This paper examines the accuracy of many of these predictions for silver and copper contracts.

*This paper is based on my doctoral thesis at the University of Rochester. I am very grateful to my dissertation committee, G. William Schwert (Chairman), Michael Jensen, John Long, and Charles Plosser, for their guidance. I have also received helpful comments from Robert Jarrow, Scott Richard, Richard Roll, Richard Ruback, Dennis Sheehan, René Stulz, Lee Wakeman, Jerold Zimmerman, and the referee, Douglas Breeden. Financial support was generously provided by the Managerial Economics Research Center, Graduate School of Management, University of Rochester; the Center for the Study of Futures Markets, Graduate School of Business, Columbia University; the Foundation for Research in Economics and Education; and the Richard D. Irwin Foundation. I would also like to thank Christopher Snyder of Data Resources, Inc., and Richard Brealey for providing data. This work was completed while I was a post-doctoral fellow at the University of California, Los Angeles.

0304-405x/83/$3.00 © 1983, Elsevier Science Publishers B.V. (North-Holland)

A forward contract is simply a sales agreement in which delivery and payment are deferred. All of the terms of the sale, such as the asset to be delivered, the time of delivery, and the purchase price (called the forward price), are specified when the contract is written. No payments are made until the contract matures. At that time the seller delivers the asset and the buyer pays the forward price. Since the asset can be purchased just before delivery and re-sold immediately afterward, a forward contract can be viewed as a bet about the maturity price of the commodity. The payoff on this bet is equal to the difference between the forward price and the maturity spot price.

A futures contract can also be viewed as a bet about the maturity price of the asset, but the parties to this bet settle-up daily.[1] At the end of each day's trading, the current futures price is compared with the closing price from the previous day. If the futures price has fallen, the investor who is long in the contract (committing himself to purchase the commodity) must pay the short investor the amount of the decrease. If the futures price has risen, the long investor receives the amount of the increase from the short investor. When the contract matures, the long investor purchases the commodity at the previous day's closing, or settlement, price. Since the commodity can be re-sold immediately at the prevailing spot price, the sum of the cashflows between the two futures traders is equal to the difference between the original futures price and the maturity spot price. This is very similar to the cashflow from the forward contract 'bet'. However, with a forward contract the profits are transferred at maturity, while the profits from a futures contract are transferred at the end of each day.[2]

Despite the differences between these contracts, most commodity traders treat futures contracts as though they are forward contracts. For example, by implicitly modelling futures contracts as forward contracts, futures traders have developed several 'arbitrage' conditions relating futures prices, spot prices, and storage costs. Many economists seem to agree that the daily settling-up has a negligible effect on futures prices. In developing their models of futures prices, Dusak (1973), Grauer (1977), and Grauer and Litzenberger (1979) abstract from the settling-up provisions of these contracts entirely. Other authors, such as Black (1976), explicitly recognize the daily settling-up, but they still conclude that futures and forward prices will be the same.

In light of this consensus about the similarity between futures and forward prices, the empirical evidence in this paper may be surprising. There are significant differences between these prices for both copper and silver contracts. For example, during the 1974–1980 sample period, the average futures–forward price differences are about 0.1%, 0.4%, and 0.8% for 3, 6, and 12 month silver contracts, respectively.

---

[1] This settling-up is often called 'marking-to-market'.
[2] Strictly speaking, each futures contract is a bet about the next day's futures price.

The next section of this paper outlines the pricing models of Cox, Ingersoll and Ross (1981), Richard and Sundaresan (1981), and French (1982). These models imply that futures and forward prices will differ in predictable ways. For example, the models predict that the price for a forward contract is related to the interest rate on a long-term bond that matures at the same time as the contract, while the futures price is related to the return from rolling over one-day bonds until the contract matures. These prices will be identically equal only if interest rates are non-stochastic.

Section 3 compares futures and forward prices for copper and silver and tests many of the predictions of the pricing models outlined in section 2. In general, the average price differences are consistent with the predictions. However, the models are not helpful in describing intra-sample variations in the futures–forward price differences. This failure is apparently caused by measurement errors in both the price differences and in the explanatory variables.

Section 4 contains a brief summary and some conclusions.

2. Models of futures and forward prices

This section uses models developed by Cox, Ingersoll and Ross (1981), Richard and Sundaresan (1981), and French (1982) to examine the theoretical differences between futures and forward prices. All of these models assume that there are no taxes or transaction costs and that individuals can borrow and lend at the same nominal interest rate.[3]

2.1. Arbitrage models

Futures and forward contracts provide a wide variety of intertemporal exchange opportunities. For example, by initiating a long forward contract and purchasing risk-free bonds, an individual can buy an asset today that will be delivered in the future. To see the mechanics of this transaction, define $f(t, T)$ as the forward price on day t for a contract that matures on day T and define $R(t, T)$ as the yield to maturity on a riskless discount bond that pays one dollar on day T. The current price of this bond is

$$B(t, T) \equiv \exp[-(T-t)R(t, T)]. \tag{1}$$

A trader can make a delayed purchase by initiating one forward contract and investing $f(t, T)B(t, T)$ dollars in riskless bonds. When the contract matures, he receives $f(t, T)$ dollars from the bonds and exchanges this for one unit of the commodity. In effect, an investment of $f(t, T)B(t, T)$ today

---

[3]The models also assume that investors will not default on any contract. This implies that there is a finite upper bound on the daily price changes and on the daily interest rates.

yields one unit of the commodity on day T. Alternatively, the trader could reverse the strategy and obtain $f(t, T) B(t, T)$ dollars today in exchange for the asset at time T.

Because this intertemporal exchange is available, investors must be marginally indifferent between $f(t, T) B(t, T)$ dollars today and one unit of the commodity on day T. By defining $\tilde{P}(T)$ as the (unknown) price of the commodity at time T, this indifference can be expressed in purely dollar terms; $f(t, T) B(t, T)$ must be the value on day t of $\tilde{P}(T)$ dollars on day T. Equivalently, the forward price must equal the present value of the maturity spot price times the gross return from a long-term bond,

$$f(t, T) = \exp[(T-t) R(t, T)] PV_{t, T}[\tilde{P}(T)]. \tag{2}$$

In eq. (2), $PV_{t, T}(\cdot)$ denotes the present value at time t of a payment received at time T.

For example, consider a forward contract on a stock that pays no dividends. Since the current stock price must be the present value of the future stock price, the forward price is equal to

$$f(t, T) = \exp[(T-t) R(t, T)] P(t). \tag{3}$$

This result is intuitively appealing. Using a forward contract to purchase the stock on day T is equivalent to purchasing the stock today, except the forward contract allows the payment to be deferred. Therefore, the forward price is equal to the deferred value of the current stock price.

The present value of the maturity spot price is not observable for most commodities; a more complete model must be introduced to evaluate the payment in (2) and to determine the forward price. However, eq. (2) is useful for highlighting the differences between futures and forward prices.

Cox, Ingersoll and Ross (1981) and French (1982) develop a similar expression for futures prices. They demonstrate that the futures price must equal the present value of the product of the maturity spot price and the gross return from rolling over one-day bonds,

$$F(t, T) = PV_{t, T} \left\{ \exp\left[\sum_{\tau=t}^{T-1} \tilde{R}(\tau, \tau+1) \right] \tilde{P}(T) \right\}. \tag{4}$$

In this equation, $F(t, T)$ is the futures price on day t for a contract that matures on day T and $R(\tau, \tau+1)$ is the continuously compounded interest rate on a one-day bond from day τ to day $\tau+1$.

Eqs. (2) and (4) indicate that the difference between forward and futures prices is related to the difference between holding a long-term bond and rolling over a series of one-day bonds. The only cashflow that is relevant to the forward trader is agreed on today and paid on the maturity date. Therefore, the relevant interest rate in determining the forward price is the known yield on a multi-period bond. On the other hand, while the futures trader knows the total payments he will have to make, the timing of these cashflows is only determined as the contract matures. Because of this uncertainty, the futures price is a function of the unknown one-day interest rates that are expected to arise over the life of contract. In general, the futures price will not equal the forward price unless these interest rates are non-stochastic.

Cox, Ingersoll and Ross use the arbitrage models in eqs. (2) and (4) to develop several propositions about the relation between forward and futures prices. In a continuous-time, continuous-state economy, they find that the difference between these prices is equal to

$$F(t,T) - f(t,T) = -PV_{t,T}\left\{\int_t^T \tilde{F}(w,T)\operatorname{cov}[\tilde{F}(w,T),\tilde{B}(w,T)]\mathrm{d}w\right\}/B(t,T). \quad (5)$$

In this equation, $\operatorname{cov}[\tilde{F}(w,T),\tilde{B}(w,T)]$ is defined as the local covariance at time w between the percentage change in the futures price and the percentage change in the bond price. This result has several implications. For example, the local covariance between the futures and bond prices is almost certainly positive for financial assets, such as treasury bills. Therefore, the forward price should be above the futures price for these assets. On the other hand, one would expect the futures price to be above the forward price for most real commodities. Unexpected inflation and changes in expected inflation probably play a major role in determining the covariance between bond prices and commodity prices. Since unexpected inflation moves bond prices and commodity prices in opposite directions, the covariance should be negative and the futures–forward price difference should be positive.[4]

Eq. (5) also implies that the difference between the futures and forward prices will be related to the variance of both the futures prices and the bond prices. Specifically, if the correlation between the futures and bond prices is constant, the absolute value of the price difference will be an increasing function of the market's expectation of both the futures and bond price variances.

Cox, Ingersoll and Ross also use the arbitrage models to show that the

---

[4]The local covariance between the futures price and the bond price may be positive for some commodities. For example, if a commodity is used in the production of a durable good, an increase in the expected real interest rate will reduce the demand for the commodity. Therefore, changes in the expected real interest rate will tend to make the commodity and bond prices move together. However, since the inflation rate is much more volatile than the expected real interest rate, the covariance is still expected to be negative for most commodities.

difference between the futures and forward prices can be expressed as

$$F(t,T)-f(t,T)=PV_{t,T}\left\{\exp\left[\int_t^T \tilde{r}(w)\,dw\right]\int_t^T [\tilde{P}(w)/\tilde{B}(w,T)]\right.$$

$$\left.\times\{\text{var}[\tilde{B}(w,T)]-\text{cov}[\tilde{P}(w),\tilde{B}(w,T)]\}\,dw\right\}, \qquad (6)$$

if the commodity is stored costlessly over the contract period. In this equation, $\tilde{r}(w)$ is the instantaneous interest rate at time w, $\text{var}[\tilde{B}(w,T)]$ is the local variance of the percentage change in the bond price, and $\text{cov}[\tilde{P}(w),\tilde{B}(w,T)]$ is the local covariance between the percentage change in the spot price and the percentage change in the bond price. This result implies that the futures–forward price difference will be a decreasing function of the market's expectation of the spot price variance if the price difference is negative and if the local correlation between the spot and bond prices is constant.

2.2. Utility based models

The relation between futures and forward prices can be explored further by assuming that markets are complete and that there is some rational individual who acts to maximize a time-additive expected utility function of the form

$$J=E_t\left\{\sum_{\tau=t}^\infty \exp[-\rho(\tau-t)]U[\tilde{C}(\tau)]\right\}. \qquad (7)$$

In eq. (7), $\tilde{C}(\tau)$ is a vector indicating the (non-negative) quantity of each good consumed on day τ, and ρ is a utility discount factor. Further, $U(\cdot)$ is a single period, von Neumann–Morgenstern utility function that is increasing, strictly quasi-concave, and differentiable. Finally, define $\tilde{\lambda}(\tau)$ as the marginal value of a dollar that is received at time τ. For notational convenience, this marginal value is discounted back to day t. In other words, $\tilde{\lambda}(\tau)$ is the discounted marginal utility of money on day τ,

$$\tilde{\lambda}(\tau)=\exp[-\rho(\tau-t)]\tilde{u}(i,\tau)/\tilde{P}(i,\tau). \qquad (8)$$

In this expression, $\tilde{P}(i,\tau)$ is the price of any commodity that is consumed on day τ and $\tilde{u}(i,\tau)$ is the marginal utility of this commodity on day τ. Notice that, unlike $\tilde{\lambda}(\tau)$, $\tilde{u}(i,\tau)$ is not discounted back to day t.

The discussion in the previous section shows that investors must be marginally indifferent between $f(t,T)$ dollars today and $\exp[(T-t)R(t,T)]\tilde{P}(T)$

dollars on day T. For an individual with the time-additive utility function in (7), this indifference can be expressed as

$$f(t,T)\lambda(t) = \exp[(T-t)R(t,T)]E_t[\tilde{P}(T)\tilde{\lambda}(T)]; \qquad (9)$$

the marginal utility of $f(t,T)$ dollars today must equal the expected marginal utility of $\exp[(T-t)R(t,T)]\tilde{P}(T)$ dollars at time T. Equivalently, the forward price must equal

$$f(t,T) = \exp[(T-t)R(t,T)]E_t[\tilde{P}(T)\tilde{\lambda}(T)/\lambda(t)]. \qquad (10)$$

If this condition were not satisfied, the individual could increase his life-time expected utility by using a portfolio of forward contracts and bonds to transfer money between day t and day T.[5]

The time-additive utility function can also be used to characterize futures prices. Eq. (4) implies that, in equilibrium,[6] investors are indifferent between $F(t,T)$ dollars today and $\exp[\sum_{\tau=t}^{T-1} \tilde{R}(\tau,\tau+1)]\tilde{P}(T)$ dollars at time T. This indifference can be expressed as

$$F(t,T)\lambda(t) = E_t\left\{\exp\left[\sum_{\tau=t}^{T-1} \tilde{R}(\tau,\tau+1)\right]\tilde{P}(T)\tilde{\lambda}(T)\right\}, \qquad (11)$$

or

$$F(t,T) = E_t\left\{\exp\left[\sum_{\tau=t}^{T-1} \tilde{R}(\tau,\tau+1)\right]\tilde{P}(T)\tilde{\lambda}(T)/\lambda(t)\right\}. \qquad (12)$$

Eqs. (10) and (12) reemphasize that the forward price is a function of the gross return from holding a long-term bond while the futures price is a function of the gross return from rolling over one-day bonds.[7]

3. A comparison of futures and forward prices

As the discussion in section 1 indicates, the similarity between futures and forward prices often leads people to view them as identical contracts. The models of futures and forward prices described in the previous section highlight the theoretical differences between these contracts. This section examines the empirical effects of these differences and tests several predictions of the models.

[5]Eq. (10) and eq. (12) below actually follow directly from eqs. (2) and (4) using the relation $PV_{t,T}(\tilde{Y}) = E_t[\tilde{Y}\tilde{\lambda}(T)/\lambda(t)]$.
[6]In equilibrium, no investor wants to make additional trades at the existing prices.
[7]The models in eqs. (10) and (12) are developed by Richard and Sundaresan (1981) and French (1982). In addition, the forward price model in (10) is similar to the futures price models in Grauer (1977) and Grauer and Litzenberger (1979).

3.1. Matching futures and forward prices

The tests in this section compare futures and forward prices for silver and copper from 1968 through 1980. Most of the organized forward activity during this period occurred on the London Metal Exchange (LME).[8] Members of this exchange trade spot and forward contracts on silver, copper, and several other metals. Although other contracts are available, the standard silver contracts have maturities of 3, 6, and 12 months and the standard copper contract has a 3-month maturity. A new set of contracts is written each day. For example, the 3-month silver contract initiated on February 10, 1977, matured on May 10, while the contract written on February 11 matured on May 11.

The futures prices reflect trading on two exchanges in the United States — the Commodity Exchange (Comex) in New York and the Chicago Board of Trade (CBT).[9] The contract maturities used in these markets follow a different convention than that used in forward markets. While forward traders write contracts with a specific time until maturity, such as 3 months, futures traders write contracts for specific maturity months. Further, futures contracts are traded continually for up to 2 years. For example, an investor could initiate a December 1978 silver contract any time from January 1977 until it matured two years later.

In comparing futures and forward prices one would like to simultaneously observe futures and forward contracts for the same commodity and the same maturity. The different maturity structures used in the futures and forward markets make this difficult. The discussion in the first two sections assumes that futures and forward contracts have precise maturity dates. While this is true for forward contracts, it is not true for most futures contracts, including those examined here. Instead, a short futures trader may choose to make delivery any time during the maturity month. The exchange's clearinghouse then assigns the shipment to the long trader with the 'oldest' contract. The tests reported in this section assume that futures contracts mature in the first week of the delivery month.[10]

The futures and forward prices have several other characteristics that make comparisons between them difficult. For example, both Comex and the CBT impose limits on the daily price movement of any futures contract that is not

---

[8] Silver contracts began trading on the LME in February 1968. The London Bullion Market prices for silver spot and forward contracts are used before 1973.

[9] The commodity price data are obtained from several sources: the Commodity Services, Inc., data bank, provided by the Center for the Study of Futures Markets at Columbia University; the Data Resources, Inc., commodities data bank; the *Wall Street Journal*; and the *Journal of Commerce*.

[10] Specifically, the tests use prices observed on Fridays. The relevant Friday for each futures contract is chosen so that the matching forward contract matures during the first week of the futures delivery month. All of the tests have been replicated using four other maturity periods: the second, third, and fourth week of the maturity month and the first business day of that month. The results are not substantially different for the different maturity assumptions.

in its delivery month. These limits constrain the futures price to lie within a range determined by the previous day's settlement price. If a limit is reached, the day's trading is effectively stopped unless the equilibrium price moves back within the limits. In other words, when a limit move occurs the reported price may be significantly different from the unobserved market-clearing price. To reduce the effect of this measurement error, any futures price that reflects a limit move is not included in the tests.

Perhaps the biggest problems encountered in trying to match futures and forward prices arise because the forward contracts are traded in Great Britain while the futures contracts are traded in the United States.[11] Ideally, the futures and forward prices should be observed simultaneously. In fact, prices from the London exchanges are recorded several hours before the American prices are observed. This difference introduces measurement error between the futures and forward prices.

Two other complications are potentially more serious. First, American futures prices are denominated in dollars while London forward contracts are denominated in pounds sterling. Before these prices can be compared, they must be converted into the same currency. Second, silver or copper in London is not exactly the same commodity as it is in New York or Chicago because of transportation costs and international trade restrictions.

One way to deal with these problems is to assume that the expected difference between the exchange-adjusted spot prices is a constant fraction of the expected spot prices,

$$E_t[\tilde{P}(T,\$)] = (1+b)E_t[\tilde{P}(T,£)\tilde{X}(T,T)]. \tag{13}$$

In this expression, $\tilde{P}(T,\$)$ is the spot price at time T denominated in dollars, $\tilde{P}(T,£)$ is the spot price in pounds, and $\tilde{X}(T,T)$ is the spot exchange rate between dollars and pounds at time T. Although the expected basis differential, b, is assumed to be constant through time, it may vary across commodities. For example, since the cost of transporting silver between London and the United States is small relative to the value of the commodity, one expects that the absolute value of the basis differential for

---

[11]The price controls imposed in the United States from August 15, 1971, through April 30, 1974, could cause more problems. Both the spot prices and the futures prices for copper and silver were subject to these controls. For example, during the first 90 days of the control period none of the futures contracts was allowed to trade above its May 25, 1970, price or the average of the prices for the 30 days preceding August 15, 1971, whichever was higher. Because of the potential distortions caused by the price controls, all of the tests have been duplicated using three separate subperiods: a pre-control period, from January 1, 1968, through August 14, 1971; a price control period from August 15, 1971, through April 30, 1974; and a post-control period from May 1, 1974, through December 31, 1980. Surprisingly, the price controls do not affect the results of these tests. For a more complete description of the price controls imposed on the copper and silver markets and some tests of the effect of these controls, see Levich and White (1981).

J.F.E.— B

silver is small. On the other hand, the basis differential for copper may be higher because the relative transportation costs are higher.

Under this constant-expected-basis-differential model, the American forward price can be estimated by the product of the London forward price, the forward exchange rate, and the basis adjustment,[12]

$$f(t, T, \$) = (1+b) f(t, T, \pounds) X(t, T). \tag{14}$$

Table 1 presents estimates of the basis differential for silver and copper as a percentage of the spot price.[13] The British spot prices used in these estimates are measured by prices from the London Metal Exchange. Explicit spot prices for copper and silver are not available from the American futures exchanges. Instead, the price for the deliverable futures contract — called the cash price — is used. For example, the December silver futures price is used to estimate the American spot price during December.

The estimates of the basis differential for silver in table 1 are very small. For example, the average differential over the full 1968–1980 sample period is less than 0.1%, with a t-statistic of 0.53.[14] This is consistent with the relatively small transportation costs for silver. The estimates for copper are much larger; the average basis differential for the full sample period is -0.34% and the average for the first subperiod, from 1968 through 1973, is -1.87%.

The forward prices that are converted from pounds to dollars in the tests below all have maturities of 3 months or more. Therefore, it is only necessary to assume that the expected basis differential is constant for forecast horizons of at least 3 months. This is weaker than assuming that the basis differential always equals b,

$$P(t, \$) = (1+b) P(t, \pounds) X(t, t). \tag{15}$$

---

[12]This conversion also assumes that, conditional on the information available at time t, the covariance of the marginal utility of a dollar with the difference between the basis-adjusted maturity spot prices is zero; $\text{cov}_t[\tilde{\lambda}(T, \$), (1+b)\tilde{P}(T, \pounds)\tilde{X}(T, T) - \tilde{P}(T, \$)] = 0$.

French (1982) demonstrates that eq. (14) holds under the assumption that this covariance is zero and that the expected basis differential, b, is zero. Extending this result to the general case of any constant expected basis differential is straightforward.

[13]Although the model in eq. (13) is specified in terms of the levels of the spot prices, these estimates and all of the tests below use the logarithms of the prices. This eliminates some heteroskedasticity.

The exchange rates used in table 1 and in the tests below are obtained from the *Bank of England Quarterly Bulletin*, the Federal Reserve Bank of New York, and Data Resources, Inc. Although daily data are available during most of the period, only the exchange rates for Friday are available from 1968 through 1970. This does not cause problems for most of the tests because they only use futures and forward prices that are observed on Friday. However, for tests involving daily data, the Friday exchange rate is used for the next four days during this period.

[14]The t-statistics in table 1 are adjusted for autocorrelation at lags one and two since these are allowed under the constant-expected-basis-differential model.

Table 1

Estimates of the basis differentials and tests of the constant-expected-basis-differential model.[a]

	Number	Mean	Std. dev.	t-stat.	$S(r_3)$	r_1	r_2	r_3	r_4	r_5	r_6
					Silver						
1/68–12/80	146	0.080	1.863	0.526	0.086	0.025	−0.044	−0.011	0.249	0.053	0.018
1/68–12/73	66	−0.015	1.533	0.056	0.160	0.446	0.179	−0.002	0.182	0.269	0.259
1/74–12/80	80	0.158	2.104	1.000	0.120	−0.149	−0.143	−0.019	0.283	0.011	−0.065
					Copper						
1/68–12/80	112	−0.349	3.558	0.605	0.178	0.795	0.520	0.576	0.428	0.376	0.400
1/68–12/73	37	−1.868	3.955	2.236	0.395	0.897	0.146	0.682	0.409	0.366	0.716
1/74–12/80	75	0.400	3.107	0.578	0.218	0.839	0.665	0.580	0.411	0.288	0.219

[a] The percentage basis differential is estimated by $\log[P(t,\$)/P(t,\pounds)X(t,t)] * 100$. Under the constant-expected-basis-differential model, the autocorrelations after lag 2 should not be significantly different from zero. The autocorrelation at lag i is denoted by r_i and $S(r_3)$ is the standard error for the autocorrelation at lag 3, estimated using Bartlett's (1946) approximation. Copper has fewer observations than silver during the first sample period because fewer copper contracts were traded during this period.

The expectational model does not rule out differences between the basis-adjusted spot prices. However, since the conditional expected value of these differences is zero, differences that are at least 3 months apart must be independent. The autocorrelations reported in table 1 provide a test of this implication.

The estimates for silver support the constant-expected-basis-differential model. Since these estimates use monthly observations, the autocorrelations should be approximately zero after the second lag. In fact, almost all of the autocorrelations for the silver price differences are close to zero. For example, only the autocorrelation at lag 4 is significant during the 1968–1980 period.[15] The results for copper are less consistent with the model. For example, all of the estimates for the 1968–1980 sample period are significantly positive. Because of these large autocorrelations, the futures and forward price comparisons involving converted copper prices should be interpreted cautiously.[16]

3.2. A preliminary look at the data

Before comparing individual futures and forward prices, it is helpful to examine the general properties of the cash, spot, futures, and forward prices that are used in the tests below. Tables 2 and 3 summarize the daily percentage changes in the prices for silver and copper contracts. These changes are equal to the daily logarithmic price relatives. For example, the daily percentage change in the spot price for London silver is equal to $\log[P(t,£)/P(t-1,£)]*100$.

Most of the tests in this paper use copper and silver prices from 1968 through 1980. However, metal prices were unusually volatile during the last two years of this sample period. For example, the cash price for silver rose from \$5.98 per ounce on January 2, 1979, to \$52.25 on January 21, 1980. By the end of 1980, the cash price had fallen back down to \$16.58. Because of this unusual behavior during 1979 and 1980, tables 2 and 3 summarize the daily price changes when these two years are included in the sample and when they are not.

Comparisons of the behavior of futures and forward prices are complicated by the price limits in the futures markets. Although limit moves are not included in the futures price series (nor in any of the tests below), the price

---

[15]The standard errors for the autocorrelations beyond the second lag are estimated using Bartlett's (1946) approximation. Under the hypothesis that the differences are uncorrelated after lag 2, these standard errors are equal to $S(r_3) = \{N^{-1}[1 + 2r_1^2 + 2r_2^2]\}^{\frac{1}{2}}$.

[16]All of the tests below were also performed using a second conversion technique. This technique assumes that the market uses the current basis differential as its forecast of the future differential, so the American forward price is estimated as $f(t,T,\$) = f(t,T,£)X(t,T)\{P(t,\$)/P(t,£)X(t,t)\}$. The results using this conversion technique are very similar to the results reported below.

limits reduce the apparent volatility of the futures prices because they make it impossible to observe large price changes. Because of this problem, tables 2 and 3 report estimates for two different sets of converted forward prices. The first set includes all of the forward prices that are available during the sample period. The second set is more restrictive; it only includes a forward price if a matching futures price is also available. In other words, a forward price is not included if the matching futures contract was not traded or if its price reflects a limit move.

The standard deviations for silver in table 2 indicate that the price limits do have a noticeable effect. For example, the estimated standard deviation for the daily change in the 3-month futures prices over the full 1968–1980 sample period is 1.5%, while the London forward prices and the first set of converted forward prices have standard deviations of approximately 2.7%. If the converted forward price series is restricted to days when non-limit futures prices are available, the estimate falls to 1.6%. However, the evidence still suggests that unconstrained American prices would be less volatile than the London or converted prices. First, the standard deviations for the restricted forward prices remain higher than the standard deviations for the futures prices. While this difference may still be caused by the price limits,[17] the second piece of evidence is not affected by this bias. Since silver (and copper) futures prices are not constrained by price limits during a contract's delivery month, the standard deviations for the cash prices are not artificially reduced. Therefore, direct comparisons between the cash and spot prices are appropriate. These comparisons indicate that the standard deviations for the American cash prices are consistently lower than the standard deviations for the London or converted spot prices.

Because of the price limits, the standard deviations for the futures prices are fairly constant through time. However, the estimates for the cash, spot and forward prices indicate that the silver price volatility increased dramatically over the sample period. For example, even if the very turbulent 1979–1980 period is excluded, the standard deviations for the spot and forward prices increased by more than 50% from the first to the second subperiod. It is also interesting that the estimated standard deviations for the forward prices do not appear to be related to the maturity of the contracts.

The summary statistics for the daily changes in the copper prices are presented in table 3. These results are slightly different from the results in

[17]Selection bias can still occur because the futures and forward prices are not perfectly correlated. A large change in the forward price can be included in the sample if it is associated with a smaller change in the futures price. However, large changes in the futures price are never included.

It may appear that the difference between the closing times of the London and American markets can also contribute to the selection bias problem. For example, if a limit move is caused by information that arrives after the London market closes on day t, this information will lead to a large change in the forward price on day $t+1$. However, a limit move on day t eliminates the price changes for both day t and day $t+1$.

Table 2

Means, standard deviations, and t-statistics of the daily percentage changes in the futures and forward prices for silver.[a]

		American prices	London prices	Converted prices	Restricted converted prices	American prices	London prices	Converted prices	Restricted converted prices
		1/68–12/80				1/68–12/78			
Cash or spot contracts	Mean	0.085	0.060	0.054	0.034	0.059	0.047	0.037	0.034
	Std. dev.	2.372	2.849	2.880	2.923	1.831	2.223	2.223	2.332
	t-stat.	1.805	1.190	1.046	0.574	1.502	1.092	0.855	0.657
	Number	2563	3145	3145	2441	2166	2662	2662	2064
3-month contracts	Mean	0.060	0.059	0.058	0.017	0.053	0.047	0.044	0.017
	Std. dev.	1.479	2.719	2.772	1.623	1.451	2.019	2.047	1.518
	t-stat.	1.941	1.225	1.164	0.480	1.662	1.199	1.101	0.491
	Number	2266	3143	3070	2167	2044	2662	2599	1955
		1/68–12/73							
Cash or spot contracts	Mean	0.022	0.045	0.042	0.025				
	Std. dev.	1.549	1.586	1.610	1.645				
	t-stat.	0.488	1.092	0.983	0.510				
	Number	1166	1456	1456	1124				
3-month contracts	Mean	0.040	0.046	0.041	0.036				
	Std. dev.	1.431	1.586	1.630	1.466				
	t-stat.	0.909	1.119	0.934	0.795				
	Number		1456	1405	1026				

		1/74–12/80				1/74–12/78			
Cash or spot contracts	Mean	0.137	0.074	0.064	0.042	0.050	0.032	0.044	
	Std. dev.	2.883	3.599	3.635	3.679	0.102	2.180	2.809	2.952
	t-stat.	1.771	0.839	0.726	0.410	2.113	0.614	0.391	0.459
	Number	1397	1689	1689	1317	1.530	1206	1206	940
						1000			
3-month contracts	Mean	0.079	0.017	0.073	−0.001	0.069	0.047	0.048	−0.005
	Std. dev.	1.522	3.406	3.454	1.753	1.472	2.442	2.449	1.573
	t-stat.	1.792	0.851	0.864	0.018	1.449	0.674	0.683	0.091
	Number	1187	1687	1665	1141	965	1206	1194	929
6-month contracts	Mean	0.020	0.086	0.089	−0.003	0.014	0.052	0.056	−0.021
	Std. dev.	1.470	3.852	3.887	2.150	1.463	3.189	3.183	2.154
	t-stat.	0.460	0.876	0.899	0.037	0.288	0.567	0.608	0.288
	Number	1159	1551	1525	1024	951	1191	1175	886
12-month contracts	Mean	0.076	0.074	0.074	0.007	0.081	0.049	0.049	0.083
	Std. dev.	1.623	3.487	3.538	2.219	1.635	2.653	2.672	2.274
	t-stat.	1.590	0.839	0.817	0.104	1.531	0.635	0.623	0.109
	Number	1167	1545	1515	1021	957	1191	1171	881

^aThe percentage price change is defined as $\log(P_t/P_{t-1})*100$. The American prices are cash and futures prices. The London prices are spot and forward prices, denominated in pounds sterling. The converted prices are London spot and forward prices converted to dollars. The estimates for the unrestricted series use all of the available converted prices, while the restricted estimates only use prices if the matching American prices are also available.

Table 3

Means, standard deviations, and t-statistics of the daily percentage changes in the futures and forward prices for copper.[a]

		American prices	London prices	Converted prices	Restricted converted prices	American prices	London prices	Converted prices	Restricted converted prices
		1/68–12/80				1/68–12/78			
Cash or spot Contracts	Mean	−0.011	0.010	0.006	−0.021	−0.023	0.012	0.004	−0.037
	Std. dev.	1.793	1.904	1.926	1.895	1.553	1.717	1.726	1.466
	t-stat.	−0.272	0.303	0.164	0.473	−0.574	0.372	0.112	0.939
	Number	1793	3216	3216	1751	1440	2728	2728	1413
3-month contracts	Mean	−0.013	0.009	0.005	−0.419	−0.018	0.011	0.003	−0.042
	Std. dev.	1.540	1.879	1.924	1.371	1.445	1.343	1.373	1.267
	t-stat.	−0.322	0.273	0.138	1.176	−0.457	0.427	0.117	1.187
	Number	1542	3215	3136	1483	1333	2727	2660	1283
		1/68–12/73							
Cash or spot contracts	Mean	0.032	0.038	0.036	−0.038				
	Std. dev.	1.500	1.863	1.869	1.594				
	t-stat.	0.484	0.781	0.733	0.542				
	Number	519	1481	1481	512				
3-month contracts	Mean	−0.013	0.035	0.029	−0.022				
	Std. dev.	1.298	1.271	1.312	1.180				
	t-stat.	0.266	1.051	0.823	0.501				
	Number	745	1482	1427	713				
		1/74–12/80				1/74–12/78			
Cash or spot contracts	Mean	−0.029	−0.013	−0.020	−0.014	−0.055	−0.018	−0.034	−0.036
	Std. dev.	1.899	1.939	1.974	2.006	1.582	1.525	1.539	1.389
	t-stat.	0.548	0.288	0.423	0.254	1.049	0.419	0.748	0.773
	Number	1274	1735	1735	1239	921	1247	1247	901
3-month contracts	Mean	−0.013	−0.013	−0.015	−0.060	−0.025	−0.017	−0.026	−0.067
	Std. dev.	1.736	2.274	2.314	1.527	1.634	1.424	1.441	1.369
	t-stat.	0.205	0.236	0.271	1.093	0.375	0.428	0.643	1.165
	Number	797	1733	1709	770	588	1245	1233	570

[a] The percentage price change is defined as $\log(P_t/P_{t-1}) \cdot 100$. The American prices are cash and futures prices. The London prices are spot and forward prices, denominated in pounds sterling. The converted prices are London spot and forward prices converted to dollars. The estimates for the unrestricted series use all of the available converted prices, while the restricted estimates only use prices if the matching American prices are also available.

table 2. For example, the standard deviations for the futures prices are approximately equal to the standard deviations for both the restricted and the unrestricted forward price series during both the 1968–1973 subperiod and the 1974–1978 subperiod. The effect of the future price limits is only noticeable when the more volatile 1979 and 1980 prices are included in the sample.[18]

The behavior of the copper price variances through time is also slightly different from the behavior for silver. The standard deviations for the copper and silver price changes are all about 1.5% during the first subperiod. However, the estimates for copper are much lower than the estimates for silver from 1974 through 1980; while silver's variance increases from the first to the second subperiod, copper's variance remains fairly constant. In fact, the standard deviations for copper do not increase unless 1979 and 1980 are added to the sample period.

Autocorrelations for the daily copper and silver price changes are presented in table 4. The autocorrelations for the spot, cash, and 3-month price series are estimated using data from 1968 through 1980, while the autocorrelations for the 6- and 12-month series are estimated from 1974 through 1980. The most striking result in table 4 is that almost all of the first-order autocorrelations are negative and relatively large. Only five of these autocorrelations are within four standard errors of zero. This serial correlation would seem to suggest a profitable trading opportunity; buy on the day after a price drop and sell after a rise. However, it is more likely that the correlation is caused by measurement error than by market inefficiency. For example, suppose the measurement error in today's reported spot price for silver is positive. This introduces a positive bias in today's price change and a negative bias in tomorrow's price change. This pattern would cause a negative first-order autocorrelation in the observed price changes. If the measurement error is negative, the pattern is reversed but the final result is the same. In view of this measurement error hypothesis, it is interesting to note that four of the five smallest first-order autocorrelations are for cash and futures prices.

To summarize the results from tables 2 through 4, there are some noticeable differences between the behavior of the futures prices and the behavior of the forward prices. For example, the evidence in tables 2 and 3 indicates that, because of the futures price limits, the variance of the observed futures prices is generally lower than the variance of the forward prices. In addition, the first-order autocorrelations in table 4 suggest that the London spot and forward prices contain more measurement error than the American cash and futures prices. The data also indicate that the variability of the daily price changes increases from 1968 to 1980. The silver price volatility

---

[18]In fact, only 3% of the 3-month copper futures prices observed from 1968 through 1978 reflect limit moves, while 9% of the prices for 1979 and 1980 are limit moves.

Table 4

Autocorrelations of the daily percent changes in the cash, spot, futures and forward prices for copper and silver.[a]

	Number	$S(r_1)$	r_1	r_2	r_3	r_4	r_5	r_6
			Silver					
Cash prices	2364	0.021	0.050	0.008	−0.026	0.018	−0.057	0.036
London spot prices	3054	0.018	−0.172	−0.025	0.052	0.020	−0.054	−0.035
Converted spot prices	3054	0.018	−0.170	−0.029	0.048	0.016	−0.052	−0.034
Restricted spot prices	2213	0.021	−0.216	0.006	0.025	0.037	−0.015	0.013
3-month contracts								
Futures prices	2081	0.022	−0.111	0.010	−0.044	0.081	−0.083	0.034
London forward prices	3051	0.018	−0.131	−0.023	0.045	0.026	−0.051	−0.045
Converted forward prices	2947	0.018	−0.133	−0.028	0.041	0.022	−0.048	−0.037
Restricted forward prices	1954	0.023	−0.203	−0.021	0.012	0.020	−0.012	0.036
6-month contracts								
Futures prices	1037	0.031	−0.148	0.020	−0.015	0.028	−0.062	0.005
London forward prices	1505	0.026	−0.195	−0.045	0.038	0.018	−0.054	−0.043
Converted forward prices	1467	0.026	−0.195	−0.042	0.026	0.026	−0.059	−0.045
Restricted forward prices	905	0.033	−0.244	0.007	−0.038	0.078	−0.028	−0.019
12-month contracts								
Futures prices	1057	0.031	−0.018	0.038	−0.015	0.017	−0.043	0.019
London forward prices	1496	0.026	−0.150	−0.028	0.038	0.034	−0.075	−0.064
Converted forward prices	1452	0.026	−0.150	−0.028	0.022	0.039	−0.079	−0.058
Restricted forward prices	906	0.033	−0.141	−0.035	0.038	0.035	−0.017	−0.018
			Copper					
Cash prices	1636	0.025	−0.023	−0.039	0.042	0.027	0.069	−0.060
London spot prices	3160	0.018	−0.106	−0.050	0.058	0.015	0.015	0.003
Converted spot prices	3160	0.018	−0.093	−0.048	0.052	0.015	0.016	0.008
Restricted spot prices	1585	0.025	−0.137	−0.062	0.054	0.036	0.056	−0.003
3-month contracts								
Futures prices	1407	0.027	−0.064	−0.039	0.007	0.001	0.081	−0.058
London forward prices	3158	0.018	−0.192	−0.020	−0.013	0.064	0.005	0.018
Converted forward prices	3043	0.018	−0.188	−0.024	−0.020	0.056	0.009	0.019
Restricted forward prices	1329	0.027	−0.053	−0.057	0.048	0.064	0.061	−0.056

[a] r_τ is the autocorrelation at lag τ; $S(r_1)$ is the standard error of the first-order autocorrelation. The cash, spot, and 3-month autocorrelations are estimated from 1/68 to 12/80. The 6- and 12-month autocorrelations are estimated from 1/74 to 12/80. The converted prices are London spot and forward prices converted to dollars. The estimates for the unrestricted series use all of the available converted prices, while the restricted estimates only use the converted prices if the matching American prices are also available.

appears to grow over the whole sample period. Although the variance of the copper prices is fairly constant from 1968 through 1978, the variances for both commodities increase significantly during the 1979–1980 period.

3.3. *The differences between futures and forward prices and tests of the Cox–Ingersoll–Ross propositions*

The simplest way to examine whether there is an empirically relevant difference between futures and forward prices is to compare them individually. Table 5 summarizes the percentage differences between matching futures and forward prices, defined as $\log[F(t, T)/f(t, T)] * 100$, for both copper and silver. These differences are measured at 3 months to maturity for the copper contracts and at 3, 6, and 12 months to maturity for the silver contracts. Since the futures contracts mature at monthly intervals, this process generates monthly observations.[19] For example, the January price difference for the 3-month silver series reflects futures and forward contracts that mature in April, while the February difference involves contracts that mature in May. The forward prices in table 5 (and in the tests below) are converted from pounds sterling to dollars using three different estimates of the basis differential for each commodity. The forward prices in the 1968–1980 comparisons are converted using the full-period estimates of the basis differential. The conversions for the subperiod tests use the basis differential estimated over the matching subperiod.

The futures–forward price differences for silver in table 5 indicate that, on average, the futures prices are larger than the forward prices. Four of the five estimates are significantly positive at the 5% level. Moreover, the difference between the futures and forward prices increases with the maturity of the contract; the average differences from 1974 through 1980 are about 0.1%, 0.4%, and 0.8% for the 3-, 6- and 12-month contracts, respectively.

The relation between the futures and forward prices for copper is less clearcut. It appears that the futures prices are lower than the forward prices during the first subperiod and higher than the forward prices during the second subperiod; the average price differences are -0.9% and 0.1%, respectively. However, the t-statistics for these estimates are only 1.55 and 0.21.[20]

Table 5 also contains some evidence about two of the propositions developed by Cox, Ingersoll and Ross (1981). They hypothesize that the futures–forward price difference is equal to

$$F(t, T) - f(t, T) = -PV_{t,T}\left\{\int_t^T \tilde{F}(w, T)\text{cov}[\tilde{F}(w, T), \tilde{B}(w, T)]dw\right\}/B(t, T), \quad (16)$$

where $\text{cov}[\tilde{F}(w, T), \tilde{B}(w, T)]$ is the local covariance at time w between the percentage change in the futures price and the percentage change in the bond price. This instantaneous covariance may be changing stochastically as the futures contract and the bond contract move toward maturity at time T.

---

[19]Futures contracts do not mature every month so some months will not be represented in these series.

[20]It is interesting that, although the average price difference for the second subperiod is positive, the t-statistic for the average difference of the full period, -1.68, is more negative than the t-statistic for the first subperiod, -1.55. This happens because different estimates of the basis differential are used for the full sample period and for each subperiod.

However, if the covariance is always positive during the contract period, the integral in (16) will be positive and the forward price should be higher than the futures price. On the other hand, if the local covariance is always negative, the futures price should be above the forward price.

Cox, Ingersoll and Ross also show that the futures–forward price difference can be expressed as

$$F(t,T) - f(t,T) = PV_{t,T} \left\{ \exp\left[\int_t^T \tilde{r}(w)\,dw\right] \int_t^T [\tilde{P}(w)/\tilde{B}(w,T)] \right.$$

$$\left. \times \{\text{var}[\tilde{B}(w,T)] - \text{cov}[\tilde{P}(w), \tilde{B}(w,T)]\}\,dw \right\}, \quad (17)$$

if the commodity is stored costlessly over the contract period. This leads to the prediction that, if the local variance of the bond price is always larger than the local covariance between the spot price and the bond price, the futures price will be above the forward price. If the variance is smaller than the covariance, the futures price should be below the forward price.

The simplest way to test these hypotheses is to assume that the local variances and covariances are constant and the same for all contracts.[21] Under this assumption the local covariance in eq. (16) is measured in two steps. First, the covariance between the daily percentage change in the futures price and the daily percentage change in the bond price is estimated for each pair of futures and forward contracts. These covariances are then averaged across contracts. The local variances and covariances in eq. (17) are estimated in the same way. The results of this process are reported in the second and third columns of table 5.[22]

Under the first CIR proposition, if the covariance between the bond prices and the futures prices is positive the futures–forward price difference should be negative. The results in table 5 provide some support for this hypothesis.

---

[21] This assumption cannot be strictly true since the local variances and covariances must converge to zero as the contracts approach maturity and the bond prices converge to one. However, estimates of the variances and covariances measured over the full contract period can be used to predict whether the relevant integrals are positive or negative. For example if the futures price is roughly constant, the average covariance between the futures price and the bond price is approximately proportional to the integral in eq. (16).

[22] All of the variances and covariances in table 5 have been multiplied by 10^6. The bond prices used to estimate these variables are measured by the 3-, 6- and 12-month treasury bill prices provided by the Federal Reserve Bank of New York and Data Resources, Inc. For example, when a futures contract has 12, 11, or 10 months to maturity, its daily price changes are compared with the price changes for treasury bills that will mature in approximately 12 months. When the futures contract has between 9 and 5 months to maturity, the 6-month treasury bill series is used. The 3-month bills are used during the last four months of the contract period. A 1-month treasury bill series is also available, but its bid/ask spread is very large. For example, the average daily spread from 1973 through 1980 is 0.32%. The average daily bid/ask spread for the 3-month series over this period is 0.025%.

Table 5

Futures–forward price differences and tests of the Cox–Ingersoll–Ross propositions.[a]

		log(fut/for)∗100	cov(F, B)	var(B)−cov(P, B)
		1968–1980		
3-month silver	Mean	0.297	0.231	0.803
	Std. dev.	1.325	1.917	4.203
	t-stat.	2.372	0.889	1.319
	Number	112	140	154
3-month copper	Mean	−0.701	0.371	0.158
	Std. dev.	3.744	1.442	0.843
	t-stat.	1.685	2.556	1.506
	Number	81	127	154
		1968–1973		
3-month silver	Mean	0.485	0.139	0.110
	Std. dev.	1.332	0.530	0.795
	t-stat.	2.651	1.193	0.653
	Number	53	68	70
3-month copper	Mean	−0.861	0.189	0.008
	Std. dev.	3.464	0.734	0.310
	t-stat.	1.552	1.195	0.150
	Number	39	56	70
		1974–1980		
3-month silver	Mean	0.136	0.318	1.380
	Std. dev.	1.325	2.630	5.595
	t-stat.	0.788	0.648	1.267
	Number	59	72	84
6-month silver	Mean	0.444	0.019	1.543
	Std. dev.	1.489	2.338	4.985
	t-stat.	2.251	0.041	1.369
	Number	57	63	84
12-month silver	Mean	0.846	−1.945	2.187
	Std. dev.	1.678	5.240	4.038
	t-stat.	3.670	1.533	2.294
	Number	53	72	79
3-month copper	Mean	0.109	0.515	0.283
	Std. dev.	3.325	1.808	1.094
	t-stat.	0.212	2.347	1.556
	Number	42	71	84

[a]Under the first CIR proposition, if the covariance between the daily percentage change in the futures price and the daily percentage change in the bond price is positive, the futures–forward price difference should be negative. If the covariance is negative, the price difference difference should be positive. Under the second CIR proposition, if the bond price variance is larger than its covariance with the spot price, the futures–forward price difference should be positive. If the variance–covariance difference is negative, the price difference should also be negative. The t-statistics for the covariances and the variance-covariance differences are adjusted for serial correlation.

For example, the average covariance for copper from 1968 through 1980 is 0.37, with a t-statistic of 2.56.[23] Using the CIR model, this implies that the futures prices will be below the forward prices. The average price difference of -0.7% is consistent with this prediction. The results for 12-month silver contracts also support the CIR hypothesis; the average covariance from 1974 through 1980 is -1.9 and, as the model predicts, the average futures–forward price difference is significantly positive. Unfortunately, the other comparisons do not provide much evidence. All but one of the other average covariances are approximately zero. The estimated covariance for 3-month copper contracts from 1974 through 1980 is significantly positive. However, since the t-statistic for the average futures–forward price difference for these contracts is only 0.21, one cannot reject the hypothesis that the true difference is negative, as the model predicts.

The results in table 5 provide more support for the second CIR proposition. Under this hypothesis, a positive difference between the variance of the bond prices and the covariance of the bond and spot prices should be associated with a positive difference between the futures and forward prices. The estimates for silver are all consistent with this model. For example, the average variance–covariance difference for 12 month silver contracts is 2.2, with a t-statistic of 2.29, and, as the model predicts, the price difference is significantly positive. Only the negative price differences for copper do not support the model.

The evidence in table 5 indicates that the average differences between the observed futures and forward prices are consistent with the CIR propositions. These propositions may also help to explain variations among the futures–forward price differences. For example, if the covariance between futures prices and bond prices in eq. (16) is not constant across contracts, changes in this covariance should be related to changes in the price differences. To examine this hypothesis, the covariance is estimated over each 3-, 6- and 12-month contract period. Then the futures contracts (and the matching forward contracts) are divided into two groups. Those contracts with negative estimated covariances are assigned to one group, while those with positive estimates are assigned to the other. Under the null hypothesis, the futures prices for the first group should be larger than the matching forward prices. In the second group, the futures prices should be below the forward prices.

The first half of table 6 describes the results of this segmentation. The 3-month contracts in this table are compared over the full 1968–1980 sample period, while the 6- and 12-month contracts are compared from 1974

---

[23]The t-statistics for the covariances and the variance–covariance differences are adjusted to reflect the serial correlation caused by the overlapping estimation periods.

Table 6

Futures–forward price differences sorted by covariances and variance–covariance differences.[a]

		$cov(F,B)<0$	$cov(F,B)>0$	Diff.	$var(B)>cov(P,B)$	$var(B)<cov(P,B)$	Diff.
3-month silver	Mean	0.328	0.270	0.058	0.363	0.236	0.127
	Std. dev.	1.097	1.522	0.260	1.119	1.499	0.251
	t-stat.	2.071	1.374	0.225	2.384	1.199	0.508
	Number	48	60	108	54	58	112
6-month silver	Mean	0.380	0.496	−0.116	0.459	0.434	0.025
	Std. dev.	1.114	2.041	0.430	1.348	1.589	0.405
	t-stat.	1.930	1.114	−0.270	1.597	1.616	0.062
	Number	32	21	53	22	35	57
12-month silver	Mean	0.662	1.255	−0.594	0.605	0.925	−0.319
	Std. dev.	1.226	2.405	0.508	1.579	1.721	0.536
	t-stat.	3.149	2.152	−1.169	1.381	3.399	−0.596
	Number	34	17	51	13	40	53
3-month copper	Mean	−0.591	−0.775	0.185	−0.661	−0.729	0.068
	Std. dev.	4.358	3.364	0.863	3.881	3.688	0.847
	t-stat.	−0.779	−1.563	0.214	−0.978	−1.369	0.080
	Number	33	46	79	33	48	81

[a] Under the first CIR proposition, the futures–forward price difference should be positive if the covariance between the bond prices and the futures prices is negative and it should be negative if the covariance is positive. The difference between the two groups should be positive.
Under the second CIR proposition, if the variance of the bond price changes is larger than the covariance between the bond price changes and the spot price changes, the futures–forward price differences should be positive. If the variance is less than the covariance, the price difference should be negative. The difference between the two groups should be positive.

through 1980.[24] In general, the covariances are not useful in discriminating among the price differences. The comparisons between the two groups are randomly distributed about zero. For example, three of the four t-statistics comparing the two groups are between -0.3 and 0.3 and none is larger than 1.2.[25]

The second CIR proposition can be tested in the same way. First, the variance of the percentage change in the bond price and the covariance between the percentage change in the bond price and the percentage change in the spot price are estimated over the life of each pair of futures and forward contracts. Then the contracts are sorted into two groups. If the bond price variance is larger than the covariance between the bond and spot prices, the futures and forward contracts are assigned to the first group. If this difference is negative, the contracts are assigned to the second group. Using the CIR model, the futures–forward price differences should be positive in the first group and negative in the second.

The results of this stratification process are summarized in the second half of table 6. Again, the 3-month contracts are compared over the full 1968–1980 sample period, while the 6- and 12-month contracts are compared from 1974 through 1980. The results in table 6 do not provide any support for the second CIR hypothesis. For example, although the model predicts that the price difference should be negative when the variance is smaller than the covariance, three of the four differences for the second group are positive. Moreover, although the average difference for the first group should be larger than the average for the second group, the comparisons between the groups are distributed randomly about zero.[26]

Although the results in table 6 do not support the CIR propositions, they are not as inconsistent with the models as they seem. First, the tests involving the 3-, 6- and 12-month silver contracts are not independent. For example, the variance–covariance difference for the 6-month contract that matures in June is estimated with bond and spot prices from January through June, while the estimate of the difference for the 3-month June

---

[24]To be included in the sample, each pair of contracts must have a futures price and a converted forward price available on the contracting date described in footnote 10. In addition, there must be at least 10 days of futures and bond price data available during each month of the contracts' life.

[25]Two other methods for stratifying the sample were also tried. One approach assigns contracts to the two groups only if the correlation between the bond and futures prices is significantly different from zero. The second method only assigns those contracts whose monthly covariances are either all positive or all negative. The results using these stratification techniques are similar to those reported.

[26]A second stratification technique was also tried. If the difference between the variance and the covariance is positive in each month during the estimation period the contract pair is assigned to the first group. If this difference is negative during each month, the contracts are assigned to the second group. All other futures–forward pairs are dropped from the sample. There is no discernible difference between the futures–forward prices differences for these two groups.

contracts uses the same data during April, May, and June. A more important problem arises because the models imply that the futures–forward price differences are related to the market's expectations of the relevant variances and covariances; these expectations are unobservable. The tests in table 6 use estimates of the realized variances and covariances as proxies for the market's expectations. Since these proxies contain measurement error, many of the price pairs may be assigned to the wrong group in table 6. This could mask the true relation between the price differences and the expected variances and covariances.

The Cox, Ingersoll, and Ross models make several other predictions that may be less sensitive to these measurement error problems. For example, if the local correlation between futures price changes and bond price changes is constant, the first CIR proposition implies that the absolute value of the futures–forward price difference is an increasing function of the market's expectation of both the futures price variance and the bond price variance. Analogously, the second proposition implies that the price difference is a decreasing function of the spot price variance if the price difference is negative and if the local correlation between the spot and bond prices is constant.

As Cox, Ingersoll and Ross demonstrate, their second proposition can be re-expressed as

$$F(t,T) - f(t,T) = -PV_t \left\{ \exp\left[\int_t^T \tilde{r}(w)\,dw \right] \int_t^T \tilde{f}(w,T) \right.$$

$$\left. \times \operatorname{cov}[\tilde{f}(w,T), \tilde{B}(w,T)]\,dw \right\}. \qquad (18)$$

This leads to one more prediction; if the local correlation between the forward price and the bond price is constant, the absolute value of the futures–forward price difference is an increasing function of the market's expectation of the forward price variance.

To test these predictions, the variances of the relevant variables are regressed against the futures–forward price differences. These variances are estimated over the life of the matching contracts.[27] For example, each futures price variance is computed using the daily price changes for an individual futures contract as it approaches maturity. The bond price variances are measured in two different ways. Under the first approach, which is also used for the forward prices, the variances for the 3-, 6- and 12-month regressions are estimated using the matching 3-, 6- and 12-month price series. Under the second approach, the bond price variances are estimated by the variance of

---

[27] These tests have been replicated using variances estimated over the period immediately before the contract date. The results from the two sets of variances are very similar.

the percentage changes in the daily federal funds return during each contract period.[28]

Table 7 presents regressions of these variances against the futures–forward price differences.[29] The 3-month regressions in this table are estimated over the full 1968–1980 sample period. The 6- and 12-month regressions are estimated from 1974 through 1980.

The results in table 7 are similar to the results in table 6; although they are consistent with the CIR propositions, they do not provide much support for these propositions. For example, the models imply that the absolute value of the price differences will increase with the variance of the futures, forward, and bond prices. Since the futures price is generally above the forward price for silver, this means that the slope coefficient in the silver regressions involving these variances should be positive. On the other hand, the price differences for copper are usually negative. Therefore, the slope coefficients for all of the copper regressions — including the spot price regression — should be negative. In fact, the estimates appear to be randomly distributed about zero.[30] These results are particularly ambiguous because only two of the twenty estimates are significantly different from zero. The results in table 7 neither support nor refute the CIR propositions.[31]

It appears that the Cox, Ingersoll and Ross propositions are useful in describing the average differences between futures and forward prices. However, without better estimates of the market's expectations of the relevant variances and covariances, neither hypothesis is able to discriminate among the individual differences.

3.4. Futures–forward price differences and interest rate differences

The models in section 2 imply that the difference between futures and forward prices should be related to the difference between short- and long-term interest rates. In fact, if the marginal utility of the commodity,

---

[28]The federal funds returns are provided by the Federal Reserve Bank of New York.

[29]The regressions in table 7 suffer from at least two econometric problems. First, the error terms are serially correlated and, second, each futures–forward price difference may be correlated with the previous error terms. Generalized least squares is usually used to solve the first problem. However, as Hansen and Hodrick (1980) demonstrate, GLS would lead to inconsistent estimates in this case. Fortunately, the ordinary least squares estimators in table 7 are consistent and asymptotically normal [see Hansen (1980)]. The usual estimated covariance matrix for the OLS coefficients, appropriately modified to reflect the serial correlation in the error terms, provides a consistent estimate of the covariance matrix of the asymptotic distribution; writing the regressions in table 7 in matrix notation, $Y = X\gamma + e$, the estimated covariance matrix for the OLS coefficients is $\hat{\Sigma} = (X'X)^{-1} X'\hat{\Omega} X (X'X)^{-1}$, where $\hat{\Omega}$ is the estimated covariance matrix for the error terms. The standard errors in table 7 are based on this estimated covariance matrix.

[30]These regressions have also been estimated using the absolute value of the futures–forward price differences. The coefficients in these regressions are very similar to the estimates reported in table 7.

[31]Part of this ambiguity may be caused by measurement errors in the observed futures–forward price differences. The effect of these measurement errors is discussed in the next section.

Table 7

Regressions of variances against futures–forward price differences.[a]

	Number	Intercept	Slope	R^2	Number	Intercept	Slope	R^2
		Treasury bill prices				Federal funds returns		
3-month silver	112	0.007 (3.893)	0.018 (0.176)	0.00	112	0.744 (5.440)	−17.733 (2.535)	0.07
6-month silver	57	0.026 (2.544)	0.139 (0.459)	0.00	57	0.339 (2.312)	2.587 (0.746)	0.01
12-month silver	51	0.102 (1.923)	−0.150 (0.087)	0.00	51	0.250 (1.961)	5.517 (1.430)	0.04
3-month copper	81	0.011 (3.598)	0.051 (0.653)	0.01	81	0.621 (4.712)	−11.520 (3.522)	0.21
		Futures prices				Converted forward prices		
3-month silver	86	0.036 (5.348)	0.335 (0.814)	0.01	90	0.270 (1.325)	−0.712 (0.062)	0.00
6-month silver	55	0.037 (2.990)	0.361 (1.006)	0.01	56	0.132 (2.527)	−0.373 (0.269)	0.00
12-month silver	54	0.042 (1.996)	0.826 (0.981)	0.10	51	0.118 (2.407)	−1.943 (1.187)	0.02
3-month copper	73	0.031 (6.953)	−0.110 (0.977)	0.02	63	0.618 (1.043)	11.655 (0.731)	0.01
		Converted spot prices						
3-month silver	111	0.266 (1.604)	0.368 (0.040)	0.00				
6-month silver	57	0.440 (1.298)	0.800 (0.084)	0.00				
12-month silver	51	0.445 (1.440)	−6.554 (0.663)	0.01				
3-month copper	80	0.031 (3.840)	−0.275 (1.424)	0.04				

[a] The dependent variable in these regressions is the variance of the indicated variable, estimated over the contract period. The independent variable is the percentage difference between the futures price and the converted forward price. The t-statistics, adjusted for the serial correlation caused by the overlapping estimation periods, are in parentheses.

$\bar{P}(T)\tilde{\lambda}(T)$, is assumed to be independent of the nominal interest rate,[32] eqs. (8) and (10) can be used to write the ratio of the futures and forward prices as

$$F(t,T)/f(t,T) = E_t\left\{\exp\left[\sum_{\tau=t}^{T-1}\tilde{R}(\tau,\tau+1)\right]\right\}\bigg/\exp[(T-t)R(t,T)]. \quad (19)$$

[32] The following set of conditions is sufficient for this assumption to hold:
(1) The price of some commodity (commodity N) is independent of the marginal utility of all commodities.
(2) The expected value of the continuously compounded real rate of return on nominal bonds is constant. This real rate is defined in terms of commodity N.

The ratio of the futures price and the forward price should equal the ratio of the expected gross return from rolling over one-day bonds and the gross return from investing in a $(T-t)$ day bond.

Since the expected return from rolling over one-day bonds is unobservable, the prediction in eq. (19) cannot be tested directly. One alternative is to use the actual return, which is observed at time T,

$$\frac{F(t,T)}{f(t,T)} = \exp\left[\sum_{\tau=t}^{T-1} R(\tau,\tau+1) - \varepsilon(t,T)\right] \Big/ \exp[(T-t)R(t,T)]. \qquad (20)$$

In this expression, $\varepsilon(t, T)$ is equal to the market's error in forecasting the cumulated one-day returns. Eq. (20) can be tested by estimating the regression

$$\sum_{\tau=t}^{T-1} R(\tau, \tau+1) - (T-t)R(t,T) = \alpha + \beta \log[F(t,T)/f(t,T)] + \varepsilon(t,T). \qquad (21)$$

Table 8 presents ordinary least squares estimates of this regression for copper and silver.[33] Under the null hypothesis, the intercept should equal zero and the slope should equal one. This hypothesis can be rejected for all of the regressions summarized in table 8. Although most of the estimates of α are not significantly different from zero, all of the estimates of β are quite significantly different from one. For example, the largest slope coefficient is estimated for the 3-month silver price regression from 1974 through 1980. The value of this coefficient is 0.058 and it has a standard error of 0.029. In other words, the largest estimate of β is more than 30 standard errors below one. The values of F-statistics testing the joint hypothesis that α equals zero and β equals one are over 50 for all of the regressions.

The evidence in table 8 indicates that the observed differences between the short- and long-term interest rates are not useful in explaining the observed differences between the futures and forward prices. However, these results do not necessarily imply that the underlying model is wrong. Instead, they may be caused by measurement errors in the observed price differences. For example, each day's forward prices are recorded in London about five hours before the futures prices are recorded in America. Many of the largest positive and negative price differences are probably caused by information that arrives after the London market closes but before the American markets do. These measurement errors in the price differences bias the slope

---

[33]The regressions in table 8 suffer from the same econometric problems as the regressions in table 7. These problems are discussed in footnote 29.

The one-day bond returns used to estimate the regressions in table 8 are measured by the overnight federal funds rate. The long-term interest rates, with maturities of 3, 6 and 12 months, are measured by the return on American treasury bills.

Table 8

Regressions of interest rate differences on futures–forward price differences.[a]

	Number	Intercept	Slope	R^2
		3-month silver		
1/68–12/80	110	0.031 (0.045)	0.035 (0.022)	0.03
1/68–12/73	53	0.109 (0.063)	0.002 (0.029)	0.00
1/74–12/80	57	−0.033 (0.057)	0.058 (0.029)	0.09
		6-month silver		
1/74–12/80	57	−0.128 (0.133)	0.006 (0.048)	0.00
		12-month silver		
1/74–12/80	53	−0.034 (0.167)	0.001 (0.055)	0.00
		3-month copper		
1/68–12/80	79	0.050 (0.047)	−0.028 (0.011)	0.12
1/68–12/73	39	−0.019 (0.067)	−0.043 (0.015)	0.27
1/74–12/80	40	0.077 (0.073)	−0.022 (0.019)	0.05

[a]The dependent variable in this regression is the cumulated one-day federal funds interest rate minus the treasury bill interest rate over the contract period. The independent variable is the percentage difference between the futures price and the converted forward price. Under the null hypothesis, the intercept should be zero and the slope coefficient should be one. The asymptotic standard errors are in parentheses.

coefficients in table 8 toward zero. This problem is particularly troublesome because, under the null hypothesis, the variation in the true, unobserved, price differences is probably small relative to the variance of the measurement errors.[34]

---

[34]Ignoring the econometric problems discussed in footnote 29, the probability limit of the estimated slope coefficient is equal to plim $\hat{\beta} = \beta/[1 + \sigma_u^2/\sigma_x^2]$, where σ_u^2 is the variance of the measurement errors and σ_x^2 is the variance of the true price differences. Therefore, the bias in the slope coefficient increases as the relative variance of the measurement errors increases.

4. Summary and conclusions

This paper uses the pricing models of Cox, Ingersoll and Ross (1981), Richard and Sundaresan (1981), and French (1982) to examine the relation between futures and forward prices for copper and silver. There are significant differences between these prices. The average differences are generally consistent with the predictions of both arbitrage and utility-based models. However, these models are not helpful in explaining intra-sample variations in the futures–forward price differences.

There are several possible reasons why the futures and forward price models do not help in discriminating among the price differences. The most obvious explanation is that the models are incomplete. For example, the models abstract from market imperfections like taxes and transactions costs. If these factors play an important role in determining the futures and forward prices, one may observe differences in these prices that are unrelated to the factors examined here.

An alternative interpretation of the evidence in this paper says that the theoretical models do describe the underlying price differences, but, because of measurement errors, the models are not useful in discriminating among the observed differences. Under this hypothesis, the models fail to capture movements in the observed price differences because measurement errors mask the variations in the true price differences. However, the models correctly predict the average observed price differences because aggregating across contracts reduces the effect of the measurement errors.

These measurement errors take two forms. First, the futures–forward price differences are measured with error. For example, the individual prices are only recorded in discrete steps, such as eighths of a dollar or tenths of a pound. Also, the prices in each pair are not matched precisely. This problem is especially acute because the forward prices are observed in London and the futures prices are observed approximately five hours later in New York and Chicago. These errors in measuring the futures–forward price differences can have a particularly large effect if the variation in the true price differences is small.

A second type of measurement error arises because all of the predictions involve variables that must be estimated. The tests involving the Cox, Ingersoll and Ross predictions provide good examples of this problem. The CIR propositions indicate that the futures–forward price differences should be related to the market's expectation of local variances and covariances. However, neither these expectations nor the realized values of the variables are observable. Although several approaches are used to estimate the variances and covariances, none of them is powerful enough to discriminate among the various price differences.

Earlier studies of the empirical relation between futures and forward prices do not provide much help in determining if the results reported here are caused by problems with the theoretical models or by problems with the data. Several papers have been written comparing the prices for treasury bill futures contracts with the forward prices implied by the interest rates on treasury bills traded in the spot market.[35] The evidence in these papers indicates that, on average, the futures prices for contracts with approximately four or more months to maturity are significantly lower than the matching forward prices. As the contracts approach maturity, this relation is reversed; the implied forward prices tend to be lower than the matching futures prices. Cornell and Reinganum (1981) compare futures and forward prices for foreign exchange contracts. Although they observe differences between individual prices, they find that the average difference is not significantly different from zero. Unfortunately, none of these papers examines the relation between the observed price differences and the theoretical models studied here. More tests are needed to support or reject these models.

The results in this paper have important implications for other research. Most commodity exchanges in the United States trade futures contracts. However, since forward contracts are easier to analyze, many economists treat the observed prices as though they were forward prices. This simplification can be misleading. The studies comparing the futures prices and implied forward prices for treasury bills provide a good example of the problems this may cause. The authors of many of these studies claim that the futures prices should equal the forward prices implied in the spot market. When they observe differences between these prices, they interpret this as evidence of market inefficiency. The results in this paper suggest that these price differences may actually be caused by differences between futures and forward contracts.

[35]See, for example, Puglisi (1978), Capozza and Cornell (1979), Rendleman and Carabini (1979), and Vignola and Dale (1980).

References

Bartlett, M.S., 1946, On the theoretical specification of sampling properties of autocorrelated time series, Journal of the Royal Statistical Society (Suppl.) 8, 27–41.
Black, F., 1976, The pricing of commodity contracts, Journal of Financial Economics 3, Jan./March, 167–179.
Capozza, D. and B. Cornell, 1979, Treasury bill pricing in the spot and futures markets, Review of Economics and Statistics 61, Nov., 513–520.
Cornell, B. and M. Reinganum, 1981, Forward and futures prices: Evidence from the foreign exchange markets, Journal of Finance 36, Dec., 1035–1045.
Cox, J., J. Ingersoll and S. Ross, 1977, A theory of the term structure of interest rates and the valuation of interest-dependent claims, Working paper (Graduate School of Business, Stanford University, Stanford, CA).
Cox, J., J. Ingersoll and S. Ross, 1981, The relation between forward prices and futures prices, Journal of Financial Economics 9, Dec., 321–346.
Dusak, K., 1973, Futures trading and investor returns: An investigation of commodity market risk premiums, Journal of Political Economy 81, Nov./Dec., 1387–1406.

French, K.R., 1982, The pricing of futures and forward contracts, Ph.D. dissertation (University of Rochester, Rochester, NY).
Grauer, F., 1977, Equilibrium in commodity futures markets: Theory and tests, Ph.D. dissertation (Stanford University, Stanford, CA).
Grauer, F. and R. Litzenberger, 1979, The pricing of commodity futures contracts, nominal bonds and other risky assets under commodity price uncertainty, Journal of Finance 34, March, 69–83.
Hansen, L., 1980, Large sample properties of generalized method of moments estimators, Working paper (Graduate School of Industrial Administration, Carnegie-Mellon University, Pittsburgh, PA).
Hansen, L. and R. Hodrick, 1980, Forward exchange rates as optimal predictors of future spot rates: An econometric analysis, Journal of Political Economy 88, Oct., 829–853.
Jarrow, R. and G. Oldfield, 1981, Forward contracts and futures contracts, Journal of Financial Economics 9, Dec., 373–382.
Levich, R. and L. White, 1981, Price controls and futures contracts: an examination of the markets for copper and silver during 1971–1974, Working paper (Center for the Study of Futures Markets, Columbia Business School, New York).
Margrabe, W., 1976, A theory of forward and futures prices, Working paper (The Wharton School, University of Pennsylvania, Philadelphia, PA).
Puglisi, D., 1978, Is the futures market for treasury bills efficient?, Journal of Portfolio Management 4, Winter, 64–67.
Rendleman, R. and C. Carabini, 1979, The efficiency of the treasury bill futures market, Journal of Finance 39, Sept., 895–914.
Richard, S.F. and M. Sundaresan, 1981, A continuous time equilibrium model of forward prices and futures prices in a multigood economy, Journal of Financial Economics 9, 347–372.
Vignola, A. and C. Dale, 1980, The efficiency of the treasury bill futures market: An analysis of alternative specifications, Journal of Financial Research 3, Fall, 169–188.

[4]

Eugene F. Fama
Kenneth R. French
University of Chicago

Commodity Futures Prices: Some Evidence on Forecast Power, Premiums, and the Theory of Storage*

I. Introduction

There are two popular views of commodity futures prices. The theory of storage of Kaldor (1939), Working (1948), Brennan (1958), and Telser (1958) explains the difference between contemporaneous spot and futures prices in terms of interest forgone in storing a commodity, warehousing costs, and a convenience yield on inventory. The alternative view splits a futures price into an expected risk premium and a forecast of a future spot price. See, for example, Cootner (1960), Dusak (1973), Breeden (1980), and Hazuka (1984).

The theory of storage is not controversial. In contrast, there is little agreement on whether futures prices contain expected premiums or have power to forecast spot prices. We use both models to study the behavior of futures prices for 21 commodities. We find that more powerful statistical tests make the response of futures prices to storage-cost variables easier to detect than evidence that futures prices contain premiums or power to forecast spot prices.

We examine two models of commodity futures prices. The theory of storage explains the difference between contemporaneous futures and spot prices (the basis) in terms of interest changes, warehousing costs, and convenience yields. We find evidence of variation in the basis in response to both interest rates and seasonals in convenience yields. The second model splits a futures price into an expected premium and a forecast of the maturity spot price. We find evidence of forecast power for 10 of 21 commodities and time-varying expected premiums for five commodities.

* This research is supported by the National Science Foundation (Fama) and the Chicago Board of Trade (French). The comments of Wayne Ferson, John Long, G. William Schwert, and workshop participants at the University of Chicago, the University of California, Los Angeles (where Fama spends winter quarters), the University of Rochester, and Yale University are gratefully acknowledged.

(*Journal of Business*, 1987, vol. 60, no. 1)
© 1987 by The University of Chicago. All rights reserved.
0021-9398/87/6001-0003$01.50

II. The Basis: Evidence on the Theory of Storage

A. The Theory of Storage

Let $F(t, T)$ be the futures price at time t for delivery of a commodity at T. Let $S(t)$ be the spot price at t. The theory of storage predicts that the return from purchasing the commodity at t and selling it for delivery at T, $F(t, T) - S(t)$, equals the interest forgone, $S(t)R(t, T)$, plus the marginal storage cost, $W(t, T)$, less the marginal convenience yield from an additional unit of inventory, $C(t, T)$:

$$F(t, T) - S(t) = S(t)R(t, T) + W(t, T) - C(t, T). \qquad (1)$$

Equivalently,

$$[F(t, T) - S(t)]/S(t) = R(t, T) + [W(t, T) - C(t, T)]/S(t). \qquad (2)$$

We call $F(t, T) - S(t)$, or $[F(t, T) - S(t)]/S(t)$, the basis.

The marginal convenience yield, $C(t, T)$, arises because inventory can have productive value. For example, there may be a convenience yield from holding inventories of some commodities (such as wheat) because they are inputs to the production of other commodities (such as flour). Or there may be a convenience yield from holding inventories to meet unexpected demand.

The theory of storage predicts a negative relation between convenience yields and inventories. Brennan (1958) and Telser (1958) provide detailed studies of the relations between convenience yields and inventories for several agricultural commodities. Since good inventory data are not available for many of the commodities studied here, we take a cruder approach. Seasonals in production or demand can generate seasonals in inventories. Under the theory of storage, inventory seasonals generate seasonals in the marginal convenience yield and in the basis. We test for seasonals in the basis.

Another implication of (2) is that, controlling for variation in the marginal storage cost and the marginal convenience yield, the $T - t$ period basis for any stored commodity should vary one-for-one with the $T - t$ period interest rate. We provide (apparently the first) systematic tests of this well-known implication of the theory of storage.

B. Data

We construct monthly observations on the basis $[F(t, T) - S(t)]/S(t)$ and the interest rate $R(t, T)$ for 1-, 3-, 6-, and 12-month maturities ($T - t$). The interest rates are beginning-of-month yields on Treasury bills calculated from the quotes in various issues of Salomon Brothers' *Analytical Record of Yields and Yield Spreads*. The sample period for interest rates is January 1967–May 1984.

Measuring the basis presents two problems. The first is that most futures contracts do not have a specific maturity. Instead, there is a delivery period of 3–4 weeks at the beginning of the maturity month. We assume that contracts mature on the first trading day of the delivery month. This means, for example, that the April 1, 1980, futures price for the May 1980 wheat contract is used as a 1-month futures price.

The second complication is that good spot-price data are not available for most commodities. We use futures prices on maturing contracts to measure spot prices. For example, the spot price for wheat on March 1 is the futures price for the contract that matures in March. Since futures contracts do not mature each month, this solution limits sample sizes. The number of observations on the basis is always less than the number of months in the sample period. On the other hand, using maturing futures prices to measure spot prices ensures that spot and futures prices are for the same commodity and are sampled at the same time.

Table 1 summarizes the structure of the commodity-price data. Each row shows the sample period for a commodity and the standard months in which contracts mature. Contracts for these standard months usually begin trading between 8 and 12 months before maturity, and they are traded every year. Copper, gold, and silver have supplemental contracts that fill in the months between the standard contracts. These supplemental contracts usually begin trading 3 or 4 months before maturity. They are useful because they augment the spot-price series.

C. Standard Deviations of the Basis

The second column of table 2 shows standard deviations of the 6-month basis for the 21 commodities. The 6-month maturity is chosen since it is available for all commodities but cotton. The 3-month basis is used for cotton. Basis standard deviations differ systematically across commodity groups. The precious metals have the lowest standard deviations—2.0% for gold, 1.5% for silver, and 4.2% for platinum. The standard deviations for the agricultural products range from 4.6% for corn to 9.7% for oats. The animal products have the largest basis standard deviations. The standard deviation for cattle is 5.6%, and the standard deviations for the other four animal products range from 10.1% for broilers to 22.2% for eggs.

The differences in the basis standard deviations for commodity subgroups are consistent with the theory of storage. One source of variation in the basis is seasonals in supply and demand. For example, spot prices for agricultural commodities usually increase between harvests and fall across harvests. Because of this pattern in the spot price, the basis is usually positive when the futures contract matures in the current crop year and negative when the futures contract matures early in the next crop year. Storage costs are important in determining the magnitude of the seasonal variation in spot prices. Higher storage costs

TABLE 1   Layout of Commodity Futures Data

Commodity	Exchange*	Sample Period	Jan.	Feb.	Mar.	Apr.	May	June	July	Aug.	Sept.	Oct.	Nov.	Dec.
Agricultural products:														
Cocoa	CSCE	3/66–7/84			✓		✓		✓		✓			✓
Coffee	CSCE	9/72–7/84			✓		✓		✓		✓			✓
Corn	CBT	3/66–7/84			✓		✓		✓		✓			✓
Cotton	CTN	3/67–7/84			✓		✓		✓			✓		✓
Oats	CBT	5/66–7/84			✓		✓		✓		✓			✓
Orange juice	CTN	2/67–7/84	✓		✓		✓		✓		✓		✓	
Soybeans	CBT	3/66–7/84	✓		✓		✓		✓	✓	✓			
Soy meal	CBT	5/66–7/84	✓		✓	✓	✓		✓	✓		✓		✓
Soy oil	CBT	5/66–7/84			✓	✓			✓	✓	✓	✓		
Wheat	CBT	5/66–7/84			✓		✓		✓		✓			✓
Wood products:														
Lumber	CME	1/70–12/82	✓		✓		✓		✓		✓		✓	
Plywood	CBT	1/70–9/83	✓		✓		✓		✓		✓		✓	
Animal products:														
Broilers†	CBT	8/68–6/81	✓		✓		✓		✓	✓		✓	✓	✓
Eggs†	CME	5/66–12/80	✓	✓	✓	✓			✓		✓	✓	✓	✓
Cattle	CME	1/72–7/84		✓		✓		✓		✓		✓		✓
Hogs	CME	3/66–7/84		✓		✓		✓	✓	✓		✓		✓
Pork bellies	CME	5/66–7/84		✓	✓		✓		✓	✓				
Metals:‡														
Copper	Comex	3/66–7/84	✓		✓		✓		✓		✓			✓
Gold	Comex	2/75–7/84		✓		✓		✓		✓		✓		✓
Platinum	NYM	1/68–7/84	✓			✓			✓			✓		
Silver	Comex	1/67–7/84	✓		✓		✓		✓		✓			✓

* CBT = Chicago Board of Trade; CME = Chicago Mercantile Exchange; Comex = Commodity Exchange; CSCE = Coffee, Sugar, and Cocoa Exchange; CTN = New York Cotton Exchange; NYM = New York Mercantile Exchange.
† The standard delivery months for broilers and eggs change toward the end of the sample period. The delivery months prevailing over most of the period are indicated here.
‡ Supplemental contracts are traded on copper, gold, and silver. These contracts fill in the months between the standard contracts.

TABLE 2 Regressions of the 6-Month Basis on the 6-Month Interest Rate and Monthly Seasonal Dummies:

$$\frac{F(t, T) - S(t)}{S(t)} = \sum_{m=1}^{12} \alpha_m d_m + \beta R(t, T) + e(t, T)$$

Commodity	Obs.	SD	β	$s(\beta)$	F	df	R_1^2	R_2^2	Storage (%)	Handling (%)
Agricultural products:										
Cocoa	35	8.1	1.16	1.44	.00	1	.00	.03	.16	.35
Coffee	30	9.6	.29	1.57	1.72	4	.06	.03	.12	.26
Corn	35	4.6	.86	.52	.01	1	.05	.07	1.41	1.73
Cotton	36	4.9	.84	1.46	1.14	2	−.02	−.02	.32	.13
Oats	34	9.7	1.06	1.27	6.55	1	.16	.01	2.65	3.26
Orange juice	102	9.2	1.39	1.21	3.32	5	.14	.04	.30	.32
Soybeans	105	7.8	1.88	.71	5.72	5	.30	.14	.64	.78
Soy meal	70	7.2	2.03	.84	.20	5	.16	.21	...	...
Soy oil	74	8.9	1.73	1.28	.79	5	.06	.07	.27	.30
Wheat	35	6.8	1.05	.86	9.03	1	.24	.05	1.39	1.71
Wood products:										
Lumber	86	13.6	2.41	2.21	1.86	5	.12	.07	1.96	3.82
Plywood	82	7.4	1.23	1.17	.71	5	.04	.06	...	...
Animal products:										
Broilers	64	10.1	1.39	1.65	5.43	11	.44	.00	...	...
Cattle	70	5.6	−.06	.57	4.48	5	.19	−.01	...	...
Eggs	80	22.2	−4.32	3.34	4.96	11	.38	.04	...	...
Hogs	102	10.9	2.21	1.36	1.79	9	.14	.08	...	...
Pork bellies	34	14.3	2.71	1.66	5.86	1	.19	.07	.98	2.54
Metals:										
Copper	89	6.5	1.39	.85	1.05	5	.14	.13	.12	.49
Gold	57	2.0	1.07	.13	.29	6	.81	.83	.01	.03
Platinum	66	4.2	1.18	.63	.28	3	.15	.18	.01	.01
Silver	101	1.5	.77	.16	.31	5	.58	.60	.03	.06

NOTE.—Obs. is the number of observations. SD is the standard deviation of the 6-month basis. df is the numerator degrees of freedom for the F-statistic test of the hypothesis that all the seasonal dummies in a regression are equal. R_1^2 is the coefficient of determination in the simple regression of the basis on the interest rate, and R_2^2 is for the regression that includes the seasonal dummies. Storage is the monthly warehousing cost per dollar of the June 1984 spot price. Handling is the total cost of loading and unloading the commodity at the warehouse per dollar of the June 1984 spot price. Storage and handling charges are from futures exchanges, dealers, elevators, and warehouses. These charges are reported only for commodities that have standard storage arrangements. The absence of such arrangements implies high storage costs. The 6-month maturity is not available for cotton. The 3-month maturity is used.

imply larger expected spot-price changes to induce storage between harvests. Thus seasonal variation in the basis should be an increasing function of storage costs.

Demand and supply shocks also generate variation in the basis. The effect of shocks on the basis depends to a large extent on the way inventories adjust to transmit the price effects of shocks through time. For example, suppose there is a spell of propitious weather before a harvest that raises expected future supplies and lowers expected future prices. The expected decline in the spot price is partly offset by the inventory response it generates. The gap between current and expected future prices is narrowed as more inventory is sold immediately. Higher inventory levels allow larger inventory responses to demand and supply shocks and thus lower variation in expected price changes. Since storage costs deter storage, the effect of demand and supply shocks on the variability of the basis should be an increasing function of storage costs. See French (1986).

The analysis predicts high basis standard deviations for seasonal, high-storage-cost commodities. Metal storage costs (table 2) are low relative to value, and the metals are not subject to seasonals in supply or demand. Thus the low basis standard deviations for the metals are consistent with the theory of storage. It is also consistent with the theory of storage that the highest basis standard deviations are observed for some of the wood and animal products (lumber, broilers, eggs, hogs, and pork bellies), where bulk and perishability make storage expensive.

D. Regression Tests

To obtain more direct tests of the theory of storage, we regress the basis against the nominal interest rate and monthly seasonal dummies:

$$\frac{F(t, T) - S(t)}{S(t)} = \sum_{m=1}^{12} \alpha_m d_m + \beta R(t, T) + e(t, T), \qquad (3)$$

where d_m equals 1.0 if the futures contract matures in month m and 0.0 otherwise. The hypothesis of the storage equation (2) is that the slope β should be 1.0 for any commodity continuously stored; that is, the basis should vary one for one with the nominal interest rate. The seasonal dummies in (3) are a crude way to capture variation in the marginal convenience yield in (2), which is due to seasonals in production or demand.

1. *Interest-rate relations.* Estimates of the slopes in regression (3) are in table 2. The metals produce the strongest evidence of variation in the basis that tracks interest rates, and gold produces the strongest evidence among the metals. The interest-rate coefficient in the 6-month gold regression is 1.07. The estimates for 1, 3, and 12 months to matu-

rity (not reported) range from 0.99 to 1.06. Table 2 shows coefficients of determination (R^2) for simple regressions of the basis on the nominal interest rate as well as for the regressions that include seasonal dummies. Nominal interest rates alone explain 83% of the 6-month basis variance for gold. The nominal interest rate explains 60% of the variance of the 6-month basis for silver. Explanatory power is lower for platinum and lower again for copper, but estimated interest rate coefficients are close to 1.0. The metals regressions for 1, 3, and 12 months to maturity (not shown) are similar. Metals prices are consistent with the hypothesis that the basis tracks nominal interest rates.

The regressions for the agricultural and wood products are also consistent with the hypothesis that the basis varies one for one with the nominal interest rate. All the interest-rate coefficients are positive, many are close to 1.0, and only two are more than 1.0 standard error from 1.0. However, the standard errors of the interest-rate coefficients for the agricultural and wood products are all greater than 0.5. This lack of precision means that the regression slopes cannot provide convincing evidence of one-for-one variation in the basis in response to nominal interest rates. The interest-rate coefficients for the animal-product regressions are even less precise. The standard errors of the coefficients are typically greater than 1.0, and the estimates are consistent with a wide range of values for the true slopes, including 0.0 as well as 1.0.

Restated in terms of (2), the regressions indicate that variation in the interest rate is a large fraction of basis variation for gold and silver. For other commodities, there is suggestive evidence of basis variation in response to the nominal interest rate, but variation in the $[W(t, T) - C(t, T)]/S(t)$ component of the basis leads to imprecise estimates of the relation between the basis and the interest rate. For agricultural, wood, and animal products, basis variation must be explained primarily in terms of economic conditions that generate variation in marginal storage costs, $W(t, T)$, and marginal convenience yields, $C(t, T)$, rather than in terms of the role of the interest rate in the storage process.

2. *Seasonals in the basis.* The seasonal dummies in (3) are evidence about seasonal variation in the basis. The F-statistics testing the hypothesis that all seasonal coefficients in a regression are equal never indicate reliable seasonals in the basis for any metal. This is not surprising since there is no presumption of seasonals in the demand or supply of metals.

As expected, there are reliable seasonals in the basis for many of the seasonally produced agricultural commodities, including corn, oats, orange juice, soybeans, and wheat. (Although the 6-month basis for corn in table 2 does not show seasonals, there are reliable seasonals in the 3-month basis.) On the other hand, it is a bit unexpected that five agricultural commodities—cocoa, coffee, cotton, soy meal, and soy oil—produce no reliable evidence of seasonals in the 6-month basis. The absence of seasonals for soy meal and soy oil is interesting given the strong seasonals in the basis for soybeans. Apparently, the production process for meal and oil reduces the effect of seasonals in the price of soybeans.

The animal products produce the strongest evidence of seasonals in the basis. The coefficients of determination in the seasonal regressions for broilers, cattle, eggs, and pork bellies are at least 0.19. The seasonals in the 6-month basis for hogs are weaker, but the coefficients of determination in the 1- and 3-month seasonal regressions for hogs (not shown) are 0.47 and 0.72, respectively. Since the nominal interest rate explains only a small fraction of the basis variation for the animal products, much of their basis variation can be attributed to seasonals.

Since the animal products are subject to seasonals in production and sometimes in demand (see Bessant 1982), and since bulk and perishability imply storage costs that are high relative to value, strong seasonals in the basis confirm the predictions of the theory of storage. On the other hand, lumber and plywood also have high storage costs and seasonals in demand due to seasonals in building activity, but the regressions for lumber and plywood produce no reliable evidence of seasonals. One possibility is that the production of wood products is more easily adapted to seasonals in demand than the production of animal products. The details of supply and demand conditions for different commodities and their implications for the behavior of the basis is interesting material for future research.

III. The Basis: Forecast Power and Premiums

The theory-of-storage view of futures prices in equation (2) is not controversial. There is another view that is the subject of long and continuing controversy. The difference between the futures price and the current spot price can be expressed as the sum of an expected premium and an expected change in the spot price:

$$F(t, T) - S(t) = E_t[P(t, T)] + E_t[S(T) - S(t)], \qquad (4)$$

where the expected premium is defined as the bias of the futures price as a forecast of the future spot price,

$$E_t[P(t, T)] = F(t, T) - E_t[S(T)]. \qquad (5)$$

Equation (4) and the theory of storage in (2) are alternative but not competing views of the basis. Variation in the expected premium or the expected change in the spot price in (4) translates into variation in the interest rate, the marginal storage cost, or the marginal convenience yield in (2). For example, the basis for agricultural commodities is often negative before a harvest when the futures price is for delivery after the harvest. Under the theory of storage, the basis is negative because inventories are low and the convenience yield is larger than interest and storage costs. In terms of (4), the explanation for negative values of the basis is that the spot price is expected to fall when a harvest will substantially increase inventories. Likewise, positive values of the basis when both the futures and the spot prices are for the period between harvests can be explained in terms of storage costs that outweigh marginal convenience yields when inventories are high, but they are equally well explained in terms of an expected increase in the spot price necessary to induce storage between harvests.

Despite research that extends from Keynes (1930), Hardy (1940), Working (1948, 1949), Telser (1958, 1967), and Cootner (1960, 1967) to Dusak (1973), Bodie and Rosansky (1980), Carter, Rausser, and Schmitz (1983), and Hazuka (1984), there is little agreement on whether the expected premium in (4) is nonzero or on whether futures prices have power to forecast future spot prices. We test for time-varying expected premiums and price forecasts in futures prices with the regression approach in Fama (1984a, 1984b). Consider the regressions of the change in the spot price and the premium on the basis:

$$S(T) - S(t) = a_1 + b_1[F(t, T) - S(t)] + u(t, T), \qquad (6)$$

$$F(t, T) - S(T) = a_2 + b_2[F(t, T) - S(t)] + z(t, T). \qquad (7)$$

Evidence that b_1 is positive means the basis observed at t contains information about the change in the spot price from t to T. Equivalently, the futures price has power to forecast the future spot price. Evidence that b_2 is positive means the basis observed at t contains information about the premium to be realized at T. Predictable variation in realized premiums is evidence of time-varying expected premiums.

A. What Can We Expect?

Regressions (6) and (7) are subject to an adding-up constraint. The sum of the premium, $F(t, T) - S(T)$, and the change in the spot price, $S(T) - S(t)$, is the basis, $F(t, T) - S(t)$. Thus the intercepts in (6) and (7) must sum to 0.0; each period's residuals must sum to 0.0; and, most important, the slope coefficients must sum to 1.0. In other words, the regressions always allocate all variation in the basis to the expected premium, the expected change in the spot price, or some mix of the two.

The point is worth emphasizing. As law-abiding financial economists, we presume that market forecasts of future spot prices are rational. Moreover, all the spot and futures prices have been checked twice. Nevertheless, even basis variance due to measurement errors and irrational forecasts of spot prices are allocated by the regressions (6)

TABLE 3 Standard Deviations of the 2-Month Basis, the Change in the Spot Price, and the Premium

Commodity	Basis $F(t, t + 2) - S(t)$	Change $S(t + 2) - S(t)$	Premium $F(t, t + 2) - S(t + 2)$
Agricultural products:			
Cocoa	4.0	14.6	15.2
Coffee	5.2	15.0	14.4
Corn	2.8	9.9	10.6
Cotton	2.4	9.0	9.0
Oats	4.4	11.7	10.5
Orange juice	4.9	13.1	13.4
Soybeans	2.8	12.2	12.0
Soy meal	4.1	13.4	13.4
Soy oil	4.7	13.5	13.7
Wheat	3.3	14.5	14.7
Wood products:			
Lumber	6.9	11.5	12.1
Plywood	3.2	9.8	10.5
Animal products:			
Broilers	5.8	11.1	8.7
Cattle	3.3	11.0	10.4
Eggs	13.2	16.3	12.6
Hogs	7.1	12.9	12.1
Pork bellies	1.9	16.9	16.4
Metals:			
Copper	2.5	12.1	12.4
Gold	.6	13.1	13.2
Platinum*	2.2	16.2	16.1
Silver	.5	18.5	18.7

* Two-month maturity is not available; 3-month maturity is used.

and (7). It is easy to show that an irrational forecast of the spot price in the futures price shows up as a time-varying expected premium (a positive value of b_2), while measurement error in the spot price shows up as forecast power (a positive value of b_1).

Although the regressions allocate all basis variation to expected premiums, expected spot-price changes, or some combination of the two, the allocation can be statistically unreliable. Since estimates of b_1 and b_2 in (6) and (7) are typically between 0.0 and 1.0, the regressions can fail to identify the source of variation in the basis—the regressions produce slope coefficients that sum to 1.0 but are not reliably different from 0.0—when basis variation is low relative to variation in realized premiums and changes in spot prices. We can get a good idea about where to place our bets in the regressions by examining variances of the basis relative to variances of premiums and changes in spot prices.

Table 3 shows standard deviations of the basis, $F(t, t + 2) - S(t)$, the change, $S(t + 2) - S(t)$, and the premium, $F(t, t + 2) - S(t + 2)$, for each commodity. The 2-month maturity is chosen because it is available for all commodities but platinum. In table 3 (and in the regressions below) all prices are measured in natural logs.

The standard deviations of spot-price changes and premiums are large, and they do not differ much across commodity groups. For example, the standard deviations of spot-price changes range from 12.1% to 18.5% for the metals, from 9.0% to 15.0% for the agricultural products, and from 11.0% to 16.9% for the animal products. It seems that futures markets exist for commodities subject to similar high levels of uncertainty about future spot prices.

In contrast, basis variability differs systematically across commodity groups. As in table 2, the basis standard deviations in table 3 are smallest for the metals, larger for the agricultural and wood products, and largest for some of the animal products. The standard deviation of the 2-month basis for gold is 0.6% versus 7.1% for hogs. For commodities such as the metals, where basis variation is low relative to the variation of premiums and spot-price changes, it is unlikely that regressions (6) and (7) can reliably assign basis variation to expected premiums or expected spot-price changes. The regressions have a better chance with commodities like the animal products, where basis variation is substantial.

B. Regression Results

Estimates of the change regression (6) and the premium regression (7) are given in table 4. Because they are the focal point of the evidence on forecast power and time-varying expected premiums, the slopes b_1 and b_2 for both (6) and (7) are reported, even though they must sum to 1.0. To limit the size of the table, only results for 2, 6, and 10 months to maturity are shown. These maturities tend to have the largest samples, and they are spaced fairly evenly among the possible maturities from 1 to 12 months.

We first categorize the regressions for different commodities according to whether futures prices show time-varying expected premiums, power to forecast spot prices, both, or neither. Then we relate the results to differences in conditions of production and storage.

Type SF—strong forecast power. Futures prices for broilers, eggs, hogs, and oats have reliable forecast power at every maturity (including those not shown in table 4), and they show no reliable evidence of time-varying expected premiums. The slopes in the change regressions for these commodities are all more than 2.6 standard errors from 0.0, and most are more than 4.0 standard errors from 0.0. Moreover, the forecast power of futures prices is nontrivial. For example, the coefficients of determination (R_1^2) in the change regressions for broilers are 0.40 and 0.42; for oats they range from 0.20 to 0.35.

Type GF—good forecast power but not for all maturities. The change regressions for cattle, pork bellies, soybeans, and soy meal indicate reliable forecast power in futures prices for at least one matu-

TABLE 4 Regressions of the Spot Price Change and the Premium on the Basis:
$S(T) - S(t) = a_1 + b_1[F(t, T) - S(t)] + u(t, T)$,
$F(t, t) - S(T) = a_2 + b_2[F(t, T) - S(t)] - u(t, T)$

		2 Months							6 Months							10 Months						
Commodity	Max.	Obs.	b_1	b_2	$t(b_1)$	$t(b_2)$	R_1^2	R_2^2	Obs.	b_1	b_2	$t(b_1)$	$t(b_2)$	R_1^2	R_2^2	Obs.	b_1	b_2	$t(b_1)$	$t(b_2)$	R_1^2	R_2^2
Agricultural products:																						
Cocoa	221	56	−.03	1.03	−.07	2.09	.00	.07	36	−.08	1.08	−.16	2.26	.00	.13	54	.24	.76	.42	1.32	.01	.08
Coffee	137	38	.86	.14	1.91	.30	.09	.00								37	.46	.54	.65	.75	.03	.04
Corn	221	56	−.40	1.40	−.84	2.93	.01	.13	36	−.59	1.59	−.81	2.20	.02	.12	54	.48	.52	.91	.98	.03	.03
Cotton	207	53	.55	.45	1.06	.87	.02	.01								50	1.10	−.10	2.27	−.21	.16	.00
Oats	217	54	1.18	−.18	3.63	−.55	.20	.01	34	1.05	−.05	4.19	−.19	.35	.00	42	1.02	−.02	3.28	−.07	.29	.00
Orange juice	207	101	.28	.72	1.07	2.69	.01	.07	100	.57	.43	1.79	1.36	.06	.04	97	1.00	−.00	2.85	−.00	.20	.00
Soybeans	221	110	.80	.20	1.95	.49	.03	.00	108	.71	.29	2.36	.95	.09	.02	106	.63	.37	1.71	1.01	.07	.03
Soy meal	217	108	.44	.56	1.26	1.59	.02	.03	68	.50	.50	1.14	1.15	.03	.03	93	.65	.35	2.85	1.56	.14	.05
Soy oil	217	112	.40	.60	1.41	2.11	.02	.04	75	−.02	1.02	−.07	2.75	.00	.16	105	.01	.99	.03	2.11	.00	.14
Wheat	219	55	.18	.82	.29	1.36	.00	.03	35	−.65	1.65	−1.33	3.39	.05	.25	52	−.78	1.78	−1.62	3.69	.07	.27
Wood products:																						
Plywood	163	81	−.00	1.00	−.02	3.42	.00	.13	79	.53	.47	1.46	1.29	.06	.05	69	1.27	−.27	3.81	−.80	.34	.02
Lumber	173	86	.35	.65	1.97	3.71	.04	.14	84	.28	.72	1.35	3.55	.05	.27	52	.16	.84	.42	2.21	.01	.24
Animal products:																						
Broilers	152	108	1.22	−.22	7.68	−1.40	.40	.02	64	.93	.07	5.39	.40	.42	.00							
Cattle	147	51	1.12	−.12	2.51	−.27	.11	.00	67	.84	.16	1.54	.30	.07	.00							
Eggs	173	145	.80	.20	8.58	2.15	.42	.04	80	.97	.03	6.24	.18	.53	.00							
Hogs	217	117	.72	.28	4.59	1.81	.16	.03	103	.66	.34	2.67	1.38	.12	.04	78	.80	.20	2.76	.70	.22	.02
Pork bellies	219	37	2.77	−1.77	1.95	−1.25	.10	.04	33	1.39	−.39	5.12	−1.43	.45	.06	36	1.12	−.12	5.08	−.53	.53	.01
Metals:																						
Copper	223	157	−.03	1.03	−.08	2.57	.00	.05	92	.64	.36	1.54	.88	.05	.02	98	.66	.34	1.36	.70	.06	.02
Gold	115	107	−2.20	3.20	−.80	1.17	.01	.02	55	−1.74	2.87	−.68	1.04	.02	.05	52	−2.83	3.83	−.89	1.20	.07	.12
Platinum	199								65	.73	.27	.82	.30	.02	.02							
Silver	211	174	−8.56	9.56	−2.45	2.73	.06	.07	100	−7.82	8.82	−2.50	2.82	.13	.16	99	−6.12	7.12	−2.03	2.36	.14	.17

NOTE.—R_1^2 and R_2^2 are the coefficients of determination for the change and premium regressions, respectively. Since the change and premium regressions have the same explanatory variable and the two residuals sum to .0, their slope coefficients have the same standard error. The t-statistics, $t(b_1)$ and $t(b_2)$, are based on standard errors adjusted for the autocorrelation of the regression residuals induced by the overlap of the observations on $S(T) - S(t)$ and $F(t, T) - S(T)$. (See Hansen and Hodrick 1980.) Obs. is the number of observations in a regression, and Max. is the number of months in the sample period.

rity and suggestive evidence of forecast power for other maturities. They show no reliable evidence of time-varying expected premiums.

Types SP and GP—expected premiums. The premium regressions for two commodities, soy oil and lumber, produce reliable evidence of time-varying expected premiums at every maturity, while three commodities—cocoa, corn and wheat—seem to have time-varying expected premiums at some but not all maturities. The evidence of time-varying expected premiums for these commodities is weaker than the evidence of forecast power for the SF and GF commodities. For example, t-statistics above 5.0 are common in the change regressions for the SF commodities, but the largest t-statistic in the premium regressions for the SP commodities is 3.71. Similarly, the coefficients of determination are often above 0.40 in the change regressions for the SF commodities, but they never exceed 0.27 in the premium regressions for the SP commodities.

Type F&P—forecast power and expected premiums. There are two commodities, orange juice and plywood, for which futures prices seem to show both forecast power and time-varying expected premiums. However, the evidence for forecast power occurs at long maturities, whereas the evidence for expected premiums is observed for shorter maturities.

Type W—weak. The regressions for coffee, copper, and cotton produce suggestive evidence that futures prices contain both time-varying expected premiums and power to forecast future spot prices; that is, for many maturities (including those not shown) the slope coefficients b_1 and b_2 for the change and premium regressions are both well above 0.0 and below 1.0. Some of the regression slopes for these commodities are more than 2 standard errors from zero, but most are not reliably different from 0.0. In short, the regressions fail to identify any commodities for which the basis shows reliable simultaneous variation in expected premiums and forecasts of spot prices.

For gold and platinum, basis variability is so low relative to the variability of realized premiums and changes in spot prices that regression coefficients equal to 1.0 would usually be less than 1 standard error from zero. For these commodities, the regressions cannot reliably identify situations in which all basis variation reflects either time-varying expected premiums or forecasts of spot-price changes. This is in contrast to the theory of storage regressions in table 2, where the basis is the dependent variable and the low basis variances of the precious metals allow the most reliable inferences that the basis tracks nominal interest rates.

The silver regressions in table 4 are puzzling. The regression slopes are more than 2.0 standard errors from zero, but the coefficients seem bizarre. For example, the estimated slope in the 2-month change regression is -8.56; taken literally, a 1.0% increase in the basis implies

TABLE 5   Regression Scoreboard

	Futures Prices Show:		
Forecast Power	Expected Premiums	Both	Neither (Weak)
Broilers* (SF) 4	Lumber (SP) 3	Orange juice* (F&P) 6	Coffee (W) 5
Eggs* (SF) 1	Soy oil (SP) 7	Plywood (F&P) 13	Copper (W) 16
Hogs* (SF) 2			Cotton (W) 17
Oats* (SF) 8	Cocoa (GP) 10		Gold (W) 21
	Corn* (GP) 15		Platinum (W) 18
Cattle* (GF) 11	Wheat* (GP) 12		Silver (W) 20
Pork bellies* (GF) 19			
Soybeans* (GF) 14			
Soy meal (GF) 9			

NOTE.—An asterisk means the commodity's basis shows reliable evidence of seasonals in the estimates of (3). The numbers after the commodities are the (reverse) order of their basis standard deviations for the 2-month maturity in table 3. For example, the 1 after eggs indicates that its basis has the highest standard deviation. The letters in parentheses after the commodity names categorize their regression results in the estimates of (5) and (6) in table 4. The categories are as follows. SF = strong forecast power: statistically reliable power to forecast changes in spot prices across all maturities; no evidence of time-varying expected premiums. GF = good forecast power: statistically reliable power to forecast changes in spot prices for most but not all maturities; no evidence of time-varying expected premiums. SP = strong expected premiums: statistically reliable evidence of time-varying expected premiums across all maturities. GP = expected premiums: statistically reliable evidence of time-varying expected premiums for most but not all maturities. F&P = forecast power and expected premiums: statistically reliable forecast power for some maturities and statistically reliable time-varying expected premiums for others. W = weak: regression evidence is unreliable or extreme.

an 8.6% drop in the expected price change. We are examining these and other metal results in more detail.

C. Interpretation of the Regressions

Table 5 summarizes the regressions, both those in table 4 and the theory of storage regressions in table 2. Commodities are allocated to the columns of table 5 depending on whether their futures prices show forecast power or time-varying expected premiums in (6) and (7). The numbers after the commodity names are the reverse order of their basis standard deviations for the 2-month maturity in table 3. An asterisk means that the commodity's basis shows seasonals in table 2.

1. *Basis variability, forecast power, and premiums.* As expected, there is a relation between basis variability and evidence that futures prices have time-varying expected premiums or power to forecast future spot prices. Of the four commodities that show strong forecast power (SF) in the estimates of (6), three—broilers, eggs, and hogs—rank in the top four in basis variability. Two commodities, lumber and soy oil, show evidence of time-varying expected premiums (SP) for all maturities; lumber ranks third in basis variability, and soy oil is seventh. At the other end of the spectrum, copper, cotton, gold, and platinum have relatively low basis variation and unreliable results in the tests for forecast power and premiums.

Since the slopes in the regressions of $S(T) - S(t)$ and $F(t, T) - S(T)$ on $F(t, T) - S(t)$ sum to 1.0 and are typically between 0.0 and 1.0, it is almost a matter of arithmetic that regression coefficients statistically far from 0.0 in (6) and (7) occur when basis variation is high relative to the variation of the changes and premiums to be explained. The interesting question is why basis variation is high for some commodities and low for others.

2. *Storage costs and forecast power.* As discussed earlier, the theory of storage predicts that storage costs are important in explaining differences in the variability of the expected spot-price change in the basis. For agricultural and animal products, which are subject to seasonals in production or demand, the amount of predictable seasonal variation in the spot price should be an increasing function of storage costs. Likewise, stored stocks act to smooth predictable adjustments in the spot price in response to demand and supply shocks. Since storage costs that are high relative to value deter storage, the theory predicts that variation in expected spot-price changes in response to shocks is also an increasing function of storage costs.

These predictions can explain broad features of the estimates of the change regression (6). The regressions for eight commodities indicate that the basis $F(t, T) - S(t)$ has reliable information about the future change in the spot price $S(T) - S(t)$ for most maturities $(T - t)$. Five of these commodities are animal products (broilers, cattle, eggs, hogs, and pork bellies), whose bulk and perishability imply high storage costs relative to value. Storage costs (table 2) are also high for the remaining three commodities (oats, soybeans, and soy meal), whose futures prices show consistent forecast power. Forecast power is not found in futures prices for gold and platinum, whose storage costs are low relative to value and basis variances are low relative to variances of spot-price changes.[1]

3. *Seasonals and forecast power.* Our analysis of storage costs and forecast power predicts that seasonal variation in the basis generates forecast power in the change regression (6). Table 5 suggests that this prediction is generally correct. The basis has reliable power to forecast changes in the spot price for eight of the 10 commodities that have reliable basis seasonals. Of the 10 commodities with reliable evidence of forecast power, eight have reliable basis seasonals.

D. *Univariate Tests for Expected Premiums*

The estimates of (7) find evidence of expected premiums for only seven of 21 commodities. The regressions, however, are designed to detect

---

1. Hazuka (1984) estimates (6) for 1-month spot-price changes and for a shorter list of commodities. His conclusions about the relation between storage costs and forecast power are similar to ours. He does not recognize that the change regression (6) has a complement, the premium regression (7).

variation in expected premiums. Failure to identify time-varying expected premiums does not imply that expected premiums are zero. To examine the issue further, we have computed average values of the premium, $F(t, T) - S(T)$, for each maturity of each commodity. This approach has no power (i) because the variances of realized premiums are so large (see table 3) and (ii) because futures contracts for a given maturity $(T - t)$ are available for only a fraction of the sample months (compare the maximum and actual observations in table 4).

Following Bodie and Rosansky (1980), we increase the power of univariate tests for expected premiums by (i) combining contracts for a commodity to ensure that an observation for the commodity is available every month and (ii) combining commodities into portfolios. Monthly returns are computed for each commodity using the shortest futures contract with at least 1 month to maturity on the first trading day of each month. A simple return is defined as the change in the futures price over the month, divided by the price of the contract at the beginning of the month. Contracts chosen generally have maturities of 1, 2, or 3 months.

The average simple returns for individual commodities (table 6) suggest that futures prices show normal backwardation—the expected return from a long futures position is positive. The average simple returns for 19 of the 21 commodities are positive, and the average returns for cocoa, coffee, orange juice, soy oil, and hogs are larger than 1.0% per month. However, the evidence for normal backwardation is weaker than these averages suggest. Standard deviations of monthly returns for individual commodities are often greater than 10.0%. As a consequence, the average simple returns for only five commodities produce t-statistics greater than 2.0. With continuous compounding, only the average return for eggs is more than 2.0 standard errors from 0.0—and that return is negative.

If normal backwardation is the normal case, combining commodities into portfolios does not smear information about expected premiums, and the power of tests for expected premiums is improved. We average the simple monthly returns on individual commodities to get equally weighted portfolio returns. A portfolio of all 21 commodities and portfolios that include natural subgroups are examined.

The average simple return on the portfolio of all commodities is 0.54% per month. Its t-statistic is 1.87. Thus on the average the monthly changes in futures prices for commodities show marginally reliable normal backwardation that is also nontrivial in magnitude. This conclusion is tempered by the continuously compounded returns. With continuous compounding the average portfolio return falls from 0.54% to 0.45% per month, and its t-statistic falls to 1.57. The nontrivial differences between average simple and continuously compounded returns are easily explained. Even the return on the portfolio of all com-

TABLE 6 Average Monthly Simple and Continuously Compounded Returns for Portfolios and Individual Commodities

	Obs.	Simple			Continuously Compounded		
		M	SD	t(M)	M	SD	t(M)
All commodities	222	.54	4.3	1.87	.45	4.2	1.57
Agricultural products:	222	.83	5.4	2.29	.69	5.2	1.97
Cocoa	220	1.59	10.1	2.33	1.10	9.8	1.67
Coffee	140	1.84	10.2	2.13	1.35	9.6	1.67
Corn	220	.12	6.6	.27	−.09	6.5	−.21
Cotton	208	.32	7.1	.66	.09	6.8	.18
Oats	218	.10	7.6	.19	−.19	7.6	−.36
Orange juice	209	1.37	11.2	1.76	.83	10.0	1.20
Soybeans	220	.66	9.7	1.01	.21	9.4	.34
Soy meal	213	.86	10.9	1.15	.31	10.3	.44
Soy oil	218	1.91	11.4	2.47	1.31	10.6	1.83
Wheat	218	.06	9.1	.10	−.30	8.4	−.54
Wood products:	177	−.23	7.5	−.42	−.51	7.5	−.91
Lumber	177	−.53	7.9	−.89	−.86	8.1	−1.40
Plywood	165	.44	8.0	.71	.13	7.8	.22
Animal products:	220	.00	6.3	.00	−.20	6.3	−.46
Broilers	151	.55	7.4	.92	.31	6.9	.56
Cattle	151	.24	7.0	.42	−.01	7.1	−.01
Eggs	175	−2.01	10.4	−2.56	−2.60	10.7	−3.20
Hogs	220	1.11	8.0	2.06	.79	8.0	1.47
Pork bellies	218	.26	10.4	.37	−.28	10.5	−.39
Metals:	222	.57	8.3	1.02	.23	8.1	.43
Copper	222	.35	8.2	.63	.01	8.2	.02
Gold	114	.32	9.0	.38	−.06	8.7	−.08
Platinum	119	.17	9.4	.26	−.26	9.4	−.40
Silver	209	.95	12.3	1.11	.25	11.8	.31

NOTE.—M is the average return. SD is the standard deviation of the return. $t(M)$ is the t-statistic for the average return.

modities has substantial variability. The standard deviations of its simple and continuously compounded returns are 4.3% and 4.2% per month.[2] Among subgroup portfolios, the highly diversified portfolio of agricultural products produces t-statistics around 2.0 in the simple and continuously compounded returns, but the t-statistics for the average returns for the remaining portfolios are 1.02 or less.

In short, large average premiums sometimes produce marginal evidence of nonzero expected premiums when the futures contracts for commodities are combined into portfolios. Even for portfolios, inference is sensitive to whether we use simple or continuously com-

---

2. Fama and Schwert (1979) report that the standard deviation of monthly rates of change in the U.S. Consumer Price Index (CPI) is about 0.25%. The standard deviations of the monthly rates of change of the nine major components of the CPI never exceed 0.62%. These numbers are trivial relative to the standard deviations in table 6. It seems safe to conclude that general inflation is a negligible component of the short-term variation in futures prices.

pounded returns, and the evidence is never strong. These results provide a good perspective on the problems of inference posed by the variability of futures prices—and on the persistence of the debate about the existence of expected premiums.

IV. Summary

Two views of commodity futures prices are common. The theory of storage summarized in equation (2) explains the difference between a futures price and the contemporaneous spot price (the basis) in terms of interest forgone in storing a commodity, warehousing costs, and a convenience yield from inventory. The alternative view of equation (4) splits a futures price into an expected premium and a forecast of the maturity spot price.

Although the two models are alternative perspectives on the same economic phenomena, developing evidence on them presents different statistical problems. Evidence on forecast power and expected premiums in futures prices is extracted from realized spot-price changes and premiums, in the manner, for example, of regressions (6) and (7). A typical characteristic of commodities traded in futures markets is highly uncertain future spot prices. For many traded commodities, basis variances that are large in absolute terms are small relative to the variances of realized premiums and spot-price changes. As a consequence, although regressions (6) and (7) allocate all basis variation to expected premiums and expected changes in spot prices, for many commodities the allocation is not statistically reliable, and nonzero variances of the two expected values in the basis cannot be separately identified.

Likewise, the large variances of realized premiums mean that average premiums that often seem economically large are usually insufficient to infer that expected premiums are nonzero, especially in the data for individual commodities. When commodities are combined into portfolios, statistical power is increased and marginal evidence of normal backwardation is obtained. But the evidence is not strong enough to resolve the long-standing controversy about the existence of nonzero expected premiums.

In contrast, regressions in which the basis is the dependent variable are used to test whether the basis varies with interest rates, warehousing costs, and convenience yields in the manner predicted by the storage-cost model of (2). Since variation in the basis is not buried in extraneous noise—even with a crude approach like the regression (3) of the basis on the nominal interest rate and seasonal dummies—the tracks of the storage-cost variables in the basis are identified more easily than variation in the basis due to expected premiums and forecasts of future spot prices.

The results for the precious metals and the animal products illustrate the different statistical problems. The low basis variances of the precious metals allow precise estimation of the interest-rate response predicted in (2), but they preclude a reliable split of the basis between the expected premium and the expected spot-price change in (4). At the other extreme, the high basis variances of the animal products preclude reliable estimates of the interest-rate coefficient in (2), but they allow us to infer that futures prices have power to forecast future spot prices.

References

Bessant, L. 1982. *Commodity Trading Manual.* Chicago: Chicago Board of Trade.
Bodie, Z., and Rosansky, V. I. 1980. Risk and return in commodity futures. *Financial Analysis Journal* 36 (May–June): 27–39.
Breeden, D. T. 1980. Consumption risks in futures markets. *Journal of Finance* 35 (May): 503–20.
Brennan, M. J. 1958. The supply of storage. *American Economic Review* 48 (March): 50–72.
Carter, C. A.; Rausser, G. C.; and Schmitz, A. 1983. Efficient asset portfolios and the theory of normal backwardation. *Journal of Political Economy* 91 (April): 319–31.
Cootner, P. H. 1960. Returns to speculators: Telser vs. Keynes. *Journal of Political Economy* 68 (August): 396–404.
Cootner, P. H. 1967. Speculation and hedging. *Food Research Institute Studies* 7, suppl.:65–106.
Dusak, K. 1973. Futures trading and investor returns: An investigation of commodity market risk premiums. *Journal of Political Economy* 81 (November–December): 1387–1406.
Fama, E. F. 1984*a*. Forward and spot exchange rates. *Journal of Monetary Economics* 14 (November): 319–38.
Fama, E. F. 1984*b*. The information in the term structure. *Journal of Financial Economics* 13 (December): 509–28.
Fama, E. F., and Schwert, G. W. 1979. Inflation, interest, and relative prices. *Journal of Business* 52 (April): 183–209.
French, K. R. 1986. Detecting spot price forecasts in futures prices. *Journal of Business* 59, pt. 2 (April): S39–S54.
Hansen, L. P., and Hodrick, R. J. 1980. Forward exchange rates as optimal predictors of future spot rates: An econometric analysis. *Journal of Political Economy* 88 (October): 829–53.
Hardy, C. 1940. *Risk and Risk Bearing.* Chicago: University of Chicago Press.
Hazuka, T. B. 1984. Consumption betas and backwardation in commodity markets. *Journal of Finance* 39 (July): 647–55.
Kaldor, N. 1939. Speculation and economic stability. *Review of Economic Studies* 7 (October): 1–27.
Keynes, J. M. 1930. *Treatise on Money.* London: Macmillan.
Salomon Brothers. Various issues. *Analytical Record of Yields and Yield Spreads.* New York: Salomon Brothers.
Telser, L. G. 1958. Futures trading and the storage of cotton and wheat. *Journal of Political Economy* 66 (June): 233–55.
Telser, L. G. 1967. The supply of speculative services in wheat, corn and soybeans. *Food Research Institute Studies* 7, suppl.:131–76.
Working, H. 1948. Theory of the inverse carrying charge in futures markets. *Journal of Farm Economics* 30 (February): 1–28.
Working, H. 1949. The theory of the price of storage. *American Economic Review* 39 (December): 1254–62.

[5]
COBWEBS, RATIONAL EXPECTATIONS AND FUTURES MARKETS

Jerome L. Stein*

Abstract—In the absence of futures markets, cobweb cycles and other behavior inconsistent with Muth Rational Expectations (MRE) persist for long periods of time. When futures markets are introduced in commodities, then these markets behave in a manner much more consistent with MRE. By contrast, despite the existence of active forward and futures markets, the MRE hypothesis is rejected in the financial and foreign exchange markets. The aim of this paper is to suggest an explanation of how futures markets change the structure of the supply response.

THERE is a growing body of evidence which suggests that, in the absence of futures markets, cobweb cycles and other behavior inconsistent with Muth Rational Expectations (MRE) persist for long periods of time. When futures markets are introduced in commodities, then these markets behave in a manner much more consistent with MRE. By contrast, despite the existence of active forward and futures markets, the MRE hypothesis is rejected in the financial and foreign exchange markets. The aim of this paper is to suggest an explanation of these phenomena.

Part I describes the evidence. Part II proposes an explanation of why non-rational behavior, such as cobwebs, tend to occur in the absence of futures. Part III explains how futures markets change the structure of the supply response.

I. Empirical Phenomena to be Explained

A. Commodities

Cobweb cycles are generated when the quantity supplied at time t depends upon the lagged price. The resulting current price $p(t)$ is then a function of the lagged price. This set of relations produces the cobweb cycle. Since the current price is negatively related to the previous price, profits could be made by producing in a countercyclical way.

1. Hog Cycles: Hayes and Schmitz (1987) examined the existence of hog cycles produced by a form of cobweb behavior. From 1902 to 1941 there was a cobweb cycle. Countercyclical production strategies would have been profitable. Futures trading in pork bellies was introduced in the early 1960s. From 1962 to 1981, the proportion of producers behaving in the manner predicted by the cobweb model became insignificant.

The hog cycle persisted for decades. Countercyclical strategies would have been profitable. The questions are why the cycle lasted so long and why it became insignificant when futures trading was introduced.

2. Potatoes: Simmons (1962) of the U.S. Department of Agriculture examined supply equations for Maine and Idaho potatoes during the periods 1931–41 and 1952–60, and his work has been analyzed by Tomek and Gray (1970), Gray (1972) and Peck (1985). There was limited futures trading in Maine potatoes during the period 1931–41, and trading was light in the immediate postwar years. Activity increased substantially in the 1952–60 period on the N.Y. Mercantile Exchange. Idaho producers made little use of this futures market in either of the two periods. Idaho potatoes are poor substitutes for Maine potatoes, and the Maine contract did not provide a good cross hedge for western grown potatoes.

Prior to the development of futures trading in Maine potatoes, the acreage planted in both Maine and Idaho was positively related to the lagged price. With the development of futures trading in Maine potatoes, the lagged price was no longer a significant determinant of acreage planted in Maine. In neither period was there a significant use of futures by Idaho producers. In Idaho, the coefficient of the acreage planted upon the lagged price increased between the two periods and was highly significant. Why did the cobweb response disappear when futures trading developed in Maine potatoes, but continued in Idaho potatoes?

Received for publication January 11, 1990. Revision accepted for publication February 5, 1991.
* Brown University.
Earlier versions were presented at the University of New South Wales, La Trobe University, Oklahoma State University, University of Bristol, Oxford Institute for Economics and Statistics, and Churchill College. I thank the participants at those seminars for their reactions. Robert Pindyck and Dermot Hayes were exceptionally helpful in the revision.

Copyright © 1992

B. Asset Market Equilibrium

When there are commodities with continuous inventories, a firm which maximizes expected profits will carry a quantity of stock such that, on the margin, the firm is indifferent between either selling a unit of stock this period or holding it and selling it at the next period. If the firm sells this period it receives the current price $p(t)$. Given the interest rate r, the firm will have $(1 + r)p(t)$ the next period. If it holds the stock it will expect to sell the stock for $p*(t + 1; t)$ the next period. The holding of the stock is expected to involve a convenience yield less non-interest carrying costs of $z*(t; t)$. The subjective expectation is taken at time t and is denoted by an asterisk.

$$p*(t + 1; t) = (1 + r)p(t) - z*(t; t). \quad (1)$$

This equation must be true when an agent optimizes and it is independent of what set of equations determines the price fundamentals and expectations. This equation is applied to commodities with continuous inventories, the stock market and the foreign exchange market.

The MRE hypothesis states that the subjective expectation of any variable $p*(t + 1; t)$ is the same as the objective expectation of the price, denoted by $Ep(t + 1; t)$, based upon the true model (i.e., the fundamentals). The difference between the realization $p(t)$ and the objective expectation $Ep(t; t - 1)$ is an i.i.d. term ϵ with a zero mean. This is (2).

$$p(t + 1) - Ep(t + 1; t) = \epsilon. \quad (2)$$

Using the MRE hypothesis (2) in the optimizing equation (1), derive equation (3). This equation describes the intertemporal price relation when continuous inventories are held, and MRE are assumed.

$$p(t + 1) = (1 + r)p(t) - z(t) + \epsilon. \quad (3)$$

The implications of the MRE hypothesis have been tested in several ways.

1. Commodities: Equation (4) is one way to test the MRE hypothesis equation (3). Regress the price $p(t)$ upon its lagged value $p(t - 1)$ and earlier values $p(t - i)$ for $i > 1$. The current price should only be related to the immediately preceding price and not to earlier prices.

$$p(t) = b(0) + b(1)p(t - 1) + \Sigma b(i)p(t - i) + \epsilon. \quad (4)$$

The null hypothesis in equation (4) is that coefficient $b(1)$ is positive and that coefficients $b(i)$, $i > 1$, are zero and ϵ is i.i.d. with a zero mean.

Cox (1976) estimated equation (4) for six commodities during two periods. The commodities were onions, potatoes, pork bellies, hogs, cattle and frozen concentrated orange juice. In the first period, there was no futures trading in the commodity. In the second, there was futures trading in the commodity. Spot prices $p(t)$ are observed on one day at weekly intervals. The F statistic measures the contribution of prices lagged by more than one period $\Sigma b(i)p(t - i)$, $i > 1$, to the explanation of the spot price $p(t)$.

The results are unambiguous that the structure of equation (4) changed drastically when futures trading was introduced. (a) When there is no futures trading, the F statistic is always significant at the 5% level. This rejects the MRE hypothesis. (b) The value of the F-statistic is always reduced when there is futures trading. (c) Except for cattle, the F-statistic is not significant when there is futures trading. The question is why the structure of the equation changed fundamentally when futures trading was introduced: i.e., why is MRE rejected before there are futures markets but not rejected when there are futures markets?

The validity of the MRE hypothesis has also been examined for financial instruments and foreign exchange. In each case, the MRE has been rejected.

2. Stock prices: Chow (1989) examined the validity of the MRE equation (3) above for the S & P 500 stocks using monthly price deflated data from 1871 to 1987. Asset market equilibrium equation (1) is valid for the stock market when z is interpreted as dividends. The variable $p(t)$ is the stock price at the beginning of period t and $z(t)$ is the dividend received during period t. The interest rate is the one month Treasury bill rate. The MRE hypothesis is that the current stock price is the rationally expected present value of the stock price dividends to be received by holding the stock one month.

If the MRE were valid, the coefficient of $p(t)$ in (3) should be $(1 + r)$ which is greater than one;

and the coefficient of $z(t)$ should be -1. Chow shows that this hypothesis using MRE must be rejected. The coefficient of $p(t)$ is significantly less than unity: and the coefficient of $z(t)$ is significantly positive.

Chow then applies to the general model (1) the adaptive expectations (AE) equation instead of the MRE equation (2). The contribution of Chow is that he tests the MRE hypothesis against the AE hypothesis on the same data set.

Using the adaptive expectations equation, instead of MRE (2), in (1). Chow obtains an equation which is consistent with the data. His conclusion is that when the asset equilibrium equation (1) is combined with the MRE hypothesis, the resulting hypothesis is rejected; but when it is combined with the adaptive expectations equation, the hypothesis is not rejected.

3. *Foreign Exchange:* In the case of foreign exchange, asset market equilibrium equation (3) becomes (5). Term $(1 + r)$ in (1) becomes $[1 + i(h)]/[1 + i(f)]$ where $i(h)$ is the home and $i(f)$ is the comparable foreign interest rate. The forward rate $q(t + 1; t)$ is equal to $[1 + i(h)]p(t)/[1 + i(f)]$. Term z is a risk premium based upon a consistent economic theory and ϵ is an i.i.d. term with a zero expectation.

$$p(t + k) = q(t + k; t) - z(t) + \epsilon. \qquad (5)$$

A standard statistical test of the uncovered interest rate parity theory with MRE is (6), where a prime denotes the logarithm. The current spot price is subtracted from both sides of (6). The hypothesis is that b is equal to unity and is not equal to zero; and ϵ is i.i.d.

$$[p'(t + 1; t) - p'(t)]$$
$$= a + b[q'(t + 1; t) - p'(t)] + \epsilon. \qquad (6)$$

Longworth, Boothe and Clinton of the Bank of Canada tested this hypothesis for six currencies relative to the U.S. dollar for the period 1970.06 through 1981.09. In each case, the U.S. dollar is viewed as the foreign currency. I have studied the data from 1981.05 to 1989.08 for the British pound (BR), Canadian dollar (CN), French franc (FR), Japanese yen (JP), Swiss franc (SW) and West German mark (WG), relative to the U.S. dollar. One day per month was used in $p(t)$; and a one month forward rate was used in $q(t + 1; t)$. The $p(t + 1)$ matches the $q(t + 1; t)$. Basically, the same results were obtained in both the earlier and our updated (Stein, 1990) studies.

Our results for the period 1981.05–1989.08 were as follows. (1) For each currency the MRE hypothesis is rejected. The coefficient b is either significantly negative or not significantly different from zero. The coefficient b almost always has a negative sign. (2) The peso problem cannot be adduced to account for the rejection of the MRE hypothesis, since the sample period contains the big changes that the market may have been anticipating: the bilateral value of the dollar rose during the first half, and declined during the second half, of the period. (3) One cannot reject the hypothesis that the monthly spot price follows a random walk. (4) The prices lagged by more than one month do not significantly add to the prediction of the subsequent spot price. (5) Except for the Japanese yen, the forecast errors $p'(t) - q'(t; t - 1)$ are not serially correlated. (6) Except for the Japanese yen, the adaptive expectations hypothesis is also rejected. (7) There is no informational content to the forward price concerning the subsequent spot price. The R-squares are as follows for the six rates: BR 0.12, CN 0.00, FR 0.02, JP 0.08, SW 0.00 and WG 0.01.

II. Cobwebs When There Are No Futures Markets

In this part, I propose an explanation of why non-rational cobweb behavior tends to exist when there are no futures markets.

When there are no futures markets, people tend to use OLS to learn the unknown parameters. Both OLS learning and myopic cobweb behavior produce the same type and speed of convergence to MRE. Thus OLS learning is no better or worse than myopic cobweb type behavior. This is consistent with the analysis of De Canio (1979).

A. *Rational Expectations, OLS Learning and Cobweb Behavior*

The model used to derive these results consists of three frequently used equations (Muth, Radner, De Canio, Bray). Equation (7) is the inverse demand for a commodity. The price $p(t)$ depends upon an output $S(t)$ brought to market. Parameter of demand $U(t)$ is the stochastic variable whose mean is unknown.

$$p(t) = U(t) - bS(t). \quad (7)$$

The demand parameter is described by equation (8). The actual parameter $U(t)$ is the sum of the expectation and an i.i.d. term ϵ which has a zero expectation. The unknown expectation $EU(t; t - 1) = \tau X(t - 1)$ is proportional to a signal $X(t - 1)$ received at time $t - 1$ when the production decision is made. The producers do not know the factor τ which maps the signal into the mean.

$$U(t) = \tau X(t - 1) + \epsilon. \quad (8)$$

Optimization by producers (equation (9)) implies that production is such that marginal cost, which is assumed to be proportional to production, $cS(t)$, be equal to the subjectively expected price $E'p(t; t - 1)$. The prime denotes the subjective expectation. It is convenient to normalize the number of producers at unity.

$$E'p(t; t - 1) = cS(t). \quad (9)$$

If there were MRE such that each producer knew the model and parameters (b, c, τ), then the rational expected price, denoted by $Ep(t; t - 1)$, is equation (10).

$$Ep(t; t - 1) = \tau c X(t - 1)/(b + c). \quad (10)$$

Production $S(t)$ is equation (11). It is just a function of the signal.

$$S(t) = [\tau/(b + c)] X(t - 1). \quad (11)$$

Substitute the production $S(t)$ from (11) into the demand (7) to obtain equation (12) for the market price $p(t)$. Define β as the unknown coefficient $[\tau c/(b + c)]$.

$$p(t) = [\tau c/(b + c)] X(t - 1) + \epsilon$$
$$= \beta X(t - 1) + \epsilon. \quad (12)$$
$$\beta = [\tau c/(b + c)]. \quad (12a)$$

Equations (10)–(12) represent the MRE solution to the model equations (7)–(9).

The MRE is a hypothesis concerning the relation between the expected and actual price, but it does not have anything to say how quickly people learn the expected price, i.e., the basic parameters (τ, b, c).

One method of learning is an OLS estimation of parameter β. The producers know the form of equation (12) but do not know parameter β. Therefore, at time $t - 1$ they form an OLS estimate of β denoted $\beta(t - 1)$ by using past observations on $p(t - h)$ and $X(t - h - 1), h > 0$.

$$\beta(t - 1) = \text{cov}(p, X)/\text{var } X. \quad (13)$$

Using the OLS estimate $\beta(t - 1)$, the subjective estimate at time $t - 1$ of the price at time t is equation (13). It must be assumed here that every producer is doing the same calculation. Therefore, every producer has the same expectation.

$$E'p(t; t - 1) = \beta(t - 1) X(t - 1). \quad (14)$$

The production $S(t)$ is equation (15), derived by substituting the expectation in (14) into the optimization equation (9).

$$S(t) = \beta(t - 1) X(t - 1)/c. \quad (15)$$

The realized price $p(t)$ in equation (16) is determined by demand equation (7) and production equation (15).

$$p(t) = [\tau - b\beta(t - 1)/c] X(t - 1) + \epsilon. \quad (16)$$

This is the price that results when each producer is using the same OLS learning model.

Each year when the output $S(t)$ is brought to market, there will be a new price $p(t)$ associated with a previous signal $X(t - 1)$ and a previous regression coefficient $\beta(t - 1)$.

The price $p(t)$, given by (16), is based upon the signal $X(t - 1)$ and the previously estimated value $\beta(t - 1)$. What is the expected value of $\beta(t)$ conditional upon $\beta(t - 1)$? Originally, the subjectively expected price $E'p(t; t - 1)$ was a multiple $\beta(t - 1)$ of the signal, i.e., $\beta(t - 1) = E'p(t; t - 1)/X(t - 1)$ from equation (14). Conditional upon this expectation, the realized price $p(t)$ is given by equation (16).

Let us hold the signal $X(t - 1)$ fixed, for a given value of $\beta(t - 1)$, and imagine repeated samples being taken. The prices $p(t)$ will vary from sample to sample of different drawings from the ϵ distribution in each sample. This process will generate a distribution of prices $p(t)$ in each period t.

The average realized price at time t, denoted by $Ep(t)$, will be a multiple $[\tau - b\beta(t - 1)/c]$ of the signal (since $E\epsilon = 0$ in equation 15). Therefore, the new value of $\beta(t) = Ep(t)/X(t - 1)$ will be equal to this multiple as described by equation (17). When (16) is used as an estimator of $\beta(t) = Ep(t; t-1)/X(t-1)$ then, with repeated sampling, the estimate of $\beta(t)$ is given by (17).

$$\beta(t) = [\tau - b\beta(t-1)/c]. \qquad (17)$$

The sampling and estimation process is repeated in each period. In period $t + 1$ there will be a new signal $X(t)$ and a new value of $\beta(t)$. Conditional upon $[X(t), \beta(t)]$, a new distribution of prices $p(t + 1)$ will result from the distribution of ϵ. A new estimate $\beta(t + 1) = Ep(t + 1; X(t), \beta(t)]/X(t)$ is obtained from the sample of ϵ drawn. Thereby, there is a dynamic process generating successive values of $\beta(t)$, $t = 1, 2, \ldots, T$, as described by closed form solution (18).

$$\beta(t) = \beta + [\beta(0) - \beta](-b/c)^t \qquad (18)$$

where

$$\beta = c\tau/(b+c). \qquad (18a)$$

There are two noteworthy propositions derived from (18). First, if the estimate of the coefficient of $X(t-1)$ in equation (16) converges to a constant, then that constant is equal to the MRE coefficient β in equation (12a).

The second proposition is more interesting. The value of $\beta(t)$ will converge to β if (b/c) is less than unity. The time T required for the absolute value of the initial deviation to fall by 50% of T is given by (19). The steeper is the supply curve (c) relative to the demand curve (b), the faster is the convergence.

$$T = 0.69/(\ln c - \ln b). \qquad (19)$$

Equation (19) describes the speed of convergence of an OLS learning model to MRE, when every producer is using the same OLS model.

The properties of the above OLS learning model are the same as those of the myopic model that leads to traditional cobwebs. This is proposition 3 that the speed of convergence to MRE is the same whether OLS learning or myopic expectations is used.

Assume that anticipations are myopic (equation (20)) so that the producers anticipate that next period's price will be the same as this period's price.

$$E'p(t; t-1) = p(t-1). \qquad (20)$$

The realized price $p(t)$ is equation (21).

$$p(t) = [\tau X(t-1) + \epsilon] - bp(t-1)/c. \qquad (21)$$

The closed form solution for the expected price $Ep(t)$ is (22), where p^* is indeed the MRE price. Price p^* can be called the stochastic equilibrium value.

$$Ep(t) = p^* + [p(0) - p^*](-b/c)^t. \qquad (22)$$
$$p^* = [c\tau/(b+c)]X(t-1). \qquad (22a)$$

This equation is exactly the same as equation (18) for $\beta(t)$. Therefore, the speed of convergence of the myopic system (the Classical Cobweb) to the MRE value is exactly the same as that for the OLS learning model. Therefore, the same type of cycles exist in the two models. The cycles will be damped if $c > b$; but if there are changes in the mean intercept of demand, there will be new cycles converging to the new equilibrium price. In such a changing world, the cobwebs will continue over any sample period.

This is the explanation of the empirical phenomena described in part I, why there tends to be cobwebs type cycles in the absence of futures markets.

III. Futures Markets and the Variance of Bayesian Errors

The difference between the rationally expected price (10), based upon the objective value of population parameter β, and the subjectively expected price, based upon the market's estimate $\beta(t-1)$, can be called a Bayesian error y. The Bayesian error reflects a deviation between the objective population mean of a distribution and the subjective estimate of the mean held by the market. It is convenient to define $W = \beta X$ and $EW(t) = \beta(t-1)X$ as the objective and subjective expectations, respectively, of the price.

$$y(t-1) = [\beta(t-1) - \beta]X(t-1),$$
$$\beta = \tau c/(b+c) \qquad (23)$$
$$y(t-1) = [EW(t) - W]. \qquad (23a)$$

The global market for the product consists of a large set of regional markets, whose prices will be eventually linked by transport costs. In each regional market, there is a beta denoted $\beta(i)$. Let $\beta(i)$ be normally distributed with a mean of β and a precision (reciprocal of the variance) of k.

This is equivalent to saying that there is a distribution of $w(i)$ around the population mean W, with a precision of k. The value of k reflects the homogeneity of the population determining the market price. The market must learn the value of β or of W.

Convergence of the price to its MRE value requires that both the expected Bayesian error $y(t)$ and its variance var y converge to zero. There is no loss of generality in assuming that the expected Bayesian error is zero: $Ey = 0$. Then the speed of convergence of a stochastic system will be measured by the speed at which the variance of the Bayesian error converges to zero.

The cobweb arose because producers used past prices to infer β or W, and their behavior affected subsequent prices. Moreover, producers do not know what other producers will supply. There is a set of people (type S) who are in direct contact with consumers and producers and can sample their demand and supply curves at low cost, before the production decision is made. In the absence of futures markets, finance costs, transactions costs and the risk of default limit the scope of type S people in speculating on the price. Their information cannot affect production, unless they are directly in the business.

With futures markets, the type S people profoundly affect the futures price: and the quantity supplied by producers is conditioned upon the futures price. The question then concerns how quickly the futures price, which reflects the market subjectively expected price, converges to the MRE value of $p* = \beta X$. The learning process is hypothesized to be as follows.

At time $t - 1$ the type S agent has a prior estimate, denoted by $EW(t - 1)$, of the parameter W. He then obtains a sample mean $m(t)$ by contacting n consumers and producers. Using a Bayesian analysis, his posterior estimate $EW(t)$ of objective parameter W is (24); and the precision $\gamma(t)$ of the subjective distribution of the mean is (24b), where the precision is the reciprocal of the variance (De Groot, 1970, p. 167).

$$EW(t) = \alpha(t)EW(t - 1)$$
$$+ (1 - \alpha(t))m(t - 1) \qquad (24)$$

$$\alpha(t) = \gamma(t - 1)/[\gamma(t - 1) + nk]. \qquad (24a)$$

Coefficient $\alpha(t)$ is the weight placed upon the prior and $(1 - \alpha(t))$ is the weight placed upon the sample.

$$\gamma(t) = \gamma(t - 1) + nk = \gamma(0) + nkt. \qquad (24b)$$

The Bayesian error $y(t) = EW(t) - W$ can be derived by subtracting the objective parameter of demand W from both sides of (24). It is difference equation (25):

$$y(t) = \alpha(t)y(t - 1) + (1 - \alpha(t))$$
$$\times [m(t - 1) - W]. \qquad (25)$$

Conditional upon information at $t = 0$, the expectation of the Bayesian error $Ey(t;0)$ is (26), and its variance var $y(t;0)$ is (27), since the expected value of the sample mean is the population mean: $E[m] = W$. (The derivation is Stein (1987) pp. 72–74, 92–93).

$$Ey(t;0) = \gamma(0) Ey(0)/[\gamma(0) + nkt] \qquad (26)$$

$$\text{var } y(t;0) = nkt/[\gamma(0) + nkt]^2. \qquad (27)$$

When the sample size is sufficiently large, then

$$\text{var } y = 1/nkt, \quad k = 1/\text{var } w(i). \qquad (27a)$$

Convergence of a stochastic system to the rational expectations solution requires that both the expectation and the variance go to zero.

The forgone profits from not knowing the objective parameter β or W is proportional to the square of the Bayesian error. For example, consider a producer. He will produce where the subjectively expected price $E_i p = E_i W$ is equal

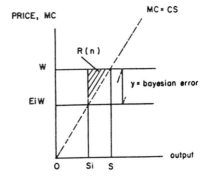

FIGURE 1.—LOSS OF PROFITS

to margin cost cs_i. Hence output $s_i = E_i W/c$. Let $Ep = W$ be the rationally expected price. Then the optimal output should be $s = W/c$. The Bayesian error $y = E_i W - W$. The loss in profits, area $R(n)$ in figure 1, resulting from the Bayesian error, is equation (28):

$$R(n) = (1/2c)y^2. \qquad (28)$$

The immediate question is why agents do not take very large sample sizes, i.e., information sets, and accelerate the convergence to MRE. The reason is that each agent has a cost function

$$G(n) = g' + (g/2)n^2 \qquad (29)$$

for information concerning parameter of demand W, where n is the number of consumers and producers sampled. Quantity $G(n)$ represents the cost per unit of time of establishing a network of n regular contacts who will reveal the information concerning parameter W.

The expected loss function $EL(t)$ is the sum of the expected forgone profits $ER(n)$ plus the cost of sampling $G(n)$. The sample size n, information set, is chosen to minimize the expected loss. When the optimal sample size is chosen, the variance of the Bayesian error is (30):

$$\text{var } y(t) = \left(2gc/k^2 t^2\right)^{1/3}. \qquad (30)$$

The height of the curve var $y(t)$ in figure 2 depends upon g/k^2 where $g = G''$ is the slope of the marginal cost of sampling and $1/k^2$ reflects the heterogeneity of the population sampled. The convex negative slope curve relating the variance to time is the process of Asymptotically Rational Expectations ARE. As time increases and the population mean W is unchanged, then ARE converges to MRE.

IV. Conclusion

Suppose that the population mean changes every T periods in figure 2. The speed of convergence to MRE is reflected by how quickly var $y(t)$ converges to zero before time T. Var $y(t)$ is positively related to the product of the convexity of the costs of sampling g and the heterogeneity of the population sampled $1/k^2 = \text{var } w$. There is a faster convergence to MRE along curve C (commodities) than along curve M (financial instruments and foreign exchange), because g/k^2 is lower for the former.

In the case of commodities, the costs of sampling prospective demand or supply are not very convex, the population sampled is not very heterogeneous, and the distribution does not change frequently. Thus the curve C converges rapidly to zero before time T.

A different situation prevails in the stock and foreign exchange markets. The rationally expected price of a stock is the rationally expected present value of the future dividends. The dividend stream depends upon future macroeconomic conditions, industry developments and idiosyncracies of the firm. The discount factor is the market interest rate. These variables are not generated by stationary processes; and both the convexity of the costs of information and the heterogeneity of the information set are very high.

The foreign exchange rate equilibrates the sum of the current account, the non-speculative capital account and the speculative capital account to zero. The speculative capital account depends upon expected short-term nominal interest rate differentials and the other two components of the balance of payments. The expected short-term interest rate differentials depend upon expected economic conditions, monetary and fiscal policies at home and abroad. The information set determining the exchange rate is very heterogeneous, the distribution changes frequently and quickly, and the costs of sampling are very convex. Therefore the var $y(t)$ curve is high for financial instruments.

Since point Vm is high and much higher than point Vc, there is a poor convergence to MRE in

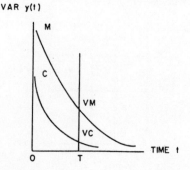

FIGURE 2.—SPEED OF CONVERGENCE OF MRE

financial instruments. Futures markets are necessary, but not sufficient, to produce a rapid convergence to MRE.

REFERENCES

Bray, M., and N. E. Savin, "Rational Expectations Equilibria, Learning and Model Specification," *Econometrica* 54 (5) (1986), 1129–1160.

Chow, Gregory, "Rational versus Adaptive Expectations in Present Value Models," this REVIEW 71 (Aug. 1989).

Cox, Charles, "Futures Trading and Market Information," *Journal of Political Economy* 84 (1976), 1215–1237.

De Canio, Stephen, "Rational Expectations and Learning from Experience," *Quarterly Journal of Economics* 93 (Feb. 1979), 47–57.

De Groot, Morris, *Optimal Statistical Decision* (New York: McGraw-Hill, 1970).

Gray, Roger W., "The Futures Market for Maine Potatoes: An Appraisal," *Food Research Institute Studies* 11 (3) (1972).

Hayes, Dermot J., and Andrew Schmitz "Hog Cycles and Countercyclical Production Response," *American Journal of Agricultural Economics* 69 (Nov. 1987), 762–770.

Longworth, David, P. Booth, and Kevin Clinton, "A Study of the Efficiency of Foreign Exchange Markets," Ottawa, Bank of Canada (1983).

Muth, R. "Rational Expectations and the Theory of Price Movements," *Econometrica* 29 (1961), 215–235.

Radner, Roy, "Equilibrium Under Uncertainty," in K. Arrow and M. Intriligator (ed.), *Handbook of Mathematical Economics*, II, ch. 20 (1982).

Simmons, W. M., "An Economic Study of the U.S. Potato Industry," U.S. Department of Agriculture, Economic Research Service, Agricultural Economic Report No. 6 (1962).

Stein, Jerome L., *The Economics of Futures Markets* (New York: Basil Blackwell, 1987).

——, "The Real Exchange Rate," *Journal of Banking and Finance, Special Issue on Real and Nominal Exchange Rates* 14 (5) (1990), 1045–1078.

Tomek, William G., and R. W. Gray, "Temporal Relations Among Prices on Commodity Futures Markets: Their Allocative and Stabilizing Roles," *American Journal of Agricultural Economics* (Aug. 1970).

Part II
Efficiency

[6]

RANDOM WALK AND PRICE TRENDS: THE LIVE CATTLE FUTURES MARKET

RAYMOND M. LEUTHOLD*

A NOTABLE and provocative development in the recent literature has been the application of the theory of random walks to the analysis of price behavior in the stock and commodity futures markets. The basic hypothesis of the random walk theory is that a particular price series behaves as a simple stochastic process. Successive price changes are independent random variables, implying that the past history of a series generates no information that would be useful in predicting future price changes.

Several authors have tested this independence hypothesis, but with mixed results. Many of the studies on stock market prices are contained in a book edited by Cootner [5], and some show evidence that stock prices behave as a random walk,[1] while others reject the theory.[2] Similar recent testing on commodity futures prices has added to the controversy. Tied to this assortment of results has been a variety of analytical techniques, each with its own justification, ranging from sophisticated statistical tools, such as spectral analysis, to mechanical trading rules which attempt to generate speculative profits.

Among the studies on commodity futures prices, Larson [13], using auto-correlograms, found evidence to support Working's [17] theory of anticipatory prices which implies that prices move randomly. Stevenson and Bear [16], who used an assortment of statistical tools and mechanical trading rules, concluded that corn and soybean futures prices move in a systematic rather than a random fashion. This tended to agree with earlier work done by Houthakker [11] who applied a stop-loss scheme to corn trading. On the other hand, Cargill and Rausser [3], utilizing spectral analysis on various futures contracts for 1967, including corn, concluded that "a simple stochastic process appears consistent with commodity markets price behavior."

A major shortcoming of the entire analysis and a possible reason for the lack of wide acceptance for any single result is the failure to subject identical data to both statistical and mechanical filter tests. The consequence has been varying results, depending upon data and tests used. Only Stevenson and Bear have attempted to apply alternative statistical tools and mechanical trading rules to similar data. However, as will be noted later, one may quarrel with their choice of statistical tools—namely, serial correlation and runs analysis. It is the purpose of this paper to rectify this void in the literature by applying both a sophisticated statistical tool and mechanical filter tests to similar data. Spectral analysis along with several mechanical filters will be employed to test whether the live cattle futures prices move in a random or a systematic fashion.

---

* Assistant Professor of Agricultural Economics at the University of Illinois, Urbana.
1. [5, pp. 85, 139, 162]. Also, see [6], [7], [8], [18] for similar results.
2. [5, pp. 231, 253, 338].

I. MODEL, DATA, AND TESTS USED

Model—If the random walk model is in fact true, then:

$$X_t - X_{t-1} = \varepsilon_t \tag{1}$$

where X_t is the discrete price series the model suggested and ε_t has mean zero and is uncorrelated with ε_{t-k}, all $k \neq 0$. The ε_t series is called white noise. Thus, if the model is correct, the series will proceed by a sequence of unconnected steps, starting each time from the previous value of the series.

Data—The data employed to investigate the random walk model are daily closing prices of 30 live beef cattle futures contracts. They start with the first contract traded,[3] April 1965, and include the subsequent June, August, October, December, and February contracts for each year, up through and including February 1970. This amounts to 6,914 observations, or an average of about 230 observations per contract. Each series is terminated the next to the last day of trading because delivery often occurs on the last trading day, creating an extreme price change.[4] If the closing price on any day was a range, the midpoint of the range was selected as the observation.[5]

Tests—Several statistical tools exist and have been used for testing the appropriateness of the random walk model as a representative of stock or commodity market prices. Among these are serial correlation tests and analysis of runs of successive price changes of the same sign. Fama [6] used these techniques on the stock market and found that they upheld the random walk model.[6] On the other hand, Stevenson and Bear [16] rejected the model after using the techniques on commodity prices.

There has been some criticism of the serial correlation and runs analysis tests, particularly by Fama himself [6]. Primarily, these approaches are too unsophisticated or too restrictive to pick up complicated patterns of price movements. Because of these weaknesses, this study employs spectral analysis as the technique for testing for independence. Spectral analysis is a powerful statistical tool which indicates whether or not a time series is random by establishing confidence intervals around its estimates.

II. SPECTRAL ANALYSIS

Spectral analysis has been used by Granger and Morgenstern [10] and Godfrey, Granger and Morgenstern [8] to test the random walk hypothesis against stock market price indices, while Cargill and Rausser [3] used the technique on selected commodity market price series. Each study found evidence to support the contention that prices behave in a random walk manner.

---

3. Trading on the first four contracts began November 30, 1964.

4. An anonymous reviewer pointed out that delivery conditions may alter the price-generating mechanism during the last few days of each series. While this may be true, a check of the data and results indicates that an earlier termination of each series would not change the basic conclusions drawn in this study.

5. The data source was [4].

6. Also see [5, pp. 85, 139].

The Live Cattle Futures Market

Theory—The spectral method decomposes a time series into a number of components, each associated with a frequency or period.[7] Frequency indicates the number of cycles per unit of time, and the period describes the length of time required for one complete cycle. This spectral decomposition of a time series yields a spectral density function and measures the relative importance of each of the frequency bands in terms of its contribution to the overall variance of the time series. Essentially, spectral analysis is an examination of the variance of a time series with respect to frequency components [14].

The power density function is based on a Fourier transformation of the autocovariance of a stationary series $(X_t, t = 1, \ldots, n)$, approximated by:

$$f(\omega) = \frac{1}{2\pi} \sum_{t=-\infty}^{\infty} \gamma(t) \cos \omega t \qquad (2)$$

where $\gamma(t)$ denotes the autocovariance function.

Before the transformation from a time domain to a frequency domain is made, the autocovariance function is weighted with the Parzen lag window. The weights are of form [12, p. 244; 9, p. 61]:

$$W(k) = \begin{cases} 1 - \dfrac{6k^2}{m^2}\left(1 - \dfrac{k}{m}\right), & 0 \leqslant k \leqslant \dfrac{m}{2} \\[2ex] 2\left(1 - \dfrac{k}{m}\right)^3, & \dfrac{m}{2} < k \leqslant m \end{cases}$$

where m is the number of lags and k is the time-span between terms in the autocovariance function.

These weights are used so that statistically consistent estimates of the power density function can be obtained. Rather than estimate the power associated with a precise frequency, this technique estimates the average power centered around the frequency in question. This is statistically equivalent to averaging over the periodogram. The Parzen weights have the advantage over alternative weighting schemes by (1) allowing for a smaller leakage between frequency bands, (2) giving only positive estimates of the spectrum, and (3) allowing for a larger number of degrees of freedom [14, pp. 111-112].

The spectral estimates are random variables for which tests of significance have been developed. Before the tests for relative peaks are made, the spectrum

---

7. For the basic theory and estimation procedures underlying spectral analysis see Granger and Hatanaka [9] and Jenkins and Watts [12]. For model development and application similar to the method used in this study, see Cargill and Rausser [3] and Rausser and Cargill [14]. This study differs from the previous two primarily by the data used and subsequent results.

is normalized by dividing it by the variance of the series [12, p. 235]. This gives a theoretical value of white noise equal to 1.0 for a normally distributed independent random series. The test of significance for a relative peak follows from a confidence band for normally distributed independent random variables and can be expressed as:

$$\Pr\left[\chi_a^2(v) \leqslant \frac{v\hat{f}(\omega)}{f(\omega)} \leqslant \chi_{1-a}^2(v)\right] = 1 - 2\alpha \qquad (3)$$

where $\chi^2(v)$ are the standard chi-squared values, $v = 3.71n/m$ is the equivalent degrees of freedom, $\hat{f}(\omega)$ is the estimated spectrum of the series, and $f(\omega) = 1.0$. A relative peak outside a confidence interval, for example, 95 per cent, is said to be significantly different from white noise at the 95 per cent level of confidence. The peak represents an important frequency component within the time series.

Results—The daily price series were transformed into first differences according to expression (1).[8] This reduces the influence of possible trends and allows for a direct test of the random walk model. If the price series is generated by the random walk model, then the spectrum will approximate the spectrum of white noise, within a certain confidence limit. The spectra for each series were estimated at 50 frequency components, unless this number violated the rule of thumb that m should not exceed one-quarter of n. When this problem occurred, the spectra were estimated at fewer frequency components, depending upon the size of n.

Two of the spectra are shown for illustrative purposes in Figures 1 and 2.

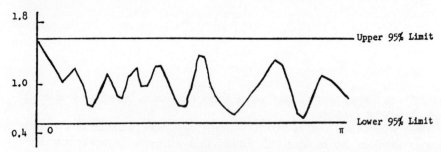

FIGURE 1
February 1968 Contract

The random walk model fits the data very well for the February 1968 contract, but the February 1970 contract indicates that a cyclical pattern exists in the data. A summary of the results of all 30 contracts is given in Table 1. Each contract was judged either random, almost random, or not random. The indefinite category of almost random was established for those contracts where a few estimated points fell slightly outside the confidence band. Since the bands were drawn at the 95 per cent level, these few points may well be within

---

8. Data were also transformed into first differences of logarithms, but subsequent analysis yielded results very similar to those reported.

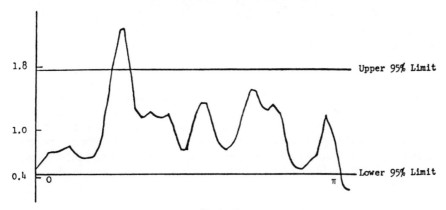

FIGURE 2
February 1970 Contract

99 per cent confidence bands. Also, spectral results have to be interpreted cautiously because $v\hat{f}(\omega)/f(\omega)$ is only approximately distributed as $\chi^2(v)$ and spectral estimates are sensitive to extreme values. Thus, unless all the points were within the bands (judged random), or a definite peak existed as in Figure 2 (judged not random), the contract was put into the almost random class. More detailed results with this classification are given later in this paper.

It is coincidental that the last 6 contracts traded were all judged not random. This occurred because each was in existence during the abnormal time period in 1969 when cattle prices rose dramatically from \$29.50/cwt. to over \$34.00/cwt., then fell back to \$29.00/cwt., all in about six months. The prices in the remaining 24 contracts are either random (13 contracts) or almost random (11 contracts), and these contracts are intermingled.

Thus, this analysis indicates that a simple stochastic process appears consistent with live beef cattle futures price behavior part of the time, but not at other times. Presumably then, drawing upon the conclusion in previous studies [3, 15], if a price series is random, it is not possible to extrapolate from these price movements a mechanism which can be used to generate profitable invest-

TABLE 1
RESULTS OF SPECTRAL ANALYSIS ON 30 LIVE CATTLE FUTURES CONTRACTS

Contract Month	Total Number of Years	Number of Years		
		Random	Almost Random	Not Random
February	5	3	1	1
April	5	2	2	1
June	5	1	3	1
August	5	2	2	1
October	5	3	1	1
December	5	2	2	1
		13	11	6

ment rules. Conversely, if prices are not a random walk, profitable mechanical rules for investment may be possible. It is to these arguments that further comparative analysis is needed.

III. FILTER RULES

Mechanical trading rules, called filters, are simulation models which test for the possibility of nonlinear dependency existing in the price data. Most statistical tools, including spectral analysis, are incapable of detecting such relationships. Many professional traders, chartists especially, claim that nonlinear patterns and dependence do exist in price data, allowing them to generate speculative profits, despite results based on the use of statistical tools indicating randomness.

Model—S. A. Alexander [1] was the first to apply mechanical filter rules to security prices; Fama and Blume [7] have added to the literature. Houthakker [11], and more recently, Stevenson and Bear [16] have applied various filters to grain commodity prices. The rules employed in this study are defined as follows: If the daily closing price of a cattle contract moves up at least x per cent, buy and hold the contract until its price moves down at least x per cent from a subsequent high, at which time simultaneously sell and go short. The short position is maintained until the daily closing price rises at least x per cent above a subsequent low, at which time one reverses position and goes long.[9]

The application of mechanical filter rules on commodity futures prices circumvents some problems that were encountered in previous studies on the stock market. For instance, (1) the rules are applied directly to prices not indices; and (2) dividends are not declared on commodities as they are on stocks, thereby eliminating possible sources of bias. The problem of determining the statistical significance of the results does remain for any price series, however. It is not possible to determine the likelihood of similar results if the process indeed has independent increments; therefore, probability statements cannot be made.

Procedure—The filter technique as defined above is applied to the same data as was the spectral analysis, the daily closing prices of 30 live cattle futures contracts. The filter rules used in this study are 1, 2, 3, 4, 5, and 10 per cent.[10] All transactions were made at the closing price which triggered the decision, and not at a price exactly x per cent from the initial price.[11] The market position held on the next to the last day of trading was liquidated at that closing price, regardless of the position or whether the price had not yet moved x per cent since the preceding transaction.

Contracts for live beef cattle traded on the Chicago Mercantile Exchange from November 1964 through February 1970 were generally for 25,000

---

9. Other mechanical filters exist, but none have proved very successful [16].
10. Prices do not often fluctuate much more than 10 per cent during the duration of a contract.
11. Buying and selling at a price exactly x per cent from an initial price introduced severe biases and problems for Alexander [2].

pounds with a commission of $36 per round-trip. Thus, profits or losses for each round-trip were based on these data and on the actual prices traded.[12] Also, the typical margin requirement requested by the broker was $300.[13] Thus, a return on investment, based on this margin and net returns, was computed for each contract-filter rule, then adjusted to an annual basis for comparisons.

Results—Table 2 indicates for each filter rule, totaled over the 30 contracts, the gross return, number of round-trips, net return after commissions, and annual net rate of return based on the $300 investment. The total gross return for each filter is positive, but the commissions for the 1 and 5 per cent rules caused their net returns to be negative. The 3 per cent rule has the largest net return, followed by the 2, 10, and 4 per cent rules. As would be expected, the smaller the filter rule, the more often the contract is traded.

TABLE 2
RESULTS OF FILTER RULES

Filter Rule	Gross Return	Number of Round-trips	Net Return	Annual Net Rate of Return (per cent)
1 per cent	+$17,390.00	657	−$6,262.00	− 76.75
2 per cent	+ 14,045.00	271	+ 4,289.00	+ 54.78
3 per cent	+ 14,515.00	161	+ 8,719.00	+115.82
4 per cent	+ 5,025.00	126	+ 489.00	+ 7.08
5 per cent	+ 872.50	101	− 2,763.50	− 44.37
10 per cent	+ 2,917.50	34	+ 1,693.50	+ 45.30

It was possible to generate gross profits much larger than those shown in Table 2 by using 5, 10, and 15 day moving averages. However, this procedure led to more frequent trading, so that after commissions the net profits indicated the scheme was far inferior to the percentage rules. Consequently, these results are not included.

The high gross return for the small filter rules indicates that trading on the basis of mechanical decisions rules can be very profitable, providing one does not have to pay commission fees. Of course, floor traders do not pay the $36 commission, only a small maintenance charge. Thus, to them prices do fluctuate so that considerable profits are available. Furthermore, profits even seem possible after commissions for the average trader for four of the six filters. But do these results deny the random walk hypothesis?

---

12. Contract size increased to 40,000 pounds effective with the August 1969 contract. However, for comparative purposes profits and losses were based on 25,000 pounds for all contracts. The effect of the larger contracts would only be to increase the amount of profit or loss per trade.

13. It is recognized that this margin may differ among brokers and over time. However, in order to determine the investment effects of just the price series itself, it is necessary to hold variables such as contract size, commission, and margin requirement constant. Little realism of actual market trading is lost by such action. Also, brokers sometimes require additional margin for their protection if the price moves in the wrong direction, but this is ignored for the same reasons as above and because investment returns are not critical to this study.

IV. Comparison of Results

Alexander [1], Fama and Blume [7] and Stevenson and Bear [16] compared their filter rules with a buy-and-hold policy, concluding that if the filter rule was more profitable than buy-and-hold, prices were not random. Such a comparison does not seem reasonable for commodity prices, however, because (1) contracts are generally only for a duration of about one year as opposed to several years for securities on the stock exchange, so no long-run trends due to inflation exist; (2) for every long position on the commodities market, there is a short position, a situation not true for the stock market; (3) there is no *a priori* reason on the commodities market to initially buy-and-hold, as opposed to sell-and-hold. Thus, the gross returns from the filters will be compared directly with the spectral results.[14]

Table 3 provides a comparison for each of the 30 contracts. As would be expected, those contracts judged not random generally generate the largest profits. Nevertheless, there were also some losses among these six. For the eleven almost random contracts the results seem to vary with both large gains and losses. However, for the thirteen random contracts gross profits on the average tend to be positive for all filter sizes, and the profits seem larger than might be expected. Some contracts, such as April 1965, June 1965, December 1965, and February 1969, generated gross profits for all six filters, while February 1967 generated some very large profits for certain filters. The October 1967, December 1967, and February 1968 contracts gave very mixed results.

These results seem to indicate that speculative profits may tend to be larger than might be expected given the spectral analysis results. Spectral analysis had already rejected, or created some doubt, about the random walk hypothesis for seventeen of the contracts, and the filter rules give additional evidence of price trends existing within the data by generating substantial profits. On the other hand, spectral analysis indicated beyond a doubt that the prices for thirteen of the contracts fluctuated randomly, but the filter rules continue to show positive gross (and often net) profits for many of these contracts. Thus, one would have to question that acceptance of the random walk hypothesis using statistical tools implies that no profits can be generated from the data by chart or mathematical devices [15]. Although we would have to concur in part, but not in general, with Cargill and Rausser [3] that "a simple stochastic process appears consistent with commodity markets price behavior," we would have to dispute their subsequent conclusion that in such instances there is no way of generating a profit by extrapolating from past changes in the prices.

This conflict is partly resolved by the fact that spectral analysis looks at time periods of fixed length (one day, in this study), while the filter rules allow the time period to vary, picking up nonlinear dependency. That is, short-run trends in the data may exist that spectral analysis cannot detect, but filter rules

---

14. It can be argued that profits after commission are not relevant to the random walk issue [5, p. 351], so using gross returns seems the most appropriate. However, the basic conclusions in this study would not be altered if net returns were used.

The Live Cattle Futures Market

TABLE 3
COMPARISON OF SPECTRAL AND FILTER RULE RESULTS

Contract		Spectral Results	Filter Rule Results[d]					
			1%	2%	3%	4%	5%	10%
April	1965	R[a]	+ .90	+ 5.17	+ 3.52	+ 5.00	+ 4.32	+ 1.62
June	1965	R	+ 4.52	+10.32	+ 5.82	+ 3.07	+ 3.32	+ 6.50
August	1965	R	+ 8.35	+ 5.92	+ 3.70	− 5.45	+ 2.92	+ 3.27
October	1965	R	+ 1.20	+ 7.80	+ 1.57	− .02	− 3.42	+ 1.50
December	1965	R	+ 3.62	+ 3.27	+ 7.15	+ 2.52	+ .75	+ .95
February	1966	A.R.[b]	− 2.17	+ 3.00	+ 4.27	− .62	− 3.12	+ 2.62
April	1966	R	− 1.20	− .87	+ 3.75	+ 1.25	+ 4.62	+ 1.60
June	1966	A.R.	+ 5.55	+ 2.82	+ 7.22	+10.20	+ 7.32	− 4.82
August	1966	R	− 2.85	− 6.07	+ 2.87	+ 2.25	− .35	+ .87
October	1966	A.R.	+ .62	+ 2.52	+ 7.27	+ 4.52	+ .87	+ 2.37
December	1966	A.R.	+13.97	+ 7.47	+ 6.60	− .37	+ 4.50	+ 5.42
February	1967	R	+11.25	+ 5.55	+ 4.52	+ 3.30	− 6.00	+ 2.17
April	1967	A.R.	+ 5.92	− 1.27	+ 3.57	+ 3.27	+ .62	+ 3.65
June	1967	A.R.	+ 9.97	+ 3.00	− 2.70	− .70	− 7.02	+ 1.20
August	1967	A.R.	+ 1.07	+ 2.55	+ 3.52	− 2.82	− 7.42	− 2.07
October	1967	R	+ 3.47	+ 1.57	+ 2.37	− 3.07	−10.37	− 1.50
December	1967	R	+ 3.42	+ 9.87	+ 2.27	− 4.40	−10.00	+ 1.67
February	1968	R	+ .02	+ 5.80	+ 4.55	− 1.40	− 5.90	− 2.97
April	1968	A.R.	+ 8.52	+ 4.47	+ 6.25	+ 4.62	+ 7.75	− 1.62
June	1968	A.R.	+ 1.55	+ 5.62	− .80	+ 1.67	+ 5.67	− 3.90
August	1968	A.R.	− 3.25	+ 1.00	+ 4.15	+ 5.15	+ 3.92	− 4.95
October	1968	R	+ 4.10	+ 2.97	− .07	− 1.95	+ 2.12	.00
December	1968	A.R.	+ 5.27	+ 8.62	+ 5.52	+ 2.10	+ 9.07	+ 2.85
February	1969	R	+ 7.07	+ 4.15	+ 5.07	+ 4.70	+ 2.75	+ 3.00
April	1969	N.R.[c]	+ 4.60	+ 7.70	+ 8.62	+ 1.32	+ 3.57	+ 7.40
June	1969	N.R.	+14.22	+ 4.97	+16.80	+16.05	+14.30	+17.17
August	1969	N.R.	+14.62	+12.65	+21.00	+12.57	+ 6.02	+ .45
October	1969	N.R.	+20.70	+ 6.65	+ 4.70	+ 1.15	+ .37	− 3.60
December	1969	N.R.	+14.65	+10.42	+ 5.60	− 2.65	−10.00	− 9.95
February	1970	N.R.	+14.15	+ 2.75	− 3.60	−11.02	−12.50	.00

[a] Random.
[b] Almost, or nearly, random.
[c] Significant variation from random walk model and judged not random.
[d] Gross returns in hundreds of dollars.

can. The lack of concurrence between the conclusions drawn from results generated by sophisticated statistical tools and mechanical filter rules in testing the random walk hypothesis on identical data demonstrates that one should be suspicious of the conclusions drawn by any researcher who used only one methodological approach and did not compare the results with an alternative approach.

For the average speculator interested in commodity futures trading, these results indicate that if he had used the 3 per cent rule on the 30 cattle contracts, substantial profits could have been generated, even after commissions. This occurs whether the price series is random or not. However, no probabilistic statement can be given as to the chances of that or any filter rule continuing to be profitable.

V. Conclusions

It has been the purpose of this paper to investigate the short-run fluctuations of the live beef cattle futures market with respect to the random walk hypothesis. Spectral analysis gave mixed results, indicating that a simple stochastic process appeared consistent with the price behavior of some of the contracts but not with others.

The same data were subjected to mechanical trading rules for further testing and comparison. These results cast serious doubt that cattle futures prices behave randomly. More importantly, the results allow one to seriously question the validity of drawing the conclusion that profitable trading is impossible after accepting the random walk hypothesis as the result of sophisticated statistical tools. Gross profits from trading rules seemed larger than might be expected where the spectral results indicated that prices behave in a random walk fashion. Prices which appear to be random as a result of statistical tests may still generate profits for the investor who relies on non-linear dependency through the use of filter rules, regardless of whether he pays commissions or not.

Thus, the conclusions drawn by any investigator who uses only one of the two basic approaches must be looked at with suspicion. This may call for using or developing alternative statistical tools to test the random walk hypothesis, especially tools that may detect the same price movements as do the mechanical filters. Also, further work is needed in investigating the accepted concept that anticipatory prices are random. Such an investigation should be made on the prices of those futures commodities where there is no inventory, such as with live cattle and hogs, being allocated over a period of time.

REFERENCES

1. S. A. Alexander. "Price Movements in Speculative Markets: Trends or Random Walks," *Industrial Management Review* 2 (May, 1961), pp. 7-26. Also in [5], pp. 199-218.
2. ———. "Price Movements in Speculative Markets: Trends or Random Walks, No. 2," *Industrial Management Review* 5 (Spring, 1964), pp. 25-46. Also in [5], pp. 338-372.
3. T. F. Cargill and G. C. Rausser. "Futures Price Behavior as a Stochastic Process," Paper presented at the American Statistical Association Meetings, New York, Aug. 19-21, 1969.
4. *Chicago Mercantile Exchange Yearbook*. Chicago, Chicago Mercantile Exchange, 1964-65 through 1969-70.
5. P. H. Cootner (ed.). *The Random Character of Stock Market Prices*. Cambridge, Mass., The M.I.T. Press, 1964.
6. E. F. Fama. "The Behavior of Stock Market Prices," *Journal of Business* 38 (January, 1965), pp. 34-105.
7. E. F. Fama and M. E. Blume. "Filter Rules and Stock-Market Trading," *Journal of Business* 39 (January, 1966), pp. 226-241.
8. M. D. Godfrey, C. W. J. Granger and O. Morgenstern. "The Random Walk Hypothesis of Stock Market Prices," *Kyklos* 17 (1964), pp. 1-30.
9. C. W. J. Granger and M. Hatanaka. *Spectral Analysis of Economic Time Series*. Princeton, N.J., Princeton University Press, 1964.
10. C. W. J. Granger and O. Morganstern. "Spectral Analysis of New York Stock Market Prices," *Kyklos* 16 (1963), pp. 1-27. Also in [5], pp. 162-188.
11. H. S. Houthakker. "Systematic and Random Elements in Short Term Price Movements," *American Economic Review* 51 (May, 1961), pp. 164-172.
12. G. M. Jenkins and D. G. Watts. *Spectral Analysis and Its Applications*. San Francisco, Holden-Day, 1968.
13. A. B. Larson. "Measurement of a Random Process in Futures Prices," *Food Research Institute Studies* 1 (November, 1960), pp. 313-324. Also in [5], pp. 219-230.

14. G. C. Rausser and T. F. Cargill. "The Existence of Broiler Cycles: An Application of Spectral Analysis," *American Journal of Agriculture Economics* 52 (February, 1970), pp. 109-121.
15. P. A. Samuelson. "Proof That Properly Anticipated Prices Fluctuate Randomly," *Industrial Management Review* 6 (Spring, 1965), pp. 41-49.
16. R. A. Stevenson and R. M. Bear. "Commodity Futures: Trends or Random Walks?" *Journal of Finance* 25 (March, 1970), pp. 65-81.
17. H. Working. "A Theory of Anticipatory Prices," *American Economic Review* 63 (May, 1958), pp. 188-199.
18. W. E. Young. "Random Walk of Stock Prices: A Test of the Variance-Time Function," Paper presented at the Econometric Society Meetings, New York, December 28-30, 1969.

[7]
Futures Trading and Market Information

Charles C. Cox
Ohio State University

This paper investigates the effect of organized futures trading on information in spot markets. First, a model is developed that relates spot-price behavior and market information. The model can be viewed as a particular efficient markets model; this connection provides additional implications about price behavior and information. Next, price series for six different commodities are investigated for an information effect of futures trading. For each commodity, the empirical evidence indicates that futures trading increases traders' information about forces affecting supply and demand.

The influence of futures trading on commodity prices has long been a controversial subject. For some 80 years, there have been farmers and other agricultural interests who have claimed that futures trading destabilizes spot prices and thereby imposes losses on producers and consumers. Congress has decided that futures trading frequently causes unreasonable price fluctuations and has enacted several laws regulating organized trading in commodity futures: trading in onion futures is prohibited, and futures trading in all other commodities is regulated by the Commodity Futures Trading Commission.[1] The congressional hearings on regulation of futures markets show that the regulators have neither a theory of destabilizing futures trading nor empirical evidence of destabilized prices. Several economists have studied futures trading and price variability by comparing price ranges or variances in a period of no

---

This paper is drawn from my doctoral dissertation ("The Regulation of Futures Trading," University of Chicago, 1975). I am indebted to George Stigler, Lester Telser, and the late Reuben Kessel for valuable advice and criticism.

[1] Trading in onion futures is prohibited by P.L. 85-839, August 28, 1958, 72 Stat. 1013. Trading in other commodities is regulated by the Commodity Futures Trading Commission Act of 1974, P.L. 93-463, 88 Stat. 1389. Prior to 1974, futures trading in most agricultural products was regulated by the Commodity Exchange Act.

futures trading and a period of active futures trading.[2] Some conclude that futures trading reduces price fluctuations; others find no difference. None of these studies offer much theoretical explanation of the empirical results.

This paper takes a different approach to the price effects of futures trading. I consider the relation between futures trading, market information, and spot prices, and I develop a model to analyze the information effect of futures trading. In the context of the model, empirical evidence on commodities' price behavior indicates that futures trading increases the information incorporated in a commodity's spot price. The results are inconsistent with the view that futures trading destabilizes spot prices in a way that is harmful to traders who handle the physical commodity.

I. Price Effects of Futures Trading

The relation between spot and futures prices together with certain characteristics of futures markets suggest that price effects of futures trading result from a change in the state of firms' price expectations. Telser (1958, 1967) shows that a futures price is an average of traders' expectations of the spot price that will prevail at the futures contract's maturity, and that for storable commodities, expected and current spot prices differ only by the net marginal cost of storage. Expected and current spot prices are determined simultaneously, and any change in expected prices induces a reallocation of the commodity between storage and current supply, thereby affecting the spot price. Futures trading can effect a state change in price expectations by altering the quantity of traders' information. Expected prices depend on current information about future supply and demand: more informed predictions are more accurate than less informed predictions. If information were free, all firms would have full knowledge of the evidence on future conditions and there would be no reason to believe that futures trading could influence price expectations. However, in real markets bits of information are dispersed among numerous individuals, the information changes frequently and is costly to acquire and communicate. Therefore, firms' price expectations reflect information that is neither complete nor perfectly

---

[2] Hieronymus (1960), Working (1960), Gray (1963), and Johnson (1973) studied onions. Working, Hieronymus, and Gray concluded that futures trading stabilized onion prices, but Johnson concluded that there was no price effect of futures trading. Naik (1970) analyzed groundnut, linseed, and hessian. He concluded that futures trading reduced the variation in groundnut and linseed prices but did not affect hessian prices. Hooker (1901) and Tomek (1971) studied wheat; both concluded that the variation in wheat prices decreased in periods with futures trading. Emery (1896) studied cotton and concluded that futures trading reduced the yearly range of cotton prices. Taylor and Leuthold (1974) investigated cattle and Powers (1970) investigated pork bellies and cattle. Both studies concluded that short-term price variations are significantly reduced when there is futures trading.

FUTURES TRADING AND MARKET INFORMATION 1217

accurate, and the introduction of futures trading can produce either more or less informed price expectations.

There are at least two reasons for believing that futures trading can alter the amount of information reflected in expected prices. First, organized futures trading attracts an additional set of traders to a commodity's market: speculators who acquire and evaluate information in order to predict prices but who do not handle the physical commodity.[3] When these speculators have either a net long or short position in the futures market, hedgers (firms that deal in the physical commodity) have a corresponding net short or long position which causes the amount of stocks held for later consumption to be different than it would have been in the absence of futures trading. With different stocks, firms' price expectations are different too. Because the speculators added by futures trading may be more or less informed about future conditions than traders who handle the physical commodity, the futures price can be consistently either a more or less accurate prediction of the spot price than the firms' expectations without futures trading. Critics of futures trading sometimes contend that speculators in futures markets are generally uninformed amateurs, while those more favorable to speculators emphasize that specialization should bring efficiency in price predictions. Relatively informed speculators would earn profits, while relatively uninformed speculators would find themselves suffering losses over time. Nevertheless, if uninformed speculators are willing to pay for the chance to earn profits from trading, and if new uninformed speculators enter the market and replace those who cannot sustain losses, a set of uninformed speculators would survive. A priori, it is impossible to determine whether speculators attracted by futures trading are more or less informed on average than other traders in the market. Empirical evidence on this question is inconclusive: the results of several studies indicate that large-scale, professional speculators can profitably forecast commodity prices, but small traders cannot.[4]

---

[3] Speculators take a long or short position in the futures market when they expect the futures price to rise or fall. Relatively low costs of transacting in futures markets make it worthwhile for these speculators to close out their positions with an offsetting sale or purchase of futures contracts rather than accepting delivery of and selling, or acquiring and delivering, the physical commodity. With futures trading, speculators can bear price risks whenever they expect profits without establishing trade connections for merchandising the commodity. This is not to say that there are no speculators trading a commodity in the absence of futures trading. Whenever stocks of a commodity are held in an uncertain world, someone speculates by bearing the price risk of stockholding. Futures trading attracts additional speculators who would not trade the commodity without a futures market.

[4] Stewart (1949) analyzed futures-trading accounts that were mainly for small-scale speculators and found that losses greatly exceeded profits. Houthakker (1957) and Rockwell (1967) used data on futures prices and traders' commitments and assumptions about trading to estimate gains and losses. Both found that large speculators earned profits and small speculators incurred losses. Using a similar method, Working (1931) estimated that speculators in wheat futures, as a group, incurred losses.

A second reason why futures trading can change the amount of traders' information concerns the cost of transacting. Without futures trading, individuals' expectations may differ widely, but often it is not worthwhile to communicate that information. A formal futures market reduces the cost of transacting because trading is completely centralized. Relative to dispersed trading and private negotiations, it is cheaper to identify potential traders, search for the best bid or offer, and negotiate a contract in a futures market. It becomes worthwhile for more individuals to trade and thereby communicate their information. The dispersed information on supply and demand is concentrated in one place and is all reflected in a single futures price.[5] All futures traders acquire this information, and because futures prices are widely publicized, the information incorporated in a futures price can be acquired cheaply by individuals who do not trade in futures markets. The magnitude of this effect depends upon the amount of the reduction in the cost of transacting. Organized futures trading should produce a larger effect the more decentralized a commodity's spot market is and the more numerous a commodity's traders are, since it is likely that the reduction in transacting cost will vary directly with these factors.

In order to investigate these effects of futures trading, it is necessary to specify the relations between information, price expectations, and the behavior of spot prices.

Market Information and Price Behavior

Consider a market with the following characteristics: Demand for the commodity fluctuates over time due to random shocks. Production is subject to a fixed lag, so the quantity produced depends on producers' price forecasts. Stocks of the commodity are held to smooth consumption over time. Information consists of a knowledge of the random shocks that affect demand, and, due to the cost of information, not all traders possess the most recent information. Expectations are formed as if the market calculates expected values conditional on the traders' information and the structure of the market. Although price expectations differ among firms—there is some distribution of price expectations—the model developed here does not take account of the dispersion of expectations. Firms' expectations are represented by a single expected price that is defined as an average of individual expected prices.[6] The following

---

[5] The role of a market price in summarizing and communicating information is discussed by Hayek (1945).

[6] Telser (1958) has used a market's expected price as an analytical device to develop an industry stockholding schedule. He suggests that the expected price can either be defined as an average or be derived from the relation between individual schedules and total market quantities. Houthakker (1968) has severely criticized the use of an expected

equations, based on a model by Muth (1961), describe the market and the effect on price behavior of a change in the quantity of traders' information:

$$C_t = \beta_0 - \beta P_t - \varepsilon_t \quad \text{(Consumption demand)}, \quad (1a)$$

$$S_t = \gamma_0 + \gamma P_t^e \quad \text{(Production)}, \quad (1b)$$

$$I_t = \alpha_0 + \alpha(P_{t+1}^e - P_t) \quad \text{(Supply of storage)}, \quad (1c)$$

$$C_t + I_t = S_t + I_{t-1} \quad \text{(Market equilibrium)}, \quad (1d)$$

where P_t is the price in period t; P_t^e is the market's expectation of the price that will prevail in period t, given the traders' information through period $t-1$; and ε_t is a random disturbance affecting demand, C_t.[7] Assume that the ε's are independent and identically distributed, and that expected prices can be expressed as linear combinations of these disturbances. The current price, then, is a linear function of the ε's,

$$P_t = \sum_{i=0}^{\infty} V_i \varepsilon_{t-i} + K. \quad (2)$$

From the expectations assumption, the expected price is the expected value of P_t conditional on the traders' information through period $t-1$.

$$\begin{aligned}P_t^e &= V_0 E(\varepsilon_t) + (1-f)V_1 E(\varepsilon_{t-1}) + f V_1 \varepsilon_{t-1} + \sum_{i=2}^{\infty} V_i \varepsilon_{t-i} + K \\ &= f V_1 \varepsilon_{t-1} + \sum_{i=2}^{\infty} V_i \varepsilon_{t-i} + K,\end{aligned} \quad (3)$$

where f is the fraction of the traders that possesses the information ε_{t-1} in period $t-1$.

In investigating a market for the effects of a change in the quantity of market information, that is, a change in f, neither the price expectations nor the random shocks can be observed directly. The actual prices,

---

price for analysis of futures trading. One of his major objections is that the procedure by which individual expected prices should be aggregated has not been specified. Furthermore, he objects to focusing exclusively on price expectations, as I do in this essay, because he argues that individual expected prices have ambiguous effects on traders' behavior unless a number of other variables, e.g., the wealth effect of price changes, are taken into account. Clearly, there are variables other than price expectations that influence price movements, and an average of expected prices is only an approximation, but my goal is to concentrate on information and the behavior of spot prices. Whether my model is useful for analyzing this problem depends on its ability to predict actual price behavior.

[7] In this model, random disturbances affect only demand because that is sufficient to make P_t a stochastic variable. Although it would seem more realistic to include a random term in production too, adding a disturbance like ε_t to (1b) neither increases nor changes the model's implications about information and price behavior. Under different assumptions about the disturbances, however, this conclusion does not hold. See Nelson (1975).

however, are observable. Therefore, to make this model operational it is necessary to solve for the expected price in terms of past prices. That is,

$$P_t^e = \sum_{j=1}^{\infty} Z_j P_{t-j} + H. \tag{4}$$

With equations (1) and (4), it is possible to derive a testable hypothesis about the effect of futures trading on the behavior of market prices. Hence, the task is to solve for the Z's of (4) in terms of the parameters of equations (1), then to find the effect of a change in f on the relation between prices. To do so, it is convenient to start by specifying the relationship between the V's implied by equations (1)–(3).

Substituting (2) and (3) into (1) yields the transformed market equilibrium equation:

$$[(\beta_0 + \alpha_0) - \beta K] - (\beta + \alpha) \sum_{i=0}^{\infty} V_i \varepsilon_{t-i} + \alpha \left(f V_1 \varepsilon_t + \sum_{i=2}^{\infty} V_i \varepsilon_{t+1-i} \right)$$
$$= [(\gamma_0 + \alpha_0) + \gamma K] + (\gamma + \alpha) \left(f V_1 \varepsilon_{t-1} + \sum_{i=2}^{\infty} V_i \varepsilon_{t-i} \right) \tag{5}$$
$$- \alpha \sum_{i=0}^{\infty} V_i \varepsilon_{t-1-i} + \varepsilon_t.$$

For (5) to hold for all possible shocks, the coefficients of the corresponding ε's must be equal, and the constant terms in brackets must be the same. Hence,

$$-(\alpha + \beta) V_0 + \alpha f V_1 = 1 \tag{6a}$$

$$\alpha V_0 - [\alpha(1 + f) + \beta + \gamma f] V_1 + \alpha V_2 = 0 \tag{6b}$$

$$\alpha V_{i-1} - (2\alpha + \beta + \gamma) V_i + \alpha V_{i+1} = 0 \quad (i = 2, 3, 4, \ldots). \tag{6c}$$

Equation (6c) is a homogeneous, second-order difference equation for which the solution is:

$$V_i = r^{i-1} V_1 \quad (i = 2, 3, 4, \ldots), \tag{7}$$

where r is the smaller root ($0 < r < 1$) of the characteristic equation for (6c) and is a function of α, β, and γ.[8]

Substituting (7) into (6b) and transforming yields

$$\phi \equiv \frac{V_1}{V_0} = \frac{\alpha}{[\alpha(1 + f - r) + \beta + \gamma f]}. \tag{8}$$

---

[8] Sufficient conditions for real and distinct roots in the characteristic equation for (6c) are $\alpha > 0$ and $(\beta + \gamma) > 0$. The roots occur in reciprocal pairs, so only one root is less than one in absolute value. From (2), it follows that (6c) is stable or P_t would be infinite. That is, the requirement that all bounded sequences of disturbances produce only bounded sequences of prices implies that (6c) is stable. Therefore, the coefficient of the larger root in the general solution must be zero.

FUTURES TRADING AND MARKET INFORMATION

Now the solution of (4) follows easily; substituting (2) and (3) into (4) yields

$$fV_1\varepsilon_{t-1} + \sum_{i=2}^{\infty} V_i\varepsilon_{t-i} = \sum_{i=1}^{\infty}\left(\sum_{j=1}^{i} Z_j V_{i-j}\right)\varepsilon_{t-i} + K\left(\sum_{j=1}^{\infty} Z_j - 1\right) + H. \quad (9)$$

Like (5), (9) must hold for all possible shocks, so the corresponding coefficients of the ε's are equal:

$$fV_1 = Z_1 V_0 \quad (10a)$$

$$V_i = \sum_{j=1}^{i} Z_j V_{i-j} \quad (i = 2, 3, 4, \ldots). \quad (10b)$$

Substituting (7), (8), into (10) and solving for Z_i gives

$$Z_1 = f\phi \quad (11a)$$

$$Z_i = (r - f\phi)\phi(r - \phi)^{i-2} \quad (i = 2, 3, 4, \ldots). \quad (11b)$$

Equations (11) produce the desired form for (4):

$$P_t^e = f\phi P_{t-1} + \sum_{j=2}^{\infty} [(r - f\phi)\phi(r - \phi)^{j-2}]P_{t-j} + H. \quad (12)$$

Combining (12) and (1), the market equilibrium equation yields

$$P_t = \frac{(\gamma_0 - \beta_0 + \gamma H)}{(\alpha f\phi - \alpha - \beta)} + \phi P_{t-1}$$

$$+ \frac{(r - f\phi)\phi[(\alpha + \gamma) - \alpha(r - \phi)]}{(\alpha f\phi - \alpha - \beta)} \sum_{j=2}^{\infty} (r - \phi)^{j-2} P_{t-j} \quad (13)$$

$$+ \frac{\varepsilon_t}{(\alpha f\phi - \alpha - \beta)}.$$

Let

$$b_0 = \frac{(\gamma_0 - \beta_0 + \gamma H)}{(\alpha f\phi - \alpha - \beta)} \quad (14a)$$

$$b_1 = \phi \quad (14b)$$

$$b_j = \frac{(r - f\phi)\phi[(\alpha + \gamma) - \alpha(r - \phi)](r - \phi)^{j-2}}{(\alpha f\phi - \alpha - \beta)} \quad (j = 2, 3, 4, \ldots) \quad (14c)$$

$$u_t = \frac{\varepsilon_t}{(\alpha f\phi - \alpha - \beta)} \quad (14d)$$

then

$$P_t = b_0 + \sum_{j=1}^{\infty} b_j P_{t-j} + u_t. \quad (15)$$

Analysis of equations (14) shows that the b_j's have the following properties:

$$b_1 > 0$$

$$b_j \begin{cases} >0 \text{ if } j \text{ is odd} \\ <0 \text{ if } j \text{ is even} \end{cases} \text{ for } 0 < f < 1 \text{ and } (j = 2, 3, 4, \ldots)$$

$$|b_j| > |b_{j+1}| \quad (j = 1, 2, 3, \ldots)$$

$$|b_j| < 1 \quad (j = 2, 3, 4, \ldots).$$

Thus the model implies that when some traders have not acquired the most recent market information, the current market price will equal a linear combination of past prices plus a random-error term, that is, equation (15). The coefficients of past prices alternate in sign starting with a positive coefficient for the price immediately preceding the current price and the earlier the price, the smaller in absolute value is its coefficient.

An increase in market information acquired by the traders is equivalent to an increase in f. The effect of increased information on the relationship between the prices is found by differentiating b_j with respect to f. By equations (14):

$$\frac{\partial |b_j|}{\partial f} < 0 \quad (j = 1, 2, 3, \ldots). \tag{16a}$$

With an increase in market information, the coefficients of past prices in equation (15) all decrease in absolute value. Also, it follows from equations (14d) and (15) that an increase in information decreases the variance of the price-forecast error.

$$\frac{\partial \sigma_u^2}{\partial f} < 0. \tag{16b}$$

In the extreme case where all traders know the latest market information, that is, in the case where $f = 1$, equation (8) shows that $\phi = r$. Therefore, by (14)

$$b_1 = r, \tag{17a}$$

$$b_j = 0 \quad (j = 2, 3, 4, \ldots), \quad f = 1. \tag{17b}$$

Equation (15) then becomes

$$P_t = b_0 + rP_{t-1} + u_t. \tag{18}$$

Why are price effects of uninformed traders not eliminated by traders with complete information? Put another way, why would fully informed traders limit their market positions instead of trading so that price is pegged at the level consistent with the unbiased estimate of the future price? One reason is related to the idea that individuals' expectations can differ for the same information set; the theory requires only that a weighted average of individual expectations based on complete information equal the expected value of the future price. Also, the fully informed traders need not be the same individuals in every period. Consequently, lack of confidence in his price forecast would limit the commitment made by each informed trader even though the completely informed traders will, as a group, earn profits at the expense of the group of traders with incomplete information. If there is no risk aversion to limit the commitments of fully informed traders, then price effects of uninformed traders would persist only to the extent that costs of transacting make it unprofitable to completely eliminate them.

Market Efficiency

The preceding implications about information and price behavior are compatible with theory developed in the efficient-markets literature—the model itself can be viewed as a particular efficient-markets model.[9] The work on efficient markets assumes that market equilibrium can be stated in terms of expected values of price changes, and that prices in an efficient market fully reflect available information. From these assumptions, it follows that the expected value of P_t conditional on all information at $t-1$ is an unbiased estimate of P_t. That is,

$$E[P_t - E(P_t \mid \text{all information at } t-1)] = 0. \qquad (19)$$

For the model developed above, the assumption that market expectations equal conditional expected values allows equilibrium to be expressed in terms of expected values; available information is fully reflected in the price when all traders are informed. So price in an efficient market is represented by (18), from which the "fair game" property (19) follows directly:

$$E\{P_t - E[P_t \mid (\varepsilon_{t-1})]\} = E(u_t) = 0. \qquad (20)$$

Implications about the sequence of observed prices in an efficient market depend upon the stochastic processes generating price changes. Several efficient-markets studies assume that successive price changes are independent, identically distributed random variables, which implies that the sequence of price changes is a random walk. In my model, however, both systematic and random factors generate price changes. Systematic changes are due to storage costs, and random changes are due to the disturbances that affect demand. Hence, successive price changes are not independent, and the sequence of price changes is not a random walk even when

[9] The efficient-markets literature is summarized in Fama (1970).

current information is fully reflected in the market price. To see this consider first differences of (18):

$$P_t - P_{t-1} = r(P_{t-1} - P_{t-2}) - u_{t-1} + u_t. \qquad (21)$$

Equation (21) shows that successive price changes are correlated, although the history of earlier price changes $(P_{t-2} - P_{t-3}, P_{t-3} - P_{t-4}, \ldots)$ adds no additional information about $P_t - P_{t-1}$. If there were no storage in the model, only the independent, identically distributed disturbances in demand (ε_t) would cause price changes and the sequence of price changes would be a random walk.

If information is not fully reflected in the price, efficient-markets theory implies only that the fair-game property will not hold. Other than this, price behavior depends on the particular price-formation process and the information that does influence price. The model in the present work focuses on differences in price behavior when more or less information is reflected in price, so it specifies both price formation and information in order to show how the relation between prices depends on the quantity of information (15). Since (15) is just one of many possible ways that a price series can behave, empirical analysis is necessary to determine if it corresponds to actual price behavior. However, (15) is consistent with efficient-markets theory in that the sequence of differences between observed and expected price is not a fair game. When P_t is given by (15), expected value conditional on *all* information at $t-1$ is the expected value of (18); hence:

$$E\{P_t - E[P_t \mid (\varepsilon_{t-1})]\} = (\phi - r)P_{t-1} + \sum_{j=2}^{\infty} b_j P_{t-j} + \text{constant}. \qquad (22)$$

The history of past prices can be used to make a price forecast that is on average more accurate than the conditional expected value. As a result, when there are uninformed traders in the market, it may be possible for a chart reader to devise a profitable trading rule based only on past spot prices.

The preceding model provides a framework for testing the hypothesis that commodity futures trading affects spot prices by increasing the market's information about forces influencing supply and demand. The coefficients of past prices in (15) reflect the quantity of the market's information, and since (15) is an autoregressive process, the coefficients can be estimated empirically from a time series of a commodity's prices. If the estimated coefficients are consistent with the implications of the model, and if there is a difference between the coefficients for periods with and without futures trading, the change can be interpreted as the contribution of futures trading to market information. Furthermore, an increase in information should decrease the returns from a trading rule. This too can be tested with a series of spot prices. The next section investigates the price behavior of six different commodities.

II. Empirical Analysis

Evidence on price effects of futures trading is presented here for onions, potatoes, pork bellies, hogs, cattle, and frozen concentrated orange juice (FCOJ). For each of these commodities, price effects of futures trading are estimated by comparing price behavior in a period with no futures trading to price behavior in a period when the commodity is traded in a formal futures market.

The most important conclusions of this empirical analysis are: (1) futures trading in a commodity increases the quantity of traders' information, (2) a spot market is more efficient in the sense that price more fully reflects available market information when there is futures trading, (3) the behavior of prices does not support the claim that producers and consumers are harmed by price effects of futures trading.

Data and Periods Examined

Price series for each commodity are compiled from trade journals that report wholesale spot prices.[10] The prices are observed on 1 day at weekly intervals in the market where futures trading occurs and are for commodities with the same specifications as the basis grade for futures trading.

Sample periods depend on the length of time that a continual price series has been reported and on the date when futures trading in a commodity began. Periods when a commodity's prices were publicly controlled are also recognized in choosing the sample periods, since reported and transaction prices often differ during times of price controls.[11] Consequently, the lengths of the sample periods vary considerably; the longest sample contains 856 observations and the shortest contains 220 observations. The commodities, markets, and periods examined are listed in table 1.

[10] Onion prices are taken from two basic sources: for the period 1928–59, prices are from the *Chicago Packer*, a trade journal for the Chicago wholesale vegetable market; for the period 1960–71, prices are from *Chicago Fresh Fruit and Vegetable Wholesale Market Prices*, a publication of the U.S. Department of Agriculture. Two data sources are used because the *Packer* frequently failed to report onion prices after 1959, and the weekly price reports made available by the USDA were only for the years 1960 and later. Potato prices are all from the *Journal of Commerce*. All prices for pork bellies, hogs, and cattle are from the *National Provisioner*. Frozen concentrated orange juice prices are taken from the *Journal of Commerce*.

[11] The series for onions and potatoes exclude the period of World War II price controls because reported prices were constant at ceiling levels and were not transaction prices. The other commodities' series start after World War II controls ended. Potatoes, pork, and cattle were subject to price controls for different periods during the Korean war, but prices for these periods are included in the samples for potatoes, pork bellies, hogs, and cattle because the periods of price control were relatively short and the data indicate that ceilings were not effective for most of those periods. After August 1971, various price-control programs at different times set ceilings on prices of all the commodities or their processed forms. Therefore, all of the price series end prior to, or at the start of, controls in 1971.

TABLE 1

COMMODITIES, MARKETS, AND SAMPLE PERIODS

Commodity	Market	Futures Trading Started	Sample Period with No Futures Trading	Sample Period with Futures Trading
Yellow onions	Chicago	Sept. 8, 1942;* terminated Nov. 6, 1959†	Sept. 1928–Apr. 1942 Nov. 1959–Apr. 1971	Sept. 1948–Oct. 1959
Maine potatoes	New York	Dec. 2, 1941‡	Oct. 1925–July 1941	Oct. 1947–July 1971
Pork bellies	Chicago	Sept. 19, 1961	Oct. 1949–Sept. 1961	Oct. 1961–Sept. 1971
Hogs	Chicago§	Feb. 28, 1966	Oct. 1949–Feb. 1966	Mar. 1966–May 1970
Cattle	Chicago‖	Nov. 30, 1964	May 1949–Nov. 1964	Dec. 1964–July 1971
Frozen concentrated orange juice (FCOJ)	New York	Oct. 26, 1966	Jan. 1957–Oct. 1966	Nov. 1966–Aug. 1971

* Onion and potato prices were subject to U.S. government price controls from November 7, 1942 to September 6, 1946.
† Public Law 85-839 prohibiting trading in onion futures became effective November 6, 1959.
‡ Futures trading in potatoes was suspended during World War II and reopened January 17, 1946.
§ Trading in live hogs at the Union Stockyards in Chicago stopped in May 1970.
‖ Trading in live cattle at the Union Stockyards in Chicago stopped in July 1971.

The Econometric Model

To investigate the impact of organized futures trading on traders' information an autoregression of the following form is estimated for periods with and without futures trading:

$$P_t = b_0 + \sum_{j=1}^{n} b_j P_{t-j} + u_t, \qquad (23)$$

where P_t is the spot price at time t, u_t is a random term, j is an interval of 1 week. The expected values of the coefficients in (23) are

$$|b_j| > |b_{j+1}|,$$
$$|b_j| < 1 \qquad (j = 2,\ldots, n)$$
$$b_j \begin{cases} >0 \text{ if } j \text{ is odd} \\ <0 \text{ if } j \text{ is even,} \end{cases}$$

for the fraction of fully informed traders $f < 1$. For $f = 1$, $0 < b_1 < 1$ and $b_j = 0$ ($j = 2,\ldots, n$). A priori, the value of b_0 is not determined. Equations (16) show that for a change in the state of traders' information

$$\frac{\partial |b_j|}{\partial f} < 0 \quad \text{and} \quad \frac{\partial \sigma_u^2}{\partial f} < 0.$$

An increase in the fraction of traders with a knowledge of the current market information decreases both the coefficients of past prices and the mean-square error of estimate. Therefore, effects of futures trading on market information can be analyzed by comparing estimates of (23) for periods with and without futures trading.

The theory in Section I shows price as an infinite-order autoregression (15), so the number of lagged prices in the econometric model (23) is determined on the empirical basis of minimum mean-square error of estimate. The best-fitting regressions for the sample periods with no futures trading are all obtained with five to 10 lagged prices. Autoregressions of the same order are then estimated for the periods with futures trading in order to compare parameters with and without futures trading.

The procedure used to estimate (23) is ordinary least squares, which yields consistent estimates of autoregressive parameters if the time series is stationary with independent and identically distributed disturbance terms. The price series investigated here are weakly stationary—they all exhibit seasonal patterns, but for periods spanning several years the prices vary about a fixed mean like a stationary series. Also, the sample correlograms damp out without peaks at the seasonal lags. Hence, the series are treated as stationary and no adjustments are made for seasonality. Analysis of residuals suggests that the disturbances are well behaved.

Only one of the regressions (FCOJ, 1957–66) has significant autocorrelation in the residuals.[12]

The price series used here are all nominal prices. This is dictated by the fact that there is no weekly price index for the entire sample period that can be used to transform the series into real prices. Deflating the prices with the monthly BLS Wholesale Price Index produces only minor changes in the regression results that are reported below. But this may result because the procedure does not change the relation between prices that are observed in the same month.

The Effect of Futures Trading on Market Information

The regressions in table 2 estimate (23) and compare spot-price behavior in the absence of futures trading to spot-price behavior during periods of futures trading. The evidence strongly supports the hypothesis that futures trading increases the quantity of traders' market information.

First, it is reasonable to interpret differences in the regression estimates as changes in information because the model is able to predict relations between prices. Estimated coefficients for each of the regressions conform to the expected values. For each of the 13 regressions, the absolute values of the coefficients b_2 through b_n are less than one and tend to conform to the prediction that $|b_j| > |b_{j+1}|$. Only one equation fits this pattern perfectly, but there are only three regressions for which half or more of the coefficients do not fit this pattern. As expected, the coefficients tend to alternate in sign, and there is a tolerable correspondence between predicted and actual signs. The regressions have, on average, 71 percent of the expected runs of signs. For one regression all of the signs are the same as predicted, and only three regressions have as many as four coefficients that differ from the predicted signs. The interval of 1 week between price observations is arbitrary, and this interval influences the actual patterns of coefficients. The agreement between the estimated and expected patterns of coefficients, therefore, suggests that the model is useful for analyzing week-to-week price behavior.

Second, for every commodity comparisons of the regression estimates with and without futures trading indicate more informed traders during periods of futures trading. As predicted for an increase in market information, the estimated coefficients during periods of futures trading are generally less in absolute value than the same coefficients in periods without futures trading. Thirty-five of the 48 coefficients decrease in absolute value, and only one of seven comparisons has an increase in as

---

[12] Residuals for each regression are tested for autocorrelation according to the procedure developed for autoregressions by Box and Pierce (1970). The Durbin-Watson statistic which is usually used to test for autocorrelated disturbances is biased toward accepting the null hypothesis of independent disturbances for any autoregression.

many as half of the coefficients.[13] However, the results are striking when significance of the coefficients is considered. In the absence of futures trading, all of the commodities have one or more of the coefficients b_2 through b_n that are significantly different from zero at the 5 percent level. For the regressions during periods of futures trading, only two of the 37 coefficients b_2 through b_n are different from zero at the 10 percent level! That is, the regression estimates not only show increased information during periods of futures trading for each commodity, for four of the commodities the estimates are consistent with all traders knowing the latest market information.

Put another way, increased market information reduces the relation between current and past prices. When all traders know the latest information, the current price "depends" only on the immediately preceding price. Therefore, the evidence reflected in comparisons of regression coefficients with and without futures trading can be conveniently summarized by testing the joint influence of P_{t-2} through P_{t-n} on P_t. The appropriate analysis-of-variance test is equivalent to testing the null hypothesis that $b_2 = b_3 = b_4 = \cdots = b_n = 0$. Table 3 reports this test for each regression. The results add evidence that futures trading increases market information. In the absence of futures trading, the set of lagged prices P_{t-2} through P_{t-n} is significant at high levels for every commodity. For periods of futures trading, all the sets of lagged prices are insignificant even at low critical levels when the regression coefficients have low t-ratios. So there is a consistent and significant decrease in the influence of past prices on the current price.

The results for onions are important because trading in onion futures is prohibited, and it is possible to analyze onion prices both prior to and after the time of futures trading. In both of the periods with no futures trading, 1928–42 and 1959–71, the current price depends significantly on lagged prices other than P_{t-1} as expected for a market with uninformed traders. But during the period of futures trading, 1948–59, lagged prices other than P_{t-1} are insignificant as predicted for a market with fully informed traders. Besides indicating increased information during the time of futures trading, this finding provides evidence that the information is due to futures trading rather than some other force that increases information over time. The same difference in significance of lagged prices is exhibited by pork bellies, hogs, and FCOJ when the periods prior to futures trading are compared to periods with futures trading. On the other hand, potatoes and cattle are noteworthy because the regression results indicate increased information with futures trading, but even then

[13] Although two-thirds of the coefficients decrease when there is futures trading, the set of coefficients $b_0, b_1, \ldots, b_n$ differs significantly (at the 5 percent level) from the set when there is no futures trading for only two of the seven tests. The significantly different regressions are for onions prior to futures trading and potatoes.

TABLE 2
Spot-Price Regressions

$$P_t = b_o + \sum_{j=1}^{n} b_j P_{t-j} + u_t$$

Commodity and Period	b_o	b_1	b_2	b_3	b_4	b_5	b_6	b_7	b_8	b_9	b_{10}	R^2	SE of Estimate	Sample Size
Onions:														
Sept. 1928– Apr. 1942	0.051 (2.281)	0.657 (13.746)	0.257 (4.355)	−0.139 (−2.335)	0.093 (1.568)	0.075 (1.524)	...	...	...	...	...	.794	0.249	473
Sept. 1948– Oct. 1959	0.131 (3.147)	0.963 (18.377)	−0.065 (−0.898)	0.021 (0.295)	−0.062 (−0.850)	0.063 (1.205)	...	...	...	...	...	.844	0.358	369
Nov. 1959– Apr. 1971	0.131 (3.366)	1.018 (19.706)	0.018 (0.250)	−0.194 (−2.728)	0.144 (2.018)	−0.052 (−1.019)	...	...	...	...	...	.889	0.259	382
Potatoes:														
Oct. 1925– July 1941	0.066 (2.850)	0.893 (22.101)	0.148 (2.744)	−0.077 (−1.441)	−0.155 (−2.894)	0.102 (1.906)	0.049 (1.235)	...	...	...	...	.918	0.256	618
Oct. 1947– July 1971	0.267 (5.093)	0.872 (24.685)	0.103 (2.196)	0.0004 (0.009)	−0.073 (−1.560)	0.023 (0.491)	−0.005 (−0.131)	...	...	...	...	.849	0.414	809

1230

TABLE 2 (Continued)

Pork bellies:									
Oct. 1949–Sept. 1961	0.804 (2.844)	1.013 (25.213)	0.003 (0.052)	−0.148 (−2.524)	0.190 (3.244)	−0.085 (−2.074)	...	...	.951 1.728 621
Oct. 1961–Sept. 1971	0.678 (2.179)	0.968 (21.865)	−0.038 (−0.622)	0.037 (0.596)	0.050 (0.810)	−0.038 (−0.852)	...	...	.956 1.708 517
Hogs:									
Oct. 1949–Feb. 1966	0.413 (3.171)	1.005 (29.267)	0.013 (0.264)	−0.001 (−0.021)	−0.046 (−0.944)	0.076 (1.574)	−0.057 (−1.178)	0.090 (1.842)	−0.102 (−2.936)	.965 0.667 848
Mar. 1966–May 1970	0.672 (1.705)	0.954 (13.617)	0.096 (0.996)	−0.020 (−0.204)	−0.084 (−0.877)	0.060 (0.624)	−0.081 (−0.841)	0.065 (0.674)	−0.020 (−0.282)	.945 0.753 212
Cattle:									
May 1949–Nov. 1964	0.358 (2.315)	0.791 (22.344)	0.116 (2.568)	0.176 (3.880)	−0.140 (−3.064)	0.132 (2.895)	−0.031 (−0.675)	0.034 (0.751)	−0.040 (−0.893)	−0.052 (−1.472)	.973 0.704 804
Dec. 1964–July 1971	0.623 (1.828)	0.787 (14.295)	0.235 (3.351)	0.057 (0.807)	−0.057 (−0.797)	0.014 (0.201)	0.004 (0.056)	−0.098 (−1.372)	−0.039 (−0.547)	0.074 (1.329)	.954 0.552 339
FCOJ:									
Jan. 1957–Oct. 1966	0.754 (2.563)	0.930 (20.793)	0.070 (1.143)	0.027 (0.443)	0.100 (1.639)	−0.204 (−3.333)	0.103 (1.691)	0.007 (0.113)	−0.049 (−0.803)	0.128 (2.101)	−0.131 (−2.957)	.976 1.772 502
Nov. 1966–Aug. 1971	0.706 (1.618)	1.013 (15.396)	−0.030 (−0.321)	0.076 (0.811)	−0.072 (−0.769)	0.001 (0.012)	−0.002 (−0.026)	0.006 (0.061)	0.044 (0.470)	−0.054 (−0.568)	−0.003 (−0.047)	.965 1.224 242

NOTE.—Figures in parentheses are t-ratios.

TABLE 3
ANALYSIS-OF-VARIANCE TEST FOR THE CONTRIBUTION OF $P_{t-2}, P_{t-3}, \ldots, P_{t-n}$ TO THE EXPLAINED SUM OF SQUARES

COMMODITY AND PERIOD	df Numerator	df Denominator	F-VALUE	SIGNIFICANCE LEVEL
Onions:				
Sept. 1928–Apr. 1942	4	467	10.674	.01
Sept. 1948–Oct. 1959	4	363	0.600	*
Nov. 1959–Apr. 1971	4	376	2.702	.05
Potatoes:				
Oct. 1925–July 1941	5	611	4.350	.01
Oct. 1947–July 1971	5	802	1.463	.25[a]
Pork bellies:				
Oct. 1949–Sept. 1961	4	615	3.050	.05
Oct. 1961–Sept. 1971	4	511	0.556	*
Hogs:				
Oct. 1949–Feb. 1966	7	839	2.321	.05
Mar. 1966–May 1970	7	203	0.456	*
Cattle:				
May 1949–Nov. 1964	8	794	7.887	.01
Dec. 1964–July 1971	8	329	2.508	.05[b]
FCOJ:				
Jan. 1957–Oct. 1966	9	491	2.918	.01
Nov. 1966–Aug. 1971	9	231	0.283	*

[a] The F-value for the contribution of $P_{t-3}, P_{t-4}, P_{t-5}, P_{t-6}$ is 1.182, which is not significant at the .25 level.
[b] The F-value for the contribution of $P_{t-3}, P_{t-4}, \ldots, P_{t-9}$ is 1.093, which is not significant at the .25 level.
* Not significant at .25 level.

all traders are not fully informed. For both commodities, P_{t-2} remains highly significant in the periods of futures trading.

Another implication of increased information is a decrease in the variance of the price-forecast error. The empirical counterpart of σ_u^2 in (16) is the standard error of estimate for the regressions in table 2. However, the levels of prices differ between the sample periods, tending to reduce the standard errors in periods of relatively low prices which correspond to periods without futures trading. To remove the price level effect, the standard errors of estimate are expressed as coefficients of variation in table 4. The results support the other evidence of increased information due to futures trading: six of the seven comparisons show a smaller coefficient of variation with futures trading. The conflicting result is for onions, where the coefficient of variation decreases when onion futures are prohibited.

In sum, the tests for each commodity strongly support the hypothesis that additional traders are informed of the latest market information due to futures trading. The evidence on the information effect of futures trading is remarkably consistent over different commodities and time

TABLE 4
Standard Errors of Estimate as Percentages of the Sample Means

Commodity and Period	SE of Estimate	Sample Mean	Coefficient of Variation
Onions:			
Sept. 1928–Apr. 1942	0.249	0.804	30.996
Sept. 1948–Oct. 1959	0.358	1.646	21.760
Nov. 1959–Apr. 1971	0.259	1.995	13.006
Potatoes:			
Oct. 1925–July 1941	0.256	1.707	15.014
Oct. 1947–July 1971	0.414	3.323	12.473
Pork bellies:			
Oct. 1949–Sept. 1961	1.728	29.947	5.771
Oct. 1961–Sept. 1971	1.708	31.881	5.357
Hogs:			
Oct. 1949–Feb. 1966	0.667	18.602	3.585
Mar. 1966–May 1970	0.753	22.445	3.355
Cattle:			
May 1949–Nov. 1964	0.704	25.730	2.737
Dec. 1964–July 1971	0.552	27.336	2.019
FCOJ:			
Jan. 1957–Oct. 1966	1.772	39.467	4.490
Nov. 1966–Aug. 1971	1.224	32.950	3.714

periods. This leads me to conclude that a significant price effect of futures trading reflects an increase in market information.

The Returns to a Trading Rule

A major empirical implication from the theory of efficient markets is that a trading rule based solely on the history of a commodity's price will not be profitable if the market's expected price fully reflects current market information. Evidence for the six commodities presented above indicates that those prices do not fully reflect available information in the absence of futures trading. In periods with futures trading, however, prices of four commodities behave as if market information is fully reflected in the price and the other two commodities show increased information. Hence, it is possible that a chartist could earn profits from a trading rule in the periods with no futures trading, but the spot markets become more efficient when there is futures trading and a chartist's profits should be eliminated or sharply reduced. There may not be actual commodity markets where price changes are random—Houthakker (1961) has shown that trading rules for wheat and corn futures are apparently profitable—but the important question for this study is whether there is a difference in profits that is consistent with the evidence on information.

The returns to one trading rule are examined here to see if the predicted change does occur. These returns are gross returns because the calculations do not include some costs such as the cost of transacting. Furthermore, this is a special test because an unlimited number of trading rules could be devised. The trading system considered is the following: Estimate an autoregression like those in table 2 for the first half of each sample period and use that equation to forecast the price 1 week hence for each observation in the last half of the sample. If the forecast is above the current price, buy one unit of the commodity and sell it at the market price 1 week hence. If the forecast is below the current price, sell one unit of the commodity and replace it at the market price 1 week hence. The return is measured as the difference between the selling and buying price.

Table 5 contains the statistics pertinent to this analysis. First, consider the average returns from the trading system. In the absence of futures trading, the average return is positive for all six commodities, but it is negative for three of the commodities when there is futures trading. The trading system is risky in every case—none of the mean returns is as much as 25 percent of the standard deviation—however, the variability of returns increases in periods of futures trading for five of the six commodities. In order to compare magnitudes, the averages are expressed as annual rates of return on the mean price for each trading period. This is approximately the rate of return on investment for a chartist using the trading system. With no futures trading, the rates of return range from 11 to 389 percent; with futures trading the range is from −13 to 25 percent. The results for onions and potatoes are remarkable. Prior to the time of futures trading, the rule yields an annual return of 389 and 108 percent for onions and potatoes, respectively. When there is futures trading in these commodities, the returns fall to −1 and 15 percent. Notice, too, that when onion futures are prohibited, the return increases substantially to 25 percent. Only one of the seven comparisons (FCOJ) shows a greater rate of return with than without futures trading. Overall, the difference in returns to the trading rule is consistent with the prediction that spot markets are more efficient because of futures trading. This result is additional support for the hypothesis that traders are more fully informed when there is organized futures trading in a commodity.

Could the markets be so imperfect that chartists would not learn of 300, 100, or even 25 percent rates of return, enter the markets, and thereby reduce the returns to more "normal" levels? The answer to this question requires a knowledge of more than the sequence of market prices. The cost of transacting in the spot markets was ignored in calculating the returns; yet costs of identifying potential traders, searching for the best price, and negotiating other terms of the exchange would lower the net returns in every case. Also, it is likely that the cost of transacting per unit of commodity traded declines enough that more than one unit would have

TABLE 5
Returns to a Trading Rule Based on the History of Prices

Commodity and Period	Average Return per Trade	SD of Returns	Annual Rate of Return	Number of Trades
Onions:				
Sept. 1935–Apr. 1942	.0607	0.261	389.886	240
Mar. 1954–Oct. 1959	−.0005	0.368	−1.782	184
Oct. 1965–Apr. 1971	.0113	0.303	25.610	191
Potatoes:				
Apr. 1933–July 1941	.0297	0.251	108.658	313
Mar. 1960–July 1971	.0106	0.421	15.652	407
Pork bellies:				
Oct. 1955–Sept. 1961	.0942	1.838	17.644	313
Oct. 1966–Sept. 1971	−.0843	1.863	−13.380	261
Hogs:				
Dec. 1957–Feb. 1966	.0385	0.607	11.216	430
Apr. 1968–May 1970	.0203	0.732	4.494	111
Cattle:				
Feb. 1957–Nov. 1964	.0864	0.581	18.188	408
Apr. 1968–July 1971	−.0187	0.634	−3.321	174
FCOJ:				
Dec. 1961–Oct. 1966	.1408	1.988	17.986	257
Apr. 1969–Aug. 1971	.1769	1.013	25.889	126

to be traded to make the system worthwhile. If so, it is important to know about the breadth of the market, that is, whether an optimum size purchase or sale would change the market price enough to eliminate any potential profits. For these reasons, the returns in table 5 do not seem unreasonably high.

III. Conclusion

The empirical evidence on price behavior clearly shows an information effect of futures trading. Both week-to-week price analysis and returns to a trading system based on the history of prices yield results consistent with increased information from futures trading. So market prices provide more accurate signals for resource allocation when there is futures trading in a commodity. Previous work on price effects of futures trading has not investigated the relation between futures trading and market information. Yet the strength and consistency of the evidence reported here suggest that price effects of futures trading result mainly from more fully informed traders.

The results in this study are directly relevant to public policy because they contradict the main argument made in behalf of legislation that prohibits trading in onion futures and regulates futures trading in other commodities. The data do not support the claim that price effects of futures trading impose costs on producers, consumers, and others who handle the physical commodity. On the contrary, spot markets seem to work more efficiently because of futures trading. The prohibition of futures trading reduces market efficiency. The other restrictions on futures trading may or may not benefit the public—we do not know the effects of this regulation—but the argument for those restrictions is incorrect.

References

Box, G. E. P., and Pierce, D. A. "Distribution of Residual Autocorrelations in Autoregressive-integrated Moving Average Time Series Models." *J. American Statis. Assoc.* 65 (December 1970): 1509–26.
Cox, C. C. "The Regulation of Futures Trading." Ph.D. dissertation, Univ. Chicago, 1975.
Emery, H. C. *Speculation on the Stock and Produce Exchanges of the United States.* New York: Columbia Univ. Press, 1896.
Fama, E. F. "Efficient Capital Markets: A Review of Theory and Empirical Work." *J. Finance* 25 (May 1970): 383–417.
Gray, R. W. "Onions Revisited." *J. Farm Econ.* 65 (May 1963): 273–76.
Hayek, F. A. "The Use of Knowledge in Society." *A.E.R.* 35 (September 1945): 519–30.
Hieronymus, T. A. "Effects of Futures Trading on Prices." In *Futures Trading Seminar.* Vol. 1. Madison, Wis.: Mimir, 1960.
Hooker, R. H. "The Suspension of the Berlin Produce Exchange and Its Effect upon Corn Prices." *J. Royal Statis. Soc.* 64 (December 1901): 574–604.
Houthakker, H. S. "Can Speculators Forecast Prices?" *Rev. Econ. and Statis.* 39 (May 1957): 143–51.
―――. "Systematic and Random Elements in Short-Term Price Movements." *A.E.R.* 51 (May 1961): 164–72.
―――. "Normal Backwardation." In *Value, Capital, and Growth: Papers in Honour of Sir John Hicks,* edited by James N. Wolfe. Chicago: Aldine, 1968.
Johnson, A. C. *Effects of Futures Trading on Price Performance in the Cash Onion Market, 1930–68.* U.S. Department of Agriculture Technical Bulletin no. 1470. Washington: Government Printing Office, 1973.
Muth, J. F. "Rational Expectations and the Theory of Price Movements." *Econometrica* 29 (July 1961): 315–35.
Naik, A. S. *Effects of Futures Trading on Prices.* Bombay: Somaiya, 1970.
Nelson, C. R. "Rational Expectations and the Predictive Efficiency of Economic Models." *J. Bus.* 48 (July 1975): 331–43.
Powers, M. J. "Does Futures Trading Reduce Price Fluctuations in the Cash Markets?" *A.E.R.* 60 (June 1970): 460–64.
Rockwell, C. S. "Normal Backwardation, Forecasting, and the Returns to Commodity Futures Traders." *Food Res. Inst. Studies* 7 (suppl.; 1967): 107–30.
Stewart, B. *An Analysis of Speculative Trading in Grain Futures.* U.S. Department of Agriculture Technical Bulletin no. 1001. Washington: Government Printing Office, 1949.
Taylor, G. S., and Leuthold, R. M. "The Influence of Futures Trading on Cash Cattle Price Variations." *Food Res. Inst. Studies* 13, no. 1 (1974): 29–35.
Telser, L. G. "Futures Trading and the Storage of Cotton and Wheat." *J.P.E.* 66, no. 3 (June 1958): 233–55.

———. "The Supply of Speculative Services in Wheat, Corn, and Soybeans." *Food Res. Inst. Studies* 7 (suppl.; 1967): 131–76.

Tomek, W. G. "A Note on Historical Wheat Prices and Futures Trading." *Food Res. Inst. Studies* 10 (1971): 109–13.

Working, H. "Financial Results of Speculative Holding of Wheat." *Wheat Studies Food Res. Inst.* 7 (July 1931): 405–35.

———. "Price Effects of Futures Trading." *Food Res. Inst. Studies* 1, no. 1 (1960): 3–31.

[8]
Can Chartists Outperform the Market? Market Efficiency Tests for "Technical Analysis"

Salih N. Neftci
Andrew J. Policano

Many traders in futures markets believe in the predictive power of technical analysis. Although many forms of technical analysis are not quantifiable, those forms which can be modeled are potentially useful in providing a framework for characterizing futures markets. This article quantifies two forms of technical analysis and assesses their ability to predict futures prices. In this sense, the article analyzes the efficiency of futures markets by focusing on the nonregression based prediction techniques that are commonly used by market participants.

It is well known that if markets are efficient, technical analysis should prove fruitless. Because an efficient market is composed of numerous well informed traders who make decisions continuously, market prices represent a reliable estimate of the intrinsic value of the commodity or asset in question. Price changes will reflect new information, and since new information arrives randomly, price changes should follow a Martingale Difference.[1] Thus, in an efficient market, any strategy which uses commonly available information cannot be profitable. However, the information set used in most forms of technical analysis, which generally consists of realized futures prices, is commonly available. Consequently, if futures markets are efficient, then the existence of traders who use technical analysis is certainly an anomaly.

---

[1] We say that ϵ_t is a Martingale Difference if

$$\epsilon_t = X_t - E\{X_t \mid I_{t-1}\}$$

where I_{t-1} is the information set available at the time $t-1$. In this sense, the error terms ϵ_t form a sequence of uncorrelated random variables.

Salih N. Neftci is Professor in the Department of Economics at the Graduate School at City University of New York.

Andrew J. Policano is a Professor in the Department of Economics at the University of Iowa.

The evidence from futures markets is mixed concerning the efficient market hypothesis.[2] Overall, however, a Martingale approximation does seem to be reasonable for most commodities and capital assets. In fact, there is general agreement in academic circles that the chartist's prediction techniques are based on unsystematic cycles that would naturally appear in any realization of a Martingale process. Thus, these cycles do exist and technical analysts do analyze them; however, the evidence suggests that the cycles are not sufficiently systematic to predict the future values of the process any better than the immediate past of the time series.

In spite of the existing evidence on efficiency, there are several reasons why a closer examination of technical analysis is warranted. First, in a recent survey of the studies of market efficiency, Kamara (1982) argues that the totality of efficiency studies concerns linear models and uses regression based procedures. In reality, traders tend to use buying and selling rules that are based on a subjective evaluation of past price performance. Thus, existing models do not correctly characterize the actual behavior of market traders. Second, the assumed linearity of the price series may be incorrect. Many time series have inherently nonlinear components, such as jump processes. Various charting techniques may be a crude way of taking these nonlinearities into account. Finally, market signals based on technical analysis can themselves have an effect of futures prices and thereby result in self-fulfilling predictions. Such effects, however, should not persist; still, they may be important in explaining temporary price fluctuations. Based on these arguments, this article attempts to extend the existing literature on (weak) efficiency by considering a market composed of traders who use technical analysis.[3]

The article models two specific forms of technical analysis; market signals are assumed to be based on either a slope or moving average method for predicting future prices. The resulting buy and sell rules are applied to the past price series in several futures markets to determine the periods in which the assumed strategy would have resulted in a buy or sell signal. The constructed series of market signals is then incorporated as a dummy variable in the usual regression analysis concerning efficiency. The results indicate that the technical analysis dummy is significant for Treasury bills, gold, and soybeans but does not seem to possess any explanatory power for copper. The moving average technique generally provides better predictive power in most cases; the slope method provides some explanatory power in only one third of the cases. Overall, the results do suggest that by characterizing the actual behavior of the market participants, improved price predictions can be obtained in several future markets.

The analysis proceeds as follows. In the next section, we model two commonly used forms of technical analysis. Section II includes a discussion of the statistical

---

[2]The hypothesis that futures price changes might be characterized as a random process was originally suggested by Working (1958). There is now a multitude of articles which examine the efficient market hypothesis; for a few examples, see Alexander (1961), Land and Raasche (1978), Rendleman and Carabine (1979), Granger and Labys (1970), Stevenson and Bear (1970), and Cargill and Rausser (1975). Kamara (1982) provides a recent survey of this literature.

[3]Several articles have examined the profitability of various trading rules as a basis for examining serial correlation in futures price series. See, for example, Stevenson and Bear (1970), Alexander (1961), Houthakker (1961), and Smidt (1965). Our study considers alternative trading algorithms and applies these algorithms to an expanded number of markets. We also employ a dummy variable technique which allows the possibility that jump processes affect the futures price series. Again, an important part of our argument is that technical analysis can be a crude way of taking these jump processes into account.

model. The empirical results are then examined in Section III. Finally, Section IV provides a summary and conclusions.

I. MODELS OF TECHNICAL ANALYSIS

A key strategy in futures markets is to trade with the trend. The trader initiates a position early in the trend and maintains that position as long as the trend continues. The trader may liquidate his position when a change in trend appears to be taking place. Thus, it is essential for each trader to adopt a strategy for determining the trend in the market.

The following analysis investigates the predictive value of two alternative strategies used by technicians; see Teweles, Harlow, and Stone (1974) for an extended discussion of technical analysis strategies. Since the technician's behavior appears to be highly subjective, it is frequently argued that it is difficult, if not impossible, to model the technician's behavior and to develop an objective test to evaluate past performance. In the following analysis, however, we develop a relatively simple mathematical formulation based on two technical analysis methods. The first is a *slope method* which assumes that traders calculate the slope of the price series (trendline) and base buy and sell decisions on the observed differences from the recent established slope of the time series. The second alternative assumes that individuals base decisions on various *moving averages* of the series.

A. The Slope Method

Traders utilizing the slope method are assumed to calculate the recent slope of the observed price series and then make market decisions when the actual price series crosses the value of the series as predicted from the established slope. The decision process entails the choice by the individual of two important parameters: one is the number of periods T over which the slope is calculated, and the other is the number of periods w to wait after the actual price series crosses the trendline before placing a buy or sell order. Basically, the idea is to determine the moment during which the observed series deviates from the established trend in some significant way.

The actual algorithm that is applied to the data to determine the signal times is outlined as follows:

(1) Choose the values for the parameters T and w.
(2) Begin at time T and calculate the current slope $\lambda(T + k)$ for each period using the first $(T + k)$ observations. Formally,

$$\lambda(T + k) = \frac{\Delta P}{\Delta t} = \frac{P(T + k) - P(0)}{T + k}, \quad 0 < k < T$$

where $P(t)$ is the actual futures price at time t and k is a time index.

(3) Based on the $\lambda(T + k)$, choose the established slope according to some previously set rule. For example, the established slope could be set according to the average of the $\lambda(t + k)$; alternatively, we assume that the established slope λ_i is chosen to equal the maximum of the $\lambda_{(t + k)}$ if the trend is positive or equal to the minimum of the $\lambda(t + k)$ if the trend is negative. This assumption results in the greatest probability that the actual price series will cross the predicted price series in any given period.

(4) Using the established slope λ_i, calculate the predicted prices $\hat{P}(T+h)$, as follows

$$\hat{P}(T+h) = P(T) + \lambda_i h, \qquad 0 < h < w$$

where h is a time index.

(5) In each period, compare the predicted value of the futures price with the actual value. If $P(T)$ crosses $\hat{P}(t)$, wait w periods before issuing a buy or sell order. Continue to compare $\hat{P}$ and P during the waiting interval to insure that the crossing was not a temporary aberration.

(6) Characterize the buy, sell, or no signal decision by constructing a dummy variable $D(t)$ as follows:

$$D(t+w) = \begin{cases} +1 \text{ if } \{\hat{P}(t+w) > P(t+w), \ldots, \hat{P}(t+w) & \text{(buy)} \\ \quad > P(t+1), \hat{P}(t) < P(t)\} & \\ -1 \text{ if } \{\hat{P}(t+w) < P(t+w), \ldots, \hat{P}(t+1) & \text{(sell)} \\ \quad < P(t+1), \hat{P}(t) > P(t)\} & \\ 0 \text{ for all other } t & \text{(no signal)} \end{cases}$$

(7) Repeat the above steps over the entire sample period to generate the dummies, $\{D(t)\}$ associated with signalling decisions based on the slope method.

The process $\{D(t)\}$ will have three values: $+1$, which represents buy orders; -1, which represents sell orders; and 0, which represents periods during which no signal was given. It is important to note that $D(t)$ is a highly nonlinear function of the observed price series $P(t)$. Specifically, $D(t)$ remains constant for a certain random period, then jumps to a new level as $P(t)$ behaves in a certain way.

Figure 1 shows an example of the type of behavior characterized by this method. The actual price series is shown by the heavy black line. The dashed line represents the calculated slope line and $\hat{P}$ represents the predicted value. In this case, the slope has been calculated over the period 0 to T. At time t, the actual price series crosses the established slope (trend) line. According to the figure the trader waits w period after $\hat{P}_t$ exceeds the actual price $P(t)$, and then enters a sell order. Consequently, $D(t)$ will be zero except for the period $t+w$, when it will be -1. Buy signals are generated in a similar way.[4]

B. The Moving Average Method

The second method of technical analysis utilizes *moving average* techniques, and is similar to the slope method but is intended to smooth out temporary aberrations in the general movement of the price series. According to this method a buy (sell) signal will be generated if the observed series $P(t)$ penetrates a moving average of the $P(t)$ from below (above). Thus, the moving average technique also indicates the trend in which a given futures price is moving. Again, because past prices are averaged, there is necessarily a lag in reflecting an actual price reversal. It can be the

---

[4] Note that the situation shown in Figure 1 is a well behaved case. In fact, it is possible for t to occur right after the time denoted by T. Also, note that the algorithm does allow for the established slope to change during the iteration. This is not shown either.

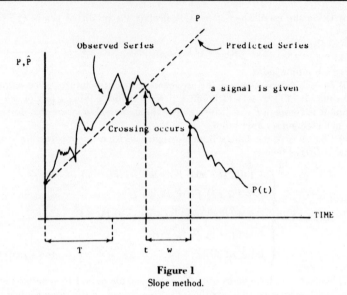

Figure 1
Slope method.

case that the lag is actually greater than would result if the slope method had been utilized. Still, the moving average technique is designed to limit losses when the trader is on the wrong side of the market. Moreover, the moving average method will automatically allow profits to run by staying with the market in sustained trands.

More precisely, the moving average method can be characterized as follows. Define

$$P^*(t) = \sum_{k=1}^{K} a_k P(t-k)$$

as a K-period, one sided moving average of the futures price $P(t)$ with the parameter K selected *a priori*. Next consider the following dummy variable process

$$D(t+w) = \begin{cases} -1 \text{ if } \{P^*(t+w) > P(t+w), \ldots, P^*(t-1) & \text{(buy)} \\ \quad > P(t-1), P^*(t) < P(t)\} \\ +1 \text{ if } \{P^*(t+w) < P(t+w), \ldots, P^*(t-1) & \text{(sell)} \\ \quad < P(t-1), P^*(t) > P(t)\} \\ 0 \text{ for all other } t & \text{(no signal)} \end{cases}$$

The process $D(t)$ will then signal w periods after the observed series penetrates the K-period moving average. It is important to note that $D(t)$ is again a highly nonlinear function of $P(t)$.

Figure 2 characterizes the individual's behavior based on the moving average technique. In this setting the individual chooses K, the averaging window, and w, the waiting period, and calculates a one-sided moving average of the price series $P(t)$. A buy order is issued w periods after the actual series crossed from below to

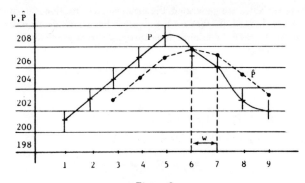

Figure 2
Moving average method.

above the moving average. Similarly, a sell order is issued w periods after the actual series crosses from above to below the moving average.

The mechanics of the two cases are similar except for the way they determine the established trend. In each case there are two parameters to be decided on: (a) the window, or the number of periods over which the established trend is calculated; and (b) the time lapse between penetration of the moving average by the actual series and the entering of a buy or sell order. The larger the window, the greater is the time lapse between an actual change in the trend and recognition of this change. Alternatively, a shorter window implies more whipsaw losses. A similar tradeoff applies to the individual's problem concerning the choice of the waiting period before entering the market. The shorter the interval, the greater is the probability of an error and the larger are total transactions costs.

It is also important to note that our buy and sell signals may not correspond to the actual buy and sell orders given by professional chartists. Technical analysts may make their buy and sell decisions subjectively without strictly following objective algorithms such as the ones listed above. Still, the strategy developed offers a reasonable first approximation to a chartist's behavior. If knowledge of this algorithm contains any predictive value, then the sequence of market signals contained in the $D(t)$ series should help predict futures prices.

II. A TEST FOR MARKET EFFICIENCY

In this section we develop a test for assessing the predictive usefulness of the two methods developed above for quantifying technical analysis. With respect to the slope method, we select several alternative values for both the interval T and the waiting period w. Next, the dummy variable series is constructed by first locating points where the actual price series crosses the calculated trend line and then by assigning the respective values of $(-1, 0, 1)$ for sell, no signal, and buy decisions. For every combination (T, w) a different $D(t)$ is generated in this way. Next, with respect to the moving average method, the analysis considers several values for the window K. Each K again generates a particular $D(t)$.

Once these variables are generated, the mean square criterion is used to test predictive accuracy. Indeed, if $\{P(t), t=1, \ldots, w\}$ is linear, nondeterministic, and covariance stationary, then the minimum mean square error prediction is obtained by solving the following:

$$\min_{\hat{P}(t) \in H_t} E\{P(t) - \hat{P}(t)\}^2, \tag{1}$$

where

$$H_t = \{P(t-1), P(t-2), \ldots, D(t-1), D(t-2), \ldots\}.$$

The solution to this prediction problem is given by

$$\hat{P}(t) = \sum_{s=1}^{m} \alpha_s P(t-s) \tag{2}$$

with:

$$P(t) - \hat{P}(t) = \epsilon(t),$$

where $\epsilon(t)$ is orthogonal to H_t and represents the smallest one step ahead prediction error. Here the equality should be interpreted as holding in the mean square sense as $m \to \infty$. This suggests that if the process $P(t)$ is linear, covariance stationary, and nondeterministic, then the autoregressive representation will yield the "best" prediction:

$$P(t) = \sum_{s=1}^{m} \alpha_s P(t-s) + \epsilon(t). \tag{3}$$

Consequently, market efficiency implies that the dummy variable $D(t)$ should not improve on the predictive ability of past prices. Specifically, the dummy variable can be incorporated in the nonlinear representation for $P(t)$ as follows:

$$P(t) = \sum_{s=1}^{m} \alpha_s P(t-s) + \sum_{u=1}^{m} \beta_u D(t-u) + \epsilon(t). \tag{4}$$

In order for Eq. (3) to be the "best" prediction we must have:

$$H_0 : \{\beta_u = 0; u = 1, \ldots, m\} \tag{5}$$

To summarize, the above analysis suggests a test for the predictive value of $\{D(t)\}$ which consists of estimating the following pair of equations:

$$P(t) = \sum_{s=1}^{m} \alpha_s P(t-s) + \sum_{u=1}^{m} \beta_u D(t-u) + \epsilon(t), \tag{6}$$

and

$$P(t) = \sum_{s=1}^{m} \alpha_s P(t-s) + \epsilon(t). \tag{7}$$

Using a standard F-test, we can then determine if $\{\beta_u\}$ are significantly different from zero.

One last point concerning the framework displayed in Eqs. (6) and (7) is the way the parameter m is going to be determined. To determine m, one could conceivably use some sort of search procedure or one could select it on an *a priori* basis. The first option is the proper way in problems dealing with forecasting. However, in testing, it may exaggerate the statistical significance of the results. For this reason we decided to select m on an a priori basis. To be on the conservative side we selected long lags.

A natural question that arises at this point concerns why the above autoregressive model is selected over the following more traditional hypothesis:

$$P_t = \beta P_{t-1} + e_t. \tag{8}$$

For example, would not the correlation in e_t imply some evidence in favor of technical analysis? We do not think so. The hypothesis that we are investigating is whether technical analysis has some predictive power over and above *optimal* predictions. It turns out that optimal prediction of stationary time series is known to be given by the autoregressive model in Eq. (6) and not by Eq. (8). That is the reason why we selected model (6).

A. Some Econometric Caveats

The estimation of equations like (6) and (7) is straightforward when the data are monthly, yearly, or quarterly series of the U.S. economy. Although problems exist, the main idea is to make sure that the series are properly transformed so that they become covariance stationary and nondeterministic. These problems have been treated in several texts; see, for example, Granger and Newbold (1977). In the present analysis, the models shown in Eqs. (6) and (7) are estimated with daily data from the futures markets.[5] The use of daily data presents additional estimation problems, which are discussed in detail by Neftci (1982) and are therefore only summarized here.

First, although the data are daily, futures markets are closed during some days of the week. Consequently, Eq. (6) holds over unequal intervals. It is not difficult to show that this can introduce a particular kind of heteroscedasticity where the variance is given by:

$$\text{Var}(\epsilon(t)) = \sigma^2 (t_2 - t_1),$$

where t_1 represents the period when the previous price was recorded and t_2 is the current period. Note that in the middle of the week $t_2 - t_1 = 1$, whereas for Mondays $t_2 - t_1 = 3$. If such heteroscedasticity is present and if no correction is made for it, then the test results may be biased.

Second, futures markets are characterized by special kinds of regulations. One of these relates to daily price limits. What is important for our purposes is that such limits are put in abeyance in some markets during the delivery period. This may be a source for another kind of heteroscedasticity.

In sum, the above issues imply that a careful analysis of residuals is necessary to detect the presence of both heteroscedasticity and deviations from normality. This analysis is discussed in conjunction with the empirical results below.

---

[5]It really does not make any sense to aggregate the data into monthly or even weekly averages, since this would destroy any predictive power technical analysis may have. In fact one should probably use intra-day data since proponents of technical analysis claim that it is used to detect abrupt changes in the observed series. Averaging would certainly destroy such changes.

III. EMPIRICAL RESULTS

The data sets used to estimate Eq. (6) consist of daily futures Price series generated in the following markets: January soybeans; February, April, June, and December gold; May and December copper; and March, June, September, and December T-bills. In organizing the data, time series on each contract are used separately and observations on the same contract for different years are stacked one after another. The data are detrended via a linear component; detrending is necessary to make the time series stationary and to allow the equation to be estimated to possess good statistical properties. The elimination of such a trend component does not affect the test of technical analysis since chartists deal mainly with short run trends and elimination of a secular component from a series will leave these trends almost intact. The results reported below pertain to the gold and Treasury bill markets; other results are mentioned briefly and are available from the authors on request.[6]

Tables I to III provide a summary of related results concerning F-tests. Two sets of results are reported; the first does not attempt any of the corrections for heteroscedasticity, but instead relates to the direct estimation of Eq. (6). The second set of results are from re-estimating the model with appropriate modifications made for eliminating heteroscedasticity.

Tables I and II display the results for gold. The lag lengths are 6 days for the technical analysis dummy and 12 days for the lagged dependent variable.

Table I indicates that with parameters $T = 12$ and $w = 4$, the dummy variables associated with the slope method fail to have any significant explanatory power. Although some individual lags do seem to be significant, Table I indicates that the

Table I
SUMMARY OF F-STATISTICS: GOLD FUTURES[a]

	Slope Method	
Variable	Slope Method Parameters $T=12$ and $w=4$	Significance Level
February Gold	0.49	80%
April Gold	0.62	75%
October Gold	1.02	60%
	Slope Method (with a Heteroscedasticity Correction)	
Variable	F-Statistic	Significance Level
February Gold	0.99	60%
April Gold	0.76	80%
October Gold	1.10	60%

[a]The Dummy Variables $D(t)$ tested in these tables are generated by the Slope method Algorithm described in the text. The Estimated Regressions are again like Eq. (6).

---

[6]The results shown here are for the price *levels*. One of the reasons we did not use logarithms or other nonlinear transformations is discussed in a manuscript by Gilbert (1982).

Table II
SUMMARY OF F-STATISTICS: GOLD FUTURES

	Moving Average Method[a]		
Variable	MA Parameter $K=25$	$K=50$	$K=100$
December Gold	1.75	—	—
February Gold	1.88	—	—
April Gold	1.93	—	—
October Gold	1.70	1.27	1.30

	Moving Average Method (with a Heteroscedasticity Correction)		
Variable	$K=25$	$K=50$	$K=100$
December Gold	1.61	—	—
February Gold	2.04	—	—
April Gold	1.98	—	—
October Gold	1.88	1.04	1.06

[a] The F Statistics in this table show the significance of dummy variables generated by the Moving Average Method. The estimated regressions correspond to Eq. (6) in the text.

Table III
SUMMARY OF F-STATISTICS: T-BILLS FUTURES

	MA Method				Slope Method	
Variable	$K=100$	Sig. Level	$K=50$	Sig. Level	F-Statistic	Sig. Level
June T-Bills	1.94	10%	—	—	0.4	85%
September T-Bills	0.67	0.75%	—	—	2.19	0.5%
December T-Bills	0.59	80%	0.10	90%	1.02	40%

	MA Method				Slope Method	
	(with a Heteroscedasticity Correction)					
Variable	$K=100$	Sig. Level	$K=50$	Sig. Level	F-Statistic	Sig. Level
June T-Bills	2.35	1%	—	—	0.6	75%
September T-Bills	0.87	45%	—	—	2.13	5%
December T-Bills	0.69	75%	0.20	90%	1.05	40%

overall F-statistics are very low. Clearly, the slope method, or at least the version used in this article, does not seem to have any predictive power over and above the own past of the gold futures prices. This result was fairly consistent for reasonable variations in the parameters T and w. The correction for the kind of heteroscedasticity mentioned above makes only a slight difference in the test statistics, since in case of gold futures such movements in residual variance seems to be minor (see Table IV).

The results concerning the moving average method are somewhat different. Table II summarizes the F-statistics for gold Futures. The dummy variables are significant for the February, April, October, and December contracts. All the F-statistics are significant at the 1% level.

Table III indicates a similar pattern with respect to futures contracts for T-bills. One difference is that, now, dummies associated with the slope method *do* seem to have a significant explanatory power in case of September contract. The moving average method, on the other hand, is significant in case of June contract. Another different result has to do with the kind of heteroscedasticity mentioned above. Table IV indicates that there is more evidence of such heteroscedastic behavior in variances for T-bills futures. As a result, F-statistics change somewhat more.

With T-bills futures we see another interesting pattern. The significance of the technical analysis dummies changes a great deal from one contract to another—while for gold the results were similar across different contracts. This suggests that if the significance that we observe is not due to sample error, then technical analysis can also be useful in predicting the "spreads."

The results for soybeans, not shown in the tables, were very similar to that of T-bills. The dummies for both the slope and moving average methods were significant in several cases. For copper, however, none of the dummies were significant.

A further implication of the results can be obtained by examining the sum of the coefficients of the lagged variables in each regression. Specifically, if a significant

Table IV
TESTS FOR HETEROSCEDASTICITY [a]

Variable	Coefficient of $d\tau_i$	Marginal Significance
March T-Bills	9.96	0.334
June T-Bills	16.67	0.018
September T-Bills	16.37	0.015
December T-Bills	−39.82	0.899
February Gold	31.58	0.51
April Gold	30.72	0.52
June Gold	37.98	0.35
October Gold	33.56	0.45
December Gold	6.24	0.94

[a] The results here display the coefficient (and the significance) of the independent variable representing the first difference of trading days, in a regression where the dependent variable was the square of residuals. The residuals themselves were obtained from a 12th-order autoregression. The variable $d\tau_i$ represents the number of days between two observations. For most of the week-days this variable has a value of one. For weekends it assumes a value of two.

number of traders use a similar form of technical analysis, then the fact that these methods signal a buy or sell may have an impact on actual prices. After a signal is given, the traders follow the technical strategy and, in so doing, may cause a change in prices even when the procedure has no predictive value in and of itself. Such effects, however, should be temporary. To test the existence of spurious trading we can test the hypothesis that the sum of the lagged coefficients is equal to zero in each equation. In general, including the cases not reported, we found that the coefficients sum to zero in very few cases. As a consequence, it appears that very little spurious trading was initiated by the signal themselves.

Finally, to see if the residuals from the estimated equations satisfy Gauss-Markov type assumptions we checked for heteroscedasticity. Table V displays the results of regressing squared residuals against the variable denoted by $(t_i - t_{i-1})$. These figures indicate that in general the variance of the residuals becomes larger as the period of observation increases. In other words, there indeed may be some heteroscedasticity in the data since the variability—measured both as the absolute value and as the square of the residuals—increases during weekends and other similar vacations as noted above. This result is obvious in the case of T-bills but such heteroscedasticity does not seem to be present for gold. However, for gold there were two large residuals which, in a sense, signalled the presence of a jump from one regime to another.

IV. CONCLUSIONS

This article quantifies two major forms of technical analysis, which we denote as moving average and trend following methods, and then examine the predictive power of each. We argue that although these procedures depend on some parameters selected on an ad hoc basis, they are still reasonable approximations to trading strategies routinely used by market participants. In the case of the moving average method the results are quite clear: there appears to be a significant relationship between the dummy variables representing the moving average signals and the futures

Table V
TESTS FOR FIRST-ORDER MARKOVNESS*

Variable	F-Test	Marginal Significance
February Gold	8.34	0.00
April Gold	8.05	0.00
June Gold	9.25	0.00
October Gold	8.79	0.00
December Gold	21.34	0.00
March T-Bills	18.21	0.00
June T-Bills	17.75	0.00
September T-Bills	21.50	0.00
December T-Bills	19.00	0.00

*The F-tests relate to the hypothesis that a 12th-order autoregression can be reduced to a first-order system without much loss of significance.

prices. This suggests some predictive power in MSE sense. In case of the slope method, the results are mixed. For some sensible values of the ad hoc parameters the dummy variables are significant in only in a third of the cases.

A disturbing point was the way results varied across commodities and across contracts for the same commodity. One set of parameters which yielded a significant dummy in one case, was found to be insignificant in other cases. This result may be explained by the importance of hedging versus speculation in different markets or even by the relative thinness of that particular market, but additional analysis is needed here.

We also discovered that the sign and sum of the coefficients were of the "right" order. Interestingly, in very few cases the coefficients of technical analysis dummies added up to zero. This indicated that there was very little spurious trading initiated by the signals given by these methods.

Finally, the empirical results displayed in this article suggest that a fair amount of heteroscedasticity may exist in models dealing with futures prices. Deviations from normality are also significant.

V. DATA

The data used in the regressions reported in this article consist of *closing* prices for various gold and T-bill futures contracts. The data were daily observations for the periods January 22, 1975 to March 6, 1980 for gold and January 12, 1976 to July 3, 1980 for most T-bills futures. The only exception to this latter was the March contract. For this series the period from August 26, 1977 to July 3, 1980 was used.

These series were seasonally unadjusted and needed to be compressed before usage since they contained gaps of zeros. In all reported regressions the contracts were used individually as a single time series and in no case were combined as a cross-section time series model.

The authors are grateful to the Columbia University Center for the Study of Futures Markets for supporting this research. In addition, the authors received numerous helpful suggestions from an anonymous referee.

Bibliography

Alexander, S. (1961): "Price Movements in Speculative Markets; Trends or Random Walks," *Industrial Management Review*.

Cargill, T., and Rausser, G. (1975): "Temporal Price Behavior in Commodity Markets," *Journal of Finance*.

Edwards, R., and Magee, J. (1948): *Technical Analysis of Stock Trends*, John Magee Inc., Springfield, MA.

Gilbert, G. C. (1982): "Some Problems in Testing the Efficient Markets Hypothesis on Foreign Exchange and Commodity Market Data," unpublished.

Granger, C. E. J., and Newbold, P. (1977): *Forecasting Economic Times Series*, Academic, New York.

Granger, C. E. J., Newbold, P., and Labys, W. C. (1970): *Speculation Hedging and Commodity Price Forecasts*.

Houthakker, H. (1961): "Systematic and Random Elements in Short Term Price Movements," *American Economic Review*.

Kamara, A. (1982): "Issues in Futures Markets: A Survey," *Journal of Futures Markets*, 2 (3): 261.

Land, R. W., and Rasche, R. H. (1978, December): "A Comparison of Yields on Futures Contracts in the International Money Market," *Federal Reserve Bank of St. Louis Review*.

Neftci, S. N. (1984): "Some Econometric Problems in Using Daily Data from Futures Markets," Manuscript in preparation.

Rendleman, R. J., and Carabine, M. (1979): "The Efficiency of the Treasury Bills Futures Market," *Journal of Finance*.

Smidt, S. (1965): "A Test of the Serial Independence of Price Changes in Soybean Futures," *Food Research Institute Studies*.

Stevenson, R., and Bear, R. (1970): "Commodity Futures: Trends or Random Walk," *Journal of Finance*.

Shiryayev, N. (1977): *"Optimal Stopping Rules,"* Springer-Verlag, New York.

Shiryayev, N., and Liptser (1979): *"Statistics of Random Processes, I and II,"* Springer-Verlag, New York.

Teweles, R. J., Harlow, C. V., and Stone, H. L. (1974): *The Commodity Futures Game*, McGraw-Hill, New York.

Working, H. (1958, May): "A Theory of Anticipatory Prices," *American Economic Review*.

[9]
Memory and Equilibrium Futures Prices

David H. Goldenberg

INTRODUCTION

Efficient market theory implies that equilibrium futures prices have no memory. This memoryless feature of futures prices in an efficient market can be incorporated into price models in a variety of ways. Perhaps the most common way is to make the Markov assumption. Indeed, Merton (1982) points out that 'the Markov assumption is almost universal among substantive models of stock price returns.' As a specific example, all diffusion-based models underlying option pricing formulas make the Markov assumption. The theory of efficient markets, therefore, leads to the empirically testable hypothesis that time series of futures prices are memoryless. The purpose of this paper is to investigate this hypothesis for the time series of transactions prices of the S&P 500 futures contracts during the years 1983 and 1984.

Specifically, this paper has three objectives. The first objective is to investigate the stationarity of intraday transaction prices of the S&P 500 futures contracts. The issue is how many differencing operations, d, are needed to render the series stationary in the usual time series sense. The hypothesized values of d are 0, 1, or 2. A value of d of zero indicates that the series is already stationary, one indicates first differencing, and two indicates second order differencing. The usual finding in time series analysis of price data is that d is one. This is also the finding of this study, but recently derived tests, called unit root tests, are used to investigate this issue [see Dickey, Bell, and Miller (1986), Doukas and Rahman (1987), Fuller (1976), and Hasza and Fuller (1979)]. Unit root tests have been applied to daily settlement prices on foreign currency futures data but not to the transactions data of other types of futures contracts.

The second objective is model selection. Here, the question is how many autoregressive and/or moving average components there are in the time series. Canonical correlation analysis and a well-founded information-theoretic criterion, called Akiake's information criterion (AIC) are used to address the question.

Finally, time series models are not, in general, Markov models; and, therefore, they appear to be inconsistent with the usual Markov models of equilibrium prices. The issue is whether this inconsistency can be removed. The statespace representation of a stationary time series removes this inconsistency. This finding removes a major theoretical inconsistency between equilibrium models and empirical models of actual price series. By doing so, it thereby removes one barrier to the empirical testing of equilibrium price models.

The results of this study may have practical application. The finding of memory in transactions futures price changes serves as a basis for the formulation of trading strategies based upon the correlation structure of transaction price data. For, under efficient

---

David H. Goldenberg is an Associate Professor of Finance in the School of Management at Rensselaer Polytechnic Institute.

market theory, there are no trading strategies guaranteed to produce profits net of transactions costs. On the other hand, if transactions price data are sufficiently correlated relative to the magnitude of transactions costs incurred in given trading strategies, then it may be possible to profit from the systematic correlation structure in the data. This is an issue which is of obvious concern to market participants [e.g., Helms, Kaen, and Rosenman (1984), and Rausser and Carter (1983)].

The organization of the paper is as follows. In the first section, the advantages and disadvantages of using linear, stationary time series as models of price data are discussed. Emphasis is placed upon unit root tests as tests of stationarity. The statespace representation at a stationary time series is presented and its equivalence to the ARMA representation is proven. Akiake's information criterion is also presented in this section as a tool for model selection. Section II describes the data in the context of time series analysis. Section III presents the empirical results and their interpretation; and Section IV summarizes the conclusions.

I. STATIONARY TIME SERIES AS MODELS OF PRICE DATA

A. Introduction

Time series models are a common method of modeling economic price series. The purpose of this mode of representation is to model the behavior of prices as a dynamic process which is both linear and stationary through time. However, time series analysis has both advantages and disadvantages when applied to economic price series. A discussion of these advantages and disadvantages helps to put the empirical work on time series analysis of prices in perspective.

Time series analysis assumes that time is discrete and that the 'state space' is continuous, where the state space of a model is defined as the range of all possibilities for prices. But price data is, in fact, discrete because in securities and in futures markets, there are minimum possible price movements. Further, the state space of time series models is $-\infty$ to $+\infty$ since the error term is assumed to be Gaussian. But prices are obviously positive. This latter problem is usually handled by taking logs of the original raw price series. However, it is not usually recognized that the use of the log function to transform the series is valid only under rather restrictive assumptions.[1] Thus time series models do not impose any boundary behavior on the price variable. In this sense, they are unconstrained stationary models.

Another defect of the usual presentation of time series models is their lack of consistency with equilibrium models from the Markov viewpoint. They are, in general, neither martingale models nor Markov models. The statespace approach is used to remove this inconsistency by redefining the state of the process so as to make the process Markov. Somewhat tautologically, if a state of the process is defined as consisting of *all* of the current information needed to predict its conditional expected future states; then the process becomes Markov, by definition, under this wider interpretation. This method is known as expansion of states.

As an example of the method of expansion of states, consider an $AR(2)$ model in which the current value of the process is determined by its lagged values to 2 lags plus a noise term. If one redefines the process as a vector-valued time series, where the state vector consists of the current state as one component and the lagged state as the second component, then the vector-process involves only lag1 dependence and is consequently

[1]Granger and Newbold (1977) point out that 'In economics it is often observed that series have similar trends in mean and standard deviation, but for the logarithmic transformation to be appropriate, these quantities have to be proportional and there is no reason to suppose that actual series have such a property.'

Markov. One can then apply the powerful analytic methods of Markov processes to the newly defined vector Markov process. The method obviously generalizes to a process for which any finite number of states is needed to define the expanded state.

The key theoretical advantage of time series analysis is that the processes modeled are not necessarily assumed to be Gaussian, although linearity and stationarity are usually assumed. However, even this theoretical advantage requires qualification, since 'most of the tests of significance used in time series analysis assume that the series is Gaussian' [see Granger and Newbold (1977)]. Further, only in the Gaussian case will the optimal, single series, least-squares forecast be a linear forecast. If the series were non-Gaussian then it is possible for a nonlinear forecast to be superior in a least-squares sense, to a linear one.

The approach to time series analysis taken in this study is different from but related to the usual ones. In order to understand this approach, a review of the methodology used in fitting time-series models is needed. The procedure outlined in most texts on time-series analysis is to first 'identify' the series through an examination of its correlation structure. This is done by examining the sample autocorrelation and the sample partial autocorrelation function estimated from the time series data. A list is provided of the respective behaviors of the *theoretical* autocorrelation functions and partial autocorrelation functions of various categories of time series models, e.g., purely autoregressive, moving-average, and mixed ARMA models. One is then expected to be able to identify the time series in hand by a matching process. This procedure is sometimes recognized to be an 'art' since one has only estimated correlation functions and not the theoretical ones. Apart from sampling error, however, there is a theoretical assumption underlying this approach that is rarely emphasized or tested. This is the problem of model multiplicity.

In order for it to be theoretically possible to identify a unique time series model representation from the correlation structure of a given set of time series data, it must be proven that each particular form of time series model is uniquely associated with a particular form of covariance generating function. This is not, in general, true. But, it can be shown that if a model is stationary, invertible, contains no common factors, and expresses a current value in terms of past history only, then it is uniquely determined by its covariance structure [see Box and Jenkins (1976), pp. 195–198]. Thus, employment of the identification technique described involves checking the data for satisfaction of the stated conditions. Under these conditions, the time series representation is nothing more, nor less, than a representation of the correlation structure of the data.[2]

The usual approach taken to these problems is to assume them away and then to continue with the estimation phase of the analysis. In this study, the focus is upon the sta-

---

[2] In another study, Goldenberg (1988), the author took a Markov chain approach to the S&P 500 time series data. In comparing the results of this study with the results of the previous study, several differences are relevant. Since futures prices have a minimum possible movement (called the tick size), the state space is in fact discrete (as it is in Markov chain models) and not continuous (as it is in ARIMA type models). A white noise error structure is not assumed in the Markov chain statistical tests but the tests are essentially nonparametric. Thus, the Markov chain models are, in fact, both more realistic than the Arima type models and they also make fewer statistical assumptions.

The approach to explaining the observed correlation structure of price changes is also different in the ARIMA vs. the Markov chain approach. In the Markov chain approach, it is possible to explain the observed negative correlation structure without dropping the Markov assumption simply by adding bounds (i.e., a finite state space) and boundary behavior at those bounds. In the Arima approach, we drop the Markov assumption by adding higher order AR and/or MA type terms. These extra terms are necessary under the ARIMA type approach to explain the negative correlation structure and their addition is forced upon the model. Because, in the specification of these types of models no boundary behavior is allowed (or specifiable): one has no choice but to add higher order AR and/or MA terms to get a model that explains the data. This may be viewed as an essential negative feature of the ARIMA type models: i.e., their specification is too restrictive.

tionarity conditions for autoregressive processes. Formal unit root tests are used to test the models for stationarity. These tests indicate how many differencing operations are needed to render the process stationary. A brief description of the stationarity conditions for different categories of models is needed in order to understand the unit root tests.

For purely autoregressive models, the stationarity conditions are that the roots of the characteristic polynomial lie outside of the unit circle. No restrictions are required on the parameters of a purely autoregressive process to ensure invertibility. For purely moving average processes, the invertibility conditions are that the roots of the characteristic polynomial lie outside the unit circle and the stationarity conditions are automatically satisfied.

In order for a mixed, autoregressive, moving average process to be stationary, all that is required is that the characteristic polynomial of the autoregressive component of the process have roots outside the unit circle. This implies that, if the stationarity conditions are satisfied for a purely autoregressive process, then they will also be satisfied if moving average terms are added to the model. On the other hand, satisfaction of the invertibility conditions for the mixed model are the same as for the purely moving average component of that model. That is, if a purely moving average model is invertible, then addition of autoregressive terms to it will not affect its invertibility. Thus, unit root tests applied to the autoregressive component of the mixed model will determine its stationarity.

In this study, the stationarity conditions for the autoregressive models, and, therefore, for the mixed ARMA models, are tested using formal unit root tests. Numerical checks of the invertibility conditions of the MA model, and, therefore, for the mixed ARMA models, are provided. It will be assumed that any common factors have been canceled. Finally, by definition, the form of the models tested involves dependence only upon past values.

B. Unit Root Tests

Begin with the second-order autoregressive model (1.1).

$$Y_t = \eta_1 Y_{t-1} + \eta_2 Y_{t-2} + \epsilon_t \tag{1.1}$$

Reparameterize the model by writing it in the form (1.2).

$$Y_t = \alpha_1 Y_{t-1} + \beta_1 (Y_{t-1} - Y_{t-2}) + \epsilon_t \tag{1.2}$$

Note that, according to this parameterization (1.3) holds.

$$\begin{aligned}\alpha_1 + \beta_1 &= \eta_1 \\ -\beta_1 &= \eta_2\end{aligned} \tag{1.3}$$

The null hypothesis of two unit roots (second-order differencing) is then (1.4).

$$H_1: \alpha_1 = \beta_1 = 1 \tag{1.4}$$

Under the null hypothesis H_1, the model reduces to (1.5).

$$Y_t = Y_{t-1} + (Y_{t-1} - Y_{t-2}) + \epsilon_t \tag{1.5}$$

and the process becomes stationary only after second order differencing since, under H_1, (1.6) holds.

$$Y_t - 2Y_{t-1} + Y_{t-2} = (1 - B)^2 Y_t = \epsilon_t \tag{1.6}$$

where B is the usual lag operator $B(Y_t) = Y_{t-1}$.

The procedure for testing the null hypothesis H_1 of double unit roots is to run an ordinary regression of the second-order difference variable $(1 - B)^2 Y_t$ on the first-order difference $Y_{t-1} - Y_{t-2}$ and on Y_{t-1} without an intercept, and then to compute the ordinary 'F' statistic from this regression. However, under the null hypothesis H_1 this statistic is not distributed as the usual F but rather is tabulated as $\phi_1(2)$ in (see Hasza and Fuller (1979), p. 1116).

If the model is modified to include an intercept term, as in (1.7),

$$Y_t = \mu_2 + \alpha_2 Y_{t-1} + \beta_2(Y_{t-1} - Y_{t-2}) + \epsilon_t \tag{1.7}$$

then the test is the same except that an intercept term must be included in the regression described and the null hypothesis becomes (1.8).

$$H_2: (\mu_2, \alpha_2, \beta_2) = (0, 1, 1) \tag{1.8}$$

and the test statistic is labeled $\phi_2(3)$. The percentiles of this statistic are given in Hasza and Fuller (1979).

If both of these tests reject the null hypothesis of double unit roots, then one can proceed to the single unit root test. Here, the model (1.7) with an intercept will be tested for the presence of a single unit root. The hypothesis is (1.9).

$$H_3: \alpha_2 = 1 \tag{1.9}$$

given that the other root is less than one in absolute value. The test procedure is similar to the t-test on a single coefficient except that, under the null hypothesis, the distribution is not that of Student's t but rather τ_μ (see Fuller (1976), p. 373).

The test procedure is to run the multiple regression of Y_t on Y_{t-1}, $Y_{t-1} - Y_{t-2}$ including an intercept and to read off the usual 't' statistic for the estimated coefficient α_2. Then, one compares it to the percentiles given in Fuller (1976). For our model the 99% point is -3.43. One expects from these tests that the null hypothesis of double unit roots for the model with and without an intercept will be rejected. On the other hand, the expectation is that the hypothesis of a single unit root will not be rejected. Further, one can not a priori reject the existence of an intercept in the model. By comparing both models, though, it is expected that the intercept will be statistically insignificantly different from zero.

Proceed now to the higher order autoregressive model tests, restricting tests to the AR(3) model. Double and single unit root tests on the AR(3) model, (1.10), follow.

$$Y_t = \eta_1 Y_{t-1} + \eta_2 Y_{t-2} + \eta_3 Y_{t-3} + \epsilon_t \tag{1.10}$$

Introduce the difference operator (1.11).

$$\Delta Y_t = Y_t - Y_{t-1} \tag{1.11}$$

Then, reparameterize the AR(3) model as (1.12).

$$Y_t = \alpha_1 Y_{t-1} + \beta_1 \Delta Y_{t-1} + \delta_1 \Delta^2 Y_{t-1} + \epsilon_t \tag{1.12}$$

Then the characteristic polynomial of the AR(3) model is (1.13).

$$m^3 - \sum_{j=1}^{2} \eta_j m^{3-j} = 0 \tag{1.13}$$

and it has two unit roots if and only if $\alpha_1 = \beta_1 = 1$.

The objective is to test the following two hypotheses (1.14) and (1.15),

$$H_1: \alpha_1 = \beta_1 = 1 \tag{1.14}$$

given that the other root of the characteristic polynomial is less than 1 in absolute value.

$$H_2: \alpha_1 = 1 \tag{1.15}$$

given that the absolute value of β_1 and that of the other root of the characteristic polynomial is less than 1. The first test is performed by constructing, through regression procedures similar to the ones described for the AR(2) model, the statistic $\phi_1(2)$. The second test for a single unit root is performed by computing τ, the 't'-statistic for the unit coefficient (see Fuller (1976)). The expectation is that the double unit root test will reject and that the single unit root test will not. If this is correct then the model reduces to an ARIMA(2, 1, 0) model since $\alpha_1 = 1$.

C. Statespace Representation of ARMA Models

Let (X_t) be a process for which a statespace or an ARMA time series representation is sought. Define v_t as (1.16), where E represents the conditional expectation.

$$v_t = \begin{pmatrix} X_t \\ E(X_{t+1}|X_t) \end{pmatrix} \tag{1.16}$$

Then (v_t) will be the state vector in the statespace representation of the process (X_t). Further, (1.17) holds by replacing t by $t + 1$ in (1.16).

$$v_{t+1} = \begin{pmatrix} X_{t+1} \\ E(X_{t+2}|X_{t+1}) \end{pmatrix} \tag{1.17}$$

The statespace representation of the process (X_t) relates the value of v_{t+1} to the value of v_t by matrices A, B, and C which define a vector AR(1) process, as in (1.18).

$$v_{t+1} = Av_t + Bu_{t+1}$$
$$X_t = Cv_t$$
$$A = \begin{pmatrix} 0 & 1 \\ \theta_2 & \theta_1 \end{pmatrix} \tag{1.18}$$
$$B = \begin{pmatrix} 1 \\ \psi_1 \end{pmatrix}$$
$$C = (1 \quad 0)$$

Then (u_t) is called a white-noise innovations process, A is called the transition matrix, B is called the innovations matrix, and C trivially defines the transformation between the original process and the newly-defined state vector (v_t).

The statespace representation given above is a Markovian representation. It can be solved for its equivalent ARMA form. The procedure follows. First, consider the characteristic polynomial (1.19).

$$\det(\lambda I - A) = \lambda^2 - \lambda\theta_1 - \theta_2 \tag{1.19}$$

The matrix A is a matrix root of the characteristic polynomial (1.19), as can be verified. Define C_1 by (1.20).

$$C_1 = C(A - \theta_1 I)B \tag{1.20}$$

Then the ARMA representation equivalent to the statespace representation given above is (1.21).[3]

$$X_t = \theta_1 X_{t-1} + \theta_2 X_{t-2} + (\psi_1 - \theta_1)u_{t-1} \tag{1.21}$$

Note that θ_1, θ_2 are the autoregressive coefficients and that the MA(1) coefficient is equal to the innovations coefficient minus the AR(1) coefficient. Thus, the statespace form (1.18) is equivalent to the ARMA form (1.21).

What is gained by considering the statespace form? The statespace form has the Markov property while the ARMA form does not. The statespace form exhibits the Markov structure of processes which are seemingly non-Markovian. This is important for both theoretical and practical reasons.

As noted, models of equilibrium prices as opposed to actual market prices, universally make the Markov assumption. The Markov assumption, however, is inconsistent with general ARMA models. By expanding the state vector, the statespace representation shows how to recover the Markov property. This representation, therefore, removes one barrier to the empirical testability of theories concerning equilibrium prices through the use of observed market prices. Further, the statespace representation can be estimated using the methods available for Markov processes. Finally, the statespace form is more easily interpretable than the ARMA form.

Before describing the statespace estimation technique, Akaike's AIC criterion is first briefly described. The AIC is the basic tool in comparing models for model selection. When a model with q independently adjusted parameters is fitted to data, the AIC is defined by (1.22).

$$\text{AIC}(q) = (-2) \log_e[\text{maximized likelihood}] + 2q \qquad (1.22)$$

This quantity can be shown to reduce to $n \log(\sigma^2) + 2q$ where n is the number of data points and σ^2 is the residual sum of squares from the fitted time series model (see Priestley (1981)). The terms defining the AIC can be interpreted as follows. The first term is a penalty for badness of fit. The second term is a penalty for introducing additional terms into the model. The idea behind the measure is that introduction of an explanatory variable into the model is justified only if its introduction is accompanied by a corresponding reduction in the residual sum of squares. An interpretation of the AIC is: $2n$ times the average information for discrimination of the assumed model from the true model.

In terms of model selection, it is important to note that in using the AIC the Markovian statespace representation is 'merely one choice of the model which will give a good approximation to an arbitrary covariance structure with a rather small number of parameters [see Akiake (1974)].

The statespace estimation procedure fits a sequence of autoregressive models using the Yule-Walker equations. It computes the AIC for each autoregressive model and selects the one for which the AIC is minimized. The next step is to select the state-vector to be used in fitting the Markovian state-space representation. This is done using the sample canonical correlation coefficients between the past value of the variable and an increasing number of steps into the future. Variables with high canonical correlations are added to the state-vector, those with small correlations are not. The size of the canonical correlation for inclusion or exclusion from the state-vector is gauged using a form of the AIC appropriate in this context. Once the state-vector has been chosen using the procedures described above, the statespace representation is estimated by maximizing an approximated likelihood function based upon the sample autocovariance matrix.

II. DATA DESCRIPTION

Transactions futures data were used to illustrate the methods discussed in the preceeding sections. The data used are time-stamped transaction prices of S&P 500 index futures contracts traded on the Index and Option Market of the Chicago Mercantile Exchange during the calendar years 1983 and 1984. This particular contract was chosen because of its extremely heavy trading volume.

Two criteria were applied to decide whether a particular contract's data should be included in the sample. The first criteria was that the contract was to be the nearby contract. These contracts have the dominant trading volume by far, with the longer maturities being relatively inactive. Given that the S&P 500 futures contracts have quarterly maturities, this first criterion implies that the sample consists of eight nonoverlapping contracts of transaction prices. However, the March 1983 contract was eliminated because it traded for part of its life in the presence of price limits. Price limits add a complication to the models tested.

The second criteria applied in screening the data was that transactions occurring during the delivery month were not to be included in the sample. In the last month of trading, futures prices may be influenced by expiration effects such as the forced convergence of the S&P 500 futures price to the S&P 500 stock index level, simultaneous expiration of S&P 500 futures and futures options contracts, and the shifting of trading interest from the nearby contract to the contract taking its place. These phenomena deserve attention but they do not fit into the framework of stationary, linear time series described in this study. Rather, such delivery month phenomena are essentially nonstationary and their description requires other modeling methods.

A further potential problem in the context of applying time series methods to transactions price data is that transactions generally occur at unequally-spaced time intervals; while the assumption usually made in time series analysis is that the data is given at equally-spaced intervals. This problem has not been resolved when there is dependence between the time series and the unequal sampling interval. This type of dependence occurs in the data used in this study because the sampling interval is *defined* by the time series as the time between price changes.

A method for dealing with unequally-spaced time series data is simply to sample the data at equally-spaced time intervals. The tests that follow were carried out on a sampled-data set consisting of ten-second by ten-second price observations sampled from the original data. This interval was chosen because a frequency distribution of intertrade times revealed that the average time between trades was approximately ten seconds. One could take longer sampling intervals but this would involve significant data loss.

III. EMPIRICAL RESULTS

Table I summarizes the correlation structure of ten-second-by-ten-second sampled futures price changes at lags 1 and 2. The critical levels of the correlation coefficients for rejection of the null hypothesis of insignificant serial correlation at the first two lags are $\pm 2/\sqrt{n}$ where n is the number of observations of the time series. For each daily data set n is 2248 and the critical values are $\pm.042$. Thus the data of sampled futures data is significantly negatively correlated at the first two lags.

The next sets of results, presented in Tables II and III, are unit root tests for stationarity of the AR(2) and AR(3) autoregressive models. These tests provide information about how many differencing operations are needed to produce a stationary time series. The AR(2) model was first considered without an intercept term and the test statistic $\phi_1(2)$ for testing the hypothesis of double unit roots was constructed. This is equivalent to the need for second-order differencing to render the series stationary. The critical 1% level, for each daily data set, is 5.18 and the hypothesis was consequently rejected for

Table I
CORRELATION STRUCTURE: SP500 FUTURES PRICE CHANGES, LAGS 1, 2

Contract	N^+	$\bar{\rho}_1^{++}$	$\bar{\rho}_2^{+++}$
Dec. 84	49	−.206	−.045
		(−.021)	(−.021)
Sept. 84	54	−.199	−.047
		(−.021)	(−.021)
June 84	52	−.216	−.047
		(−.021)	(−.021)
Mar. 84	51	−.215	−.051
		(−.021)	(−.021)
Dec. 83	51	−.206	−.075
		(−.021)	(−.021)
Sept. 83	53	−.188	−.055
		(−.021)	(−.021)
June 83	51	−.202	−.056
		(−.021)	(−.021)
MEAN	51.6	−.205	−.054
		(−.021)	(−.021)

$^+$N: Number of trading days in the sample.
$^{++}$Average first-order serial correlation coefficient between successive price changes (approximate standard error in parentheses).
$^{+++}$Average first-order serial correlation coefficient between price changes separated by one price change (average standard error in parentheses).

all contracts. The AR(2) model with an intercept was also tested using the statistic $\phi_2(3)$ and the null hypothesis of two unit roots was also rejected.

Next, the AR(2) model was tested for a single unit root using the test statistic τ_μ and the hypothesis was not rejected at the 1% significance level since the critical value of the

Table II
UNIT ROOT TESTS: AR(2) MODEL

Contract	τ_μ^+	$\phi_1(2)^{++}$ (no-intercept)	$\phi_2(3)^{+++}$ (with intercept)
Dec. 84	−2.075	1672.	1680.
Sept. 84	−2.001	1653.	1660.
June 84	−2.065	1722.	1728.
Mar. 84	−2.156	1722.	1731.
Dec. 83	−1.903	1686.	1691.
Sept. 83	−2.174	1590.	1598.
June 83	−1.843	1646.	1653.
MEAN	−2.031	1424.	1677.

$^+$Critical τ_μ value at 1% significance level, $(n = \infty) = -3.43$ [Fuller (1976), Table 8.5.2, p. 373].
$^{++}$Critical $\phi_1(2)$ value at 1% significance level, $(n = \infty) = 5.14$ [Hasza-Fuller (1979), Table 4.1, p. 1116].
$^{+++}$Critical $\phi_2(3)$ value at 1% significance level, $(n = \infty) = 5.76$ [Hasza-Fuller (1979), Table 4.1, p. 1116].

Table III
UNIT ROOT TESTS: AR(3) MODEL

Contract	τ^+	$\phi_1(2)^{++}$
Dec. 84	−.085	800.
Sept. 84	.134	801.
June 84	−.159	824.
Mar. 84	−.116	832.
Dec. 83	−.024	854.
Sept. 83	−.036	786.
June 83	.175	806.
MEAN	−.159	815.

$^+$Critical τ values at 1% significance level, $(n = \infty) = -2.58$ (lower 1%) and 2.00 (upper 1%) [Fuller (1976), Table 8.52, p. 373].
$^{++}$Critical $\phi_1(2)$ value at 1% significance level, $(n = \infty) = 5.14$.

test statistic is −3.43. One may conclude from these results that the AR(2) model has a single unit root and therefore, that first-order differencing is sufficient to render it stationary. Further, the existence of an intercept cannot be rejected *a priori*. To investigate this issue, the significance of the intercept in the AR(2) model was examined and it was found to be uniformly insignificant.

Table III reports the unit root tests for the higher order AR(3) model. The model was run without an intercept and the test statistics $\phi_1(2)$ and τ were computed. The same result obtained for the AR(2) model was also obtained for the AR(3) model: the hypothesis of double unit roots was rejected but that of a single unit root was not. With this information in hand, the statespace model may be estimated and the issue of model selection addressed.

The statespace representation was estimated using the procedures discussed in Section II and the test results are reported in Table IV. The statespace representation is equivalent to an ARIMA $(p, 1, p-1)$ model for some p. That is, the form is an autoregressive-moving average model with p autoregressive terms and p-1 moving average terms on first differences as required to render the series a linear, stationary time-series. The statespace representation was estimated freely as described in section II. But, the desire was to obtain a state-vector of low dimension. Therefore, for each contract, the number of days for which a low-order statespace representation fit the daily data was computed. The results given in Table IV indicate that a statespace representation with a state-vector of dimension 2 fit 75% of the daily data on average. The average transition matrix A, and the average innovations matrix B, are also reported in Table IV. A represents the evolution of the two-dimensional state vector v_t. B represents how the white-noise error terms u_t affect the evolution of the state vector.

For comparison, the equivalent ARIMA(2, 1, 1) model was also estimated and its estimates are presented in Table V. Here, the autoregressive and the moving average coefficients and their approximate standard errors are explicitly exhibited. Since the two forms are equivalent, no new information is contained in Table V.

When a low order statespace representation fit the daily data, it is important to examine the residuals from the fitted model to see if they contain any systematic patterns. This was done using Bartlett's Kolmogorov Statistic (see Priestley (1981), and the test results are reported in Table VI. The test is based upon the normalized cumulative periodogram and compares it to the uniform (0, 1) distribution. The 99% point for this test is approxi-

Table IV
STATESPACE REPRESENTATION OF DAILY TRANSACTIONS DATA

Contract	AIC	N^*	N_1^{**}	N_1/N	A^+	B^{++}
Dec. 84	5673	49	35	.71	$\begin{bmatrix} 0 & 1 \\ -.018 & .137 \\ (.045) & (.165) \end{bmatrix}$	$\begin{bmatrix} 1 \\ -.236 \\ (.021) \end{bmatrix}$
Sept. 84	5627	54	39	.72	$\begin{bmatrix} 0 & 1 \\ -.017 & .175 \\ (.043) & (.157) \end{bmatrix}$	$\begin{bmatrix} 1 \\ -.238 \\ (.021) \end{bmatrix}$
June 84	5464	52	39	.75	$\begin{bmatrix} 0 & 1 \\ -.002 & .209 \\ (.044) & (.150) \end{bmatrix}$	$\begin{bmatrix} 1 \\ -.245 \\ (.021) \end{bmatrix}$
Mar. 84	5055	51	43	.84	$\begin{bmatrix} 0 & 1 \\ .0011 & .251 \\ (.040) & (.126) \end{bmatrix}$	$\begin{bmatrix} 1 \\ -.510 \\ (.021) \end{bmatrix}$
Dec. 83	5104	51	40	.78	$\begin{bmatrix} 0 & 1 \\ -.021 & .254 \\ (.037) & (.112) \end{bmatrix}$	$\begin{bmatrix} 1 \\ -.249 \\ (.021) \end{bmatrix}$
Sept. 83	5843	53	37	.70	$\begin{bmatrix} 0 & 1 \\ -.024 & .173 \\ (.041) & (.160) \end{bmatrix}$	$\begin{bmatrix} 1 \\ -.214 \\ (.021) \end{bmatrix}$
June 83	5883	51	39	.76	$\begin{bmatrix} 0 & 1 \\ -.007 & .250 \\ (.041) & (.138) \end{bmatrix}$	$\begin{bmatrix} 1 \\ -.228 \\ (.021) \end{bmatrix}$
MEAN	5521	51.6	38.9	.75	$\begin{bmatrix} 0 & 1 \\ -.013 & .207 \\ (.042) & (.144) \end{bmatrix}$	$\begin{bmatrix} 1 \\ -.274 \\ (.021) \end{bmatrix}$

*Number of trading days in the sample.
**Number of days a two-dimensional statespace representation (2.1) fit the data.
+Average transition matrix (standard errors in parentheses).
++Average innovations matrix (standard errors in parentheses).

mated by $1.63/\sqrt{m-1}$ where m is the number of periodogram ordinates used in constructing the periodogram. For each daily data set, m is 1123 and the critical 99% point is .0486. Thus, according to the results in Table VI, the residuals from the fitted low-order statespace representation are indistinguishable from white noise.

Before interpreting the tests results, the final issue of model selection is considered. Note that the statespace representation forces a mixed model upon the data. But, it is theoretically possible that either a pure autoregressive or a pure moving average model may fit the data better. This issue was investigated by running pure AR(2) and MA(2) models upon first differences of the data. Then the AIC was computed for each model. The model with the minimum AIC was selected as providing the best fit to the data. The results are presented in Tables VII, VIII, and IX. The AR(2) model results are in Table VII, the MA(2) in Table VIII, and the minimum AIC model results in Table IX. Generally, the ARIMA(2, 1, 1) model provided the best fit to the data as measured by the AIC. But there are exceptions: the AR(2) model fit the September 1984 data better and the MA(2) model fit the June 1983 data better than the mixed model. One may conclude

Table V
EQUIVALENT ARIMA (2, 1, 1)[+] REPRESENTATION

Contract	N_1/N	θ_1	θ_2	ψ_1
Dec. 84	.71	.137	−.018	.373
		(.165)	(.045)	(.159)
Sept. 84	.72	.175	−.017	.413
		(.157)	(.043)	(.229)
June 84	.75	.209	−.002	.454
		(.150)	(.044)	(.151)
Mar. 84	.84	.251	+.0011	.761
		(.126)	(.040)	(.175)
Dec. 83	.78	.254	−.021	.503
		(.112)	(.037)	(.110)
Sept. 83	.70	.173	−.024	.387
		(.160)	(.041)	(.141)
June 83	.76	.250	−.007	.478
		(.138)	(.041)	(.133)
MEAN	.75	.207	−.013	.481
		(.144)	(.042)	(.157)

[+]Model: $x_t = \theta_1 x_{t-1} + \theta_2 x_{t-2} - \psi_1 u_{t-1} + u_t$.
*Approximate standard errors in parentheses.

from these results that S&P 500 sampled futures data appears to contain both autoregressive and moving average terms.

Finally, the invertibility conditions for the MA(2) model and consequently for the ARIMA(2, 1, 1) model were checked from the estimated autoregressive coefficients given in Table VIII. The invertibility conditions are given in (1.23) [see Box and Jenkins (1976), p. 70].

$$\psi_2 + \psi_1 < 1$$
$$\psi_2 - \psi_1 < 1$$
$$-1 < \psi_2 < 1 \qquad (1.23)$$

Table VI
WHITE NOISE TEST FOR RESIDUALS OF STATESPACE MODEL

Contract	N	N_1[+]	N_1/N	Bartlett's K-S Statistic
Dec. 84	49	35	.71	.0158
Sept. 84	54	39	.72	.0153
June 84	52	39	.75	.0387
Mar. 84	51	43	.84	.0151
Dec. 83	51	40	.78	.0150
Sept. 83	53	37	.70	.0151
June 83	51	39	.76	.0145
MEAN	51.6	38.9	.75	.0185

[+]N_1: The number of trading days for which a low-order statespace representation fit the data.

Table VII
AR(2) MODEL ESTIMATION

Contract	N	N_1[+]	N_1/N	θ_1[++]	θ_2	AIC[+++]
Dec. 84	49	46	.94	−.228 (−10.81)	−.098 (−4.65)	5715.05
Sept. 84	54	46	.85	−.233 (−11.07)	−.107 (−5.08)	5577.02
June 84	52	52	1.00	−.239 (−11.31)	−.100 (−4.76)	5497.49
Mar. 84	51	48	.94	−.246 (−11.65)	−.110 (−5.21)	5129.79
Dec. 83	51	51	1.00	−.232 (−10.98)	−.124 (−5.89)	5144.79
Sept. 83	53	50	.94	−.209 (−9.91)	−.099 (−4.70)	5843.51
June 83	51	51	1.00	−.222 (−10.54)	−.102 (−4.82)	5886.33
MEAN	51.6	49.1	.95	−.230 (−10.90)	−.106 (−5.02)	5542.01

[+]N_1: The number of days an AR(2) model provided a lower AIC than an AR(1) model.
[++]θ_i: Average autoregressive parameter estimate $i = 1, 2$ (t-statistic in parentheses).
[+++]AIC: Average of the AIC over N_1.

These conditions are satisfied since $\psi_1 = .235$ and $\psi_2 = .064$. The signs must be reversed in order to interpret the coefficients correctly.

Table VIII
MA(2) MODEL ESTIMATION

Contract	N	ψ_1[+]	ψ_2	AIC[++]
Dec. 84	49	−.233 (−11.04)	−.053 (−2.51)	5747.90
Sept. 84	54	−.226 (−10.72)	−.054 (−2.55)	5776.82
June 84	52	−.245 (−11.61)	−.054 (−2.58)	5492.15
Mar. 84	51	−.253 (−11.98)	−.070 (−3.32)	5383.71
Dec. 83	51	−.244 (−11.55)	−.089 (−4.24)	5133.67
Sept. 83	53	−.212 (−10.08)	−.062 (−2.93)	5884.02
June 83	51	−.231 (−10.96)	−.069 (−3.25)	5878.77
MEAN	51.6	−.235 (−11.13)	−.064 (−3.05)	5613.86

[+]ψ_i: Average moving average estimate $i = 1, 2$ (t-statistic in parentheses).
[++]: Average of the AIC over N.

Table IX
MINIMUM AIC MODEL

Contract	Minaic Model
Dec. 84	ARIMA(2, 1, 1)
Sept. 84	AR(2)
June 84	ARIMA(2, 1, 1)
Mar. 84	ARIMA(2, 1, 1)
Dec. 83	ARIMA(2, 1, 1)
Sept. 83	ARIMA(2, 1, 1)
June 83	MA(2)

IV. SUMMARY AND CONCLUSIONS

This study has considered the issues associated with modeling empirical price series as linear, stationary time series. Such models have frequently been estimated but the assumptions that they impose upon the data rarely discussed. The viewpoint taken here is that, excepting first-order autoregressive models, linear, stationary, time series models have little convincing economic arguments to support them. On the other hand, if certain conditions are satisfied, then there is a one-to-one correspondence between the correlation structure of a given data set and an autoregressive-moving average time series model. This fact makes such models one convenient way to capture the correlation structure of a given data set of empirical price series. If this is all that one wishes to do, then time series models justify their application. Other objectives such as forecasting would require additional justification.

This study took S&P 500 futures transactions data during 1983 and 1984 as an example, although other data sets could have been tested. The stationarity of daily data sets of ten-second by ten-second sampled S&P 500 futures prices was examined by conducting formal unit root tests. These tests found that first-order differencing is sufficient to render each data set of daily data stationary. The invertibility conditions for the model were checked numerically.

A basic problem in modeling market prices is that they are inconsistent with the Markov assumption usually made in modeling equilibrium prices in frictionless markets. To remedy this inconsistency, the method of expansion of states was employed. The method produces an empirically tractable Markov statespace representation. Further, it provides an estimation procedure for seemingly non-Markov processes which minimizes an information criterion known as Akiake's AIC.

Using the state-space representation and estimation techniques it was found that, over the entire extensive data base of transactions prices, the best fit was provided by the equivalent ARIMA(2, 1, 1) model for an average of 75% of the data. Further when this model fit the data, nonparametric white-noise tests failed to distinguish its residuals from those generated by white noise.

Purely autoregressive and moving average models of low order were also globally fit to the data and these have the possible advantage that they almost always provide estimates. However, there was a deterioration in the fit as measured by the AIC on a global basis. It thus seems that an appropriate model is mixed: there are, in general, *both* autoregressive and moving average components of the transactions time series.

Another approach to modeling futures data would be to take a discrete time, discrete state-space Markov chain approach and to impose economically meaningful boundary constraints on the futures price data. But this approach lies beyond the scope of linear, stationary, time series analysis.

Bibliography

Akiake, H. (1974): "Markovian representations of stochastic processes and its application to autoregressive moving average processes," *Ann. Inst. Statistic. Math.*, 26:363–387.

Box, G., and Jenkins, G. (1976): *Time Series Analysis, Forecasting and Control*, revised edition, Oakland, CA: Holden-Day.

Dickey, D., Bell, W., and Miller, R. (1986, February): "Unit Root Tests in Time Series Models: Tests and Implications," *American Statistician*, 40(1):12–26.

Doukas, J., and Rahman, A. (1987, March): "Unit Root Tests: Evidence from the Foreign Exchange Futures Market," *Journal of Financial and Quantitative Analysis*, 22(1):101–108.

Fuller, W. (1976): *Introduction to Statistical Time Series*, John Wiley, New York.

Goldenberg, D. H. (1988): "Trading Frictions and Futures Price Movements," *Journal of Financial and Quantitative Analysis*, 23(4):465–481.

Granger, C., and Newbold, P. (1977): *Forecasting Economic Time Series*, New York: Academic.

Hasza, D., and Fuller, W. (1979): "Estimation for Autoregressive Processes with Unit Roots," *Annals of Statistics*, 7(5):1106–1120.

Helms, B., Kaen, F., and Rosenman, R. (1984): "Memory in Commodity Futures Contracts," *The Journal of Futures Markets*, 4(4):559–567.

Merton, R. (1982): "On the mathematics and economic assumptions of continuous time models," in W. Sharpe and C. Cootner, Eds., *Financial Economics, Essays in honor of Paul Cootner*, Englewood Cliffs, NJ: Prentice-Hall.

Priestley, M. B. (1981): *Spectral Analysis and Time Series*, Vol. 1, New York: Academic.

Rausser, G. C. and Carter, C. (1983): "Futures Market Efficiency in the Soybean Complex," *Review of Economics and Statistics*, 65(3):469–478.

[10]
Testing Rationality in Futures Markets

Christopher K. Ma
William H. Dare
Darla R. Donaldson

INTRODUCTION

In recent years, the possibility of market irrationality has generated significant discussion among financial economists. One area of interest concerns the path of the reaction of security prices to new information. This issue has been examined from different perspectives. Shiller (1981, 1984) claimed that the observed volatility in stock returns is excessive in the sense that it cannot be solely explained by the uncertainty of future real dividends. French and Roll (1986) formulated testable hypotheses to identify three possible causes of market volatility: the release of public information, the production of private information, and trading noise. The trading noise hypothesis suggests that traders tend to overreact to others' trading and this overreaction creates noise in the market. French and Roll (1986), Makihija and Nachmann (1988), and Ma, Rao, and Sears (1988) have all provided empirical evidence of such overreaction in financial markets.

The second form of testing market rationality is based on the overreaction of securities prices *per se* to the release of unexpected information. A study in experimental psychology by Kahneman and Tversky (1981) showed that people tend to overreact to unexpected and dramatic events. They argued for the so-called "overreaction hypothesis" that individuals tend to overweight recent information and underweight prior information when revising their beliefs. This violates the basic Bayesian rule that the extremeness of predictions must be moderated with considerations of probability of its occurrence. Based on this hypothesis, DeBondt and Thaler (1985, 1987) reported that large abnormal returns can be earned by the contrarian investment strategy in the stock

---

The authors wish to thank Don Chance, Luc Soneon, Chip Peterson, Scott Hein, and participants of Research Seminar in Texas Tech University.

Christopher K. Ma is an Associate Professor in the College of Business Administration, Texas Tech University.

William H. Dare is a Ph.D. Student in the College of Business Administration, Texas Tech University.

Darla R. Donaldson is a Ph.D. Student in the College of Business Administration, Texas Tech University.

market. They concluded that market participants consistently overreact to substantive news of any nature. Their findings have raised subsequent debate.[1]

On the other hand, some totally "rational" explanations for the seemingly irrational overreaction in the stock market have been offered by several other studies. Brown, Harlow, and Tinic (1988) proposed the uncertain information hypothesis that, in the presence of imperfect information, rational, risk-averse investors will respond by initially overreacting to bad news and underreacting to good news. This is due to the fact that subsequent to the news of a dramatic financial event, both the risk level and the expected return of the affected companies will increase as a result of the information uncertainty. Consequently, the immediate price changes of significantly favorable events will ostensibly be followed by positive returns during the post-event period. The post-announcement price adjustment, while not rejecting market rationality, suggests that the market reacts to uncertain information in an efficient, if not instantaneous, manner.

Similarly, DeLong, Shleifer, Summers, and Waldmann (1987) found that noise traders with erroneous and stochastic beliefs can earn higher returns than do rational investors since they bear a large amount of risk. Their presence raises overall expected returns because sophisticated investors dislike bearing the "noise trader risk", i.e., the risk that noise traders may be irrationally pessimistic and push asset prices down in the future. Given this additional risk in asset markets, the average price of assets will be below fundamental values in the short run. This divergence, however, will decrease once the noise is reduced, giving rise to the patterns of mean reversion in stock and bond prices as noted by Fama and French (1986), and the price reversals in the empirical literature of overreaction.

The third possible explanation is called "the overshooting hypothesis." Dornbush (1976) argued that while interest rates can adjust to new information instantaneously, the money supply cannot. The different adjustment speeds lead exchange rates to overshoot in the short run. At the new equilibrium, the exchange rate reverses itself when the money supply is eventually able to adjust. Using the same argument in the stock market, Fabozzi, Ma, and Lindsley (1988) claimed that securities prices generally adjust to information faster than trading volume. The latent trading volume induced by investors' portfolio revisions will reverse the price pattern which creates a short run price overreaction.

The issue of price overreaction is particularly relevant in the futures markets. Since the two major functions of futures prices are to provide information discovery and resolution to cash traders, the speed and the nature of futures price adjustments to new information suggest important welfare considerations. This article investigates the adjustment process of futures prices in reaction to significant events. Contrary to previous studies, statistically significant price changes are used as proxies for the arrival of significant events. The evidence indicates that, in general, futures prices of agricultural commodities tend to overreact to significant events, while financial futures prices tend to underreact to significant events. The fact that the price does not adjust to information instantaneously seems to imply that either there is information asymmetry among traders in the market and/or that traders do not have homogenous risk attitudes. The contribution of this study goes beyond the academic interest on the efficiency of futures markets. The findings of this study provide strong (dis)justifications to the design and implementation of most regulatory devices in futures markets, especially if the effectiveness of

---

[1]For details, See Brown, Harlow, and Tinic (1988), Chan (1988), DeBondt and Makhija (1988), Delong, Shleifer, Summers, and Waldmann (1987), Dyl and Maxfield (1987), Gandar, Zuber, O'Brien, and Russo (1988), Jones (1987), and Summers (1986).

EMPIRICAL DESIGN

Sample

Since there is not an *a priori* reason why the price adjustment process subsequent to significant events should be uniform across different futures contracts, the same procedure of testing rationality is repeated across twelve different types of futures contracts. In Table I, the sample is briefly described. There are six futures contracts for agricultural commodities, two metal futures contracts, and four financial futures contracts.[2] Daily closing prices for the nearby contract were collected.[3] Note that the varying lengths of the sample period are restricted by the data availability and the life of the specific futures market.

Daily prices, rather than prices with a longer time horizon (used in earlier studies) are used for testing rationality because of the nature of futures markets. Since liquid futures trading is uniquely characterized by the short maturity of the asset and by the aggressive basis and spread arbitrage that occurs, the time to respond to significant daily events is expected to be relatively short. Using market price data of longer time intervals will not allow us to observe reactions of the type under study.

Methodology

Significant price changes are used in this study as proxies for the occurrence of significant events which is different from previous studies where information is often characterized by a specific event. A significant price change is defined in a statistical sense. Since the time series of historical prices is invariably affected by the underlying fundamental trend of each commodity, identifying an abnormal price movement is only possible when the "normal" price movement is ascertained. That is, the return-generating process can be described as follows:

$$R_{it} = E(R_{it} \mid I_{t-1}) + \varepsilon_{it}$$

where R_{it} is the actual daily return measured by the logarithm of price changes during period t for the ith futures contract, and $E(R_{it} \mid I_{t-1})$ is the expected ("normal") rate of return, given the information set, I_{t-1} at time $t - 1$. The issue of market irrationality may only be examined after a certain form of rationality is defined. The rationality of market expectations, as shown by $E(R_{it} \mid I_{t-1})$, is determined under the condition that the estimation error, ε_{it}, is a result of the assumption that the market formulates expected returns on a rational expectation basis. Specifically, using all currently available information, rational trading agents will not consistently make biased estimates. Under this

---

[2]21 futures contracts serve as the preliminary sample. The sample was screened according to the number of the observations and significant events for each contract. The final sample consisted of 12 different contracts.

[3]The potential problems of using closing prices instead of actual transaction prices are acknowledged. However, the extent and the relevance of possible biases can vary depending on the issues investigated. If the purpose of identifying irrationality is to explore trading profit, the testing is better served by actual transaction prices. Since it is the price adjustment process after significant events that is of interest, the bias is considered not to be crucial to the conclusion. Note that the bias attributed to the thin trading of certain contracts is further reduced in this study, since only nearby contracts are used.

Table I
SAMPLE DESCRIPTION

Futures Contract	Sample Period	Number of Obs.	ARIMA Model	Chi-Square Lags: 6	12	18	Min. Days
Commodities Futures							
Corn	Jan. 1977–Dec. 1987	2528	$R_t = -7.39E\text{-}05 + .0092\,R_{t-1} + \varepsilon_t$	7.84	15.97	25.75	3
Coffee	Jan. 1977–Dec. 1987	2514	$R_t = -.00022 - .0387\,R_{t-1} + \varepsilon_t$	15.86	21.03	31.87	72
Pork Bellies	Jan. 1977–Dec. 1987	2531	$R_t = -.0454 - .00003\,t = .1102\,R_{t-1} + .0585\,R_{t-10} + \varepsilon_t$	8.57	16.16	18.27	3
Soybean	Jan. 1977–Dec. 1987	2528	$R_t = -3.322E\text{-}06 - .0253\,R_{t-1} + \varepsilon_t$	8.39	18.83	25.01	6
Soymeal	Jan. 1977–Dec. 1987	2527	$R_t = -.00011 - .0123\,R_{t-1} + \varepsilon_t$	5.33	11.77	17.00	4
Wheat	Jan. 1977–Dec. 1987	2528	$R_t = .0001 - .0180\,R_{t-1} + \varepsilon_t$	5.54	12.65	24.42	26
Metal Futures							
Gold	Jan. 1975–July 1987	2899	$R_t + .1138 - .0001\,t = -.0719\,R_{t-1} - .0908\,R_{t-4} + .039\,R_{t-10} + .0592\,R_{t-12} + .0575\,R_{t-13} + \varepsilon_t$	4.05	6.61	24.09	9
Silver	Jan. 1975–July 1988	3149	$R_t + .0804 - .00004\,t = .0583\,R_{t-1} - .0569\,R_{t-4} - .0602\,R_{t-5} + .0698\,R_{t-8} + .0498\,R_{t-12} + .0411\,R_{t-13} + \varepsilon_t$	1.35	4.40	18.13	13
Financial Futures							
Treasury Bond	July 1977–July 1988	2744	$R_t = -6.349E\text{-}05 - .0505\,R_{t-1} + \varepsilon_t$	11.42	17.65	21.79	1
Muni Bond	June 1985–July 1988	775	$R_t = -1.679E\text{-}0.6 + .0226\,R_{t-1} + \varepsilon_t$	6.14	14.82	20.72	33
S&P 500	April 1982–July 1988	1568	$R_t = -.2539 + .0003\,t + \varepsilon_t$	2.36	2.74	3.14	10
Value Line	Aug. 1985–July 1988	1584	$R_t = .0004 - .0109\,R_{t-1} + \varepsilon_t$	16.87	21.98	24.73	8

*: All chi-square statistics are insignificant at one percent level.
Min. Days: The minimum number of days between two consecutive significant events.

assumption, ε_{it} is the white noise which represents the unexpected, abnormal component of the return-generating process[4], with the following properties:

$$E(\varepsilon_{it} | I_{t-1}) = 0, \quad V(\varepsilon_{it} | I_{t-1}) = \sigma_i^2, \quad \text{and } \text{Cov}(\varepsilon_{it}, \varepsilon_{it-1}) = 0.$$

Undoubtedly, there may be numerous possible candidates for the expectation scheme in each market. Since it is the unexpected component of market reaction being investigated, one must first identify the expected component of the return-generating process of each futures contract with the most parsimonious model of the autoregressive integrated moving average process (ARIMA) using the Box and Jenkins' method.[5] The values of the parameters for the ARIMA model are estimated to minimize the deviation of actual returns from returns predicted by the specified model, subject to the condition that the resulting estimation error follows a white-noise process. The exact estimation procedure starts by identifying any trend, linear or not, inherent in the return series. Once the seasonal component is removed, the remaining return is estimated for the ARIMA model. The relevance (fitness) of any specific model is tested by comparing the forecasted returns based on the model with the actual returns in the testing sample. The residual between the forecasted return and the actual return is tested for randomness. The most parsimonious model is defined by the simplest model which results in residuals of white noise.

In Table I, the ARIMA model for each contract and the chi-square statistics for the fitness of the process are presented.[6] It is noted that most contracts can be described by a simple autoregressive (AR) model. For simplicity, only the chi-square statistics of lags 6, 12, and 18 are reported. It appears that each return series well fits by the model specified, given the insignificant chi-square statistics at the one percent level. The series of each residual, ε_{ijk}, in the form of white noise, therefore, may be considered the abnormal component of the price movement.

Statistically, a significant price change can be identified by the statistical significance of the residual return generated by the above procedure. A significant positive (negative) event is identified by the residual which is statistically positive (negative), significant at the five percent level. After using this guideline to select significant price changes, a

---

[4]Since the purpose of the article is to examine the unexpected component of the return-generating process, the specific form of the model for each series is not as important as the resulting residual being white noise. This identification is similar to Flannery and James (1984).

[5]The expected component of the return-generating process of each futures contract can be described by the general form ARIMA (p,d,q)

$$\varphi(B)R_t = \phi(B)\Delta^d R_t = \theta_o + \theta(B)\varepsilon_t$$

where

$$\phi(B) = 1 - \phi_1 B - \phi_2 B^2 \ldots \ldots \ldots -\phi_p B^p$$
$$\theta(B) = 1 - \theta_1 B - \theta_2 B^2 \ldots \ldots \ldots -\theta_q B^q$$

and Δ^d is the dth difference operator. In what follows:

(1) $\phi(B)$ is called the autogressive operator; it is assumed to be stationary, that is the roots of $\phi(B) = 0$ lie outside the unit circle.
(2) $\varphi(B) = \Delta^d \phi(B)$ is called generalized autogressive operator; it is a nonstationary operator with d of the roots of $\varphi(B) = 0$ equal to unity.
(3) $\theta(B)$ is called the moving average operator; it is assumed to be invertible, that is, the roots of $\theta(B) = 0$ lie outside the unit circle.

[6]Again, there may have been other fitted models for each series. However, for the purpose of this article, the simplest form is used.

sample of positive and negative event dates are identified. Standard event methodology is employed to examine the price adjustment process subsequent to these event dates, that is, a cumulative average residual return (*CAR*) is computed for each observation period after an event date as follows:

$$CAR_{it} = \sum_{j=1}^{t} \sum_{k=1}^{n} \varepsilon_{ijk}/n$$

and

    i: the ith futures contract
    j: the jth day after the significant event date
    k: the kth significant event
    t: the tth in the observation period
    n: the total number of significant events for the ith contract

where ε_{ijk} is the residual return for the ith futures contract the jth day after the kth significant positive (negative) event date. The CAR_{it} measures the cumulative average residual return for the ith contract from one day after the event date up to the tth day after each event. The pattern of the *CAR* subsequent to event dates will reveal the process by which futures prices adjust to significant events. An overreaction of futures prices is observed when the *CAR* reverses itself shortly after the event date. An underreaction is observed when the *CAR* exhibits persistent increasing movement after the event date. In either case, the market price does not adjust to the event instantaneously.

Standard event study test statistics are employed to examine the statistical significance of the price reversal and dependence following the event dates (see Brown and Warner (1985)). For a given day t after the event date, the statistical significance for the residual return, ε_{ijk}, can be tested by the following Z statistics:

$$Z_{ijk} = \varepsilon_{ijk}/[(1 + \sum_{j=1}^{t-1} \varphi_j^2)^{1/2} s_\varepsilon/n]$$

where

$$s_\varepsilon = (1 - \phi^2)R_1^2 + \sum_{t=2}^{n}(R_t - \phi R_{t-1})^2$$

where $\varphi(B)$ and $\phi(B)$ are the autoregressive operators described in Footnote 4, and Z_{ijk} is the test statistic for the residual return on the jth day from the kth event date for the ith futures contract.[7] The test statistic for the significance of the *CAR* for the ith futures contract over a given time interval, i.e., t days from the event date, is given by:

$$CZ_{it} = \sum_{j=1}^{t} \sum_{k=1}^{n} Z_{ijk}/(nt)^{1/2}$$

where n is the number of significant events in the sample for a given day t.[8] The level of CZ_{it} determines if the cumulative average residual t days from event date is significantly

---

[7] See Box and Jankins (1976) for details.
[8] The number of cases, n, may vary in the post-event period. If there is no trading or the closing price is not available, the number of cases will be reduced.

different from zero. This allows one to test whether there is a significant price reversal or a price dependence t days after an event date.

The determination of the length of an observation period after each significant price change for individual futures contract warrants further explanation. Since the length of the reaction period may not be uniform across different futures contracts, the minimum time period between two consecutive significantly positive (negative) daily residuals is first determined in each sample. In Table I, the length of the minimum time period between any two consecutive significant events for each contract is reported. The length of the minimum time period ranges from one day (Treasury Bond) to seventy-two days (Coffee). However in the empirical testing of this study, five days was used as the minimum observation period. That is, significant events which are at least five days apart are considered independent cases in the sample. Any significant events identified within five days after the first event is not treated as a separate case to avoid overlapping observation periods. For any time period longer than fifteen days, fifteen days was used as the observation period.[9] When the length of the observation period is determined by this procedure, the biases resulting from overlapping observation periods and insufficient degrees of freedom are reduced.

EMPIRICAL RESULTS AND IMPLICATIONS

Based on the methodology described in the last section, the daily average residuals and cumulative average residuals after the event day (Day 0) and the corresponding test statistics are presented in Table II(A) (positive events) and II(B) (negative events). The significance on the *CAR* level over any time interval after the event day allows one to examine the *duration* of the price adjustment. The pattern of individual average daily residual (*AR*) provides a view of the *process* of that adjustment. For most of the contracts, there are statistically significant price reactions after an event date. Specifically, there are significant price reversals for the contracts on Coffee, Corn, Soybeans, Wheat, Gold, and Silver following positive events. For negative events, Coffee, Soymeal, Wheat, Pork Bellies, and Silver contracts also show some overreaction. On the other hand, the Muni-Bond, Treasury Bond, Value Line Index, and S&P 500 futures prices demonstrate some dependence after either positive or negative events. The reaction starts as early as one day after the event (Wheat, Pork Bellies, Muni-Bond, Soybeans, etc.) to as late as seven days after the event (Gold). The duration of the reactions lasts from one day (Corn) to thirteen days (Wheat). It is easy to note that in most of the contracts, the price movement after an event date violates the random walk hypothesis; price levels do not adjust to the new equilibrium instantaneously. Further insights are evident from the often reversing price movements which are evident by the significant test statistics for average daily residual returns in the post-event period. It appears that the price level moves toward a pattern of random walk, but the process takes longer than one day.

Essentially, price reversals following event dates imply overreaction of market participants, while price dependences suggest underreaction. While there is strong evidence of noninstantaneous price adjustments, the direction of reaction is not uniform across different futures contracts. In general, financial futures prices tend to underreact to significant information.

---

[9]The test is replicated using observation periods other than the minimum 5 days and the maximum 15 days. The conclusion is not sensitive to these parameters.

Table II(A)
THE PRICE ADJUSTMENT PROCESS FOR POSITIVE EVENTS-AGRICULTURAL FUTURES

Days	COFFEE AR	Z	n = 39 CAR	CZ	PORK BELLIES AR	Z	n = 15 CAR	CZ
Days	−0.0000	−00.000[b]	−0.000	−00.000[b]	−0.000	−00.000[b]	−0.0000	−00.000[b]
0	6.055	17.673[a]	0.000	17.673[a]	8.717	13.836[a]	0.000	13.836[a]
1	−1.014	−2.959[a]	−1.014	−2.959[a]	−0.644	−1.023[a]	−0.644	−1.023[a]
2	0.429	1.251	−0.585	−1.208	0.454	0.720	−0.191	−0.214
3	−0.116	−0.338	−0.701	−1.182	−0.287	−0.455	−0.477	−0.437
4	0.341	0.995	−0.360	−0.526	0.671	1.065	0.194	0.154
5	0.204	0.597	−0.156	−0.203	1.021	1.621[b]	1.215	0.862

Days	CORN AR	Z	n = 44 CAR	CZ	SOYBEANS AR	Z	n = 40 CAR	CZ
0	3.635	18.046[a]	0.000	18.046[a]	3.655	16.723[a]	0.000	16.723[a]
1	−0.491	−2.438[a]	−0.491	−2.438[a]	−0.319	−1.458	−0.319	−1.458
2	0.175	0.866	−0.317	−1.111	−0.036	−0.164	−0.355	−1.147
3	0.296	1.471	−0.020	−0.058	−0.313	−1.431	−0.667	−1.763[b]
4	0.032	0.160	0.012	0.030	0.184	0.842	−0.483	−1.106
5	0.146	0.727	0.158	0.352	−0.351	−1.607[b]	−0.835	−1.708[b]
6	−0.557	−2.766[a]	−0.399	−0.808	0.446	2.041[b]	−0.388	−0.725
7	0.155	0.768	−0.244	−0.458	−0.110	−0.504	−0.499	−0.862
8	−0.059	−0.293	−0.303	−0.532	0.201	0.920	−0.298	−0.481
9	0.139	0.689	−0.164	−0.272	0.166	0.760	−0.131	−0.200
10	−0.205	−1.019	−0.370	−0.580	0.200	0.914	0.068	0.099
11	0.114	0.565	−0.256	−0.383	0.239	1.092	0.307	0.423
12	−0.086	−0.428	−0.342	−0.490	−0.067	−0.307	0.240	0.317
13	0.115	0.570	−0.227	−0.313	−0.213	−0.973	0.027	0.035
14	−0.131	−0.652	−0.358	−0.476	−0.254	−1.162	−0.227	−0.277
15	−0.249	−1.238	−0.608	−0.779	0.048	0.220	−0.179	−0.211

Days	SOYMEAL AR	Z	n = 78 CAR	CZ	WHEAT AR	Z	n = 38 CAR	CZ
0	4.228	24.740[a]	0.000	24.740[a]	4.298	16.578[a]	0.000	16.578[a]
1	−0.199	−1.164	−0.199	−1.164	−0.967	−3.731[a]	−0.967	−3.731[a]
2	−0.050	−0.291	−0.249	−1.029	−0.299	−1.153	−1.266	−3.454[a]
3	−0.190	−1.111	−0.439	−1.482	−0.334	−1.288	−1.600	−3.563[a]
4	0.358	2.097[b]	−0.080	−0.235	0.032	0.124	−1.568	−3.024[a]
5	−0.165	−0.966	−0.245	−0.642	0.095	0.366	−1.473	−2.541[a]
6	−0.125	−0.732	−0.370	−0.885	−0.147	−0.568	−1.620	−2.551[a]
7	0.064	0.372	−0.031	−0.678	−0.192	−0.741	−1.812	−2.642[a]
8	−0.003	−0.017	−0.310	−0.641	0.408	1.575[b]	−1.404	−1.915[b]
9	−0.045	−0.251	−0.354	−0.691	−0.113	−0.437	−1.517	−1.951[b]
10					0.074	0.286	−1.443	−1.760[a]
11					0.372	1.436	−1.071	−1.245
12					−0.015	−0.059	−1.086	−1.209
13					−0.153	−0.589	−1.239	−1.325

Days	S&P 500 AR	Z	n = 14 CAR	CZ	VALUE LINE AR	Z	n = 20 CAR	CZ
0	3.936	9.745^a	0.000	9.745^a	3.694	12.580^a	0.000	12.580^a
1	1.111	2.750^a	1.111	2.750^a	−0.035	−0.120	−0.035	−0.120
2	0.318	0.788	1.429	2.502^a	0.380	1.292	0.344	0.829
3	0.646	1.599^b	2.075	2.966^a	−0.515	−1.755^b	−0.171	−0.336
4	0.079	0.195	2.154	2.666^a	0.369	1.257	0.198	0.337
5	−0.104	−0.258	2.050	2.269^a	−0.067	−0.230	0.131	0.199

Days	T-BONDS AR	Z	n = 41 CAR	CZ	MUNI-BONDS AR	Z	n = 13 CAR	CZ
0	2.496	16.687^a	0.000	16.687^a	2.394	10.498^a	0.000	10.498^a
1	0.139	0.927	0.139	0.927^a	0.347	1.521^b	0.347	1.521
2	0.211	1.409	0.349	1.652	0.595	2.607^a	0.941	2.919
3	0.113	0.756	0.463	1.785	0.269	1.184	1.211	3.067^a
4	0.209	1.396	0.671	2.244	−0.240	−1.052	0.971	2.130^b
5	0.300	2.002^b	0.971	2.903	−0.702	−3.078^a	0.270	0.529
6	0.355	2.372^a	1.326	3.618				
7	0.113	0.754	1.439	3.635				
8	0.078	0.520	1.516	3.584				
9	0.195	1.303	1.711	3.813				
10	0.113	0.755	1.824	3.856				
11	0.081	0.538	1.905	3.882				
12	0.092	0.615	1.997	3.894				
13	−0.332	−2.220^a	1.665	3.126				
14	0.217	1.451	1.882	3.400				
15	0.083	0.555	1.965	3.428				

Days	GOLD AR	Z	n = 39 CAR	CZ	SILVER AR	Z	n = 35 CAR	CZ
0	4.738	17.884^a	0.000	17.884^a	7.322	16.648^a	0.000	16.648^a
1	0.350	1.320	0.350	1.320	−1.106	−2.515^a	−1.106	−2.515^a
2	−0.203	−0.765	0.147	0.392	0.276	0.628	−0.830	−1.334
3	0.059	0.222	0.206	0.449	1.172	2.666^a	0.343	0.450
4	−0.207	−0.781	−0.001	−0.002	−0.744	−1.691^b	−0.401	−0.456
5	0.057	0.216	0.056	0.095	−0.298	−0.678	−0.699	−0.711
6	−0.922	−3.480^a	−0.866	−1.334	−0.295	−0.670	−0.994	−0.923
7	0.705	2.660^a	−0.161	−0.230	0.835	1.898^b	−0.159	−0.137
8	0.680	2.566^a	0.519	0.693	0.06	0.137	−0.099	−0.080
9	−0.367	−1.383	0.152	0.192				
10	−0.362	−1.366	−0.210	−0.250				
11	0.407	1.536	0.197	0.225				
12	−0.581	−2.192^a	−0.383	−0.418				
13	−0.137	−0.517	−0.520	−0.545				
14	−0.025	−0.093	−0.545	−0.550				
15	−0.039	−0.148	−0.584	−0.569				

n: # of Significant events. ^{b}Significant at the 5% level. Z: Test Statistic for AR. CZ: Test Statistic for CAR.
^{a}Significant at the 1% level. AR: Average Residual. CAR: Cumulative Average Residual.

Table II(B)
THE PRICE ADJUSTMENT PROCESS FOR NEGATIVE EVENTS-AGRICULTURAL FUTURES

Days	COFFEE AR	Z	n = 35 CAR	CZ	PORK BELLIES AR	Z	n = 16 CAR	CZ
0	−6.856	−18.956^a	0.000	−18.956^a	−8.768	−14.374^a	0.000	−14.374^a
1	−0.099	−0.274	−0.099	−0.274	0.948	1.554	0.948	1.554
2	1.007	2.783^a	0.908	1.775^b	0.358	0.586	1.306	1.514
3	0.746	2.062^b	1.654	2.640^a	1.185	1.943^b	2.491	2.357^a
4	−0.019	−0.053	1.635	2.260^b	0.808	1.325	3.299	2.704^a
5	0.222	0.613	1.856	2.295^b	0.856	1.403	4.155	3.046^a

Days	CORN AR	Z	n = 36 CAR	CZ	SOYBEANS AR	Z	n = 47 CAR	CZ
0	−4.820	−21.645^a	0.000	−21.645^a	−3.600	−17.855^a	0.000	−17.855^a
1	0.030	0.136	0.030	0.136	−0.097	−0.48	−0.097	−0.480
2	0.042	0.187	0.072	0.228	0.033	0.164	−0.064	−0.223
3	0.020	0.090	0.092	0.239	0.337	1.671^b	0.273	0.782
4	−0.149	−0.670	−0.057	−0.129	−0.051	−0.252	0.222	0.551
5	−0.092	−0.413	−0.149	−0.299	0.139	0.691	0.362	0.802
6	−0.102	−0.456	−0.251	−0.459	0.233	1.155	0.595	1.204
7	0.090	0.405	−0.160	−0.272	−0.184	−0.913	0.411	0.770
8	−0.130	−0.583	−0.290	−0.460	−0.485	−2.406^a	−0.074	−0.131
9	0.245	1.101	−0.045	−0.067	0.276	1.370	0.202	0.334
10	0.013	0.059	−0.032	−0.045	−0.346	−1.718^b	−0.145	−0.227
11	−0.173	−0.774	−0.204	−0.276	−0.215	−1.066	−0.360	−0.538
12	0.109	0.490	−0.095	−0.123	−0.315	−1.562^b	−0.675	−0.966
13	0.192	0.860	0.097	0.120	0.075	0.372	−0.600	−0.825
14	0.000	−0.002	0.096	0.115	0.010	0.051	−0.589	−0.781
15	0.162	0.728	0.258	0.300	0.101	0.499	−0.489	−0.626

Days	SOYMEAL AR	Z	n = 76 CAR	CZ	WHEAT AR	Z	n = 30 CAR	CZ
0	−4.071	−23.511^a	0.000	−23.511^a	−5.953	−20.404^a	0.000	−20.404^a
1	0.128	0.738	0.128	0.738	0.521	1.784	0.521	1.784^b
2	0.159	0.918	0.287	1.171	0.020	0.067	0.540	1.309
3	0.214	1.238	0.501	1.671^b	0.114	0.390	0.654	1.294
4	0.364	2.103^b	0.865	2.498^a	−0.345	−1.183	0.309	0.529
5	0.403	2.329^a	1.268	3.276^a	−0.046	−0.158	0.263	0.403
6	0.046	0.264	1.314	3.099^a	−0.116	−0.397	0.147	0.205
7	−0.453	−2.614^a	0.861	1.881^a	0.478	1.639^b	0.625	0.810
8	−0.330	−1.906^b	0.531	1.085	0.301	1.031	0.926	1.122
9	−0.127	−0.732	0.405	0.779	0.067	0.228	0.992	1.134
10					0.038	0.131	1.031	1.117
11					0.018	0.063	1.049	1.084
12					−0.454	−1.554^b	0.596	0.589
13					0.359	1.229	0.954	0.907
14					0.329	1.127	1.283	1.175
15					0.195	0.668	1.478	1.308

	S&P 500		$n = 21$		VALUE LINE		$n = 32$	
Days	AR	Z	CAR	CZ	AR	Z	CAR	CZ
0	−5.749	−17.432[a]	0.000	−17.432[a]	−4.386	−18.872[a]	0.000	−18.872[a]
1	−0.859	−2.603[a]	−0.859	−2.603[a]	−0.669	−2.881[a]	−0.669	−2.881[a]
2	−0.217	−0.659	−1.076	−2.307[b]	−0.069	−0.300	−0.739	−2.250[b]
3	−0.407	−1.507	−1.573	−2.754[a]	0.060	0.258	−0.679	−1.688[b]
4	0.305	0.925	−1.268	−1.922[b]	−0.133	−0.574	−0.812	−1.749[b]
5	0.99	3.001[a]	−0.278	−0.377	0.185	0.799	−0.627	−1.207

	T-BONDS		$n = 48$		MUNI-BONDS		$n = 13$	
Days	AR	Z	CAR	CZ	AR	Z	CAR	CZ
0	−2.460	−17.792[a]	0.000	−17.792[a]	−2.387	−10.467[a]	0.000	−10.467[a]
1	−0.174	−1.258	−0.174	−1.258	−0.309	−1.355	−0.309	−1.355
2	−0.337	−2.436[a]	−0.511	−2.612[a]	−0.279	−1.222	−0.588	−1.823[b]
3	0.281	2.003	−0.230	−0.959	0.084	0.366	−0.504	−1.277
4	0.278	2.010	0.048	0.175	0.199	0.874	−0.305	−0.699
5	0.263	1.901	0.311	1.007	0.433	1.899[b]	0.128	0.251

	GOLD		$n = 50$		SILVER		$n = 41$	
Days	AR	Z	CAR	CZ	AR	Z	CAR	CZ
0	−4.445	−18.997[a]	0.000	−18.997[a]	−7.417	−18.253[a]	0.000	−18.253[a]
1	−0.359	−1.536	−0.359	−1.536	0.187	0.460	0.187	0.460
2	0.297	1.267	−0.063	−0.190	0.084	0.208	0.271	0.472
3	−0.087	−0.373	−0.150	−0.370	0.359	0.883	0.630	0.895
4	0.004	0.015	−0.147	−0.313	0.105	0.258	0.735	0.904
5	0.616	2.632[a]	0.469	0.897	0.456	1.123	1.191	1.311
6	0.051	0.219	0.521	0.908	−0.098	−0.240	1.094	1.099
7	0.622	2.658[a]	1.143	1.846[b]	0.286	0.703	1.379	1.283
8	−0.324	−1.383	0.819	1.237	0.492	1.211	1.872	1.628[b]
9	−0.052	−0.224	0.766	1.092				
10	−0.697	−2.980[a]	0.069	0.093				
11	0.217	0.926	0.286	0.368				
12	−0.115	−0.491	0.171	0.211				
13	0.124	0.529	0.295	0.349				
14	0.118	0.503	0.412	0.471				
15	−0.045	−0.190	0.368	0.406				

n: # of Significant events.
[a]Significant at the 1% level.
[b]Significant at the 5% level.
AR -:- Average Residual.
Z: Test Statistic for AR.
CAR: Cumulative Average Residual.
CZ: Test Statistic for CAR.

Some Conjectures

The differential price adjustment process of agricultural futures versus financial futures to significant events, while puzzling, can possibly be attributed to the idiosyncrasies in each market. Several possible conjectures for the observed market irrationality follow There is a different mix of informed and uninformed traders in the agricultural and financial futures environments. Informed traders are distinguished by their superior estimation ability resulting in fewer prediction errors, and smaller biases between the predicted equilibrium level and the true equilibrium level. Consider a market which is composed of a queue of agents with different information sets. Since a rational informed trader will not trade instantly to the predicted equilibrium level if the trading counterpart is not yet informed, the deviation between the initial clearing price and the predicted equilibrium level is thus determined by the difference in information sets between two trading agents. Given the nonuniform information sets, the trading will be triggered on a sequential basis; with the more informed agents trading first; and then the less informed agents trading later. The sequential arrival and revelation of information will set a motion in action which results in a noticeable price dependence.

At the other extreme, when the market is predominantly occupied by informed traders, the mere competition among informed traders to trade with a limited number of uninformed traders will lead to a price so close to the upper range of the new predicted equilibrium level which may be beyond the true equilibrium level in the short run. Once the uninformed traders become informed, and this "disequilibrium" price level is well known, subsequent arbitraging behavior will reverse the price to the true equilibrium level. Therefore, a price reversal or an overreaction may have been a result of the dominating market power of informed traders. Note that the differential reaction in price movements found in various futures markets may be consistent with this hypothesis. Obviously, it is presumptuous to argue that there are more informed traders in agricultural futures markets than in financial futures markets without further supporting evidence. Since the degree of informativeness is not readily observable, and therefore not comparable across different markets, the empirical evidence that financial futures prices and agricultural futures prices react to information differently does not provide a direct test of the hypothesis.

Another possible explanation for the overreaction/underreaction of futures prices is the impact of price limit rules on futures markets. Price limits have been deemed necessary by exchange officials because limiting the magnitude of daily price changes is believed to reduce excessive market volatility, thus enabling the market to move in an orderly fashion. However, opponents of price limits contend that such restrictions produce, rather than eliminate, significant price discontinuities by preventing the price from reaching its new, anticipated equilibrium level. Consider a market where the futures price and its volatility are driven by the arrival of information. Assume all traders are equally informed with respect to both the information and the true equilibrium level. If the price limits are present and the true equilibrium price falls outside the current day's price limit range, the futures price will move to the appropriate price limit and all trading will suspend. The trading resumes when the equilibrium price lies within the newly established trading limits. If this scenario is correct, the futures price and its related volatility will reflect no information during the limit move; the price limit merely serves to delay trading to the next tradeable period. Because the futures price was not allowed to trade at its true equilibrium level during the current session, the price adjustment process is lengthened to subsequent periods. Therefore, a price dependence will emerge especially when the market hits limits consecutively.

To test this possibility, the actual limit moves of each contract during the sample period is identified. In Table III(A), the daily price limit for each futures contract is presented. Daily high and low prices along with the closing price of the previous trading session of each contract are used to identify the days when limit moves may have occurred. In Table III(A), the numbers of days when the futures price reached the up limit

Table III(A)
PRICE LIMIT RULES AND NUMBER OF LIMIT MOVES

Futures Contracts	Daily Limit	Number of Up Limits	Number of Down Limits
Coffee	4 cent	10	12
Corn	10 cent	31	24
Pork Bellies	2 points	396	393
Soybeans	30 cent	32	48
Soymeal	1 cent	22	28
Wheat	20 cent	18	13
Gold	50 dollar	9	5
Silver	1 dollar	58	61
Muni-Bond	2 points*	6	9
S&P 500	NA**	NA	NA
Treasury Bond	2 points*	92	74
Value-Line Index	NA**	NA	NA

*Changed to 3 points since August 1987.
**No price limits until early 1988.
(A variable limit rule (150%) applies when three consecutive limit moves occur.)

level or the down limit level are reported. The original sample is screened by removing significant event dates which are also limit dates. The same testing procedure is replicated on this sample which is now free from the possible impact of limit moves. This screening procedure only affects four futures contracts. Table III(B), and III(C) present the results of these four futures contracts. First, only one of the four financial futures (Treasury Bonds) had limit moves at all in the original sample while all four exhibit price dependence. In some cases, the reaction after the event day may have been weakened by the removal of days of limit moves; however, the same statistically significant patterns of reactions still prevail as before. This implies that while the price limit rules may explain partially the underreaction in financial futures, it is not the only cause for price dependence. One more puzzling point on the impact of price limit rules is that it is inconsistent with the overreaction in agricultural futures. Even considering the possibility that limit moves may have occurred more often in financial futures markets than in agricultural futures markets, the lack of limit moves should not result in overreaction.

CONCLUSIONS

This article examines market rationality in futures pricing and, in particular, the adjustment process of futures prices subsequent to the occurrence of significant events. Using statistically significant price changes as proxies of significant events, futures price adjustments demonstrate significant deviations from the prediction of market rationality. Specifically, the evidence suggests that futures prices of agricultural commodities tend to overreact to significant events, whereas financial futures prices tend to underreact to significant events.

The fact that the price does not adjust to information instantaneously is consistent with that either all traders do not share the same information set, or they do not have the same analytical abilities. The findings of this study provide fruitful implications to regulators, exchanges, and traders. The success of a number of regulatory devices in curbing excessive volatility and speculation depends on the understanding of the nature of a mar-

Table III(B)
THE PRICE ADJUSTMENT PROCESS FOR POSITIVE EVENTS WITHOUT LIMIT MOVES

Days	COFFEE AR	Z	n = 37 CAR	CZ	T-BONDS AR	Z	n = 39 CAR	CZ
0	6.058	17.221[a]	0.000	17.221[a]	2.479	16.160[a]	0.000	16.160[a]
1	−0.889	−2.526[a]	−0.889	−2.526[a]	0.145	0.937	0.143	0.937
2	0.441	1.253	−0.448	−0.901	0.252	1.644[b]	0.396	1.825[b]
3	−0.079	−0.224	−0.527	−0.865	0.112	0.728	0.508	1.910[b]
4	0.268	0.762	−0.259	−0.368	0.157	1.024	0.665	2.166[b]
5	0.094	0.267	−0.161	−0.210	0.232	1.511[b]	0.896	2.613[a]

Days	WHEAT AR	Z	n = 18 CAR	CZ	SOYBEANS AR	Z	n = 33 CAR	CZ
0	4.202	11.158[a]	0.000	11.158[a]	3.630	15.083[a]	0.000	15.083[a]
1	−2.262	−6.007[a]	−2.262	−6.007[a]	−0.499	−2.074[b]	−0.499	−2.074[b]
2	−0.274	−0.729	−2.537	−4.763[a]	−0.110	−0.456	−0.609	−1.789[b]
3	−0.054	−0.146	−2.591	−3.971[a]	−0.349	−1.448	−0.957	−2.297[b]
4	0.292	0.775	−2.299	−3.052[a]	0.242	1.005	−0.715	−1.486
5	−0.245	−0.650	−2.544	−3.020[a]	−0.386	−1.604[b]	−1.101	−2.047[b]
6	−0.079	−0.210	−2.623	−2.843[a]	0.583	2.423[a]	−0.518	−0.879
7	−0.406	−1.076	−3.029	−3.039[a]	−0.216	−0.896	−0.734	−1.153
8	0.188	0.498	−2.841	−2.667[a]	0.407	1.692[b]	−0.327	−0.480
9	0.053	0.141	−2.788	−2.467[a]	0.247	1.028	−0.079	−0.110
10	0.400	1.061	−2.388	−2.005[b]	0.123	0.509	0.043	0.057
11	0.165	0.440	−2.222	−1.779[b]	0.114	0.472	0.157	0.196
12	−0.153	−0.407	−2.376	−1.821[b]	0.041	0.170	0.198	0.237
13	−0.269	−0.714	−2.644	−1.947[b]	−0.335	−1.474	−0.157	−0.181
14	−0.099	−0.262	−2.744	−1.947[b]	−0.293	−1.219	−0.450	−0.500
15	−0.424	−1.127	−3.168	−2.172[b]	0.119	0.494	−0.331	−0.356

n: # of Significant events.
[a]Significant at the 1% level.
[b]Significant at the 5% level.
AR: Average Residual.
Z: Test Statistic for AR.
CAR: Cumulative Average Residual.
CZ: Test Statistic for CAR.

ket's price movement. In particular, the design and the justification of margin requirements, price limit rules, and position limits rely heavily on the assumption that the futures market overreacts to information in the short run. For example, price limits will prove futile if the market price always adjusts to equilibrium instantaneously. On the other hand, frequent changes in margin requirements and position limits to control default risks of traders may mean only illiquidity and obstacles to trading if the market price tends to overreact in the short run.

The tendency of the market to overreact/underreact to significant events also suggests trading implications for traders. If the market tends to overreact to information and the price reverses in the near future, a contrarian strategy may prove profitable in the short

Table III(C)
THE PRICE ADJUSTMENT PROCESS FOR NEGATIVE EVENTS WITHOUT LIMIT MOVES

Days	COFFEE AR	Z	n = 33 CAR	CZ	T-BONDS AR	Z	n = 46 CAR	CZ
0	−6.964	−18.699[a]	0.000	−18.699[a]	−2.446	16.687[a]	0.000	−17.321[a]
1	−0.176	−0.472	−0.176	−0.472	−0.169	−1.193	−0.169	−1.193
2	0.799	2.145[a]	0.623	1.183	−0.255	−1.805[b]	−0.423	−2.120[b]
3	−0.541	1.454	1.165	1.805[b]	0.226	1.601	−0.197	−0.806
4	0.111	0.297	1.275	1.712[b]	0.290	2.055[b]	0.093	0.329
5	0.116	0.312	1.391	1.671[b]	0.272	1.926[b]	0.365	1.156

Days	WHEAT AR	Z	n = 19 CAR	CZ	SOYBEANS AR	Z	n = 37 CAR	CZ
0	−5.399	−14.727[a]	0.000	−14.727[a]	−3.655	−15.389	0.000	−15.723[a]
1	0.739	2.015[b]	0.739	2.015	0.021	0.092	0.021	0.092
2	0.139	0.380	0.878	1.694	0.128	0.563	0.149	0.463
3	0.033	0.091	0.911	1.435	0.334	1.470	0.483	1.227
4	−0.760	−2.073[b]	0.151	0.206	−0.174	−0.765	0.309	0.680
5	0.296	0.806	0.447	0.545	0.264	1.161	0.573	1.128
6	−0.0636	−0.173	0.383	0.427	0.284	1.250	0.867	1.640
7	0.372	1.014	0.755	0.778	−0.015	−0.067	0.842	1.400
8	0.270	0.737	1.025	0.989	−0.387	−1.704	0.455	0.708
9	0.319	0.869	1.344	1.222	0.195	0.859	0.650	0.953
10	0.169	0.460	1.512	1.305	−0.367	−1.615	0.283	0.394
11	0.009	0.024	1.521	1.251	−0.552	−2.427[a]	−0.269	0.394
12	−0.507	−1.384	1.014	0.798	−0.473	−2.080[b]	−0.742	−0.356
13	0.530	1.445	1.544	1.168	−0.143	−0.627	−0.884	−0.942
14	0.479	1.307	2.023	1.474	0.045	0.199	−0.888	−1.079
15	0.344	0.939	2.367	1.667	−0.109	−0.488	−0.948	−0.986

n: # of Significant events.
[a]Significant at the 1% level.
[b]Significant at the 5% level.
AR: Average Residual.
Z: Test Statistic for AR.
CAR: Cumulative Average Residual.
CZ: Test Statistic for CAR.

run. On the other hand, if the price underreacts to information, a strategy of "jumping on the bandwagon" may generate significant short-term profit.[10]

Bibliography

Box, G., and Jenkins, G. (1976): *Time Series Analysis Forecasting and Control*, San Francisco: Holden-Day.

[10]The potential of profiting from the market overreaction/underreaction identified in this study is currently under study.

Brown, K., Harlow W., and Tinic, S. (1988): "Risk Aversion, Uncertain Information, and Market Efficiency," *Journal of Financial Economics*, forthcoming.

Brown, S., and Warner, J. (1985): "Using Daily Returns," *Journal of Financial Economics*, 14:3–31.

Chan, K. C. (1988): "On the Return of the Contrarian Investment Strategy," *Journal of Business*, 61, no. 2, 147–163.

DeBondt, W. E., and Thaler, R. (1985): "Does the Stock Market Overreact?," *Journal of Finance*, 40:793–804.

DeBondt, W. E. (1987): "Further Evidence of Investor Overreaction and Stock Market Seasonality," *Journal of Finance*, 42:557–582.

DeBondt, W. E., and Makhija, A. (1988): "Throwing Good Money After Bad?: Nuclear Power Plant Investment Decisions and the Relevance of Sunk Costs," *Journal of Economic Behavior and Organization*, forthcoming.

DeLong, J., Shleifer A., Summers, L., and Waldman, R. (1987): "The Economic Consequences of Noise Traders," Working paper, Boston University and NBER.

Dornbush, R. (1976): "Expectations and Exchange Rate Dynamics," *Journal of Political Economy*, 84:1161–1176.

Dyl, E., and Maxfield, K. (1987): "Does the Market Overreact? Additional Evidence," Working paper, University of Arizona.

Fabozzi, F., Ma, C., and Linksley, D. (1988): "Overreaction, Rational Expectation, and the Relationship Between Trading Volume and Security Price Changes," *Research in Finance*, Andrew Chen, Ed., JAI Press, forthcoming.

Fama, E., and French, K. (1986): "Permanent and Temporary Components of Stock Prices," Chicago: University of Chicago xerox.

Flannery, M., and James, C. (1984): "The Effect of Interest Rate Changes on Common Stock Returns of Financial Institutions," *Journal of Finance*, 39:1141–1154.

French, K., and Roll, R. (1986): "Stock Return Variances: The Arrival of Information and the Reaction of Traders," *Journal of Financial Economics*, 17:5–26.

Gandar, J., Zuber, R., O'Brien, T., and Russo, B. (1988): "Testing Rationality in the Point Spread Betting Market," *Journal of Finance*, 43:995–1008.

Jones, S. (1987): "Reaction to the Overreaction Hypothesis," Working paper, Purdue University.

Kahneman, D., and Tversky, A. (1981): "Intuitive Prediction: Biases and Corrective Procedures," in *Judgement Under Uncertainty: Heuristics and Biases*, Kahneman, Slovic, and Tversky, Eds., Cambridge University Press.

Ma, C., Rao, R., and Sears, S. (1989): "Limit Moves and Price Resolution: The Case in Treasury Bond Futures Market," *Journal of Futures Markets*, 9:321–335.

Makhija, A., and Nachtmann, R. (1988): "Is Trading Self-Generated?: The Case of NYSE-ASE Listed Stocks," Working paper, University of Pittsburgh.

Shiller, R. (1981): "Do Stock Prices Move Too Much to be Justified by Subsequent Changes in Dividends?," *American Economic Review*, 71:421–350.

Shiller, R. (1984): "Theory of Aggregate Stock Price Movements," *Journal of Portfolio Management*, 10:28–37.

Summers, L. H. (1986): "Does the Stock Market Rationally Reflect Fundamental Values?" *Journal of Finance*, 41:591–601.

Part III
Price Distributions

[11]

THE VARIATION OF CERTAIN SPECULATIVE PRICES*

BENOIT MANDELBROT[†]

I. INTRODUCTION

THE name of Louis Bachelier is often mentioned in books on diffusion process. Until very recently, however, few people realized that his early (1900) and path-breaking contribution was the construction of a random-walk model for security and commodity markets.[1] Bachelier's simplest and most important model goes as follows: let $Z(t)$ be the price of a stock, or of a unit of a commodity, at the end of time period t. Then it is assumed that successive differences of the form $Z(t + T) - Z(t)$ are independent, Gaussian or normally distributed, random variables with zero mean and variance proportional to the differencing interval T.[2]

Despite the fundamental importance of Bachelier's process, which has come to be called "Brownian motion," it is now obvious that it does not account for the abundant data accumulated since 1900 by empirical economists, simply because *the empirical distributions of price changes are usually too "peaked" to be relative to samples from Gaussian populations.*[3] That

---

* The theory developed in this paper is a natural continuation of my study of the distribution of income. I was still working on the latter when Hendrik S. Houthakker directed my interest toward the distribution of price changes. The present model was thus suggested by Houthakker's data; it was discussed with him all along and was first publicly presented at his seminar. I therefore owe him a great debt of gratitude.

The extensive computations required by this work were performed on the 7090 computer of the I.B.M. Research Center and were mostly programmed by N. J. Anthony, R. Coren, and F. L. Zarnfaller. Many of the data which I have used were most kindly supplied by F. Lowenstein and J. Donald of the Economic Statistics section of the United States Department of Agriculture. Some stages of the present work were supported in part by the Office of Naval Research, under contract number Nonr-3775(00), NR-047040.

† Harvard University and Research Center of the International Business Machines Corporation.

[1] The materials of this paper will be included in greater detail in my book tentatively titled *Studies in Speculation, Economics, and Statistics*, to be published within a year by John Wiley and Sons.

The present text is a modified version of my "Research Note," NC-87, issued on March 26, 1962 by the Research Center of the International Business Machines Corporation. I have been careful to avoid any change in substance, but certain parts of that exposition have been clarified, and I have omitted some less essential sections, paragraphs, or sentences. Sections I and II correspond roughly to chaps. i and ii of the original, Sections III and IV correspond to chaps. iv and v, Sections V and VI, to chap. vi, and Section VII, to chap. vii.

[2] The simple Bachelier model implicitly assumes that the variance of the differences $Z(t + T) - Z(t)$ is independent of the level of $Z(t)$. There is reason to expect, however, that the standard deviation of $\Delta Z(t)$ will be proportional to the price level, and for this reason many modern authors have suggested that the original assumption of independent increments of $Z(t)$ be replaced by the assumption of independent and Gaussian increments of $\log_e Z(t)$.

Since Bachelier's original work is fairly inaccessible, it is good to mention more than one reference: "Théorie de la spéculation" (Paris Doctoral Dissertation in Mathematics, March 29, 1900) *Annales de l'Ecole Normale Supérieure*, ser. 3, XVII (1900), 21–86; "Théorie mathématique du jeu," *Annales de l'Ecole Normale Supérieure*, ser. 3, XVIII (1901), 143–210; *Calcul des probabilités* (Paris: Gauthier-Villars, 1912); *Le jeu, la chance et le hasard* (Paris, 1914 [reprinted up to 1929 at least]).

[3] To the best of my knowledge, the first to note this fact was Wesley C. Mitchell, "The Making and Using of Index Numbers," Introduction to *Index Numbers and Wholesale Prices in the United States and Foreign Countries* (published in 1915 as Bulletin No. 173 of the U.S. Bureau of Labor Statistics, reprinted in 1921 as Bulletin No. 284). But unquestionable proof was only given by Maurice Olivier in "Les Nombres indices de la variation des prix" (Paris doctoral dissertation, 1926), and Frederick C. Mills in *The Behavior of Prices* (New York: National Bureau of Economic Research, 1927). Other evi-

is, the histograms of price changes are indeed unimodal and their central "bells" remind one of the "Gaussian ogive." But there are typically so many "outliers" that ogives fitted to the mean square of price changes are much lower and flatter than the distribution of the data themselves (see, e.g., Fig. 1). The tails of the distributions of price changes are in fact so extraordinarily long that the sample second moments typically vary in an erratic fashion. For example, the second moment reproduced in Figure 2 does not seem to tend to any limit even though the sample size is enormous by economic standards, and even though the series to which it applies is presumably stationary.

It is my opinion that these facts warrant a radically new approach to the problem of price variation.[4] The purpose of this paper will be to present and test such a new model of price behavior in speculative markets. The principal feature of this model is that starting from the Bachelier process as applied to log. $Z(t)$ instead of $Z(t)$, I shall replace the Gaussian distributions throughout by another family of probability laws, to be referred to as "stable Paretian," which were first described in Paul Lévy's classic

---

dence, referring either to $Z(t)$ or to $\log_e Z(t)$ and plotted on various kinds of coordinates, can be found in Arnold Larson, "Measurement of a Random Process in Future Prices," *Food Research Institute Studies*, I (1960), 313-24; M. F. M. Osborne, "Brownian Motion in the Stock Market," *Operations Research*, VII (1959), 145-73, 807-11; S. S. Alexander, "Price Movements in Speculative Markets: Trends of Random Walks?" *Industrial Management Review of M.I.T.*, II, pt. 2 (1961), 7-26.

[4] Such an approach has also been necessary—and successful—in other contexts; for background information and many additional explanations see my "New Methods in Statistical Economics," *Journal of Political Economy*, Vol. LXXI (October, 1963).

I believe, however, that each of the applications should stand on thèir own feet and have minimized the number of cross references.

Calcul des probabilités (1925). In a somewhat complex way, the Gaussian is a limiting case of this new family, so the new model is actually a generalization of that of Bachelier.

Since the stable Paretian probability laws are relatively unknown, I shall begin with a discussion of some of the more

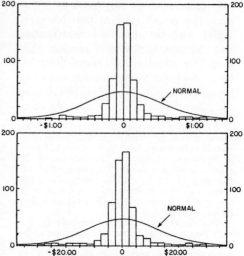

FIG. 1.—Two histograms illustrating departure from normality of the fifth and tenth difference of monthly wool prices, 1890-1937. In each case, the continuous bell-shaped curve represents the Gaussian "interpolate" based upon the sample variance. Source: Gerhard Tintner, *The Variate-Difference Method* (Bloomington, Ind., 1940).

important mathematical properties of these laws. Following this, the results of empirical tests of the stable Paretian model will be examined. The remaining sections of the paper will then be devoted to a discussion of some of the more sophisticated mathematical and descriptive properties of the stable Paretian model. I shall, in particular, examine its bearing on the very possibility of implementing the stop-loss rules of speculation (Section VI).

II. MATHEMATICAL TOOLS: PAUL LEVY'S STABLE PARETIAN LAWS

A. PROPERTY OF "STABILITY" OF THE GAUSSIAN LAW AND ITS GENERALIZATION

One of the principal attractions of the modified Bachelier process is that the logarithmic relative

$$L(t, T) = \log_e Z(t + T) - \log_e Z(t)$$

is a Gaussian random variable for *every* value of T; the only thing that changes with T is the standard deviation of $L(t, T)$. This feature is the consequence of the following fact:

Let G' and G'' be two independent Gaussian random variables, of zero means and of mean squares respectively equal to σ'^2 and σ''^2. Then, the sum $G' + G''$ is also a Gaussian variable, of mean square equal to $\sigma'^2 + \sigma''^2$. In particular, the "reduced" Gaussian variable, with zero mean and unit mean square, is a solution to

(S) $\qquad s'U + s''U = sU$,

where s *is a function of* s' *and* s'' *given by the auxiliary relation*

(A$_2$) $\qquad s^2 = s'^2 + s''^2$.

It should be stressed that, from the viewpoint of equation (S) and relation (A$_2$), the quantities s', s'', and s are simply scale factors that "happen" to be closely related to the root-mean-square in the Gaussian case.

The property (S) expresses a kind of stability or invariance under addition, which is so fundamental in probability theory that it came to be referred to simply as "stability." The Gaussian is the only solution of equation (S) for which the second moment is finite—or for which the relation (A$_2$) is satisfied. When the variance is allowed to be infinite, however, (S) possesses many other solutions. This was shown constructively by Cauchy, who considered the random variable U for which

$$Pr(U > u) = Pr(U < -u)$$
$$= \tfrac{1}{2} - (1/\pi) \tan^{-1}(u) ,$$

so that its density is of the form

$$dPr(U < u) = [\pi(1 + u^2)]^{-1} .$$

For this law, integral moments of all orders are infinite, and the auxiliary relation takes the form

(A$_1$) $\qquad s = s' + s''$,

where the scale factors s', s'', and s are not defined by any moment.

As to the general solution of equation

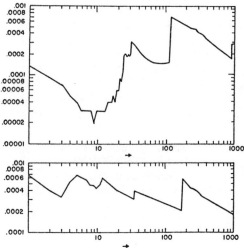

Fig. 2.—Both graphs are relative to the sequential sample second moment of cotton price changes. Horizontal scale represents time in days, with two different origins $T°$: on the upper graph, $T°$ was September 21, 1900; on the lower graph $T°$ was August 1, 1900. Vertical lines represent the value of the function

$$(T - T°)^{-1} \sum_{t=T°}^{t=T} [L(t,1)]^2 ,$$

where $L(t, 1) = \log_e Z(t + 1) - \log_e Z(t)$ and $Z(t)$ is the closing spot price of cotton on day t, as privately reported by the United States Department of Agriculture.

(S), discovered by Paul Lévy,[5] the logarithm of its characteristic function takes the form

(PL) $\log \int_{-\infty}^{\infty} \exp(iuz)\,dPr(U<u) = i\delta z$
$- \gamma |z|^a [1 + i\beta(z/|z|)\tan(a\pi/2)]$,

It is clear that the Gaussian law and the law of Cauchy are stable and that they correspond to the cases ($a = 2$) and ($a = 1; \beta = 0$), respectively.

Equation (PL) determines a family of distribution and density functions $Pr(U < u)$ and $dPr(U < u)$ that depend continuously upon four parameters which also happen to play the roles usually associated with the first four moments of U, as, for example, in Karl Pearson's classification.

First of all, the a is an index of "peakedness" that varies from 0 (excluded) to 2 (included); if $a = 1$, β must vanish. This a will turn out to be intimately related to Pareto's exponent. The β is an index of "skewness" that can vary from -1 to $+1$. If $\beta = 0$, the stable densities are symmetric.

One can say that a and β together determine the "type" of a stable random variable, and such a variable can be called "reduced" if $\gamma = 1$ and $\delta = 0$. It is easy to see that, if U is reduced, sU is a stable variable having the same values for a, β and δ and having a value of γ equal to s^a: this means that the third parameter, γ, is a scale factor raised to the power a. Suppose now that U' and U'' are two independent stable variables, reduced and having the same values for a and β; since the characteristic function

[5] Paul Lévy, *Calcul des probabilités* (Paris: Gauthier-Villars, 1925); Paul Lévy, *Théorie de l'addition des variables aléatoires* (Paris: Gauthier-Villars, 1937 [2d ed., 1954]). The most accessible source on these problems is, however, B. V. Gnedenko and A. N. Kolmogoroff, *Limit Distributions for Sums of Independent Random Variables*, trans. K. L. Chung (Reading, Mass.: Addison-Wesley Press, 1954).

of $s'U' + s''U''$ is the product of those of $s'U'$ and of $s''U''$, the equation (S) is readily seen to be accompanied by the auxiliary relation

(A) $\qquad s^a = s'^a + s''^a$.

If on the contrary U' and U'' are stable with the same values of a, β and of $\delta = 0$, but with different values of γ (respectively, γ' and γ''), the sum $U' + U''$ is stable with the parameters a, β, $\gamma = \gamma' + \gamma''$ and $\delta = 0$. Thus the familiar additivity property of the Gaussian "variance" (defined by a mean-square) is now played by either γ or by a scale factor raised to the power a.

The final parameter of (PL) is δ; strictly speaking, equation (S) requires that $\delta = 0$, but we have added the term $i\delta z$ to (PL) in order to introduce a location parameter. If $1 < a \leq 2$ so that $E(U)$ is finite, one has $\delta = E(U)$; if $\beta = 0$ so that the stable variable has a symmetric density function, δ is the median or modal value of U; but δ has no obvious interpretation when $0 < a < 1$ with $\beta \neq 0$.

B. ADDITION OF MORE THAN TWO STABLE RANDOM VARIABLES

Let the independent variables U_n satisfy the condition (PL) with values of a, β, γ, and δ equal for all n. Then, the logarithm of the characteristic function of

$S_N = U_1 + U_2 + \ldots U_n + \ldots U_N$

is N times the logarithm of the characteristic function of U_n, and it equals

$i\delta Nz - N\gamma|z|^a [1 + i\beta(z/|z|)\tan(a\pi/2)]$,

so that S_N is stable with the same a and β as U_n, and with parameters δ and γ multiplied by N. It readily follows that

$U_n - \delta$ and $N^{-1/a} \sum_{n=1}^{N} (U_n - \delta)$

have identical characteristic functions and thus are identically distributed random variables. (This is, of course, a most familiar fact in the Gaussian case, $\alpha = 2$.)

The generalization of the classical "$T^{1/2}$ Law."—In the Gaussian model of Bachelier, in which daily increments of $Z(t)$ are Gaussian with the standard deviation $\sigma(1)$, the standard deviation of the change of $Z(t)$ over T days is equal to $\sigma(T) = T^{1/2} \sigma(1)$.

The corresponding prediction of my model is the following: consider any scale factor such as the intersextile range, that is, the difference between the quantity U^+ which is exceeded by one-sixth of the data, and the quantity U^- which is larger than one-sixth of the data. It is easy to find that the expected range satisfies

$$E[U^+(T) - U^-(T)] = T^{1/\alpha} E[U^+(1) - U^-(1)].$$

We should also expect that the deviations from these expectations exceed those observed in the Gaussian case.

Differences between successive means of $Z(t)$.—In all cases, the average of $Z(t)$ over the time span $t^0 + 1$ to $t^0 + N$ can then be written as

$$(1/N) [Z(t^0 + 1) + Z(t^0 + 2) + \ldots$$
$$Z(t^0 + N)] = (1/N) \{ N Z(t^0 + 1)$$
$$+ (N - 1) [Z(t^0 + 2) - Z(t^0 + 1)] + \ldots$$
$$+ (N - n) [Z(t^0 + n + 1) - Z(t^0 + n)]$$
$$+ \ldots [Z(t^0 + N) - Z(t^0 + N - 1)]\}.$$

On the contrary, let the average over the time span $t^0 - N - 1$ to t^0 be written as

$$(1/N) \{N Z(t^0) - (N - 1) [Z(t^0) - Z(t^0 - 1)] - \ldots - (N - n) [Z(t^0 - n + 1)$$
$$- Z(t^0 - n)] - \ldots [Z(t^0 - N + 2)$$
$$- Z(t^0 - N + 1)]\}.$$

Thus, if the expression $Z(t + 1) - Z(t)$ is a stable variable $U(t)$ with $\delta = 0$, the difference between successive means of values of Z is given by

$$U(t^0) + [(N - 1)/N] [U(t^0 + 1)$$
$$+ U(t^0 - 1)] + [(N - n)/N] [U(t^0 + n)$$
$$+ U(t^0 - n)] + \ldots [U(t^0 + N - 1)$$
$$+ U(t^0 - N + 1)].$$

This is clearly a stable variable, with the same α and β as the original U, and with a scale parameter equal to

$$\gamma^0(N) = [1 + 2(N - 1)^\alpha N^{-\alpha} + \ldots$$
$$2(N - n)^\alpha N^{-\alpha} + \ldots + 2] \gamma(U).$$

As $N \to \infty$, one has

$$\gamma^0(N)/\gamma(U) \to 2N/(\alpha + 1),$$

whereas a genuine monthly change of $Z(t)$ has a parameter $\gamma(N) = N\gamma(U)$; thus the effect of averaging is to multiply γ by the expression $2/(\alpha + 1)$, which is smaller than 1 if $\alpha > 1$.

C. STABLE DISTRIBUTIONS AND THE LAW OF PARETO

Except for the Gaussian limit case, the densities of the stable random variables follow a generalization of the asymptotic behavior of the Cauchy law. It is clear for example that, as $u \to \infty$, the Cauchy density behaves as follows:

$$u \, Pr(U > u) = u \, Pr(U < -u) \to 1/\pi.$$

More generally, Lévy has shown that the tails of *all* non-Gaussian stable laws follow an asymptotic form of the law of Pareto, in the sense that there exist two constants $C' = \sigma'^\alpha$ and $C'' = \sigma''^\alpha$, linked by $\beta = (C' - C'')/(C' + C'')$, such that, when $u \to \infty$, $u^\alpha Pr(U > u) \to C' = \sigma'^\alpha$ and $u^\alpha Pr(U < -u) \to C'' = \sigma''^\alpha$.

Hence *both* tails are Paretian if $|\beta| \neq 1$, a solid reason for replacing the term "stable non-Gaussian" by the less negative one of *"stable Paretian."* The two numbers σ' and σ'' share the role of the standard deviation of a Gaussian variable and will be designated as the "standard positive deviation" and the "standard negative deviation."

In the extreme cases where $\beta = 1$ and hence $C'' = 0$ (respectively, where $\beta = -1$ and $C' = 0$), the negative tail (respectively, the positive tail) decreases faster than the law of Pareto of index a. In fact, one can prove[6] that it withers away even faster than the Gaussian density so that the extreme cases of stable laws are practically J-shaped. They play an important role in my theory of the distributions of personal income or of city sizes. A number of further properties of stable laws may therefore be found in my publications devoted to these topics.[7]

D. STABLE VARIABLES AS THE ONLY POSSIBLE LIMITS OF WEIGHTED SUMS OF INDEPENDENT IDENTICALLY DISTRIBUTED ADDENDS

The stability of the Gaussian law may be considered as being only a matter of convenience, and it is often thought that the following property is more important.

Let the U_n be independent, identically distributed, random variables, with a finite $\sigma^2 = E[U_n - E(U)]^2$. Then the classical central limit theorem asserts that

[6] A. V. Skorohod, "Asymptotic Formulas for Stable Distribution Laws," *Dokl. Ak. Nauk SSSR*, XCVIII (1954), 731–35, or *Select. Tranl. Math. Stat. Proba. Am. Math. Soc.* (1961), pp. 157–61.

[7] Benoit Mandelbrot, "The Pareto-Lévy Law and the Distribution of Income," *International Economic Review*, I (1960), 79–106, as amended in "The Stable Paretian Income Distribution, When the Apparent Exponent Is near Two," *International Economic Review*, IV (1963), 111–15; see also my "Stable Paretian Random Functions and the Multiplicative Variation of Income," *Econometrica*, XXIX (1961), 517–43, and "Paretian Distributions and Income Maximization," *Quarterly Journal of Economics*, LXXVI (1962), 57–85.

$$\lim_{N \to \infty} N^{-1/2} \sigma^{-1} \cdot \sum_{n=1}^{N} [U_n - E(U)]$$

is a reduced Gaussian variable.

This result is of course the basis of the explanation of the presumed occurrence of the Gaussian law in many practical applications relative to sums of a variety of random effects. But the essential thing in all these aggregative arguments is not that $\Sigma[U_n - E(U)]$ is weighted by any special factor, such as $N^{-1/2}$, but rather that the following is true:

There exist two functions, $A(N)$ *and* $B(N)$, *such that, as* $N \to \infty$, *the weighted sum*

(L) $$A(N) \sum_{n=1}^{N} U_n - B(N)$$

has a limit that is finite and is not reduced to a non-random constant.

If the variance of U_n is not finite, however, condition (L) may remain satisfied while the limit ceases to be Gaussian. For example, if U_n is stable non-Gaussian, the linearly weighted sum

$$N^{-1/a} \Sigma (U_n - \delta)$$

was seen to be *identical in law* to U_n, so that the "limit" of that expression is already attained for $N = 1$ and is a stable non-Gaussian law. Let us now suppose that U_n is asymptotically Paretian with $0 < a < 2$, but not stable; one can show that the limit exists in a real sense, and that it is the stable Paretian law having the same value of a. Again the function $A(N)$ can be chosen equal to $N^{-1/a}$. These results are crucial but I had better not attempt to rederive them here. There is little sense in copying the readily available full mathematical arguments, and experience shows that what was intended to be an illuminating heuristic explanation often looks like another instance in which far-reaching conclusions are based on loose thoughts. Let me therefore just quote the facts:

The problem of the existence of a limit for $A(N)\Sigma U_n - B(N)$ can be solved by introducing the following generalization of the asymptotic law of Pareto:[8]

The conditions of Pareto-Doeblin-Gnedenko.—Introduce the notations

$$Pr(U > u) = Q'(u)u^{-a};$$

$$Pr(U < -u) = Q''(u)u^{-a}.$$

The conditions of P-D-G require that (a) *when* $u \to \infty$, $Q'(u)/Q''(u)$ *tends to a limit* C'/C'', (b) *there exists a value of* $a > 0$ *such that for every* $k > 0$, *and for* $u \to \infty$, *one has*

$$\frac{Q'(u) + Q''(u)}{Q'(ku) + Q''(ku)} \to 1.$$

These conditions generalize the law of Pareto, for which $Q'(u)$ and $Q''(u)$ themselves tend to limits as $u \to \infty$. With their help, and unless $a = 1$, the problem of the existence of weighting factors $A(N)$ and $B(N)$ is solved by the following theorem:

If the U_n *are independent, identically distributed random variables, there may exist no functions* $A(N)$ *and* $B(N)$ *such that* $A(N) \Sigma U_n - B(N)$ *tends to a proper limit. But, if such functions* $A(N)$ *and* $B(N)$ *exist, one knows that the limit is one of the solutions of the stability equation* (S). *More precisely, the limit is Gaussian if and only if the* U_n *has finite variance; the limit is stable non-Gaussian if and only if the conditions of Pareto-Doeblin-Gnedenko are satisfied for some* $0 < a < 2$. *Then* $\beta = (C' - C'')/(C' + C'')$ *and* $A(N)$ *is determined by the requirement that*

$$N Pr[U > u A^{-1}(N)] \to C'u^{-a}.$$

[8] See Gnedenko and Kolmogoroff, *op. cit.*, n. 4, p. 175, who use a notation that does not emphasize, as I hope to do, the relation between the law of Pareto and its present generalization.

(Whichever the value of a, the P-D-G condition (b) also plays a central role in the study of the distribution of the random variable max U_n.)

As an application of the above definition and theorem, let us examine the product of two independent, identically distributed Paretian (but not stable) variables U' and U''. First of all, for $u > 0$, one can write

$$Pr(U'U'' > u) = Pr(U' > 0; \quad U'' > 0$$

and $\log U' + \log U'' > \log u)$

$$+ Pr(U' < 0; \quad U'' < 0 \text{ and}$$

$$\log |U'| + \log |U''| > \log u).$$

But it follows from the law of Pareto that

$$Pr(U > e^z) \sim C' \exp(-az) \text{ and}$$

$$Pr(U < -e^z) \sim C'' \exp(-az),$$

where U is either U' or U''. Hence, the two terms P' and P'' that add up to $Pr(U'U'' > u)$ satisfy

$$P' \sim C'^2 az \exp(-az) \quad \text{and}$$

$$P'' \sim C''^2 az \exp(-az).$$

Therefore

$$Pr(U'U'' > u) \sim a(C'^2 + C''^2)(\log_e u) u^{-a}.$$

Similarly

$$Pr(U'U'' < -u) \sim a2C'C'' (\log_e u) u^{-a}.$$

It is obvious that the Pareto-Doeblin-Gnedenko conditions are satisfied for the functions $Q'(u) \sim (C'^2 + C''^2)a \log_e u$ and $Q''(u) \sim 2C'C''a \log_e u$. Hence the weighted expression

$$(N \log N)^{-1/a} \sum_{n=1}^{N} U'_n U''_n$$

converges toward a stable Paretian limit with the exponent a and the skewness

$$\beta = (C'^2 + C''^2 - 2C'C'')/(C'^2 + C''^2 + 2C'C'') = [(C' - C'')/(C' + C'')]^2 \geq 0.$$

In particular, the positive tail should always be bigger than the negative.

E. SHAPE OF STABLE PARETIAN DISTRIBUTIONS OUTSIDE ASYMPTOTIC RANGE

The result of Section IIC should not hide the fact that the asymptotic behavior is seldom the main thing in the applications. For example, if the sample size is N, the orders of magnitude of the largest and smallest item are given by

$$N \, Pr[U > u^+(N)] = 1,$$

and

$$N \, Pr[U < -u^-(N)] = 1,$$

and the interesting values of u lie between $-u^-$ and u^+. Unfortunately, except in the cases of Gauss and of Cauchy and the case ($\alpha = \frac{1}{2}; \beta = 1$), there are no known closed expressions for the stable densities and the theory only says the following: (a) the densities are always unimodal; (b) the densities depend continuously upon the parameters; (c) if $\beta > 0$, the positive tail is the fatter—hence, if the mean is finite (i.e., if $1 < \alpha < 2$), it is greater than the most probable value and greater than the median.

To go further, I had to resort to numerical calculations. Let us, however, begin by interpolative arguments.

The symmetric cases, $\beta = 0$.—For $\alpha = 1$, one has the Cauchy law, whose density $[\pi(1 + u^2)]^{-1}$ is always *smaller* than the Paretian density $1/\pi u^2$ toward which it tends in relative value as $u \to \infty$. Therefore,

$$Pr \, (U > u) < 1/\pi \, u,$$

and it follows that for $\alpha = 1$ the doubly logarithmic graph of $\log_e [Pr(U > u)]$ is entirely on the left side of its straight asymptote. By continuity, the same shape must apply when α is only a little higher or a little lower than 1.

For $\alpha = 2$, the doubly logarithmic graph of the Gaussian $\log_e [Pr(U > u)]$ drops down very fast to negligible values.

Hence, again by continuity, the graph for $\alpha = 2 - \epsilon$ must also begin by a rapid decrease. But, since its ultimate slope is close to 2, it must have a point of inflection corresponding to a maximum slope greater than 2, and it must begin by "overshooting" its straight asymptote.

Interpolating between 1 and 2, we see that there exists a smallest value of α, say α^0, for which the doubly logarithmic graph begins by overshooting its asymptote. In the neighborhood of α^0, the asymptotic α can be measured as a slope even if the sample is small. If $\alpha < \alpha^0$, the asymptotic slope will be underestimated by the slope of small samples; for $\alpha > \alpha^0$ it will be overestimated. The numerical evaluation of the densities yields a value of α^0 in the neighborhood of 1.5. A graphical presentation of the results of this section is given in Figure 3.

The skew cases.—If the positive tail is fatter than the negative one, it may well happen that its doubly logarithmic graph begins by overshooting its asymptote, while the doubly logarithmic graph of the negative tail does not. Hence, there are two critical values of α^0, one for each tail; if the skewness is slight, α is between the critical values and the sample size is not large enough, the graphs of the two tails will have slightly different over-all apparent slopes.

F. JOINT DISTRIBUTION OF INDEPENDENT STABLE PARETIAN VARIABLES

Let $p_1(u_1)$ and $p_2(u_2)$ be the densities of U_1 and of U_2. If both u_1 and u_2 are large, the joint probability density is given by

$$p^0(u_1, u_2) = \alpha C_1' u_1^{-(\alpha+1)} \alpha C_2' u_2^{-(\alpha+1)}$$
$$= \alpha^2 C_1' C_2' (u_1 u_2)^{-(\alpha+1)}.$$

Hence, the lines of equal probability are portions of the hyperbolas

$$u_1 u_2 = \text{constant}.$$

In the regions where either U_1 or U_2 is large (but not both), these bits of hyperbolas are linked together as in Figure 4. That is, the isolines of small probability have a characteristic "plus-sign" shape. On the contrary, when both U_1 and U_2 are small, $\log_e p_1(u_1)$ and $\log_e p_2(u_2)$ are near their maxima and therefore can be locally approximated by $a_1 - (u_1/b_1)^2$ and $a_2 - (u_2/b_2)^2$. Hence, the probability isolines are ellipses of the form

$$(u_1/b_1)^2 + (u_2/b_2)^2 = \text{constant}.$$

The transition between the ellipses and the "plus signs" is, of course, continuous.

G. DISTRIBUTION OF U_1, WHEN U_1 AND U_2 ARE INDEPENDENT STABLE PARETIAN VARIABLES AND $U_1 + U_2 = U$ IS KNOWN

This conditional distribution can be obtained as the intersection between the surface that represents the joint density $p^0(u_1, u_2)$ and the plane $u_1 + u_2 = u$. Hence the conditional distribution is unimodal for small u. For large u, it has two sharply distinct maxima located near $u_1 = 0$ and near $u_2 = 0$.

More precisely, the conditional density of U_1 is given by $p_1(u_1)p_2(u - u_1)/q(u)$, where $q(u)$ is the density of $U = U_1 + U_2$. Let u be positive and very large; if u_1 is small, one can use the Paretian approximations for $p_2(u_2)$ and $q(u)$, obtaining

$$p_1(u_1)p_2(u - u_1)/q(u)$$
$$\sim [C_1'/(C_1' + C_2')]p_1(u_1).$$

If u_2 is small, one similarly obtains

$$p_1(u_1)p_2(u - u_1)/q(u)$$
$$\sim [C_2'/C_1' + C_2')]p_2(u - u_1).$$

In other words, the conditional density $p_1(u_1)p_2(u - u_1)/q(u)$ looks as if two unconditioned distributions scaled down in the ratios $C_1'/(C_1' + C_2')$ and $C_2'/(C_1' + C_2')$ had been placed near $u_1 = 0$ and $u_1 = u$. If u is negative but $|u|$ is very large, a similar result holds with C_1'' and C_2'' replacing C_1' and C_2'.

For example, for $\alpha = 2 - \epsilon$ and $C_1' = C_2'$, the conditioned distribution is made up of two almost Gaussian bells, scaled down to one-half of their height. But, as α tends toward 2, these two bells become

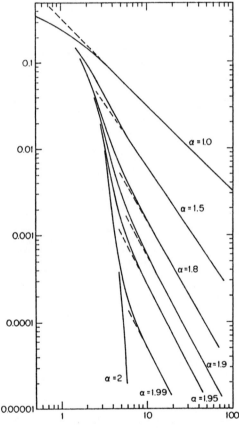

FIG. 3.—The various lines are doubly logarithmic plots of the symmetric stable Paretian probability distributions with $\delta = 0$, $\gamma = 1$, $\beta = 0$ and various values of α. Horizontally, $\log_e u$; vertically, $\log_e \Pr(U > u) = \log_e \Pr(U < -u)$. Sources: unpublished tables based upon numerical computations performed at the author's request by the I.B.M. Research Center.

smaller and a third bell appears near $u_1 = u/2$. Ultimately, the two side bells vanish and one is left with a central bell which corresponds to the fact that when the sum $U_1 + U_2$ is known, the conditional distribution of a Gaussian U_1 is itself Gaussian.

III. EMPIRICAL TESTS OF THE STABLE PARETIAN LAWS: COTTON PRICES

This section will have two main goals. First, from the viewpoint of statistical economics, its purpose is to motivate and develop a model of the variation of speculative prices based on the stable Paretian laws discussed in the previous section. Second, from the viewpoint of statistics considered as the theory of data analysis, I shall use the theorems concerning the sums ΣU_n to build a new test of the law of Pareto. Before moving on to the main points of the section, however, let us examine two alternative ways of treating the excessive numbers of large price changes usually observed in the data.

A. EXPLANATION OF LARGE PRICE CHANGES BY CAUSAL OR RANDOM "CONTAMINATORS"

One very common approach is to note that, a posteriori, large price changes are usually traceable to well-determined "causes" that should be eliminated before one attempts a stochastic model of the remainder. Such preliminary censorship obviously brings any distribution closer to the Gaussian. This is, for example, what happens when one restricts himself to the study of "quiet periods" of price change. There need not be any observable discontinuity between the "outliers" and the rest of the distribution, however, and the above censorship is therefore usually undeterminate.

Another popular and classical procedure assumes that observations are generated by a mixture of two normal distributions, one of which has a small weight but a large variance and is considered as a random "contaminator." In order to explain the sample behavior of the moments, it unfortunately becomes necessary to introduce a larger number of contaminators, and the simplicity of the model is destroyed.

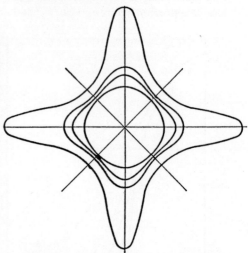

Fig. 4.—Joint distribution of successive price relatives $L(t, 1)$ and $L(t + 1, 1)$ under two alternative models. If $L(t, 1)$ and $L(t + 1, 1)$ are independent, they should be plotted along the horizontal and vertical coordinate axes. If $L(t, 1)$ and $L(t + 1, 1)$ are linked by the model in Section VII, they should be plotted along the bisectrixes, or else the above figure should be rotated by 45° before $L(t, 1)$ and $L(t + 1, 1)$ are plotted along the coordinate axes.

B. INTRODUCTION OF THE LAW OF PARETO TO REPRESENT PRICE CHANGES

I propose to explain the erratic behavior of sample moments by assuming that the population moments are infinite, an approach that I have used with success in a number of other applications and which I have explained and demonstrated in detail elsewhere.

This hypothesis amounts practically to the law of Pareto. Let us indeed assume that the increment

$$L(t, 1) = \log_e Z(t + 1) - \log_e Z(t)$$

is a random variable with infinite population moments beyond the first. This implies that its density $p(u)$ is such that $\int p(u) \, u^2 du$ diverges but $\int p(u) \, u du$ converges (the integrals being taken all the way to infinity). It is of course natural, at least in the first stage of heuristic motivating argument, to assume that $p(u)$ is somehow "well behaved" for large u; if so, our two requirements mean that as $u \to \infty$, $p(u)u^3$ tends to infinity and $p(u)u^2$ tends to zero.

In words: $p(u)$ must somehow decrease faster than u^{-2} and slower than u^{-3}. From the analytical viewpoint, the simplest expressions of this type are those with an asymptotically Paretian behavior. *This was the first motivation of the present study.* It is surprising that I could find no record of earlier application of the law of Pareto to two-tailed phenomena.

My further motivation was more theoretical. Granted that the facts impose a revision of Bachelier's process, it would be simple indeed if one could at least preserve the convenient feature of the Gaussian model that the various increments,

$$L(t, T) = \log_e Z(t + T) - \log_e Z(t),$$

depend upon T only to the extent of having different scale parameters. From all other viewpoints, price increments over days, weeks, months, and years would have the same distribution, which would also rule the fixed-base relatives. This naturally leads directly to the probabilists' concept of stability examined in Section II.

In other terms, the facts concerning moments, together with a desire to have a simple representation, suggested a check as to whether the logarithmic price relatives for unsmoothed and unprocessed time series relative to very active speculative markets are stable Paretian. Cotton provided a good example, and the present paper will be limited to the examination of that case. I have, however, also established that my theory applies to many other commodities (such as wheat and other edible grains), to many securities (such as those of the railroads in their nineteenth-century heyday), and to interest rates such as those of call or time money.[9] On the other hand, there are unquestionably many economic phenomena for which much fewer "outliers" are observed, even though the available series are very long; it is natural in these cases to favor Bachelier's Gaussian model—known to be a limiting case in my theory as well as its prototype. I must, however, postpone a discussion of the limits of validity of my approach to the study of prices.

C. PARETO'S GRAPHICAL METHOD APPLIED TO COTTON-PRICE CHANGES

Let us begin by examining in Figure 5 the doubly logarithmic graphs of various kinds of cotton price changes as if they were independent of each other. The theoretical $\log Pr(U > u)$, relative to $\delta = 0$, $\alpha = 1.7$, and $\beta = 0$, is plotted (*solid curve*) on the same graph for comparison. If the various cotton prices followed the stable Paretian law with $\delta = 0$, $\alpha = 1.7$ and $\beta = 0$, the various graphs should be horizontal translates of each other, and a cursory examination shows that the data are in close conformity with the predictions of my model. A closer examination suggests that the positive tails contain systematically fewer data than the negative tails, sug-

[9] These examples were mentioned in my 1962 "Research Note" (*op. cit.*, n. 1). My presentation, however, was too sketchy and could not be improved upon without modification of the substance of that "Note" as well as its form. I prefer to postpone examination of all the other examples as well as the search for the point at which my model of cotton prices ceases to predict the facts correctly. Both will be taken up in my forthcoming book (*op. cit.*, n. 1).

gesting that β actually takes a small negative value. This is also confirmed by the fact that the negative tails alone begin by slightly "overshooting" their asymptotes, creating the bulge that should be expected when a is greater than the critical value a° relative to one tail but not to the other.

D. APPLICATION OF THE GRAPHICAL METHOD TO THE STUDY OF CHANGES IN THE DISTRIBUTION ACROSS TIME

Let us now look more closely at the labels of the various series examined in the previous section. Two of the graphs refer to daily changes of cotton prices, near 1900 and near 1950, respectively. It is clear that these graphs do not coincide but are horizontal translates of each other. This implies that between 1900 and 1950 the generating process has changed only to the extent that its scale γ has become much smaller.

Our next test will be relative to monthly price changes over a longer time span. It would be best to examine the actual changes between, say, the middle of one

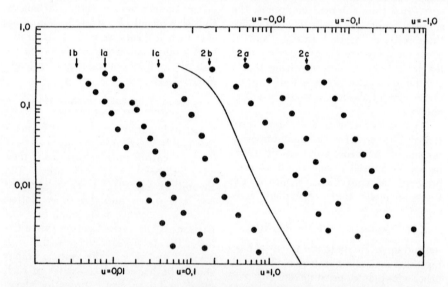

Fig. 5.—Composite of doubly logarithmic graphs of positive and negative tails for three kinds of cotton price relatives, together with cumulated density function of a stable distribution. Horizontal scale u of lines $1a$, $1b$, and $1c$ is marked only on lower edge, and horizontal scale u of lines $2a$, $2b$, and $2c$ is marked along upper edge. Vertical scale gives the following relative frequencies: ($1a$) $Fr[\log_e Z(t + \text{one day}) - \log_e Z(t) > u]$, ($2a$) $Fr[\log_e Z(t + \text{one day}) - \log_e Z(t) < -u]$, both for the daily closing prices of cotton in New York, 1900–1905 (source: private communication from the United States Department of Agriculture).

($1b$) $Fr[\log_e Z(t + \text{one day}) - \log_e Z(t) > u]$, ($2b$) $Fr[\log_e Z(t + \text{one day}) - \log_e Z(t) < -u]$, both for an index of daily closing prices of cotton in the United States, 1944–58 (source: private communication from Hendrik S. Houthakker).

($1c$) $Fr[\log_e Z(t + \text{one month}) - \log_e Z(t) > u]$, ($2c$) $Fr[\log_e Z(t + \text{one month}) - \log_e Z(t) < -u]$, both for the closing prices of cotton on the 15th of each month in New York, 1880–1940 (source: private communication from the United States Department of Agriculture).

The reader is advised to copy on a transparency the horizontal axis and the theoretical distribution and to move both horizontally until the theoretical curve is superimposed on either of the empirical graphs; the only discrepancy is observed for line $2b$; it is slight and would imply an even greater departure from normality.

month to the middle of the next. A longer sample is available, however, when one takes the reported monthly averages of the price of cotton; the graphs of Figure 6 were obtained in this way.

If cotton prices were indeed generated by a stationary stochastic process, our graphs should be straight, parallel, and uniformly spaced. However, each of the 15-year subsamples contains only 200-odd months, so that the separate graphs cannot be expected to be as straight as those relative to our usual samples of 1,000-odd items. The graphs of Figure 6 are, indeed, not quite as neat as those relating to longer periods; but, in the absence of accurate statistical tests, they seem adequately straight and uniformly spaced, except for the period 1880–96.

I conjecture therefore that, since 1816, the process generating cotton prices has changed only in its scale, with the possible exception of the Civil War and of the periods of controlled or supported prices. Long series of monthly price changes should therefore be represented by *mixtures* of stable Paretian laws; such mixtures remain Paretian.[10]

E. APPLICATION OF THE GRAPHICAL METHOD TO STUDY EFFECTS OF AVERAGING

It is, of course, possible to derive mathematically the expected distribution of the changes between successive monthly means of the highest and lowest quotation; but the result is so cumbersome as to be useless. I have, however, ascertained that the empirical distribution of these changes does not differ significantly from the distribution of the changes between the monthly means obtained by averaging all the daily closing quotations within months; one may therefore speak of a single average price for each month.

[10] See my "New Methods in Statistical Economics," *Journal of Political Economy*, October, 1963.

We then see on Figure 7 that the greater part of the distribution of the averages differs from that of actual monthly changes by a horizontal translation to the left, as predicted in Section IIC (actually, in order to apply the argument of that section, it would be necessary to rephrase it by replacing $Z(t)$ by $\log_e Z(t)$ throughout; however, the geometric and arithmetic averages of daily $Z(t)$ do not differ much in the case of medium-sized over-all monthly changes of $Z(t)$).

However, the largest changes between successive averages are smaller than predicted. This seems to suggest that the dependence between successive daily changes has less effect upon actual monthly changes than upon the regularity with which these changes are performed.

F. A NEW PRESENTATION OF THE EVIDENCE

Let me now show that my evidence concerning daily changes of cotton price strengthens my evidence concerning monthly changes and conversely.

The basic assumption of my argument is that successive daily changes of log (price) are independent. (This argument will thus have to be revised when the assumption is improved upon.) Moreover, the population second moment of $L(t)$ seems to be infinite and the monthly or yearly price changes are patently not Gaussian. Hence the problem of whether any limit theorem whatsoever applies to $\log_e Z(t + T) - \log_e Z(t)$ can also be answered *in theory* by examining whether the daily changes satisfy the Pareto-Doeblin-Gnedenko conditions. *In practice*, however, it is impossible to ever attain an infinitely large differencing interval T or to ever verify any condition relative to an infinitely large value of the random variable u. Hence one must consider that a month or a year is infinitely

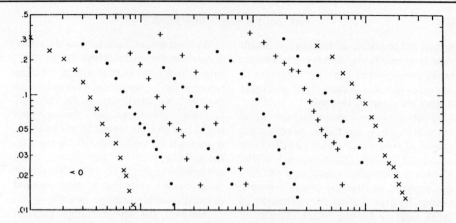

Fig. 6.—A rough test of stationarity for the process of change of cotton prices between 1816 and 1940. Horizontally, negative changes between successive monthly *averages* (source: *Statistical Bulletin* No. 99 of the Agricultural Economics Bureau, United States Department of Agriculture.) (To avoid interference between the various graphs, the horizontal scale of the kth graph from the left was multiplied by 2^{k-1}.) Vertically, relative frequencies $Fr(U < -u)$ corresponding respectively to the following periods (from left to right): 1816–60, 1816–32, 1832–47, 1847–61, 1880–96, 1896–1916, 1916–31, 1931–40, 1880–1940.

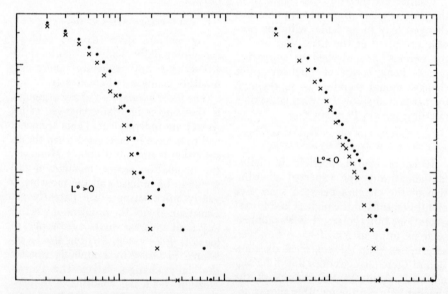

Fig. 7.—These graphs illustrate the effect of averaging. Dots reproduce the same data as the lines $1c$ and $2c$ of Fig. 5. The x's reproduce distribution of $\log_e Z^0(t+1) - \log_e Z^0(t)$, where $Z^0(t)$ is the average spot price of cotton in New York during the month t, as reported in the *Statistical Bulletin* No. 99 of the Agricultural Economics Bureau, United States Department of Agriculture.

long, and that the largest observed daily changes of $\log_e Z(t)$ are infinitely large. Under these circumstances, one can make the following inferences.

Inference from aggregation.—The cotton price data concerning daily changes of $\log_e Z(t)$ surely appear to follow the weaker condition of Pareto-Doeblin-Gnedenko. Hence, from the property of stability and according to Section IID, one should expect to find that, as T increases,

$$T^{-1/\alpha} \{\log_e Z(t+T) - \log_e Z(t) - T\,E[L(t,1)]\}$$

tends toward a stable Paretian variable with zero mean.

Inference from disaggregation.—Data seem to indicate that price changes over weeks and months follow the same law up to a change of scale. This law must therefore be one of the possible non-Gaussian limits, that is, it must be a stable Paretian. As a result, the inverse part of the theorem of Section IID shows that the daily changes of $\log Z(t)$ must satisfy the conditions of Pareto-Doeblin-Gnedenko.

It is pleasant to see that the inverse condition of P-D-G, which greatly embarrassed me in my work on the distribution of income, can be put to use in the theory of prices.

A few of the difficulties involved in making the above two inferences will now be discussed.

Disaggregation.—The P-D-G conditions are weaker than the asymptotic law of Pareto because they require that limits exist for $Q'(u)/Q''(u)$ and for $[Q'(u) + Q''(u)]/[Q'(ku) + Q''(ku)]$, but not for $Q'(u)$ and $Q''(u)$ taken separately. Suppose, however, that $Q'(u)$ and $Q''(u)$ still vary a great deal in the useful range of large daily variations of prices. If so, $A(N)\Sigma U_n - B(N)$ will not approach its own limit until *extremely* large values of N are reached. Therefore, if one believes that the limit is rapidly attained, the functions $Q'(u)$ and $Q''(u)$ of daily changes must vary very little in the regions of the tails of the usual samples. In other words, it is necessary after all that the asymptotic law of Pareto apply to daily price changes.

Aggregation.—Here, the difficulties are of a different order. From the mathematical viewpoint, the stable Paretian law should become increasingly accurate as T increases. Practically, however, there is no sense in even considering values of T as long as a century, because one cannot hope to get samples sufficiently long to have adequately inhabited tails. The year is an acceptable span for certain grains, but only if one is not worried by the fact that the long available series of yearly prices are ill known and variable averages of small numbers of quotations, not prices actually quoted on some market on a fixed day of each year.

From the viewpoint of economics, there are two much more fundamental difficulties with very large T. First of all, the model of independent daily L's eliminates from consideration every "trend," except perhaps the exponential growth or decay due to a non-vanishing δ. Many trends that are negligible on the daily basis would, however, be expected to be predominant on the monthly or yearly basis. For example, weather might have upon yearly changes of agricultural prices an effect different from the simple addition of speculative daily price movements.

The second difficulty lies in the "linear" character of the aggregation of successive L's used in my model. Since I use natural logarithms, a small $\log_e Z(t+T) - \log_e Z(t)$ will be undistinguishable from the relative price change $[Z(t+$

$T) - Z(t)]/Z(t)$. The addition of small L's is therefore related to the so-called "principle of random proportionate effect"; it also means that the stochastic mechanism of prices readjusts itself immediately to any level that $Z(t)$ may have attained. This assumption is quite usual, but very strong. In particular, I shall show that, if one finds that log $Z(t +$ one week$) - \log Z(t)$ is very large, it is very likely that it differs little from the change relative to the single day of most rapid price variation (see Section VE); naturally, this conclusion only holds for independent L's. As a result, the greatest of N successive daily price changes will be so large that one may question both the use of $\log_e Z(t)$ and the independence of the L's.

There are other reasons (see Section IVB) to expect to find that a simple addition of speculative daily price changes predicts values too high for the price changes over periods such as whole months.

Given all these potential difficulties, I was frankly astonished by the quality of the predictions of my model concerning the distribution of the changes of cotton prices between the fifteenth of one month and the fifteenth of the next. The negative tail has the expected bulge, and even the most extreme changes are precise extrapolates from the rest of the curve. Even the artificial excision of the Great Depression and similar periods would not affect the general results very greatly.

It was therefore interesting to check whether the ratios between the scale coefficients, $C'(T)/C'(1)$ and $C''(T)/C''(1)$, were both equal to T, as predicted by my theory whenever the ratios of standard deviations $\sigma'(T)/\sigma'(s)$ and $\sigma''(T)/\sigma''(s)$ follow the $T^{1/\alpha}$ generalization of the "$T^{1/2}$ Law" referred to in Section IIB. If the ratios of the C parameter are different from T, their value may serve as a measure of the degree of dependence between successive $L(t, 1)$.

The above ratios were absurdly large in my original comparison between the daily changes near 1950 of the cotton prices collected by Houthakker and the monthly changes between 1880 and 1940 of the prices communicated by the USDA. This suggested that the supported prices around 1950 varied less than their earlier counterparts. Therefore I repeated the plot of daily changes for the period near 1900, chosen haphazardly but not actually at random. The new values of $C'(T)/C'(1)$ and $C''(T)/C''(1)$ became quite reasonable, equal to each other and to 18. In 1900, there were seven trading days per week, but they subsequently decreased to 5. Besides, one cannot be too dogmatic about estimating $C'(T)/C'(1)$. Therefore the behavior of this ratio indicated that the "apparent" number of trading days per month was somewhat smaller than the actual number.

IV. WHY ONE SHOULD EXPECT TO FIND NONSENSE MOMENTS AND NONSENSE PERIODICITIES IN ECONOMIC TIME SERIES

A. BEHAVIOR OF SECOND MOMENTS AND FAILURE OF THE LEAST-SQUARES METHOD OF FORECASTING

It is amusing to note that the first known non-Gaussian stable law, namely, Cauchy's distribution, was introduced in the course of a study of the method of least squares. In a surprisingly lively argument following Cauchy's 1853 paper, J. Bienaymé[11] stressed that a method based upon the minimization of the sum

[11] J. Bienaymé, "Considérations a l'appui de la découverte de Laplace sur la loi de probabilité dans la méthode des moindres carrés," *Comptes rendus, Académie des Sciences de Paris*, XXXVII (August, 1853), 309–24 (esp. 321–23).

of squares of sample deviations cannot be reasonably used if the expected value of this sum is known to be infinite. The same argument applies fully to the problem of least-squares smoothing of economic time series, when the "noise" follows a stable Paretian law other than that of Cauchy.

Similarly, consider the problem of least-squares forecasting, that is, of the minimization of the expected value of the square of the error of extrapolation. In the stable Paretian case this expected value will be infinite for every forecast, so that the method is, at best, extremely questionable. One can perhaps apply a method of "least ζ-power" of the forecasting error, where $\zeta < a$, but such an approach would not have the formal simplicity of least squares manipulations; the most hopeful case is that of $\zeta = 1$, which corresponds to the minimization of the sum of absolute values of the errors of forecasting.

B. BEHAVIOR OF THE KURTOSIS AND ITS FAILURE AS A MEASURE OF "PEAKEDNESS"

Pearson's index of "kurtosis" is defined as

$$-3 + \frac{\text{fourth moment}}{\text{square of the second moment}}.$$

If $0 < a < 2$, the numerator and the denominator both have an infinite expected value. One can, however, show that the kurtosis behaves proportionately to its "typical" value given by

$$\frac{(1/N) \text{ (most probable value of } \Sigma L^4)}{[(1/N) \text{ (most probable value of } \Sigma L^2)]^2}$$

$$= \frac{\text{const. } N^{-1+4/a}}{[\text{const. } N^{-1+2/a}]^2} = \text{const. } N.$$

In other words, the kurtosis is expected to increase without bound as $N \to \infty$. For small N, things are less simple but presumably quite similar.

Let me examine the work of Cootner in this light.[12] He has developed the tempting hypothesis that prices vary at random only as long as they do not reach either an upper or a lower bound, that are considered by well-informed speculators to delimit an interval of reasonable values of the price. If and when ill-informed speculators let the price go too high or too low, the operations of the well-informed speculators will induce this price to come back within a "penumbra" à la Taussig. Under the circumstances, the price changes over periods of, say, fourteen weeks should be smaller than would be expected if the contributing weekly changes were independent.

This theory is very attractive a priori but could not be generally true because, in the case of cotton, it is not supported by the facts. As for Cootner's own justification, it is based upon the observation that the price changes of certain securities over periods of fourteen weeks have a much smaller kurtosis than one-week changes. Unfortunately, his sample contains 250-odd weekly changes and only 18 fourteen-week periods. Hence, on the basis of general evidence concerning speculative prices, I would have expected a priori to find a smaller kurtosis for the longer time increment, and Cootner's evidence is not a proof of his theory; other methods must be used in order to attack the still very open problem of the possible dependence between successive price changes.

C. METHOD OF SPECTRAL ANALYSIS OF RANDOM TIME SERIES

Applied mathematicians are frequently presented these days with the task of describing the stochastic mecha-

[12] Paul H. Cootner, "Stock Prices: Random Walks vs. Finite Markov Chains," *Industrial Management Review of M.I.T.*, III (1962), 24–45.

nism capable of generating a given time series $u(t)$, known or presumed to be random. The response to such questions is usually to investigate first what is obtained by applying the theory of the "second-order random processes." That is, assuming that $E(U) = 0$, one forms the sample covariance

$$r(\tau) = \left(\frac{1}{N-\tau}\right) \cdot \sum_{t=T^\circ+1}^{t=T^\circ+N-\tau} u(t)u(t+\tau),$$

which is used, somewhat indirectly, to evaluate the population covariance

$$R(\tau) = E[U(t)U(t+\tau)].$$

Of course, $R(\tau)$ is always assumed to be finite for all; its Fourier transform gives the "spectral density" of the "harmonic decomposition" of $U(t)$ into a sum of sine and cosine terms.

Broadly speaking, this method has been very successful, though many small-sample problems remain unsolved. Its applications to economics have, however, been questionable even in the large-sample case. Within the context of my theory, there is unfortunately nothing surprising in such a finding. The expression $2E[U(t)U(t+\tau)]$ equals indeed $E[U(t) + U(t+\tau)]^2 - E[U(t)]^2 - E[U(t+\tau)]^2$; these three variances are all infinite for time series covered by my model, so that spectral analysis loses its theoretical motivation. I must, however, postpone a more detailed examination of this fascinating problem.

V. SAMPLE FUNCTIONS GENERATED BY STABLE PARETIAN PROCESSES; SMALL-SAMPLE ESTIMATION OF THE MEAN "DRIFT" OF SUCH A PROCESS

The curves generated by stable Paretian processes present an even larger number of interesting formations than the curves generated by Bachelier's Brownian motion. If the price increase over a long period of time happens a posteriori to have been usually large, in a stable Paretian market, one should expect to find that this change was mostly performed during a few periods of especially high activity. That is, one will find in most cases that the majority of the contributing daily changes are distributed on a fairly symmetric curve, while a few especially high values fall well outside this curve. If the total increase is of the usual size, the only difference will be that the daily changes will show no "outliers."

In this section these results will be used to solve one small-sample statistical problem, that of the estimation of the mean drift δ, when the other parameters are known. We shall see that there is no "sufficient statistic" for this problem, and that the maximum likelihood equation does not necessarily have a single root. This has severe consequences from the viewpoint of the very definition of the concept of "trend."

A. CERTAIN PROPERTIES OF SAMPLE PATHS OF BROWNIAN MOTION

As noted by Bachelier and (independently of him and of each other) by several modern writers,[13] the sample paths of the Brownian motion very much "look like" the empirical curves of time variation of prices or of price indexes. At closer inspection, however, one sees very well the effect of the abnormal number of

[13] See esp. Holbrolk Working, "A Random-Difference Series for Use in the Analysis of Time Series," *Journal of the American Statistical Association*, XXIX (1934), 11–24; Maurice Kendall, "The Analysis of Economic Time-Series—Part I: Prices," *Journal of the Royal Statistical Society*, Ser. A, CXVI (1953), 11–34; M. F. M. Osborne, "Brownian Motion in the Stock Market," *op. cit.*; Harry V. Roberts, "Stock-Market 'Patterns' and Financial Analysis: Methodological Suggestions," *Journal of Finance*, XIV (1959), 1–10; and S. S. Alexander, "Price Movements in Speculative Markets: Trends or Random Walks," *op. cit.*, n. 3.

large positive and negative changes of $\log_e Z(t)$. At still closer inspection, one finds that the differences concern some of the economically most interesting features of the generalized central-limit theorem of the calculus of probability. It is therefore necessary to discuss this question in detail, beginning with a reminder of some classical facts concerning Gaussian random variables.

Conditional distribution of a Gaussian L(t), *knowing* $L(t, T) = L(t, 1) + \ldots + L(t + T - 1, 1)$.—Let the probability density of $L(t, T)$ be

$$(2\pi\sigma^2 T)^{-1/2} \exp[-(u - \delta T)^2/2T\sigma^2].$$

It is then easy to see that—if one knows the value u of $L(t, T)$—the density of any of the quantities $L(t + \tau, 1)$ is given by

$$[2\pi\sigma^2(T-1)/T]^{-1/2}$$

$$\exp\left[-\frac{(u'-u/T)^2}{2\sigma^2(T-1)/T}\right].$$

We see that each of the contributing $L(t + \tau, 1)$ equals u/T plus a Gaussian error term. For large T, that term has the same variance as the unconditioned $L(t, 1)$; one can in fact prove that the value of u has little influence upon the size of the largest of those "noise terms." One can therefore say that, whichever its value, u is roughly uniformly distributed over the T time intervals, each contributing negligibly to the whole.

Sufficiency of u *for the estimation of the mean drift* δ *from the* $L(t + \tau, 1)$.—In particular, δ has vanished from the distribution of any $L(t + \tau, 1)$ conditioned by the value of u. This fact is expressed in mathematical statistics by saying that u is a "sufficient statistic" for the estimation of δ from the values of all the $L(t + \tau, 1)$. That is, whichever method of estimation a statistician may favor, his estimate of δ must be a function of u alone.

The knowledge of intermediate values of $\log_e Z(t + \tau)$ is of no help to him. Most methods recommend estimating δ by u/T and extrapolating the future linearly from the two known points, $\log_e Z(t)$ and $\log_e Z(t + T)$.

Since the causes of any price movement can be traced back only if it is ample enough, the only thing that can be explained in the Gaussian case is the mean drift interpreted as a trend, and Bachelier's model, which assumes a zero mean for the price changes, can only represent the movement of prices once the broad causal parts or trends have been removed.

B. SAMPLE FROM A PROCESS OF INDEPENDENT STABLE PARETIAN INCREMENTS

Returning to the stable Paretian case, suppose that one knows the values of γ and β (or of C' and C'') and of α. The remaining parameter is the mean drift δ, which one must estimate starting from the known $L(t, T) = \log_e Z(t + T) - \log_e Z(t)$.

The unbiased estimate of δ is $L(t, T)/T$, while the maximum likelihood estimate matches the observed $L(t, T)$ to its a priori *most probable* value. The "bias" of the maximum likelihood is therefore given by an expression of the form $\gamma^{1/\alpha} f(\beta)$, where the function $f(\beta)$ must be determined from the numerical tables of the stable Paretian densities. Since β is mostly manifested in the relative sizes of the tails, its evaluation requires very large samples, and the quality of one's predictions will depend greatly upon the quality of one's knowledge of the past.

It is, of course, not at all clear that anybody would wish the extrapolation to be unbiased with respect to the mean of the change of the *logarithm* of the price. Moreover, the bias of the maximum likelihood estimate comes principally from an underestimate of the size of changes that are so large as to be catastrophic. The forecaster may therefore very well wish to treat such changes separately and to take account of his private feelings about many things that are not included in the independent-increment model.

C. TWO SAMPLES FROM A STABLE PARETIAN PROCESS

Suppose now that T is even and that one knows $L(t, T/2)$ and $L(t + T/2, T/2)$ and their sum $L(t, T)$. We have seen in Section II G that, when the value $u = L(t, T)$ is given, the conditional distribution of $L(t, T/2)$ depends very sharply upon u. This means that the total change u is not a sufficient statistic for the estimation of δ; in other words, the estimates of δ will be changed by the knowledge of $L(t, T/2)$ and $L(t + T/2, T/2)$.

Consider for example the most likely value δ. If $L(t, T/2)$ and $L(t + T/2, T/2)$ are of the same order of magnitude, this estimate will remain close to $L(t, T)/T$, as in the Gaussian case. But suppose that *the actually observed* values of $L(t, T/2)$ and $L(t + T/2, T/2)$ are very unequal, thus implying that at least one of these quantities is very different from their common mean and median. Such an event is most likely to occur when δ is close to the observed value either of $L(t + T/2, T/2)/(T/2)$ or of $L(t, T/2)/(T/2)$.

We see that as a result, the maximum likelihood equation for δ has two roots, respectively close to $2L(t, T/2)/T$ and to $2L(t + T/2, T/2)/T$. That is, the maximum-likelihood procedure says that one should neglect one of the available items of information, any weighted mean of the two recommended extrapolations being worse than either; but nothing says which item one should neglect.

It is clear that few economists will accept such advice. Some will stress that the most likely value of δ is actually nothing but the most probable value in the case of a uniform distribution of a priori probabilities of δ. But it seldom happens that a priori probabilities are uniformly distributed. It is also true, of course, that they are usually very poorly determined; in the present problem, however, the economist will not need to determine these a priori probabilities with any precision: it will be sufficient to choose the most likely *for him* of the two maximum-likelihood estimates.

An alternative approach to be presented later in this paper will argue that successive increments of $\log_e Z(t)$ are not really independent, so that the estimation of δ depends upon the order of the values of $L(t, T/2)$ and $L(t + T/2, T/2)$ as well as upon their sizes. This may help eliminate the indeterminacy of estimation.

A third alternative consists in abandoning the hypothesis that δ is the same for both changes $L(t, T/2)$ and $L(t + T/2, T/2)$. For example, if these changes are very unequal, one may be tempted to believe that the trend δ is not linear but parabolic. Extrapolation would then approximately amount to choosing among the two maximum-likelihood estimates the one which is chronologically the latest. This is an example of a variety of configurations which would have been so unlikely in the Gaussian case that they should be considered as non-random and would be of help in extrapolation. In the stable Paretian case, however, their probability may be substantial.

D. THREE SAMPLES FROM A STABLE PARETIAN PROCESS

The number of possibilities increases rapidly with the sample size. Assume now that T is a multiple of 3, and consider $L(t, T/3)$, $L(t + T/3, T/3)$, and $L(t + 2T/3, T/3)$. If these three quantities are of comparable size, the knowledge of log $Z(t + T/3)$ and log $Z(t + 2T/3)$ will again bring little change to the estimate based upon $L(t, T)$.

But suppose that one datum is very large and the other are of much smaller and comparable sizes. Then, the likelihood equation will have two local maximums, having very different positions and sufficiently equal sizes to make it impossible to dismiss the smaller one. The absolute maximum yields the estimate $\delta = (3/2T)$ (sum of the two small data); the smaller local maximum yields the estimate $\delta = (3/T)$ (the large datum).

Suppose finally that the three data are of very unequal sizes. Then the maximum likelihood equation has *three* roots.

This indeterminacy of maximum likelihood can again be lifted by one of the three methods of Section VC. For example, if the middle datum only is large, the method of non-linear extrapolation will suggest a logistic growth. If the data increase or decrease—when taken chronologically—one will rather try a parabolic trend. Again the probability of these configurations arising from chance under my model will be much greater than in the Gaussian case.

E. A LARGE NUMBER OF SAMPLES FROM A STABLE PARETIAN PROCESS

Let us now jump to a very large number of data. In order to investigate the predictions of my stable Paretian model, we must first re-examine the meaning to be attached to the statement that, in order that a sum of random variables follow a central limit of probability, it is necessary that each of the addends be negligible relative to the sum.

It is quite true, of course, that one can speak of limit laws only if the value of the sum is not *dominated* by any single addend known in advance. That is, to study the limit of $A(N)\Sigma U_n - B(N)$, one must assume that (for every n) $Pr|A(N) U_n - B(N)/N| > \epsilon)$ tends to zero with $1/N$.

As each addend decreases with $1/N$, their number increases, however, and the condition of the preceding paragraph does not by itself insure that the largest of the $|A(N) U_n - B(N)/N|$ is negligible in comparison with their sum. As a matter of fact, the last condition is true only if the limit of the sum is Gaussian. In the Paretian case, on the contrary, the following ratios,

$$\frac{\max |A(N) U_n - B(N)/N|}{A(N)\Sigma U_n - B(N)}$$

and

$$\frac{\text{sum of } k \text{ largest } |A(N) U_n - B(N)/N|}{A(N)\Sigma U_n - B(BN)}$$

tend to non-vanishing limits as N increases.[14] If one knows moreover that the sum $A(N)\Sigma U_n - B(N)$ happens to be large, one can prove that the above ratios should be expected to be close to *one*.

Returning to a process with independent stable Paretian $L(t)$, we may say the following: If, knowing α, β, γ, and δ, one observes that $L(t, T = \text{one month})$ is *not* large, the contribution of the day of largest price change is likely to be non-negligible in relative value, but it will remain small in absolute value. For large but finite N, this will not differ too much from the Gaussian prediction that even the largest addend is negligible.

Suppose however that $L(t, T = \text{one month})$ is *very* large. The Paretian theory

[14] Donald Darling, "The Influence of the Maximum Term in the Addition of Independent Random Variables," *Transactions of the American Mathematical Society*, LXX (1952), 95–107; and D. Z. Arov and A. A. Bobrov, "The Extreme Members of Samples and Their Role in the Sum of Independent Variables," *Theory of Probability and Its Applications*, V (1960), 415–35.

then predicts that the sum of a few largest daily changes will be very close to the total $L(t, T)$; if one plots the frequencies of various values of $L(t, 1)$, conditioned by a known and very large value for $L(t, T)$, one should expect to find that the law of $L(t + \tau, 1)$ contains a few widely "outlying" values. However, if the outlying values are taken out, the conditioned distribution of $L(t + \tau, 1)$ should depend little upon the value of the conditioning $L(t, T)$. I believe this last prediction to be very well satisfied by prices.

Implications concerning estimation.—Suppose now that δ is unknown and that one has a large sample of $L(t + \tau, 1)$'s. The estimation procedure consists in that case of plotting the empirical histogram and translating it horizontally until one has optimized its fit to the theoretical density curve. One knows in advance that this best value will be very little influenced by the largest outliers. Hence "rejection of the outliers" is fully justified in the present case, at least in its basic idea.

F. CONCLUSIONS CONCERNING ESTIMATION

The observations made in the preceding sections seem to confirm some economists' feeling that prediction is feasible only if the sample size is both very large and stationary, or if the sample size is small but the sample values are of comparable sizes. One can also predict when the sample size is one, but here the unicity of the estimator is only due to ignorance.

G. CAUSALITY AND RANDOMNESS IN STABLE PARETIAN PROCESSES

We mentioned in Section V A that, in order to be "causally explainable," an economic change must at least be large enough to allow the economist to trace back the sequence of its causes. As a result, the only causal part of a Gaussian random function is the mean drift δ. This will also apply to stable Paretian random functions when their changes happen to be roughly uniformly distributed.

Things are different when $\log_e Z(t)$ varies greatly between the times t an $t + T$, changing mostly during a few of the contributing days. Then, these largest changes are sufficiently clear-cut, and are sufficiently separated from "noise," to be traced back and explained causally, just as well as the mean drift.

In others words, a careful observer of a stable Paretian random function will be able to extract causal parts from it. But, if the total change of $\log_e Z(t)$ is neither very large nor very small, there will be a large degree of arbitrariness in this distinction between causal and random. Hence one could not tell whether the predicted proportions of the two kinds of effects are empirically correct.

To sum up, the distinction between the causal and the random areas is sharp in the Gaussian case and very diffuse in the stable Paretian case. This seems to me to be a strong recommendation in favor of the stable Paretian process as a model of speculative markets. Of course, I have not the slightest idea why the large price movements should be represented in this way by a simple extrapolation of movements of ordinary size. I came to believe, however, that it is very desirable that both "trend" and "noise" be aspects of the same deeper "truth," which may not be explainable today, but which can be adequately described. I am surely not antagonistic to the ideal of economics: eventually to decompose even the "noise" into parts similar to the trend and to link various series to each other. But, until we can approximate this ideal, we can at least represent some trends as being similar to "noise."

H. CAUSALITY AND RANDOMNESS IN AGGREGATION "IN PARALLEL"

Borrowing a term from elementary electrical circuit theory, the addition of successive daily changes of a price may be designated by the term "aggregation in series," the term "aggregation in parallel" applying to the operation

$$L(t, T) = \sum_{i=1}^{I} L(i, t, T),$$

$$= \sum_{i=1}^{I} \sum_{\tau=0}^{T-1} L(i, t+\tau, 1),$$

where i refers to "events" that occur simultaneously during a given time interval such as T or 1.

In the Gaussian case, one should, of course, expect any occurrence of a large value for $L(t, T)$ to be traceable to a rare conjunction of large changes in all or most of the $L(i, t, T)$. In the stable Paretian case, one should on the contrary expect large changes $L(t, T)$ to be traceable to one or a small number of the contributing $L(i, t, T)$. It seems obvious that the Paretian prediction is closer to the facts.

To add up the two types of aggregation in a Paretian world, a large $L(t, T)$ is likely to be traceable to the fact that $L(i, t + \tau, 1)$ happens to be very large for one or a few sets of values of i and of τ. These contributions would stand out sharply and be causally explainable. But, after a while, they should of course rejoin the "noise" made up by the other factors. The next rapid change of $\log_e Z(t)$ should be due to other "causes." If a contribution is "trend-making" in the above sense during a large number of time-increments, one will, of course, doubt that it falls under the same theory as the fluctuations.

VI. PRICE VARIATION IN CONTINUOUS TIME AND THE THEORY OF SPECULATION

The main point of this section is to show that certain systems of speculation, which would have been advantageous if one could implement them, cannot in reality be followed in the case of price series generated by a Paretian process.

A. INFINITE DIVISIBILITY OF STABLE PARETIAN LAWS

Whichever N, it is possible to consider that a stable Paretian increment

$$L(t, 1) = \log_e Z(t+1) - \log_e Z(t)$$

is the sum of N independent, identically distributed, random variables, and that those variables differ from $L(t)$ only by the value of the constants γ, C' and C'', which are N times smaller.

In fact, it is possible to interpolate the process of independent stable Paretian increments to continuous time, assuming that $L(t, dt)$ is a stable Paretian variable with a scale coefficient $\gamma(dt) = dt\,\gamma(1)$. This interpolated process is a very important "*zero*th" order approximation to the actual price changes. That is, its predictions are surely modified by the mechanisms of the market, but they are very illuminating nonetheless.

B. PATH FUNCTIONS OF A STABLE PROCESS IN CONTINUOUS TIME

It is almost universally assumed, in mathematical models of physical or of social sciences, that all functions can safely be considered as being continuous and as having as many derivatives as one may wish. The functions generated by Bachelier are indeed continuous ("almost surely almost everywhere," but we may forget this qualification); although they have no derivatives ("almost surely almost nowhere"), we need not be concerned because price quotations are always rounded to simple fractions of the unit of currency.

In the Paretian case things are quite different. If my process is interpolated to continuous t, the paths which it generates become everywhere discontinuous (or rather, they become "almost surely almost everywhere discontinuous"). That is, most of their variation is performed through non-infinitesimal "jumps," the number of jumps larger than u and located within a time increment T, being given by the law $C'T|d(u^{-\alpha})|$.

Let us examine a few aspects of this discontinuity. Again, very small jumps of $\log_e Z(t)$ could not be perceived, since price quotations are always expressed in simple fractions. It is more interesting to note that there is a non-negligible probability that a jump of price is so large that "supply and demand" cease to be matched. In other words, the stable Paretian model may be considered as predicting the occurrence of phenomena likely to force the market to close. In a Gaussian model such large changes are so extremely unlikely that the occasional closure of the markets must be explained by non-stochastic considerations.

The most interesting fact is, however, the large probability predicted for medium-sized jumps by the stable Paretian model. Clearly, if those medium-sized movements were oscillatory, they could be eliminated by market mechanisms such as the activities of the specialists. But if the movement is all in one direction, market specialists could at best transform a discontinuity into a change that is rapid but progressive. On the other hand, very few transactions would then be expected at the intermediate smoothing prices. As a result, even if the price Z^0 is quoted transiently, it may be impossible to act rapidly enough to satisfy more than a minute fraction of orders to "sell at Z^0." In other words, a large number of intermediate prices are quoted even if $Z(t)$ performs a large jump in a short time; but they are likely to be so fleeting, and to apply to so few transactions, that they are irrelevant from the viewpoint of actually enforcing a "stop loss order" of any kind. In less extreme cases—as, for example, when borrowings are oversubscribed—the market may have to resort to special rules of allocation.

These remarks are the crux of my criticism of certain systematic methods: they would perhaps be very advantageous if only they could be enforced, but in fact they can only be enforced by very few traders. I shall be content here with a discussion of one example of this kind of reasoning.

C. THE FAIRNESS OF ALEXANDER'S GAME

S. S. Alexander has suggested the following rule of speculation: "if the market goes up 5%, go long and stay long until it moves down 5%, at which time sell and go short until it again goes up 5%."[15]

This procedure is motivated by the fact that, according to Alexander's interpretation, data would suggest that "in speculative markets, price changes appear to follow a random walk over time; but . . . if the market has moved up $x\%$, it is likely to move up more than $x\%$ further before it moves down $x\%$." He calls this phenomenon the "persistence of moves." Since there is no possible persistence of moves in any "random walk" with zero mean, we see that if Alexander's interpretation of facts were confirmed, one would have to look at a very early stage for a theoretical improvement over the random walk model.

In order to follow this rule, one must of course watch a price series continu-

[15] S. S. Alexander, *op. cit.* n. 3.

ously in time and buy or sell whenever its variation attains the prescribed value. In other words, this rule can be strictly followed if and only if the process $Z(t)$ generates continuous path functions, as for example in the original Gaussian process of Bachelier.

Alexander's procedure cannot be followed, however, in the case of my own first-approximation model of price change in which there is a probability equal to one that the first move *not smaller* than 5 per cent is *greater* than 5 per cent and *not equal* to 5 per cent. It is therefore mandatory to modify Alexander's scheme to suggest buying or selling when moves of 5 per cent are *first exceeded*. One can prove that the stable Paretian theory predicts that this game also is fair. Therefore, the evidence—as interpreted by Alexander—would again suggest that one must go beyond the simple model of independent increments of price.

But Alexander's inference was actually based upon the discontinuous series constituted by the closing prices on successive days. He assumed that the intermediate prices could be interpolated by some continuous function of continuous time—the actual form of which need not be specified. That is, whenever there was a difference of *over* 5 per cent between the closing price on day F' and day F'', Alexander implicitly assumed that there was at least one instance between these moments when the price had gone up *exactly* 5 per cent. He recommends buying at this instant, and he computes the empirical returns to the speculator as if he were able to follow this procedure.

For price series generated by my process, however, the price actually paid for a stock will almost always be greater than that corresponding to a 5 per cent rise; hence the speculator will almost always have paid more than assumed in Alexander's evaluation of the returns. On the contrary, the price received will almost always be less than suggested by Alexander. Hence, at best, Alexander overestimates the yield corresponding to his method of speculation and, at worst, the very impression that the yield is positive may be a delusion due to overoptimistic evaluation of what happens during the few most rapid price changes.

One can of course imagine contracts guaranteeing that the broker will charge (or credit) his client the actual price quotation nearest by excess (or default) to a price agreed upon, irrespective of whether the broker was able to perform the transaction at the price agreed upon. Such a system would make Alexander's procedure advantageous to the speculator; but the money he would be making on the average would come from his broker and not from the market; and brokerage fees would have to be such as to make the game at best fair in the long run.

VII. A MORE REFINED MODEL OF PRICE VARIATION

Broadly speaking, the predictions of my main model seem to me to be reasonable. At closer inspection, however, one notes that large price changes are not isolated between periods of slow change; they rather tend to be the result of several fluctuations, some of which "overshoot" the final change. Similarly, the movement of prices in periods of tranquillity seem to be smoother than predicted by my process. In other words, large changes tend to be followed by large changes—of either sign—and small changes tend to be followed by small changes, so that the isolines of low probability of $[L(t, 1), L(t - 1, 1)]$ are X-shaped. In the case of daily cotton prices,

Hendrik S. Houthakker stressed this fact in several conferences and private conversation.

Such an X shape can be easily obtained by rotation from the "plus-sign shape" which was observed in Figure 4 to be applicable when $L(t, 1)$ and $L(t - 1, 1)$ are statistically independent and symmetric. The necessary rotation introduces the two expressions:

$S(t) = (1/2)[L(t, 1) + L(t - 1, 1)]$

$\quad = (1/2) [\log_e Z(t + 1) - \log_e Z(t - 1)]$

and

$D(t) = (1/2) [L(t, 1) - L(t - 1, 1)]$

$\quad = (1/2) [\log_e Z(t + 1) - 2 \log_e Z(t)$
$\quad\quad + \log_e Z(t - 1)] \, .$

It follows that in order to obtain the X shape of the empirical isolines, it would be sufficient to assume that the first and second finite differences of $\log_e Z(t)$ are two stable Paretian random variables, independent of each other and naturally of $\log_e Z(t)$ (see Fig. 4). Such a process is invariant by time inversion.

It is interesting to note that the distribution of $L(t, 1)$, conditioned by the known $L(t - 1, 1)$, is asymptotically Paretian with an exponent equal to $2a + 1$.[16] Since, for the usual range of a, $2a + 1$ is greater than 4, it is clear that no stable Paretian law can be associated with the conditioned $L(t, 1)$. In fact, even the kurtosis is finite for the conditioned $L(t, 1)$.

Let us then consider a Markovian process with the transition probability I have just introduced. If the initial $L(T^0, 1)$ is small, the first values of $L(t, 1)$ will be weakly Paretian with a high exponent $2a + 1$, so that $\log_e Z(t)$ will begin by fluctuating much less rapidly than in the case of independent $L(t, 1)$. Eventually, however, a large $L(t^0, 1)$ will appear. Thereafter, $L(t, 1)$ will fluctuate for some time between values of the orders of magnitude of $L(t^0, 1)$ and $-L(t^0, 1)$. This will last long enough to compensate fully for the deficiency of large values during the period of slow variation. In other words, the occasional sharp changes of $L(t, 1)$ predicted by the model of independent $L(t, 1)$ are replaced by oscillatory periods, and the periods without sharp change are less fluctuating than when the $L(t, 1)$ are independent.

We see that, for the correct estimation of a, it is mandatory to avoid the elimination of periods of rapid change of prices. One *cannot* argue that they are "causally" explainable and ought to be eliminated before the "noise" is examined more closely. If one succeeded in eliminating all large changes in this way, one would have a Gaussian-like remainder which, however, would be devoid of any significance.

---

[16] Proof: $Pr[L(t, 1) > u$, when $w < L(t - 1, 1) < w + dw]$ is the product by $(1/dw)$ of the integral of the probability density of $[L(t - 1, 1)L(t, 1)]$, over a strip that differs infinitesimally from the zone defined by

$$S(t) > (u + w)/2 \, ;$$
$$w + S(t < D(t) < w + S(t) + dw \, .$$

Hence, if u is large as compared to w, the conditional probability in question is equal to the following integral, carried from $(u + w)/2$ to ∞.

$\int C' a s^{-(a+1)} C' a (s + w)^{-(a+1)} \, ds$

$\sim (2a + 1)^{-1} (C')^2 a^2 2^{-(2a+1)} u^{-(2a+1)} \, .$

The Distribution of Futures Prices: A Test of the Stable Paretian and Mixture of Normals Hypotheses

Joyce A. Hall, B. Wade Brorsen, and Scott H. Irwin*

Abstract

Two alternate hypotheses, the stable Paretian and mixture of normals, have been proposed to explain the observed thick-tailed distributions of futures price movements. The two hypotheses are tested by applying the stability-under-addition test of stable distribution parameters to twenty lengthy time series of changes in daily closing futures prices. Tests are conducted on both the original data series and randomized data. The results offer support for the mixture of normals hypothesis.

I. Introduction

The distribution of daily commodity futures price movements is important in economic modeling. For example, portfolio models of asset allocation and option pricing models are typically derived assuming price changes are normally distributed with a constant variance.[1] Furthermore, statistical tests of the efficient market hypothesis that use the random walk model are based on the same assumption. If speculative price movements are not distributed normally, variance may not be an appropriate measure of dispersion, and statistical tests based on finite variance are likely to give misleading results (Fama (1965)). If distributions are normal, but variance is nonconstant, then an adjustment for heteroskedasticity must be made before conducting statistical tests (Taylor (1985)).

While the distribution of daily speculative price movements is often assumed to have a normal distribution, research on stock prices (Fama (1963), Officer (1972), Teichmoeller (1971), and Barnea and Downes (1973)) and futures prices (Cornew, et al. (1984), Hudson et al. (1987), and Gordon (1985)) has found distributions that are leptokurtic relative to the normal distribution (i.e., having more values near the mean and in the extreme tails than a normal distribution).[2] Two hypotheses frequently proposed to explain the observed departures

---

* First two authors, Department of Agricultural Economics, Purdue University, West Lafayette, IN 47907; third author, Department of Agricultural Economics and Rural Sociology, The Ohio State University, Columbus, OH 43210. The authors thank the two anonymous *JFQA* referees for helpful comments.

[1] More specifically, option pricing models are derived assuming logarithmic price relatives are normally distributed with a constant variance.

[2] The references cited are by no means an exhaustive list. Mandelbrot (1963) cited studies that observed the "fat-tailed" phenomena as early as 1915.

from normality are the stable Paretian and the mixture of normals distributions.[3] Under the stable Paretian hypothesis, distributions conform to nonnormal members of the stable Paretian family with infinite variance (Mandelbrot (1963)). Under the mixture of normals hypothesis, distributions are combinations of normal distributions with different variances (Fama (1965)).

Recent research on the distribution of stock prices provides reasonably strong evidence in favor of the mixture of normals hypothesis, either through tests of subordinated stochastic process models of prices and trading volumes (Epps and Epps (1976), Morgan (1976), Westerfield (1977), and Harris (1987)), tests based on sample variances for successively larger sample sizes (Perry (1983)), or tests based on the stability-under-addition property of stable distributions (Fielitz and Rozelle (1983)). Research on futures prices has not been as exhaustive or conclusive. Clark (1973) and Tauchen and Pitts (1983) applied subordinated stochastic process models to cotton and U.S. Treasury bill futures prices, respectively, and both reported results supportive of the mixture of normals hypothesis.[4]

The stable Paretian and mixture of normals hypotheses are tested in this paper by applying the stability-under-addition test of stable distribution parameters. This study uses daily futures price movements of 20 commodities. Financial, metal, and agricultural futures are included in the sample. A continuous series of nearby futures price changes is used; thus, relative to past research that only considered one contract at a time, a longer time series of data is available. The longer time series should be able to remove much of the effects of seasonality or differing maturities. As the stability-under-addition property of stable distributions holds only for independent random variables and evidence suggests variance may be correlated over time, the statistical procedure is applied to two different series. The first, which is the original series, is in chronological order. The second series uses the same data but the order is random. Estimates from the randomly ordered series are compared to the estimates from the original series. This randomization procedure has been applied by Fielitz and Rozelle (1983) to stock returns but has not been applied to futures prices.

II. The Alternate Hypotheses

Either the mixture of normals or stable Paretian hypotheses can explain the observed leptokurtic distributions. While the stable Paretian family includes the normal distribution, the stable Paretian hypothesis refers to distributions conforming to nonnormal members of the family. Stable Paretian distributions are the only possible limiting distributions for sums of independent, identically distributed, random variables (Fama (1963)). By definition, a stable Paretian distribution is invariant under addition (Fama (1963)).

---

[3] While this dichotomy is commonly found in the literature, Blattberg and Gonedes (1974) show that the stable distribution can itself be derived as mixtures of a normal distribution. In this case, if the variance of the normal distribution follows a strictly positive (asymmetric) stable distribution with $\alpha < 1$, then the unconditional distribution is symmetric stable with $\alpha < 2$.

[4] Mann and Hiefner (1976) conducted a stability-under-addition test of stable distribution parameters for nine commodity futures price series. However, their results are of questionable value due to computational errors (Hudson, et al. (1987)).

The logarithm of the characteristic function for the family of stable Paretian distributions is

(1) $$\log f(t) = i\delta t - \gamma |t|^\alpha (1 + i\beta(t/|t|) \tan(\pi\alpha/2)),$$

where t is any real number and i is $\sqrt{-1}$. Stable Paretian distributions can be described by the four parameters, α, β, δ, and γ. The parameter γ, or c where $\gamma = c^\alpha$, is the scale parameter, δ is the location parameter, β is a measure of skewness, and α is the characteristic exponent. The characteristic exponent, α, determines the total probability in the extreme tails (Fama (1963)).

The characteristic exponent, α, is the most important parameter for determining the type of distribution. Values of the characteristic exponent are limited to the interval $0 < \alpha \leq 2$. When $\alpha = 2$, the distribution is normal and the variance exists. When $\alpha < 2$, there are more observations in the tails than under the normal distribution and the variance is not defined. The smaller the value of α, the thicker the tails of the distribution (Fama (1963)).

The mixture of normal distributions hypothesis suggests commodity futures price movements are combinations of normal distributions with different variances. Nonconstant variance could arise, for example, if variance were proportional to the actual number of days rather than trading days. This would result from the variance of weekend and holiday price changes being greater than the variance of price changes during the week (Fama (1965)). Doukas and Rahman (1986) point out that the differing maturity of adjacent closing prices may cause differences in variability. Cornew (1984), however, argues that differences in maturity will be unimportant in a data set like the one used here. So (1987) recently estimated parameters of stable Paretian distributions for currency futures prices and tested whether nonstationarity of scale, attributable to a relationship between time-to-maturity and variability, could explain the observed distributions. He concluded that the nonnormality of foreign currency futures prices was not caused by nonstationarity of scale and that the stable Paretian distribution adequately described price changes for most currencies and most contracts. Results of Anderson (1985) and Kenyon, et al. (1987) suggest that seasonality also may have an influence in the grains. For example, Anderson (1985) found that the seasonality effect exceeded the maturity effect by a wide margin in explaining the variance of nine futures price series; in four of the nine studied, by a factor of at least ten-to-one. Anderson (1985) and Brorsen and Irwin (1987) also found significant differences in variance across years for some commodities.

Both hypotheses can be tested by estimating the characteristic exponent, α, for the entire sample, and for nonoverlapping sums of observations from the sample (Fama and Roll (1971)). The test arises from the stability-under-addition property of stable distributions. That is, as the stable Paretian distribution is invariant under addition, the distribution of sums of a stable Paretian distribution is stable Paretian with the same values of α and β (Fama (1963)). Therefore, if the underlying distribution is nonnormal stable, the value of the estimated characteristic exponent, $\hat{\alpha}$, should tend to equality across the sums (Fama and Roll (1971)). If the underlying distribution is a mixture of normals, the values of $\hat{\alpha}$ for the sums should be closer to 2 than for the entire sample (Fama and Roll (1971)).

A mixture of nonnormal stable distributions with different scale parameters also will display the property of $\hat{\alpha}$ rising across the sums (Brenner (1974), Barnea and Downes (1973)). However, if the mixture is drawn from a population with infinite variance ($\alpha < 2$), $\hat{\alpha}$ will stop rising across the sums before it reaches 2 (Barnea and Downes (1973)).

III. Procedure and Data

Following the procedure suggested by Fama and Roll (1971), the two alternate hypotheses, the mixture of normals and the stable Paretian, are tested by estimating α for the entire sample and for nonoverlapping sums of observations from the sample. Monte Carlo studies describing the behavior of $\hat{\alpha}$ under differing distributional assumptions are documented by several authors including Fama and Roll (1971), Barnea and Downes (1973), Blattberg and Gonedes (1974), and Fielitz and Rozelle (1983). As indicated previously, the hypothesis of the mixture of normals is supported if the values of $\hat{\alpha}$ for the sums are closer to 2 than for the entire sample. If the alternate hypothesis of the stable Paretian distribution is appropriate, $\hat{\alpha}$ should tend to equality across the sums. The procedure suggested by Fama and Roll (1971) assumes symmetry and gives results similar to more complex methods that estimate all four parameters if asymmetry is not present. Leitch and Paulson (1975) compared estimating parameters with and without the assumption that β, the measure of skewness, equaled zero and found the effect of β on α was small and decreased as α approached 2.

Logarithms of commodity futures price changes based on daily closing prices are used. The daily closing prices were obtained from the Dunn & Hargitt Commodity Data Bank. Log changes in closing prices of the futures contract nearest delivery are used until approximately two weeks before the delivery date. Then log changes in closing prices for the next nearest delivery month are used. The procedure is repeated as each "nearby" contract reaches its delivery month.[5] This gives a long time series and minimizes differences in maturity.[6] The number of years of data and total number of observations vary by commodity (see Table 1).

The characteristic exponent is calculated for distributions based on all data available and for distributions including data for the six years, 1979–1984. The 1979–1984 period provides a sample of the same size for comparisons between commodities and allows for a comparison within commodities as the size of the sample is increased. Adjacent price movements are summed into groups of increasing size and the characteristic exponent estimated for each distribution. Due to the large amount of data, the inclusion of larger sums is possible. Sum sizes for the full data set are 2, 4, 10, 20, and 30. The larger sums should be able to detect effects due to differing maturities. However, sample size decreases as the sum size increases and, therefore, estimates for larger sums are subject to greater variance. For this reason, the largest sum size for the 1979–1984 subset is 20.

---

[5] To avoid a discontinuity on the date of switch-over between contracts, the first price change of the new series is calculated as the logarithmic price relative of the closing price of the new contract on the day of the switch-over and the day previous to the switch-over.

[6] This is similar to the procedure used by Cornew, et al. (1984).

TABLE 1
Commodities, Years of Data, and Total Number of Observations in Sample

Commodity	(Years)	Total Number of Observations of Daily Returns	Number of Observations of Daily Returns in 6-Year Subset (1979–84)
Financials			
Treasury Bills	(1976–84)	2263	1514
Treasury Bonds	(1978–84)	1764	1513
Deutsche Mark	(1977–84)	2015	1514
Swiss Franc	(1977–84)	2015	1514
British Pound	(1977–84)	2012	1513
Japanese Yen	(1977–84)	2014	1513
Metals			
Copper	(1960–84)	6236	1510
Gold	(1975–84)	2511	1512
Silver	(1964–84)	5234	1509
Agricultural			
Corn	(1960–84)	6287	1511
Soybeans	(1960–84)	6282	1511
Wheat	(1960–84)	6288	1511
Sugar	(1962–84)	5720	1508
Cocoa	(1960–84)	6225	1509
Cotton	(1960–84)	6246	1510
Pork Bellies	(1965–84)	5028	1512
Live Cattle	(1966–84)	4778	1514
Live Hogs	(1970–84)	3773	1512
Lumber	(1974–84)	2769	1513
Coffee	(1979–84)	1507	1507

Note: Data source is the Dunn & Hargitt Commodity Data Bank, Lafayette, IN, Dunn & Hargitt, Inc.

Although subject to greater sampling error, Monte Carlo results of Fama and Roll (1971) show estimates of α to be relatively free of bias with a slight downward bias for small ($N \leq 99$) sample sizes.

As the stability-under-addition property of stable distributions holds only for independent random variables and variance may be correlated over time, daily futures price movements are also randomized. Sums are taken again over the randomized series and the characteristic exponent estimated for each of these distributions. If adjacent price changes in the original series are independent and variance is not correlated over time, the estimated α's for the randomized series should follow the same pattern as those for the original series.

Fama and Roll (1971) suggest estimating α based on order statistics. Their procedure uses the fact that stable distributions are more thick-tailed the smaller the value of α, and thus a given fractile increases as α gets smaller over the interval $1 \leq \alpha \leq 2$. Once the fractile (f) is determined, this measure is compared to known mappings of f and α, $G(f,\alpha)$, to estimate α. Fama and Roll (1968) present tables of $G(f,\alpha)$ for standardized symmetric variables. A standardized variable is defined as $u = (x - \delta)/c$. If x is symmetric stable with parameters α, δ, and $\gamma = c^\alpha$, it follows from the properties of stable distributions that u is stable with parameters α (unaffected by the transformation), $\delta = 0$, and $\gamma = c = 1$. As the value of α is unaffected by the transformation, the tables presented by Fama and Roll (1968) for standardized symmetric variables may be used to provide information about the distribution of x. If x is a symmetric stable variable with characteristic exponent α and scale c, an estimate of α may be found by calculating an estimate of the f fractile, where f is in the tail region, of the standardized symmetric stable distribution with characteristic exponent α.

First, an estimate of c is required. An estimate of c, is the semi-interquartile range (i.e., ½ of $[X_{0.75} - X_{0.25}]$). However, an approximation to the semi-interquartile range, but having lower asymptotic bias (< 0.4 percent), is based on the 0.72 fractile. As the 0.72 fractile of a standardized symmetric stable distribution is in the interval 0.827 ± 0.003 for $1 \leq \alpha \leq 2$ (Fama and Roll (1968), p. 285), Fama and Roll (1968), (1971) suggest an estimator of c as

$$(2) \qquad \hat{c} = (1/2)\left[\left(\hat{X}_{0.72} - \hat{X}_{0.28}\right)/0.827\right],$$

where $\hat{X}_{0.72}$ and $\hat{X}_{0.28}$ are used to estimate the 0.72 and 0.28 fractiles of the distribution of x. An estimate of the f fractile of the standardized symmetric stable distribution with characteristic exponent α is (Fama and Roll (1971))

$$(3) \qquad \hat{Z}_f = (1/2)\left[\left(\hat{X}_f - \hat{X}_{1-f}\right)/\hat{c}\right].$$

Substituting for $\hat{c}$, $\hat{Z}_f$ becomes

$$(4) \qquad \hat{Z}_f = (0.827)\left[\hat{X}_f - \hat{X}_{1-f}/\hat{X}_{0.72} - \hat{X}_{0.28}\right].$$

Fama and Roll (1971) conclude that estimates of α using $0.95 \leq f \leq 0.97$ were robust and relatively free of bias with a slight downward bias for $\alpha > 1.7$ due to the truncation of the sampling distribution at $\hat{\alpha} = 2$. For this study, $f = 0.96$ is used. Thus, the estimate of the 0.96 fractile of the standardized symmetric variable ($\hat{Z}_{0.96}$) can be used to find the appropriate α value for the distribution of x. The estimate of α is from a table of standardized symmetric stable cumulative density functions whose 0.96 fractile matches $\hat{Z}_{0.96}$. The 0.96 fractile monotonically decreases from 7.916 to 2.477 for the interval $1 \leq \alpha \leq 2$ (Fama and Roll (1968), p. 822).[7]

IV. Empirical Results

Estimates of α for the original data series (Tables 2 and 3) present a varied picture. Within the financials group, the two interest rate contracts, Treasury bills and bonds, exhibit rising $\hat{\alpha}$'s across the sums for the full data set and the 1979–1984 sample, but the $\hat{\alpha}$'s do not approach 2. The four currency contracts, for both the full data set and the 1979–1984 sample, exhibit patterns of rising $\hat{\alpha}$'s that approach 2. In the metals group, gold shows a slight tendency for $\hat{\alpha}$ to increase across the sums, but $\hat{\alpha}$ does not approach 2 for either data set. Copper exhibits rising $\hat{\alpha}$'s over the full data set and rising $\hat{\alpha}$'s that approach 2 for the

---

[7] As the value of α must be in the interval $0 < \alpha \leq 2$, following Fama and Roll (1971), any $\hat{Z}_{0.96} \leq 2.477$ is assigned the value of $\hat{\alpha} = 2$. Of the $\hat{\alpha}$ values reported as 2 in Tables 2–5, 58 percent were within 0.20 and 92 percent were within 0.40 of 2.477. Any $\hat{Z}_{0.96}$ value less than 2.477 would arise due to sampling error.

1979–1984 sample. Silver shows no tendency for $\hat{\alpha}$ to increase for the full data set. For the 1979–1984 sample, silver has larger $\hat{\alpha}$ estimates than for the full sample, but there is no tendency for $\hat{\alpha}$ to rise across the sums.

TABLE 2
Estimates of the Characteristic Exponent (α) for Daily Returns in Chronological Order
(All Data)

Commodity	Sum Sizes					
	1	2	4	10	20	30
Financials						
Treasury Bills	1.21	1.25	1.33	1.42	1.43	1.26
Treasury Bonds	<1.00	<1.00	1.11	1.31	1.31	1.50
Deutsche Mark	1.51	1.66	1.69	1.74	1.72	1.92
Swiss Franc	1.67	1.71	1.64	2.00	2.00	1.78
British Pound	1.50	1.51	1.53	1.59	1.99	1.82
Japanese Yen	1.58	1.63	1.57	1.99	2.00	1.94
Metals						
Copper	1.49	1.52	1.51	1.59	1.63	1.84
Gold	1.45	1.50	1.49	1.47	1.39	1.73
Silver	1.34	1.29	1.30	1.36	1.33	1.31
Agricultural						
Corn	1.36	1.40	1.38	1.39	1.49	1.43
Soybeans	1.26	1.23	1.26	1.21	1.21	1.23
Wheat	1.38	1.41	1.39	1.49	1.55	1.45
Sugar	1.69	1.60	1.67	1.78	1.63	1.55
Cocoa	1.75	1.62	1.60	1.80	1.85	1.54
Cotton	1.15	1.21	1.27	1.35	1.32	1.19
Pork Bellies	2.00	1.74	1.82	1.89	1.82	1.55
Live Cattle	1.53	1.50	1.60	1.62	1.63	2.00
Live Hogs	1.65	1.68	1.71	2.00	2.00	1.95
Lumber	2.00	1.90	1.97	1.95	1.71	2.00

Note: The characteristic exponent α measures the total probability in the extreme tails of a distribution. The range for α is $0 < \alpha \leq 2$, with $\alpha = 2$ indicating a normal distribution. Estimates were calculated following Fama and Roll (1971). These estimates are based on finding an estimate of the 0.96 fractile of a standardized symmetric variable and "matching" this to tables of known fractiles and α values.

Within the agricultural group, corn, cocoa, soybeans, wheat, sugar, and cotton show little evidence of rising $\hat{\alpha}$'s over the full data sample. When the sample is restricted to the 1979–1984 period, the $\hat{\alpha}$ estimates are larger but show little tendency to increase over the sums. The other agricultural commodities, pork bellies, live cattle, live hogs, and lumber, exhibit patterns of rising $\hat{\alpha}$'s that approach or equal 2 for both the full sample and the 1979–1984 sample periods. Again, however, lower $\hat{\alpha}$'s are shown for the full data set. Coffee, for which data are only available from 1979–1984, shows a slight tendency for $\hat{\alpha}$ to rise across the sums.

The results for the original data series offer some suppport for the mixture of normal distributions hypothesis. Differences in maturity appear to be relatively unimportant in explaining the observed leptokurticity in futures prices. If nonstationarity in variance due to maturity is present, the summing should remove most of these effects. Therefore, the larger sums would be expected to be much closer to 2 than smaller sums and this is not the case. The estimates of α for the random-

TABLE 3
Estimates of the Characteristic Exponent (α) for Daily Returns in Chronological Order (1979–1984)

Commodity	Sum Sizes				
	1	2	4	10	20
Financials					
Treasury Bills	1.33	1.43	1.35	1.49	1.53
Treasury Bonds	1.04	1.00	1.21	1.48	1.77
Deutsche Mark	1.55	1.69	1.65	2.00	1.45
Swiss Franc	1.67	1.70	1.88	2.00	1.71
British Pound	1.64	1.74	1.81	1.85	1.65
Japanese Yen	1.62	1.60	1.58	1.75	2.00
Metals					
Copper	1.61	1.61	1.78	1.85	2.00
Gold	1.46	1.36	1.45	1.49	1.54
Silver	1.77	1.59	1.52	1.57	2.00
Agricultural					
Corn	1.65	1.73	1.61	1.94	1.58
Soybeans	1.58	1.76	1.74	1.49	1.50
Wheat	1.70	1.75	1.66	1.98	2.00
Sugar	1.95	1.65	1.72	1.92	1.67
Cocoa	1.83	1.82	1.76	2.00	2.00
Cotton	1.61	1.67	2.00	1.58	1.61
Pork Bellies	2.00	1.95	1.95	1.76	2.00
Live Cattle	1.74	1.79	1.88	2.00	2.00
Live Hogs	1.76	1.73	1.80	2.00	1.80
Lumber	2.00	2.00	2.00	1.94	2.00
Coffee	1.51	1.56	1.57	1.66	1.70

Note: The characteristic exponent α measures the total probability in the extreme tails of a distribution. The range for α is $0 < \alpha \leq 2$, with $\alpha = 2$ indicating a normal distribution. Estimates were calculated following Fama and Roll (1971). These estimates are based on finding an estimate of the 0.96 fractile of a standardized symmetric variable and "matching" this to tables of known fractiles and α values.

ized series (Tables 4 and 5), however, are consistent with the mixture of normals hypothesis. The tendency for $\hat{\alpha}$ to approach 2 is much more dramatic for the randomized series. For example, 52 percent of the $\hat{\alpha}$'s for both the full randomized sample and the 1979–1984 randomized sample are between 1.9 and 2.0.

These results support the hypothesis that commodity price movements are mixtures of normals with differing variances (other distributions with a finite variance are also consistent with these results). This conclusion is generally only valid after the data are randomized. That the mixture of normals hypothesis is supported after the data are randomized suggests that adjacent price movements in the original series are not independent, which leads to the observed leptokurtic distributions. Autocorrelation in futures price changes is small. Therefore, the probable cause of the dependence in the distribution is the presence of serially-correlated variances in the original series. As the values of $\hat{\alpha}$ do reach 2 across the sums, it is unlikely that the underlying distributions are nonnormal stable with changing scale.

TABLE 5
Estimates of the Characteristic Exponent (α) for Daily Returns in Randomized Order (1979–1984)

Commodity	\multicolumn{5}{c}{Sum Sizes}
	1	2	4	10	20
Financials					
Treasury Bills	1.33	1.78	1.78	1.86	2.00
Treasury Bonds	1.04	2.00	1.98	1.87	2.00
Deutsche Mark	1.55	2.00	2.00	2.00	2.00
Swiss Franc	1.67	2.00	2.00	2.00	2.00
British Pound	1.64	2.00	2.00	2.00	2.00
Japanese Yen	1.62	1.87	2.00	1.51	1.90
Metals					
Copper	1.61	2.00	1.98	1.90	2.00
Gold	1.46	1.82	1.51	1.93	2.00
Silver	1.77	1.82	1.90	1.85	2.00
Agricultural					
Corn	1.65	2.00	2.00	1.94	2.00
Soybeans	1.58	2.00	1.98	2.00	1.74
Wheat	1.70	1.75	1.88	1.94	2.00
Sugar	1.95	2.00	2.00	2.00	1.90
Cocoa	1.83	1.73	1.77	2.00	2.00
Cotton	1.61	1.74	1.64	1.72	1.29
Pork Bellies	2.00	1.69	1.70	1.63	1.62
Live Cattle	1.74	2.00	1.98	1.81	1.89
Live Hogs	1.76	2.00	1.77	2.00	2.00
Lumber	2.00	2.00	2.00	2.00	1.69
Coffee	1.51	1.83	2.00	1.86	1.75

Note: The characteristic exponent α measures the total probability in the extreme tails of a distribution. The range for α is $0 < \alpha \leq 2$, with $\alpha = 2$ indicating a normal distribution. Estimates were calculated following Fama and Roll (1971). These estimates are based on finding an estimate of the 0.96 fractile of a standardized symmetric variable and "matching" this to tables of known fractiles and α values.

the data. Second, the process generating the nonconstant variance is likely to be complex, responding to seasonal effects, structural shifts in demand and/or supply parameters, changes in government policies, etc., and represents a promising area for future study. Third, option pricing models that assume a constant or deterministically changing variance are likely to exhibit biases in predicting futures options premiums. It is possible though, if the variance changes slowly enough, that for a given option, the assumption of constant variance may be adequate. However, recently proposed models that allow variance to change stochastically (Johnson and Shanno (1987), Hull and White (1987)) represent a promising improvement.

TABLE 4
Estimates of the Characteristic Exponent (α) for Daily Returns in Randomized Order
(All Data)

Commodity	Sum Sizes					
	1	2	4	10	20	30
Financials						
Treasury Bills	1.21	1.71	1.80	1.77	1.94	2.00
Treasury Bonds	<1.00	1.84	1.79	2.00	2.00	1.62
Deutsche Mark	1.51	2.00	1.92	2.00	1.74	1.68
Swiss Franc	1.67	2.00	2.00	2.00	2.00	1.86
British Pound	1.50	2.00	1.98	2.00	2.00	2.00
Japanese Yen	1.58	1.95	2.00	2.00	2.00	2.00
Metals						
Copper	1.49	1.44	1.40	1.55	1.58	1.36
Gold	1.45	1.66	1.90	1.50	1.49	2.00
Silver	1.34	1.66	1.70	1.54	1.64	1.58
Agricultural						
Corn	1.36	1.97	1.86	2.00	2.00	1.80
Soybeans	1.26	2.00	2.00	2.00	2.00	2.00
Wheat	1.38	1.97	1.79	1.92	1.90	1.94
Sugar	1.69	2.00	2.00	2.00	2.00	2.00
Cocoa	1.75	1.79	1.91	1.77	1.88	1.87
Cotton	1.15	2.00	2.00	2.00	2.00	2.00
Pork Bellies	2.00	1.66	1.75	1.64	1.65	1.46
Live Cattle	1.53	1.89	1.93	1.94	1.98	1.68
Live Hogs	1.65	2.00	2.00	2.00	2.00	2.00
Lumber	2.00	1.71	1.80	2.00	2.00	2.00

Note: The characteristic exponent α measures the total probability in the extreme tails of a distribution. The range for α is $0 < \alpha \leq 2$, with $\alpha = 2$ indicating a normal distribution. Estimates were calculated following Fama and Roll (1971). These estimates are based on finding an estimate of the 0.96 fractile of a standardized symmetric variable and "matching" this to tables of known fractiles and α values.

V. Concluding Comments

Two hypotheses, the stable Paretian and mixture of normals, have been proposed to explain the leptokurticity in observed distributions of futures price movements. The two hypotheses are tested by applying the stability-under-addition test of stable distribution parameters to twenty long series of the change in daily futures price closes. This paper improves upon past research by including a larger number of commodities, longer time series, and by randomly ordering the data. For log changes in the original series, the results were suggestive of the mixture of normals. But, even with sum sizes larger than those in past research, the sums still were not distributed normally. The results with the randomized data were strikingly different. Sums of the randomized data did appear normally distributed. This suggests that the observed leptokurtic distribution can be explained by price changes not being independent. The most likely reason for rejecting independence is that variance is serially correlated.

If the variance is serially correlated as our results suggest, there are important implications. First, classical statistical methods may be validly applied to most daily futures price series if an adjustment for heteroskedasticity is made to

References

Anderson, R. W. "Some Determinants of the Volatility of Futures Prices." *Journal of Futures Markets*, 5 (Fall 1985), 331–348.
Barnea, A., and D. H. Downes. "A Re-examination of the Empirical Distribution of Stock Price Changes." *Journal of the American Statistical Association*, 168 (June 1973), 348–350.
Blattberg, R. C., and N. J. Gonedes. "A Comparison of the Stable and Student Distributions as Statistical Models for Stock Prices." *Journal of Business*, 47 (April 1974), 244–280.
Brenner, M. "On the Stability of the Distributions of the Market Component in Stock Price Changes." *Journal of Financial and Quantitative Analysis*, 9 (Dec. 1974), 945–961.
Brorsen, B. W., and S. H. Irwin. "Futures Funds and Price Volatility." *The Review of Futures Markets*, 6 (No. 2, 1987), 118–138.
Clark, P. K. "A Subordinated Stochastic Process Model with Finite Variance for Speculative Prices." *Econometrica*, 41 (Jan. 1973), 135–155.
Cornew, R. W. "Response to a Comment on 'Stable Distributions, Futures Prices, and the Measurement of Trading Performance'." *Journal of Futures Markets*, 6 (Winter 1986), 677–680.
Cornew, R. W.; D. E. Town; and L. D. Crowson. "Stable Distributions, Futures Prices, and the Measurement of Trading Performance." *The Journal of Futures Markets*, 4 (Fall 1984), 531–557.
Doukas, J., and A. Rahman. "Stable Distributions, Futures Prices, and the Measurement of Trading Performance: A Comment." *The Journal of Futures Markets*, 6 (Winter 1986), 505–506.
Dunn & Hargitt Commodity Data Bank. Lafayette, IN, Dunn & Hargitt, Inc.
Epps, T. W., and M. L. Epps. "The Stochastic Dependence of Security Changes and Transaction Volumes: Implications for the Mixtures-of-Distributions Hypothesis." *Econometrica*, 44 (March 1976), 305–321.
Fama, E. F. "Mandelbrot and the Stable Paretian Hypothesis." *Journal of Business*, 36 (Oct. 1963), 420–429.
──────. "The Behavior of Stock Market Prices." *Journal of Business*, 38 (Jan. 1965), 34–105.
Fama, E. F., and R. Roll. "Some Properties of Symmetric Stable Distributions." *Journal of the American Statistical Association*, 63 (Sept. 1968), 817–836.
──────. "Parameter Estimates for Symmetric Stable Distributions." *Journal of the American Statistical Association*, 66 (June 1971), 331–338.
Ficlitz, B. D., and J. P. Rozelle. "Stable Distributions and the Mixtures of Distributions Hypotheses for Common Stock Returns." *Journal of the American Statistical Association*, 78 (March 1983), 28–36.
Gordon, J. D. "The Distribution of Daily Changes in Commodity Futures Prices." Technical Bulletin No. 1702, ERS, USDA (July 1985).
Harris, L. "Transaction Data Tests of the Mixture of Distributions Hypothesis." *Journal of Financial and Quantitative Analysis*, 22 (June 1987), 127–141.
Hudson, M. A.; R. M. Leuthold; and G. F. Sarassoro. "Commodity Futures Price Changes: Recent Evidence for Wheat, Soybeans, and Live Cattle." *Journal of Futures Markets*, 7 (June 1987), 287–301.
Hull, J., and A. White. "The Pricing of Options on Assets with Stochastic Volatilities." *Journal of Finance*, 62 (June 1987), 281–300.
Johnson, H., and D. Shanno. "Option Pricing when Variance is Changing." *Journal of Financial and Quantitative Analysis*, 22 (June 1987), 143–151.
Kenyon, D.; K. Kling; J. Jordan; W. Seale; and N. McCabe. "Factors Affecting Agricultural Futures Price Variance." *Journal of Futures Markets*, 7 (Feb. 1987), 73–91.
Leitch, R. A., and A. S. Paulson. "Estimation of Stable Law Parameters: Stock Price Behavior." *Journal of the American Statistical Association*, 70 (Sept. 1975), 690–697.
Mandelbrot, B. "The Variation of Certain Speculative Prices." *Journal of Business*, 36 (Oct. 1963), 394–419.
Mann, J. S., and R. G. Heifner. "The Distribution of Short-Run Commodity Price Movements." Technical Bulletin No. 1536, ERS, USDA (1976).
Morgan, I. G. "Stock Prices and Heteroskedasticity." *Journal of Business*, 49 (Oct. 1976), 496–508.
Officer, R. "The Distribution of Stock Returns." *Journal of the American Statistical Association*, 67 (Dec. 1972), 807–812.
Perry, P. R. "More Evidence on the Nature of the Distribution of Security Returns." *Journal of Financial and Quantitative Analysis*, 18 (June 1983), 211–221.
So, J. C. "The Sub-Gaussian Distribution of Currency Futures: Stable Paretian or Nonstationary?" *Review of Economics and Statistics*, 69 (Feb. 1987), 100–107.

Tauchen, G., and M. Pitts. "The Price Variability-Volume Relationship on Speculative Markets." *Econometrica*, 51 (March 1983), 485–505.

Taylor, S. J. "The Behavior of Futures Prices over Time." *Applied Economics*, 17 (Aug. 1985), 713–734.

Teichmoeller, J. "A Note on the Distribution of Stock Price Changes." *Journal of the American Statistical Association*, 66 (June 1971), 282–284.

Westerfield, R. "The Distribution of Common Stock Price Changes: An Application of Transactions Time and Subordinated Stochastic Models." *Journal of Financial and Quantitative Analysis*, 12 (Dec. 1977), 743–765.

[13]

Futures Prices Are not Stable-Paretian Distributed

Donald W. Gribbin
Randy W. Harris
Hon-Shiang Lau

INTRODUCTION

The (unconditional) distribution of stock and futures prices has been considered by many researchers [e.g., see review in Badrinath and Chatterjee (1988)]. One major theory asserts that these prices follow the stable (Pareto–Levy) distribution. This article uses a newly developed statistical methodology [Lau, Lau, and Wingender (1990)] to show conclusively that the stable distribution is unsuitable as a general model for futures price changes.

BRIEF LITERATURE REVIEW

The characteristic function of a stable distribution is

$$\log \phi(t) = i\delta t - c|t|^\alpha \cdot [1 + i\gamma(t/|t|) \tan(\pi\alpha/2)] \quad \text{for } 0 < \alpha \leq 2 \quad (1)$$

c and δ are the scale and location parameters, respectively. Parameter γ measures asymmetry, $-1 \leq \gamma \leq 1$. Parameter α controls tail thickness, smaller α gives thicker tails. If $\alpha \leq 1$, the distribution's mean is undefined; if $1 < \alpha \leq 2$, the distribution has a finite mean but infinite second- and higher-order moments.

Mandelbrot (1963) and Fama (1965) claimed that prices of many financial instruments should be modeled by stable distributions with $1 < \alpha \leq 2$. Since then numerous studies have presented evidence for and against this claim. Most of the studies consider only stock prices [e.g., see review in Akgiray and Booth (1988)]. For futures prices, Cornew, Town, and Crowson (1984) show that stable distributions provide a better fit than the normal distribution for various types of commodities. Similarly, So (1987) claims that the stable distribution is suitable for most currency futures and spot rates. In contrast, Hudson, Leuthold, and Sarassoro (1987) and Hall, Brorsen, and Irwin (1989) use the "stability-under-addition" test to show that futures prices do not appear to be stable distributed. Note that all preceding four

---

Donald W. Gribbin is an Assistant Professor at the School of Accountancy at Southern Illinois University.

Randy W. Harris is a Management Analyst at the Oklahoma Medical Center, Oklahoma City.

Hon-Shiang Lau is Regents Professor of Management at Oklahoma State University.

futures studies consider only the hypothesis of identically distributed stable-Paretian price changes.

This study explains why a test stronger than the stability-under-addition test is needed to resolve the controversy of whether futures prices are stable distributed. Further, such a test is presented, applied and analyzed.

A CRITIQUE OF THE "STABILITY-UNDER-ADDITION" TEST

Review of the "Stability-Under-Addition" Test

Fama and Roll (1971) propose the following "stability-under-addition" method for testing whether a given series is stable distributed:

If an n-element series $\{X\} = \{x_1, x_2, \ldots x_n\}$ is stable distributed with a given α-value [see eq. (1)], then if one forms an m-element series $\{Y\} = \{y_1, y_2, \ldots y_m\}$ by summing up k consecutive elements in $\{X\}$; i.e., $m = n/k$ and:

$$y_1 = \sum_{i=1}^{k} x_i \quad y_2 = \sum_{i=k+1}^{2k} x_i \quad y_3 = \sum_{i=2k+1}^{3k} x_i \quad \text{etc.} \tag{2}$$

then $\{Y\}$ should have the same α-value. However, if $\{X\}$ is not stable distributed, then $\{Y\}$ will have increasingly larger α-values for increasingly larger k-values [see eq. (2)] used to construct $\{Y\}$.

Applying this test to futures prices of various commodities, both Hudson et al. (1987) and Hall et al. (1989) conclude that, for a large percentage of these commodities, the α-values of their $\{Y\}$-series increase with k. Therefore, they conclude that the stable model may not be generally valid.

However, two points, as explained below, can be used to defend the stable model against "unfavorable" results from the stability-under-addition test.

Defense Using Fielitz and Rozelle's (1983) Results

First, Fielitz and Rozelle (1983) show that [see Fielitz and Rozelle (1983, Tables 8 and 9)] if series $\{X\}$ is formed by mixtures of stable distributions with different c-and γ-values [see eq. (1)], the estimated α-values from the $\{Y\}$-series will also increase with k [k defined in eq. (2)]. In other words, the results observed by Hudson et al. (1987) and Hall et al. (1989) can be explained by the alternative hypothesis that the futures prices are generated by mixtures of stable distributions. In fact, Fielitz and Rozelle (1983, p. 34) conclude that their "simulations indicate that the more general nonnormal *stable* mixtures model may be preferred (over the normal mixture model)." This conclusion is not addressed by Hudson et al. (1987).

Defense Based on the Sampling Error of α-Estimates

The second defense for the stable distribution is the fact that α-estimates are affected by sampling errors, and one cannot be sure whether an observed change (or trend) in α-estimates is merely a random fluctuation or due to actual changes in the α-parameter. Table I presents examples of the Koutrouvelis method's sampling error properties as reported by Koutrouvelis (1980).

For example, the last row of Table I means that, from a stable population with $\alpha = 1.3$ and $\gamma = 0$, a sample of $n = 200$ observations is drawn from it, and α is estimated from this sample using the Koutrouvelis method. This procedure is repeated

Table I
EXTRACTS FROM KOUTROUVELIS (1980, TABLE 3): STATISTICAL
CHARACTERISTICS OF α-ESTIMATES FROM KOUTROUVELIS' METHOD

Population (α, γ)	# of Observations Used to Estimate an α-Value	# of α-Estimates	Statistics of α-Estimates		
			Max.	Min.	SD
(1.9, 0)	1600	50	1.96	1.82	0.037
(1.9, 0)	200	160	2.00	1.70	0.083
(1.7, 0)	1600	50	1.79	1.59	0.042
(1.7, 0)	200	160	1.95	1.45	0.107
(1.5, 0)	1600	50	1.58	1.39	0.041
(1.5, 0)	200	160	1.81	1.16	0.119
(1.3, 0)	1600	50	1.38	1.19	0.044
(1.3, 0)	200	160	1.65	1.04	0.130

160 times. The values of the resultant 160 α-estimates range from 1.04–1.65, and the estimates' S.D. is 0.130. For smaller n, the range of probable α-estimate will be larger. Also, compared with the more recent and sophisticated Koutrouvelis (1980) method, the older Fama and Roll (1971) method of estimating α is less reliable, and hence, will produce a wider range of α-estimates [Akgiray and Lamoureux (1989)].

Consider now the extracts shown in Table II from Hall et al.'s (1989) "best" results (i.e., their Table 4). Table II shows only one example (gold) that purports to reject the stable hypothesis, and one example (copper) that does not. For gold, although Table II indicates that the initial number of observations is 2511, when $k = 4, 10, 20,$ or 30, the effective sample size is reduced to, respectively, 627, 251, 125, or 83.

Referring back to Table I, it is apparent that gold's various α-estimates, shown in Table II, could have been generated from a stable population with, say, $\alpha = 1.55$. In other words, the variation of gold's α-estimates (including the fact that the α-estimate reaches 2 when $k = 30$) can be explained as sampling errors from a genuine stable population. Similarly, Copper's α-estimates shown in Table II could have been generated from a stable population with, say, $\alpha = 1.5$. Also, under the stability-under-addition logic, Copper's α-estimates seem to indicate that copper's futures are clearly stable distributed.

The Need to Specify a Significance Level in Hypothesis Testing

The sampling error factor discussed above reinforces the basic statistical concept that, in testing a hypothesis, one should have a test that can reject the hypothesis at a specified significance level (denoted in this study by "AL" instead of the conventional "α" symbol). However, this concept is not (and cannot be) implemented in the stability-under-addition test. To implement this concept, it is necessary to know the

Table II
EXTRACTS FROM TABLE IV IN HALL ET AL. (1989)
ESTIMATE OF α-VALUE AT DIFFERENT k

Commodity	# of Observations in $\{X\}$-Series	k-Value					
		1	2	4	10	20	30
Gold	2511	1.45	1.66	1.90	1.50	1.49	2.00
Copper	6236	1.49	1.44	1.40	1.55	1.58	1.36

statistical characteristics of the sampling distributions of α-estimates obtained from stable distributions with: (i) various (α, γ)-parameters; (ii) at different sample sizes, n; and (iii) using various methods [e.g., those by Fama and Roll (1971) or Koutrouvelis (1980)]. Of course, this information is currently unavailable and is also very difficult to compile. In contrast, the method described below enables one to test (and reject) the stable hypothesis at a specified AL.

BRIEF SUMMARY OF THE LAU ET AL. (1990) METHOD FOR TESTING THE STABLE HYPOTHESIS

Basic Definitions and Properties

For a random variable x, let μ_x be its expected value, $\mu_k(x) = E(x - \mu_x)^k$ be its kth central moment, $\beta_1(x) = \mu_3(x)/\mu_2(x)^{1.5}$, $\beta_2(x) = \mu_4(x)/\mu_2(x)^2$, $\beta_4(x) = \mu_6(x)/\mu_2(x)^3$. β_1 and β_2 are, respectively, the standardized skewness and kurtosis indicators for finite μ_k distributions. The sample estimates of $\mu_i(x)$ and $\beta_i(x)$ are, respectively, m_i and b_i. To compute these estimates with n sample observations x_is ($i = 1$ to n), set

$$m_1(x) = \Sigma x_i/n, \quad m_k(x) = \Sigma(x_i - m_1)^k/n \quad \text{for } k \geq 2 \quad (3)$$

$$b_2(x) = m_4(x)/[m_2(x)]^2, \quad b_4(x) = m_6(x)/[m_2(x)]^3 \quad (4)$$

When the identity of the random variable is obvious, the qualifier "x" is omitted.

A normal distribution has $\beta_1 = 0$ and $\beta_2 = 3$. Distributions with $\beta_2 > 3$ have "thick tails" and are called leptokurtic.

Brief Description of the Lau et al. Test

A new method developed by Lau et al. (1990) for testing whether a reasonably large sample of (say) futures price changes comes from a stable population is based on the following simple principle: If a population has finite higher-order moments, the b_2 and b_4 computed with a sample of size n from this population should approach the population's finite β_2 and β_4 when n is large. On the other hand, if the population is stable distributed, and hence has infinite higher moments (therefore, infinite β_2 and β_4), the b_2 and b_4 computed from large samples will tend to increase without bound as n increases. Therefore, if the b_2 and b_4 of a sample of future prices are much smaller than the expected magnitudes of b_2 and b_4 from an equal-sized sample of a stable population, one can conclude that the sample of future prices does not come from a stable population.

For example, from a stable population with $\alpha = 1.7$, a sample of $n = 5000$ observations are computer simulated and a pair of (b_2, b_4) is computed (say, $b_2 = 46$ and $b_4 = 8772$). This process is repeated 500 times. From the resultant 500 (b_2, b_4) values, the statistical characteristics of b_2 and b_4 obtained for 5000-observation samples from a stable population with $\alpha = 1.7$ are shown in Table III.

Lau et al. (1990) show that the above characteristics are applicable for stable populations of $\alpha = 1.7$ with any skewness. Therefore, if a sample of 5000 observations of a commodity's futures price changes has a fitted $\alpha = 1.7$, and if these observations have one of the following characteristics: (a) a $b_2 = 14$ (say) which is lower than the 1st percentile of b_2 (equal to 30 from Table III) from a stable population, or (b) a $b_4 = 1070$ (say) which is lower than the 1st percentile of b_4 (equal to 3278 from Table III) from a stable population, then, one can reject, at $AL = 0.01$, the null hypothesis (H_0) that futures price changes are stable distributed, regardless of whether

Table III
MEAN, SD, AND LOWER PERCENTILES OF b_2 AND b_4 ESTIMATED FROM SAMPLES WITH $n = 5000$ FROM A STABLE ($\alpha = 1.7$) POPULATION

Statistic	Mean	SD	Lower Percentiles			
			1st	2nd	5th	10th
b_2	598	880	30	35	46	67
b_4	1,520,861	3,873,438	3278	4561	8772	14768

the population is skewed. If both characteristics (a) and (b) are observed, H_0 is rejected at an $AL < 0.01$, but not at $AL = 0.01 \times 0.01$, since b_2 and b_4 are closely correlated.

Applicability of the Lau et al. Test to Dependent Variables

Fama–Roll's stability-under-addition test is for a series with independent elements. However, as shown in Fielitz (1983) and Hall et al. (1989), the test can be easily adapted for a dependent series by simply randomizing the series. Note that the series' (unconditional) distribution (the issue considered in this and earlier related studies) is not affected by the ordering of the series' individual elements. In using the Lau et al. test with dependent series, even the randomizing step necessary to Fama–Roll's test can be eliminated, since the values of b_2 and b_4 of a series are not affected by the ordering of the individual elements (in contrast, the fitted α-value in Fama–Roll's test *is* affected by the ordering). In other words, if the Lau et al. test concludes that a series' distribution is not stable-Paretian, this conclusion holds, regardless of whether the series' elements are dependent.

DATA AND PROCEDURES

Let P_t be the price of a financial instrument at day t (e.g., the closing price of a futures contract). Define:

"price change" as $PC_t = P_t - P_{t-1}$ (5a)

"price ratio" as $PR_t = P_t/P_{t-1}$ (5b)

"log of price ratio" as $LPR_t = \text{Log}(PR_t)$ (5c)

Mandelbrot's (1963) theoretical arguments for stable-distributed price changes are based on the *arithmetic* price difference (i.e., PC_t), but practically all previous empirical studies supporting the stable hypothesis for futures prices [e.g., Cornew, Town, and Crowson (1984); So (1987)] consider LPR_t. However, it is far from obvious (and nobody has shown) how Mandelbrot's arguments based on the arithmetic price differences can also be valid for price ratios (i.e., PR_t or LPR_t). For more conclusive results, this empirical study tests the validity fo the stable hypothesis for both PC_t and LPR_t.

Futures prices for 13 commodities are from the Center for the Study of Futures Markets (CSFM) at Columbia University. Following the procedure of Cornew et al. (1984) and Hall et al. (1989), for each commodity and each contract, the values of PC_ts are compiled for consecutive trading days until approximately two weeks before the contract's delivery date. For each commodity, the first 5000 PC_ts generated by the CSFM data are collected. Although more than 5000 PC_ts can be obtained

Table IV
VALUES OF ESTIMATED α, b_2, AND b_4 PC_tS FOR 13 FUTURES ($n = 5000$)

Commodity	α-Estimate	b_2	b_4
1. Treasury bill, 91-day (IMM)	1.615	6.71	103.9
2. Treasury bonds (Day Night)	0.443	6.14	68.1
3. Swiss franc (IMM)	1.362	8.27	252.7
4. Japanese yen (IMM)	0.524	28.35	5395.6
5. British pound (IMM)	0.880	11.74	801.3
6. Copper (COMEX)	1.682	3.84	31.3
7. Silver (COMEX)	1.677	4.54	50.0
8. Gold (COMEX)	1.634	6.08	88.9
9. Corn (CBOT)	1.609	8.82	240.7
10. Soybeans (CBOT)	1.294	13.68	316.1
11. Wheat (CBOT)	1.722	7.07	136.9
12. Live cattle (MIDAM)	1.676	14.19	1708.0
13. Live hogs (MIDAM)	1.641	10.25	885.4

Table V
ESTIMATED LOWER PERCENTILES OF STABLE DISTRIBUTIONS' b_2 AND b_4 WHEN $n = 5000$ (BASED ON 500 SIMULATIONS PER α-VALUE)

Percentile	$\alpha = 1.5$		$\alpha = 1.6$		$\alpha = 1.7$		$\alpha = 1.8$		$\alpha = 1.9$	
	b_2	b_4	b_2	b_4	b_2	b_4	b_2	b_4	b_2	b_4
1st	79	15,814	51	7,539	30	3,278	14.7	925	5.8	145
2nd	88	21,934	59	10,681	35	4,561	17.1	1,229	6.4	178
5th	121	37,560	79	20,017	46	8,772	22.5	2,529	7.7	337
10th	175	74,489	112	37,104	67	14,768	30.4	4,524	9.6	552

from the CSFM data for most commodities, it will be apparent later that the sample size of 5000 is more than adequate for the purpose.

For each commodity, the Koutrouvelis (1980) method is used to estimate the α-value of the 5000 PC_ts; Akgiray and Lamoureux (1989) show that the Koutrouvelis method is the best among several alternatives. The values of b_2 and b_4 [see eq. (4)] are also computed for these PC_ts. The results are shown in Table IV. The Lau et al. (1990) Table III is represented here as Table V. This table gives the lower percentiles of the sampling distributions of b_2 and b_4 computed with 5000 observations from stable populations.

RESULTS: PRESENTATION AND INTERPRETATION

Interpreting Table IV for PC_ts Distribution

Table IV shows that the 5000 PC_t observations for commodity 1 (IMM 91-day Treasury bill) has a fitted α of 1.615. Table V has entries for only $\alpha = 1.6$ and 1.7, but not for $\alpha = 1.615$. Table V also shows that the lower percentiles of stable-distribution's b_2 and b_4 decrease as α increases. Therefore, to be conservative, commodity 1's b_2 and b_4 are compared with the entries for $\alpha = 1.7$ in Table V. Since commodity 1's b_2 (= 6.74) and b_4 (104.4) are both considerably smaller than their corresponding 1st-percentile values (30 and 3278) in Table V, the stable distribution null hypothesis for commodity 1's PC_t can be rejected at $AL < 0.01$.

Consider now commodity 3 (IMM Swiss Franc), with $\alpha = 1.362$. Table V has no entries for $\alpha = 1.3$ or 1.4, but since the percentiles in Table V increase with decreasing α, the entries of $\alpha = 1.5$ in Table V can be used to benefit the position of the stable distribution null hypothesis. Even with this benefit, commodity 3's sample b_2 and b_4 again reject this null hypothesis at $AL < 0.01$ by using the entries for $\alpha = 1.5$ in Table V.

Using the above approach, it can be verified that the stable hypothesis can be rejected at $AL < 0.01$ for all the 13 commodities shown in Table IV. In contrast, recall from Table II that the Hall et al. (1989) results indicate that, for example, copper's (commodity 6) futures are stable distributed. The four groupings of commodities shown in Table IV include all major categories of futures markets.

Explanation for Cases with $\alpha < 1$

Table IV shows that commodities 2, 4, and 5 have $\alpha < 1$. Although the entries for $\alpha = 1.5$ in Table V (as in commodity 3) can be used to reject the stable hypothesis with a wide margin, one might question whether the appearance of cases with $\alpha < 1$ implies something wrong with the α-fitting procedure. Note that a stable distribution with $\alpha < 1$ has an infinite mean, and earlier advocates of the stable distribution suggest (though without clear justifications) that financial variables such as futures price changes come from populations with $\alpha > 1$. It might be argued that if one is willing to believe that these populations have infinite variances, there is no reason why one should not also believe that these populations have infinite means. Nevertheless, those empirical PC_t distributions with $\alpha < 1$ are examined closely.

Table VI shows the frequency distributions of the PC_ts that generate the results in Table IV for commodities 2 (Treasury bonds, with $\alpha = 0.443$) and 7 (silver, with $\alpha = 1.677$). The frequency distribution for commodity 7 is unimodal with tails stretching out at both ends. This is the expected form for a stable distribution. In contrast, commodity 2's frequency distribution exhibits an upturn at the end of the right-hand tail which is a distinctive nonstable characteristic. Other distributions with fitted α-values less than 1 are found to have similar nonstable characteristics.

Table VI
FREQUENCY DISTRIBUTIONS OF PC_tS OF COMMODITIES 2 AND 7

Commodity 2 (Treasury Bonds)		Commodity 7 (Silver)	
Interval	Frequency	Interval	Frequency
> −312.0 to −258.7	1	> −230.0 to −192.6	1
> −258.7 to −205.4	2	> −192.6 to −155.2	0
> −205.4 to −152.1	52	> −155.2 to −117.8	0
> −152.1 to −98.8	94	> −117.8 to −80.4	76
> −98.8 to −45.5	648	> −80.4 to −43.0	351
> −45.5 to 7.8	3054	> −43.0 to −5.6	1497
> 7.8 to 61.1	512	> −5.6 to 31.8	2369
> 61.1 to 114.4	565	> 31.8 to 69.2	556
> 114.4 to 167.7	9	> 69.2 to 106.6	146
> 167.7 to 221.0	63	> 106.6 to 144.0	4

Since Koutrouvelis' procedure is designed to estimate stable's α for a distribution that is *actually* stable (so are other α-estimation procedures), one can now understand why the procedure produces unrealistic estimates when it is forced to produce an α-estimate for a distribution that is clearly nonstable. Hall et al. (1989) also report (without explanation) a few α-estimates less than 1 with the Fama–Roll (1971) α-estimation procedure.

Distributions of Log of Price Ratios

Table VII is the counterpart of Table IV for the variable LPR_t [see eq. (5c)]. The same conclusion is reached: the stable hypothesis is rejected for all commodities at a very low AL.

Price Limits as a Possible Factor Limiting the Magnitudes of b_2 and b_4

While it is the purpose of this study to test *whether* empirical futures price changes are actually stable-Paretian, the fact that many commodities have imposed price-change limits may explain *why* the b_2s and b_4s of these price changes do not attain the large magnitudes expected from stable-Paretian populations. Therefore, if the stable-Paretian model is convenient, one might attempt to salvage it by conjecturing that futures price changes *could have been* stable-Paretian in a modified world that has no imposed price-change limits. However, it is shown later that the stable-Paretian model is unnecessarily troublesome compared to other currently available alternatives and is not worth salvaging. Incidentally, Akgiray and Booth (1988) and Lau et al. (1990) have shown that stock prices that have no price-change limits are not stable-Paretain.

CONSIDERATION OF NONSTATIONARY PARAMETERS

The conclusions in the preceding section are based on the implicit assumption that the PC_ts (or LPR_ts) are identically (though not necessarily independently) distrib-

Table VII
VALUES OF ESTIMATED α, b_2, AND b_4 OF LOG(P_t/P_{t-1})s FOR 13 FUTURES ($n = 5000$)

Commodity	α-Estimate	b_2	b_4
1. Treasury bill, 91-day (IMM)	1.617	6.67	102.4
2. Treasury bonds (DayNight)	0.442	8.06	116.9
3. Swiss franc (IMM)	1.382	8.78	273.9
4. Japanese yen (IMM)	0.549	27.61	5195.5
5. British pound (IMM)	0.817	12.12	535.6
6. Copper (COMEX)	1.825	3.37	18.3
7. Silver (COMEX)	1.748	4.08	37.5
8. Gold (COMEX)	1.610	5.86	68.2
9. Corn (CBOT)	1.675	7.57	158.9
10. Soybeans (CBOT)	1.366	11.27	225.5
11. Wheat (CBOT)	1.812	5.83	102.9
12. Live cattle (MIDAM)	1.645	12.54	1260.6
13. Live hogs (MIDAM)	1.686	9.93	769.1

uted, since Koutrouvelis' α-estimation procedure assumes a homogeneous population, and the b_2/b_4 characteristics tabulated in Table V are for homogeneous stable populations. However, it is suggested [e.g., see Samuelson (1965) and Doukas and Rahman (1986)] that the PC_ts and LPR_ts come from a mixture of different stable distributions due to one or more of the following reasons: (i) economic and trading environments go through fundamental changes during the long time span required to generate 5000 observations; (ii) prices become more volatile as a contract's maturity approaches; (iii) price changes over two consecutive calendar days are different from price changes over two consecutive trading days separated by a weekend or holiday. Therefore, the applicability of the Lau et al. (1990) procedure when the PC_ts and LPR_ts have nonstationary parameters is considered now.

The Lau et al. Experiment

Lau et al. (1990) generate 100 theoretical PC_t series with 5000 elements per series. Each series is composed of 10 subseries, with 500 stable-distributed elements per subseries. The parameters δ, c, α and γ [see eq. (1)] in each subseries of each series are generated randomly, and the ranges of these parameters are much wider than what can be reasonably expected from empirical distributions of stock prices. They find that the b_2s and b_4s obtained from these simulated stable series with heterogeneous parameters are still very large and correspond closely to those depicted in Table V, but not as small as those observed in empirical price-change distributions (as in Tables IV and VII). Therefore, the small b_2s and b_4s observed from empirical PC_t distributions are still effective indicators for rejecting the type of *exaggerated* parameter heterogeneity considered in the Lau et al. experiment.

Stable Populations with Heterogeneous Scale Parameters

A reviewer has suggested that "a stable distribution with $\alpha = 1.9$ and a time-varying scale parameter remains a viable model" for the empirical data depicted in Tables IV and VII. To systematically study the effect of mixing two stable populations with the same α of 1.9 but with different scale parameters, consider now two stable populations, A and B, with identical $\delta (= 0)$, $\gamma (= 0)$, and $\alpha (= 1.9)$. The following procedure is used to generate PC_t series: Let populations A and B have c (scale parameter) $= 1$ and K, respectively, and let the "mixing proportion" be $(1 - p)$ and p. That is, for each PC_t series, $5000(1 - p)$ elements are generated from population A with $\alpha = 1.9$ and $c = 1$, and $5000p$ elements are generated from population B with $\alpha = 1.9$ and $c = K$.

For each pair of (p, K), 200 PC_t series (each with 5000 elements) are generated. For each series, its b_2 and b_4 are computed and its α is estimated by the Koutrouvelis method. From the 200 sets of values of b_2s, b_4s, and α-estimates, the α-estimates' mean and standard deviation are computed, as well as the 10th, 30th, and 50th percentiles of the b_2s and the b_4s. Thus, Table VIII shows that, with $p = 0.01$ and $K = 3$, the average of the 200 α-estimates is 1.87; the 10th, 30th, and 50th percentiles of the b_2s are 10.4, 21.6, and 16,132, respectively; and the corresponding percentiles of the b_4s are 573, 3307, and 16,132. Table VIII also gives the corresponding values for other (p, K) combinations. For each (p, K) combination, only the average of the α-estimates is given, because it is found that the standard deviation is about 0.02 for all combinations; i.e., within each (p, K) combination the variation of the α-estimates is small, as would be expected since the "sample size" here is 5000. Note that the high α-value of 1.9 is chosen here to give the stable-distribution null

Table VIII
CHARACTERISTICS OF b_2S, b_4S AND α-ESTIMATES FROM MIXTURES OF TWO STABLE $\alpha = 1.9$ SUBPOPULATIONS

	K = 3			K = 10			K = 50		
	α	b_2	b_4	α	b_2	b_4	α	b_2	b_4
$p = 0.01$	1.87	10.4	573	1.78	53.5	7,730	1.78	214	65,899
		21.6	3307		72.7	14,964		254	100,035
		53.9	16,132		92.8	25,554		293	137,821
$p = 0.1$	1.68	13.3	691	1.23	29.4	1,740	1.13	35.0	2,210
		22.8	2,438		36.0	3,406		42.3	4,413
		41.3[a]	10,185		49.8	8,770		58.7	11,536
$p = 0.3$	1.50	13.3	696	0.75	16.0	734	0.51	16.8	795
		21.8	2,914		26.4	3,500		27.5	3,636
		41.5	9,691[a]		47.8	12,002		49.7	12,262
$p = 0.5$	1.52	10.7	474[a]	0.68	11.6	560	0.15	11.8	578
		19.2	1,982[a]		20.0	2,194		20.4	2,274
		45.7	14,419		52.8	16,613		53.9	17,253
$p = 0.7$	1.67	10.0	524	1.26	10.6	553	1.19	10.7	561
		21.7	3,276		22.2	2,890		22.4	2,968
		44.1	11,820		45.9	11,665		46.3	11,785
$p = 0.9$	1.84	9.5	488	1.81	9.7	502	1.80	9.8	504
		21.1	3,823		21.3	3,950		21.4	3,962
		44.7	10,841		45.0	11,179		45.1	11,212
$p = 0.99$	1.89	8.8[a]	476	1.89	8.8	478	1.89	8.8	478
		20.9[a]	3,655		20.9	3,665		20.9	3,666
		56.2	19,357		56.3	19,393		56.3	19,396

[a] Indicates lowest percentile value among all (p, K) combinations.

hypothesis a favorable position, since a higher α gives lower expected b_2s and b_4s (as depicted in Table V), thus making it more difficult to reject a stable-population null hypothesis.

The most glaring phenomenon depicted in Table VIII is that the estimated α of a large sample from a mixture of populations can be much smaller than the true α of the component populations. In the extreme case, where $p = 0.5$ and $K = 50$, even though the two component populations have $\alpha = 1.9$, the average estimated α of samples from the mixture is only 0.15 (the actual range of estimated α values from the 200 series is from 0.13 to 0.16). However, for the purpose of this study, a more relevant and important observation is that, for any (p, K) combination, the b_2s and b_4s of the 5000-element samples are still very large. For example, b_2s 10th percentile is as large as 214 when $p = 0.01$ and $K = 50$ but, even in the smallest case, it is 8.8 when $p = 0.99$ and $K = 3$.

Consider now commodity 1 (Treasury bill in Table VII) with its α-estimate of 1.617 and $b_2 = 6.67$. The 1st-percentile b_2 entry for $\alpha = 1.7$ in Table V was used earlier to reject the identically distributed stable hypothesis. At this point, however, one might argue that the low estimated α of 1.617 may arise from the following model:

Hypothesis X: The commodity's PC_is come from a mixture of two stable populations with different scale parameters but identical $\alpha = 1.9$.

However, under Model X, the b_2s 10th percentile should still be *at least* 8.8 (if $p = 0.99$) but could be much higher (say, when $p = 0.01$ and $K = 50$). Therefore, Hypothesis X can be rejected very comfortably at $AL = 0.1$, no matter what (p, K) combination a Hypothesis X proponent wants to assume.

In Table VIII, for each set of percentiles (say, the 10th percentiles of b_2), the *lowest* percentile value among all (p, K) combinations is identified with an "a". Noting now that the lowest 10th percentile for b_4 in Table VIII is 474 (when $p = 0.5$ and $K = 3$), the preceding logic can be used to reject Hypothesis X at $AL = 0.1$ for 9 of the 13 commodities in Table IV (i.e., commodities 1, 2, 3, 6, 7, 8, 9, 10, and 11). Of the remaining four commodities, since the lowest 30th percentile is 20.9 for b_2 (at $p = 0.99$ in Table VIII), and is 1982 for b_4 (at $p = 0.5$ and $K = 3$), the null hypothesis can be rejected very comfortably at $AL = 0.3$ for three of them (commodities 5, 12, and 13). Therefore, the null Hypothesis X cannot be rejected for only one commodity (4). However, so far, the null Hypothesis X is considered as a model for each *individual* commodity. Next, the null Hypothesis X is considered as a general model for *all* commodities.

It is well known that, setting up a certain hypothesis as a null hypothesis puts it at a great advantage over the alternative hypothesis. Therefore, in setting up the null hypothesis, one should have ascertained from other considerations that the null hypothesis is more likely to be true than the alternative hypothesis. Table VIII illustrates that nine of the 13 commodities have either their b_2s or b_4s (most have both) below the *lowest* 10th-percentile b_2 and b_4 and three of the remaining four commodities have either their b_2s or b_4s below the *lowest* 30th-percentile b_2 and b_4. It should be obvious that Model X is not a suitable general model for all commodities. Therefore, Hypothesis X should not be given the status of a null hypothesis. Since commodity 4's b_2 and b_4 are smaller then the *lowest* 50th-percentile b_2 and b_4 (see Table VIII) there is no reason to assume that commodity 4's PC_is are stable distributed.

It is impossible to test all the possible variations of mixtures of stable distributions that one can propose as possible models for the PC_is depicted in Table IV. However, the experiments described in this section illustrate a simple principle: if the population is composed of several different stable subpopulations, the sample b_2 and b_4 will still be as large as those shown in Table V (or even larger), but not as small as those observed in Tables IV and VII.[1]

CONCLUSION

This study shows conclusively that the stable distribution (with or without dependence and/or parameter stationarity) is unsuitable as a *general* model for futures prices. Although one or two commodities have price changes that are not totally

---

[1] On a related factor, Lau et al. (1990) have shown that the b_2/b_4 test is robust against special events such as the stock market's 1987 "Black Monday" effect, which may be considered as a form of parameter heterogeneity of the generating distributions.

inconsistent with a model of stable distribution with nonstationary parameters, it is shown below that simpler alternative models are available for these cases. The high b_2 values shown in Tables VI and VII do confirm the well-known fact that prices of financial instruments are typically nonnormal.

Many models have been proposed to explain the nonnormal and eptokurtic nature of futures prices. These models include, among others: the stable-Paretian, the mixture of normals or exponentials, time series, four-parameter general distribution functions, etc. Besides the stable-Paretian model, all other alternatives make use of finite-moment distributions that have explicit density functions and much more tractable fitting and computational procedures. In contrast, the stable-Paretian model requires the queer notion of infinite variance and higher moments, has no explicit density function, and is generally difficult to handle. The earlier literature advocating stable-Paretian models concentrates on the version of i. i. d. stable-Paretian variables because this version requires the determination of only four parameters. However, if a mixture of stables has to be used, then not only is there no developed procedure for fitting empirical data to a mixture of stable-Paretian distributions, but the model would involve more parameters than (say) a mixture-of-normals model. Since this study shows only very weak evidence for the mixture-of-stables hypothesis (and then only for a small minority of the commodities considered), there appears to be very little reason to attempt to salvage the stable-Paretian models.

The belief in stable-distributed stock and futures prices has spurred a considerable amount of effort to develop supporting investment decision models for stable-Paretian markets [e.g., Samuelson (1967); Ohlson (1975); Chamberlain et al. (1990), to name but a few]. It is hoped that the conclusions of this study will help to spur research in other directions.

Bibliography

Akgiray, V., and Booth, G. (1988): "The Stable Law Model of Stock Returns," *Journal of Business & Economic Statistics*, 6:51–57.

Akgiray, V., and Lamoureux, C. (1989): "Estimation of Stable-Law Parameters: A Comparative Study," *Journal of Business and Economic Statistics*, 7:85–93.

Badrinath, S., and Chatterjee, S. (1988): "On Measuring Skewness and Elongation in Common Stock Return Distributions: The Case of the Market Index," *Journal of Business*, 61:451–472.

Bollerslev, T. (1987): "A Conditional Heteroscedastic Time Series Model for Speculative Prices and Rates of Return," *Review of Economics and Statistics*, 69:542–547.

Bookstaber, R., and McDonald, J. (1987): "A General Distribution for Describing Security Price Returns," *Journal of Business*, 60:401–424.

Chamberlain, T., Cheung, C., and Kwan, C. (1990): "Optimal Portfolio Selection Using the General Multi-Index Model: A Stable Paretian Framework," *Decision Sciences*, 21:563–571.

Cornew, R., Town, D., and Crowson, L. (1984): "Stable Distribution, Futures Prices, and the Measurement of Trading Performance," *The Journal of Futures Markets*, 4:531–557.

Doukas, J., and Rahman, A. (1986): "Stable Distributions, Futures Prices, and the Measurement of Trading Performance: A Comment," *The Journal of Futures Markets*, 6:505–506.

Fama, E., (1965): "The Behavior of Stock Market Prices," *Journal of Business*, 38:34–105.

Fama, E., and Roll, R. (1971): "Parameter Estimates for Symmetric Stable Distributions," *Journal of the American Statistical Association*, 66:331–338.

Fielitz, B., and Rozelle, J. (1983): "Stable Distributions and the Mixtures of Distributions Hypotheses for Common Stock Returns," *Journal of the American Statistical Association*, 78:28–36.

Hall, J., Brorsen, B., and Irwin, S. (1989): "The Distribution of Future Prices: A Test of the Stable Paretian and Mixture of Normals Hypotheses," *Journal of Financial and Quantitative Analysis*, 24:105–116.

Hudson, M., Leuthold, R., and Sarassoro, G. (1987): "Commodity Futures Price Changes: Recent Evidence for Wheat, Soybeans, and Live Cattle," *The Journal of Futures Markets*, 7:287–301.

Kon, S. (1984): "Models of Stock Returns—A Comparison," *Journal of Finance*, 39:147–165.

Koutrouvelis, I. (1980): "Regression-Type Estimation of the Parameters of Stable Laws," *Journal of the American Statistical Association*, 75:918–928.

Lau, A., Lau, H., and Wingender, J. (1990): "The Distribution of Stock Returns: New Evidence Against the Stable Model," *Journal of Business & Economic Statistics*, 8:217–223.

Mandelbrot, B. (1963): "The Variation of Certain Speculative Prices," *Journal of Business*, 36:394–419.

Ohlson, J. (1975): "Portfolio Selection in a Log-Stable Market," *Journal of Financial and Quantitative Analysis*, 10:285–298.

Samuelson, P. (1965): "Proof that Properly Anticipated Prices Fluctuate Randomly," *Industrial Management Review*, 8:41–49.

Samuelson, P. (1967): "Efficient Portfolio Selection for Pareto–Levy Investments." *Journal of Financial and Quantitative Analysis*, 2:107–117.

So, J. (1987): "The Sub-Gaussian Distribution of Currency Futures: Stable Paretian or Nonstationary?" *Review of Economics and Statistics*, 69:100–107.

Part IV
Chaos

Part IV
Cases

[14]

"Chaos" in Futures Markets? A Nonlinear Dynamical Analysis

Steven C. Blank

INTRODUCTION AND OBJECTIVES

Commodity market analysts constantly seek better explanations of price behavior in the form of economic models. Such models are used for many types of forecasting. However, the various linear models developed to date do not always work very well [Just and Rausser (1981)]. Some cases of short-term forecasting success of time series and econometric models imply that futures and spot prices are not always generated by a "random" process, but the long-term failure of these models to explain price behavior indicates they have not captured the true nature of the underlying generating process. For example, residuals in commodity price models may not be random, as assumed, but the result of a nonlinear process. It may be time to change existing theoretical assumptions and/or empirical approaches.

A new methodology, called nonlinear dynamics (or "chaos"), evolving recently in physics and other natural sciences, may offer an alternative explanation for behavior of economic phenomena [Brock (1988a)]. Based on the assumption that at least part of the underlying process is nonlinear, chaos analysis evaluates whether that process is a deterministic system [Jensen (1987)].[1] Deterministic processes that look random under statistical tests such as spectral analysis and the autocovariance function are called "deterministic chaos" in nonlinear science. In practice, some economists argue that separating deterministic and stochastic processes may be very difficult due to the "noisy" nature of economic data [Mirowski (1990)]. Although applications of chaos analysis in economics are still very rare [examples include Baumol and Benhabib; (1989) Brock (1986); Brock and Sayers (1988); Candela and Gardini (1986); Day (1983); Goodwin (1990); Lorenz (1987); Melese and Transue (1986)], there may be potential for its use in some markets.

In markets for undifferentiated commodities, intuition leads to expectations of multiple sources for chaos or nonlinear feedback [Savit (1988)]. Cyclical and seasonal patterns are often visible in charts of both prices and trade volumes. The futures price-setting process is similar to that in many financial spot markets where

---

This study was partially funded by a grant from the Center for the Study of Futures Markets, Columbia University. This is Giannini Foundation Research Paper No. 976.

[1]Compared to linear methods, nonlinear dynamics may be a less restrictive approach to modeling economic systems simply because of the assumptions it does *not* make, concerning the distribution, for example, as discussed later.

Steven C. Blank is an extension economist, Department of Agricultural Economics, University of California, Davis.

evidence of chaos has been found [see Brock (1988b); Frank and Stengos (1989); Hinich and Patterson (1985); Scheinkman and LeBaron (1989); van der Ploeg, (1986]. Also, there are a number of marketing strategies based, at least implicitly, upon behavioral and structural aspects of commodity markets. In sum, futures markets appear to be a logical place to expand the analysis of chaos hypotheses.

Applying a new methodology to any problem raises many questions. The first question is usually "why bother?" It is sometimes claimed that if a model gives a "reasonable approximation" of reality, it is good enough. This implies that the cost of developing a more complex model may not be well spent. Considering the adequate performance of some linear economic models, some analysts may be satisfied to continue using them. But are those models "good enough" only because methods are not yet advanced enough to know that the world is round (nonlinear), not flat (linear)? It may be that BLUE (Best Linear Unbiased Estimate) is not always the relevant "color" for economic models. If the real structure of prices is nonlinear, using linear models may give noisy results; however, a completely deterministic nonlinear function may explain prices with no noise, meaning that forecasting may be possible. While the goal of improving forecasting models through the use of chaotic parameters may seem out of reach at present, the possibility makes studies such as this necessary.

The general objectives of this study are to (i) evaluate commodity futures markets using the methodology of nonlinear dynamics to detect whether there are any signs of a deterministic system underlying prices over time; and (ii) while doing so, to illustrate the empirical procedures and their limitations. Specific objectives of this study are to determine whether (a) there is a difference between chaotic analysis results for cash and futures markets of financials; (b) there is a difference between results for futures markets of financials and agricultural products; and (c) chaos is detectable over a period lengthy enough to justify development of forecasting models. The presentation begins with a summary of related studies. That is followed by a section introducing the basic concepts in chaos analysis. Empirical procedures are outlined then and the results from analyses of two heavily traded futures markets, the S&P 500 index and soybeans, are presented as examples.

SUMMARY OF PREVIOUS WORK

Applying chaos analysis methods to commodity futures prices raises questions ranging from behavioral to structural issues.[2] One motivation for considering chaos as a possible explanation for commodity spot and futures price behavior is the poor results produced by studies using traditional methods. For example, using regression analysis, Roll (1984) explains only 1–3% of the daily variation in orange juice futures prices. If deterministic models can be developed with the assistance of chaos methods, forecasting of futures prices could be improved.

Empirical applications of nonlinear dynamical analysis techniques in economics are few in number. They are concentrated in two areas: assessments of the business cycle [Brock and Sayers (1988); Day (1983); Lorenz (1987)] and financial markets [Hinich and Patterson (1985); Savit (1989); Scheinkman and LeBaron (1989); van

---

[2]For example, "Can nonlinear dynamics explain speculative bubbles?" or "Do trading rules, such as those imposed on futures markets, create price patterns similar to patterns generated by 'strange attractors' (defined in the next section)?" Intuitively, there is reason to believe chaos may contribute to the debate over "bubbles" and structural aspects of commodity trading may provide some of the explanation.

der Ploeg (1986)]. The results are somewhat mixed, possibly due to the nature of data used. Studies of macroeconomic variables, such as the business cycle, do not generate results as strong as micro-level analyses of some specific markets [Barnett and Chen (1988)]. Therefore, evaluating data characteristics should be an early stage of any empirical study.

The first indication that relying on traditional analysis methods alone may be inadequate come from studies evaluating the characteristics of futures market data. Cornew et al. (1984) find that futures prices are not normally distributed, creating error in traditional trading performance measures, all of which are based on the normality assumption. Helms and Martell (1985) also reject the normality assumption concerning the distribution of futures price changes. However, they find that the normal distribution fit their data better than other members of the stable Paretian class of distribution. They note that the underlying generating process does *not* appear to be stationary, possibly being a subordinated stochastic or compound process requiring a more sophisticated approach to determine its exact nature. Garcia et al. (1988) use nonparametric tests and find more "nonrandomness" in livestock futures prices than are found using traditional tests. They suggest that the nonrandomness may be nonlinear in nature. These conclusions are similar to those reached by Hinich and Patterson (1985) regarding stock market returns.

These results are significant because traditional, linear models assume the data are normally distributed [Stevenson and Bear (1970); Kenyon et al. (1987)], while nonlinear dynamics makes no a priori assumptions concerning data distributions. In fact, distributions are hypothesized to change across nonlinear systems of differing degrees of chaotic behavior.

The usual way of looking for order in a time series entails spectral analysis. [Economic applications are illustrated by Shumway (1988) and Talpaz (1974).] The process involves transforming a series into a number of independent components associated with different frequencies. If the series includes periodic motion, the resulting power spectrum corresponds to the fundamental frequency. At the opposite extreme is white noise; all frequencies contribute equally. Unfortunately, the presence of sharp spectral peaks in a time series does not necessarily indicate a periodic attractor, nor does the absence of such peaks exclude the possibility of deterministic dynamics [Barnett and Hinich (1991)]. Therefore, other methods of analysis must be used to identify chaos in economic time series data.

An intermediate step is illustrated by Ashley and Patterson's (1989) use of the bispectral nonlinearity test. They test for a linear generating mechanism for both an aggregate stock market index and an aggregate industrial production index, rejecting the hypothesis in both cases. They conclude that their results strongly suggest that nonlinear dynamics should be an important feature of any macroeconomic model. The general state-dependent models outlined by Priestly (1988) could be one of the practical ways of pursuing nonlinear modeling in the future.

In microeconomic analysis, one method used to test the speculative efficiency hypothesis is called rescaled range analysis, which is capable of identifying persistent or irregular cyclic dependence in time series data. The hypothesis that respective price changes are independent of previous price changes is rejected in applications of rescaled range analysis to the foreign exchange market [Booth et al. (1982a)], the gold market [Booth et al. (1982b)], and the stock market [Greene and Fielitz (1977)]. Long-term persistent dependence is found in each study. A similar study of soybean futures markets finds nonperiodic cycles (persistent dependence) in both daily and intraday futures prices [Helms et al. (1984)].

Mandelbrot (1977) evaluates cotton prices and finds patterns which match across *scales* of time (daily, monthly). This raises the question, "is scaling a problem or an answer?" [Feigenbaum (1983)]. Economists use different data aggregations in their analyses (annual, quarterly, monthly, weekly, daily, and for futures—intraday). In particular, futures and spot price data for commodities give the appearance of having what Mandelbrot (1977) called *fractal dimensions*. Empirical studies for gold and silver [Frank and Stengos (1989); Scheinkman and LeBaron (1989)] and T-bills [Brock (1988b)] consider only the spot market but the fact that each undifferentiated product tested produces positive results indicates that further investigation is warranted.

CONCEPTS IN CHAOS ANALYSIS

As explained by Brock and Sayers (1988), a data time series (a_t) can be characterized as deterministically chaotic if there exists a system, (h, F, x_0), such that h maps R^n to R, F maps R^n to R^n, $a_t = h(x_t)$, $x_{t+1} = F(x_t)$, and x_0 is the initial condition at time $t = 0$. In this case, the map F is deterministic, the state space is n-dimensional, all trajectories (x_t) lie on an attractor A, and two nearby trajectories on A locally diverge. The variable h is a general function of the unknown state vector x, and F is an unknown dynamic that governs the evolution of the state. Also, x_0 is, in general, unknown. The goal of analysis is to discover information about the system (h, F, x_t) from observations (a_t).

An *attractor*, A, is a subset of the n-dimensional phase space, R^n. Attractors, i.e., collections of points to which initial conditions tend, can be loosely defined as having the following property. Solutions (trajectories) originating at points on the attractor remain there forever; solutions based at points *not* on the attractor, but within a region called the attractor's "basin of attraction," approach the attractor to an arbitrary degree of closeness. In the case of price data, an attractor might be particular (equilibrium?) price levels or patterns.

Chaos theory deals with deterministic processes which appear to be random (stochastic), but whose dimension is finite. Specifically, a "random process" is defined to have a "high" dimension, while a "deterministic process" has a "low" dimension. The object of analysis is to distinguish between the two. To do so, "dimension" must be defined and measured. In chaos analysis, the focus is on *fractal dimensions:* similar patterns across different (time) scalings.

One of the three types of probabilistic fractal dimension[3] is the "correlation dimension" (hereafter CD). It and the Lyapunov exponent (LE) (defined below) have become the most popular measures of nonlinear systems [Abraham et al. (1984); Grassberger and Procaccia (1983); Lorenz (1987)]. It is a measure of the minimal number of nonlinear "factors" needed to describe the data [Brock and Sayers (1988)]. To estimate the correlation dimension it is first necessary to compute the distances between all the points of a time series and then to determine what fraction of those distances are less than a series of predetermined length scales. This gives a measure called the "correlation integral," which is defined for different scale lengths, g, by the equation

$$C(g) = \lim_{N \to \infty} \left[\frac{1}{N(N-1)} \right] \sum_{i \neq j}^{N} (g, X_i, X_j) \quad (1)$$

---

[3]Probabilistic dimensions explicitly consider the frequency distribution with which points on the attractor are visited.

where N is the sample size, X_i and X_j are (vector-valued) observations in the time series and

$$(g, X_i, X_j) = \begin{cases} 1 \text{ if } |X_i - X_j| < g \\ 0 \text{ if } |X_i - X_j| > g \end{cases}$$

Grassberger and Procaccia (1983) argue that for small g

$$C(g) = \text{Constant} \cdot g^n \qquad (2)$$

where the exponent n is the CD. Empirical procedures used to estimate the CD are discussed in the methodology section later in this paper.

Low-dimensional chaos involves instability and "overshooting," while stochastic processes are infinite dimensional [Brock and Dechert (1991); van der Ploeg (1986)]. The few economic applications of this measure involve a stock returns index and gold and silver spot prices, all of which have CD estimates of about 6 (considered to be low) using weekly data [Frank and Stengos (1989); Scheinkman and LeBaron (1989)], and Treasury bill returns which have a dimension around 2 [Brock (1988b)].

Lyapunov exponents are simply generalized eigenvalues averaged over the entire attractor. They measure the average rate of contraction (when negative) or expansion (when positive) on an entire attractor. They can be positive or negative, but at least one must be positive for an attractor to be classified as chaotic or "strange" [Wolf (1986)]. In the one-dimensional case, where $x_{i+1} = F(x_i)$, the Lyapunov exponent, λ, is defined as

$$\lambda = \lim_{N \to \infty} \left(\frac{1}{N}\right) \sum \log_2 \left|\frac{dF}{dx}\right| \qquad (3)$$

where the derivative is evaluated at each point on the trajectory and logarithms are taken to the base 2. Usually, LEs are reported in units of bits per observation. Positive exponents can be viewed as measuring the rate at which new information is created; specifically, the rate at which unmeasurable (because they are too small) variations are magnified to the point where they can be observed.

In summary, Savit (1988) lists three features a deterministic sequence should have to be chaotic:

1. It should sample all regions of its domain (eventually).
2. It is practically unpredictable in the long term (if there is any indeterminacy in one's knowledge or ability to compute.[4]
3. There are many initial prices, P_o, called periodic points,[5] and the sequence of prices generated by the chaotic map is periodic, i.e., over time the sequence of prices P_t eventually repeats itself.

This list makes it clear that chaos analysis must begin with a detailed description of the data involving a set of statistics new to most market analysts.

GENERAL METHODOLOGY

Empirical methods derived from those applied in previous economic studies of chaotic systems [Brock (1986); Deneckere and Pelikan (1986)] are used here. To ac-

[4]For example, rounding errors accumulate rapidly in the calculations involved in estimating fractal dimensions, thus reducing precision in distant forecasts.

[5]The existence of a large number of periodic points is just one example of hidden regularities in a chaotic system.

complish this study's first general objective, this three-step process of dynamical analysis is followed:

1. Calculate the Grassberger-Procaccia correlation dimension for various embedding dimensions [Abraham et al. (1984); Swinney (1983)].
2. Apply a residual test for the presence of deterministic chaos as an alternate for the best-fitting linear model of prices [Brock and Sayers (1988)].
3. Estimate the largest Lyapunov exponent for various embedding dimensions [Abraham et al. (1984); Swinney (1983); Wolf (1986); Wolf and Swift (1984); Wolf et al. (1985)].

Operationally, the correlation dimension [n in eq. (2)] is the slope, k, of the regression: log $C(g)$ versus log g for small values of g. To estimate the CD from a single variable time series, the procedure is as follows:

1. The data are embedded in successively higher dimensions as prescribed by Takens (1985).
2. For each embedding, $C(g)$ is computed and the scaling factor, k, is estimated.
3. The procedure is repeated until the estimates of k converge.

The correlation dimension is therefore expected to equal whatever value at which k remains stable over a number of embedding dimensions.

Lyapunov exponents are local quantities which are averaged over the attractor. To compute the largest LE from a time series, the program by Wolf et al. (1985) is used which suggests choosing a so-called "fiducial" trajectory and estimating the rate at which it and a nearby test trajectory diverge. When the distance between the two points becomes large, a new point is chosen near the fiducial trajectory and the procedure is repeated. The entire time series is stepped through in this way and the stretchings and contractions are averaged.

In practice, estimating Lyapunov exponents in this way requires experimentation on the part of an analyst. Wolf's algorithm requires that the following information be provided:

- an embedding dimension and time lag for the reconstruction of the attractor;
- the time interval over which the two pieces of the trajectory are followed (called the "evolution");
- the minimum acceptable separation between points that are to be followed; and
- the maximum acceptable separation.

As a result of this flexibility in inputs, an analyst must simply experiment. The goal of the experimentation is to find a region in parameter space over which the estimate is approximately constant. Clearly, this portion of the analysis is rough, hence the reluctance of previous authors to report exact LE values for economic data series.

The data used in this study are futures prices for the S&P 500 index and soybeans. These products are selected as examples to represent, respectively, financial and agricultural futures markets because they are traded heavily and each market has been studied previously by analysts using a variety of methods, which provides a base for comparison. The S&P index, in particular, is selected because it is the product traded on futures markets which is closest to the variables studied in earlier chaotic analyses of the cash stock market. This enables direct comparison between results from previous studies of the cash stock market and the results produced here for the futures index. For each product, daily closing price data for recent individual futures contracts and nearby contracts are evaluated. For soybeans, the November 1986 and November 1987 contracts are used. The data for each contract begins during July of the previous calendar year, giving 337 and 335 observations, respectively. The nearby futures price series, constructed from the closing prices of the futures contract closest to its maturity date at each point in time, covers the period from March 1966 through June 1988, with 5823 observations. The December 1986 and December 1987 S&P 500 contracts are used. Each contract has 250 observations covering the previous calendar year. The S&P 500 nearby series begins in May 1982, ends in December 1987, and has 1420 observations.

Before conducting nonlinear dynamical analysis, the data are detrended using ordinary least squares and autoregressive methods, deseasonalized and transformed (if necessary) as described by Baumol and Benhabib (1989). If a time series has a deterministic explanation, fitting a smooth time series model with a finite number of leads and lags will generate a residual series with the same CD and largest LE as the original series. The key is to first make the residuals as close to "white noise" as possible with traditional linear methods. In this way, if nonlinear models find significant traces of a deterministic system in the residuals, the hypothesis of a linear generating system can be rejected.

Brook and Sayers (1988) evaluate the H_o: whiteness tests and diagnostics do not alter chaotic systems and can be used to test residuals from the best linear model. They use a new "W" statistic to test for independence. Based on the correlation integral, the W statistic for embedding dimension m is defined as

$$W_m(g, N) \equiv \sqrt{N}\left(\frac{D_m(g, N)}{b_m(g, N)}\right) \tag{4}$$

where $D_m = C_m - (C_1)^m$, and b_m is an estimate of the standard deviation

$$b_m = (1, -mC_{m-1})' \sum (1, -mC_{m-1}) \tag{5}$$

as discussed by Brock (1988a). The W test detects misspecification caused by a linear model fit to nonlinear data and indicates such by giving a nonzero value. Brock and Dechert (1991) show that $D_m(g, N)$ converges to a nonzero number if evaluated using the residuals from a misspecified model, while the residuals from a correctly fitted linear model are independent and identically distributed and are characterized by $D_m(g, \infty) \equiv D_m(g) = 0$ for all m and all $g > 0$. This means that a W value of 0 indicates a stochastic process and a large W is evidence of a misspecified (nonlinear) model. Statistically significant nonlinearity appears to exist at the 5% level when the W value is greater than 1.96 [Brock and Dechert (1991)]. W statistics are reported below for the data series evaluated.

Due to the weakness of the standard CD empirical processes in some cases, it is desirable to calculate the correlation dimension for "random" numbers generated to provide a basis for comparison and to report the W statistic for those values [Brock (1986)]. The random numbers used are the residuals "scrambled" as described by Scheinkman and LeBaron (1989). If the data are stochastic, the CD estimates for the residuals and the "scrambled" residuals will be identical; if the scrambled data generate higher CD estimates, this is evidence of hidden (nonlinear) structure in the residuals. The scrambled residuals test is conducted in this study.

Also, the small sample distribution of the CD and LE statistics are illustrated here by presenting values calculated from 100 series of random numbers. The series are drawn using random number generators based on the following distributions: normal, log, chi-square, exponential, double exponential, geometric, poisson, F-distribution, T-distribution, and beta. Ten series are drawn from each distribution since no a priori assumption is made concerning which distribution is "best". Each series includes 250 observations. The 100 CD values estimated are averaged to provide a benchmark representing stochastic processes. As in the scrambled residual test, deterministic CD values must be below those estimated from the random numbers. For LEs, two sets of estimates are reported: average values for the 100 series and the highest of the 100 LEs observed for each group of experiments. The average values for the random series can be compared against the values estimated from the actual futures price data to establish the general case for evidence of deterministic processes in the LE values. A qualitative assessment of the degree of significance of actual LE values can be made by a second comparison involving the highest of the 100 random estimates. This means that an LE for futures price data must be both positive and greater than the average LE from the random data to be considered evidence of a chaotic process; but, in addition, it must be greater than the highest of the 100 random LE values to be convincing evidence.

EMPIRICAL RESULTS AND IMPLICATIONS

Estimates of correlation dimensions and Lyapunov exponents are both given below, along with a discussion of the results. First, measures used to "prewhiten" the data are noted.

A generalized autoregressive conditional heteroscedasticity (GARCH) model is used to generate the residuals used in the analysis. The GARCH procedure, developed by Bollerslev (1986), is applied in studies of exchange rates [Hsieh (1989)] and stock market returns using spot market data [Baillie and DeGennaro (1990); Scheinkman and LeBaron (1989)] and futures market data [Cheung and Ng (in press)] as well as in studies of commodity markets [Aradhyula and Holt (1988)]. GARCH methods are found to be useful in detecting nonlinear patterns in variance while not destroying any signs of deterministic structural shifts in a model [Lamoureux and Lastrapes (1990)]. Therefore, it serves as a good filter for studies of chaos.

Brock and Sayers (1988) demonstrate that the power of the W statistic is weak if an autoregressive [AR(q)] model is applied with a high order (q) and, therefore, q should be set as low as possible in GARCH whitening processes. In this study, if conventional criteria finds that a GARCH(1, 1) model produces white noise residuals, it is used. If a GARCH(1, 1) model fails this test, a GARCH(2, 2) model would be fitted next, and so forth until white noise is found.

The data for the two S&P 500 contracts cover years during which prices generally trended. Prices of the December 1986 S&P 500 contract fluctuate around an upward-sloping trendline. As a result, the GARCH(1, 1) model for the December 1986 S&P 500 contract price at time t is

$$x_t = 0.207 - 0.024 x_{t-1} + 0.013 x_{t-2} + \delta_t \tag{6a}$$
$$(0.192) \quad (0.011) \qquad (0.011)$$

$$h_t = 6.592 + 0.633\delta_{t-1}^2 + 0.566h_{t-1} \quad (6b)$$
$$(0.847) \quad (0.459) \quad (0.490)$$

where the x_t's are first differences, δ is a residual, h is the conditional variance of the residuals, and the standard errors are in parentheses. Stock prices are lower during 1987 due to the "Crash" in October. The uptrend-ending jolt gives the December 1987 S&P 500 contract a model of

$$x_t = 0.008 - 0.252x_{t-2} - 0.120x_{t-4} + 0.109x_{t-5} + \delta_t \quad (7a)$$
$$(0.455) \quad (0.064) \quad (0.064) \quad (0.062)$$
$$h_t = 49.072 + 0.696\delta_{t-1}^2 + 0.752h_{t-1} \quad (7b)$$
$$(33.831) \quad (0.391) \quad (0.359)$$

using the same notation.

The data for the two soybean contracts cover the same two years, but display trends for those years with slopes opposite to those in the S&P 500 data. Whereas stock prices rise during 1986, soybean prices trend downward that year. The GARCH(2, 2) model of the November 1986 soybean contract price at time t is

$$x_t = -0.143 - 0.108x_{t-2} + 0.065x_{t-3} + \delta_t \quad (8a)$$
$$(0.258) \quad (0.055) \quad (0.055)$$
$$h_t = 21.793 + 0.143\delta_{t-1}^2 - 0.541\delta_{t-2}^2 + 0.365h_{t-1} + 0.507h_{t-2} \quad (8b)$$
$$(2.883) \quad (0.343) \quad (0.166) \quad (0.343) \quad (0.182)$$

On the other hand, during 1987 stock prices are lower on the year, while soybean prices rise. The price of the November 1987 soybean contract at time t is

$$x_t = 0.197 - 0.093x_{t-1} - 0.086x_{t-5} + \delta_t \quad (9a)$$
$$(0.349) \quad (0.055) \quad (0.055)$$
$$h_t = 39.964 - 0.738\delta_{t-1}^2 - 0.853\delta_{t-2}^2 - 0.703h_{t-1} - 0.515h_{t-2} \quad (9b)$$
$$(6.867) \quad (0.050) \quad (0.049) \quad (0.080) \quad (0.079)$$

The fact that both soybean models have GARCH(2, 2) processes while both S&P 500 series have GARCH(1, 1) processes may indicate a difference in time series properties of commodity and financial futures.

The two nearby futures contract price series produce models more similar to each other. The price of the nearby S&P 500 contract at time t is

$$x_t = 0.075 + 0.451x_{t-1} - 0.220x_{t-2} - 0.094x_{t-4} + 0.095x_{t-5} + \delta_t \quad (10a)$$
$$(0.240) \quad (0.044) \quad (0.045) \quad (0.045) \quad (0.044)$$
$$h_t = 28.011 + 0.701\delta_{t-1}^2 + 0.773h_{t-1} \quad (10b)$$
$$(18.136) \quad (0.181) \quad (0.159)$$

Stock prices steadily rise during the period covered by the S&P 500 index futures contract data, despite some "corrections." The nearby soybean contract price data have a spiky pattern in which numerous periods of trending prices are evident. As a whole, the GARCH(1, 1) model for the data is

$$x_t = 0.831 - 0.154x_{t-2} + 0.168x_{t-3} + 0.191x_{t-4} - 0.141x_{t-5} + \delta_t \quad (11a)$$
$$(0.415) \quad (0.048) \quad (0.053) \quad (0.054) \quad (0.054)$$
$$h_t = 45.168 + 0.849\delta_{t-1}^2 + 1.107h_{t-1} \quad (11b)$$
$$(13.266) \quad (0.027) \quad (0.013)$$

Correlation Dimension Results

Correlation dimension estimates made from the residuals, δ, of eqs. 6–11 are presented in Table I. Observations which can be made from the results in the table include:

1. Both the S&P index and soybeans have "low" CDs in absolute terms and in comparison to CDs reported in earlier cash stock market studies.
2. Both nearby series have lower CDs than the contract series.
3. All series pass both the "scrambled residuals" and random number tests: their CDs are lower than those of the scrambled and random data.

The general implication of these results is that both the S&P index and soybeans appear to have nonlinearities in their underlying generating processes. More detailed observations are made below before presenting the W statistic results from tests of the nonlinear hypothesis.

Table I presents results for the first ten embedding dimensions to enable the reader to see how the CDs stabilize. The CD estimates are rounded to one decimal point from the regression output for each embedding dimension. Despite this imprecision, it appears that the estimates converge after the fourth or fifth embedding dimension in the case of each data series. Convergence does not occur in most of the scrambled series, nor in the random series.

It appears that the CDs in Table I are lower for soybeans than for the S&P index and that both futures markets evaluated have CDs lower than those Scheinkman and LeBaron (1989) report for cash stock market returns, although no statistic is

Table I
CORRELATION DIMENSION ESTIMATES
FOR S&P 500 AND SOYBEAN FUTURES PRICES

	Embedding Dimension									
	1	2	3	4	5	6	7	8	9	10
Contract Series										
S&P 12/86	1.0	1.5	2.1	2.2	2.4	2.5	2.3	2.7	2.4	2.3
S&P 12/86[a]	1.1	1.9	2.8	3.2	4.1	4.2	4.5	5.3	6.1	5.8
S&P 12/87	1.0	1.6	2.1	2.1	2.3	2.0	2.0	2.3	2.7	2.8
S&P 12/87[a]	1.0	2.0	2.9	3.6	4.3	4.4	4.4	5.1	4.8	4.9
Soybean 11/86	0.9	1.4	1.7	1.9	1.9	2.0	1.6	1.7	1.4	1.4
Soybean 11/86[a]	0.9	1.8	2.8	3.0	3.4	3.7	4.5	4.8	5.3	5.8
Soybean 11/87	0.9	1.3	1.6	1.9	2.0	2.2	1.9	2.1	2.2	2.1
Soybean 11/87[a]	0.9	2.0	2.7	4.0	4.4	4.8	5.1	5.5	5.6	6.2
Nearby Series										
S&P nearby	0.9	1.3	1.4	1.6	1.6	1.7	1.5	1.6	1.5	1.4
S&P nearby[a]	1.0	2.1	3.2	3.8	4.1	5.2	6.0	7.2	7.9	8.3
Soybean nearby	0.9	1.0	1.2	1.2	1.3	1.3	1.3	1.3	1.3	1.3
Soybean nearby[a]	0.9	2.2	3.4	3.9	4.4	5.8	6.4	7.1	8.0	9.2
Random Series[b]	0.9	2.1	3.6	4.5	5.1	6.3	7.8	8.9	9.6	10.3

[a]Results from a "scrambled" series created for comparison.
[b]Average results from 100 series of random numbers generated from various distributions for comparison.

available to aid in determining whether one CD estimate is significantly different than another. The difference between stock and soybean futures results is more apparent for the contract price series than for the nearby series. The general CDs for the November 1986 and 1987 soybean contracts, respectively, seem to be 1.7–2.0 and 1.9–2.2. The CDs for both S&P contracts are 2.3–2.7. The nearby soybean series has a CD of 1.3, while the S&P nearby data have a CD of 1.5–1.7. These values may not be significantly different from each other, but it is expected that they are significantly lower than the CDs of 6–7 which Scheinkman and LeBaron (1989) report.

The level and stability of the CD estimates in Table I give rise to the question of sample size effects. Ramsey and Yuan (1987) show that CDs may be underestimated from small data sets. In this case, estimates are lower and more stable for larger samples. For example, the nearby soybean series is the largest with 5823 observations and it has the lowest, most stable CD estimates across embedding dimensions. This indicates that no conclusions can be reached concerning the relative differences in CDs between the two markets noted above. Nevertheless, the fact that even the smallest data sets (the S&P contract series) generated CDs that are "low," compared to the CDs for the scrambled and random series, supports the hypothesis that nonlinearity exists in all six series. To resolve the question of significance, W statistics are calculated.

Table II presents W statistics for each of the six series, their respective scrambled counterparts, and the random series. For each price series the statistic exceeds the 1.96 value needed (at the 95% confidence level) to reject the null hypothesis of a linear process. For the soybean nearby series, in particular, the results are strong. This indicates that nonlinearities are present in the data. However, although the W statistic can distinguish between a linear and nonlinear generating process, it can-

Table II
W STATISTICS FOR S&P 500 AND SOYBEAN FUTURES PRICE SERIES

		Embedding Dimension		
	Observations (n)	4	5	6
Contract Series				
S&P 12/86	250	4.21	5.81	5.95
S&P 12/86[a]	250	1.27	1.55	1.80
S&P 12/87	250	6.99	7.76	8.12
S&P 12/87[a]	250	3.03	3.62	4.15
Soybean 11/86	335	5.86	6.07	7.23
Soybean 11/86[a]	335	1.17	1.31	1.43
Soybean 11/87	337	4.66	5.40	6.92
Soybean 11/87[a]	337	1.05	1.11	1.31
Nearby Series				
S&P nearby	1420	6.61	7.22	8.10
S&P nearby[a]	1420	0.75	0.99	1.31
Soybean nearby	5823	12.32	13.00	14.26
Soybean nearby[a]	5823	1.27	1.37	1.52
Random Series[b]	250	0.92	1.06	1.15

[a]Results from a "scrambled" series created for comparison.
[b]Average results from 100 series of random numbers.

not detect whether that process is stochastic or deterministic. Therefore, additional evidence, such as LE estimates, is needed to make this distinction.

Lyapunov Exponent Results

Lyapunov exponent estimates for soybean and S&P 500 prices are presented, respectively, in Tables III and IV. In the absence of statistics for use in determining the significance level of these estimates, only qualitative observations can be made, using the random number results presented in Table V, including:

1. Both the S&P index and soybeans have positive, stable LEs across embedding dimensions, implying the presence of chaos.
2. LEs for the S&P nearby series appear to be of similar magnitude to those for S&P contract series and are higher than the random number LEs in many cases, while the LEs for the soybean nearby series are consistently lower than both the soybean contract series' LEs and the highest of the random number LEs.
3. For all series, LE values decline as evolution lengths increase, as expected.

The general conclusion is that these results support those of the correlation dimension analysis: both the S&P index and soybeans appear to have chaotic nonlinearities in their underlying generating processes. More detailed observations are made below.

Tables III and IV present estimates of the largest Lyapunov exponent calculated for different embedding dimensions using different evolution lengths. Dimensions 3, 5, and 9 are selected to illustrate results across the range that has stable CDs. For

Table III
LYAPUNOV EXPONENTS FOR SOYBEAN FUTURES PRICE SERIES

Price Series	Evolution[a]	Embedding Dimension		
		3	5	9
November 1986 Contract	5	0.0430	0.0613	0.0484
	10	0.0401	0.0525	0.0401
	21	0.0308	0.0337	0.0180
	42	0.0112[b]	0.0136	0.0172
	63	0.0109[b]	0.0129[b]	0.0067[b]
November 1987 Contract	5	0.0382[b]	0.0517	0.0410
	10	0.0285	0.0431	0.0402
	21	0.0240	0.0366	0.0180
	42	0.0233	0.0137	0.0126
	63	0.0263	0.0128[b]	0.0122
Nearby Contract	5	0.0002[b]	0.0051[b]	0.0067[b]
	10	0.0001[b]	0.0050[b]	0.0057[b]
	21	0.0000[b]	0.0031[b]	0.0045[b]
	42	−0.0011[b]	0.0039[b]	0.0037[b]
	63	−0.0012[b]	0.0042[b]	0.0035[b]

[a]Number of observations over which the two pieces of the trajectory are followed.
[b]Values fall between the average and highest estimates for the relevant entry in Table V.
Note: The minimum and maximum scale lengths used here are 1 and 45 cents per bushel, respectively.

Table IV
LYAPUNOV EXPONENTS FOR S&P 500 FUTURES PRICE SERIES

Price Series	Evolution[a]	Embedding Dimension		
		3	5	9
December 1986 Contract	5	0.0334	0.0316[b]	0.0339
	10	0.0316	0.0261[b]	0.0317
	21	0.0245	0.0232	0.0168
	42	0.0149	0.0195	0.0097[b]
	63	0.0081[b]	0.0058[b]	0.0183
December 1987 Contract	5	0.0960	0.0978	0.0695
	10	0.0623	0.0930	0.0550
	21	0.0708	0.0647	0.0216
	42	0.0012[b]	−0.0018[b]	0.0100[b]
	63	−0.0027[b]	0.0009[b]	0.0065[b]
Nearby Contract	5	0.0216[b]	0.0465	0.0423
	10	0.0211[b]	0.0336	0.0280
	21	0.0199[b]	0.0120[b]	0.0202
	42	0.0066[b]	0.0077[b]	0.0149
	63	0.0071[b]	0.0129[b]	0.0138

[a]Number of observations over which the two pieces of the trajectory are followed.
[b]Values fall between the average and highest estimates for the relevant entry in Table V.
Note: The minimum and maximum scale lengths used here are 1 and 25 index points, respectively.

Table V
LYAPUNOV EXPONENTS FOR 100 SERIES OF RANDOM NUMBERS

Price Series	Evolution[a]	Embedding Dimension		
		3	5	9
Average Estimates	5	−0.0123	0.0032	−0.0037
	10	−0.0191	0.0006	−0.0112
	21	−0.0265	−0.0069	−0.0131
	42	−0.0281	−0.0080	−0.0143
	63	−0.0254	−0.0101	−0.0162
Highest Estimates	5	0.0238	0.0456	0.0070
	10	0.0223	0.0286	0.0141
	21	0.0185	0.0160	0.0117
	42	0.0140	0.0108	0.0105
	63	0.0152	0.0182	0.0102

[a]Number of observations over which the two pieces of the trajectory are followed.

each of those dimensions, LEs are calculated for evolution lengths equaling one week (five observations), two weeks (ten observations), one month (21 observations), two months (42 observations), and three months (63 observations).

This cross section of LEs is estimated in a "bootstrapping" effort to add robustness to any conclusions reached concerning the presence of chaos and to provide for a preliminary test of the hypothesis that futures prices are detectably deterministic over a long enough time period to make (short-term) price forecasting models possible. As noted by Frank and Stengos (1989, p. 555), "A chaotic system will be quite predictable over very short time horizons. If however the initial conditions are only known with finite precision, then over long intervals the ability to predict the time path will be lost." This means that if chaos can be detected at an evolution interval, the deterministic system generating prices has not been overwhelmed by stochastic noise and the development of forecasting models may be possible. If the largest LE is never positive in experiments across evolution lengths, the system is stochastic. However, if LEs are positive for short evolutions and turn negative at some longer length, the implication is that at that time interval stochastic noise becomes dominant and deterministic forecasting models are not empirically viable, even though the underlying system may be completely deterministic in nature. In summary, experimenting with evolution lengths provides a way in which analysts can assess the potential for developing forecasting models.

Table V provides results for the random numbers for the same cross section of LE experiments. These results illustrate the small sample distribution of the LE statistic and provide a basis for assessing the effects of noise on the estimates. The "Average Estimates" reported in Table V are the mean estimates of the LE from the 100 series of random numbers. The fact that all but two of the values reported are negative indicates that Wolf et al.'s (1985) procedure for calculating LEs does a good job of detecting stochastic processes in general. However, in any particular case there is some chance of mislabeling a stochastic process as being deterministic due to the effects of noise in the small sample (of 250 observations). This is evident in Table V as the "Highest Estimates" are positive for each experiment. In other words, at least one of the 100 random series produces a positive LE for each combination of evolution length and embedding dimension. Therefore, actual data which produce LE estimates falling between the average and highest value reported for the relevant experiment in Table V may or may not have a deterministic generating process.

In Table III all but two LEs are positive, strongly supporting the conclusion that soybean futures prices have a chaotic nonlinear generating process. Also, that process may be predictable over periods as long as the three-month evolutions evaluated here. However, a closer look leads to some interesting issues for future research. For example, the LEs for the two contract price series are very similar across embedding dimensions and evolution lengths, but they differ from LEs for the nearby series. LEs for nearby prices are approximately zero at dimension 3 and, although they stabilize at higher dimensions, no actual estimate exceeds the relevant "Highest Estimate" from Table V. One hypothesis is that the two types of series will have different generating systems because contract series have less noise (possibly indicated by a lower coefficient of variation) and fewer trends, compared to more volatile nearby series which contain multiple trends.

One explanation for this hypothesis comes from expectations concerning the two types of data series. Futures contract price series reflect increasing amounts of information about the relatively few factors known to influence prices expected at one point in time (the contract maturity date). Over the life of a particular contract, trade volume tends to rise as information changes become easier to interpret, making the market more liquid and, hence, more efficient in its reaction to information flows. On the other hand, nearby futures contract prices reflect a liquid market's interpretation of information concerning many supply and demand factors for different points in time. Trading volume in whatever contract is "nearby" at the moment tends to remain high and be closely correlated with spot prices of the commodity [Blank et al. (1991)].

The results in Table III indicate that compared to contract series, nearby soybean futures prices have a more complex generating system requiring analysis at a higher embedding dimension before the effects of chaos (if any) can be captured. The differences in LEs between dimensions may also mean that more complex models will be required for forecasting, making successful specification of those models less likely.

Table IV presents LE estimates for S&P 500 futures prices which, in general, are surprisingly similar to those for soybeans, but which have two subtle differences raising additional issues for future research. First, the LEs for the December 1986 contract and the nearby series are similar to the soybean contracts' LEs. One hypothesis for this phenomenon is that the S&P nearby series is like many contract series in that the data have a single trend around which prices demonstrate relatively low levels of noise (at least at higher embedding dimensions). If multiple trends are present, the S&P nearby series might produce a more complex set of results, as in the case of soybeans.

Second, the LE results for the December 1987 S&P contract are unique compared to the other three contract series studied, drawing attention to the effects of the sharp market correction in October 1987. The LE values for all embedding dimensions are noticeably higher than those of any other series at evolution lengths of 5–21 days, yet for evolutions of 42 and 63 days the LEs are low and occasionally negative. It is hypothesized that the strong uptrend in S&P prices prior to the "crash" had so little noise in it that forecasting was quite possible for periods of up to one month (21 trading days), but longer forecasts necessitate more complex models to account for the effects of "Black Monday," which are interpreted as noise by simple models. This illustrates the frustration which will no doubt continue to face modelers: even if a system such as that underlying stock prices is deterministic, forecasting models cannot be expected to detect every trend or turning point. As long as initial conditions are not perfectly identified, analysts will not know whether a model is correctly specified until it fails. In other words, no matter how complex a deterministic model is, additional complexity may be required to avoid forecasting errors so large as to question the modeling effort's value.

SUMMARY AND CONCLUDING COMMENTS

This study provides results of nonlinear dynamical analysis of two commodity futures markets. It illustrates what type of methodological and empirical procedures must be used to evaluate these markets. It also raises and attempts to address issues concerning identification and measurement of nonlinear generating systems in economic data, providing a guide for research in the future. Although chaos analyses in economics are still very rare, the results presented here and elsewhere give reason for expecting use of these methods to expand, but with difficulty.

Results from analyses of a financial, the S&P 500 index, and an agricultural product, soybeans, are presented as examples. All empirical results in this study are consistent with those of markets with underlying generating systems characterized by deterministic chaos. Comparing results for the stock index and soybean futures reveals surprising similarity, yet the CDs for the index are noticeably different than those reported in earlier stock market studies which use cash price data. Both futures markets are shown to have a "low" correlation dimension of about two, while CDs are slightly lower for soybeans and for nearby series compared to contract series. The statistical significance of this difference in CDs between product types is unclear, but statistical tests do indicate the presence of nonlinearities in both markets. Estimates of Lyapunov exponents indicate that these nonlinearities are (at least partially) deterministic, rather than stochastic in nature. However, the absence of any tests for the statistical significance of estimated LEs makes the results of this study necessary, but not sufficient conditions to prove the existence of deterministic chaos.

Although providing just an introduction to the study of nonlinear dynamics in future markets, the results of this analysis may be useful for commodity market analysts in industry, academia, and government. The fact that futures prices appear to have a nonlinear generating process of a type not recognized previously raises the possibility that short-term forecasting models may be improved by incorporating these new factors. This, in turn, has significant implications for resource allocation and marketing strategies for firms trading in these product markets. Ultimately, the discovery of a nonlinear, nonrandom process in commodity futures markets could raise the level of debate in the economic literature concerning "random walk" hypotheses and definitions of pricing efficiency. However, from a practical viewpoint, chaos analysis procedures provide another test for (deterministic) nonlinearity, but do not easily lend themselves to direct applications in forecasting model construction.

Bibliography

Abraham, N., Gollub, J., and Swinney, H. (1984): "Testing Nonlinear Dynamics," *Physica*, 11D:252–264.

Aradhyula, S., and Holt, M. (1988): "GARCH Time-Series Models: An Application to Retail Livestock Prices," *Western Journal of Agricultural Economics*, 13:365–374.

Ashley, R., and Patterson, D. (1989): "Linear Versus Nonlinear Macroeconomies: A Statistical Test," *International Economic Review*, 30:685–704.

Baillie, R., and DeGennaro, R. (1990): "Stock Returns and Volatility," *Journal of Financial and Quantitative Analysis*, 25:203–214.

Barnett, W., and Chen, P. (1988): "The Aggregation-Theoretic Monetary Aggregates Are Chaotic and Have Strange Attractors: An Econometric Application of Mathematical Chaos," in *Dynamical Econometric Modeling*, Barnett, Berndt, and White (eds.). Cambridge: Cambridge University Press, pp. 199–246.

Barnett, W., and Hinich, M., (1991): "Has Chaos Been Discovered with Economic Data?" in *Evolutionary Dynamics and Nonlinear Economics*, Chen and Day (eds.), Oxford University Press.

Baumol, W., and Benhabib, J. (1989): "Chaos: Significance, Mechanism, and Economic Applications," *The Journal of Economic Perspectives*, 3:77–105.

Blank, S., Carter, C., and Schmiesing, B. (1991): *Futures and Options Markets: Trading Commodities and Financials*. Englewood Cliffs, NJ: Prentice Hall, Chapter 3.

Bollerslev, T. (1986): "Generalized Autoregressive Conditional Heteroscedasticity," *Journal of Econometrics* 31:307–327.

Booth, G., Kaen, F., and Koveos, P. (1982a): "R/S Analysis of Foreign Exchange Rates under Two International Monetary Regimes," *Journal of Monetary Economics*, 10:407–415.

Booth, G., Kaen, F., and Koveos, P. (1982b): "Persistent Dependence in Gold Prices," *Journal of Financial Research*, 85–93.

Brock. W. A. (1986): "Distinguishing Random and Deterministic Systems: Abridged Version," *Journal of Economic Theory,* 40: 168–195.

Brock, W. A. (1988a): "Introduction to Chaos and Other Aspects of Nonlinearity," in *Differential Equations, Stability, and Chaos in Dynamic Economics,* Brock, W., and Malliaris, A., New York: North Holland.

Brock, W. A. (1988b): "Nonlinearity and Complex Dynamics in Economics and Finance," in *The Economy as an Evolving Complex System,* Addison-Wesley Publishing Company: New York.

Brock, W., and Dechert, W. (1991): "Theorems on Distinguishing Deterministic from Random Systems," in *Dynamic Econometric Modeling,* Barnett, Berndt, and White (eds.). Cambridge: Cambridge University Press.

Brock, W., and Sayers, C. (1988): "Is the Business Cycle Characterized by Deterministic Chaos?" *Journal of Monetary Economics,* 22:71–90.

Candela, G., and Gardini, A. (1986): "Estimation of a Non-Linear Discrete-Time Macro Model," *Journal of Economic Dynamics & Control,* 10:249–255.

Cheung, Y., and Ng, L. (in press): "The Dynamics of S&P 500 Index and S&P 500 Futures Intraday Price Volatilities," *The Review of Futures Markets.*

Cornew, R., Town, D., and Crowson, L. (1984): "Stable Distributions, Futures Prices, and the Measurement of Trading Performance," *The Journal of Futures Markets,* 4:531–557.

Day, R. H. (1983): "The Emergence of Chaos from Classical Economic Growth," *The Quarterly Journal of Economics,* 98:201–213.

Deneckere, R., and Pelikan, S. (1986): "Competitive Chaos," *Journal of Economic Theory,* 40:13–25.

Feigenbaum, M. J. (1983): "Universal Behavior in Nonlinear Systems," *Physica,* 7D:16–39.

Frank, M., and Stengos, T. (1989): "Measuring the Strangeness of Gold and Silver Rates of Return," *Review of Economic Studies,* 56:553–567.

Garcia, P., Hudson, M., and Waller, M. (1988): "The Pricing Efficiency of Agricultural Futures Markets: An Analysis of Previous Research Results," *Southern Journal of Agricultural Economics* 20:119–130.

Goodwin, R. (1990): *Chaotic Economic Dynamics.* Oxford: Oxford University Press.

Grassberger, P., and Procaccia, I. (1983): "Measuring the Strangeness of Strange Attractors," *Physica,* 9D:189–208.

Greene, M., and Fielitz, B. (1977): "Long Term Dependence in Common Stock Returns," *Journal of Financial Economics,* 4:339–349.

Helms, B., and Martell, T. (1985): "An Examination of the Distribution of Futures Price Changes," *The Journal of Futures Markets,* 5:259–272.

Helms, B., Kaen, F., and Rosenman, R. (1984): "Memory in Commodity Futures Contracts," *The Journal of Futures Markets,* 4:559–567.

Hinich, M., and Patterson, D. (1985): "Evidence of Nonlinearity in Daily Stock Returns," *Journal of Business and Economic Statistics,* 3:69–77.

Hsieh, D. (1989): "Testing for Nonlinear Dependence in Daily Foreign Exchange Rate Changes," *Journal of Business,* 62:339–368.

Jensen, R.V. (1987): "Classical Chaos," *American Scientist,* 75:168–181.

Just, R., and Rausser, G. (1981): "Commodity Price Forecasting with Large Scale Econometric Models and the Futures Market," *American Journal of Agricultural Economics,* 63:197–208.

Kenyon, D., Kling, K., Jordan, J., Seale, W., and McCabe, N. (1987): "Factors Affecting Agricultural Futures Price Variance," *The Journal of Futures Markets,* 7:73–91.

Lamoureux, C., and Lastrapes, W. (1990): "Persistence in Variance, Structural Change, and the GARCH Model," *Journal of Business and Economic Statistics,* 8:225–234.

Lorenz, H.-W. (1987): "Strange Attractors in a Multisector Business Cycle Model," *Journal of Economic Behavior & Organization,* 8:397-411.

Mandelbrot, B. (1977): *The Fractal Geometry of Nature.* New York: Freeman.

Melese, F., and Transue, W. (1986): "Unscambling Chaos through Thick and Thin," *The Quarterly Journal of Economics,* 101:419-423.

Mirowski, P. (1990): "From Mandelbrot to Chaos in Economic Theory," *Southern Economic Journal,* 57:289-307.

Priestly, M. B. (1988): *Non-Linear and Non-Stationary Time Series Analysis,* San Diego: Academic Press.

Ramsey, J., and Yuan, H. (1987): "The Statistical Properties of Dimension Calculations Using Small Data Sets." New York: C. V. Starr Center for Applied Economics, New York University.

Roll, R. (1984): "Orange Juice and Weather," *American Economic Review,* 74:861-880.

Savit, R. (1988): "When Random is Not Random: An Introduction to Chaos in Market Prices," *The Journal of Futures Markets,* 8:271-289.

Savit, R. (1989): "Nonlinearities and Chaotic Effects in Options Prices," *The Journal of Futures Markets,* 9:507-518.

Scheinkman, J., and LeBaron, B. (1989): "Nonlinear Dynamics and Stock Returns," *Journal of Business* 62:311-337.

Shumway, R. H. (1988): *Applied Statistical Time Series Analysis.* Englewood Cliffs, NJ: Prentice-Hall.

Stevenson, R., and Bear, R. (1970): "Commodity Futures: Trends or Random Walks?" *Journal of Finance,* 25:65-81.

Swinney, H. L. (1983): "Observations of Order and Chaos in Nonlinear Systems," *Physica,* 7D:3-15.

Takens, F. (1985): "On the Numerical Determination of the Dimension of an Attractor," in *Dynamical Systems and Bifurcations,* Braaksma, N., Broer, H., and Takens, F. (eds.). Berlin: Springer-Verlag, pp. 99-106.

Talpaz, H. (1974): "Multi-Frequency Cobweb Model: Decomposition of the Hog Cycle," *American Journal of Agricultural Economics* 56:38-49.

van der Ploeg, F. (1986): "Rational Expectations, Risk and Chaos in Financial Markets," *Economic Journal,* 96:151-161.

Wolf, A. (1986): "Quantifying Chaos with Lyapunov Exponents," in *Nonlinear Science: Theory and Applications,* Holden, A. (ed.) Manchester: Manchester University Press.

Wolf, A., and Swift, J. (1984): "Progress in Computing Lyapunov Exponents from Experimental Data," in *Statistical Physics and Chaos in Fusion Plasmas,* Horton, C., and Reichl, L. (eds.). New York: John Wiley & Sons.

Wolf, A., Swift, J., Swinney, H., and Vastano, J. (1985): "Determining Lyapunov Exponents from a Time Series," *Physica,* 16D:285-317.

Part V
Theories of Hedging

The Hedging Performance of the New Futures Markets

LOUIS H. EDERINGTON*

ORGANIZED FUTURES MARKETS in financial securities were first established in the U.S. on October 20, 1975 when the Chicago Board of Trade opened a futures market in Government National Mortgage Association 8% Pass-Through Certificates. This was followed in January, 1976 by a 90 day Treasury Bill futures market on the International Monetary Market of the Chicago Mercantile Exchange. In terms of trading volume both have been clear commercial successes and this has led to the establishment, in 1977, of futures markets in Long Term Government Bonds and 90-day Commercial Paper and, in 1978, of a market in One-Year Treasury notes and new GNMA markets.

The classic economic rationale for futures markets is, of course, that they facilitate hedging—that they allow those who deal in a commodity to transfer the risk of price changes in that commodity to speculators more willing to bear such risks. The primary purpose of the present paper is to evaluate the GNMA and T-Bill futures markets as instruments for such hedging. Obviously it is possible to hedge by entering into forward contracts outside a futures market, but, as Telser and Higinbotham [19] point out, an organized futures market facilitates such transactions by providing a standardized contract and by substituting the trustworthiness of the exchange for that of the individual trader.

In the futures market, price change risk can be eliminated entirely by making or taking delivery on futures sold or bought, but few hedges are concluded in this manner.[1] The major problem with making or taking delivery is that there are only four delivery periods per year for financial security futures so it is often

---

* Associate Professor, Georgia State University. The author would like to acknowledge the helpful comments of Bruce Fielitz, Ed Ulveling, and Jerome Stein. This research was supported in part by the Bureau of Business and Economic Research of Georgia State University.

[1] It should perhaps be noted that in the GNMA market there would, however, be some uncertainty regarding the amount one would need to hold to make delivery. The futures contract is for $100,000 of GNMA 8% Pass-Through Certificates. Since prepayment on these certificates might occur prior to delivery, there is some uncertainty regarding the quantity one would need to hold at present in order to deliver $100,000 of certificates. This is mitigated by the fact that one can deliver certificates of between $97,500 and $102,500 face value with the deficiency or excess to be settled in cash but some uncertainty remains. In addition, the person who accepts delivery of GNMA futures faces uncertainty regarding the type and relative market value of the certificates to be received. While trading is in 8% certificates, certificates of any mortgage rate can be delivered as long as the quantity delivered is equivalent to $100,000 of 8% certificates assuming a thirty year certificate with total prepayment at the end of twelve years. Since the market doesn't always accept such arbitrary prepayment assumptions, it may be cheaper to deliver 6½% or 9% or some other certificates. Indeed, it has generally been cheaper to deliver 9% certificates [6]. Consequently, those accepting delivery may not receive $100,000 of 8% certificates or their market equivalent. This also means that at delivery the futures price for GNMA's will generally remain somewhat below the cash price.

It should also be noted that over the observed period, January 1976 through July 1977, futures prices were below cash prices except for a few occasions within a few weeks of delivery. Purchasers of

impossible to hedge in this manner over the desired time period. Moreover, the desired time period may change or may be uncertain. The most common hedge, therefore, is one in which the seller (buyer) of the futures contract cancels his delivery commitment by buying (selling) a contract of the same future prior to delivery. It is this type of hedge, in which futures positions are liquidated by offsetting trades, which has received the most attention in the hedging literature and is examined in this paper.

In order to illustrate such a hedge and the potential of the new markets for risk avoidance, let us suppose that on September 16, 1977 a mortgage lending institution committed itself to a future loan at a set interest rate. Suppose, further, it was the lender's intention to finance this loan by issuing or selling $100,000 of 30 year GNMA Pass-Through Certificates with an 8% coupon rate which were selling at that time (September 16, 1977) at $99,531 or an effective yield of 8.02%.[2] Fearing that interest rates would rise and GNMA prices would fall by the time it actually sold its certificates, the mortgagor decided to hedge against this risk by selling December 1977 GNMA futures which were trading at $98,219 or an effective yield of 8.20% on September 16.[3] This transaction is summarized in the top half of Table 1.

In this particular case, our firm's fears of an interest rate rise were realized and the hedge was successful. By October 14, 1977, when the firm closed its loan and sold the GNMA certificates, cash market yields had risen 17 basis points to 8.19%. However, futures market yields had also risen 15 basis points to 8.30% so, as shown in Table 1, the futures market gain largely offset the cash market loss. This is a short hedge. If an individual or firm plans to purchase GNMA's, T-Bills, or some other security in the future, it could attempt to protect against the contingency of a decline in interest rates by buying GNMA or T-Bill futures, i.e., entering a long hedge. In this particular example, the hedge was successful because cash and futures prices both fell, but this may not always be the case.

There is not perfect agreement in the futures market literature as to what hedging is or why it is undertaken. The paper begins in Part I, therefore, with a survey of three major theories of hedging: the traditional theory, the theories of Holbrook Working, and the portfolio theory. The portfolio theory, which the author finds superior to the other two, suggests a method for measuring the hedging effectiveness of a futures market and this measure is used in Part II to evaluate the GNMA and T-Bill futures markets. These financial security futures are compared with each other and with two more established and heavily traded

---

GNMA or T-Bill futures could therefore lock-in a lower price as well as a certain price but sellers of futures would have to be willing to lock-in a loss. On GNMA's, for example, the futures price averaged 1.9 below the cash price two months before delivery over the observed period and ranged from 1.1% below the cash price to 2.5% below.

[2] GNMA yields are calculated on the assumption of a prepayment after 12 years. The published market yields also take into account, as the face yields do not, that there is an interest free delay of 15 days in payments of principal and interest.

[3] Note that if the firm were to wait until December and make delivery, it would lock in exactly this price and yield but if it closes the hedge prior to delivery the price and yield are still somewhat uncertain.

At the present time there is no good data on what sort of firms are hedging in the market so this example is hypothetical. In addition, there are regulatory constraints on the participation of banks and S & L's (See Ederington and Plumly, 1976).

Table 1
A Possible Short Hedge Based on Actual Prices

Cash Market	Futures Market
September 16, 1977	
Makes mortgage commitment and makes plan to sell $100,000 face value of GNMA 8% Certificates	Sells one December futures contract at $98,219
Current price $99,531	
October 14, 1977	
Sells GNMA 8% certificates ($100,000 face value)	Buys one December futures contract at $97,156
Current price $98,281	

Results:	
Loss from delay on cash market	$1250
Gain on futures market	1063
Net Loss	$ 187

futures markets: corn and wheat. The portfolio theory also provides a method for measuring the costs of hedging and these costs are examined for the two financial security futures. The article closes with a summary of the conclusions and some observations on possible future research in futures in Part III.

I. Theories of Hedging

A. *Traditional Hedging Theory*

While traditional hedging theory predates the work of Working and the application of portfolio theory to hedging, it continues to be important. Indeed, it is the traditional theory which underlies almost all the early "How To" articles on hedging which accompanied the establishment of the GNMA and T-Bill futures markets.[4]

Traditional hedging theory emphasizes the risk avoidance potential of futures markets. Hedgers are envisioned as taking futures market positions equal in magnitude but of opposite sign to their position in the cash market as in the example in Table 1. For instance, holders of an inventory of X units would protect themselves against the loss from a decline in the cash price by selling X futures of the same commodity or security. When the inventory is sold, futures contracts would be purchased canceling both positions.

If the cash or spot prices at times t_1 and t_2 are P_s^1 and P_s^2 respectively, the gain or loss on an unhedged position, U, of X units is $X[P_s^2 - P_s^1]$, but the gain or loss on a hedged position, H, is $X\{[P_s^2 - P_s^1] - [P_f^2 - P_f^1]\}$ where the f subscript denotes the futures price. Traditional theory argues that spot and futures prices generally move together so that the absolute value of H is less than U or that $\text{Var}(H) < \text{Var}(U)$. This question is often discussed in terms of the change in the cash price versus the change in the "Basis," where the basis is defined as the difference between the futures and spot prices so that the change in the basis is

---

[4] Examples are the Chicago Board of Trade's "Hedging in GNMA Interest Rate Futures" (1975) and articles by Smith [6], Jacobs and Kozuch [10], Sandor [5], Stevens [8], and Duncan [5].

$\{(P_f^2 - P_s^2) - (P_f^1 - P_s^1)\}$ or $-\{(P_s^2 - P_s^1) - (P_f^2 - P_f^1)\}$. A hedge is viewed as perfect if the change in the basis is zero. It is commonly argued that the basis and changes in the basis are small because of the possibility of making or taking delivery, hence $\mathrm{Var}(H) < \mathrm{Var}(U)$. The question of smallness is, of course, relative. While it is true that delivery possibilities limit changes in the basis, a range for variation obviously remains.

Certainly, the familiar theory of adaptive expectations implies that if futures prices reflect market expectations they should not normally match changes in cash prices. According to the theory of adaptive expectations

$$E_n^2 - E_n^1 = a[P_s^2 - E_2^1] + u$$

where E_n^2 and E_n^1 represent the cash prices expected to prevail in period n as of periods 2 and 1 respectively and E_2^1 represents the price which had in period 1, been expected to prevail in period 2. If one assumes that $P_f^2 = E_n^2$ and $P_f^1 = E_n^1$, one obtains

$$P_f^2 - P_f^1 = a[P_s^2 - P_s^1] - a[E_2^1 - P_s^1]$$

If, therefore, no change in spot prices is expected between periods 1 and 2 ($E_2^1 = P_s^1$) and a $\neq$ 1, this theory implies that any change in the spot price will be accompanied by a proportional but unequal movement of the futures price. If, on the other hand, cash prices change in exactly the manner which had been expected ($P_s^2 = E_2^1$), then certainly there will be no change in futures prices.

While it is clear that the basis changes so that most traditional hedges are not perfect, Working [20] complained that many writers of the time were conveniently ignoring this fact:

> A major source of mistaken notions of hedging is the conventional practice of illustrating hedging with a hypothetical example in which the price of the future bought or sold as a hedge is supposed to rise or fall by the same amount that the spot price rises or falls. [20, pp. 320-321.]

In perusing articles and pamphlets on hedging in GNMA's and T-Bills, I have been surprised to note that many continue to follow the same practice almost 25 years later. This includes not only publications of the exchanges and brokerage houses and articles in trade publications, such as *Savings and Loan News* [16] and *The Mortgage Banker* [10], but also articles in the *Review of the Federal Reserve Bank of St. Louis* [18] and the *Federal Home Loan Bank Board Journal* [15]. In these articles, any caveat that cash and futures price changes may not be equal is relegated to a footnote or a discussion of cross-hedging.

B. *Working's Hypothesis*

Working [20 and 21] challenged the view of hedgers as pure risk minimizers and emphasized expected prfit maximization. In his view hedgers functioned much like speculators, but, since they held positions in the cash market as well, they were concerned with relative not absolute price changes. Instead of expecting cash and futures prices to move together, he argued that "most hedging is done in expectation of a change in spot-futures price relations [20]." Holders of a long position in the cash market would, according to Working, hedge if the basis was expected to fall and would not hedge if the basis was expected to rise.

C. *Portfolio and Hedging Theory*

By viewing hedging as a simple application of basic portfolio theory Johnson [11] and Stein [17] were able to integrate the risk avoidance of traditional theory with Working's expected profits maximization. Johnson and Stein argued that one buys or sells futures for the same risk-return reasons that one buys any other security. While traditional theory argued that hedgers should always be completely hedged and Working's hypothesis indicated (though he realized such was not always the case) that hedgers would be completely hedged or unhedged, the application of portfolio theory allowed Johnson and Stein to explain why hedgers would hold both hedged and unhedged commodity stocks.

While the portfolio model of hedging may contain nothing which is new to those in the finance field, it is less familiar to analysts of commodity futures markets and has experienced a somewhat slower acceptance in this field. Since we will use this model to evaluate the GNMA and T-Bill futures as hedging instruments in the next section, let us briefly summarize its important characteristics.

One difference between this and the more familiar portfolio model is that cash and futures market holdings are not viewed as substitutes. Instead, spot market holdings, X_s, are viewed as fixed and the decision is how much of this stock to hedge. Following Johnson and Stein, let us restrict our attention to the case in which the potential hedger holds only one spot market commodity or security. Since spot market holdings are exogenous, any interest payments may also be viewed as predetermined and therefore irrelevant to the hedging decision. Letting U represent once again the return on an unhedged position,

$$E(U) = X_s E[P_s^2 - P_s^1] \qquad (1)$$

$$\text{Var}(U) = X_s^2 \sigma_s^2 \qquad (2)$$

Let R represent the return on a portfolio which includes both spot market holdings, X_s, and futures market holding[5], X_f.

$$E(R) = X_s E[P_s^2 - P_s^1] + X_f E[P_f^2 - P_f^1] - K(X_f) \qquad (3)$$

$$\text{Var}(R) = X_s^2 \sigma_s^2 + X_f^2 \sigma_f^2 + 2 X_s X_f \sigma_{sf} \qquad (4)$$

where

X_s and X_f represent spot and futures market holdings.

$K(X_f)$ are brokerage and other costs of engaging in futures transactions including the cost of providing margin.

σ_s^2, σ_f^2, σ_{sf} represent the subjective variances and the covariance of the possible price changes from time 1 to time 2.

Note that the portfolio, whose returns are represented by R, may be a portfolio which is either completely are partially hedged. There is no presumption, as in traditional theory, that $X_f = -X_s$ (in which case $R = H$). Indeed cash and futures market holdings may even have the same sign.

Let $b = -X_f/X_s$ represent the proportion of the spot position which is hedged. Since in a hedge X_s and X_f have opposite signs, b is usually positive.

$$\text{Var}(R) = X_s^2 \{\sigma_s^2 + b^2\sigma_f^2 - 2b\sigma_{sf}\} \quad \text{and} \tag{5}$$

$$E(R) = X_s\{E(P_s^2 - P_s^1) - bE(P_f^2 - P_f^1)\} - K(X_s, b)$$

$$= X_s\{(1 - b)E(P_s^2 - P_s^1) + bE(P_s^2 - P_s^1) - bE(P_f^2 - P_f^1)\}$$

$$- K(X_s, b) \tag{6}$$

or, letting $E(\Delta b) = E\{P_f^2 - P_s^2 - (P_f^1 - P_s^1)\}$ represent the expected change in the basis,

$$E(R) = X_s[(1 - b) E(S) - b E(\Delta B)] - K(X_s, b) \tag{7}$$

where $E(S) = E(P_s^2 - P_s^1)$ is the expected price change on one unit of the spot commodity.

If the expected change in the basis is zero, then clearly the expected gain or loss is reduced as $b \to 1$. It is also obvious that expected changes in the basis may add to or subtract from the gain or loss which would have been expected on an unhedged portfolio $\{E(U) = X_s E(S)\}$.

Holding X_s constant, let us consider the effect of a change in b, the proportion hedged, on the expected return and variance of the portfolio R.

$$\frac{\partial \text{Var}(R)}{\partial b} = X_s^2\{2b\sigma_f^2 - 2\sigma_{sf}\} \tag{8}$$

so the risk minimizing b, b^*, is

$$b^* = \frac{\sigma_{sf}}{\sigma_f^2} \tag{9}$$

$$\frac{\partial E(R)}{\partial b} = -X_s[E(\Delta B) + E(S)] - \frac{\partial K(X_s, b)}{\partial b} \tag{10}$$

Since $E(\Delta B)$ and $E(S)$ may be either positive or negative, the opportunity locus of the possible combinations of $E(R)$ and $\text{Var}(R)$, which are shown in figure 1, may lie in either the first or second quadrant or both. Moreover, as b increases one moves either clockwise or counterclockwise around the locus depending on the sign of equation 10.

In this model there is no riskless asset. Treasury bills, which are usual candidate for a riskless asset, are themselves being hedged. One may wish to liquidate a position in bills prior to maturity in which case there is a price risk however small. Consequently, the optimal b, $\hat{b}$, will be that associated with the point on the indifference curve which is just tangent to the highest indifference curve, II'. Not only need $\hat{b}$ not equal one as traditional hedging theory presumed, but $\hat{b}$ may be greater than one, in which case one takes a greater position in the futures than in the cash market, or $\hat{b}$ may be less than zero, in which case one takes the same position (either short or long) in both the spot and futures markets.[5]

[5] Since one would normally assume that $\sigma_{sf} > 0$, $b^* > 0$ but since b may be either increasing or decreasing as one moves counterclockwise around the opportunity locus, the portion of the locus above b^* may represent either $b < b^*$ or $b < b^*$.

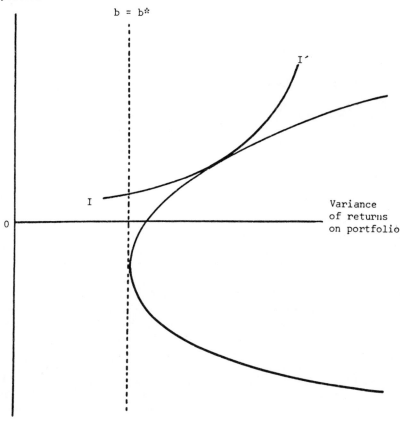

Figure 1

II. Evaluating the GNMA and T-Bill Futures Markets

The purpose of this section is to estimate the effectiveness of the new futures markets in reducing the risk associated with a cash position in GNMA's or T-Bills based on the market experience to date and to estimate the costs of hedging (the impact on expected returns).

While traditional theory indicates that the risk reduction to be achieved by hedging can be measured by comparing the variance of the change in the basis to the variance of the change in the cash price, this presumes that $b = 1$ which as shown above may not be the case. Fortunately, portfolio theory also provides a measure of hedging effectiveness. While the risk reduction achieved by any one hedger depends on the chosen b, the futures markets' potential for risk reduction can be measured by comparing the risk on an unhedged portfolio with the minimum risk that can be obtained on a portfolio containing both spot and forward securities. This minimum risk is represented by the left most point of the opportunity locus in figure 1, and corresponds to the variance of the return on a portfolio where b equals the b^* defined in equation 9. The measure of hedging effectiveness used in this paper is, therefore, the percent reduction in the variance or

$$e = 1 - \frac{\text{Var}(R^*)}{\text{Var}(U)}$$

where varR^* denotes the minimum variance on a portfolio containing security futures.

Substituting equation 9 into equation 5 yields

$$\text{Var}(R^*) = X_s^2 \left\{ \sigma_s^2 + \frac{\sigma_{sf}^2}{\sigma_f^2} - 2\frac{\sigma_{sf}^2}{\sigma_f^2} \right\} = X_s^2 \left(\sigma_s^2 - \frac{\sigma_{sf}^2}{\sigma^2 f} \right)$$

Consequently

$$e = \frac{\sigma_{sf}^2}{\sigma_s^2 \sigma_f^2} = \rho^2$$

where ρ^2 is the population coefficient of determination between the change in the cash price and the change in the future's price.

In order to judge the market's effectiveness at reducing risk, we estimated e using the sample coefficient of determination, r^2, for hedges of two arbitrary lengths (two and four weeks) and using the sample variances and sample covariance of the two and four week price changes over the observed period to estimate b^* as well as σ_s^2, σ_f^2 and σ_{sf}. As noted above, the GNMA and T-Bill markets were established in October 1975 and January 1976 respectively. Since it seemed prudent to allow the markets to gain some depth before analyzing them, weekly data collection for the GNMA market began in January 1976 and for the T-Bill market in March 1976. Both data sets were continued through December 1977. For comparison purposes we also collected data (January 1976—December 1977) and calculated e for two established and heavily traded futures: corn and wheat.[6]

For T-Bill cash prices, 90-day T-Bill prices were consistently used because they were readily available. This ignores the fact that over the hedge period the term to maturity of any T-Bills held will decline. Actual hedgers would need to adjust their b according to the term of the T-Bills held and the length of the hedge [5].

Since a hedger can buy futures with near or distant delivery dates, hedges in futures with a delivery date in 3 months or less (the nearby contract), in 3 to 6 months, in 6 to 9 months, and in 9 to 12 months were evaluated separately.[7] It could be argued that one's expectations of the near future will be affected more by unexpected changes in the cash price than one's expectation of the more distant futures, and this is supported by some work on adaptive expectations using forward rates from the term structure [12]. Consequently, we hypothesize that e will decline as one considers more distant contracts.

---

[6] The futures prices were weekly closing prices as reported in the *Wall Street Journal*. For the spot price of wheat, we used the price of #2 Kansas City hard and for corn we used the price of #2 Chicago yellow as reported in the *Journal*.

[7] Two or four week periods in which the nearby contract expired were dropped from the sample. During the harvest season, futures contracts are available for every other month for corn and wheat, so the time periods for these differ somewhat from those for GNMA's and T-Bills.

The New Futures Market

Table 2
Two Week Hedges

The Futures Contract	Estimated e	Estimated b*
8% GNMA's (46 observations)		
The Nearby Contract	.664	.801*
3 to 6 Month Contract	.675	.832
6 to 9 Month Contract	.677	.854
9 to 12 Month Contract	.661	.852
90 Day Treasury Bills (41 observations)		
The Nearby Contract	.272	.307*
3 to 6 Month Contract	.256	.237*
6 to 9 Month Contract	.178	.143*
9 to 12 Month Contract	.140	.116
Wheat (45 observations)		
The Nearby Contract	.898	.864*
2 to 6 Month Contract	.889	.815*
4 to 8 Month Contract	.868	.784*
6 to 10 Month Contract	.841	.778*
Corn (45 observations)		
The Nearby Contract	.649	.915
2 to 6 Month Contract	.605	.905
4 to 8 Month Contract	.541	.868
6 to 10 Month Contract	.450	.764

* Significantly different from 1 at .05 level.

In addition, it is hypothesized that e will be greater for four week than for two week hedges because absolute changes in cash prices should generally be greater and futures prices would have more time to respond (if there is a lag) over the longer period.

The results for two week hedges are shown in Table 2 and the results for four week hedges are shown in Table 3. The most striking result is the marked superiority of the GNMA market to the T-Bill market particularly for the shorter hedges. While it appears less effective than the wheat market, the GNMA market compares quite favorably with the corn market as a hedging instrument. With the puzzling exception of hedges in the nearby contract for a four week period, the T-Bill market appears rather ineffective in reducing exposure to price change risk particularly over the shorter period. Indeed, if one followed the prescription of traditional theory and set $b = 1$, the hedged T-Bill portfolio would have been more risky than the unhedged portfolio in all cases except for four week hedges in the nearby contract. The author feels that this may be due to the fact that the T-Bill rate is closely related to the federal funds rate which, given current Federal Reserve operating procedures, is basically controlled by the Fed over short periods. If short-run changes in T-Bill rates are viewed as induced by monetary authorities, market participants may see no need to adjust their expectations of future rates.

While the author is unaware of any way to statistically test this hypothesis, the

Table 3
Four Week Hedges

The Futures Contract	Estimated e	Estimated b*
8% GNMA's (23 observations)		
The Nearby Contract	.785	.848
3 to 6 Month Contract	.817	.993
6 to 9 Month Contract	.799	1.019
9 to 12 Month Contract	.780	1.035
90 Day Treasury Bills (21 observations)		
The Nearby Contract	.741	.651*
3 to 6 Month Contract	.571	.427*
6 to 9 Month Contract	.406	.242*
9 to 12 Month Contract	.369	.228*
Wheat (21 observations)		
The Nearby Contract	.918	.917
2 to 6 Month Contract	.921	.862*
4 to 8 Month Contract	.909	.840*
6 to 10 Month Contract	.887	.843*
Corn (21 observations)		
The Nearby Contract	.725	1.021
2 to 6 Month Contract	.666	1.011
4 to 8 Month Contract	.608	.969
6 to 10 Month Contract	.560	.887

* Significantly different from 1 at .05 level.

results in Tables 1 and 2 are certainly consistent with the hypothesis that e will be larger for the longer hedges. This difference in hedging effectiveness appears particularly pronounced for the financial security futures.

The hypothesis that short-term hedges in nearby contracts are more effective than hedges in more distant contracts appears to hold for all except the GNMA market.

In estimating e we also estimated b^*.[8] These estimates, which are also reported in the Tables, are themselves of interest since traditional theory implies that $b^* = 1$. In most cases b^* was significantly different from 1 and in general was less than 1. The hypothesis that $b^* = 1$ is therefore rejected.

Since these are ex-post estimates of b^* and since hedgers may be unable because of the individuality of the futures contract to achieve the desired b, the question of the sensitivity of e to the chosen b is one of some importance. To address this question, we calculated e or r^2 for b's ten percent greater and lower than those shown in Tables 1 and 2. For hedges in either GNMA's or T-Bills, in either the nearby or the next closest contract, and over either a two or four week period, raising or lowering b ten percent from the estimated b^* resulted in a reduction in e of approximately 1%. We conclude, therefore, that these results are not very sensitive to small deviations in b.

[8] Let us note again that hedgers in T-Bills must adjust these estimates of b^* to reflect the term to maturity and the hedging period of their own portfolio.

While real cross-hedging was not considered, the effectiveness of the GNMA futures market in hedging positions in 6½% and 9% certificates was examined. As mentioned earlier, one can deliver these certificates to satisfy a futures contract and an earlier study (Ederington and Plumly, 1976) indicated that, at least in 1976, it would have been cheaper to deliver 9% certificates than 8% certificates and more expensive to deliver 6½% certificates. For this reason we expected e to be higher for 9% than for either 8 or 6½% certificates. This proved to be the case for all two-week hedges. Indeed, for all futures contracts e was highest for a hedge against 9% certificates, lower for 8% certificates, and lowest for 6½% certificates. For hedges in the nearby contract over a two week period, for instance, the measures of e were .820, .664, and .662 respectively.

Having found that, at least for GNMA's, one can lower the risk (as measured by the variance) associated with holding securities by holding futures, attention is now turned to the impact of hedging on expected returns. Two points are clear from equation 7. One, expected returns are lowered by the amount of the brokerage and other costs associated with the futures. Two, if the expected change in the basis is zero and $0 < b < 1$, partial hedging reduces the gain or loss associated with an unhedged position $\{X_s E(S)\}$. Attention is therefore centered on the term, $E(\Delta B)$. The important question is whether over the long run $E(\Delta B)$ will tend to be consistently negative or positive i.e., whether the expected value of the expected change in the basis is positive or negative. Since the basis must be approximately zero at the delivery date,[9] $E(\Delta B)$ will generally be positive if the current cash price exceeds the current futures price and will generally be negative if the futures price exceeds the cash price.

The longer the hedge and the closer the delivery date, the closer this relationship between $E(\Delta B)$ and the initial basis should be. The question basically reduces, therefore, to whether there is any reason to anticipate that in the long-run futures prices will generally be above or below cash prices.

Over the observed period, cash prices on GNMA's and T-Bills consistently exceeded futures prices (except occasionally at delivery). To provide an idea of what changes in the basis might have been expected during this period, the average change in the basis as a percent of the cash price (for comparison) was calculated for four week hedge periods.[10] The results are shown in Table 4.[11] As expected, the average change in the basis was positive so that over this period the change in the basis tended to add to (subtract from) the expected returns of those taking a long (short) position in the futures market.[12] In addition, it is interesting to note that for GNMA's the average change in the basis tended to vary inversely with the length of the futures contract. Since the risk reduction

---

[9] If it is cheaper to deliver GNMA certificates with a mortgage rate other than 8%, the basis for GNMA's will not be eliminated completely. A negative basis remains depending on the difference in costs.

[10] The average change for four weeks is not exactly double the change for two weeks because the periods do not completely overlap since periods in which the nearby contract matured were eliminated.

[11] The author does not feel that corn and wheat provide a meaningful comparison in this case because the basis on these varies with the time till harvest and storage costs.

[12] Note that when the basis is negative, those who take a long position in the futures market and take delivery lock in the lower buying price and higher interest rate. Those who are short and make delivery lock-in a selling price which is below the current selling price.

Table 4

Average Change in the Basis
Over 4 Week Periods
January 1976 (March for T-Bills)—December 1977

Futures Contract	Average Change in the Basis as a % of the Cash Price	
	GNMA Certificates	Treasury Bills
The Nearby Contract	.271%	.184%
3 to 6 Month Contract	.162%	.220%
6 to 9 Month Contract	.133%	.161%
9 to 12 Month Contract	.098%	.164%

was approximately the same for all four contracts, this suggests that long (short) hedgers would have been well advised to hedge in the nearby (distant) contract.

While over the observed period cash prices on GNMA's and T-Bills consistently exceeded futures prices so that positive changes in the basis could generally be expected, this was not always the case in 1978 and may not be the case in the future. The author is much more reluctant to accept Table 4 as a guide to the future than Tables 2 and 3. The crucial question is whether futures prices are unbiased measures of market expectations of future spot rates or whether they are biased downward by "normal-backwardation." There isn't enough data to answer this question since the lower futures prices to date could simply reflect consistent expectations of rising interest rates.

There continues to be a theoretical and empirical debate over "normal backwardation," the Keynes-Hick argument from which the liquidity premium theory of the term structure was developed.[13] However, it is questionable whether evidence from other futures markets is applicable to GNMA and T-Bill markets. Hick's argument [8, pp. 136–139] was that most hedgers of agricultural commodities maintain a long position in the cash and a short position in the futures market so that there is a weakness on the demand side of the futures market which speculators will not step in and absorb until the futures price is sufficiently low so that the expected favorable price change will compensate for the risk. Since it is an open question whether hedgers in GNMA's and T-Bills are generally long or short, the existence and sign of any liquidity premium in these markets is less certain.

For the T-Bill market there is an additional consideration. Since one can satisfy the delivery commitment by delivering longer T-Bills on which all but three months have elapsed, the possibility of riskless arbitrage should theoretically keep the futures rates close to the forward rates implicit in the term structure.[14] If, therefore, there are liquidity premiums in the term structure they should be reflected in the futures market. While there is still debate on this point, the bulk of recent evidence indicates that the term structure does contain liquidity premiums [7 and 9]. For T-Bills, therefore, it may be that futures prices normally tend to be below cash prices so that $E(\Delta B)$ is generally positive.

[13] See Peck, Section 1 [4], Burger, Lang and Rasche [3], Fama [7], and Cornell [4].
[14] While this should theoretically be the case, surprisingly large differences between future and forward rates have been observed [2].

III. Conclusions and Observations

The conclusions of this study may be summarized as follows:

1. The decision to hedge a cash or forward market position in the futures market is no different from any other investment decision—investors hedge to obtain the best combination of risk and return. Basic portfolio theory, which best explains when and how much holders of financial portfolios will wish to hedge, encompasses both the traditional hedging theory and Working's theory as special cases.
2. The implication of many "How-To" articles in the popular financial press that hedges in GNMA's and T-Bills are perfect because cash and futures prices change by equal amounts is completely indefensible.
3. Contrary to traditional hedging theory (but consistent with the theory of adaptive expectations), our empirical results indicate that even pure risk-minimizers may wish to hedge only a portion of their portfolios. In most cases the estimated b^* was less than one.
4. Based on the experience to date, the GNMA futures market appears to be a more effective instrument for risk avoidance than the T-Bill market particularly for short-term (i.e., two-week) hedges.
5. Both the GNMA and the T-Bill market appear to be more effective in reducing the price change risk over long (four-week) than over short (two-week) periods.
6. While changes in the basis were generally positive over the observed period (adding to the return on long hedges and subtracting from that on short hedges), the financial futures markets have not been in existence long enough to tell whether this is the usual case because of "normal backwardation" or whether it merely reflects expectations during the observed period.

A number of unanswered questions and topics for future research regarding futures markets in financial securities obviously remain. One which the author regards as particularly important is the effectiveness of the new futures markets for cross-hedging, i.e., for reducing the risk of portfolios containing securities other than GNMA's or T-Bills. Since mortgage lenders must often commit themselves months before the funds are lent, the effectiveness of the GNMA future in hedging against changes in conventional mortgage rates (or in the cost of funds) seems to be an important unanswered question. [However, our results are appropriate if the lender plans to finance the mortgages by issuing GNMA Pass-Through Certificates as in Table 1.] Unfortunately, the only data series for local mortgage rates of which the author is aware—the Federal Home Loan Bank Board series—measures the rate on loans made and these loans may reflect commitments made months ago. What are needed are localized data on new commitments.

REFERENCES

1. P. W. Bacon, and R. E. Williams, 1976. "Interest Rate Futures: New Tool for the Financial Manager," *Financial Management* (Spring, 1976), pp 32–38.
2. B. Branch, 1978. "Testing the Unbiased Expectations Theory of Interest Rates." Paper presented at 1978 annual meeting of the Eastern Finance Association.
3. A. E. Burger, R. W. Lang, and R. H. Rasche, 1977. "The Treasury Bill Futures Market and Market Expectations of Interest Rates," *Review* of the Federal Reserve Bank of St. Louis, Vol 59, No. 6, pp 2–11.

4. Bradford Cornell, 1977. "Spot Rates, Forward Rates and Exchange Market Efficiency," *Journal of Financial Economics* (August, 1977), pp 55–60.
5. W. H. Duncan, 1977. "Treasury Bill Futures—Opportunities and Pitfalls," *Review* of the Federal Reserve Bank of Dallas (July, 1977).
6. L. E. Ederington, and W. E. Plumly, 1976. "The New Futures Market in Financial Securities," Futures Trading Seminar Proceedings, Vol IV, Chicago Board of Trade.
7. E. F. Fama, 1976. "Forward Rates as Predictors of Future Spot Rates," *Journal of Financial Economics* (Oct., 1976), pp 361–378.
8. J. R. Hicks, 1946. *Value and Capital* (London: Oxford University Press) second edition.
9. T. E. Holland, 1965. "A Note on the Traditional Theory of the Term Structure of Interest Rates on Three-and-Six-Month Treasury Bills," *International Economic Review* (September, 1965), pp 330–36.
10. S. F. Jacobs, and J. R. Kozuch, 1975. "Is There a Future for a Mortgage Futures Market," *The Mortgage Banker*.
11. L. L. Johnson, 1960. "The Theory of Hedging and Speculation in Commodity Futures," *Review of Economic Studies*. Vol 27, No. 3, pp 139–51.
12. J. B. Michaelsen, 1973. *The Term Structure of Interest Rates* (New York: Interest Educational Publishers).
13. J. H. McCulloch, 1975. "An Estimate of the Liquidity Premium," *Journal of Political Economy* (February, 1975), pp 95–119.
14. A. E. Peck, 1977. *Selected Writings on Futures Markets*, Vol II (Chicago: Board of Trade of the City of Chicago).
15. R. L. Sandor, 1975. "Trading Mortgage Interest Rate Futures," *Federal Home Loan Bank Board Journal* (September, 1975), pp 2–9.
16. B. Smith, 1976. "Trading Complexities, FHLBB Rules Impede Association Activity," *Savings and Loan News* (January, 1976).
17. J. L. Stein, 1961. "The Simultaneous Determination of Spot and Futures Prices," *American Economic Review*, Vol LI, No. 5.
18. N. A. Stevens, 1976. "A Mortgage Futures Market: Its Development, Uses, Benefits and Cost," *Review* of the Federal Reserve Bank of St. Louis (April, 1976).
19. L. G. Telser, and H. N. Higinbotham, 1977. "Organized Futures Markets: Costs and Benefits," *Journal of Political Economy* (October, 1977), Vol 85, pp 969–1000.
20. H. Working, 1953. "Futures Trading and Hedging," *American Economic Review* (June, 1953), pp 314–343.
21. ———. 1962. "New Concepts Concerning Futures Markets and Prices," *American Economic Review* (June, 1962), pp 431–459.

[16]

Optimal Hedging under Price and Quantity Uncertainty: The Case of a Cocoa Producer

Jacques Rolfo
International Bank for Reconstruction and Development

After devising expectational measures of production and price uncertainty, this paper presents a model that derives an optimal hedging strategy for a producing country that is subject to variability in both the price and the production of its output. The analysis is then used to derive the optimal hedging for representative cocoa producers of Ghana, Nigeria, Ivory Coast, and Brazil, four countries which account for close to 80 percent of world production. While the traditional definition of hedging recommends a hedge ratio of one, this paper shows that the ratio of optimal hedge to expected output should be below unity. To arrive at this result, individual preferences are represented by a logarithmic utility function (and also by a quadratic utility function for values of the risk parameter which are inferior to 0.001). Thus, limited usage of the futures market may be superior to a full short hedge of expected output when there is production variability. This result is a warning for developing countries whose agricultural produce is subject to high price and quantity volatility and should aid them in deciding upon the use of futures trading as a hedging instrument.

Futures trading originates in part from merchants' desire to be protected from price variability. It is argued that futures trading allows a

In the preparation of this paper the author received strong encouragement from Mr. Singh, Division Chief, Commodities and Export Projections Division, IBRD. The author is extremely grateful to Professor Litzenberger of Stanford University, to the late Professor Cootner, and to Dr. H. Sosin of Bell Laboratories for numerous discussions on the topic, and to Messrs. E. Grilli, P. Yeung, P. Pollack, and C. Chung, IBRD, for the valuable comments and criticism they offered on earlier drafts of the paper. Helpful comments of two anonymous referees are also thankfully acknowledged. Ultimately, the author wishes to take full responsibility for the views and conclusions expressed in this paper as well as for its shortcomings. The views expressed are those of the author and not necessarily those of the IBRD.

transfer of price risk from merchants to speculators. The traditional recommendation is to protect an established long position of known magnitude in the physical product with a short position of *equal* size in the futures market. It is also suggested that the opportunity to hedge on futures markets may be useful to farmers of developing countries which depend upon the sale or export of their crop as a major source of income or foreign exchange, and are therefore deeply concerned by high variability in the price of their crop. However, while there is a long tradition of futures trading by merchants, the participation of farmers has been extremely limited.

The reason for the lack of interest in futures markets on the part of farmers and developing countries may be attributed to the fact that their situation is more complex than that of a merchant. While the merchant can regulate the size of his inventory, the farmer cannot accurately forecast the size of his harvest even after all production decisions have been made. Thus the farmer suffers from *both* price and quantity uncertainty.[1]

This paper derives the optimal hedge for a producer who is subject to both price and quantity uncertainties. The major result of the analysis is that, in this environment, a minimal usage of a futures market (or none at all) may be superior to a full short hedge. These results are established explicitly for the case of a risk-averse cocoa producer.

Cocoa was chosen for analysis because historically it has had one of the highest price and quantity volatilities among primary commodities. Further, all cocoa producers are tropical developing countries whose revenues (especially for West Africa) rely to a large extent on the export of cocoa.[2]

Section I presents two models of optimal hedging assuming that there are different price distributions on the physical (cash) market and futures market and that both price and quantity uncertainty exist. The first model uses a mean-variance framework; the second assumes that preferences are represented by a logarithmic utility function. In the latter case, it is shown that "reverse hedging" (i.e., the situation where a producer would benefit from being long in both physical and

---

[1] As noted by a reviewer, multiple uncertainty can be found in problems of international trade and forward exchange markets. The reviewer gives the example of an importer who is subject to foreign exchange risk and domestic price uncertainty. The same framework could be applied to this problem. However, if a futures market on the imported produce exists, the importer should look for simultaneous optimal hedges in *both* the futures and the foreign exchange markets.

[2] Five countries (Ghana, Nigeria, Brazil, the Ivory Coast, and Cameroon) account for about 80 percent of world production. Cocoa is consumed mainly in the developed countries. The United States, the European Economic Community, and the Soviet Union represent about two-thirds of world consumption.

futures markets) may be optimal. Section II introduces measures of price and production uncertainties, respectively. These measures are based on the difference between forecasts that incorporate all information available before the harvest and realized values. These should be contrasted with measures based solely on historical variability as has been assumed by other authors. Section III tests the unbiasedness of price and quantity forecast errors. Sections IV and V analyze the correlation between price and quantity and between revenue and both price and quantity uncertainty, respectively. The corresponding variances and covariances are then used in following sections to determine the optimal hedge. Specifically, Section VI presents empirical evidence that illustrates that (for a logarithmic utility function) hedging only a limited fraction of expected output is optimal. Section VII calculates the optimal hedge in the mean-variance framework (as described in Section I) and relates it to the producer's risk-aversion parameter.

I. The Mean-Variance and Logarithmic Models

This section introduces two models of optimal hedging for a producer who is subject to both price and quantity uncertainties on his production. First, a mean-variance representation of preferences is assumed, and then a logarithmic utility function is assumed. To simplify the paradigm, the continuous production cycle is divided into two periods: before the harvest and the harvest. During the preharvest period, both price and production to be realized are assumed to be unknown. All uncertainty is resolved at the harvest. Ex ante distributions of price and quantity are empirically determined (as explained in a later part of the paper) and are based on the difference between a price forecast before harvest and the realized price. This paper differentiates the price distribution on the physical market, $\tilde{p}$, from the price distribution on the futures markets, $\tilde{p}_f$.[3] Holding n futures contracts enables the farmer to modify his end-of-period income distribution—from $\tilde{p}\tilde{Q}$ to $\tilde{W} = \tilde{p}\tilde{Q} + n(f - \tilde{p}_f)$, where $\tilde{Q}$ is the output distribution and f is the futures price that is quoted before the harvest.[4]

A mean-variance framework assumes that the farmer's expected utility is a function of only expected income, $E(\tilde{W})$, and variance of income, var $(\tilde{W})$, that is, $EU = E(\tilde{W}) - m[\text{var}(\tilde{W})]$ where m is the farmer's risk parameter.[5]

---

[3] The physical market, or market on actuals, refers to the market on which the physical commodity is traded; futures contracts are traded on the futures markets.
[4] Futures prices are determined according to individual preferences (and risk aversions) in a market equilibrium setting.
[5] The expression $E(\tilde{W}) - m[\text{var}(\tilde{W})]$ can also be interpreted as part of the Lagrangian in a maximization problem where expected income is maximized at a given level of

OPTIMAL HEDGING

The optimal hedge n^* is a solution of the first-order condition $dEU/dn = 0$:

$$n^* = \frac{\text{cov}(\tilde{p}\tilde{Q}, \tilde{p}_f)}{\text{var}(\tilde{p}_f)} + \frac{f - E(\tilde{p}_f)}{2m \cdot \text{var}(\tilde{p}_f)}.[6] \quad (1)$$

The first component of n^*, cov $(\tilde{p}\tilde{Q}, \tilde{p}_f)/\text{var}(\tilde{p}_f)$, is the coefficient of $\tilde{p}_f$ in a linear regression where $\tilde{p}_f$ is the independent variable and $\tilde{p}\tilde{Q}$ (i.e., the farmer's nominal revenue generated by his output $\tilde{Q}$), the dependent variable; it is proportional to the covariance between revenue and futures price (see Section V). The second component of n^*, $[\tilde{f} - E(\tilde{p}_f)]/[2m \cdot \text{var}(\tilde{p}_f)]$, is proportional to the bias in the futures price (i.e., the difference between futures price and expected future spot price) and inversely proportional to the measure of risk aversion, m. If the futures contract is priced above the expected future spot price, the farmer benefits by selling ahead more of his crop. The second component of n^* disappears if either the futures price is an unbiased estimate of the future spot price or if an individual is infinitely risk averse ($m \to \infty$). In the latter case, the optimal hedge is independent of whether the futures price is (or is not) a biased estimate of future spot price (see McKinnon 1967).

A mean-variance framework assumes either that the producer has constant absolute risk aversion or that his preferences are defined only on expected value and variance of income (i.e., his utility function is quadratic and his risk aversion increases with wealth). Both of these preference structures have been criticized as unrealistic. They are, however, computationally convenient since they lead to a simple closed-form expression for the optimal hedge.

A logarithmic (Bernoulli) utility function allows for the more realistic assumption of decreasing absolute risk aversion and constant

---

variance of income. The first interpretation corresponds to a representation of preferences by an exponential utility function for jointly normal distributions and implies a constant absolute risk aversion at all levels of wealth. The risk parameter, m, is then the price, measured in units of expected income, paid in order to maintain the same expected utility as the variance of income changes:

$$m = \frac{d\,[E(\tilde{W})]}{d\,[\text{var}(\tilde{W})]} \bigg| \text{ at constant expected utility.}$$

The higher the required payoff, measured in terms of expected income, to compensate the increase in variance, the more risk averse the individual. Consequently, a greater (smaller) m depicts a more risk-averse (less risk-averse) attitude. At $m = 0$, the individual is risk neutral; he is indifferent to the variance of his income distribution and derives utility only from his expected income. Note that the trade-off between expected income and variance of income is independent of the level of expected income. This is a consequence of the underlying assumption of exponential utility function which implies that individuals' attitude toward risk does not depend on their wealth level.

[6] Recall that m has the dimension of $(pQ)^{-1}$; n^* has the dimension of production.

relative risk aversion. It implies an optimal holding of futures contracts, n_1^*, defined by

$$E\left[\frac{\tilde{p}_f - f}{\tilde{p}\tilde{Q} + n_1^*(f - \tilde{p}_f)}\right] = 0. \tag{2}$$

It is not possible to derive a closed form expression for n_1^* because relation (2) involves the ratio of distributions. Numeric solutions to (2) are provided in Section VI and are compared in Section VII with those derived for the mean-variance framework.

It is traditionally assumed that a merchant who wants to hedge his inventory should be short in futures contracts ($n^* > 0$) (i.e., sell his inventory ahead). For instance, Hieronymus (1971) defines hedging as follows:

> Risks are shifted by the process of hedging. To hedge is to take a position in futures equal and opposite to an existing cash position. If a merchant has a stock of 100,000 bushels of corn in his elevator, he is long cash corn. If the price goes up, he makes money. If it goes down, he loses money. He is subject to the risk of a price decline. He can offset this risk by selling 100,000 bushels of futures contracts. As he sells he becomes short futures. He is long cash and short futures; thus he is hedged. So long as cash and futures move up and down together, what the hedger makes on the one position he will lose on the other; consequently he will neither gain nor lose from a change in price. [P. 106]

In the absence of production uncertainty, Hieronymus's analysis is straightforward. However, once production uncertainty is introduced, the situation is more complex. The solution of relations such as (1) and (2) is not even unambiguously positive. The farmer benefits from selling futures contracts on his crop only if his marginal expected utility with respect to the holding of futures contracts at $n = 0$ is positive; otherwise he should be long.

II. Measure of Price and Quantity Uncertainty

Officially, a new cocoa season starts on the first of October of each year (i.e., when the main crop begins in the major producing countries of West Africa and also in Brazil). In the remainder of this paper, preharvest refers to late September and harvest refers to March, when most elements of cocoa demand and supply are known.

As noted earlier, this paper differentiates the price distribution on the physical market, $\tilde{p}$, from the price distribution on the futures market, $\tilde{p}_f$.[7] Futures contracts are held as instruments of portfolio adjustment by producers who are subject to income volatility. That is, producers take a preharvest position in the futures market in order to increase their welfare as measured in terms of expected utility. To undo their positions, contract holders typically do not take delivery of (or tender) the commodity but rather, close to maturity, reverse in the futures market the position they initially assumed.

Three price series are used concurrently in the analysis: the March futures prices reported on the last day of September (price predictors), the March futures prices reported on the first Friday of March (futures prices at settlement date), and the shipment prices reported on the last day of March (prices on "actuals") (see the Appendix for remarks on the price series). The three price series were collected from the *London Financial Times* for 24 seasons (1952–53 to 1975–76). Forecast errors are defined as the difference between realized and forecast prices divided by the forecast price:[8]

$$e^p(t) = [p(t) - p_0(t)]/p_0(t), \; t = 1, 24, \tag{3}$$

and

$$e_f^p(t) = [p_f(t) - p_0(t)]/p_0(t), \; t = 1, 24, \tag{4}$$

where $p_0(t)$ is the price forecast, $p(t)$, the shipment price, and $p_f(t)$, the futures price at delivery, for the tth season.

As was the case for prices, the measure of production uncertainty used in this paper is based on the difference between the last forecast available before the beginning of harvest and the realized production at the harvest and is computed for each country.[9] This procedure, of measuring production uncertainty using expectational data rather than historical data, is preferred because the pattern of cocoa production changes with time, in spite of the extended productive life of cocoa trees—up to 45 years. Aggregate production depends on the age structure of cocoa trees, which is not homogeneous; yield distributions are conditional on the ages of the trees; technical progress contributes to higher yields; tree diseases are more threatening at certain times; new acreage is planted, etc. All these factors contribute

---

[7] The price of the futures contract at maturity and the spot price on the cash market may differ, implying the existence of basis risk.

[8] Dividing by the price forecast allows for different historical rates of inflation.

[9] As noted earlier, the official harvest season for cocoa starts on the first of October of every year and coincides with the beginning of the main crop harvest. The summer crop is quite secondary (except in the case of Brazil where the Temperao crop is often larger than its main crop), and represents less than 5 percent of aggregate production. The production of cocoa is very volatile and the amount of uncertainty is large, even just before (i.e., a few days) harvest starts.

to the high volatility of cocoa production and influence the information that is available before harvest and which is incorporated into the production forecast.

This paper utilizes a set of outputs (forecast and realized) provided by Gill and Duffus[10] covering 24 seasons (1952–53 to 1975–76) for the four largest cocoa producers who account for about 80 percent of world production: three in West Africa (Ghana, Nigeria, and the Ivory Coast), and Brazil. (The production statistics correspond to the total crop for Nigeria and to the main crops for the other countries.)

The forecasts are assumed to incorporate all available information before harvest as by the last day of September. The forecast output of country i[11] for the tth season is denoted by $Q_i^e(t)$ and the realized output by $Q_i(t)$. Quantity uncertainty for every country and every season is measured by the forecast error $e_i^Q(t)$, which is defined as the difference between realized and forecast production divided by forecast production:[12]

$$e_i^Q(t) = [Q_i(t) - Q_i^e(t)]/Q_i(t).\text{[13]} \tag{5}$$

III. Unbiasedness of Price and Quantity Forecasts

Table 1 displays the sample means, sample standard deviations, and the corresponding t-values for price and quantity forecast error distributions (see tables A1–A3 for series on prices, productions, and forecast errors on production, respectively). The hypothesis of a consistent bias in price and output forecasting (i.e., that the mean values of price and quantity forecast errors are different from zero) is rejected at the 5 percent level for price distributions on both the futures and the physical markets for Ghana, Nigeria, and the Ivory Coast.[14] The only exception is Brazil: Gill and Duffus deal primarily in West African cocoa and are therefore likely to expend more effort

---

[10] It is generally believed in the trade that Gill and Duffus have the best information on the prevailing conditions of cocoa production. Here, it is assumed that the output forecast circulated by Gill and Duffus incorporates all available information, and that no other forecast is perceived to be more accurate for the period under study.

[11] 1 refers to Ghana, 2 to Nigeria, 3 to the Ivory Coast, and 4 to Brazil.

[12] This measurement procedure is applied to a situation in which the crop investment has already been made. It is the residual uncertainty on production (due, for instance, to the vagaries of weather) which farmers have to cope with before harvest. This paper emphasizes the fact that agricultural production functions are stochastic even after the investment decision has been made. It focuses on the uncertainty of production facing the representative farmer of a producing country. Local differences within a country would add an extra element of uncertainty that is not considered in this paper.

[13] t varies from 1 for 1952–53 to 24 for 1975–76.

[14] Note that the possibility of a systematic but random bias averaging to zero over the crop seasons is not tested by this procedure.

TABLE 1
Summary Statistics for Price and Quantity Forecast Error Distributions

	Price Forecast Error		Production Forecast Error of			
	Shipment Prices	Futures Prices	Ghana	Nigeria	Ivory Coast	Brazil
Sample mean	.075	.022	.014	.031	.068	.137
Sample SD	.29	.24	.14	.16	.18	.25
t-value	1.25	.45	.49	.96	1.84	2.68

and resources in forecasting the production of West Africa than of Brazil. This may explain why their production forecasts are better for Africa than for Brazil.

The unbiasedness in forecasting is tested by analyzing whether the forecast errors have means of zero. This test is a modified version of a test based on the linear regression of realized prices and quantities against their respective forecasts: the test is performed in such a way as to abstract from changes in nominal price levels and variations in cocoa-producing acreage during the 24 years covered by the study.[15]

IV. Correlation between Price and Quantity Uncertainty

Table 2 presents the variance-covariance and correlation matrices of production uncertainties between producing countries. Within West Africa, production uncertainties are strongly correlated: the correlation coefficient is .66 between Ghana and Nigeria, .46 between Ghana and Ivory Coast, and .39 between Ivory Coast and Nigeria. Climatic conditions play a major role in output variability and clearly present more similarity between the three West African neighbor countries than between West Africa and Brazil. As expected, the correlation between production uncertainties in West African countries and Brazil is small: .1 with Ghana, .24 with Nigeria, and .2 with the Ivory Coast.

Table 3 presents the covariances and correlations between production uncertainties and price uncertainty of markets in "actuals." The correlation coefficient between quantity uncertainty and price uncertainty is higher for the West African countries (−.47 for Ghana, −.5 for Nigeria, and −.22 for the Ivory Coast) than for Brazil, for which it

---

[15] The efficiency of foreign exchange markets has been tested using similar procedures (see Levich 1978 for a review). Note that futures market efficiency does not necessarily generate unbiased forecasts. See Grauer, Litzenberger, and Stehle (1976) for an illustration when risk aversion is introduced.

TABLE 2
Variance-Covariance and Correlation Matrices of Forecast Errors in Cocoa Production

	PRODUCTION			
	Ghana	Nigeria	Ivory Coast	Brazil
Ghana	.019828*	.014826	.011725	.003487
	(1.000000)†	(.660835)	(.463789)	(.099392)
Nigeria	.014826	.025386	.011029	.009498
	(.660835)	(1.000000)	(.385575)	(.239264)
Ivory Coast	.011725	.011029	.032232	.009037
	(.463789)	(.385575)	(1.000000)	(.202033)
Brazil	.003487	.009498	.009037	.062070
	(.099392)	(.239264)	(.202033)	(1.000000)

* Variance-covariance.
† Correlation.

is positive, although negligible: .008. This result is not surprising because West Africa as a block is by far the largest producer of cocoa, and consequently its production has a stronger impact on world prices than does Brazil's.

V. Correlation between Forecast Error of Revenue and Price and Quantity Uncertainties

Table 4 displays the correlations between forecast errors of revenue[16] per country and price uncertainty of markets in actuals and production uncertainty. It shows a significant positive correlation between the uncertainty of regional revenue and price uncertainty: .2 for Ghana, .19 for Nigeria, .23 for the Ivory Coast, and .27 for Brazil. The results imply that, if the realized price is higher (lower) than forecast, then realized revenue is also likely to be higher (lower) than

TABLE 3
Covariance and Correlation between Forecast Errors in Cocoa Production and Forecast Errors on Shipment Prices

	PRODUCTION			
	Ghana	Nigeria	Ivory Coast	Brazil
Covariance	−.019392	−.023253	−.011725	.000573
Correlation	−.471111	−.499256	−.223416	.007871

[16] Defined as $[e^p(t) + e_t^q(t) + e^p(t)e_t^q(t), t = 1, 24]$.

TABLE 4

CORRELATION MATRIX OF ERRORS IN FORECAST REVENUE (per Country)
AND ERRORS IN FORECAST QUANTITY AND SHIPMENT PRICE

REVENUE	PRODUCTION				PRICE
	Ghana	Nigeria	Ivory Coast	Brazil	
Ghana	−.006367	−.058993	−.013926	.010113	.200061
Nigeria	−.041290	.006255	−.019452	−.028991	.185840
Ivory Coast	−.063318	−.082783	.079802	−.029854	.232519
Brazil	−.096921	−.078814	−.015984	.182633	.265524

forecast. This result is independent of the difference between forecast and realized output.

Conversely, the correlation between a country's revenue uncertainty and its production uncertainty is smaller than between revenue and price: .006 for Nigeria, .08 for the Ivory Coast, and, for Ghana, it is negative (−.006). This result holds for all countries but Brazil where the correlation of revenue with production is of the same order as that with revenue and price (.18).

The correlation between one country's revenue uncertainty and another country's output uncertainty is always small and negative.

VI. Empirical Evidence: The Case of a Logarithmic Utility Function

The optimal hedge for a producer with a logarithmic utility function facing uncertainty in both price and output is the solution n_i^* of equation (2). In the case of country i, and replacing $\bar{p}, \bar{p}_f$, and $\bar{Q}$ by $f(1 + \tilde{e}^p), f(1 + \tilde{e}_f^p)$, and $Q_i^e(1 + \tilde{e}_i^Q)$, respectively, condition (2) is rewritten as

$$E\left[\frac{\tilde{e}_f^p}{(1 + \tilde{e}^p)(1 + \tilde{e}_i^Q) - (n_i^*/Q_i^e)\tilde{e}_f^p}\right] = 0. \quad (6)$$

Equation (6) shows that, given the assumptions of the logarithmic model, the proportion of expected output to be hedged, n_i^*/Q_i^e, is independent of the levels of both output and price forecasts, Q_i^e and f, respectively, and depends only on the distributions of the forecast error terms.

In order to estimate n_i^*/Q_i^e, it is assumed that the set of observations $[e^p(t), e_f^p(t), e_i^Q(t), t = 1, 24]$ are independent drawings from distribution $[\tilde{e}^p, \tilde{e}_f^p, \tilde{e}_i^Q]$, respectively. Equation (6) is then approximated by

$$\sum_{t=1}^{24} e^p(t)/\{[1 + e^p(t)][1 + e_i^Q(t)] - e^p(t)n_i^*/Q_i^e\} = 0. \quad (7)$$

TABLE 5
LOGARITHMIC OPTIMAL HEDGING

Country	Marginal Expected Utility	Optimal Hedge Ratio
Ghana	.0070	.151
Nigeria	.0059	.134
Ivory Coast	.0128	.303
Brazil	.0184	.452

A search program to solve equation (7) is easily designed. Table 5 gives the estimates of the marginal expected utility at $n = 0$ and the optimal hedge for each country. Marginal expected utilities at $n = 0$ have small positive values. Consequently, the optimal hedge ratios are well below unity. Although, for the 24 seasons covered by this study, the smallest negative (or largest in absolute value) production forecast error has been -0.21 for Ghana, -0.27 for Nigeria, -0.2 for the Ivory Coast, and -0.18 for Brazil,[17] the logarithmic hedging model recommends that cocoa producers take short positions in the futures market that are equal to only part of their forecast outputs: 0.15 for Ghana, 0.13 for Nigeria, 0.3 for the Ivory Coast, and 0.45 for Brazil.[18] A correlation between price and quantity distributions close to zero for Brazil (see table 3) explains why the optimal hedge ratio is higher for Brazilian than for West African producers.[19]

VII. Empirical Evidence: The Mean-Variance Framework

With $\tilde{p} = f(1 + \tilde{e}^p)$, $\tilde{Q}_i = Q_i^e(1 + \tilde{e}_i^q)$, $\tilde{p}_f = f(1 + \tilde{e}_f^p)$, the optimal hedge ratio for the ith country in a mean-variance framework is rewritten as

$$\frac{n_i^*}{Q_i^e} = \frac{\text{cov}\,[(1 + \tilde{e}^p)(1 + \tilde{e}_i^q), \tilde{e}_f^p]}{\text{var}\,(\tilde{e}_f^p)} - \frac{E(\tilde{e}_f^p)}{2mfQ_i^e\,\text{var}\,(\tilde{e}_f^p)}. \quad (8)$$

The optimal hedge ratio (n^*/Q_i^e) is an explicit function of the quantity and price distributions and of the output forecast Q_i^e; furthermore, (n^*/Q_i^e) is an increasing function of the risk parameter m.[20]

---

[17] It means that the realized output for none of the four countries has ever been below 70 percent of its preharvest forecast (which would correspond to a production forecast error of -0.3).

[18] When price and quantity distributions are statistically independent, a mean-variance framework à la McKinnon implies an optimal hedge ratio of one.

[19] Using hypothetical distributions, it can be shown that even when the price predictor (i.e., the futures price) is an upward-biased estimate of future spot price (i.e., $f > e[\tilde{p}]$ in this paper), reverse hedging may be optimal. This result for Brazil is certainly due to some "noise" between the U.S. dollar and pound sterling price distributions.

[20] This is true because the sample mean of the futures price forecast error is positive.

TABLE 6
Optimal Hedge: Mean-Variance Framework

Risk-Aversion Parameter m	Ghana	Nigeria	Ivory Coast	Brazil
∞	.609	.654	.778	.935
1,000	.609*	.654	.778	.935
	(.000)†	(.000)	(.000)	(.000)
100	.609	.654	.778	.935
	(.000)	(.000)	(.000)	(.000)
10	.609	.654	.778	.935
	(.000)	(.000)	(.000)	(.000)
1	.609	.654	.777	.935
	(.000)	(.000)	(.000)	(.000)
.1	.608	.652	.773	.935
	(.000)	(.000)	(.002)	(.000)
.01	.599	.633	.737	.932
	(.004)	(.009)	(.022)	(.001)
.001	.502	.446	.370	.904
	(.041)	(.095)	(.222)	(.013)
.0001	−.461	−1.431	−3.295	.622
	(.410)	(.946)	(2.217)	(.126)
.00001	−10.090	−20.201	−39.949	−2.195
	(4.100)	(9.459)	(22.171)	(1.264)

*Average optimal hedge as a proportion of expected output.
†Standard deviation of optimal hedge.

Reverse hedging becomes optimal for values of m under $E(\tilde{e}_f^p)/2fQ_i^e \cdot \text{cov}[(1 + \tilde{e}_i^Q)(1 + \tilde{e}^p), \tilde{e}_f^p]$.

Table 6 displays the optimal hedge ratios of the four producing countries for values of the risk parameter between ∞ and 0.00001. For $m = \infty$ the second term of n^*/Q_i^e is zero, and the optimal hedge ratios are 0.61 for Ghana, 0.65 for Nigeria, 0.78 for the Ivory Coast, and 0.94 for Brazil. For m between ∞ and 1, the optimal hedge ratios do not vary significantly. However, they drop drastically for m below unity, with reverse hedging recommended for the West African countries at $m = 0.0001$ and for Brazil at $m = 0.00001$.

Peck's 1975 analysis of the optimal hedge of an egg producer does not consider the case of production uncertainty. Instead, her study concentrates on price uncertainties, that is, on the cash market and on the basis on delivery date, assuming m in the range $(0.1 \geq m \geq 0.001)$, and finds that, without production uncertainty, a producer should hedge between 75 and 95 percent of his output, although "a total hedging scheme compares very favorably with the optimal routine." This is to be contrasted with the result of this paper in which production uncertainty is introduced and where reverse hedging becomes optimal for values of m less than 0.0001.

The levels at which reverse hedging becomes optimal are 0.000175,

TABLE 7
Threshold for Reverse Hedging

	Ghana	Nigeria	Ivory Coast	Brazil
m (in thousandths)	.175	.319	.523	.033
$m \cdot$ mean $(\tilde{p}\tilde{Q}_i)$	19.019	19.665	24.209	16.206

TABLE 8
Risk Parameters Implied by Logarithmic Optimal Hedge

	Ghana	Nigeria	Ivory Coast	Brazil
m (in thousandths)	.234	.401	.857	.065
$m \cdot$ mean $(\tilde{p}\tilde{Q}_i)$	25.388	24.736	39.651	31.371

0.000319, 0.000523, and 0.000033 for Ghana, Nigeria, Ivory Coast and Brazil, respectively (see table 7). The risk parameters yielding the optimal hedges of Section VII are 0.000234, 0.000401, 0.000857, and 0.000065, respectively (see table 8). It is clear from tables 7 and 8 that the differences between results dwindle when risk parameters are multiplied by the average revenue, that is, by the mean of $\tilde{p}\tilde{Q}$ (recall that risk parameters have the dimension of [revenue]$^{-1}$).

VIII. Conclusion

After devising expectational measures of production and price uncertainties, this paper shows how the optimal hedging strategy of a producing country subject to the variability of both the price and the production of its output can be calculated and presents cocoa as a case study. It finds that the ratio of optimal hedge to expected output should be well below unity: the traditional definition of hedging which recommends a ratio of unity needs to be broadened to account for production uncertainty, an important characteristic of agricultural crops. The preceding result is obtained for a model where preferences are represented by a logarithmic utility function. Similar results are obtained with a quadratic utility function for values of the risk parameter less than 0.0001.

The lack of interest among U.S. farmers for futures trading (in contrast with merchants' attitude) has traditionally been observed. Farmers have also been known to remain in a net long position in the physical product by keeping part of their output unhedged. Although the empirical evidence presented is limited to cocoa, quantity uncertainty may provide a partial explanation to these two observations.

Further support for this conclusion is the observation that I have not detected any evidence of major or systematic involvement in cocoa futures trading by the four countries covered in the study. I have not found any publicly available information on the subject, and the inference is based on private conversations.

Appendix

Empirical Measure of Price Uncertainty

The two largest cocoa markets are the London Cocoa Terminal and the New York Cocoa Exchange. Western Europe is the destination of most West

TABLE A1

Cocoa Prices (London)

Season	Futures Prices*	Futures Prices in March†	Forecast Error on Futures Prices‡	Shipment Prices§	Forecast Error on Shipment Prices‖
1952–53	242.0	239.5	−.010331	247.5	.022727
1953–54	261.0	450.0	.724138	470.0	.800766
1954–55	373.0	336.5	−.097855	302.5	−.189008
1955–56	256.0	203.5	−.205078	195.0	−.238281
1956–57	215.0	170.0	−.209302	183.75	−.145349
1957–58	262.0	350.0	.335878	332.5	.269084
1958–59	268.5	290.0	.080074	282.5	.052142
1959–60	256.5	209.0	−.185185	212.0	−.173489
1960–61	216.5	147.0	−.321016	164.0	−.242494
1961–62	165.0	157.5	−.045455	166.0	.006061
1962–63	163.0	190.0	.165644	190.0	.165644
1963–64	201.0	175.5	−.126866	174.0	−.134328
1964–65	190.0	126.0	−.336842	126.0	−.336842
1965–66	139.0	175.5	.262590	182.0	.390353
1966–67	190.5	216.0	.133858	228.5	.199475
1967–68	228.0	267.5	.173246	262.0	.149123
1968–69	346.0	401.0	.158960	400.0	.156069
1969–70	394.5	292.0	−.259823	384.5	−.025349
1970–71	303.0	243.5	−.196370	225.0	−.257426
1971–72	213.0	210.0	−.014085	226.5	.063380
1972–73	316.5	322.0	.017378	408.0	.289100
1973–74	572.5	659.0	.151092	975.0	.703057
1974–75	697.0	734.5	.053802	681.0	−.022956
1975–76	600.5	771.0	.283930	826.0	.375520
Mean	...	...	.022183	...	.074832
SD	...	...	.240712	...	.292318
t-value	...	...	.451461	...	1.254121
Square root of mean square error	...	...	.244843	...	.288655

*Futures prices (closing) on the last day of September for the March futures contract on the London Cocoa Terminal (*London Financial Times*).
†Futures prices (closing) on the first Friday of March for the March futures contracts on the London Cocoa Terminal (*London Financial Times*).
‡Futures price in March minus futures price, divided by futures price.
§Shipment prices on the last day of March (*London Financial Times*).
‖Shipment price minus futures price divided by futures price.

TABLE A2

Cocoa Production (Forecast and Realized)*

Season	Ghana†		Nigeria‡		Ivory Coast§		Brazil‖	
	Forecast	Realized	Forecast	Realized	Forecast	Realized	Forecast	Realized
1952–53	240.0	243.779	100.0	109.0	55.0	58.0	1,000.0	1,258.0
1953–54	236.0	205.793	100.0	97.0	58.0	55.0	850.0	920.0
1954–55	225.0	206.445	110.0	89.0	57.0	70.0	750.0	1,026.0
1955–56	212.0	218.017	100.0	114.0	60.0	65.0	700.0	1,282.0
1956–57	212.0	261.063	120.0	135.0	75.0	68.0	1,100.0	1,231.0
1957–58	205.0	194.637	95.0	81.0	50.0	40.0	1,000.0	1,000.0
1958–59	237.0	225.856	130.0	140.0	60.0	54.0	1,400.0	1,480.0
1959–60	247.0	291.671	130.0	155.0	65.0	60.0	1,400.0	1,615.0
1960–61	295.0	420.647	150.0	195.0	55.0	83.5	800.0	926.0
1961–62	375.0	397.133	190.0	191.0	75.0	77.5	1,500.0	1,272.0
1962–63	450.0	381.947	210.0	176.0	85.0	91.702	1,100.0	906.0
1963–64	390.0	416.754	190.0	216.0	70.0	88.493	950.0	905.0
1964–65	450.0	542.073	225.0	294.0	90.0	126.811	1,000.0	926.0
1965–66	500.0	396.143	250.0	182.0	110.0	108.698	1,400.0	1,553.0
1966–67	400.0	369.399	210.0	263.0	135.0	139.302	1,100.0	1,491.0
1967–68	400.0	389.686	320.0	235.0	115.0	130.222	1,500.0	1,365.0
1968–69	360.0	297.908	200.0	189.0	125.0	129.356	900.0	871.0
1969–70	355.0	375.897	200.0	219.0	140.0	157.5	1,100.0	1,529.0
1970–71	370.0	359.0	250.0	303.0	170.0	159.322	800.0	945.0
1971–72	400.0	444.0	265.0	251.0	200.0	205.383	1,350.0	1,511.0
1972–73	400.0	405.0	250.0	237.0	205.0	172.746	1,500.0	1,791.0
1973–74	325.0	337.28	240.0	212.0	170.0	205.635	2,000.0	2,376.0
1974–75	387.0	361.379	225.0	211.0	210.0	241.51	1,450.0	1,613.0
1975–76	400.0	382.455	240.0	213.0	232.0	231.069	1,620.0	1,899.0

*Gill and Duffus statistics.
†Thousand long tons—main crop only.
‡Thousand long tons—total crop.
§Thousand long tons—main crop; all figures metric except prior to 1962–63.
‖Thousand bags (one bag = 60 kg)—main crop.

TABLE A3
Forecast Errors on Cocoa Production*

Season	Ghana	Nigeria	Ivory Coast	Brazil
1952–53	.015746	.090000	.054545	.258000
1953–54	−.127996	−.030000	−.051724	.082353
1954–55	−.082467	−.190909	.228070	.368000
1955–56	.028382	.140000	.083333	.831429
1956–57	.231429	.125000	−.093333	.119091
1957–58	−.050551	−.147368	−.200000	.000000
1958–59	−.047021	.076923	−.100000	.057143
1959–60	.180854	.192308	−.076923	.153571
1960–61	.425922	.300000	.518182	.157500
1961–62	.059021	.005263	.033333	−.152000
1962–63	−.151229	−.161905	.078847	−.176364
1963–64	.068600	.136842	.264186	−.047368
1964–65	.204607	.306667	.409011	−.074000
1965–66	−.207714	−.272000	−.011836	.109286
1966–67	−.091503	.252381	.031866	.355455
1967–68	−.025785	.068182	.132365	−.090000
1968–69	−.172478	−.055000	.034848	−.032222
1969–70	.058865	.095000	.125000	.390000
1970–71	−.029730	.212000	−.062812	.181250
1971–72	.110000	−.052830	.026915	.119259
1972–73	.012500	−.052000	−.157337	.194000
1973–74	.037785	−.116667	.209618	.188000
1974–75	−.066204	−.062222	.150048	.112414
1975–76	−.043863	−.112500	−.004013	.172222
Mean	.014049	.031132	.067591	.136542
SD	.140812	.159329	.179533	.249139
t-value	.488768	.957230	1.844381	2.684917
Square root of mean square error	.143123	.159618	.169901	.212873

*Realized production minus forecast divided by forecast.

African cocoa. Brazilian cocoa is mostly shipped to the United States. The spot prices reported in the financial newspapers (e.g., the *Wall Street Journal* and the *Journal of Commerce*) of the United States apply to only a very limited volume of transactions. At times, reported spot prices are at best nominal estimates. Although spot prices have been, and still are, widely used in econometric analyses (e.g., Weymar 1968), this study instead uses the shipment prices (c.i.f. prices, ex-warehouses [Western Europe]) as reported in the *Reuter Cocoa Bulletin*, in the bimonthly report of Gill and Duffus, the largest cocoa dealer on the London Cocoa Terminal Market, and in the *London Financial Times*. This price series was chosen because it provides estimates of the effective transaction prices corresponding to a given date. Thus, the harvest spot price is defined as the shipment price on the last day of March as reported in the *London Financial Times*.

The December, March, and May futures contracts are all quoted on the futures exchanges as of the end of September, just before the new cocoa season starts, and their settlement months are included in the new season.

The futures contract most appropriate for this study is the March contract since it terminates at a time when most uncertainty on production is resolved. The study assumes that positions in the futures market are liquidated on the first Friday of March at the closing price on that day. It is also assumed that the March futures price as reported on the London Cocoa Terminal Exchange at the close of the last day of September just before the official harvest begins is the most efficient market forecast for both the future cocoa spot (shipment) price and the futures price that will prevail in March. When no quotation is available for the last day of September (which occurred mostly because markets were closed on that day), the closing price of the first day of October was chosen.

The controversy concerning the interpretation of futures prices as predictors of future spot prices is not discussed in this paper. It is assumed that the futures price is a market-determined price corresponding to a consensus on expected prices based on all available information.

References

Gill and Duffus. *Bimonthly Report.* London: Gill & Duffus, various years.
Grauer, F. L. A.; Litzenberger, Robert H.; and Stehle, R. E. "Sharing Rules and Equilibrium in an International Capital Market under Uncertainty." *J. Financial Econ.* 3, no. 3 (June 1976): 233–56.
Hieronymus, T. "Economics of Futures Trading." New York: Commodity Research Bureau, 1971.
Levich, Richard M. "In the Efficiency of Markets for Foreign Exchange." In *International Economic Policy: Theory and Evidence*, edited by Rudiger Dornbusch and Jacob A. Frenkel. Baltimore: Johns Hopkins Univ. Press, 1978.
McKinnon, Ronald I. "Futures Markets, Buffer Stocks, and Income Instability for Primary Producers." *J.P.E.* 75, no. 6 (December 1967): 844–61.
Peck, A. "Hedging and Income Stability: Concepts, Implications, and an Example." *American J. Agricultural Econ.* 57, no. 3 (August 1975): 410–19.
Weymar, F. Helmut. *The Dynamics of the World Cocoa Market.* Cambridge, Mass.: M.I.T. Press, 1968.

[17]
Estimating Time-Varying Optimal Hedge Ratios on Futures Markets

Robert J. Myers

An optimal hedge ratio is usually defined as the proportion of a cash position that should be covered with an opposite position on a futures market. Under certain simplifying assumptions discussed below, optimal hedge ratios can be characterized by a simple rule: set the hedge ratio equal to the ratio of the covariance between cash and futures prices to the variance of the futures price (see Anderson and Danthine (1981) and Benninga, Eldor, and Zilcha (1984)). The conventional approach to implementing this rule is to regress historical cash prices, price changes, or returns on futures prices, price changes, or returns. The resulting slope coefficient is then used as the estimated optimal hedge ratio (see Ederington, (1979) and Kahl (1983)).

There are two problems with the conventional regression approach to optimal hedge ratio estimation. First, it generally fails to take proper account of all of the relevant conditioning information available to hedgers when they make their hedging decision (see Myers and Thompson (1989)). Second, it implicitly assumes that the covariance matrix of cash and futures prices, and hence optimal hedge ratios, are constant over time. There is evidence, however, that commodity price volatility changes as markets move through cycles of high and low uncertainty about future economic conditions (see Anderson (1985) and Fackler (1986)). For example, there was a clear jump in commodity price volatility during the boom of 1973, and during the recent 1988 drought. This suggests that the conditional covariance matrix of cash and futures prices, and hence optimal hedge ratios, may vary substantially over time. A recent article by Cecchetti, Cumby, and Figlewski (1988) estimates time-varying optimal hedge ratios for Treasury bonds using the autoregressive conditional heteroscedastic (ARCH) framework of Engle (1982). They find substantial fluctuations in the time path of optimal hedge ratios.

This article outlines and compares two approaches for estimating time-varying optimal hedge ratios on futures markets. Both methods take account of relevant conditioning information but they differ in their degree of sophistication and ease of estimation. The first method involves calculating moving sample variances and covariances of past prediction errors for cash and futures prices. This method is simple and easy to apply, but is also *ad hoc* and imposes questionable restrictions on the time pattern of commodity price volatility. The second method is the general-

Acknowledgement is made to the Michigan Agricultural Experiment Station for its support of this research. Thanks are due to Paul Fackler, Steve Hanson, Jim Oehmke, and two anonymous reviewers for helpful comments on an earlier version of this article.

Robert Myers is an Assistant Professor, Department of Agricultural Economics, Michigan State University.

ized autoregressive conditional heteroscedastic (GARCH) model of Bollerslev (1986). This model provides a flexible and consistent framework for estimating time-varying optimal hedge ratios, but requires a nonlinear maximum likelihood estimator. The GARCH model generalizes the univariate ARCH framework, used by Cecchetti, Cumby, and Figlewski (1988) to estimate time-varying optimal bond hedges, by allowing for much more flexible patterns of persistence in the conditional covariance matrix of cash and futures prices.

These time-varying methods are applied to an example of wheat storage hedging and results are compared with no hedge and constant hedge outcomes using both in-sample and post-sample performance evaluations. There is strong evidence supporting time-varying optimal hedge ratios for wheat but it is found that time-varying optimal hedge ratio estimates computed from the GARCH model perform only marginally better than constant estimates obtained using conventional regression techniques. Thus, in this application the extra expense and complexity of the GARCH model do not appear to be warranted. Of course, this is not a general result and the GARCH model may provide significantly better performance in other applications.

A MODEL WITH TIME-VARYING OPTIMAL HEDGE RATIOS

Hedging behavior is modeled in the one-period portfolio selection framework outlined in Merton (1982). A consumption based intertemporal portfolio model could have been used (e.g., Stulz (1984) and Adler and Detemple (1988)). However, the one-period model is simpler and, in the context of the present article, provides virtually identical hedging rules as the intertemporal model.

An individual investor wants to determine the optimal allocation of initial wealth among two investment opportunities: purchase of a risky asset whose return at the end of the period is stochastic; and purchase of a risk-free bond. There is a futures market in the risky asset and the investor can therefore hedge by selling contracts which mature at or after the end of the period. The margin requirements on futures contracts can be satisfied with interest bearing government securities so that taking out futures positions requires no initial outlay of wealth. An example of this type of investment problem is a commodity trader who allocates initial wealth between purchasing a commodity for storage and later resale, and investing in a risk free bond.

The investor has a von Neumann-Morgenstern utility function, U, defined over end-of-period wealth. Utility is assumed to be increasing, strictly concave and twice differentiable. Given this setup, the portfolio selection problem can be formally stated as

$$\max_{q_{t-1}, b_{t-1}} E[U(W_t) | \Omega_{t-1}] \quad (1)$$

subject to

$$W_t = (1 + r)[W_{t-1} - p_{t-1}q_{t-1}] + p_t q_{t-1} + (f_t - f_{t-1})b_{t-1} \quad (2)$$

where W_t is end-of-period wealth; W_{t-1} is initial wealth; Ω_{t-1} is the set of information available at the beginning of the period; r is the risk-free interest rate; p_{t-1} is the initial price of the risky asset; p_t is the (stochastic) end-of-period price of the risky asset; q_{t-1} is the quantity of the risky asset purchased; f_{t-1} is the initial futures price; f_t is the (stochastic) end-of-period futures price; and b_{t-1} is the quantity of futures purchased (sold if negative). A dividend (or storage cost) on the risky asset could be incorporated into the model without changing the substance of the hedging analysis.

Choosing how much to invest in the risky asset implicity defines the optimal investment in the risk free bond because of the wealth constraint. The two first-order conditions can therefore be written as

$$E[U'(W_t)|\Omega_{t-1}]\mu_t^p + \text{Cov}[U'(W_t), p_t|\Omega_{t-1}] = 0 \tag{3}$$

$$E[U'(W_t)|\Omega_{t-1}]\mu_t^f + \text{Cov}[U'(W_t), f_t|\Omega_{t-1}] = 0 \tag{4}$$

where μ_t^p and μ_t^f are the conditional expectations of returns to holding cash and futures positions, respectively:

$$\mu_t^p = E(p_t|\Omega_{t-1}) - (1+r)p_t \tag{5}$$

$$\mu_t^f = E(f_t|\Omega_{t-1}) - f_{t-1}. \tag{6}$$

A result proven in Rubinstein (1976) is helpful in analyzing these first-order conditions further. Rubinstein shows that if two random variables X and Y are joint normally distributed, and g is a differentiable function, then

$$\text{Cov}[g(X), Y] = E[g'(X)]\text{Cov}(X, Y).$$

Thus, assuming the joint distribution of (W_t, p_t, f_t) conditional on Ω_{t-1} is multivariate normal then (3) and (4) can be expressed[1]

$$\mu_t^p + \frac{U''}{U'}\text{Cov}(W_t, p_t|\Omega_{t-1}) = 0 \tag{7}$$

$$\mu_t^f + \frac{U''}{U'}\text{Cov}(W_t, f_t|\Omega_{t-1}) = 0 \tag{8}$$

where it is understood that $U'' = E[U''(W_t)|\Omega_{t-1}]$ and $U' = E[U'(W_t)|\Omega_{t-1}]$. The covariance terms can be evaluated easily using the budget constraint (2). This leads to the pair of equations

$$H_t \begin{bmatrix} q_{t-1} \\ b_{t-1} \end{bmatrix} = -\frac{U'}{U''}\begin{bmatrix} \mu_t^p \\ \mu_t^f \end{bmatrix} \tag{9}$$

where H_t is the covariance matrix of $(p_t, f_t)'$ conditional on the information set Ω_{t-1}.

Premultiplying both sides of (9) by the inverse of H_t gives the asset and futures demand functions

$$\begin{bmatrix} q_{t-1} \\ b_{t-1} \end{bmatrix} = -\frac{U'}{U''}H_t^{-1}\begin{bmatrix} \mu_t^p \\ \mu_t^f \end{bmatrix}. \tag{10}$$

The usual assumption is that the conditional covariance matrix H_t is constant over time. Here, however, the time subscript indicates that time-varying volatility is allowed for explicitly in the model.

The optimal hedge ratio is the proportion of the long cash position which should be covered by futures selling. Dividing $-b_{t-1}$ by q_{t-1} gives

$$\frac{-b_{t-1}}{q_{t-1}} = \frac{h_t^{11}\mu_t^f - h_t^{21}\mu_t^p}{h_t^{21}\mu_t^f - h_t^{22}\mu_t^p} \tag{11}$$

where h_t^{ij} is the element in the ith row and jth column of H_t. In general, asset demands depend on investor risk preferences as well as on the probability distribution

---

[1] While there is evidence that the unconditional distributions of asset and commodity prices are not normal, conditional normality is a more reasonable assumption (see Baillie and Myers (1989)). Conditional normality combined with time-varying volatility can lead to unconditional distributions with unstable variances and fatter tails than the normal. These are precisely the characteristics which have been found in studies of the unconditional distribution of asset prices.

of asset prices. However, the optimal hedge ratio is preference free under the assumptions of this model.

It is often assumed that the expected return to trading futures is approximately zero, $\mu_t^f = 0$ for all t, so that (11) reduces to

$$\frac{-b_{t-1}}{q_{t-1}} = \frac{h_t^{21}}{h_t^{22}} \qquad (12)$$

and the optimal hedge ratio equals a simple ratio of the conditional covariance between cash and futures prices to the conditional variance of futures. Equation (12) is also the hedge ratio which minimizes the variance of the investors total return (see Kahl (1983)). The remainder of the article focuses on estimation of this simplified hedging rule.

ESTIMATION

To operationalize the hedging rule, the conditional covariance matrix of cash and futures prices must be estimated. To begin, price realizations are separated into two components: an expectation conditioned on information available at time $t - 1$ and a random shock that is unpredictable. Formally, this can be expressed

$$p_t = E(p_t|\Omega_{t-1}) + u_t \qquad (13)$$

$$f_t = E(f_t|\Omega_{t-1}) + v_t \qquad (14)$$

where u_t is the prediction error for the cash price; and v_t is the prediction error for the futures price. The prediction errors are assumed to be serially uncorrelated with expected value zero (conditional on the information set). However, the conditional covariance matrix of the prediction errors is allowed to vary over time in response to changing market conditions.

Estimation requires specifying a model for the conditional means of cash and futures prices. If the expected return to holding futures is zero then the conditional mean of the futures price can be specified $E(f_t|\Omega_{t-1}) = f_{t-1}$. Despite its simplicity, there is considerable evidence supporting this model for commodity futures price data (see Gordon (1985) and Hudson, Leuthold, and Sarassoro (1987)). A model for the conditional mean of cash prices is $E(p_t|\Omega_{t-1}) = \alpha + p_{t-1}$. For storable seasonally-produced commodities, the constant term is a drift reflecting carrying charges and convenience yield over the course of the crop year. These are very simple models for the conditional means of cash and futures prices but they seem to fit the data well in the application to wheat storage hedging below. Extending the approach to more general models of the conditional mean for cash prices is straightforward. But when the expected return on futures is nonzero and/or cash commodity holdings are stochastic, then (12) is no longer the expected utility-maximizing hedge ratio and a different framework is required.[2]

These conditional mean models imply that (13) and (14) can be re-written

$$\Delta p_t = \alpha + u_t \qquad (15)$$

$$\Delta f_t = v_t \qquad (16)$$

where Δ is the first difference operator. The prediction errors have a time-varying covariance matrix

[2]See Rolfo (1980) and Cecchetti, Cumby, and Figlewski (1988) for examples of how to proceed in these circumstances.

$$H_t = E(\epsilon_t \epsilon_t' | \Omega_{t-1}) \tag{17}$$

where $\epsilon_t = (u_t, v_t)'$. Operationalizing the hedging rule (12) requires a model for H_t. Three alternative conditional covariance models are considered here.

Constant Conditional Covariance Matrix

The usual assumption is that the conditional covariance matrix is constant over time,

$$H_t = C \quad \text{for all } t. \tag{18}$$

In this case, an estimate of the conditional covariance matrix, C, is easy to obtain using least squares methods (see Myers and Thompson, (1989)). Once C has been estimated, the constant optimal hedge ratio can be computed as the ratio (12). This approach is very easy to apply but takes no account of the time-varying volatility that appears to characterize many cash and futures price series.

Moving Sample Variances and Covariances

Time-varying volatility can be incorporated into the estimation procedure in a naive way using moving sample variances and covariances of past price prediction errors. Suppose that the conditional covariance matrix at t depends on the past n prediction errors according to

$$H_t = \frac{1}{n} \sum_{i=1}^{n} \epsilon_{t-i} \epsilon_{t-i}'. \tag{19}$$

This implies that squared forecast errors are autocorrelated and the conditional covariance matrix therefore changes over time.

Once n is chosen there are no unknown parameters in the model for H_t. Therefore, the model can be estimated by first applying ordinary least squares to (15). This provides an estimate of the conditional mean parameter, α. Using the regression residuals and data on futures price changes, then compute moving sample variances and covariances of past prediction errors using some arbitrary value for n. Once H_t is estimated over the sample in this way, time-varying optimal hedge ratios can be estimated by computing the ratio (12) at each period.

Moving sample variances and covariances are easy to estimate but have two serious disadvantages. First, even if (19) is the appropriate model for H_t the simple two-step estimation procedure is inefficient. Least squares estimation of the conditional mean parameter, α, does not provide optimal inference when the conditional covariance matrix changes over time. Thus, improved inference generally results from maximum likelihood estimation. Second, (19) is a very restrictive model for H_t. It allows for autocorrelation in the squared prediction errors, so that price volatility may change over time, but the weights on past squared prediction errors are equal through lags n and zero thereafter. This imposes an extremely inflexible structure on the relationship between past volatility and current volatility. The GARCH model provides a more flexible mechanism for accounting for time-varying volatility in commodity prices.

The GARCH Model

A more formal way to introduce time-varying volatility is through the GARCH model of Engle (1982) and Bollerslev (1986). Suppose that H_t can be specified

$$\text{vech}(H_t) = C + \sum_{i=1}^{m} A_i \text{vech}(\epsilon_{t-i}\epsilon'_{t-i}) + \sum_{j=1}^{q} B_j \text{vech}(H_{t-j}) \qquad (20)$$

where C is a (2×1) vector of parameters; the A_i are (3×3) matrices of parameters for $i = 1, 2, \ldots, m$; the B_j are (3×3) matrices of parameters for $j = 1, 2, \ldots, q$; and vech is the column stacking operator that stacks the lower triangular portion of a symmetric matrix. This is a bivariate GARCH(m, q) model and it allows autocorrelation in the squared prediction errors (i.e., volatility) to be modeled flexibly, in much the same way that an ARIMA specification provides a flexible means of modeling the autocorrelation in the levels of time series.

Assuming that the conditional distributions of the prediction errors are normal, the log-likelihood function for a sample of T observations on cash and futures prices is

$$L(\Theta) = -T \log 2\pi - 0.5 \sum_{t=1}^{T} \log|H_t(\Theta)| - 0.5 \sum_{t=1}^{T} \epsilon_t(\Theta)' H_t^{-1}(\Theta) \epsilon_t(\Theta) \qquad (21)$$

where $\Theta = \{\alpha, C, A_1, A_2, \ldots, A_m, B_1, B_2, \ldots, B_q\}$ is the set of all conditional mean and variance parameters. Notice that H_t and ϵ_t are functions of the sample data on cash and futures prices and the parameter vector, Θ. Thus, given a sample, estimation proceeds by maximizing the log-likelihood with respect to the unknown parameters.

Estimating Θ by maximum likelihood involves a complex nonlinear optimization problem. Once this has been accomplished, however, the time path of optimal hedge ratios can be computed easily by taking the ratio of h_t^{21} to h_t^{22} at each time period in the sample. The algorithm used for the estimation results in this article is based on Berndt, Hall, Hall, and Hausman (1974).

The GARCH model represents a flexible specification for modeling time-varying volatility in asset prices, and maximum likelihood is an optimal approach to inference. Thus, the GARCH model has significant theoretical advantages over moving sample variances and covariances. On the other hand, the GARCH model is much more difficult and demanding to estimate. A natural question is whether the additional effort required to estimate the GARCH model provides a significantly improved hedging performance, compared to simpler approaches. This question is investigated with an example because results will invariably depend on the particular application under study.

AN APPLICATION

Optimal hedge ratios are estimated for storage hedging of wheat to illustrate and test the time-varying methods. Wheat is an important commodity in many parts of the U.S. and wheat futures contracts maturing in various months are traded at the Chicago Board of Trade, Kansas City, and Minneapolis. Here, attention is focused on the May and December contracts at the Chicago Board of Trade.

Consider an investor that takes out long positions in wheat. That is, the investor buys and stores wheat for later resale at a price which is unknown at the time of purchase. The investor can hedge the long cash position by selling futures. Hedging in two contract months, May and December, is allowed in the analysis. It is assumed that the investor takes out futures positions in one of these contracts and reevaluates his or her portfolio on a weekly basis. Each week the portfolio may be adjusted to reflect changing information and economic conditions. When a contract matures, futures positions are rolled over into the same contract month of the next year.

Because portfolio adjustment is assumed to occur on a weekly basis, weekly data are used in the empirical analysis. Cash prices are for the Saginaw market in Michigan and are from Mid-States Terminals, Toledo, Ohio. Futures prices are for the May and December contracts on the Chicago Board of Trade and are from various issues of the Chicago Board of Trade Statistical Annual. All data are the mid-week (Wednesday) closing price and the sample period runs from June 1977 to May 1983, a total of six years. However, the data are split into two segments, the first for estimation and in-sample performance evaluation and the second for post-sample testing. The estimation period runs from June 1977 to May 1983, leaving two years of data for post-sample tests.

Separate bivariate GARCH models are estimated for cash and May futures prices, and for cash and December futures prices. Preliminary results suggest that a GARCH(1,1) model, with one lag on the squared prediction errors and one lag on past conditional covariance matrices, provides an adequate representation of wheat price volatility. This is consistent with the findings of a number of other studies on the conditional distribution of asset prices (see Engle and Bollerslev (1986)). Even in the GARCH(1,1) model, however, there are 21 conditional covariance matrix parameters to estimate, suggesting that the model may be over-parameterized. Following Bollerslev, Engle, and Wooldridge (1988), a more parsimonious representation can be obtained by assuming that the A and B matrices are diagonal. This is a natural simplification because it implies that each variance and covariance depends only on its own past values and prediction errors. The diagonal restrictions reduce the number of conditional covariance matrix parameters to nine.

Estimation results for the two diagonal GARCH(1,1) models are shown in Table I (May Contract) and Table II (December Contract). For purposes of comparison, results from estimating constant conditional covariance matrix models are also included in the tables. The only unknown parameter in the conditional covariance matrix of the moving sample variances and covariances model is n, the number of periods to include in the moving sample calculation. In the analysis which follows, $n = 10$ is used.

The GARCH parameter estimates in Tables I and II are all highly significant, and a likelihood ratio test of the constant covariance matrix model versus the GARCH model rejects the former in favor of the latter at essentially any significance level. For the May (December) contract the $\chi^2(6)$ statistic is 31.98 (69.53) and the critical value for the test at the 0.005 significant level is 18.55. Thus, there is strong evidence of time-varying volatility in wheat prices.

Optimal hedge ratio estimates from the constant conditional covariance matrix and moving sample variances and covariances models are computed using standard techniques. For the GARCH model, in-sample hedge ratios are constructed using the in-sample estimates of the time-varying conditional covariance matrices $\hat{H}_t$. Post-sample hedge ratios are computed using the parameter estimates in Tables I and II, along with realized values of cash and futures prices available up to the time the portfolio is being adjusted. These post-sample estimates are therefore based only on information that is available at the time each hedging decision is made. More efficient use of available information can be achieved by updating the GARCH model's parameter estimates as each new observation becomes available. However, this is very costly and is not attempted here.

Table I
ESTIMATION RESULTS FOR THE MAY CONTRACT

Constant Conditional Covariance Matrix Model

$$\Delta p_t = 0.009 + \hat{u}_t; \quad \Delta f_t = \hat{v}_t$$
$$(2.228)$$

$$\hat{H}_t = \begin{bmatrix} 0.018 & 0.013 \\ (13.131) & (12.827) \\ 0.013 & 0.014 \\ (12.827) & (15.757) \end{bmatrix} \text{ for all } t.$$

Log-likelihood = 884.176

GARCH(1, 1) Model

$$\Delta p_t = 0.009 + \hat{u}_t; \quad \Delta f_t = \hat{v}_t$$
$$(2.142)$$

$$\text{vech}(\hat{H}_t) = \begin{bmatrix} 0.002 \\ (3.680) \\ 0.001 \\ (3.462) \\ 0.001 \\ (2.566) \end{bmatrix} + \begin{bmatrix} 0.128 & 0.0 & 0.0 \\ (4.486) & & \\ 0.0 & 0.073 & 0.0 \\ & (3.311) & \\ 0.0 & 0.0 & 0.075 \\ & & (3.476) \end{bmatrix} \begin{bmatrix} \hat{u}_{t-1}^2 \\ \hat{v}_{t-1}\hat{u}_{t-1} \\ \hat{v}_{t-1}^2 \end{bmatrix}$$

$$+ \begin{bmatrix} 0.762 & 0.0 & 0.0 \\ (18.523) & & \\ 0.0 & 0.851 & 0.0 \\ & (25.700) & 0.0 \\ 0.0 & 0.0 & 0.861 \\ & & (23.479) \end{bmatrix} \begin{bmatrix} \hat{h}_{t-1}^{11} \\ \hat{h}_{t-1}^{21} \\ \hat{h}_{t-1}^{22} \end{bmatrix}$$

Log-likelihood = 900.164

Note: Values in parentheses are asymptotic *t*-ratios.

Estimated optimal hedge ratio paths for hedging in the May and December contracts are illustrated in Figures 1 and 2, respectively. In each figure, the upper graph shows the hedge ratio path estimated with moving sample variances and covariances, and also displays the constant optimal hedge ratio estimates of 0.93 (May contract) and 0.92 (December contract) as a reference point. The lower graph shows the hedge ratio path estimated with the GARCH model, again compared to the constant estimates as a reference point. Estimated hedge ratios from the two time-varying methods have a tendency to move together, and they both fluctuate consid-

Table II
ESTIMATION RESULTS FOR THE DECEMBER CONTRACT

Constant Conditional Covariance Matrix Model

$\Delta p_t = 0.007 + \hat{u}_t; \Delta f_t = \hat{y}_t$
(1.500)

$$\hat{H}_t = \begin{bmatrix} 0.017 & 0.012 \\ (12.793) & (12.633) \\ \\ 0.012 & 0.013 \\ (12.633) & (15.868) \end{bmatrix}$$

Log-likelihood = 884.737

GARCH(1, 1) Model

$\Delta p_t = 0.009 + \hat{u}_t; \Delta f_t = \hat{v}_t$
(2.447)

$$\text{vech}(\hat{H}_t) = \begin{bmatrix} 0.002 \\ (5.187) \\ 0.001 \\ (4.525) \\ 0.001 \\ (3.421) \end{bmatrix} + \begin{bmatrix} 0.150 & 0.0 & 0.0 \\ (7.489) & & \\ 0.0 & 0.086 & 0.0 \\ & (7.243) & \\ 0.0 & 0.0 & 0.106 \\ & & (5.490) \end{bmatrix} \begin{bmatrix} \hat{u}_{t-1}^2 \\ \hat{v}_{t-1}\hat{u}_{t-1} \\ \hat{v}_{t-1}^2 \end{bmatrix}$$

$$+ \begin{bmatrix} 0.736 & 0.0 & 0.0 \\ (33.994) & & \\ 0.0 & 0.834 & 0.0 \\ & (92.489) & \\ 0.0 & 0.0 & 0.810 \\ & & (30.555) \end{bmatrix} \begin{bmatrix} \hat{h}_{t-1}^{11} \\ \hat{h}_{t-1}^{21} \\ \hat{h}_{t-1}^{22} \end{bmatrix}$$

Log-likelihood = 919.502

Note: Values in parentheses are asymptotic *t*-ratios.

erably over time. However, fluctuations in the moving sample variances and covariances hedge ratios are clearly more pronounced than in the GARCH hedge ratios. This suggests that futures positions would have to be adjusted by much greater amounts when using the moving sample variances and covariances model compared to the GARCH model.

Figures 1 and 2 demonstrate that in many periods there is a wide divergence between hedge ratios estimated assuming a constant conditional covariance matrix for cash and futures prices, and hedge ratios estimated with the GARCH model. As

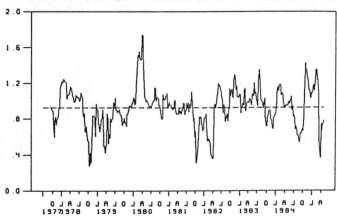

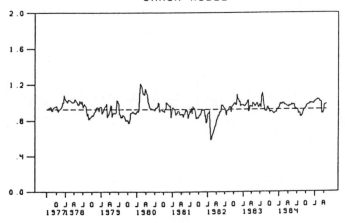

Figure 1
Time-varying optimal hedge ratios using the May contract.

yet, however, no evidence has been presented on the hedging performance of the alternative rules. Performance testing is necessary to determine whether the additional complexity of the GARCH approach is justified.

Performance tests are carried out using a simulation study. An investor is assumed to hold one bushel of wheat continuously over the sample period. The investor hedges fluctuations in his or her wealth (caused by fluctuating cash prices) by selling either May or December futures. The investor's wealth at the end of the

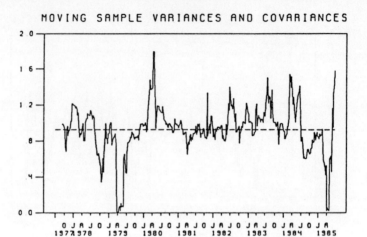

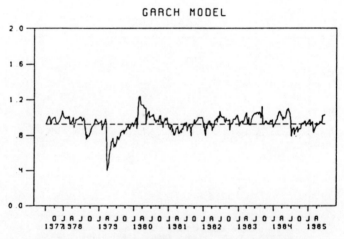

Figure 2
Time-varying optimal hedge ratios using the December contract.

week equals the cash value of the bushel of wheat plus or minus any gain or loss on futures. The futures position can be adjusted on a weekly basis. As the futures contract matures, futures positions are rolled over into the same contract month of the next year. Performance is evaluated in terms of effects on the mean and variance of the investor's wealth position.

Ex-ante evaluation proceeds by assuming that the GARCH specification is the correct probability model for wheat cash and futures prices. Then using this model, the *ex-ante* conditional expectation and conditional standard deviation of wealth are constructed for each date under four different hedging rules, no hedge, the constant hedge, the moving sample variances and covariances hedge, and the GARCH hedge. The results for each date are then averaged over the relevant period to provide a summary measure of hedging performance. *Ex-post* evaluation proceeds by constructing the actual *ex-post* wealth levels that would have been achieved under each hedging rule. The *ex-post* wealth levels for each date are then averaged over the relevant period to provide a summary measure.

Performance test results are reported in Tables III and IV. Table III assumes all hedging is done in the May contract while Table IV assumes all hedging is done in the December contract. Results are expressed in dollars per bushel, as well as percentage deviations from the no hedge outcomes. Furthermore, results are provided for the in-sample and post-sample periods separately as well as for the two periods combined.

Tables III and IV give very similar results, indicating that hedging performance is insensitive to the contract month used to implement the hedge. Within each table, the *ex-ante* conditional means of wealth are the same irrespective of which hedging rule is used, because of the assumption that the expected return from holding futures is zero. But, of course, the *ex-ante* conditional standard deviation of wealth does change with the hedging rule. The GARCH hedge reduced this conditional standard deviation by between 45% and 48%, compared to no hedging, depending on which contract month and sample period are being considered. The GARCH hedge ratio performs marginally better in terms of variance reduction than either the constant hedge or the moving sample variances and covariances hedge.

While the *ex-ante* results illustrate what can be expected from using each hedging rule over the long run, actual *ex-post* performance during any particular sample period could be quite different. Therefore, *ex-post* incomes are calculated for each date in the *in-sample* and *post-sample* periods under the same four hedging rules.

Table III
HEDGE RATIO PERFORMANCE EVALUATIONS FOR THE MAY CONTRACT

	In-Sample Average	Post-Sample Average	Combined Sample Average
Ex-Ante Evaluation			
$E(W_t|\Omega_{t-1})$	3.4120	3.2689	3.3752
$\sigma(W_t|\Omega_{t-1})$			
-No hedge	0.1296 (0%)	0.1095 (0%)	0.1244 (0%)
-Constant hedge	0.0717 (−44.7%)	0.0578 (−47.2%)	0.0681 (−45.3%)
-Moving hedge	0.0731 (−43.6%)	0.0599 (−45.3%)	0.0697 (−44.0%)
-GARCH hedge	0.0710 (−45.2%)	0.0575 (−47.5%)	0.0675 (−45.7%)
Ex-Post Evaluation			
W_t			
-No hedge	3.4089 (0%)	3.2604 (0%)	3.3706 (0%)
-Constant hedge	3.4138 (0.14%)	3.2693 (0.27%)	3.3765 (0.18%)
-Moving hedge	3.4156 (0.20%)	3.2660 (0.17%)	3.3770 (0.19%)
-GARCH hedge	3.4134 (0.13%)	3.2686 (0.25%)	3.3760 (0.16%)

Note: $\sigma(W_t|\Omega_{t-1})$ is the conditional standard deviation of wealth and numbers in parentheses are percentage deviations from the no hedge outcome.

Table IV
HEDGE RATIO PERFORMANCE EVALUATIONS FOR THE DECEMBER CONTRACT

	In-Sample Average	Post-Sample Average	Combined Sample Average
Ex-Ante Evaluation			
$E(W_t\|\Omega_{t-1})$	3.4105	3.2709	3.3735
$\sigma(W_t\|\Omega_{t-1})$			
-No hedge	0.1293 (0%)	0.1091 (0%)	0.1240 (0%)
-Constant hedge	0.0718 (−44.5%)	0.0599 (−45.1%)	0.0686 (−44.7%)
-Moving hedge	0.0727 (−43.8%)	0.0638 (−41.5%)	0.0704 (−43.2%)
-GARCH hedge	0.0709 (−45.2%)	0.0595 (−45.5%)	0.0679 (−45.2%)
Ex-Post Evaluation			
W_t			
-No hedge	3.4069 (0%)	3.2619 (0%)	3.3684 (0%)
-Constant hedge	3.4087 (0.05%)	3.2686 (0.21%)	3.3715 (0.09%)
-Moving hedge	3.4121 (0.15%)	3.2664 (0.14%)	3.3734 (0.15%)
-GARCH hedge	3.4093 (0.07%)	3.2682 (0.19%)	3.3719 (0.10%)

Note: $\sigma(W_t|\Omega_{t-1})$ is the conditional standard deviation of wealth and numbers in parentheses are percentage deviations from the no hedge outcome.

Results are reported in the second part of Tables III and IV and indicate that, on average, *ex-post* income levels are not very sensitive to the hedging rule used. This is exactly what is expected if the average return to holding futures is zero.

A striking feature of these results is that the constant hedge, the moving sample variances and covariances hedge, and the GARCH hedge all provide a remarkably similar hedging performance. Thus, while the GARCH model performs best in terms of *ex-ante* variance reduction, the simple constant optimal hedge ratio estimate performs almost as well. Furthermore, the constant estimate (marginally) outperforms the moving sample variances and covariances estimate. If the hedger is extremely risk averse, then the extra cost of working with a GARCH model may still be warranted. However, since the GARCH model performs only marginally better, is much more complex to estimate, and since the continual futures adjustments that it requires entails extra commission charges, a strong case can be made for using the constant optimal hedge ratio estimate. Of course, this conclusion applies only to the wheat storage hedging example studied here and quite different results may be found in other applications.

CONCLUSIONS

This article outlines two methods for estimating time-varying optimal hedge ratios on futures markets and compares them to traditional regression methods, which implicitly assume hedge ratios are constant over time. It is argued that the GARCH model has distinct theoretical advantages over alternative methods, and that improved optimal hedge ratio estimates should therefore arise from GARCH models of the conditional distributions of cash and futures prices.

In an application to wheat storage hedging in Michigan, there is strong evidence for rejecting the constant conditional covariance model in favor of a GARCH model of wheat price volatility. It is also found that the GARCH model provides superior hedging performance than either the constant hedge ratio model or the moving sample variances and covariances model. However, the GARCH model performs only marginally better than a simple constant hedge ratio estimate. This suggests that assuming constant optimal hedge ratios, and using linear regression approaches to optimal hedge ratio estimation, may be an adequate approximation in this application. Whether similar conclusions will emerge from other applications of these methods to optimal hedge ratio estimation remains a question for future research.

Bibliography

Adler, M., and Detemple, J. (1988): "Hedging with Futures in an Intertemporal Portfolio Context," *Journal of Futures Markets*, 8:249–269.

Anderson, R.W. (1985): "Some Determinants of the Volatility of Futures Prices," *Journal of Futures Markets*, 5:332–348.

Anderson, R.W., and Danthine, J. P. (1981): "Cross Hedging," *Journal of Political Economy*, 81:1182–1196.

Baillie, R.T., and Myers, R. J. (1989): "Modeling Commodity Price Distributions and Estimating the Optimal Futures Hedge," Working Paper CSFM 201, Center for the Study of Futures Markets, Columbia Business School.

Benninga, S., Eldor, R., and Zilcha, I. (1984): "The Optimal Hedge Ratio in Unbiased Futures Markets," *Journal of Futures Markets*, 4:155–159.

Berndt, E. K., Hall, B. H., Hall, R. E., and Hausman, J. A. (1974): "Estimation and Inference in Nonlinear Structural Models," *Annals of Economic and Social Measurement*, 4:653–665.

Bollerslev, T. (1986): "Generalized Autoregressive Conditional Heteroscedasticity," *Journal of Econometrics*, 31:307–327.

Bollerslev, T., Engle, R. F., and Wooldridge, J. M. (1988): "A Capital Asset Pricing Model with Time-Varying Covariances," *Journal of Political Economy*, 96:116–131.

Cecchetti, S. G., Cumby, R. E., and Figlewski, S. (1988): "Estimation of the Optimal Futures Hedge," *Review of Economics and Statistics*, 70:623–630.

Ederington, L. H. (1979): "The Hedging Performance of the New Futures Markets," *Journal of Finance*, 34:157–170.

Engle, R. F. (1982): "Autoregressive Conditional Heteroscedasticity with Estimates of the Variance of U.K. Inflation," *Econometrica*, 50:987–1008.

Engle, R. F., and Bollerslev, T. (1986): "Modeling the Persistence of Conditional Variances," *Econometric Reviews*, 5:1–50.

Fackler, P. L. (1986): *Futures Price Volatility: Modeling Non-Constant Variance*, Paper presented at the Annual Meeting of the American Agricultural Economics Association, Reno, Nevada, July 27–30.

Gordon, D. J. (1985): *The Distribution of Daily Changes in Commodity Futures Prices*, Technical Bulletin No. 1702, Economic Research Service, USDA.

Hudson, M. A., Leuthold, R. M., and Sarassoro, G. F. (1987): "Commodity Futures Price Changes: Recent Evidence for Wheat, Soybeans and Live Cattle," *Journal of Futures Markets*, 7:287–301.

Kahl, K. H. (1983): "Determination of the Recommended Hedging Ratio," *American Journal of Agricultural Economics*, 65:603–605.

Merton, R. C. (1982): "On the Microeconomic Theory of Investment Under Uncertainty," Chapt. 13 of K. J. Arrow and M. D. Intriligator, Eds., *Handbook of Mathematical Economics*, Vol. II, Amsterdam, North-Holland.

Myers, R. J., and Thompson, S. R. (1989): "Generalized Optimal Hedge Ratio Estimation," *American Journal of Agricultural Economics*, 71:858–868.

Rolfo, J. (1980): "Optimal Hedging Under Price and Quantity Uncertainty: The Case of the Cocoa Producer," *Journal of Political Economy*, 88:100–116.

Rubinstein, M. (1976): "The Valuation of Uncertain Income Streams and the Pricing of Options," *Bell Journal of Economics*, 7:407–425.

Stulz, R. M. (1984): "Optimal Hedging Policies," *Journal of Financial and Quantitative Analysis*, 19:127–140.

Part VI
Portfolio Selection with Futures

[18]
Hedging with Futures in an Intertemporal Portfolio Context

Michael Adler
Jerome Detemple

I. INTRODUCTION

The traditional hedging model (THM) posits investors with undiversified portfolios, each consisting of a cash position with a definite maturity and one or more futures.[1] The identity of the cash position is not a question in the THM. For the farmer, it is the value of his crop at harvest time; for the institutional investor, it is the value of a future foreign-currency cash flow. The main problem posed in the futures market literature to date is to determine the optimal hedge, defined as the quantity of futures that either minimizes the variance of the cash-cum-futures position or that maximizes its expected utility.[2] A variance-minimizing hedge generally appears as a component of an expected-utility maximizing strategy.

The purpose of this paper is to explore the intertemporal structure of the optimal hedging decision when, in addition to a single cash position, investors can also hold (a portfolio of) freely shortable, traded assets. Among the major implications of this extension are that futures generally will not be used exclusively for hedging purposes; that the existence of a futures contract that is perfectly correlated with the price of the nontraded position will not generally be sufficient for a perfect, zero-variance hedge; and that the conditions for optimal hedges to be preference-free and, therefore, implementable, will rarely be met in practice.

Demands for assets for hedging purposes in an intertemporal portfolio choice framework were first identified by Merton (1971 and 1973). What gen-

---

The support of the Center for the Study of the Futures Markets is gratefully acknowledged. Professor M. Sundaresan suggested what turned out to be the focus of the paper and commented valuably on the first draft. Proofs of all propositions are available in a separate Appendix that is available from the authors.

[1] We mean nothing invidious by this characterization. The term "traditional" does not mean obsolete and is used here simply as a short-hand device. The literature on hedging using the THM is long and distinguished. It contains the classics in the field: Working (1953 and 1962), Johnson (1960), Telser (1955 and 1958) and Stein (1961). Recently, with the growth of organized futures markets, the topic has been fruitfully revisited: In one-period models by Ederington (1979), Stoll (1979), Rolfo (1980), Anderson and Danthine (1981), and Benninga, Eldor, and Zilcha (1985); and in intertemporal models, following Merton (1971 and 1973), and Breeden (1979 and 1984), by Ho (1984), and Stulz (1984).

[2] Variance-minimizing hedging rules generally will not maximize expected utility, a point clearly recognized by Ederington (1979) and Anderson and Danthine (1981) and those who came after them. See also Section 6, below.

Michael Adler is a Professor and Jerome Detemple is an Associate Professor at the Graduate School of Business, Columbia University, New York.

erates hedging behavior in Merton's model is the possibility of shifts in the opportunity set. More specifically, investors demand financial assets for hedging purposes when the future consumption of each depends on economic state variable in addition to the level of his wealth. State variables are best described as information processes that cause the future means and variances of traded asset returns and, therefore, the opportunity set, to be random: they may include the asset prices themselves. The presence of state variables in the specification of traded-asset return-diffusions is tantamount to the assumption of an imperfection, in the form of incomplete information about the future local moments of asset-return distributions. The only kind of hedging that arises in Merton's model or in that of Breeden (1979 and 1984) is of this information-based variety.

To obtain hedging in the THM sense, that is, the use of one or more assets and futures to hedge a pre-designated position, three further requirements must be met. The position cannot be continuously revisable; it must be correlated with existing assets; and it must appear as the source of an identifiable future cash flow that affects the investor's welfare. Merton and Breeden did not find any THM hedging demands because their investors did not take positions in state variables directly. However, Mayers (1972) obtained a (variance-minimizing) hedging term in a one-period portfolio-choice model due to his introduction of nontraded assets that affect end-of-period consumption and that are correlated with traded assets. A puzzle in the literature, which we resolve below, is why, when Ho (1984) replaced the freely traded assets in Merton's model with a nontraded position, he did not obtain the intertemporal counterpart of Mayers' minimum-variance hedge while Stultz (1984), working in a very similar setting, did.

As a device for generating traditional hedging decisions, nonmarketability is sufficient and convenient. The nontradedness paradigm may indeed capture empirically relevant aspects of reality. The liabilities that pension managers are locked into may legitimately be viewed as non-traded. So may other financial assets such as unregistered stock or privately-placed corporate and municipal securities. Empirically, however, observed hedging behavior is often directed at positions that are not permanently nonmarketable, like large managed portfolios that are subject to short selling constraints but that can be liquidated at a cost. Even farmers may add to or sell off part of their holdings before the harvest season. What generates hedging in these latter cases is high liquidation costs and costly restrictions on short-selling that produce discontinuities in trading for some assets. The imperfections that give rise to what might be called temporary nontradedness are unduly hard to model in any detail. For simplicity we therefore proxy their effects in what follows by allowing some positions to be completely nontradeable.

The structure of the paper is as follows. Section II sets forth our assumptions. Section III demonstrates the equivalence between alternative formulations of the investor's expected-utility maximization program, presents the optimal demands for traded assets and futures, and decomposes these demands into speculative and hedging components. Section IV establishes that futures will be preferred to traded assets as hedging instruments only under conditions where the hedging demand for traded assets disappears. Section V explores the feasibility of perfect, zero-variance hedges. Section VI investigates implementable hedges and shows that they will rarely also be optimal for general utility structures. Conclusions and final remarks appear in Section VII.

II. ASSUMPTIONS

Assumption 1. The investor is endowed at time-0 with the right to an uncertain quantity, $\tilde{Q}_T$, of a specific commodity or asset that will be received at time T. Costless information about this delivery is gathered continuously and allows the agent to revise his beliefs. The continuous information process, $\{Q_t\}$ satisfies the stochastic differential equation:

$$dQ_t = \mu_q(Q, t)dt + \sigma(Q, t)dz_q(t), \qquad (1)$$

where $\{z_q(t); 0 \leq t \leq T\}$ is a standard Brownian motion process (BMP). The process $\{Q_t\}$ may be interpreted as a weather report that causes a farmer to update his forecast of his field's yield at harvest-time. Alternatively, take the case of a common stock, traded on a foreign exchange and quoted in a foreign currency, that the investor either cannot or does not want to liquidate or sell short before time T; $\tilde{Q}_T$ then represents the random foreign-currency value of the stock at time T while $\{Q_t\}$ is the current foreign-currency price of the stock.

Assumption 2, (Nontradedness). The initial endowment is fixed and cannot be revised or altered between times 0 to T, even parsimoniously.

Assumption 3. The spot price of the nontraded position is specified exogenously and satisfies the stochastic differential equation:

$$dP_t = \mu_p(P, t) + \sigma_p(P, t)dz_p(t), \qquad (2)$$

where $\{z_p(t); 0 \leq t \leq T\}$ is a standard BMP and the instantaneous correlation between the price and quantity processes is given by: $\rho_{p,q}dt = dz_p \cdot dz_q$.

Assumption 4. The investor has free and unrestricted access to a financial market in which a number, A, of financial assets are traded continuously. The $A \times 1$ vector of prices, P_a, of these assets satisfies the stochastic differential equation:[3]

$$dP_{a,t} = I_a[\mu_a dt + \sigma_a dz_a(t)] \qquad (3)$$

where I_a is an $A \times A$ diagonal matrix whose diagonal is the vector of prices; μ_a represents the constant vector of mean rates of return on these assets and

---

[3]Notice that while the price dynamics of the information processes, P and Q, are written in terms of their levels, the dynamics of traded-assets' prices are specified in terms of their percentage changes. For the ith traded asset: $dP_{ai}/P_{ai} = \mu_{ai}dt + \sigma_{ai}dz_{ai}(t)$, where the moments are at most deterministic functions of time.

$V_{aa} \equiv \sigma_a \sigma_a'$ is the constant instantaneous variance-covariance matrix. The ith component, z_{a_i} of the vector Wiener process, z_a, has instantaneous correlations, $\rho_{a_i,p}$ and $\rho_{a_i,q}$, with the processes z_p and z_q, respectively.

Assumption 5. An instantaneously riskless bond is available. Its rate of return, r, is constant over the period $[O, T]$. The investor may borrow or lend freely at this rate.

Assumption 6. The investor also has free and unrestricted access to a futures market. One of the futures contracts is written on the nontraded position. It promises delivery at time T of a fixed amount of Q at a futures price fixed at time 0. This contract is marked to market continuously leaving its net value equal to zero. The settlement price of the contract, F_t, is assumed to satisfy:

$$dF_t = \mu_f(P, t)dt + \sigma_f(P, t)dz_f(t), \qquad (4)$$

where the BMP, $\{z_f(t); 0 \leq t \leq T\}$ has correlations $\rho_{f,p}$ and $\rho_{f,q}$ with the processes z_p and z_q that in general are not perfect due, possibly, to random convenience yields.[4] When the futures contract is priced by arbitrage and the convenience yield is proportional to the spot price ($c(P, t) = cP$), $F_t = P_t e^{(r-c)(T-t)}$ and $\rho_{f,p} = 1$. When, in addition, the contract is assumed, following Breeden (1984), to mature instantaneously, $F_t = P_t$.

In what follows, we contemplate at several points the introduction of a separate futures contract that is perfectly correlated with Q.[5] In the case of a foreign stock, for instance, where Q represents its foreign currency price, the contract would promise the delivery of one share at time T, at the futures price fixed at time-0. Perfect correlation is obtained if the variations in the settlement price of this contract are spanned by the variations in the foreign currency price and in the riskless (constant interest rate) instantaneous foreign bond.

Assumption 7. The investor chooses a consumption stream $\{c_t\}$, a trading strategy in futures $\{x_t\}$ and in traded assets $\{w_t, W_t\}$ adapted to his information, so as to maximize his expected lifetime utility. For simplicity, we shall suppose that the life of the investor corresponds to the delivery interval $[O, T]$. During his lifetime, the investor instantaneously consumes an amount of the good c_t and trades in the asset market so as to secure future consumption. At maturity, he consumes his terminal wealth consisting of the cash amount generated by his past trading strategies and of the proceeds of his nontraded posi-

---

[4] For instance, if the convenience yield satisfies the stochastic differential equation $dc = \mu_c(P, t)dt + \sigma_p(P, t)dz_c$ where $\{z_c(t); 0 \leq t \leq T\}$ is a BMP distinct from the process $\{z_p(t); 0 \leq t \leq T\}$, an arbitrage argument involving only the commodity, the futures contract and the riskless bond cannot be implemented. In this instance the futures settlement price is imperfectly correlated with the commodity price. Obviously the assumption that the correlation between the futures and spot price is imperfect and the representation of the futures settlement price process assumed in Equation (4) raise questions of compatibility with a full-fledged equilibrium model.

[5] Such a contract would be written much like index contracts are now. At maturity they promise delivery of an amount of cash equal to some pre-set multiple times Q. For a farmer, for example, to view the contract as perfectly correlated with his yield, it would have to be written on quantity of his specific harvest.

tion $P_T Q_T$. The instantaneous utility function $u(c_t, t)$ and the terminal utility function $B(W_T + P_T Q_T, T)$ are assumed to satisfy the usual assumptions.

Assumption 8. In the course of his life, it is quite possible that the investor may adopt strategies that will deplete his cash resources or that will generate a positive probability of obtaining a negative cash-flow at the maturity date T. For the purpose of this paper, we shall not deal explicitly with this bankruptcy problem and its consequences in terms of decision rules. We will instead suppose that the structure of the economy produces a positive cash flow with certainty at date T along the optimal path.

III. THE OPTIMAL HEDGING DECISION

This section investigates the investor's program for optimally hedging his nontraded position in the presence of traded assets and futures. A main result is that two apparently competing specifications of the intertemporal budget constraint are, in fact, equivalent and lead to the same optimal decision. This proposition serves to identify the minimum-variance component of the optimal hedge as an intertemporal demand in the sense of Merton (1971). Following Assumption 7, the investor's program is:

$$\underset{\{c_t, (wW_t), x_t\}}{\text{Maximize}} E\left[\int_0^T u(c_t, t) + B(Y_T, T)\right] \qquad (5)$$

where W_T represents the cash position at the target date; $P_T Q_T$ is the unique cash flow generated by the nontraded position at time T and total wealth at maturity is given by their sum: $Y_T = W_T + P_T Q_T$.

To solve this intertemporal consumption-investment-hedging problem, the investor must maximize Equation (5) subject to a dynamic budget constraint. Two different formulations of this constraint are possible. The first is a constraint on the cash-balance:

$$dW = w'W \frac{dP_a}{P_a} + xdF + [(1 - w'l)rW - c]dt \qquad (6)$$

where $w'l = \Sigma_{i=1}^{A} w_i$ is the sum of the portfolio weights of traded assets. Alternatively, the constraint may be expressed in terms of total wealth at time t; $Y_t = W_t + P_t Q_t$:

$$dY = d(PQ) + w'W \frac{dP_a}{P_a} + xdF + [(1 - w'l)rW - c]dt \qquad (7)$$

Except for the inclusion of the cash flows from traded assets, Equation (6) is the form used by Ho (1984), and Equation (7) is the one employed by Stulz (1984). The difference between the two formulations is that Equation (7) contains $d(PQ)_t$ while Equation (6) does not. This apparent difference is illusory.

In the cash balance constraint formulation, Equation (6), the investor chooses a trading strategy in traded assets and futures so as to guarantee optimal consumption and to control the level of the cash balance position. Although there are no intermediate cash flows associated with the nontraded position, its presence causes the investor to modify his intertemporal trading. The boundary condition, which stipulates that the value function at time-T be equal to the terminal utility of the cash balance plus the cash flow generated by the nontraded position, is what produces this effect.

In the wealth constraint formulation, Equation (7), $P_t Q_t$ is the present value of $P_T Q_T$. As the position is nontraded, $d(PQ)_t$ does not represent a cash flow and does not have a direct control variable associated with it. Consequently, $d(PQ)_t$ operates in Equation (7) as a pure information process. The investor using this formulation of the constraint in effect trades in assets and futures to adjust the cash balance, using information on the current value of the nontraded position, so as to maximize his expected lifetime utility. What may not be obvious is that the trading strategy of an investor who uses the cash balance formulation of the constraint is identical. A straightforward generalization of Adler and Detemple (1986) yields,

Proposition 1. The optimal trading strategies for futures and traded assets and the investor's expected utility based on the cash balance constraint, Equation (6), and those based on the wealth constraint Equation (7) are the same.

What drives the proof is the fact that the information conveyed by the processes $\{Y_t, P_t, Q_t\}$ and the processes $\{W_t, P_t, Q_t\}$ is identical, as wealth and cash balances are linked by the additive relationship, $Y_t = W_t + P_t Q_t$. Conservation of information suggests that the solution not be modified by moving from one formulation to the other. Consequently, the optimal hedges obtained by Ho and Stulz should have been, despite any apparent difference, the same.

The proof of Proposition 1 in the appendix also enables us to write out the optimal vector asset demands for traded assets and futures as:

$$\begin{pmatrix} wW \\ x \end{pmatrix} = -\frac{J_y}{J_{yy}} V^{-1} \begin{pmatrix} \mu_a - rl \\ \mu_f \end{pmatrix} - V^{-1} \left\{ \begin{pmatrix} V_{a,p} \\ V_{f,p} \end{pmatrix} \left(\frac{J_{py}}{J_{yy}} + Q \right) + \begin{pmatrix} V_{a,q} \\ V_{f,q} \end{pmatrix} \left(\frac{J_{qy}}{J_{yy}} + P \right) \right\}$$

(8)

where, in addition to notation already introduced, J is the indirect utility or value function and subscripts denote its partial derivatives; $V_{a,p}$ and $V_{a,q}$ are respectively the $(A \times 1)$ vectors of the covariances, $\sigma_{a_i,p}$ and $\sigma_{a_i,q}$, between the traded assets and the price or quantity of the nontraded position; $V_{f,p}$ and $V_{f,q}$ are the (scalar) covariances between the futures price and, respectively, the spot price and the quantity; and V is the $(A + 1) \times (A + 1)$ variance-covariance matrix with the (single) futures contract appearing in the $(A + 1)$st position.

Equation (8) decomposes the demand for assets and futures into two parts, a locally speculative demand in the first term on the right hand side (RHS) and a hedging demand in the second. To see this interpretation, notice first that the speculative demand consists of the mean-variance-efficient portfolio, weighted by the investor's risk tolerance, that solves the problem:[6]

$$\underset{\{wW,x\}}{\text{Max }} E(dW) \text{ subject to Var}(dW) = \text{a constant}$$

As in Anderson and Danthine (1981), the THM result, reached first by Working (1953) and McKinnon (1967) and repeated more recently by Rolfo (1980) and by Benninga, Eldor and Zilcha (1985), that the sign of μ_f automatically determines the sign of the weight of the futures position in the speculative demand portfolio, breaks down in our model. Whether the investor is long or short in futures depends, in general, not only on the expected change in the futures price but also, via the inverse of the variance-covariance matrix, on its correlations with every other traded asset. Finally, we note that the speculative demand would be the only demand were there no nontraded position (or other exogenous state variables). This observation illustrates the point, implied also in Merton (1973), that investors will not hedge at all when all assets can freely be sold short and there are no shifts in the opportunity set.[7]

---

[6] As pointed out also in Stulz (1984), the problem is:

$$\underset{\{wW,x\}}{\text{Max }} [\mu_{pq} + w'W(\mu_a - rI) + x'\mu_f] + \lambda[k - (W^2 w'V_{aa}w + x'V_{ff}x + 2Ww'V_{a,f}x)].$$

The first order conditions are:

$$\mu_a - rI = \lambda(V_{aa}wW + V_{a,f}x)$$

$$\mu_f = \lambda(V_{f,a}wW + V_{ff}x)$$

which, after manipulation, provides up to a scalar multiple:

$$\begin{pmatrix} wW \\ x \end{pmatrix} = \begin{bmatrix} V_{aa} & V_{af} \\ V_{fa} & V_{ff} \end{bmatrix}^{-1} \begin{pmatrix} \mu_a - rI \\ \mu_f \end{pmatrix}$$

This portfolio is also called a speculative demand because it depends on the direction in which securities' and futures' prices are expected to move.

[7] Notice that as an interim step in obtaining the mean-variance efficient portfolio in footnote 6 one could have written the demand as:

$$wW^m = [V_{aa} - \beta'V_{ff}\beta]^{-1}[(\mu_a - rI) - \beta'\mu_f]$$

$$x^m = V_{ff}^{-1}(\mu_f - V_{f,a}wW)$$

where $\beta' = V_{a,f}V_{ff}^{-1}$ = the matrix of regression coefficients of a on f, and $V_{aa} - \beta'V_{ff}\beta$ = the matrix of the residuals of these regressions. Following Sercu (1980), the equation for wW^m can conceivably be interpreted as a demand for traded assets "hedged by futures" and x^m is then the sum of the demand for futures to hedge traded assets plus a demand for futures as part of the efficient portfolio. The point to stress, however, is that the notion of hedging traded assets with futures is completely arbitrary. It is an artifact, due purely to an arbitrary partitioning of the variance-covariance matrix: other partitions would produce different "hedging" demands. It is meaningless to define hedging in the absence of state variables that shift the opportunity set.

The hedging expression, the second term on the RHS of Equation (8), represents (twice) the portfolio that maximizes the covariance between the controllable cash balance component of wealth and the relative change in the marginal utility of total wealth; that is, it is (two times) the portfolio that solves the unconstrained program:[8]

$$\underset{\{wW,x\}}{\text{Max}} \text{Cov}\left[dW, \frac{dJ_y}{J_y}(Y, P, Q, t)\right]$$

It is useful to decompose the hedging term one stage further. Denoting the hedge portfolio by h, we obtain from Equation (8):

$$\begin{pmatrix} wW \\ x \end{pmatrix}^h = -V^{-1}\left\{\begin{pmatrix} V_{a,p} \\ V_{f,p} \end{pmatrix}\frac{J_{py}}{J_{yy}} + \begin{pmatrix} V_{a,q} \\ V_{f,q} \end{pmatrix}\frac{J_{qy}}{J_{yy}}\right\} - V^{-1}\left\{\begin{pmatrix} V_{a,p} \\ V_{f,p} \end{pmatrix}Q + \begin{pmatrix} V_{a,p} \\ V_{f,q} \end{pmatrix}P\right\}$$

(9)

The two preference weighted portfolios in the first term on the RHS of Equation (9) replicate the Merton-Breeden dynamic hedges in this case with two state variables. The second term on the RHS of Equation (9) is the one that did not emerge in their setting as it is due to the introduction of a nontraded position into Equation (5). Since the stochastic part of $d(PQ)$ equals the stochastic

---

[8]The program is $\underset{\{wW,x\}}{\text{Max}} \text{Cov}[dW, (dJ_y/J_{yy})(Y, P, Q, t)]$, where

$$dJ_y = \pounds J_y(\cdot) + J_{yy}[wW\sigma_a dz_a + x\sigma_f dz_f + Q\sigma_p dz_p + P\sigma_q dz_q] + J_{yp}\sigma_p dz_p + J_{yq}\sigma_q dz_q$$

and where $\pounds$ is the instantaneous mean operator. This program is equivalent to

$$\underset{\{wW,x\}}{\text{Max}} \frac{J_{yy}}{J_y}\left\{(w'W, x')V\begin{pmatrix} wW \\ x \end{pmatrix} + (w'W, x')\left[\begin{pmatrix} V_{a,p} \\ V_{f,p} \end{pmatrix}Q + \begin{pmatrix} V_{a,q} \\ V_{f,q} \end{pmatrix}P\right]\right\}$$

$$+ (w'W, x')\left[\begin{pmatrix} V_{a,p} \\ V_{f,p} \end{pmatrix}\frac{J_{py}}{J_y} + \begin{pmatrix} V_{a,q} \\ V_{f,q} \end{pmatrix}\frac{J_{qy}}{J_y}\right]$$

for which the first order conditions are:

$$2V\begin{pmatrix} wW \\ x \end{pmatrix} + \begin{pmatrix} V_{a,p} \\ V_{f,p} \end{pmatrix}\left(\frac{J_{py}}{J_{yy}} + Q\right) + \begin{pmatrix} V_{a,q} \\ V_{f,q} \end{pmatrix}\left(\frac{J_{qy}}{J_{yy}} + P\right) = 0$$

$$\Rightarrow \begin{pmatrix} wW \\ x \end{pmatrix} = -\frac{1}{2}\left[V^{-1}\begin{pmatrix} V_{a,p} \\ V_{f,p} \end{pmatrix}\left(\frac{J_{py}}{J_{yy}} + Q\right) + V^{-1}\begin{pmatrix} V_{a,q} \\ V_{f,q} \end{pmatrix}\left(\frac{J_{qy}}{J_{yy}} + P\right)\right]$$

part of $QdP + PdQ$, it is immediate that this term represents the portfolio that solves the program:[9]

$$\operatorname*{Min}_{\{wW, x\}} \operatorname{Var}(dY) = (w'W, x) \begin{bmatrix} V_{aa} & V_{af} \\ V_{fa} & V_{ff} \end{bmatrix} \begin{pmatrix} wW \\ x \end{pmatrix}$$

$$+ 2(w'W, x) \begin{pmatrix} V_{a,pq} \\ V_{f,pq} \end{pmatrix} + \operatorname{Var}[d(PQ)], \quad (10)$$

where $V_{i,pq}$ = covariance of asset i with the value of the nontraded position.

In what follows, we shall refer to this portfolio as the minimum-variance hedge. As the sequence of decompositions indicates, it is a component of the intertemporal demand for assets and futures, for hedging shifts in the opportunity set. As distinct from all the other components of the optimal demand, it is preference-free and is, therefore, potentially implementable by regression analysis. Finally, it is the one term that distinguishes hedging in the sense of the THM from the more general problem of determining the optimal intertemporal demand for assets.

IV. ON THE EXCLUSIVE USE OF FUTURES FOR HEDGING

This section addresses the question of whether futures will be preferred to other traded assets as hedging instruments when transactions costs are zero. An immediate implication of the construction of the minimum-variance hedge is that, in general, neither will be preferred and both will be used together. To see this, we write out the first order conditions for Equation (10), denoting the minimum-variance hedge portfolio by v, as follows:

$$(wW)^v = -V_{aa}^{-1} V_{af} x^v - V_{aa}^{-1} V_{a,pq}$$

$$x^v = -V_{ff}^{-1} V_{fa} (wW)^v - V_{ff}^{-1} V_{f,pq}$$
(11)

---

[9] $\operatorname*{Min}_{\{wW,x\}} (\operatorname{Var}[d(PQ)] + W^2 w' V_{aa} w + x' V_{ff} x + 2Ww' V_{a,pq} + 2x' V_{f,pq} + 2Ww' V_{a,f} x)$ provides the first order conditions:

$$V_{aa} wW + V_{af} x + V_{a,pq} = 0$$

$$V_{fa} wW + V_{ff} x + V_{f,pq} = 0, \quad \text{so that}$$

$$\begin{pmatrix} wW \\ x \end{pmatrix}^v = -V^{-1} \begin{pmatrix} V_{a,pq} \\ V_{f,pq} \end{pmatrix} = -V^{-1} \left[\begin{pmatrix} V_{a,p} \\ V_{f,p} \end{pmatrix} Q + \begin{pmatrix} V_{a,q} \\ V_{f,q} \end{pmatrix} P \right]$$

The second term in each line of Equation (11) reveals that the nontraded position will be hedged by both traded assets and futures. The first terms in each line reveal further that the variance-minimizing demands for traded assets and futures each respectively depends on the other. It follows that futures will be the preferred hedging instrument under conditions that set the variance-minimizing demand for traded assets, $(wW)^v$, equal to zero. These conditions are summarized in the following sequence of linked propositions.

Proposition 2. If there exists for a given state variable a futures price that is perfectly correlated with it, then: (i) only that futures contract will be used for hedging it; and (ii) a portfolio of the future and other assets will, in general, be used to hedge other state variables.

Proposition 2 implies directly that, where a futures is perfectly correlated with the underlying asset, it and it alone will be used to hedge the underlying asset. The proposition generalizes readily. When there are many state variables and futures contracts, each state variable will be hedged exclusively by the one futures that is perfectly correlated with it.[10]

In general, however, the perfect correlation requirements of Proposition 2 may be violated. Random convenience yields can produce imperfect correlations between futures prices and the associated spot prices. In addition, there may exist no futures contracts at all for such variables as the weather in various locations, foreign GNPs and interest rates or, for that matter, for the quantity component of the nontraded position in our model. Under what conditions will futures be preferred over traded assets for hedging in these more general circumstances? In the presence of many futures and state variables (or nontraded positions), the answer has two parts. The first is:

Proposition 3. The hedging demand for traded assets will disappear and only futures will be used for hedging if the return on each traded asset is independent of each futures price and of each state variable, including the spot prices and quantities of each nontraded position.

Proposition 3 incorporates the possibility, discussed by Anderson and Danthine (1981), that a given nontraded position will be cross-hedged by more than one future in a world with no perfect correlations. Moreover, it generalizes their result. The hedge portfolio will include also traded assets unless the latter are independent of both the futures and the nontraded position. Finally, Proposition 3 leads naturally to the statement of the very strong conditions to be met if the routine, one-position, one-futures hedge of the THM is to arise in this case.

---

[10]See Breeden (1984) for the complete markets case with instantaneously maturing futures that are perfectly correlated with each and every state variable. Due to these perfect correlations and with spanning, the demand for traded securities to hedge state variables disappears. Under more general conditions where correlation is imperfect, however, the link that Breeden forges between risk aversion and the $J_\eta/J_{\eta\eta}$ terms and his subsequent result, that the logarithmic utility separates "long" hedgers from "reverse" hedgers, both break down. Logarithmic utility does not produce myopia in this instance when the underlying cash position is nontraded, as we show in Adler and Detemple (1986).

Proposition 4. Each nontraded position will be hedged exclusively by the one, imperfectly correlated futures contract written on it if each nontraded position is correlated with only one futures price (independently of all other security prices) and each such futures price is independent of all other futures and asset prices.

To sum up this section, futures can be said to be preferred over other assets as hedging instruments in the absence of transaction-cost differentials only under conditions where the hedging-demand for traded assets disappears. The notion of futures being better for the purpose of hedging when traded assets also appear in the hedging demands is vacuous. The two sets of conditions in which futures only are used for hedging involve a trade-off. Propositions 3 and 4 allow futures to be imperfectly correlated with (the components of) the nontraded position but then require these two sources of uncertainty to be orthogonal to all other traded assets. Proposition 2 is more restrictive in that it requires perfect correlation between a futures contract and each component of the nontraded position, but is less restrictive in that it allows all sources of uncertainty to be correlated.

In practice, transaction cost differences may account for what casual empiricism suggests is a market preference for hedging with futures. To short a stock, for example, one initially borrows and sells it; puts the proceeds after paying a commission in escrow at zero interest; and simultaneously posts a 50%, interest-earning margin. Subsequently, with maintenance margins set at 30%, margin calls are satisfied by cash payments. When shorting a future, there are no initial proceeds on which interest income is lost. In other respects, the cost structure is similar: Commissions must be paid; margin of between 2% and 6% can be posted with T-bills; and margin calls are paid in cash. The main cost advantages of futures are the lower margins and the avoidance of the lost interest on short-sale proceeds, and these may be substantial. However, if transactions costs distort pricing in equilibrium in such a way as to remove the advantage of futures, investors in general will use all traded assets for hedging purposes except under circumstances like those described above.

V. THE FEASIBILITY OF ZERO-VARIANCE HEDGES

We maintain the setting of Section 3, with many traded assets, one nontraded position and no state variables other than P and Q. The question in this section is: When will minimum-variance hedges also be zero-variance, or what have been called perfect, hedges in the presence of quantity uncertainty? As anticipated, it is enough to have access to futures whose prices are perfectly correlated with P and Q, respectively.[11] This is the immediate implication of the following proposition.

---

[11] The possibility of perfect insurance in continuous time models where futures contracts based on each of the sources of uncertainty and perfectly correlated with these sources are available is discussed in Ho (1984). In the BEZ (1985) one-period model a perfect hedge is possible, but the hedge ratio for the exchange rate depends on the hedge ratio for the quantity. This dependence arises because the multiplicative uncertainty faced in the single-period setting cannot be linearized as in a continuous time model.

Proposition 5. A perfect hedge, which reduces the variance of changes in total wealth to zero, exists if there are futures that are perfectly correlated with changes in P and changes in Q, respectively.

It is of interest to note that the additive combination of the two futures contracts described in the proposition provides the investor with perfect insurance against the product of two variables, PQ. This follows from the fact that, in continuous-time models with diffusion processes, the local uncertainty faced is linear-additive. That is, the stochastic part of the change in the product PQ is a linear combination of the stochastic parts of the change in P and of the change in Q. As long as the investor can trade continuously, he can then locally offset each of these sources of uncertainty by the selection of an appropriate trading strategy in the two futures, thereby achieving a perfect hedge.

It is perhaps notable that Proposition 5 is unaffected by the presence of traded assets, other than the two assumed futures, that may be partially correlated with the nontraded position. This is a reflection of Proposition 2 above, which establishes that the demand for traded assets for hedging any state variable that has a perfectly correlated future written on it will be zero. As a result, the vector zero-variance demand for the two futures may be written simply as:

$$\begin{pmatrix} x \\ y \end{pmatrix}^{v=0} = -\begin{pmatrix} Q\sigma_p/\sigma_f \\ P\sigma_q/\sigma_y \end{pmatrix} \tag{12}$$

where y denotes the position in the futures that is perfectly correlated with dQ and σ_y is the standard deviation of its price, while σ_p, σ_q and σ_f are the standard deviations, respectively, of the spot price, the quantity and the price of the future that is perfectly correlated with dP.

Of course, futures contracts on the quantities of nontraded positions are, with rare exceptions, not available. The usual situation is that of having to hedge a position where, at best, there is a contract perfectly correlated with the spot price. The following proposition summarizes all the circumstances, mentioned at various points in the literature, in which a zero-variance hedge is available in this case.[12]

Proposition 6. When there is one futures contract whose price changes are perfectly correlated with dP and no other asset or futures that is perfectly correlated with dQ, a perfect hedge exists either:

(i) if quantity is deterministic ($\sigma_q = 0$), where the zero-variance hedge is given by $x^{v=0} = -Q\sigma_p/\sigma_f$; or

(ii) if quantity is random but is perfectly instantaneously correlated with the price ($\rho_{pq} = \pm 1$), where the hedge is given by $x^{v=0} = -(Q\sigma_p \pm P\sigma_q)/\sigma_f$.

---

[12]See, especially, Anderson and Danthine (1981) and Ho (1984).

This is perhaps the appropriate point to compare the zero-variance hedges of Proposition 6 with the "delta" hedges of the futures and options literature. A delta hedge is defined as the number of futures (or options) required to insure perfectly a unitary position in the underlying commodity or asset, where perfect insurance means that the insured position has zero variance and returns the riskless rate. Delta hedge ratios are derived assuming that $F = F(P, t)$, that is, that the futures price (and the convenience yield) is a function of at most the current spot price and time. A delta hedge then involves going short F_p^{-1} futures contracts for each unit of the commodity purchased.

To obtain the relationship between delta and zero-variance hedges, notice that when $F = F(P, t)$, $\sigma_f = F_p \sigma_p$. Consequently, the hedge ratio in case (i) of Proposition 6 may be written as: $(x^{v=0}/Q) = -F_p^{-1}$. When quantity is nonrandom, the zero-variance hedge is a delta hedge. In case (ii), where quantity is random but perfectly correlated with price, the zero-variance hedge ratio becomes: $(x^{v=0}/Q) = -F_p^{-1}[1 \pm (P\sigma_q/Q\sigma_p)]$. In this case, the zero-variance hedge is proportional but not equal to the delta hedge, where the proportionality constant depends on the ratio of the normalized standard deviations, σ_q/Q and σ_p/P. In general, a minimum-variance hedge that is not perfect is neither equal to nor proportional to a delta hedge.

To close this section, we explore the conditions for the zero-variance hedge ratio to be constant, that is, not to require revision, over time. Clearly, this is impossible in case (ii) of Proposition 6, where quantity may fluctuate, or under Proposition 5, where both P and Q may vary. In case (i) of Proposition 6, the hedge ratio will at least be deterministic. When the futures is priced by arbitrage, as in Black (1976), Brennan and Schwartz (1985), and Richard and Sundaresan (1981), and in the absence of a convenience yield, $F_t = P_t e^{r(T-t)}$, and the perfect-hedge ratio, $F_p^{-1} = e^{-r(T-t)}$, is at most a function of time to maturity: it is constant for Breeden-type futures that mature instantaneously.

VI. IMPLEMENTABLE HEDGES

For our final purpose, we define as implementable those hedges that are preference-free and that depend (for all preference structures) only on the measurable characteristics of the opportunity set. Under what conditions, we then ask, will preference-free hedges be optimal, that is, expected-utility maximizing, for arbitrary preferences? The answer to this question is of considerable practical interest.

The only preference-free hedge in our framework is the minimum-variance hedge. To see this, we need only rewrite Equation (8), following Equation (9), as:

$$\begin{pmatrix} wW \\ x \end{pmatrix} = -\frac{J_y}{J_{yy}} V^{-1} \begin{pmatrix} \mu_a - rI \\ \mu_f \end{pmatrix} - V^{-1} \left[\begin{pmatrix} V_{a,p} \\ V_{f,p} \end{pmatrix} \frac{J_{py}}{J_{yy}} + \begin{pmatrix} V_{a,q} \\ V_{f,q} \end{pmatrix} \frac{J_{qy}}{J_{yy}} \right] - V^{-1} \begin{pmatrix} V_{a,pq} \\ V_{f,pq} \end{pmatrix} \quad (13)$$

Clearly, the only preference-free term is the last. There is widespread recognition throughout the literature that the minimum-variance hedge is potentially nonoptimal (even for quadratic preferences). What is perhaps less well-known is the precise set of conditions under which it will be optimal.

Restated, the question can now be asked in two ways. First, what are the conditions that set both of the first two, preference-laden terms on the RHS of Equation (13) equal to zero? This is the subject of Proposition 7, below. Alternatively, can we determine conditions under which: Only futures appear in the hedge portfolio; only traded assets feature in the speculative portfolio; and the middle, Merton-Breeden hedging term on the RHS of Equation (13) drops out? This is the subject of Proposition 8. Both are proved in the appendix.

For simplicity, we maintain the following assumptions throughout this section: (a) there is one traded asset, one nontraded position, and a single futures contract; (b) there is no quantity uncertainty; (c) the futures contract promises delivery of one unit of the nontraded position and is perfectly correlated with it (i.e., $\rho_{pf} = 1$); and (d) the traded asset is distinct from the futures (i.e., $\rho_{fa} \neq \pm 1$). Under these assumptions, we have the following sufficient conditions.

Proposition 7. Under assumptions (1)-(4) above, the optimal demands for traded assets and futures consist only of the minimum-variance demands if:

(i) $\mu_f = 0$; the futures price is a pure martingale, and
(ii) $\mu_a = r$; the risky traded asset is dominated by the riskless asset for all risk-averse investors.

Proposition 7 merits further discussion. The condition, $\rho_{af} \neq \pm 1$, in principle permits both the traded asset and the futures to appear in the optimal demand. However, following Proposition 2 above, only the futures contract will actually be used for hedging as it is perfectly correlated with the spot price. Together, conditions (i) and (ii) reduce the speculative, mean-variance demand to zero. And, as the appendix demonstrates, they are sufficient also to set the cross-partial derivative of the value function, $J_{py} = 0$. Thus, the first two terms on the RHS of Equation (13) become equal to zero and the optimal demands, denoted by an asterisk, are given in this case by:

$$\begin{pmatrix} wW^* \\ x^* \end{pmatrix} = -\begin{pmatrix} 0 \\ Q\sigma_p/\sigma_f \end{pmatrix} \quad (14)$$

Notably, the traded asset, which is dominated in the mean-variance sense, also serves no useful hedging purpose. The hedging demand for futures, as before, can be computed as a regression coefficient, as $Q\sigma_p/\sigma_f = Q\sigma_{fp}/\sigma_f^2$ when $\rho_{fp} = 1$. Following Proposition 6, the hedge is perfect.

Notice further that conditions (i) and (ii) of Proposition 7 would be met were assets priced in the capital markets as if aggregate risk-tolerance were infinite, that is, risk-neutrally. These conditions are therefore inconsistent with any single-agent model of capital market equilibrium where the representative individual is risk-averse. They are at best consistent with a multiple-agent equilibrium in which risk-averters are dominated at the level of pricing by the presence of at least one risk-neutral agent who would end up holding all assets in positive net supply. There is sufficient evidence of risk-premia in the mean returns on capital assets in general to suggest that the two conditions of Proposition 7 are violated empirically.[13]

The question then remains: Can the minimum-variance hedging demand for futures be optimal under less restrictive circumstances? In the next proposition, the traded asset's expected returns can differ from the riskless rate: it is, therefore, not dominated. Proposition 8 identifies the condition under which there is a separation of functions: only the traded asset is held for speculative purposes; only the futures is used for hedging; and the hedging demand is implementable.

Proposition 8. Under the assumptions preceding Proposition 7 and with $\mu_a \neq r$, the optimal speculative demand contains only the traded asset and the optimal hedging demand is a minimum-variance portfolio containing only the future if: $\mu_f = (\mu_a - r)\sigma_{fa}/\sigma_a^2$.

In this case, the optimal demands for traded assets and futures are given, as the proof of the proposition in the appendix implies, by:

$$\begin{pmatrix} wW^* \\ x^* \end{pmatrix} = -\frac{J_y}{J_{yy}} \begin{pmatrix} (\mu_a - r)/\sigma_a^2 \\ 0 \end{pmatrix} - \begin{pmatrix} 0 \\ Q\sigma_p/\sigma_f \end{pmatrix} \quad (15)$$

where, by virtue of Proposition 6, the hedge again is perfect, i.e., zero-variance.

The intuition behind Proposition 8 is straightforward. A risk-averse investor who owns a nontraded position will, in the absence of a perfect hedging instrument, diversify his portfolio in a distorted way, so as to offset the imbalance due to that position. In the limiting case where there exists a future whose returns are perfectly correlated with those of the nontraded asset, the investor first hedges by shorting the future in a manner that exactly cancels the presence of the nontraded position. He then proceeds to choose an efficient portfolio from among the remaining traded assets (or, in this case, that consists of the traded asset). Three-fund separation is achieved. The optimal portfolio consists of combinations of the riskless asset, the risky traded asset and the hedge portfolio. The condition that the future be priced so that its excess expected returns are linearly related to those of the traded asset, that is, that

---

[13] Here we are taking exception to the thrust of the argument in Benninga, Eldor, and Zilcha (1984) who assume "unbiased capital markets," i.e., risk neutrality, as an empirically verified proposition. Their paper also assumes "regressivity," that is, that the spot price is a linear function of the futures price plus some error term of the form: $\tilde{P}_t = a + b\tilde{F}_t + \tilde{e}_t$. This formulation is hard to motivate on the basis of existing theory. Linearity holds under arbitrage pricing but with no error. When the futures price depends on the spot price plus additional (imperfectly hedgable) state variables, there is no prior reason for a linear relationship to materialize.

$\mu_f = (\mu_a - r)\sigma_{fa}/\sigma_a^2$, is what guarantees that the future will not be held for mean-variance efficiency purposes.[14]

What is perhaps less obvious but true nonetheless is that the same pricing condition (combined with the same perfect hedging opportunity) also removes the preference-dependent component of the hedging demand for futures. Intuitively, at the point where the nontraded position is hedged perfectly and the pricing condition is met, changes in wealth are independent of the futures price and, therefore, of the nontraded position, so that $J_{py} = 0$.[15]

The discussion of Proposition 8 reveals also its fragility. Following Proposition 2 above, its desirable, function-separating properties break down in the presence of quantity uncertainty that cannot separately be covered by a perfectly correlated futures contract. More generally, one would expect that incomplete hedging opportunities would render the pricing condition of the proposition inconsistent with a capital market equilibrium with nontraded assets. In short, the conditions for implementable, variance-minimizing hedges also to be optimal are likely to be breached empirically.

VII. CONCLUDING REMARKS

Hedging in the sense of the THM does not occur in perfect financial markets. For a demand to appear, for some assets to hedge other, predesignated assets,

---

[14]To see this last point more precisely, note that the speculative component of the demand for the asset and the future, denoted by m, is:

$$\begin{pmatrix} wW \\ x \end{pmatrix}^m = -\frac{J_y}{J_{yy}} V^{-1} \begin{pmatrix} \mu_a - r \\ \mu_f \end{pmatrix}$$

In this two-by-two case, we also have:

$$V^{-1} = D^{-1} \begin{pmatrix} \sigma_f^2 & -\sigma_{af} \\ -\sigma_{fa} & \sigma_a^2 \end{pmatrix}, \quad \text{where} \quad D = \sigma_a^2 \sigma_f^2 (1 - \rho_{af}^2).$$

Substituting, the mean variance demand becomes:

$$\begin{pmatrix} wW \\ x \end{pmatrix}^m = -\frac{J_y}{J_{yy}} D^{-1} \begin{bmatrix} (\mu_a - r)\sigma_f^2 - \mu_f \sigma_{af} \\ -(\mu_a - r)\sigma_{fa} + \mu_f \sigma_a^2 \end{bmatrix} = -\frac{J_y}{J_{yy}} \begin{bmatrix} (\mu_a - r)/\sigma_a^2 \\ 0 \end{bmatrix}$$

since the condition of Proposition 8 implies that the bottom term in the square bracket equals zero and, rewritten as $\mu_f/\sigma_f = \rho_{af}(\mu_a - r)/\sigma_a$, that the top term is given by $(\mu_a - r)\sigma_f^2 - (\sigma_{af}^2/\sigma_a^2)(\mu_a - r) = (\mu_a - r)\sigma_f^2(1 - \rho_{af}^2)$.

[15]Note the proof in the appendix. Another way of seeing this is to write out the wealth budget constraint as:

$$dY = \{(Q\mu_p + x\mu_f - rPQ)dt + Q\sigma_p dz_p + x\sigma_f dz_f\} + \{(wW(\mu_a - r) + rY)dt + wW\sigma_a dz_a\}.$$

where the first bracketed term is zero by arbitrage. What remains is the second bracketed expression, changes in which can be associated with the total returns on the mean-variance portfolio of traded assets. When futures are priced by the condition that $\mu_f = (\mu_a - r)\sigma_{fa}/\sigma_a^2$, these returns are independent of the moments of the futures price and, therefore, of the spot price, as footnote 13 shows. Consequently, dY is similarly independent of P.

some imperfection that causes trading discontinuities in the pre-identified assets is required.[16] Taking some positions as completely nontraded most closely conforms to the fixed-cash-position assumption of the THM. When perfect hedges are infeasible, investors will generally hedge their nontraded positions with portfolios that contain both traded assets and futures.

The only implementable hedges are minimum-variance hedges. They can be estimated by ordinary least squares (OLS) techniques provided that the regression coefficients are intertemporally constant. If the regression coefficients depend on exogenous state variables, OLS procedures at best provide an approximation and more complex statistical techniques are required. In general, minimum-variance hedges must be rebalanced continuously. Only if there is no quantity uncertainty and a perfect hedge is possible can the hedge ratio be constant. In any event, minimum or zero-variance hedges will seldom be optimal in the expected-utility-maximizing sense.

The main limitation of the model on which these results are based is, as was implied in the introduction, its assumption of complete nonmarketability for the positions that investors choose to hedge. By virtue of this assumption, this paper, along with most of the hedging literature, considers only the problem of hedging a given exposure. Over time, of course, each exposure, that is, the size of each temporarily nontraded position, can in principle be varied. Were this position instantaneously and costlessly modifiable in any direction, the hedging model would reduce once more to the general portfolio model. Only shifts in the opportunity set would be left to motivate hedging behavior as the direct hedging term, which reflects THM-type hedging, would disappear. A full theory of hedging therefore lies between the two extremes: Of the complete nontradedness of target positions that underlies the THM on the one hand, and pure portfolio theory with freely variable spot positions on the other.

A notable line of contributions, including Stein (1961), Stoll (1979), Rolfo (1980), Anderson and Danthine (1981), and Benninga, Eldor, and Zilcha (1985), all in a one-period framework; and Ho (1984) in an intertemporal model, have explored the interaction between hedging and an initial, once-off production decision. Their analyses are most clearly applicable to circumstances like those of a farmer who, once his field is cultivated and planted, may be unable thereafter to increase his acreage or liquidate part of it. However, this approach cannot capture the essence of hedging behavior in financial markets where exposures themselves (i.e., production decisions) are periodically revisable. What is required is a theory of the optimal choice of spot positions that can be adjusted, perhaps sluggishly, over time. Explicitly modelling this problem will undoubtedly require the introduction of transactions costs, short-selling constraints and stopping times. While this task is formidable, hedging theory will remain incomplete until the work is done.

---

[16] The assumption of nontradedness of an asset or position, however, also raises the issue of its compatibility with a continuous process for that asset, i.e., the existence of a market with continuous trading. This apparent conflict is resolved as follows. First a market with continuous trading may exist, but access to the market may be restricted for various reasons: divisibility problems, minimum transaction size requirements, discrimination among classes of investors, and so on. Second, investors may trade at discrete points in time in some markets, but the arrival process of orders to the market may still produce continuous trading. In both cases a continuous price process at the aggregate level coexists with barriers to continuous trading at the individual level.

Appendix

Proof of Proposition 7

Under the maintained assumptions (1)-(4) in the text, the demand functions are:

$$\begin{pmatrix} wW \\ x \end{pmatrix} = -\frac{J_y}{J_{yy}} \begin{pmatrix} \sigma_a^2 & \sigma_{af} \\ \sigma_{fa} & \sigma_f^2 \end{pmatrix}^{-1} \begin{pmatrix} \mu_a - r \\ \mu_f \end{pmatrix} - \begin{pmatrix} 0 \\ \sigma_p/\sigma_f \end{pmatrix} \frac{J_{py}}{J_{yy}} - \begin{pmatrix} 0 \\ Q\sigma_p/\sigma_f \end{pmatrix}$$

and substituting in the Bellman equation leads to,

$$-J_t = J_y[Q\mu_p + rW - c] + J_p\mu_p + \tfrac{1}{2} J_{pp}\sigma_p^2 + u(c,t)$$

$$+ \tfrac{1}{2} J_{yy}\sigma_p^2 Q^2 + J_{yp}\sigma_p^2 Q - \tfrac{1}{2}\left[\frac{J_y^2}{J_{yy}}(\mu_a - r, \mu_f)V^{-1}\begin{pmatrix} \mu_a - r \\ \mu_f \end{pmatrix}\right.$$

$$+ 2J_y(\mu_a - r, \mu_f)V^{-1}\begin{pmatrix} \sigma_{ap} \\ \sigma_{fp} \end{pmatrix}\frac{J_{py}}{J_{yy}} + J_{yp}(\sigma_{pa}, \sigma_{pf})V^{-1}\begin{pmatrix} \sigma_{ap} \\ \sigma_{fp} \end{pmatrix}\frac{J_{py}}{J_{yy}}$$

$$+ J_{yy}Q^2(\sigma_{pa}, \sigma_{pf})V^{-1}\begin{pmatrix} \sigma_{ap} \\ \sigma_{fp} \end{pmatrix} + 2J_y(\mu_a - r, \mu_f)V^{-1}\begin{pmatrix} \sigma_{ap} \\ \sigma_{fp} \end{pmatrix} Q$$

$$\left. + 2J_{yp}(\sigma_{pa}, \sigma_{pf})V^{-1}\begin{pmatrix} \sigma_{ap} \\ \sigma_{fp} \end{pmatrix}\right]$$

Further noticing that:

$$\sigma_p^2 - (\sigma_{pa}, \sigma_{pf})V^{-1}\begin{pmatrix} \sigma_{ap} \\ \sigma_{fp} \end{pmatrix} = 0$$

$$(\mu_a - r, \mu_f)V^{-1}\begin{pmatrix} \sigma_{ap} \\ \sigma_{fp} \end{pmatrix} = (\sigma_p/\sigma_f)\mu_f$$

and that by arbitrage:

$$\mu_p - (\sigma_p/\sigma_f)\mu_f = rP$$

we obtain:

$$-J_t = J_y(rY - c) + J_p\mu_p + 1/2 J_{pp}\sigma_p^2 + u(c, t)$$

$$- 1/2 \frac{J_y^2}{J_{yy}} (\mu_a - r, \mu_f) V^{-1} \begin{pmatrix} \mu_a - r \\ \mu_f \end{pmatrix} - J_y(\sigma_p/\sigma_f)\mu_f \frac{J_{py}}{J_{yy}}$$

$$- 1/2 J_{yp}(\sigma_{pa}, \sigma_{pf}) V^{-1} \begin{pmatrix} \sigma_{ap} \\ \sigma_{fp} \end{pmatrix} \frac{J_{py}}{J_{yy}}$$

Now the mean variance demands are zero if:

(C1) $\begin{cases} \sigma_f^2(\mu_a - r) - \sigma_{fa}\mu_f = 0 \\ -\sigma_{fa}(\mu_a - r) + \sigma_a^2\mu_f = 0 \end{cases}$

and the value function J is of the separable form $J[Y, P, t] = \psi(Y, t) + \phi(P, t)$ (so that $J_{yp} = 0$) if:

$(\mu_a - r, \mu_f) V^{-1} \begin{pmatrix} \mu_a - r \\ \mu_f \end{pmatrix}$ is independent of P.

and there exist two functions ψ and ϕ satisfying

(C2) $-\psi_t = \psi_y(rY - c) + u(c, t) - 1/2 \frac{\psi_y^2}{\psi_{yy}} (\mu_a - r, \mu_f) V^{-1} \begin{pmatrix} \mu_a - r \\ \mu_f \end{pmatrix}$

$$-\phi_t = \phi_p\mu_p + 1/2\phi_{pp}\sigma_p^2$$

$\phi(P, T) = 0;\quad \psi(Y, T) = B[Y, T]$ where $c = u_c^{-1}(\psi_y)$.

Now if conditions (*i*) and (*ii*) of the proposition are satisfied, we immediately get (C1) and the first condition of (C2) holding. Thus, the result is obtained if in addition there exists a solution ψ and ϕ of the system:

$$-\psi_t = \psi_y(rY - c) + u(c, t)$$

$$-\phi_t = \phi_p \mu_p + 1/2 \phi_{pp} \sigma_p^2$$

$$\phi(P, T) = 0; \quad \psi(Y, T) = B[Y, T]$$

where $c = u_c^{-1}(\psi_y)$

In the statement of the proposition we omit these existence conditions. That is, we implicitly suppose that there exists a space of utility functions, U, for which these conditions are met.

Proof of Proposition 8

Following the proof of proposition 7, we need the conditions:

(C'1) $\quad\quad -\sigma_{fa}(\mu_a - r) + \sigma_a^2 \mu_f = 0$

and (C2) to be satisfied. Under the condition of the proposition, (C'1) is trivially satisfied and the first condition of (C2), namely:

$$[(\mu_a - r)^2 \sigma_f^2 - 2\sigma_{af}(\mu_a - r)\mu_f + \mu_f^2 \sigma_a^2][\sigma_a^2 \sigma_f^2 (1 - \rho_{af}^2)]^{-1} \quad \text{independent of } P$$

becomes

$$[(\mu_a - r)^2 / \sigma_a^2] \quad \text{independent of } P$$

This condition is clearly satisfied. Assuming away the existence problem mentioned earlier completes this proof of Proposition 8.

Bibliography

Adler, M., and Detemple, J. B. (1986): "On the Optimal Hedge of a Non-Traded Cash Position." Working Paper, Columbia University, *Journal of Finance*, March 1988.

Anderson, R. W., and Danthine, J-P. (1981, December): "Cross Hedging." *Journal of Political Economy*, 89:1182-1196.

Benninga, S., Eldor, R., and Zilcha, I. (1984): "The Optimal Hedge Ratio in Unbiased Futures Markets." *Journal of Futures Markets,* 4:155-159.

Benninga, S., Eldor, R., and Zilcha, I. (1985, December): "Optimal International Hedging in Commodity and Currency Forward Markets." *Journal of International Money and Finance,* 4:537-552.

Black, F. (1976, January-March): "The Pricing of Commodity Contracts," *Journal of Financial Economics,* 3:167-179.

Breeden, D. T. (1979, September): "An Intertemporal Asset Pricing Model with Stochastic Consumption and Investment Opportunities." *Journal of Financial Economics,* 7:265-296.

Breeden, D. T. (1984, April): "Futures Markets and Commodity Options: Hedging and Optimality in Incomplete Markets." *Journal of Economic Theory,* 32:275-300.

Brennan, M. J., and Schwartz, E. S. (1985, April): "Evaluating Natural Resource Investments." *Journal of Business,* 58:135-157.

Ederington, L. E. (1979, March): "The Hedging Performance of the New Futures Markets." *Journal of Finance,* 34:157-170.

Ho, T. S. Y. (1984, June): "Intertemporal Commodity Futures Hedging and the Production Decision." *Journal of Finance,* 34:351-376.

Johnson, L. L. (1960, June): "The Theory of Hedging and Speculation in Commodity Futures." *Review of Economic Studies,* 27:139-151.

Mayers, D. (1972): "Non-Marketable Assets and Capital Market Equilibrium under Uncertainty," in M. C. Jensen, ed. *Studies in the Theory of Capital Markets* (New York: Praeger Publishers Inc.): 223-248.

McKinnon, R. I. (1967, December): "Futures Markets, Buffer Stocks and Income Stability for Primary Producers." *Journal of Political Economy,* 75:844-861.

Merton, R. C. (1971, December): "Optimum Consumption and Portfolio Rules in a Continuous Time Model." *Journal of Economic Theory,* 3:373-413.

Merton, R. C. (1973, September): "An Intertemporal Capital Asset Pricing Model." *Econometrica,* 41:867-887.

Richard, S. F. and Sundaresan, M. "A Continuous Time Equilibrium Model of Forward Prices and Futures Prices in a Multigood Economy." *Journal of Financial Economics,* 9:347-371.

Rolfo, J. (1980, February): "Optimal Hedging Under Price and Quantity Uncertainty." *Journal of Political Economy,* 88:100-116.

Sercu, P. (1980, June): "A Generalization of the International Asset Pricing Model." *Revue de l'Association Francaise de Finance,* 1:91-135.

Stein, J. L. (1961, December): "The Simultaneous Determination of Spot and Futures Prices." *American Economic Review,* 51:1012-1025.

Stoll, H. (1979, November): "Commodity Futures and Spot Price Determination and Hedging in Capital Market Equilibrium." *Journal of Financial and Quantitative Analysis,* 14:873-894.

Stulz, R. M. (1984, June): "Optimal Hedging Policies." *Journal of Financial and Quantitative Analysis,* 19:127-140.

Telser, L. (1955): "Safety First and Hedging." *Review of Economic Studies,* 23:1-16.

Telser, L. (1958, June): "Futures Trading and the Storage of Cotton and Wheat." *Journal of Political Economy,* 66:233-255.

Working, H. (1953, June): "Futures Trading and Hedging." *American Economic Review,* 43:314-343.

Working, H. (1962, June): "New Concepts Concerning Futures Markets and Prices." *American Economic Review,* 52:431-459.

[19]
A Multiperiod Model for the Selection of a Futures Portfolio

John F. Marshall
Anthony F. Herbst

INTRODUCTION

Traditional portfolio theory selects an optimal portfolio from a universe of securities using a mean/variance approach to return–risk measurement and a well-behaved, usually quadratic, utility function. Unfortunately, the traditional model, developed by Markowitz (1952, 1959), is inadequate for portfolio optimization when applied in the context of a futures portfolio. There are at least five reasons for this inadequacy. First, futures positions are taken without "investment" in the usual sense. Second, futures trading involves considerable leverage, but the leverage multiplier, that is, the commodity value covered by a contract divided by the margin required to carry it, varies over time. Third, the symmetry of futures markets allows for long and short positions, but the margin requirement is positive in both cases. The optimization technique must explicitly recognize this peculiarity of futures trading by requiring all portfolio weights to be positive. Traditional optimization techniques built around the Markowitz model treat short positions as having negative weights. Fourth, the Markowitz model is single period while the futures portfolio problem is decidedly multiperiod. Finally, the traditional utility criterion is too abstract for most practical applications.[1]

As a side point, the capital market line (CML) extension of the Markowitz model does not hold in a futures portfolio framework, because the required separation theorem does not apply to a futures portfolio. The separation theorem, Tobin (1958), applicable in a securities portfolio context, allows for the investor to move wealth freely between a risky market portfolio and a risk-free asset. Thus, the size of the risk-free position is determined by the size of the risky market position. In a futures portfolio, trading capital is held in the form of risk-free securities, and these

---

The research represented by this article was jointly funded by the Chicago Board of Trade Educational Research Foundation, the Business Research Institute, and Brandywine Asset Management. The authors are indebted to Wade Brorsen, Jacky So, Alan Tucker, Matthew Wong, and several anonymous referees for constructive comments on an earlier draft.

[1] Others who have looked at the problems with modeling a futures portfolio include Brorsen and Lukac (1990) and Lukac and Brorsen (1990). Related issues involving cost and performance of futures funds have been addressed by Elton, Gruber, and Rentzler (1990).

John F. Marshall *is a Professor of Finance at St. John's University, New York.*
Anthony F. Herbst *is a Professor of Finance at the University of Texas at El Paso.*

same securities are used to meet margin requirements. The size of the risk-free position is, therefore, not determined by the size of the futures position.

This article offers a model for portfolio optimization in the context of a diversified futures portfolio and an illustration of its application. With the exception of the choice criteria, the model is a generalization of the Markowitz model. This article is targeted, first and foremost, to futures fund managers, but also to managers of other types of futures portfolios, and managers of portfolios that have a futures component.

This study is structured as follows: The next section lays out the model assumptions, introduces the bulk of the notation, and defines a number of underlying relationships. The underlying relationships are deliberately crafted to mimic, as closely as possible, actual trading practice. The third section formulates the optimization problem and solves for the minimum variance set in a single-period context. The fourth section adds a multiperiod dimension to the model and describes two equivalent multiperiod choice criteria to determine the optimal position sizes. The final section applies the model to data provided by a fund manager, obtains optimized values, and interprets these values.

ASSUMPTIONS, NOTATION, AND UNDERLYING RELATIONSHIPS

Since this article is directed to the futures fund manager, it is written in language as near to the industry as possible, while retaining its academic perspective. For simplicity, it is assumed that the fund manager employs "technical" methods of price analysis in the design of trading strategies.[2]

Define a "trading regime" to be a set of trading rules. Define a "strategy" to be a trading regime applied to a specific futures contract series. The same trading regime applied to two different futures series constitutes two different strategies. Similarly, two different regimes applied to the same futures series constitutes two different strategies.

Next, define a daily strategy return as the unlevered per-unit profit from that day to the next expressed as a percentage of that day's settlement price. That is, the return from strategy i on day t, denoted $R(i, t)$, is given by equation (1)

$$R(i, t) = 100 \times \frac{D(i, t) \cdot (Z(i, t + 1) - P(i, t)) + D(i, t + 1) \cdot (P(i, t + 1) - Z(i, t + 1))}{P(i, t)} \quad (1)$$

where $D(i, t)$ and $D(i, t + 1)$ denote the side of the market strategy i is on on days t and $t + 1$, respectively. These "dummy" variables take the values $+1$ when long, -1 when short, and 0 when neutral (out of the market). $Z(i, t + 1)$ denotes the transaction price on day $t + 1$ if a trade is made on day $t + 1$. If no trade is made on day $t + 1$ then $Z(i, t + 1)$ is the settlement price on day $t + 1$. $P(i, t)$ and $P(i, t + 1)$ are the settlement prices on days t and $t + 1$, respectively. This formulation allows for trading strategies that transact close-to-close, open-to-open, or any other time of the

---

[2] As shown by Brorsen and Irwin (1987), Irwin and Brorsen (1985); and Lukac, Brorsen, and Irwin (1988), most futures fund managers employ technical methods of price analysis in the design of trading rules and in the selection of their funds' positions.

day, provided that a strategy transacts no more than once per day.[3] This calculation is repeated daily to generate a sufficiently long daily strategy-return series. It is also repeated for each strategy the futures fund might employ.

The mean and variance of the return series i, denoted $\mu(i)$ and $\sigma^2(i)$, are assumed to be unbiased estimates of future strategy performance.[4] It is further assumed that each return series is mean/variance stationary, and that the successive returns in the return series are mutually independent—both within and across strategies. That is, $R(i, t)$ and $R(j, t + s)$ ($s \neq 0$) are independent for all i and for all j. The covariance of daily returns on series i and series j is denoted $\sigma(i, j)$. It is important to appreciate that the means, variances, and covariances of the strategy returns will generally not be equal to the means, variances, and covariances of the various underlying price series.[5]

It is assumed that the size of a continuing position, that is, the number of contracts, can be adjusted without cost on any given day.[6] The portfolio manager possesses trading capital in the amount of $C(t)$ at time t, and the bulk of this trading capital is invested in interest-bearing securities. For purposes of this study, it is assumed that the interest-bearing securities are some form of overnight money—overnight repos, for example.[7] The fraction of $C(t)$ held in this form on day t is denoted by $a(t)$. The remaining portion of trading capital, $1 - a(t)$, is held as cash to provide for variation margin, that is, cash transfers to and from the margin ac-

---

[3] The notation in equation (1) can be modified to allow for multiple trades (intraday trading) between time t and time $t + 1$. For example, partially suppress the day index (t) and the strategy index (i) and let k denote the kth trade made on day t, $k = 0, 1, 2, \ldots, T$. The return on the kth trade is given by:

$$R(k) = \frac{D(i,k) \cdot [Z(k + 1) - Z(k)]}{P(i,t)} \quad k = 0, 1, 2, 3, \ldots, T$$

where, if $k = 0$ then $Z(k) = P(i, t)$ and if $k = T$ then $Z(k + 1) = P(i, t + 1)$. The daily return for strategy i on day t is then given by:

$$R(i, t) = \sum_{k=0}^{T} R(k)$$

The remaining notation is the same as that employed in equation (1).

[4] This is not a trivial assumption. As noted elsewhere, many technical "systems" developers employ faulty development techniques that seriously bias the return–risk parameters of their strategies (Marshall, 1989). Others who have addressed these concerns, although in a different context, include Bodie and Rosansky (1980), Caudill and Holcombe (1987), Denton (1985), and Neftci (1983). In addition, if the individual return series are not normal, the unbiasedness property will not hold. Empirical evidence, discussed later, suggests that the individual return series are not normal. However, as also shown later, empirical evidence suggests that portfolio returns are approximately normal. In this study, it is the portfolio returns that are the key, and thus, the assumption of unbiasedness of the individual return parameters does no harm.

[5] The exception is a benchmark strategy that is always long.

[6] This is not to imply that there is no cost to trading. Transaction costs, including both commissions and market impact costs, are assumed to already be reflected in the return–risk parameters of each strategy. The proper handling of transaction costs is discussed later.

[7] While T-bills are a more common vehicle in which to hold trading capital, T-bill returns violate the serial independence assumption. As an operational matter, this violation is probably of little practical importance as the capital return component is a relatively small portion of total daily return. Furthermore, if the T-bill maturities precisely match the investment horizon, it would not be inappropriate to view the T-bill return as having zero variance and to be uncorrelated with the strategy return series.

count as a consequence of daily marking-to-market.[8] The daily return on invested trading capital held to meet margin requirements is denoted $R(c,t)$, and the mean and variance of this return are denoted $\mu(c)$ and $\sigma^2(c)$, respectively. The covariance of the daily return on invested trading capital and the return series for strategy i is denoted $\sigma(i,c)$.

The number of units covered by a futures contract, that is, contract size, is denoted $S(i)$. Contract value for strategy i on day t is then $P(i,t) \cdot S(i)$. The leverage multiplier for strategy i on day t, denoted $L(i,t)$, is given by equation (2)

$$L(i,t) = \frac{P(i,t) \cdot S(i)}{M(i,t)} \quad (2)$$

where $M(i,t)$ is the per-contract dollar margin required for a speculative position in the futures involved in strategy i on day t.[9] Finally, the portion of total trading capital committed to strategy i on day t, denoted $w(i,t)$, is given by equation (3a), which is equivalent to equation (3b)

$$w(i,t) = \frac{M(i,t) \cdot N(i,t)}{C(t)} \quad (3a)$$

$$N(i,t) = \frac{C(t) \cdot w(i,t)}{M(i,t)} \quad (3b)$$

where $N(i,t)$ denotes the number of strategy i futures held on day t. The notation used in this article is summarized in Appendix A.

THE OPTIMIZATION PROBLEM AND MINIMUM VARIANCE SET

Let there be $n - 1$ strategies available for inclusion in the futures portfolio and let there be one additional strategy defined to be the "null strategy." The null strategy is a strategy having a zero mean and a zero variance. The weight assigned to this strategy represents that portion of total trading capital not committed as margin on a futures position and may be regarded as trading capital held in reserve. The leverage multiplier for the null strategy is, by definition, 1.

The 1-day portfolio return for day t, denoted $R_p(1)$, is given by equation (4)

$$R_p(1) = \sum_{i=1}^{n} w(i,t) \cdot L(i,t) \cdot R(i,t) + a(t) \cdot R(c,t) \quad (4)$$

where $\sum w(i,t) = 1$ and $a(t) \le 1$.

The mean 1-day portfolio return is given by equation (5).

$$\mu_p(1) = \sum_{i=1}^{n} w(i,t) \cdot L(i,t) \cdot \mu(i,t) + a(t) \cdot \mu(c,t) \quad (5)$$

The variance of the 1-day portfolio return is given by equation (6).

---
[8] As a practical matter, the value $a(t)$ will generally be close to 1.
[9] As reported by Brorsen and Irwin (1987), initial margins generally approximate 5% of contract value. This implies a leverage multiplier of about 20. Nevertheless, this varies from day to day because exchange margins are changed infrequently but contract value changes daily.

$$\sigma_p^2(1) = \sum_{i=1}^{n} w^2(i,t) \cdot L^2(i,t) \cdot \sigma^2(i)$$

$$+ 2 \sum_{i>j}^{n} \sum^{n} w(i,t) \cdot w(j,t) \cdot L(i,t) \cdot L(j,t) \cdot \sigma(i,j)$$

$$+ 2 \sum_{i=1}^{n} w(i,t) \cdot a(t) \cdot L(i,t) \cdot \sigma(c,i)$$

$$+ a^2(t) \cdot \sigma^2(c) \qquad (6)$$

The requirement that $\Sigma w(i,t) = 1$ in equation (4) is overly restrictive. It only applies as an absolute condition if no two strategies involve the same commodity. When two strategies involve the same commodity *and* the two strategies happen to be on opposite sides of the market, then the margin requirements are partially offsetting.[10] Thus, in such situations, the sum of the weights can exceed 1. A more inclusive treatment would distinguish between regimes and commodities. For example, let $w(k,l)$ denote the weight on regime k applied to commodity l. Let there be $G(l)$ regimes applicable to commodity l and let there be H commodities. Then the constraint has the form given by equation (7) (in which the time subscript is suppressed but understood)

$$\text{ABS}\left[\sum_{k=1}^{G(1)} D(k,1) \cdot w(k,1)\right] + \text{ABS}\left[\sum_{k=1}^{G(2)} D(k,2) \cdot w(k,2)\right] + \ldots$$

$$\ldots + \text{ABS}\left[\sum_{k=1}^{G(H)} D(k,H) \cdot w(k,H)\right] + w(\text{null}) = 1 \quad (7)$$

where ABS[—] denotes the absolute value of the term in brackets and w(null) denotes the weight on the null strategy. This less restrictive form of the constraint only needs to be considered in those optimization cases in which the weight on the null strategy is binding in the more restrictive form. In simple terms, if, when employing equation (4), the weight on the null strategy (reserve trading capital) is found to be zero, then the less restrictive form of the constraint, given by equation (7), should be employed instead. The more restrictive form given in equation (4) is used in the remainder of this study and in the computer program employed to solve the model.

The first term in the variance equation [equation (6)] is unsystematic risk. It is directly analogous to the unsystematic risk associated with holding a stock portfolio. It differs, however, from the latter in two ways: (1) excluding the weight assigned to the null strategy, the weights need not sum to 1.0 (and generally will not); and (2) the leverage multiplier term is included to account for the leverage provided by futures.

The second term in the variance equation is systematic risk. It is also analogous to the systematic risk of a stock portfolio. Again, it is modified to account for the presence of leverage.

---

[10] Suppose, for example, that strategy 1 requires a long position in three July wheat futures and strategy 2 requires a short position in two July wheat futures. Then, the net margin requirement is for one wheat futures. The lower margins on intracommodity spreads also present a problem. For example, if strategy 1 is long one July wheat and Strategy 2 is short one September wheat, then the margin requirements may again be regarded as partially offsetting.

The third and fourth terms are unique to a futures portfolio. The third term represents a special form of systematic risk. The presence of this risk is explained by the fact that a portion of trading capital is held in the form of an interest-bearing asset. A priori, one might expect the correlation between the returns on a trading strategy and the returns on invested trading capital to be near zero. However, this might not be the case for all futures strategies, particularly those involving short-term interest rate futures such as T-bill and Eurodollar futures. The fourth term is a special form of unsystematic risk. Unlike the unsystematic risk of a stock portfolio, this risk does not necessarily get smaller with increasing portfolio diversification since the weight, $a(t)$, on this return component is independent of the degree of diversification.

When the leverage multiplier, $L(i,t)$, equals 1 for all i, $a(t)$ equals 0, and $D(t,i) = +1$ for all i, then the model presented here reduces, in all of its dimensions, to the Markowitz model. It is for this reason, that the futures model may be viewed as a generalization of the Markowitz model.

While equations (5) and (6) provide the mean and variance of the one-day portfolio return, the distribution of this return is not clear due to the heavy weighting given to the $R(c,t)$ term. Fortunately, when extended to a multiperiod context, the distribution becomes clear. (This is explained in the next section.)

The single-period optimization problem can be defined now. The first step seeks to identify the weights $w(i)$, $i = 1, 2, 3, \ldots, n$, such that the portfolio variance is minimized for any required portfolio return. To simplify the notation, suppress the time subscript and make the following substitutions:

$$s(i,j) = L(i) \cdot L(j) \cdot \sigma(i,j)$$

$$x(i,c) = a \cdot L(i) \cdot \sigma(i,c)$$

$$v(i) = L(i) \cdot \mu(i)$$

Equation (8) is obtained by combining terms 1 and 2 of equation (6), and substituting the notation above.

$$\sigma_p^2(1) = \sum_i \sum_j w(i) \cdot w(j) \cdot s(i,j) + 2\sum_i w(i) \cdot x(i,c) + a^2 \cdot \sigma^2(c) \qquad (8)$$

To map the efficient set, portfolio variance must be minimized subject to the following two constraints:

$$\sum w(i) = 1$$

$$\sum w(i) \cdot v(i) + a \cdot \mu(c) = b$$

where b is the expected overall portfolio return (including any interest earned on trading capital). Formulate the appropriate Lagrangian with $h(1)$ and $h(2)$ denoting the Lagrangian multipliers:

$$\begin{aligned} \text{MIN } L(\mathbf{w}, \mathbf{h}) = {} & \sum\sum w(i) \cdot w(j) \cdot s(i,j) + 2\sum w(i) \cdot x(i,c) \\ & + a^2 \cdot \sigma^2(c) + h(1) \cdot (b - \sum w(i) \cdot v(i) - a \cdot \mu(c)) \\ & + h(2) \cdot (1 - \sum w(i)) \end{aligned}$$

The first order conditions with respect to the vectors **w** and **h** are as follows:

$$1 \cdot s(1,1) \cdot w(1) + 2 \cdot s(1,2) \cdot w(2) + \cdots + 2 \cdot s(1,n) \cdot w(n) + 2 \cdot x(1,c) - v(1) \cdot h(1) - 1 \cdot h(2) = 0$$
$$2 \cdot s(2,1) \cdot w(1) + 1 \cdot s(2,2) \cdot w(2) + \cdots + 2 \cdot s(2,n) \cdot w(n) + 2 \cdot x(2,c) - v(2) \cdot h(1) - 1 \cdot h(2) = 0$$
$$\vdots$$
$$2 \cdot s(n,1) \cdot w(1) + 2 \cdot s(n,2) \cdot w(2) + \cdots + 1 \cdot s(n,n) \cdot w(n) + 2 \cdot x(n,c) - v(n) \cdot h(1) - 1 \cdot h(2) = 0$$
$$-v(1) \cdot w(1) + \quad -v(2) \cdot w(2) + \cdots + \quad -v(n) \cdot w(n) + b - a \cdot \mu(c) \quad\quad\quad = 0$$
$$-1 \cdot w(1) + \quad -1 \cdot w(2) + \cdots + \quad -1 \cdot w(n) + 1 \quad\quad\quad = 0$$

If a solution to this system of linear equations exists, that is, a feasible solution, it must be that which minimizes the original variance term. This is assured by the concavity of the original objective function. However, the solutions for the weights must be restricted to nonnegative values. This can be handled by employing a linear programming algorithm in which both the **w** and **h** values are restricted to be nonnegative. This approach requires formulating a new, yet null, objective function—with a dummy variable added for each strategy.[11] These dummy variables are denoted $d(1), d(2), \ldots d(n)$. The new problem to be solved is then maximize:

$$0 \cdot w(1) + 0 \cdot w(2) + \cdots + 0 \cdot w(n) + 0 \cdot h(1) + 0 \cdot h(2) + -d(1) + -d(2) + \cdots + -d(n)$$

subject to:

$$1 \cdot s(11) \cdot w(1) + 2 \cdot s(12) \cdot w(2) + \cdots + 2 \cdot s(1n) \cdot w(n) - v(1) \cdot h(1) - 1 \cdot h(2) + 1 \cdot d(1) + 0 \cdot d(2) + \cdots + 0 \cdot d(n) = -2 \cdot x(1,c)$$
$$2 \cdot s(21) \cdot w(1) + 1 \cdot s(22) \cdot w(2) + \cdots + 2 \cdot s(2n) \cdot w(n) - v(2) \cdot h(1) - 1 \cdot h(2) + 0 \cdot d(1) + 1 \cdot d(2) + \cdots + 0 \cdot d(n) = -2 \cdot x(2,c)$$
$$\vdots$$
$$2 \cdot s(n1) \cdot w(1) + 2 \cdot s(n2) \cdot w(2) + \cdots + 1 \cdot s(nn) \cdot w(n) - v(n) \cdot h(1) - 1 \cdot h(2) + 0 \cdot d(1) + 0 \cdot d(2) + \cdots + 1 \cdot d(n) = -2 \cdot x(n,c)$$
$$v(1) \cdot w(1) + \quad v(2) \cdot w(2) + \cdots + \quad v(n) \cdot w(n) + \quad 0 \cdot h(1) + 0 \cdot h(2) + 0 \cdot d(1) + 0 \cdot d(2) + \cdots + 0 \cdot d(n) = b - a \cdot \mu(c)$$
$$1 \cdot w(1) + \quad 1 \cdot w(2) + \cdots + \quad 1 \cdot w(n) + \quad 0 \cdot h(1) + 0 \cdot h(2) + 0 \cdot d(1) + 0 \cdot d(2) + \cdots + 0 \cdot d(n) = 1$$

$$w(i) \geq 0 \quad \text{and} \quad d(i) \geq 0 \quad (i = 1,2,3,\ldots,n) \quad \text{and} \quad h(i) \geq 0 \quad (i = 1,2)$$

For any selected value of b, the solution to the model will provide a point on the single-period (one-day) minimum variance set—provided of course that a solution exists. By varying b, the entire minimum variance set can be mapped (i.e., plotted in risk–return space).

THE MULTIPERIOD DIMENSION

The problem with the formulation thus far is that it is single-period and the length of a single period is but one day. If the portfolio manager's horizon is indeed one-day long, then the model, except for the final selection criteria, is complete as is. Alternatively, if the selection criteria are independent of the length of the horizon, then the length of the horizon is irrelevant to the selection decision, and again, the model is complete as is. Unfortunately, neither of these conditions generally hold. The

---

[11] This is essentially the quadratic programming procedure first described by Wolfe (1969), and applicable whenever the original objective function is concave.

portfolio manager's horizon is far more likely to be several months or even several years in length; and, the selection of an optimal portfolio by an individual with a well-behaved utility function is very much influenced by the length of the investment horizon.[12] This point is very often neglected in both theoretical discussions of portfolio theory and in applications by portfolio managers.

As shown by Tobin (1965), the single-period minimum variance set and the multi-period minimum variance set are identical, although the single-period efficient set is a subset of the multiperiod efficient set. The portfolio return–risk measures for a length-T horizon are related to the portfolio return–risk measures for a length-1 horizon by equations (9) and (10). These relationships assume daily portfolio rebalancing.[13]

$$\mu_p(T) = (1 + \mu_p(1))^T - 1 \tag{9}$$

$$\sigma_p^2(T) = ((1 + \mu_p(1))^2 + \sigma_p^2(1))^T - (1 + \mu_p(1))^{2T} \tag{10}$$

The lognormal law assures that the length-T return, $R_p(T)$, will have a lognormal distribution (shifted left by 1). This will hold precisely if $R_p(1)$ has a lognormal distribution and approximately if $R_p(1)$ has any other type of distribution. The longer T, the better the approximation.[14] In any practical application (in which T is more than a few days in length), the approximation to the lognormal distribution should be quite good under the assumptions made.[15]

Knowledge of the distribution of $R_p(T)$ allows the construction of a confidence channel for any portfolio on the single-period minimum variance set. A confidence channel is defined by the upper and lower bounds of an appropriately specified confidence interval when the interval is computed for a continuum of investment horizons, that is, $T = 1, 2, \ldots, N$. The construction of a confidence channel is straightforward. In brief, the effective return for a one-day horizon is converted to its normally distributed return equivalent, that is, the continuous return. The mean and standard deviation of this distribution are easily inferred from the mean and standard deviation of the effective return. The confidence interval for the one-day horizon is then computed in the usual manner. Finally, the upper and lower bounds of the interval are converted back to their effective equivalents. This procedure is repeated for a two-day horizon, a three-day horizon, and so on, out to some preset

---

[12] The importance of the investment horizon in optimal portfolio selection has been considered by Gressis, Philippatos, and Hayya (1976); Lloyd and Haney (1980); Gilster (1983); and, more recently, Marshall and Wynne (1990). It is not unreasonable to expect that portfolio managers will have at least intermediate horizons that correspond to the frequency of their reports to their investors.

[13] For a discussion of the importance of the rebalancing assumption in multiperiod portfolio analysis see Marshall (1989, chap. 6).

[14] The lognormal law holds that any variable defined as the product of independently and identically distributed random variables will have a distribution which converges, as the number of variables included increases, to a lognormal distribution. For further discussion, see Aitchison and Brown (1957).

[15] Evidence from Fama (1965) and others have demonstrated that return series for assets traded in competitive markets often exhibit leptokurtic behavior. Studies by Hall, Brorsen, and Irwin (1989) and Lukac and Brorsen (1990) have shown that *individual* returns series for futures traders using technical trading models also exhibit leptokurtic behavior. However, Lukac and Brorsen have shown that *diversified* futures portfolios, even those employing technical trading systems, do not exhibit this perverse behavior when the portfolio returns are measured monthly. This finding justifies, to some degree, the assumptions of unbiasedness made earlier in this article.

limit.[16] For purposes of computing such a channel, and all other computations reported in this study, it is assumed that a month consists of 21 trading days and a year consists of 252 trading days. A typical confidence channel is depicted in Figure 1.

The confidence channel is important for two reasons. First, the mean of the channel is a direct measure of the "expected" performance of the portfolio over the continuum of possible horizons. Second, the lower bound of the channel represents the maximum loss of trading capital (called drawdown here) that might occur and the temporal frame within which this loss might occur for the chosen level of confidence.

The fact that the lower bound of a confidence channel represents the maximum drawdown at a prescribed level of confidence suggests a useful criterion for choosing an optimal portfolio. Call this criterion "drawdown criterion."[17] In using drawdown criterion, *the fund manager specifies the maximum acceptable drawdown of initial trading capital over some specified horizon.* For example, the maximum acceptable drawdown might be 25% and the horizon might be six months. Finally, the fund manager specifies some level of significance (say 5%). The level of significance, as employed here, is interpreted as the likelihood that actual drawdown of initial trading capital will exceed the maximum acceptable level of drawdown *at any point in time over the entire length of the trading horizon* as perceived at the start of the trading horizon. The goal for the fund manager is then to *find the efficient one-day port-*

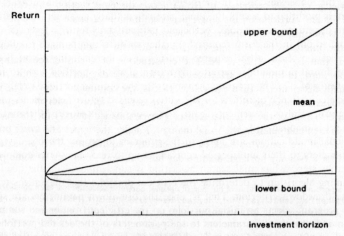

Figure 1
Confidence channel.

---

[16] The procedure for calculating a confidence channel when the return variable has a lognormal distribution is discussed more fully in Marshall (1989, chap. 16).

[17] Ad hoc measures and various rules-of-thumb with this same name have long been used by fund managers in designing portfolios; for example, see LaPorte Asset Allocation System, Burlington Hall Asset Management, or Managed Accounts Reports Quarterly Performance Reports. One such drawdown-based measure is the Sterling Ratio developed and used by Deane S. Jones, a futures portfolio manager, in Reno, Nevada. Many of these ad hoc measures, however, suffer from the defect that they are sample-size dependent. The drawdown criterion employed in this article is statistically stable in the sense that it is not dependent on the size of a sample.

folio that maximizes expected return over the trading horizon while not exceeding the drawdown limitation.[18]

An equivalent, but more intuitive, criterion for the selection of an optimal portfolio is "ruin criterion." Ruin criterion begins by selecting an *explicit percentage of trading capital that, if lost over some specified period of time, would constitute "ruin."* This might be 20% or 30%, or whatever percentage the portfolio manager deems appropriate. Then, using the multiperiod math described in the preceding section, and the properties of the lognormal distribution, the precise probability that a given single-period (one-day) portfolio will result in a loss of this magnitude or greater for each trading horizon from one day to the length of the actual horizon is determined. Call the graph of this probability of ruin (over the continuum from one day to the actual horizon) a "ruin curve." The goal for the manager using this criterion is to *maximize expected return while not exceeding some specified probability of ruin.*

While drawdown and ruin criteria are extremely attractive in terms of their appeal to a practitioner, they are also extremely tedious criteria to employ from a computational perspective. Fortunately, however, both readily lend themselves to a programming solution.

AN APPLICATION

To apply the model described in the preceding sections, a quadratic programming algorithm is modified to accept the input parameters (daily mean returns, standard deviations of returns, correlations coefficients between daily returns, leverage multipliers, and so on) in the form required. Further modification is made to allow for the specification of an initial required return and an incrementing factor. For example, an initial minimum required daily return of $z\%$ is specified with an incrementing factor of $x\%$. The program then solves for the optimal portfolio weights and the associated variance of return for the initial required return, increments the required return, resolves, increments again, and so on. By this process, the minimum variance set is mapped.

Additional modifications are made to the program to project the one-day portfolio parameters to their multiperiod equivalents up to one year. After completion of this latter step, a binomial search algorithm is superimposed on the quadratic programming algorithm to determine the efficient portfolio that maximizes return under the drawdown criterion. That is, once the drawdown parameters are specified, the program selects an initial portfolio on the efficient frontier and compares its return and drawdown parameters to the parameters of the desired portfolio. If the initial portfolio's drawdown is too high (low), relative to the specified drawdown, then the program increments downward (upward) on the efficient set until it finds a portfolio having too low (high) a drawdown, relative to the specified drawdown. Once two efficient portfolios are found, one having too high a drawdown and one having too low a drawdown, the returns on those two portfolios are averaged to generate a new required return. The efficient portfolio having this return is then solved for. The process is repeated until the optimal portfolio—that is, the one having the precise drawdown characteristics indicated—is found. This usually takes

---

[18] Zelney (1982) has shown that most institutional investors perceive risk as the probability of not achieving a minimum level of return. This is precisely what both the drawdown criterion and the ruin criterion, discussed later, measure.

from 12–15 iterations. The program is later altered to search, in the same manner, for the optimal portfolio using ruin criterion.

As a final step, two companion programs are developed. One generates confidence channels for any portfolio on the efficient set. The other generates a ruin curve for any portfolio on the efficient set.[19]

To test the efficacy of the portfolio model and the portfolio selection criteria, the assistance of a futures fund management firm was enlisted.[20] The fund managers provided return series data from 11 of their proprietary trading strategies.

The data cover the period January 23, 1973 through July 29, 1977 and represent in-sample return data adjusted for transaction costs.[21,22] There are a total of 1135 daily return observations on each series. These series are used to generate the required daily means, standard deviations, and correlation coefficients. For simplicity, margin requirements are assumed to be 5% of contract value for each contract traded under each strategy. Thus, the leverage multipliers are all 20.0. It is assumed that margin is held in the form of interest-earning securities that return 8.325% a year or 0.031746% per day compounded daily (252 trading days in a year), and that 90% of trading capital is held in this form, with the remainder held as cash. The return on trading capital is assumed to have zero variance and to be uncorrelated with each of the trading strategies. The commodities, together with the associated daily parameters, are reported in Table I.

The program noted in Table I then sequentially maps the portfolios on the efficient set. The same efficient set is mapped for investment horizons of one day, one month, three months, six months, and one year (these horizons were identified by fund managers to be of particular interest). A portion of the efficient set for a horizon of one year is depicted in Figure 2. Sample output from this program, for portfolio A on the efficient set, appears as Appendix B.

The drawdown criterion is tested next. The drawdown values are provided by the same futures fund managers that supplied the data. Specifically, the maximum accept-

---

[19] Interested parties may obtain copies of these programs from the authors.

[20] This was Brandywine Asset Management, Inc., which manages several futures funds.

[21] It is well understood that the use of in-sample return data—return data representing the same period on which the trading strategies were developed—will, generally, upwardly bias estimates of return performance. This problem has been extensively discussed elsewhere [see, e.g., Marshall (1989, chap. 16)]. The objective of this study, however, is not to judge system performance but rather to model portfolio behavior in a multiperiod context and to introduce practical selection criteria. No model can accurately predict portfolio performance if the input parameters of the individual trading strategies are biased. For these reasons, no claim is made that the portfolio performance presented here is at all realistic for this fund manager or for any other fund manager.

[22] For purposes of generating the return series, the fund managers assume a $50 per contract transaction cost. The correct adjustment for transaction costs is a two-step process. First, some assumption must be made as to per-contract transaction costs. After a trade is completed, the number of market days spanned by the trade is determined. The transaction cost is then restated on a per-unit per-day basis in the same monetary units as the futures price. In the case of soybean oil, for example, this is cents per pound and each contract covers 60,000 pounds. This value is computed as follows:

$$\text{PTC}(t) = \frac{\text{Transaction cost (in dollars)} \times 100}{\text{Number of units} \times \text{number of days in trade}}$$

The value PTC(t) is then deducted from the numerator of equation (1) (for each day spanned by the trade) to arrive at the adjusted strategy return series as below (individual series subscript suppressed).

$$R(t) = 100 \times \frac{D(t) \cdot (Z(t+1) - P(t)) + D(t+1) \cdot (P(t+1) - Z(t+1)) - \text{PTC}(t)}{P(t)}$$

Table I
STRATEGY RETURN PARAMETERS EMPLOYED AS INPUT VALUES TO THE SIMULATION

Commodity	Strategy	1	2	3	4	5	6	7	8	9	10	11
Deutsche mark	1	1.000	0.541	0.759	0.705	0.751	0.736	0.521	0.663	0.486	0.432	0.636
Swiss franc	2		1.000	0.550	0.509	0.536	0.653	0.589	0.575	0.277	0.266	0.747
British pound	3			1.000	0.906	0.820	0.750	0.554	0.661	0.422	0.400	0.722
Canadian dollar	4				1.000	0.818	0.745	0.525	0.653	0.450	0.413	0.701
Japanese yen	5					1.000	0.818	0.588	0.659	0.468	0.417	0.734
Silver	6						1.000	0.630	0.673	0.442	0.427	0.777
Live cattle	7							1.000	0.837	0.322	0.286	0.620
Live hogs	8								1.000	0.439	0.395	0.628
Sugar	9									1.000	0.703	0.340
Soybeans	10										1.000	0.281
Corn	11											1.000
Mean		0.062	0.077	0.097	0.093	0.083	0.079	0.072	0.074	0.061	0.070	0.079
St. dev.		0.632	0.681	0.670	0.661	0.643	0.631	0.507	0.516	0.630	0.664	0.682
Lev. multiplier		20.0	20.0	20.0	20.0	20.0	20.0	20.0	20.0	20.0	20.0	20.0
$a(t)$		0.90										
$R(c, t)$		0.031746%										

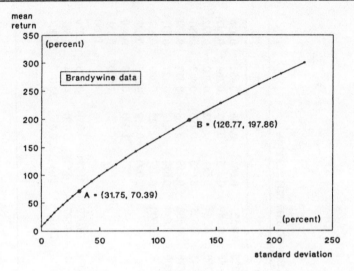

Figure 2
Efficient set of portfolios (one-year horizon).

able drawdown is set at 20% of trading capital over a one-year horizon with a level of significance of 1%. The algorithm then determines that the portfolio which maximizes return subject to drawdown not exceeding 20% at a 1% level of significance has the weights indicated in Table II. This particular portfolio has a mean annual return of 197.86% and a standard deviation of 126.77%. It is indicated as portfolio B on the mapping of the efficient set in Figure 2. The actual program output appears as Appendix C.

The percentage commitments indicated in Table II can be translated into the appropriate number of futures contracts using equation (3b). Suppose, for example, that the current per-contract margin requirements for silver, live cattle, and soybeans are $1000, $1500, and $1200, respectively. Suppose further that the fund has trading capital of $2 million. Then, the weights obtained suggest that the fund should hold 36.98 silver contracts, 209.82 live cattle contracts, and 178.22 soybean contracts.

A total of 28.3% of trading capital is committed as margin. The remainder of trading capital is uncommitted, as implied by the null strategy. As a practical mat-

Table II
OPTIMAL PORTFOLIO COMPOSITION USING DRAWDOWN CRITERION

Commodity	Strategy Number	Weight
Silver	6	1.849%
Live cattle	7	15.737%
Soybeans	10	10.693%
All others		0.000%
	Null	71.721%

ter, the indivisibility of futures contracts requires that the optimal size of the futures positions be rounded to the nearest integer value.[23]

As a next step, the ruin criterion is employed to select the optimal portfolio. In this case, ruin is defined as a loss of 20% of trading capital at any time over a one-year trading horizon. A maximum acceptable probability of ruin of 1% is indicated. As one would expect, the algorithm produces a portfolio identical to that produced under the drawdown criterion; thereby confirming the mathematical equivalence of the two criteria. The ruin curve, which is defined as the probability of ruin for any given trading horizon, is depicted in Figure 3. Notice that the probability of ruin rises for a time and then declines significantly. As defined, however, the probability of ruin is the maximum probability of experiencing ruin over the entire course of the trading horizon.

As a final step, the companion program is employed to generate a 90% confidence channel for the optimized portfolio. This is depicted in Figure 4. The lower bound of the confidence channel may be interpreted as a drawdown curve, at a 5% level of significance in this particular case.

SUMMARY AND CONCLUSION

This article discusses a portfolio model that allows for the determination of the efficient set of futures portfolios using the well-tested mean–variance approach. It extends the traditional Markowitz model by allowing for daily portfolio adjustments,

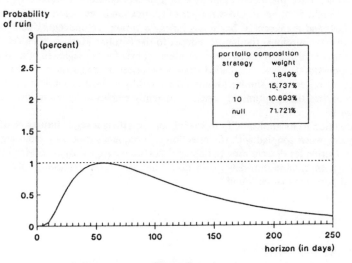

Figure 3
Ruin curve for portfolio B.

[23] The indivisibility of futures contracts requires that, after the weights are ascertained and translated into a given number of futures contracts, the number of futures should be rounded to the nearest integer value. It is well-known that an integer programming solution such as a Gomory cutting plane modification to a linear programming model can lead to a better solution than simple rounding. The use of such a procedure, however, requires considerable modification of the model and an extra layer of complexity. In repeated trials of the procedure on several data sets, no economically meaningful improvement is found by using integer programming over simple rounding. Nevertheless, some improvement might be obtained from such a modification for a different data set.

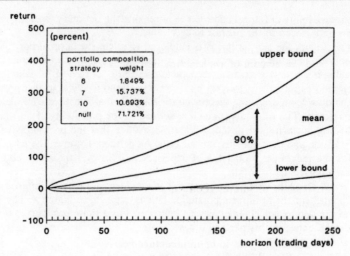

Figure 4
Confidence channel for portfolio B.

leverage, long and short positions, and multiperiod trading horizons. These enhancements make the model applicable in a futures portfolio context and, for this reason, should be of interest to managers of futures funds, managers of other futures portfolios, and managers of portfolios having a futures component. Under certain restrictive assumptions, the model reduces to the familiar Markowitz model.

This article also introduces two equivalent criteria for the selection of an optimal futures portfolio. These are called drawdown criterion and ruin criterion. These optimizing criteria are similar to, but more formally defined and have nicer statistical properties than, optimizing criteria currently employed by many futures fund managers.

In addition to its applicability in solving for the efficient set of futures portfolios, the model, when coupled with the selection criteria, lends itself to a rapid binomial search solution for determining the optimal portfolio weights. By specifying either a maximum acceptable drawdown or a maximum acceptable probability of ruin, an optimal portfolio can be found.

Appendix A

SUMMARY OF NOTATION

$P(i, t)$: the settlement price of the futures underlying strategy i on day t.

$Z(i, t + 1)$: the transaction price for the futures underlying the ith strategy on day $t + 1$ if a transaction has been made; otherwise $Z(i, t + 1) = P(i, t + 1)$.

$R(i, t)$: the return on strategy i for day t.

$\mu(i)$: the mean daily return for strategy i.

$\sigma(i)$: the standard deviation of daily return for strategy i.

$R(c, t)$: the daily return on overnight money on day t.

$\mu(c)$: the mean daily return on invested trading capital.

$\sigma(c)$: the standard deviation of daily return on trading capital.
$\sigma(i, j)$: the covariance of daily returns for strategies i and j.
$\sigma(i, c)$: covariance of daily return for strategy i and trading capital.
$C(t)$: the dollar amount of available trading capital on day t.
$M(i, t)$: the dollar amount of required margin on one futures contract for strategy i.
$S(i)$: the contract size for a specific futures contract (i.e., number of units covered by the contract).
$D(i, t)$: dummy variable representing the side of the market suggested by strategy i on day t. $D(i, t)$ is $+1$ for a long position, -1 for a short position, and 0 if flat.
$L(i, t)$: the leverage multiplier for strategy i on day t.
$N(i, t)$: the number of futures contracts constituting a position in strategy i on day t (for modeling purposes, contracts are assumed infinitely divisible).
$a(t)$: the fraction of trading capital held in interest-bearing form on day t. Remainder assumed to be in nonreturn-bearing cash.
$w(i, t)$: fraction of trading capital committed to strategy i on day t.
$R_p(T)$: the portfolio return for a T-day trading horizon.

Appendix B

SAMPLE OUTPUT FROM EFFICIENT SET MAPPING ALGORITHM (PORTFOLIO A)

	Return and Volatility Analysis (all values are percentages)				
	1-Day	1-Month	3-Months	6-Months	1-Year
Return	0.2117	4.541	14.252	30.53	70.39
Volatility	1.1661	5.580	10.577	17.13	31.75

	Drawdown Analysis (all values are percentages)				
	1-Day	1-Month	3-Months	6-Months	1-Year
LOS 10%	−1.28	−2.67	−2.67	−2.67	−2.67
LOS 5%	−1.69	−4.37	−4.37	−4.37	−4.37
LOS 1%	−2.47	−7.78	−8.55	−8.55	−8.55

		Portfolio Composition (all weights are percentages)			

Strategy Number	Strategy Name	Weight	Strategy Number	Strategy Name	Weight
1	ST01	0.000	7	ST07	7.108
2	ST02	0.000	8	ST08	0.000
3	ST03	0.000	9	ST09	0.000
4	ST04	0.000	10	ST10	4.830
5	ST05	0.000	11	ST11	0.000
6	ST06	0.835	12	Null	87.227

Appendix C

**SAMPLE OUTPUT FROM DRAWDOWN CRITERION
RETURN-MAXIMIZING ALGORITHM**

Return and Volatility Analysis
(all values are percentages)

	1-Day	1-Month	3-Months	6-Months	1-Year
Return	0.4341	9.522	31.372	72.59	197.86
Volatility	2.5818	12.945	27.082	50.85	126.77

Drawdown Analysis
(all values are percentages)

LOS 1%: Maximum drawdown from 1-day to 1-year is 20.00%.

Portfolio Composition
(all weights are percentages)

Strategy Number	Strategy Name	Weight	Strategy Number	Strategy Name	Weight
1	ST01	0.000	7	ST07	15.737
2	ST02	0.000	8	ST08	0.000
3	ST03	0.000	9	ST09	0.000
4	ST04	0.000	10	ST10	10.693
5	ST05	0.000	11	ST11	0.000
6	ST06	1.849	12	Null	71.721

Bibliography

Aitchison, J., and Brown, J. A. (1957): *The Lognormal Distribution.* Cambridge, UK: Cambridge University Press.

Bodie, Z., and Rosansky, V. I. (1980): "Risk and Return in Commodity Futures," *Financial Analysts Journal,* 36:27–39.

Brorsen, B.W., and Irwin, S. H. (1987): "Futures Funds and Price Volatility," *Review of Futures Markets,* 6:118–135.

Brorsen, B.W., and Lukac, L. P. (1990): "Optimal Portfolios for Futures Funds," *The Journal of Futures Markets,* 10:247–258.

Caudill, S. B., and Holcombe, R. G. (1987): "Coefficient Bias Due to Specification Search in Econometric Models, *Atlantic Economic Journal,* 15:30–34.

Denton, F.T. (1985): "Data Mining as an Industry," *Review of Economics and Statistics,* 67:124–127.

Elton, E. J., Gruber, M. J., and Rentzler, J. (1990): "The Performance of Publicly Offered Commodity Funds," *Financial Analysts Journal,* 43:23–30.

Fama, E. F. (1965): "The Behavior of Stock Market Prices," *Journal of Business,* 38:34–105.

Gilster, J.A. (1983): "Capital Market Equilibrium with Divergent Investment Horizon Length Assumptions," *Journal of Financial and Quantitative Analysis,* 18:257–268.

Gressis, N., Philippatos, C., and Hayya, J. (1976): "Multiperiod Portfolio Analysis and the Inefficiency of the Market Portfolio," *Journal of Finance,* 31:1115–1126.

Hall, J. A., Brorsen, B.W., and Irwin, S. H. (1989): "The Distribution of Futures Prices: A Test of the Stable Paretian and Mixture of Normals Hypothesis," *Journal of Finanical and Quantitative Analysis,* 24:105–116.

Irwin, S. H., and Brorsen, B.W. (1985): "Public Futures Funds," *The Journal of Futures Markets,* 5:149–172.

Lloyd, W. P., and Haney, R. L. (1980): "Time Diversification: Surest Route to Lower Risk," *Journal of Portfolio Management,* 6:5–9.

Lukac, L. P., and Brorsen, B.W. (1990): "A Comprehensive Test of Futures Market Disequilibrium," *The Financial Review,* 25:593–622.

Lukac, L. P., Brorsen, B.W., and Irwin, S. H. (1988): "Similarity of Computer-Guided Technical Trading Systems," *The Journal of Futures Markets,* 8:1–14.

Markowitz, H. (1952): "Portfolio Selection," *Journal of Finance,* 7:77–91.

Markowitz, H. (1959): *Portfolio Selection: Diversification of Investments.* New York: Wiley.

Marshall, J. F. (1989): *Futures and Option Contracting: Theory and Practice.* Cincinnati, OH: South-Western.

Marshall, J. F., and Wynne, K. J. (1990): "The Role of the Investment Horizon in the Portfolio Decision." Working paper, Center for Applied Research, Pace University, New York.

Neftci, S. N. (1983): "Some Econometric Problems in Using Daily Futures Price Data." Working paper #55, Center for the Study of Futures Markets, Columbia University, New York.

Tobin, J. (1958): "Liquidity Preference as Behavior Towards Risk, *Review of Economic Studies,* 25:65–85.

Tobin, J. (1965): "The Theory of Portfolio Selection," in *The Theory of Interest Rates,* Hahn, F., and Breechling, F. (eds.). London: Macmillan.

Wolfe, P. (1967): "Methods of Nonlinear Programming," in Abadie, J. (ed.). *Nonlinear Programming.* Amsterdam: North Holland.

Zelney, M. (1982): *Multiple Criteria in Decision Making.* New York: McGraw-Hill.

Part VII
Various Markets

[20]

Orange Juice and Weather

By RICHARD ROLL*

Frozen concentrated orange juice is an unusual commodity. It is concentrated not only hydrologically, but also geographically; more than 98 percent of U.S. production takes place in the central Florida region around Orlando.[1] Weather is a major influence on orange juice production and unlike commodities such as corn and oats, which are produced over wide geographical areas, orange juice output is influenced primarily by the weather at a single location. This suggests that frozen concentrated orange juice is a relatively good candidate for a study of the interaction between prices and a truly exogenous determinant of value, the weather.

The relevant weather for OJ production is easy to measure. It is reported accurately and consistently by a well-organized federal agency, the National Weather Service of the Department of Commerce. Forecasts of weather are provided by the same agency and this makes it possible to assess the predictive ability of OJ futures prices against a rather exacting standard.

Geographic concentration is the most important attribute of orange juice for our empirical purposes, but the commodity also possesses other convenient features. It seems unlikely to be sensitive to *non*weather influences on supply and demand. For example, although the commodity is frozen and not very perishable, only a small amount is carried over in inventory from one year to the next. During 1978, for example, inventory declined to about 20 percent of the year's "pack" of new juice.[2]

Data on short-term variability in demand are nonexistent, but there is little reason to suspect much. Orange juice demand might very well respond to price variation in substitutes such as, say, apple juice; but national income and tastes probably do not fluctuate enough to explain a significant part of the *daily* OJ juice movement[3] (which is substantial, as we shall see).

Short-term variations in supply induced by planting decision must also be quite low because of the nature of the product. Oranges grow on trees that require five to fifteen years

---

*Graduate School of Management, University of California, Los Angeles, CA 90024. I am grateful for discussions with Eugene Fama and Stephen Ross, for comments on an earlier draft by Gordon Alexander, Thomas Copeland, Michael Darby, David Mayers, Huston McCulloch, and Sheridan Titman, for the cooperation of Paul Polger of the National Oceanographic and Atmospheric Administration, and for comments in seminars from the finance faculties of the universities of British Columbia, Alberta, and Illinois. Kathy Gillies provided excellent research assistance. Financial assistance was provided by Allstate, the Center for Research in Financial Markets and Institutions at UCLA and by the Center for the Study of Futures Markets at Columbia.

[1] The proportion produced in Florida is now close to 100 percent. Indeed, the annual publication, *Agricultural Statistics*, by the U.S. Department of Agriculture, no longer gives a breakdown by area, reporting the production only for Florida (presumably because production elsewhere is so small). The last breakdown by area was for 1961 (see *Agricultural Statistics*, 1972, Table 324). In 1961, Florida produced 115,866,000 gallons while California and Arizona combined produced 2,369,000 gallons. It may surprise the reader to know that OJ production for frozen concentrate is mainly a Florida industry; many *table* oranges do come from California. This difference between Florida and California oranges is attributable to differences in their sugar and juice content and in their exteriors. Florida oranges are sweeter and make better-tasting juice. California oranges, being less sweet, have a longer shelf life and they also tend to have less juice but more appealing skins. Apparently, there is not as much substitutability as might have been imagined. Actually, Florida produces the bulk of all oranges for both table and juice. In 1972–73, for example, Florida orange production by weight was about 80 percent of the U.S. total. (See *Florida Agricultural Statistics*, Table 3, p. 4.)

[2] See Tables 380 and 382 of *Agricultural Statistics* (1979, pp. 252 and 254).
[3] A rough indication of exogenous shifts in demand due to income and tastes can be obtained from U.S. consumption of all citrus fruit which has hovered closely around 27 pounds per capita for a number of years (see Table 384, p. 255, *Agricultural Statistics*, 1979).

to mature.[4] Thus, any vagaries in farmers' planting decisions are felt much later and do not impact the current year's crop. There might, however, be short-term effects from farming decisions concerning fertilizer use or harvesting methods. These could be influenced by the prices of fertilizer and energy.

It should be emphasized that even unstable conditions of demand and supply would not eliminate the influence of weather, they would simply make that influence harder to measure empirically. The main argument in favor of studying orange juice instead of other commodities is the geographical concentration of OJ production. The fact that nonweather influences seem unlikely to generate much empirical noise is simply an added benefit.

I. Data

A. Orange Juice Futures

Futures contracts in frozen concentrated orange juice are traded by the Citrus Associates of the New York Cotton Exchange. There are usually nine contracts outstanding with deliveries (expirations) scheduled every second month, January, March, etc., the most distant delivery being 17 to 18 months from the present. A contract is for 15,000 pounds of orange solids standardized by concentration (termed "degrees Brix") and with minimum "scores" for color, flavor, and defects.[5]

Price data[6] are available for each day since the exchange began OJ trading in the early 1970's. However, the weather data are available only for October 1975 through December 1981, so this constitutes the sample period. There were 1,564 trading days during this period.

As is typical of many commodities, trading volume in OJ futures tends to be concentrated in the near-maturity contracts. The open interest of distant contracts, say 8 to 18 months maturity, is often only 10 percent or less of the open interest in nearer contracts, say from 2 to 6 months maturity. Because of well-known problems in price data from thin markets,[7] the fourth and longer maturities were discarded in the following empirical work.

The nearest-maturity contract was also discarded after a close examination of its price behavior around the maturity date. Volume of trading is quite high in the nearest contract until just a few days before expiration. But in the last several days of the contract's life, open interest declines and price volatility increases substantially. A good example of the ensuing econometric problem involved the contract which matured on November 16, 1977. During the last fifteen minutes before expiration, its price rose from $1.30 to $2.20 per pound, an annualized rate of return of about 1.8 *million* percent. Such events would seem to have little to do with the weather.

This leaves us with two contracts having, respectively, between 2 and 4 months and between 4 and 6 months to maturity; an equally weighted average of the daily returns on these two contracts was chosen as the basic OJ return for use in all subsequent analysis. (Using either contract separately gives virtually identical results. This is to be expected because the correlation between their returns is .97.)

On a contract expiration day, the shorter of these two contracts is dropped and a new contract, previously the fourth-from-

---

[4] See John McPhee (1967) for a fascinating and entertaining description of orange tree propagation and of the citrus business in general.

[5] The contract quality is specified as follows: "U.S. Grade A with a Brix value of not less than 51° having a Brix value to acid ratio of not less than 13 to 1 nor more than 19.0 to 1 and a minimum score of 94, with the factor of color and flavor each scoring 37 points or higher, and defects at 19 or better..., provided that [OJ] with a Brix value of more than 66° shall be calculated as having 7.278 pounds of solids per gallon" (*Citrus Futures*, undated). "Degrees Brix" is a term used in honor of a nineteenth-century German scientist, Adolf F. W. Brix (McPhee, p. 129).

[6] The price used here is the "settlement" price. This price (which may or may not reflect an actual transaction) is determined by members of the exchange at the close of each day's trading. It is the price reported in the financial press.

[7] See Myron Scholes and Joseph Williams (1977), Elroy Dimson (1979), Marshall Blume and Robert Stambaugh (1983).

TABLE 1—OJ FUTURES DAILY RETURNS BY DAY OF WEEK AND BY SEASON
OCTOBER 1975–DECEMBER 1981

Day of Week	Mean Returns[a]				
	Winter[b]	Spring	Summer	Autumn	All Seasons
Monday[c]	−.256	−.321	−.107	.0309	−.158
	(2.58)	(1.84)	(1.52)	(1.84)	(1.96)
Tuesday	.224	.269	.199	−.107	.146
	(2.11)	(1.37)	(.147)	(1.48)	(1.62)
Wednesday	.301	.188	−.102	−.169	.0540
	(1.72)	(1.54)	(1.40)	(1.36)	(1.52)
Thursday	.167	−.219	.113	.153	.0518
	(2.14)	(1.16)	(1.21)	(1.35)	(1.51)
Friday	.290	.0227	−.125	.242	.108
	(1.98)	(1.55)	(1.63)	(1.53)	(1.68)
Post-Holiday	−.0554	.311	.278	−.0817	.0102
	(1.78)	(1.72)	(1.25)	(1.37)	(1.52)
All Days	.141	−.00741	−.00079	.0253	.0392
	(2.09)	(1.51)	(1.51)	(1.52)	(1.66)

Notes: Levene's test (see Morton Brown and Alan Forsythe, 1974) for equal variances: $F = 3.59$; tail probability $\cong 0$. Dummy variable regression:

$$R_t = \underset{(1.86)}{.0886} - \underset{(-2.30)}{.247} d_m - \underset{(.328)}{.0784} d_h \qquad R^2 = .00211$$

where d_m is 1 on Monday, 0 otherwise, and d_h is 1 on post-holiday day, zero otherwise.
[a]Average of the second- and third-nearest maturity contracts' returns. The mean returns (standard deviations) of the two contracts separately were .0388(1.70) and .0397(1.65), respectively; their correlation was .969. The returns are shown in percent; standard deviations are shown below in parentheses.
[b]Winter is defined as December, January, February, inclusive. Spring, Summer, and Autumn include, respectively, each subsequent three months.
[c]Monday returns are from settlement price Friday to settlement price Monday. Other days are from settlement on previous day. Post-Holiday returns are from settlement on day before holiday to close on day after holiday.

the-shortest maturity, starts to be used in construction of the return series. The return on the new contract over the expiration date replaces the return on what has become the shortest maturity contract.[8]

[8]Specifically, let $R_{T,t}$ be the continuously compounded return on day t of a contract which matures on calendar date T. Say that contracts mature on days $T = 60, 120, 180, 240, 360$. The return series ($R_t^*$) used here is calculated as follows

$$R_t^* = (R_{120,t} + R_{180,t})/2 \qquad t \leq 60$$

$$R_t^* = (R_{180,t} + R_{240,t})/2 \qquad 120 \geq t > 60$$

$$R_t^* = (R_{240,t} + R_{360,t})/2 \qquad 180 \geq t > 120,$$

and similarly as times goes on and contracts mature.

Table 1 gives information about OJ returns over the sample period. The grand mean return is .0392 percent per day, about 10.3 percent per annum. The rather large volatility of these returns is shown by the fact that the standard error of the mean daily return is $1.66/(1563)^{1/2} = .0420$. The standard error is larger than the mean despite the large sample size.

In the body of the table, means and standard deviations are broken down by season and by day of the week. The seasonal pattern shows a larger mean and larger variability during winter. This might have been anticipated on the grounds that colder temperatures and the risk of freezing make investments in orange juice more hazardous during the winter months. A finer breakdown indicates, however, that the larger winter mean OJ return is due to January alone, perhaps for the same reason that equities of small firms have larger January returns.[9] (Compare Donald Keim, 1983.)

The day-of-the-week results can be compared to recent work on equity returns (Kenneth French, 1980; Michael Gibbons and Patrick Hess, 1981) which found a significantly negative Monday effect. A similar pattern is observed here in the means.[10] Thus, insofar as mean returns are concerned, OJ futures seem to display annual and weekly seasonals similar to equities.

The intraweek pattern of standard deviations is interesting for what it does *not* display. Since Monday's return covers a three-day period, while other days of the week cover only 24 hours, one might have thought that Monday's variance of returns would be approximately three times as large as the other days. Yet the ratio of Monday's to the average of the other days' variances is only about $(1.96/1.58)^2 = 1.54$. Monday's return has too low a variance. (Note that post-holiday returns, which are always for at least two calendar days, also have too low a variance.) Because of this pattern of variances across days, it must be admitted that weather may not be the only relevant factor for OJ returns after all. If weather alone were moving OJ prices, Monday's return volatility should be larger because weather surprises must occur just as readily on a weekend as on any other day. Nevertheless, since no one has yet discovered just what factors *are* causing day-of-the-week patterns, I shall proceed with an examination of weather, which is at least a known factor.

The OJ futures exchange imposes limits on price movements. These limit rules (see Table 2) prevent the price from moving by

---

[9] January's average daily OJ return was .701 percent (standard error = .238) while all other months combined had an average daily return of −.0193 percent (standard error = .0402).

[10] When compared against other days of the week in an analysis of variance, Monday's return is found to be significantly lower (*F*-statistic of 5.20 and tail probability of .0228). Monday's mean return is, however, only marginally significantly negative; the standard error of the mean (of −.158) is .114 percent. The dummy variable regression reported at the bottom of the table shows that the Monday effect is significant but that the explained variance is low.

TABLE 2—LIMIT RULES OF THE CITRUS ASSOCIATES OF THE NEW YORK COTTON EXCHANGE AFTER (BEFORE) JANUARY 1, 1979

General Rule: Prices may move no more than 5 (3) cents per pound, $750 ($450) per contract, above or below the settlement price of the previous market session.
Increased Limit Rule: When three or more contract months have closed at the limit in the same direction for three successive business days, the limit is raised to 8 (5) cents per pound for those contract months. The limit remains at 8 (5) cents until fewer than three contract months close at the limit in the same direction, then the limit reverts to 5 (3) cents on the next business day.
Current Rule for Near Contract: On the last three days before the near contract's expiration, its limit is 10 cents per pound. If that limit is reached during the market session, trading is suspended on *all* contracts for fifteen minutes. Then another 10 cents is added to or deducted from the near contract's limit and trading recommences. Limit moves and fifteen-minute suspensions can be repeated until the market's close. If this happens on the last day before expiration, trading hours are extended.

more than a certain amount from the previous day's settlement price. When a significant event, such as a freeze in Florida, causes the price to move the limit, the settlement price on that day cannot fully reflect all available information. In other words, limit rules cause a type of market information inefficiency (but not a profit opportunity). This might be inconsequential if limit moves occurred rarely; unfortunately, they are rather common. During the October 1975–December 1981 period, one or both of the two contracts being used here moved the price limit on 160 different trading days, slightly over 10 percent of the trading days in the sample. This implies that about 10 percent of the recorded prices in the sample are known in advance not to reflect all relevant available information.

Limit rules might be suspected as the reason why Monday's variance is too low since these rules would be more frequently applied to limit the three-day weekend/Monday return. It turns out, however, that only 40 of the 160 limit moves in the sample occurred on Monday. This frequency is slightly higher than the frequency of 20 percent which would be expected if all five weekday returns

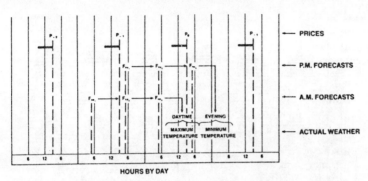

FIGURE 1. TIMING SCHEMATIC OF OJ FUTURES MARKET, WEATHER FORECASTS, AND ACTUAL PERIOD OF WEATHER AT ORLANDO

Note: ▬ indicates market trading hours

covered the same number of hours. The ratio of Monday's return variance to the average variance on the other days is only 1.75 even when all limit move observations are excluded.

B. Central Florida Weather

The U.S. Weather Service reporting station in Orlando issues a variety of different weather bulletins. The most relevant information for oranges involve temperature and rainfall; the data[11] used here consist of daily information on these two variables.

Each 24-hour interval is divided into 12-hour daytime and evening periods. The daytime period begins at 7:00 A.M., eastern standard time, and ends at 7:00 P.M. on the same day. The evening period begins at 7:00 P.M. and ends at 7:00 A.M. the following day. For the daytime period, the weather service reports actual rainfall and the *maximum* temperature, while for the evening period, the rainfall and *minimum* temperature are reported.

Three different forecasts of both rainfall and temperature are also provided. They correspond to periods 36 hours, 24 hours, and 12 hours in advance of the 12-hour period to which the forecast applies. For example, say that the forecast is of the maximum temperature on January 5 (which could occur anytime from 7:00 A.M. until 7:00 P.M.). The first forecast is issued about 5:00 A.M. on January 4. (I call this the 36-hour-ahead forecast because it is developed and issued during the third 12-hour period prior to the 12-hour observation period of the actual maximum temperature.) A second forecast applying to the maximum January 5 temperature is issued at 5:00 P.M. on January 4; then, the third forecast is issued at 5:00 A.M. on January 5. This same cycle, but delayed by 12 hours, is used to issue forecasts of the minimum temperature on January 5 (from 7:00 P.M. January 5 until 7:00 A.M. January 6). Rainfall forecasts for the daytime and evening periods are issued along with the temperature forecasts.

Figure 1 gives a timing schematic of the actual weather, the forecasts of weather, and the trading times of orange juice futures. The symbol p_0 indicates the OJ settlement price on a particular calendar date. Note that p_0 is observed during the 12-hour daytime period, well before the evening period begins, and even before the last forecast of evening weather issued by the weather service. For this reason, we might anticipate that surprises in daytime weather would be

---

[11] The cooperation of Paul Polger of the National Oceanographic and Atmospheric Administration, who provided these data and provided a detailed explanation, is gratefully acknowledged.

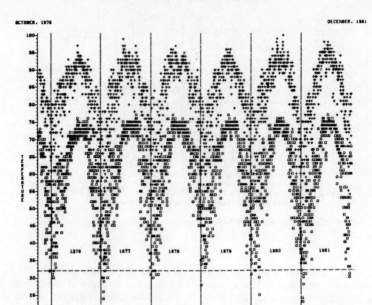

FIGURE 2. MAXIMUM AND MINIMUM DAILY TEMPERATURES AT ORLANDO

associated with price movements of p_{-1} to p_0 while evening weather surprises would influence price changes p_0 to p_{+1}.

The actual daily temperatures are plotted for the sample period in Figure 2 (+ indicates daily maximum and □ indicates minimum). The figure shows that temperatures in central Florida are not only lower during the winter season, they are also more variable. Damage to orange trees occurs if the temperature drops below freezing and stays there for a period of several hours. Thus, the minimum (P.M.) temperature during the winter months would seem to be an important factor influencing the size of the crop and the price of futures.

Table 3 shows that the Weather Service's short-term forecasts of temperature are quite accurate on average and that the forecast improves as its period approaches.[12] The OJ futures market has access to both the 36-hour-ahead and the 24-hour-ahead forecast of that day's P.M. minimum temperature (compare Figure 1). These two forecasts are issued prior to the market's opening. Thus, even aside from whatever private weather forecasts are made by OJ futures traders, two reasonably accurate forecasts of the day's

---

[12]However, there is a curiosity in these forecasts. Note that the A.M. level regressions tend to have slopes

($\hat{b}$) below 1.0. This could be due to errors in the data (rather than in the forecasts). The data were filtered and obvious transcription errors were corrected as detected. Of course, there may still be errors remaining. Errors-in-variables-induced attenuation bias cannot, however, explain why the P.M. forecast intercept is significantly negative. The Theil inequality proportions indicate significant bias in the P.M. forecasts. Note that the low Durbin-Watson statistics on the 36-hour-ahead forecasts are to be expected since there is an intervening actual between this forecast and the actual to which the forecast applies. (See Figure 1.) In other words, the 36-hour-ahead forecast on day t is issued before the forecast error is known for the 36-hour-ahead forecast from day $t-1$. This induces positive dependence in adjacent forecast errors.

TABLE 3—TEMPERATURE FORECAST ACCURACY FOR ORLANDO
OCTOBER 1975–DECEMBER 1981

Hours Forecast is Ahead[a]	Temperature Level				Temperature Change			
	$\hat{a}$ (1)	$\hat{b}$ (2)	R^2 (3)	U^m (4)	$\hat{a}$ (1)	$\hat{b}$ (2)	R^2 (3)	U^m (4)
Maximum (A.M.) Temperature Forecast								
36	4.23	.953	.872	1.15	.357	.832	.604	.777
(2,040)	(6.34)	(118.)	(1.53)	(1.60, 97.3)	(3.34)	(55.7)	(1.81)	(5.82, 93.4)
24	4.60	.951	.896	3.24	.667	.912	.663	2.57
(2,049)	(7.79)	(133.)	(1.81)	(2.16, 94.6)	(6.73)	(63.4)	(1.97)	(1.75, 95.7)
12	4.32	.952	.911	1.90	.511	.984	.708	1.55
(2,048)	(7.96)	(145.)	(1.91)	(2.46, 95.6)	(5.56)	(70.3)	(1.90)	(.061, 98.4)
Minimum (P.M.) Temperature Forecast								
36	−1.48	1.01	.884	6.14	−1.62	.771	.495	6.28
(2,048)	(−2.93)	(125.)	(1.42)	(.035, 93.8)	(−9.24)	(44.8)	(1.64)	(7.49, 86.2)
24	−2.71	1.03	.907	8.88	−1.89	.823	.575	8.86
(2,038)	(−5.92)	(141.)	(1.58)	(.532, 90.6)	(−11.7)	(52.5)	(1.64)	(5.35, 85.8)
12	−.852	1.00	.922	6.23	−1.49	.902	.648	5.92
(2,048)	(−2.11)	(155.)	(1.76)	(0.0, 93.8)	(−10.2)	(61.3)	(1.82)	(2.01, 92.1)

Notes: Regression: Actual = $\hat{a} + \hat{b}$ (forecast). The "actual" is the minimum or maximum temperature observed during a 12-hour period. In the "changes" regression, the dependent variable is the actual percentage change from the previous day's corresponding 12-hour period and the explanatory variable is the predicted percentage change.

Cols. (1),(2): *t*-statistics are shown in parentheses.
Cols. (3): Durbin-Watson statistics are shown in parentheses.
Cols. (4): U^r, U^d are shown in parentheses. The inequality proportions are shown in percent. See Henri Theil (1966, pp. 32–34). U^m = bias, U^r = regression, U^d = disturbance, proportions of mean squared prediction error due to, respectively, bias, deviation of regression slope from 1.0, and residuals.

[a] Sample size is shown in parentheses. There were 2,284 calendar days in the sample. However, the data contain numerous missing observations.

crucial minimum temperature are publicly available during trading hours.

Rainfall is also predicted by the Weather Service, but the form of the forecast is less useful for our purposes than in the case of temperature. The forecast "probability" of rain is always an even decile such as 30 percent and it rarely exceeds 60 percent. Weather service officials have told me that this forecast is intended to convey the chance of *any* measurable precipitation.

Table 4 reports the complete sample distribution of rainfall forecasts and actuals (the latter are provided in categories only). As shown, high forecast probabilities of rain are unusual even though there is measurable rainfall during about 28 percent of the reporting periods. The last column shows that the actual frequency of the rain is not far from the forecast probability. There is not a strong connection between the forecast probability and the *amount* of rain, but the Weather Service forecast is not intended to predict the amount, simply the chance of rain in *any* amount.

As shall be shown in the next section, there is an obvious relation between temperature and the price of OJ futures. The relation between rainfall and price is much more difficult to detect, if it is there at all. Perhaps this is due to temperature being a more important variable for the crop. Perhaps it is due to less useful weather data regarding rainfall.

TABLE 4—FORECAST PROBABILITY OF RAIN VS. ACTUAL RAINFALL BY CATEGORY IN ORLANDO
OCTOBER 1975–DECEMBER 1981

Forecast Probability of Rain[a]	Actual Rainfall (inches)								Total	Frequency of Measurable Precipitation[a]
	0	.001–.009	.01–.120	.121–.25	.251–.50	.501–1.0	1.01–2.0	2.01–3.0	3.01–4.0		
	Frequency (All Forecasts)										
0	3157	79	28	12	3	1	1	0	0	3281	3.78
10	2439	216	100	39	29	14	9	1	0	2847	16.7
20	1401	266	153	51	34	17	11	2	0	1935	27.6
30	904	260	180	83	39	34	17	2	0	1519	40.5
40	420	178	156	68	58	56	35	7	1	979	57.1
50	279	133	177	80	72	59	40	6	5	851	67.2
60	116	70	120	63	48	37	30	0	3	487	76.2
70	18	22	29	22	16	23	7	1	0	138	87.0
80	8	4	6	2	5	12	3	1	0	41	80.5
90	1	1	7	3	0	5	1	0	0	18	94.4
100	0	0	1	0	0	1	1	0	0	3	100.
Total	8743	1229	957	423	304	259	155	20	9	12099	

Note: χ^2 Test of Dependence:

	χ^2	Tail Probability	Forecasts	χ^2	Tail Probability
All Forecasts	4151	$p = 0.0$	36-Hours-Ahead	1185	$p = 0.0$
All A.M. Forecasts	2277	$p = 0.0$	24-Hours-Ahead	1421	$p = 0.0$
All P.M. Forecasts	1559	$p = 0.0$	12-Hours-Ahead	1744	$p = 0.0$

[a]Shown in percent.

II. Empirical Results

A. Temperature

Cold weather is bad for orange production. Orange trees cannot withstand freezing temperatures that last for more than a few hours. Florida occasionally has freezing weather and the history of citrus production in the state has been marked by famous freezes. In 1895, almost every orange tree in Florida was killed to the ground on February 8, production declined by 97 percent, and 16 years passed before it recovered to its previous level.[13] Farmers have since learned how to counter freezes with hardier trees, smudge pots, water spraying,[14] and air circulation by large fans; but although the trees are now more likely to survive a freeze, the crop can be severely damaged. Even a mild freeze will prompt the trees to drop significant amounts of fruit.

Figure 3 illustrates the impact of freezing weather on OJ futures prices during the sample period. The actual minimum temperature at Orlando is plotted along with the OJ price level.[15] Freezing level is indicated by the horizontal dashed line.

During this 6¼-year period, there were 27 recorded freezing temperatures (below 32°) at Orlando out of 2284 calendar days. However, only four periods registered temperatures below 30°. These occurred on January 17–21, 1977, January 2, 1979, March 2, 1980, January 11–13 and 18, 1981. (See Figure 2 also.) Figure 3 shows that these episodes were accompanied by significant price increases. The January freezes in 1977 and 1981 were particularly harsh in that six successive days and three successive nights,

---

[13]McPhee (p. 101).
[14]Spraying trees with water during a freeze can protect them under certain conditions. The water, freezing on the trees' leaves and buds, gives off heat in the process of changing from a liquid to a solid.

[15]Thirty cents has been added to the OJ price in order to keep the plots apart. The price is an average of the second and third shortest-maturity contracts. (See Section I.)

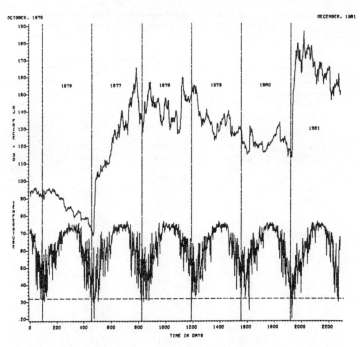

FIGURE 3. OJ FUTURES PRICES AND MINIMUM TEMPERATURES AT ORLANDO

respectively, had freezing temperatures. The most severe freeze during this sample, and the largest accompanying price increase, occurred during the latter period, on January 11, 12, and 13, 1981, when successive daily minimum temperatures were 24°, 23°, and 20°. During the week of January 12-16, OJ futures prices were up the limit on all five trading days.

Market participants realize, of course, that severe freezes are more likely during winter, so the price of OJ futures in the autumn should be high enough to reflect the probability of a freeze during the coming season. Each day thereafter that passes without a freeze should be accompanied by a slight price decline, a relief that winter is one day closer to being over. Also, harvesting of oranges begins in the fall and lasts until early summer, and inventories typically increase over the winter months.

For both of these reasons: freezes that do not occur and inventory build-up; there is a downtrend in futures prices during a typical nonfreeze winter. This pattern can be seen in every year of the sample (Figure 3), except 1977. A general downward movement with small fluctuations is interrupted by occasional sharp price increases sufficient to bring positive returns, on average, to those with long positions.[16] The distribution of returns is very skewed to the right.

If the OJ futures market is an efficient information processor, it should incorporate all publicly available long-term and short-term weather forecasts. Any private forecasts should be incorporated to the extent that traders who are aware of those forecasts are also in command of significant resources. The futures price should, therefore, incorporate the predictable part of weather in advance. Unpredicted weather alone should be

---

[16] An extensive theoretical discussion of this phenomenon is given by Benoit Mandelbrot (1966).

TABLE 5—OJ FUTURES RETURNS AND TEMPERATURE FORECAST ERRORS
WITH AND WITHOUT WEIGHTING, OCTOBER 1975–DECEMBER 1981

Seasons	Hours Forecast is Ahead[a]	Return Lead/Lag (Days)				
		b_{-2}	b_{-1}	b_0	b_{+1}	b_{+2}
Maximum (A.M.) Temperature Forecast						
Unweighted	36	.105	−.00414	−.0463	−.00397	−.322
	(1,391)	(1.31)	(−.0507)	(−.567)	(−.0487)	(−3.91)
Weighted		.102	−.0558	−.0894	−.0600	−.490
		(1.15)	(−.624)	(−1.00)	(−.673)	(−5.37)
Unweighted	24	.0639	−.0497	−.0113	.0379	−.247
	(1,408)	(.872)	(−.673)	(−.154)	(.510)	(−3.36)
Weighted		.0374	−.0615	.0224	.0585	−.379
		(.461)	(−.750)	(.275)	(.714)	(−4.71)
Unweighted	12	.000123	−.0715	−.000467	.0565	−.123
	(1,400)	(.00186)	(−1.07)	(−.00699)	(.838)	(−1.84)
Weighted		−.0851	−.0905	.00691	.0295	−.191
		(−1.17)	(−1.23)	(.0936)	(.398)	(−2.62)
Minimum (P.M.) Temperature Forecast						
Unweighted	36	.0822	−.104	−.154	.136	.0570
	(1,407)	(.632)	(−.791)	(−1.17)	(1.03)	.436
Weighted		.101	−.198	−.379	.133	.0561
		(.664)	(−1.30)	(−2.49)	(.874)	(.374)
Unweighted	24	.0412	−.139	−.352	−.238	−.0404
	(1,399)	(.357)	(−1.20)	(−3.03)	(−2.03)	(−.348)
Weighted		.0593	−.220	−.673	−.544	−.139
		(.442)	(−1.62)	(−4.96)	(−3.99)	(−1.09)
Unweighted	12	−.0698	−.152	−.263	−.0849	.104
	(1,398)	(−.677)	(−1.47)	(−2.52)	(−.807)	(.991)
Weighted		−.0796	−.231	−.549	−.217	.133
		(−.678)	(−1.97)	(−4.62)	(−1.83)	(1.13)

Notes: The regression equation is $\log(A/F)_t = a + b_{-2}R_{t-2} + b_{-1}R_{t-1} + b_0 R_t + b_1 R_{t+1} + b_2 R_{t+2}$, where A is actual temperature, F is forecast temperature and R_t is the return on day t of an equally weighted sum of two futures contracts.

T-statistics are shown in parentheses. All Durbin-Watson statistics were in the range 1.6–1.9. Adjusted R^2s were between 1 and 3 percent.

The weighting scheme is January = 7, February = 6, March = 5, April = 4, May = 3, June = 2, July = 1, August = 2, September = 3, October = 4, November = 5, December = 6.

[a] Sample size is shown in parentheses.

contemporaneously correlated with price movements.

To examine the market's information processing ability, a series of empirical tests were carried out relating surprises in temperature to OJ futures price changes. The temperature forecast error, the percentage difference between the actual temperature and the forecast temperature provided by the National Weather Service, was taken as a measure of surprise. Price change was measured by the average of the daily returns on the second- and the third-shortest maturity contracts (see Section I).

Table 5 presents the first results. The regressions there use the temperature forecast error as the dependent variable. The independent variables are the same day's OJ return plus the returns on two leading and two lagged days. (There is no causality implied or intended by choosing the "dependent" and "independent" variables in this way. Causality actually runs from weather to prices.) Results are given separately in Table 5 for the daily maximum and minimum temperatures, for each of the three available forecasts, and for observations weighted and unweighted by season.

TABLE 6—OJ FUTURES RETURNS AND TEMPERATURE FORECAST ERRORS WITH AGGREGATION OF LIMIT MOVES, OCTOBER 1975–DECEMBER 1981, OBSERVATIONS WEIGHTED BY SEASON

Hours Forecast is Ahead	Return Lag/Lead (Days)				
	b_{-2}	b_{-1}	b_0	b_{+1}	b_{+2}
Maximum (A.M.) Temperature Forecast					
36	.0692	.0671	−.102	.0449	−.0341
(1.257)	(1.46)	(1.25)	(−2.31)	(1.01)	(−.686)
24	.0654	−.00721	−.111	.0234	−.0545
(1.272)	(1.48)	(−.165)	(−2.74)	(.570)	(−1.33)
12	.0518	.0196	−.0121	.0482	−.0368
(1.263)	(1.30)	(.495)	(−.327)	(1.30)	(−.987)
Minimum (P.M.) Temperature Forecast					
36	.0542	−.101	−.236	.167	.0291
(1.272)	(.652)	(−1.23)	(−3.08)	(2.16)	(.377)
24	−.0955	−.00879	−.622	−.0395	−.00346
(1.263)	(−1.32)	(−.122)	(−9.25)	(−.584)	(−.0510)
12	−.00910	.0641	−.143	.0226	.106
(1.262)	(−.138)	(.981)	(−2.37)	(.375)	(1.74)

Notes: For regression and weights, see Table 5. All Durbin-Watson statistics were in the range 1.50–1.95. Adjusted R^2s were between 1 and 4 percent.

Given the preceding discussion, it might seem that the only relevant temperature observations would be for winter evenings (since freezes do not occur at other times); but the futures market deals in anticipations, so forecast errors during the morning hours or even errors during the summer months could conceivably contain meaningful information about the *probability* of a freeze later. The unweighted regressions with A.M. temperature errors do indeed contain some statistical significance. But the P.M. regressions weighted[17] by season are more significant. In the P.M. weighted cases, the contemporaneous OJ return is always statistically significant with the anticipated negative sign.

The P.M. temperature results indicate that the OJ futures price on a given day at the close of trading (2:45 P.M.) is a statistically significant predictor of the forecast *error* of the minimum temperature later that evening (from 7:00 P.M. until 7:00 A.M. the following morning). The price appears to be a slightly better predictor of the error in the forecast issued by the National Weather Service at 5:00 A.M. that same morning than of the errors made by the two other forecasts (5:00 P.M. the previous evening and 5:00 P.M. later the same day).

The futures price is not informationally efficient, however, because several later returns are statistically significant in some regressions. The significant negative coefficient b_{+1} in the P.M. 24-hour ahead case might be consistent with efficiency since trading ceases on day zero before the evening period begins and recommences on day +1 after the evening period ends (see Figure 1). However, the significant two-day later negative coefficients (b_{+2}) for the A.M. temperatures cannot be so easily dismissed.

There is ample a priori reason to suspect some effective informational inefficiency induced by limit move rules. There were 160 limit moves during the sample and prices on these days cannot reflect all information (see Section I). In a first attempt to eliminate this source of inefficiency, limit moves were "aggregated." The results are given in Table 6. For data used in this table, if a particular day registered a limit price move, the "eco-

---

[17] The weighting scheme is rather arbitrary but is was the only one I tried. January observations, in the middle of winter, receive the highest weight; July observations, in the middle of summer, receive the lowest. January observations are weighted seven times more heavily than July observations, intervening months are weighted linearly between January and July; i.e., February = 6, March = 5,...June = 2,...December = 6.

nomic" closing price for that day was assumed to be the price on the next subsequent day which did not have a limit move.

On Tuesday, January 6, 1976, for example, the March contract closed at 59.75 cents per pound. The next day registered a limit move of 3 cents; the reported closing price was 62.75 cents. On Thursday (January 8), which was not a limit move day, the settlement price was 64.4 cents. This was taken as an estimate of what the price would have been the preceding day (January 7) if the exchange had imposed no limits. Thus, the daily return for January 7 used in the regression was $\log_e(64.4/59.75) = 7.5$ percent. There was no observation used for January 8.

Limit moves often occur one after another. In such cases, the price on the first day with no limit move was brought back to the day of the first limit move and all intervening days were discarded.[18]

This procedure obviously overestimates the ability of the market to predict temperatures. Hindsight was used in that no one could know for sure on the first limit move day how many additional days with limit moves would follow. Thus, the results in Table 6 are biased in favor of finding market efficiency, as opposed to those in Table 5 that are biased against finding efficiency because of the exchange's own rules.

In Table 6, there is no longer a significant negative relation of temperature forecast error and later OJ returns. This indicates that the statistical significance of the lagging coefficients found in Table 5 was indeed due to the exchange's limit rules and not to some other possible source of informational inefficiency.[19] Notice that five of the six contemporaneous coefficients are significant and negative.[20]

To estimate the predictive content of OJ prices without resorting to hindsight, while at the same time including the extra information known to market participants that particular days had limit moves, the regressions in Table 7 were computed. A contemporaneous return and a lagged daily return were included as predictors along with slope dummies for limit move days.

Slope dummies are more appropriate than intercept dummies because the size of a limit move changed during the sample period (see Table 2).[21] Before January 1, 1979, the limit was 3 cents while it was 5 cents thereafter. As a consequence, only 39 out of 160 limit move days occurred during 1979–81 even though almost one-half of the sample observations were in those years. Thus, during 1979–81, the settlement price was more informationally efficient and the news that a particular day displayed a limit move constituted more material information. Slope dummies may not perfectly capture the greater importance of limit moves in the last three years of the sample, but at least they do weight these observations more heavily (by approximately 67 percent).

The F-statistics for these regressions indicate that the A.M. forecast errors cannot be

---

[18] If an up limit was followed by a down limit (or vice versa), day 1 was treated as if the return were zero and day 2 was discarded. The next included observation was then for day 3 (if it was not a limit move). In other words, for any sequence of limit moves followed immediately by another sequence in the opposite direction, the first closing price after reversal was brought back to the first day of the initial sequence. Then the price on the first day with no limit move is brought back to the first day of the second sequence.

[19] The one anomalous coefficient, b_{+1} in the 36-hour P.M. regression, has a positive sign. A single "significant" coefficient such as this is to be expected by chance among so many possibilities.

[20] The reader may notice that the number of observations differs by only one, 1263 to 1262, between the P.M. 24- and 12-hour regressions; yet the t-statistics on the contemporaneous returns are -9.25 and -2.37. Could this be caused by a single observation out of more than 1200? The answer is no. There are actually 138 observations that differed in these two regressions (due to missing data), but almost exactly one-half were missing from each regression. (There were other *common* missing observations.)

[21] Also, a slope dummy preserves the sign of the price change. This could be done, too, with intercept dummies, for example, using $+1$, 0, and -1 for up limit, normal, and down limit, but the slope dummy accomplishes this feat automatically while allowing for the nonstationarity in the size of a limit move.

TABLE 7—PREDICTIVE MODEL OF TEMPERATURE FORECAST ERRORS USING SLOPE DUMMY VARIABLES FOR LIMIT MOVE DAYS OCTOBER 1975–DECEMBER 1981, WEIGHTING BY SEASONS

Hours Forecast is Ahead	Contemporaneous		Lagged One Day		
	b_0	d_0	b_{-1}	d_{-1}	F^a
Maximum (A.M.) Temperature Forecast					
36	−.0636	−.0839	.0750	−.348	2.80
(1,391)	(−.495)	(−.475)	(.580)	(−1.91)	
24	.0992	−.213	−.0989	.0422	.897
(1,408)	(.835)	(−1.34)	(−.845)	(.254)	
12	.0198	−.0581	−.0807	−.0859	1.16
(1,400)	(.186)	(−.386)	(−.766)	(−.576)	
Minimum (P.M.) Temperature Forecast					
36	−.672	−.418	.0282	−.276	2.71
(1,407)	(−.329)	(−1.39)	(.131)	(−.898)	
24	.119	−1.55	.184	−.588	23.9
(1,399)	(.616)	(−5.82)	(.961)	(−2.17)	
12	−.119	−.643	.217	−.781	14.7
(1,398)	(−.697)	(−2.78)	(1.30)	(−3.32)	

Notes: The regression equation is $\log(A/F)_t = a + b_0 R_t + d_0 \delta_t R_t + b_{-1} R_{t-1} + d_{-1} \delta_{t-1} R_{t-1}$, where A is actual temperature, F is forecast temperature, R_t is return on day t, $\delta_t = 1$ if there was a limit move on day t and zero otherwise.

See weighting scheme in Table 5.

T-statistics are shown in parentheses. Durbin-Watsons were in the range 1.59 to 1.99. Adjusted R^2s were in the range .0018 to .038.

[a] F-statistics for the regressors having no effect. The 95 percent fractile is approximately 5.6.

predicted by the current and lagged OJ returns plus a limit move slope dummy. This is also true for the P.M. 36-hour ahead forecasts. However, both the 24- and 12-hour ahead forecast errors can be improved by prior OJ returns.

The lack of predictive content of A.M. temperatures is, perhaps, not all that surprising because A.M. temperatures are relevant only to the extent that they predict freezes that evening. Apparently, this link is too weak to be picked up with statistical reliability by OJ returns.

The low predictive content for P.M. temperatures may be a disappointment until one reflects upon the scope of *possible* predictive ability. As shown in Table 3, about 90 percent of the variability in temperature is removed by the National Weather Service's forecast. The OJ prices predict a very small but still significant part of the remaining 10 percent.[22]

[22] It should be noted that all of the contemporaneous slope dummies (d_0) have negative signs. Also, the differences between the last two regressions in the table are intriguing but puzzling. The lagged slope dummy (d_{-1}) is more important for the 12-hour forecast error than for the 24-hour forecast error. Could this be related to the fact that the 12-hour forecast is not issued until after the market closes, while the 24-hour forecast is issued before it opens?

B. *Rainfall*

Orange juice prices are replotted in Figure 4 along with the day's total rainfall[23] (in tenths of inches) at Orlando. Unlike the earlier plot of price and temperature (Figure 3), no relation between the two series in Figure 4 is apparent to the naked eye.

The effect of rainfall on the crop is much less obvious than the effect of temperature. Most of the groves in Florida are not irrigated, so a long dry spell might be damag-

[23] Rainfall data are available only in the categories shown in Table 4. To construct Figure 4, the midpoint of each category was used as an estimate of the actual rainfall in inches. The A.M. and P.M. figures were added to obtain the total precipitation for the day.

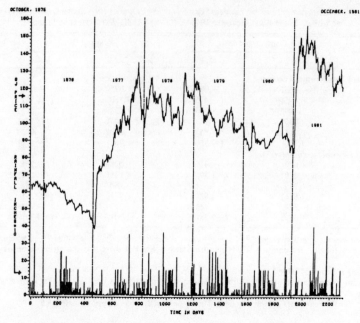

FIGURE 4. OJ FUTURES PRICES AND DAILY RAINFALL AT ORLANDO

ing. On the other hand, the crop could be reduced by extremely heavy rain or by wind damage from tropical storms (that appear in the rainfall time series because they also drop a lot of water).

For example, on November 6, 1981, the *Wall Street Journal* reported higher orange juice prices "...on news of a hurricane off the Florida coast," and on February 18, 1983, prices were purportedly higher due to "...talk of heavy rain." Some confusion about the effect of rainfall is disclosed in the latter story; it included a statement from the Florida Citrus Commission that the orange crop was "unscathed" by the rain. " 'Our oranges are enjoying the weather,' said a department spokesman, 'oranges need a lot of moisture.' " A commodities "analyst" stated that OJ traders drove up prices because they were confused by reports of rain damage to strawberries and tomatoes!

Whether or not the futures market understands the effect of rainfall is rather moot if the empiricist does not understand it well enough to develop a measure of rainfall surprise. With this admission in mind, let us plunge ahead into this turbid subject.

As shown previously in Section II (Table 4), National Weather Service rainfall forecasts are statistically significant but imperfect predictors of actual precipitation. I experimented with several different models of rainfall forecasts (including "probit" and logarithmic models), in order to find the most reliable predictor. It turned out that the largest reduction in variance was obtained with the simplest of regression models,

$$A_t = a + bF_t,$$

where $A_t = 1, \ldots, 9$ is the actual rainfall by category on day t and F_t is the forecast "probability of rain." The adjusted R^2 of this regression ranged between .118 and .332 (see Table 8). It is interesting to note that predictive ability for rainfall rises more rapidly as the prediction period approaches than it does in the case of temperature (compare Table 3).

Table 8 contains F-statistics from regressions relating the rainfall forecast error to

TABLE 8—PREDICTIVE MODEL OF RAINFALL FORECAST ERRORS USING SLOPE DUMMY VARIABLES FOR LIMIT MOVE DAYS OCTOBER 1975–DECEMBER 1981, NO WEIGHTING

Hours Forecast is Ahead	Adjusted R^2 of Weather Service Forecast[a]	F-Statistic of OJ Return Predictive Power[b,c]
A.M. Rainfall		
36	.239	.362
(1,371)		
24	.265	.410
(1,393)		
12	.332	.417
(1,372)		
P.M. Rainfall		
36	.118	.388
(1,393)		
24	.165	.230
(1,374)		
12	.225	.629
(1,384)		

[a] Actual rainfall A_t, by category, ($A_t = 1, 2, \ldots 9$), was predicted by the Weather Service's "probability of rain," F_t, in the simple regression model $A_t = \hat{a} + \hat{b}F_t + \varepsilon_t$; the forecast error ε_t was then used as the dependent variable in another regression model with OJ returns as predictors (see fn. c below).
[b] The 95 percent fractile of the F-statistic is approximately 5.6.
[c] The regression model was $\varepsilon_t = a + b_0 R_t + d_0 \delta_t R_t + b_{-1} R_{t-1} + d_{-1} \delta_{t-1} R_{t-1}$, where ε_t is the Weather Service's rainfall prediction error, R_t is the OJ return on day t and δ_t is +1 if day t had a limit move, otherwise zero. No coefficient was significant and coefficients are not reported for reasons of space.

the contemporaneous and lagged OJ return plus a slope dummy for limit moves, that is, the same purely predictive model as the one for temperature in Table 7. As might have been anticipated in light of the preceding discussion, OJ returns appear to have no significant predictive power for rainfall.[24] There was not a single significant coefficient

[24] A similar model was computed with a dependent variable defined as the *absolute value* of the rainfall forecast's prediction error. Of course, this would not be a legitimate model from an efficient markets perspective since it would not imply predictive ability of the direction of error (even if it had worked). It is, however, suggested by the possibility that either too much or too little rain is bad for the orange crop. As it turned out, the model had even lower explained variance than the model in Table 8 which preserved the sign of the rainfall prediction error.

out of the 24 possible and no F-statistic is significant in any of the six regressions.

C. *Nonweather Influences on OJ Prices*

The small predictive power for temperature and rainfall seems to imply that influences other than weather are affecting OJ returns. What might they be? In an attempt to find out, news stories in the financial press were systematically examined.

From October 1, 1975 through December 31, 1981 (the sample period of the paper), a total of 91 articles related to oranges appeared in the *Wall Street Journal*; 26 articles reported either results of weather (17) or forecasts of weather (9). Of the 26 weather articles, 25 concerned temperature and 1 concerned rainfall. There were 22 articles disclosing crop forecasts by the U.S. Department of Agriculture, 15 articles reporting price movements with no explanation, 7 articles about international conditions (Canadian and Japanese imports and Brazilian exports), 6 articles about supermarket supplies, and 15 miscellaneous articles. In this last category, the subjects ranged from product quality (4) and new products (1) through antitrust action against the Sunkist cooperative in California (3), to such truly unclassifiable stories as orange rustlers in Florida and advertising contracts with Anita Bryant.

The number and content of weather stories shows that weather is considered important and that rainfall is a relatively minor factor compared to temperature. Among the other topics, *ex post* stories about futures price movements per se and most of the miscellaneous stories could not possibly have been about true influences on earlier OJ price variation. Agricultural crop forecasts, though, would seem likely to have moved prices in some direction. Perhaps international news, reports of supermarket supplies, and antitrust actions are also relevant. The variability of returns was computed for periods ending on the *Wall Street Journal* publication date of such articles and including two prior trading days (to allow for news leakage). This variability is compared in Table 9 to the variability of returns on dates with no orange juice news.

TABLE 9—VARIABILITY OF OJ FUTURES RETURNS ON DAYS WITH NEWS ABOUT
ORANGE JUICE IN THE WALL STREET JOURNAL, OCTOBER 1975–DECEMBER 1981

	No News (1)	Weather (2)	Crop Forecast (3)	Supplies, Antitrust, International (4)	Miscellaneous (5)
Standard Deviation of Returns	1.53 (1361)	2.86 (64)	2.01 (60)	1.97 (34)	1.37 (34)

	Comparisons Among	F-Statistic	Tail Probability
Levene's Test for Equal Variances[a]	Cols. (1)–(5)	22.5	0.0000
	Cols. (1), (3), (4), (5)	9.83	.0018
	Cols. (2), (3), (4).	8.99	.0033

Notes: Standard deviation of returns are shown in percent per day, with sample size shown in parentheses; returns on an equally weighted index of the second and third from the shortest maturity contracts on the day of the news story and on the two preceding trading days.

Sample sizes are smaller than the number of possible days because of overlapping dates among articles. For overlapping dates, returns were assigned hierarchically to category (2) (Weather) first, then to categories (3), (4), and (5), respectively.

[a] See Brown and Forsythe.

The miscellaneous category has a low volatility. It is even lower than the variability of returns on days with no news stories. Volatility of returns is highest during periods when stories about weather were published. During periods associated with stories about crop forecasts, retail supplies, antitrust actions, and international events, volatility is higher than during "no news" periods. However, it is significantly *lower* than during periods with weather-related news stories.

From this evidence, weather remains as the most important identifiable factor influencing OJ returns. Crop forecasts and other newsworthy events have an influence, but their frequency is too small and their impact too slight to explain a material part of the variability in returns left unexplained by weather. As Table 9 shows, there is substantial volatility (a daily standard deviation of returns of 1.53 percent per day), on days that are not associated with *any* story about oranges in the *Wall Street Journal*; and these days constitute about 87 percent of the sample observations.

In addition to events important enough to appear in special orange juice stories in the financial press, other influences on supply and demand might be directly measurable. For instance, stock market returns could measure general economic activity and thus provide a proxy for consumer demand. Canada is the largest customer for U.S. orange juice, so the Canadian dollar/U.S. dollar exchange rate might have a measurable impact on orange juice because it would proxy for Canadian demand. Energy prices could affect short-term supply because they influence the cost of operating farm equipment and the costs of processing and distributing the product. Petroleum is also a direct ingredient of fertilizer and a major component of fertilizer production costs.

Table 10 offers evidence about the influence of these and other variables on OJ price movements. Two regressions were computed. The first involves the OJ return as dependent variable. It shows that cold temperatures indeed cause OJ price movements, but general stock market returns, changes in the Canadian dollar exchange rate, and oil stock returns (a measure of energy prices), have no significant influence.

The second regression in Table 10 uses the squared OJ return as dependent variable. This was done because the objective here is merely to identify sources of price movements in either direction, as opposed to test-

TABLE 10—T-STATISTICS OF EXPLANATORY FACTORS FOR OJ RETURNS, NO CONSIDERATION OF LIMIT MOVES, DAILY DATA, OCTOBER 1975–DECEMBER 1981

	Dependent Variable	
Explanatory Variable	OJ Return	Squared OJ Return
Max $(32 - T_{-1}, 0)^a$	5.40	7.99
Max $(32 - T_{-0}, 0)$	3.69	8.09
(Oil Stock Return)$_{-1}$^{b}	−.618	.385^g
(Oil Stock Return)$_0$	.624	2.11^g
(VW Market Return)$_{-1}$^{c}	.525	−1.05^g
(VW Market Return)$_0$	−.120	−1.53^g
(Δ CDN exch. Rate)$_{-1}$^{d}	−.417	−.759^g
(Δ CDN exch. Rate)$_0$	.577	.938^g
Monday^e	−2.18	4.23
Weather-Related News Story^f	–	9.36
Crop Forecast News Story^f	–	3.35
Supplies or Int'l News Story^f	–	−.563
Miscellaneous News Story^f	–	−1.47
Multiple Adjusted R^2	.0668	.268
F-Statistic for Regression	13.4	45.0
Durbin-Watson	1.81	1.39
Number of Observations	1,559	1,559

$^a T_t$ is the minimum temperature at Orlando on day t.
^{b} Return on an equally weighted portfolio of oil stocks listed on the NYSE and the AMEX, consisting of up to 45 firms. The sample consisted of all listed oil firms covered in the 1982 *Value Line* service.
^{c} Value-weighted index of all NYSE and AMEX stocks.
^{d} Percentage change in the Canadian/U.S. dollar exchange rate.
^{e} Dummy variable; 1 if Monday, 0 otherwise.
^{f} Dummy variable; 1 if news story in this category in the *Wall Street Journal* on day t or $t+1$, zero otherwise.
$^g T$-statistic for the squared explanatory variable.

ing the direction of influence of particular variables. Using the squared return permits the inclusion of dummy variables on news story dates without having to decide whether the story should be associated with a positive or negative price change. To illustrate the problem, take the case of crop forecast stories. It would be very hard to know whether a particular forecast by the Department of Agriculture is above or below the previously expected production level without looking at the OJ price movement itself.

In this second regression, cold weather remains very significant and stories related to weather and to crop forecasts are significant as well (the latter result confirms the implications drawn from Table 9). The contemporaneous squared oil stock return is also significant, though its t-statistic indicates a much lower level of influence. (This is something of a curiosity in that oil stock returns are unrelated in direction to OJ returns in the first regression.) Finally, notice that only 27 percent of the variability in squared OJ returns is explained by all of these variables combined. Most of the variability remains unexplained.[25]

D. *Supply Shocks vs. Demand Shocks*

Variability in OJ prices could be caused by shifts in demand induced by changes in the prices of substitute products. The prices of apple juice, tomato juice, and soft drinks, inter alia, should influence the demand for orange juice. We have seen already in Table 10 that general consumer demand and the demand of the largest foreign customer (Canada) are not important relative to the supply shocks of weather, energy prices, and crop forecasts. Table 11 provides information about the relative importance of more micro demand shocks.

For firms in the orange juice business and for certain firms producing substitutes, daily stock returns were related, firm by firm, to OJ returns. In each case, the firm's return was regressed on the contemporaneous OJ return, plus two leading and two lagged OJ returns, plus slope dummies for limit move days on the OJ exchange. The F-statistics of the regression were examined for significance. In cases where significance was indicated, the coefficients were examined for direction of comovement between equity and OJ returns.

Two basic types of firms were examined. The first type consists of firms whose SIC (standard industrial classification) code on the CRSP tape indicated that it was in some aspect of the orange juice or a related food-processing business. (It had the same SIC

---

[25] These regressions are obviously misspecified (for example, notice the Durbin-Watson statistics in the second regression). However, they are intended merely to characterize the data, not to test any particular theory, so it seems doubtful that much can be learned by using more sophisticated econometric methods.

TABLE 11—RETURNS ON AGRICULTURE RELATED EQUITIES AND RETURNS ON ORANGE JUICE FUTURES[a]

Company[b]	Line of Business	Relation to OJ Returns[c]
American Agronomics	Owns 9200 acres of Fl. citrus; Produces and markets OJ	None (+)
CHB Foods	Produces and markets pet food, fish, vegetables and fruit	None
Castle & Cooke	Produces and markets pineapples, bananas, fish, broccoli, sugar; Owns Hawaii land	Positive
Consolidated Foods	Manufactures and distributes coffee, candy, sugar, soft drinks	Positive
Curtice-Burns	Processes and packs fruits and vegetables, soft drinks, Mexican food, frozen vegetables	None
Del Monte[d]	Produces fresh bananas and pineapples; processes seafood	None
Di Giorgio	Diversified food processor including citrus, Italian food, sells OJ in Europe; Has some Fl. land	None
Green Giant[d]	Produces canned and frozen vegetables	None
Norton Simon	Produces tomato-based food products, popcorn, cooking oil, liquor	None (−)
Orange-Co. Inc.	Owns 8100 acres of Fl. citrus; Produces and markets OJ	None
J. M. Smucker	Produces jellies, condiments, syrups, and canned fruit drinks	None (−)
Stokeley Van Camp	Produces Gatorade and canned and frozen vegetables	None
Tropicana[d]	Processes citrus juice; Owns a few Fl. groves which are experimental plantings	Negative
United Foods	Produces frozen vegetables	None

[a] Equities with the standard industrial classification of food manufacturers and processors with the same four-digit SIC codes as Di Giorgio, Orange-Co. or Tropicana, and with at least 100 daily return observations in the period October 1975–December 1981.
[b] In addition to these companies, regressions were also run with soft drink equities, Coca-Cola, Dr. Pepper, MEI, Pepsi Cola, and Royal Crown. None of these regressions were significant.
[c] "Positive" or "Negative" indicates that the regression's F-statistic was significant at the 5 percent level. The regression's dependent variable is the equity's return and independent variables are two leading, contemporaneous, and two lagged orange juice futures returns plus corresponding slope dummies for limit moves. A symbol in parentheses indicates a marginally significant regression (at the 10 percent level).
[d] Companies no longer listed on the New York or American Exchange.

code as Di Giorgio, Tropicana, or Orange-Co., three companies known in advance to be in the orange juice business.) All such companies are listed by name in Table 11.

The second type of company produced soft drinks (see Table 11, fn. b). No soft drink producer had a significant relation to orange juice. So changes in OJ demand due to changes in soft drink prices are not revealed in the data.[26]

Turning back to the first type of firm, Table 11 indicates that many were not related to OJ prices. This was true even for such companies as Orange-Co., whose principal business is growing oranges and producing juice. There are several possible explanations for the lack of significant comovement in such a firm. First, consider the impact of supply shocks: an increase in OJ prices due to, say, cold weather, would not affect the firm if the gain in the value of its Florida land were offset by a reduction in the value of its processing and distribution divisions, or if the firm had hedged its own supply by selling OJ futures.

A demand shock, however, should affect the firm unequivocally unless it overhedged in the futures market. For example, an exogenous increase in OJ demand raises the value of its land and, if there are fixed costs, also raises the value of its production and distribution facilities. Thus, the lack of significant comovement between OJ prices and firms such as Orange-Co., Di Giorgio, and Amer-

[26] One of these companies, Coca-Cola, also produces orange juice, so a lack of comovement due to shifts in prices of orange juice substitutes might be expected for this particular firm; roughly, what it gains in the soft drink business might be lost in the orange juice business, or vice versa.

ican Agronomics, who grow *and* process juice, suggests that most of the OJ price volatility is due to supply shocks instead of demand shocks.

This is reinforced by the case of Tropicana, a processor owning virtually no land. It is the only such firm and also the only firm whose equity comoves negatively and significantly with OJ prices. It is conceivable, of course, that this negative relation is induced by a combination of demand shocks and Tropicana purchasing too many futures contracts (more than its own anticipated requirements), but it seems more plausible that the relation is induced directly by supply shocks that squeeze Tropicana's profit margin.

Two companies, Castle & Cooke and Consolidated Foods, produce OJ substitutes and have positive comovement with OJ prices (as is expected if OJ prices move because of supply shocks). One firm, Smucker, buys oranges for jam and has a marginally negative comovement (also explainable by OJ supply shocks). The only anomalous firm is Norton Simon, a producer of substitutes such as tomato juice and liquor (but its negative comovement is of only marginal significance). Some wits have suggested that Norton-Simon actually produces a complement, not a substitute, product. Vodka, one of its biggest sellers, is often consumed with orange juice.

Overall, the evidence in Table 11 supports the view that supply shocks are the principal cause of OJ price movements. Unfortunately, the identity of such shocks remains at least a partial mystery. Weather is important, but measured weather explains only a small fraction of the volatility in OJ prices.

III. Summary and Conclusion

The market price of frozen concentrated orange juice is affected by the weather, particularly by cold temperatures. A statistically significant relation was found between OJ returns and subsequent errors in temperature forecasts issued by the National Weather Service for the central Florida region where most juice oranges are grown. Orange juice prices are much less related to errors in rainfall prediction. Indeed, no significant statistical association was found between these variables.

The OJ futures price is rendered informationally inefficient by the existence of exchange-imposed limits on price movements. This inefficiency manifests itself in the data by allowing temperature surprises to have apparent predictive power for *later* price changes. When limit moves are taken into account, however, temperature has no remaining predictive content.

There is, nevertheless, a puzzle in the OJ futures market. Even though weather is the most obvious and significant influence on the orange crop, weather surprises explain only a small fraction of the observed variability in futures prices. The importance of weather is confirmed by the fact that it is the most frequent topic of stories concerning oranges in the financial press and by the ancillary fact that other topics are associated with even less price variability than is weather.

Possible sources of orange juice demand and supply movements such as substitute product prices, general demand, export demand, and production costs were also examined here. Yet *no* factor was identified that can explain more than a small part of the daily price movement in orange juice futures. There is a large amount of inexplicable price volatility.

REFERENCES

Blume, Marshall, E., and Stambaugh, Robert F., "Biases in Computed Returns: An Application to the Size Effect," *Journal of Financial Economics*, November 1983, *12*, 387–404.

Brown, Morton B. and Forsythe, Alan B., "Robust Tests for the Equality of Variances," *Journal of the American Statistical Association*, June 1974, *69*, 364–67.

Dimson, Elroy, "Risk Measurement When Shares are Subject to Infrequent Trading," *Journal of Financial Economics*, June 1979, *7*, 197–226.

French, Kenneth R., "Stock Returns and the Weekend Effect," *Journal of Financial Economics*, March 1980, *8*, 55–69.

Gibbons, Michael R. and Hess, Patrick, "Day of the Week Effects and Asset Returns,"

Journal of Business, October 1981, *54*, 579–96.

Hopkins, James T., *Fifty Years of Citrus: The Florida Citrus Exchange: 1909–1959*, Gainesville: University of Florida Press, 1960.

Keim, Donald B., "Size Related Anomalies and Stock Return Seasonality: Further Empirical Evidence," *Journal of Financial Economics*, June 1983, *12*, 13–32.

Mandelbrot, Benoit, "Forecasts of Future Prices, Unbiased Markets, and 'Martingale' Models," *Journal of Business*, January 1966, *39*, 242–55.

McPhee, John, *Oranges*, New York: Farrar, Straus, and Giroux, 1967.

Scholes, Myron and Williams, Joseph, "Estimating Betas from Nonsynchronous Data," *Journal of Financial Economics*, December 1977, *5*, 309–27.

Theil, Henri, *Applied Economic Forecasting*, Amsterdam: North-Holland, 1966.

Citrus Associates of the New York Cotton Exchange, *Citrus Futures*, Four World Trade Center, NY 10048, undated.

Florida Department of Agriculture, *Florida Agricultural Statistics Summary*, Tallahassee: Florida Department of Agriculture, various years.

U.S. Department of Agriculture, *Agricultural Statistics*, Washington: USGPO, various years.

Business Cycles and the Behavior of Metals Prices

EUGENE F. FAMA and KENNETH R. FRENCH*

ABSTRACT

The theory of storage says that the marginal convenience yield on inventory falls at a decreasing rate as inventory increases. The authors test this hypothesis by examining the relative variation of spot and futures prices for metals. As the hypothesis implies, futures prices are less variable than spot prices when inventory is low, but spot and futures prices have similar variability when inventory is high. The theory of storage also explains inversions of "normal" futures-spot price relations around business-cycle peaks. Positive demand shocks around peaks reduce metal inventories and, as the theory predicts, generate large convenience yields and price inversions.

THE THEORY OF STORAGE of Brennan [2], Telser [6], and Working [7] is the dominant model of commodity forward and futures prices. Following Brennan and Telser, many tests of the theory use inventory data to test the hypothesis that the marginal convenience yield on inventory falls at a decreasing rate as aggregate inventory increases. Inventory data are always a problem in this approach. It is usually unclear how aggregate inventory should be defined. For example, how should one treat government stocks? Moreover, like the metals we study, many commodities are produced, consumed, and traded internationally, and the accuracy of aggregate inventory data is questionable.

Our tests of the theory of storage are also based on the hypothesis that the marginal convenience yield declines at higher inventory levels but at a decreasing rate. Rather than test the hypothesis by examining the inventory-convenience yield relation directly, however, we test its implications about the relative variation of spot and futures prices. These implications can be viewed as refinements of Samuelson's [5] much-tested proposition that futures prices vary less than spot prices and that the variation of futures prices is a decreasing function of maturity.

Thus, the theory of storage leads us to predict that futures prices are less variable than spot prices (the Samuelson hypothesis holds) when inventory is low. When inventory is high, however, the theory predicts that spot and futures prices have roughly the same variability. Using a simple proxy for the level of inventory, our tests on the industrial metals, aluminum, copper, lead, tin, and zinc, consistently support our refinement of the Samuelson proposition. The results are in contrast to the evidence on the simple version of the Samuelson hypothesis, which is often inconclusive. See Anderson [1] and the references therein.

* Both authors from Graduate School of Business, University of Chicago. The comments of M. Hartzmark, a referee, and workshop participants at the University of Chicago, the University of Michigan, and the University of Utah are gratefully acknowledged. This research is supported by the National Science Foundation (Fama) and the Center for Research in Security Prices (French).

The theory of storage and the concept of a declining marginal convenience yield on inventory were developed to explain the seasonal behavior of spot and futures prices for agricultural commodities—in particular, futures prices that are below spot prices before harvests, when inventories are low and the marginal convenience yield on inventory is high. Metal inventories and prices are not affected by such seasonals, but they are affected by general business conditions, at least during the 1972 to 1983 sample period. Our evidence suggests that metal production does not adjust quickly to positive demand shocks around business-cycle peaks. As a consequence, inventories fall, forward prices are below spot prices, and spot prices are more variable than forward prices around business-cycle peaks, all in the manner predicted by the theory of storage. The success of the theory in describing metals prices over the business cycles in our sample is interesting because the predicted price behavior is generated by general business conditions rather than by the harvest seasonals that motivated the development of the theory.

Our data include the dramatic swing in the price of silver and the inversion of "normal" futures-spot price relations in 1979 and 1980, which many view as evidence of a squeeze in silver markets. We offer an alternative to the squeeze hypothesis, suggested by the similar behavior of other metals prices during the same period. In particular, the large price swing and the inversion of futures-spot price relations for silver may just reflect the workings of the theory of storage over the business cycle.

I. The Relation between Forward and Spot Prices: Theory

Let $F(t, T)$ be the forward (or futures) price at time t for delivery of a commodity at T. Let $S(t)$ be the spot price. The theory of storage says that the return from purchasing the commodity at t and selling it for delivery at T, $F(t, T) - S(t)$, equals the interest foregone during storage, $S(t)R(t, T)$, plus the marginal warehousing cost, $W(t, T)$, minus the marginal convenience yield, $C(t, T)$:

$$F(t, T) - S(t) = S(t)R(t, T) + W(t, T) - C(t, T). \quad (1)$$

The intuition of the convenience yield is that an uncompensated carrying cost—a futures price that does not exceed the spot price by enough to cover interest and warehousing costs—implies that storers get some other return from inventory. For example, a convenience yield can arise when holding inventory of an input lowers unit output costs and replenishing inventory involves lumpy costs. Alternatively, time delays, lumpy replenishment costs, or high costs of short-term changes in output can lead to a convenience yield on inventory held to meet customer demand for spot delivery.

The storage equation (1) implies that the difference between the basis, $[F(t, T) - S(t)]/S(t)$, and the interest rate, $R(t, T)$, is

$$[F(t, T) - S(t)]/S(t) - R(t, T) = [W(t, T) - C(t, T)]/S(t). \quad (2)$$

We observe $F(t, T)$, $S(t)$, and $R(t, T)$. Thus, the observed quantity on the left-hand side of (2)—the interest-adjusted basis—is the difference between the relative warehousing cost, $w(t, T) = W(t, T)/S(t)$, and the relative convenience yield, $c(t, T) = C(t, T)/S(t)$, on the right. We use this observation to develop testable hypotheses about the convenience yield and the relative variation of spot and forward prices.

We assume that marginal warehousing costs for metals are roughly constant over the relevant range of inventory, and variation in $C(t, T)$ dominates variation in $W(t, T)$. The relative convenience yield $c(t, T)$ falls with increases in inventory, but at a decreasing rate; $\partial c/\partial I < 0$ and $\partial^2 c/\partial I^2 > 0$. Figure 1 shows $c(t, T)$ and the interest-adjusted basis as functions of inventory. At low inventory levels, the convenience yield $c(t, T)$ is larger than the warehousing cost $w(t, T)$, and the interest-adjusted basis is negative. At higher inventory levels, $c(t, T)$ falls toward 0.0; the interest-adjusted basis becomes positive and rises toward $w(t, T)$.

The assumption of Figure 1 that the marginal convenience yield declines with increases in inventory but at a decreasing rate is intuitive and common in empirical work on the theory of storage. (See, for example, Brennan [2] and Telser [6].) It allows us to make predictions about the impact of demand and supply shocks on spot and forward prices.

For example, suppose there is a permanent (current and future) increase in some industry's demand for copper. Because the shock increases current and expected spot prices, other consumers progressively substitute away from copper and producers increase planned outputs of copper. (Demand and supply elastic-

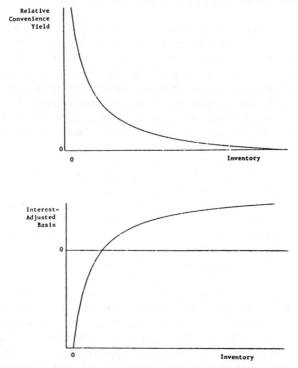

Figure 1. The Relative Convenience Yield and the Interest-Adjusted Basis as Functions of Inventory

ities increase with the horizon.) These demand and supply responses partly offset the effect of the shock on expected prices. Although the demand shock is permanent, the current spot price increases more than expected spot prices because anticipated supply and demand responses mean that part of the effect of the shock on the spot price is temporary.

The relative impact of the permanent demand shock on current and expected spot prices also depends on inventory and the shape of the convenience-yield function for copper. At high inventory levels, the convenience-yield function is almost flat. There can be a large inventory response to the demand shock without a large change in the convenience yield or the interest-adjusted basis. The inventory response dampens the effect of the demand shock on the current spot price, and the change in the current spot price is not much larger than the changes in expected spot prices in forward prices. Most of the change in the spot price is anticipated to be permanent.

In contrast, at low inventory levels, the convenience yield rises faster when inventory is used to meet an increase in demand. As a consequence, the inventory response is smaller, and the shock has a large impact on the current spot price. The change in expected spot prices in forward prices is smaller because the market anticipates future demand and supply responses. Thus, when inventories are low, less of the change in the spot price shows up in forward prices, and the spread of forward over spot prices is more variable than when inventories are high.

French [4] develops formally the implications of the assumed shape of the convenience-yield function in Figure 1. Predictions about relative changes in spot and forward prices in response to (a) permanent (current and future) shocks to supply conditions or (b) temporary shocks that affect only current demand or supply are similar to those for a permanent demand shock. The shocks generate relatively larger changes in spot prices than in forward prices when inventory is low, but changes in spot and forward prices are roughly equal when inventory is high. Moreover, when inventory is high, the theory again predicts roughly equal changes in spot and forward prices in response to shocks that affect only future demand or supply. When inventory is low, however, shocks to future demand or supply cause larger changes in forward prices than in the current spot price.

We assume throughout that, for the metals, shocks that affect only future demand or supply are rare relative to (a) permanent shocks to both current and future demand or supply and (b) temporary current shocks. We recognize that the assumption would be questionable for agricultural products where information about future supply—harvests—is more important.

Our analysis refines Samuelson's [5] hypothesis about the relative variation of spot and forward prices. In essence, he shows that, if (a) the forward price is the expected spot price and (b) the spot price is a stationary (mean-reverting) process, then forward prices vary less than spot prices, and the variation of forward prices is a decreasing function of maturity. The theory of storage leads us to the hypothesis that the relative variation of spot and forward prices is also a function of inventory. The tracks of the Samuelson hypothesis that forward prices vary less than spot prices are likely to be more identifiable when inventory is low.

II. Data

The data include daily observations from the London Metals Exchange (LME) on spot and three-month forward prices for aluminum, cooper, lead, tin, and zinc and spot, three-, six-, and twelve-month forward prices for silver. The sample also includes futures prices for copper and gold from the New York Commodity Exchange (Comex) and futures prices for platinum from the New York Mercantile Exchange (NYM). The futures prices are for maturities to twelve months. Prices are available from 1972 to 1983 for all commodities except aluminum, which begins in 1979, and gold futures, which being in 1975.

The LME data have two advantages. First, there are no limits on LME spot and forward price changes. In futures markets, trading stops when price changes hit daily limits. We drop limit days from the futures data because quoted prices are not equilibrium prices. The second advantage of the LME data is that there aer simultaneous spot and forward prices, for fixed forward maturities, every business day. In contrast, a futures contract does not have a fixed maturity. Instead, there is a three- to four-week delivery period at the beginning of the maturity month. Also, good spot price quotes for the close of futures trading are not available. We use futures prices on maturing contracts as spot prices. For example, March spot prices are closing prices for contracts that mature in March. This solution to the spot price problem limits sample sizes since futures contracts do not mature every month.

III. Evidence on Demand and Supply Shocks and the Theory of Storage

A natural approach would be to test directly the hypotheses about inventory and the variation of spot and forward prices. The metals we study are produced and consumed internationally, however, and the accuracy of data on short-term variation in aggregate inventory is questionable. We use a proxy for inventory suggested by the storage equation (2). When inventory is high, the marginal convenience yield on inventory is low and the interest-adjusted basis is positive. When inventory is low, the convenience yield is high and the interest-adjusted basis is negative. Thus, the sign of the interest-adjusted basis is a proxy for high (+) and low (−) inventory.

A. The Variability of the Interest-Adjusted Basis

For example, the theory of storage prediction that shocks produce more independent variation in spot and forward prices when inventory is low implies that the interest-adjusted basis is more variable when it is negative. This prediction is confirmed by the standard deviations of daily changes in the interest-adjusted basis for the LME industrial metals (Table I). The standard deviations for aluminum, copper, lead, tin, and zinc are at least forty-five percent larger when the interest-adjusted basis is negative. F-tests (not shown) for the industrial

Table I
Standard Deviations of Daily Changes in the Interest-Adjusted Basis and Averages of Daily Values of the Interest-Adjusted Basis[a]

	Industrial Metals					Precious Metals			
		Positive	Negative	All			Positive	Negative	All
Part A: Standard Deviations of Daily Changes in the Interest-Adjusted Basis									
Aluminum	3 Mo Fwd	0.17	0.52	0.79	Gold	3 Mo Fut	0.10	0.09	0.08
Copper	3 Mo Fwd	0.18	0.41	0.59	Gold	6 Mo Fut	0.16	0.15	0.14
Lead	3 Mo Fwd	0.31	0.55	0.68	Gold	12 Mo Fut	0.25	0.23	0.21
Tin	3 Mo Fwd	0.24	0.56	0.57					
Zinc	3 Mo Fwd	0.26	0.63	0.89	Platinum	3 Mo Fut	0.30	0.39	0.47
					Platinum	6 Mo Fut	0.38	0.39	0.39
Copper	3 Mo Fut	0.27	0.44	0.73	Platinum	12 Mo Fut	0.52	0.54	0.54
Copper	6 Mo Fut	0.28	0.41	0.66	Silver	3 Mo Fwd	0.26	0.28	0.31
Copper	12 Mo Fut	0.36	0.54	0.72	Silver	6 Mo Fwd	0.46	0.48	0.51
					Silver	12 Mo Fwd	0.47	0.58	0.68

Part B: Averages of Daily Values of the Interest-Adjusted Basis

Aluminum	3 Mo Fwd	0.79	−4.21	−1.21	Gold	3 Mo Fut	0.23	−0.34	−0.14
Copper	3 Mo Fwd	0.51	−2.51	−0.80	Gold	6 Mo Fut	0.57	−0.50	0.01
Lead	3 Mo Fwd	1.07	−3.30	−1.42	Gold	12 Mo Fut	1.03	−0.73	0.29
Tin	3 Mo Fwd	0.26	−2.86	−2.76					
Zinc	3 Mo Fwd	0.61	−3.10	−1.03	Platinum	3 Mo Fut	0.78	−1.21	−0.14
					Platinum	6 Mo Fut	1.26	−2.09	−0.36
Copper	3 Mo Fut	0.57	−4.37	−0.76	Platinum	12 Mo Fut	1.66	−4.02	−2.81
Copper	6 Mo Fut	1.12	−4.65	−0.33					
Copper	12 Mo Fut	2.00	−5.94	−1.37	Silver	3 Mo Fwd	0.28	−0.39	0.00
					Silver	6 Mo Fwd	0.47	−0.84	−0.05
					Silver	12 Mo Fwd	0.79	−1.78	−0.37

*Statistics are for all days (All), days when the interest-adjusted basis is positive, and days when the interest-adjusted basis is negative. Spot and three-month forward prices for aluminum, copper, lead, tin, and zinc, and spot, three-, six-, and twelve-month forward prices for silver are from the London Metals Exchange (LME). The LME spot and forward prices are not subject to limits on daily changes. Futures prices for copper and gold are from the New York Commodity Exchange (Comex), and futures prices for platinum are from the New York Mercantile Exchange (NYM). The sample period is 1972 to 1983 for all commodities except aluminum, which begins in 1979, and gold, which begins in 1975. To put all prices in the same units, LME spot and forward prices are translated into dollars using spot and forward dollar/pound exchange rates (from the Federal Reserve Bank of New York, Data Resources, Inc., and International Monetary Market Exchange yearbooks). Spot and three-month forward exchange rates are available for the 1972 to 1983 sample period. The six- and twelve-month forward rates needed to translate six- and twelve-month LME forward prices for silver into dollars are not available until June 1973. The interest-adjusted basis is a percentage of the spot price. Interest rates in the interest-adjusted basis are yields on U.S. Treasury bills, from the Federal Reserve Bank of New York. Metals prices are from Data Resources, Inc, Comex and NYM year books, the *Wall Street Journal*, and the *Financial Times* of London. Sample sizes are in Table II.

metals reject the hypothesis that the variance of the interest-adjusted basis does not depend on its sign at the 0.995 probability level.

The evidence for the precious metals is weaker. The standard deviations of the interest-adjusted basis for silver and platinum are only slightly larger when the interest-adjusted basis is negative. The interest-adjusted basis for gold is slightly more variable when it is positive than when it is negative. The precious metals produce weak results in all the tests. We leave the explanation until later.

B. *The Relative Variability of Spot and Forward Prices*

The theory of storage and the assumed shape of the convenience-yield function in Figure 1 predict that demand and supply shocks produce roughly equal changes in spot and forward prices when the interest-adjusted basis is positive (inventory is high), but shocks cause spot prices to change more than forward prices when the interest-adjusted basis is negative (inventory is low). This prediction is confirmed by the ratios of the standard deviation of daily percent forward price changes to the standard deviation of percent spot price changes for the LME industrial metals in Table II. The ratios for aluminum, copper, lead, tin, and zinc are close to 1.0 (0.96 or greater) when the interest-adjusted basis is positive. The ratios are lower, from 0.78 (aluminum) to 0.91 (lead), when the interest-adjusted basis is negative.

When the interest-adjusted basis is positive, the variances of spot price changes and three-month forward price changes for the industrial metals are never reliably different at the 0.95 probability level. The variances of spot and three-month forward price changes are always reliably different at the 0.99 probability level when the interest-adjusted basis is negative.

The theory of storage also predicts that demand and supply shocks produce larger changes in near-term expected spot prices than in more distant expected spot prices because the shocks are progressively offset by demand and supply responses. The ratios of the standard deviation of futures price changes to the standard deviation of spot price changes for copper (the only industrial metal with more than one maturity) are roughly consistent with this prediction. The ratios for positive interest-adjusted bases fall from 1.02 at three months to 0.97 at six months and 0.92 at twelve months. The ratios for negative interest-adjusted bases are 0.92, 0.93, and 0.85. The twelve-month ratios are reliably different from 1.0 at the 0.95 probability level. This evidence is consistent with Samuelson's [5] general proposition that the difference between the variability of spot and futures prices increases with the maturity of the futures price.

C. *The Response of Forward Prices to Changes in Spot Prices*

The theory of storage and the shape of the convenience-yield function in Figure 1 imply a more precise prediction about the response of spot and forward prices to demand and supply shocks. Consider the regression of the percent change in the forward price on the percent change in the spot price:

$$\ln[F(t, T)/F(t - 1, T - 1)] = a + b\ln[S(t)/S(t - 1)] + e(t). \qquad (3)$$

Table II
Ratios of the Standard Deviation of Daily Forward (or Futures) Price Changes to the Standard Deviation of Daily Spot Price Changes[a]

		Industrial Metals				Precious Metals		
		Positive	Negative	All		Positive	Negative	All

Part A: Ratios of Forward Standard Deviation to Spot Standard Deviation

Aluminum	3 Mo Fwd	0.98	0.78*	0.88	Gold 3 Mo Fut	1.00	1.00	1.00
Copper	3 Mo Fwd	0.98	0.88*	0.92	Gold 6 Mo Fut	0.99	1.00	1.00
Lead	3 Mo Fwd	0.96	0.91*	0.92	Gold 12 Mo Fut	0.99	0.99	0.99
Tin	3 Mo Fwd	1.01	0.86*	0.86				
Zinc	3 Mo Fwd	0.96	0.86*	0.89	Platinum 3 Mo Fut	0.95	0.97	1.00
					Platinum 6 Mo Fut	0.97	0.97	0.98
					Platinum 12 Mo Fut	0.93	0.94	0.94
Copper	3 Mo Fut	1.02	0.92*	0.98	Silver 3 Mo Fwd	1.00	1.00	1.00
Copper	6 Mo Fut	0.97	0.93*	0.95	Silver 6 Mo Fwd	0.99	0.99	0.99
Copper	12 Mo Fut	0.92**	0.85*	0.88	Silver 12 Mo Fwd	0.97	0.97	0.96

Part B: Number of Observations

Aluminum	3 Mo Fwd	689	460	1149	Gold 3 Mo Fut	217	394	611
Copper	3 Mo Fwd	1596	1222	2818	Gold 6 Mo Fut	398	446	844
Lead	3 Mo Fwd	1215	1603	2818	Gold 12 Mo Fut	435	313	748
Tin	3 Mo Fwd	91	2727	2818				
Zinc	3 Mo Fwd	1570	1248	2818	Platinum 3 Mo Fut	243	208	451
					Platinum 6 Mo Fut	233	219	452
					Platinum 12 Mo Fut	48	178	226
Copper	3 Mo Fut	262	97	359	Silver 3 Mo Fwd	1647	1176	2823
Copper	6 Mo Fut	522	176	698	Silver 6 Mo Fwd	1513	982	2495
Copper	12 Mo Fut	529	390	919	Silver 12 Mo Fwd	1364	1119	2483

[a] Statistics are for all days (All), days when the interest-adjusted basis is positive, and days when the interest-adjusted basis is negative. Spot and three-month forward prices for aluminum, copper, lead, tin, and zinc, and spot, three-, six-, and twelve-month forward prices for silver are from the London Metals Exchange (LME). The LME spot and forward prices are not subject to limits on daily changes. Futures prices for copper and gold are from the New York Commodity Exchange (Comex), and futures prices for platinum are from the New York Mercantile Exchange (NYM). The sample period is 1972 to 1983 for all commodities except aluminum, which begins in 1979, and gold, which begins in 1975. To put all prices in the same units, LME spot and forward prices are translated into dollars using spot and forward dollar/pound exchange rates. Spot and three-month forward exchange rates are available for the 1972 to 1983 sample period. The six- and twelve-month forward rates needed to translate six- and twelve-month LME forward prices for silver into dollars are not available until June 1973.

*, ** An F-test rejects the hypothesis that the variances of daily spot and forward price changes are equal at the 0.95 (*) or 0.99 (**) probability level.

At high inventory levels, the marginal convenience yield in (2) is not sensitive to changes in inventory. Large inventory responses mean that shocks produce roughly equal changes in current and expected spot prices. The slope b in (3) is close to 1.0. At lower inventory levels, the convenience-yield function is steeper. Smaller inventory responses mean that shocks have a larger effect on the current spot price than on expected spot prices. Changes in the spot price are associated with less than one-for-one changes in the expected spot prices in forward prices because the market forecasts future production and demand responses to the shock. If we use the sign of the interest-adjusted basis to proxy for high and low inventory, the slope b in (3) should be smaller when the interest-adjusted basis is negative.

The slopes for the LME industrial metals in Table III confirm this prediction. When the interest-adjusted basis is positive, the slopes range from 0.95 (lead and zinc) to 1.00 (tin). Moreover, spot and forward prices move almost in lock step; the regression R^2 ranges from 0.96 to 0.99. In contrast, when the interest-adjusted basis is negative, the slopes are much lower, ranging from 0.69 (aluminum) to 0.86 (lead). There is also more independent variation in spot and forward prices; the regression R^2 ranges from 0.77 to 0.92. The slope when the interest-adjusted basis is negative is always at least 5.0 standard errors smaller than when the interest-adjusted basis is positive. The behavior of spot and forward prices for the LME industrial metals is consistent with the theory of storage prediction that expected spot prices change roughly one for one with the current spot price when inventory is high, but expected spot prices move less than the current spot price when inventory is low.

The theory of storage also predicts that shocks have less impact on longer maturity futures prices because demand and supply responses are larger for longer planning horizons. Thus, the slopes in (3) should be lower for longer maturity futures prices. The regressions for copper are roughly consistent with this prediction. The slopes when the interest-adjusted basis is positive fall from 1.00 at three months to 0.95 at six months and 0.90 at twelve months, and the six- and twelve-month slops are more than 5.0 standard errors from 1.0. The slopes when the interest-adjusted basis is negative are 0.83, 0.88, and 0.78.

D. *The Precious Metals*

The regressions for the precious metals in Table III are less support for the theory of storage. Slopes and R^2 in (3) for gold, platinum, and silver are close to 1.0, and they are not consistently lower when the interest-adjusted basis is negative. Likewise, spot prices for gold, platinum, and silver are not consistently more variable than futures (or forward) prices when the interest-adjusted basis is negative (Table II), and the basis itself is about as variable when it is positive as when it is negative (Table I).

A simple explanation is that storage costs for the precious metals that are low relative to value, and the demand for gold and silver as investment assets, lead to inventories sufficient to limit variation in convenience yields and thus in the interest-adjusted basis. The averages and standard deviations of the interest-adjusted basis in Table I are consistent with this view. Differences between

Table III
Regressions of Daily Changes in Forward or Futures Prices on Contemporaneous Daily Changes in Spot Prices:[a]

$$\ln[F(t,T)/F(t-1,T-1)] = a + b\ln[S(t)/S(t-1)] + e(t)$$

		Positive			Negative			All		
		b	s(b)	R^2	b	s(b)	R^2	b	s(b)	R^2
Industrial Metals										
Aluminum	3 Mo Fwd	0.970	0.004	0.99	0.687	0.018	0.77	0.822	0.009	0.87
Copper	3 Mo Fwd	0.969	0.003	0.98	0.849	0.007	0.92	0.888	0.004	0.94
Lead	3 Mo Fwd	0.949	0.004	0.97	0.863	0.007	0.91	0.890	0.005	0.93
Tin	3 Mo Fwd	0.997	0.020	0.96	0.777	0.007	0.82	0.782	0.007	0.82
Zinc	3 Mo Fwd	0.945	0.004	0.97	0.806	0.008	0.88	0.844	0.005	0.90
Copper	3 Mo Fut	1.000	0.012	0.96	0.833	0.041	0.81	0.925	0.016	0.90
Copper	6 Mo Fut	0.952	0.008	0.97	0.876	0.024	0.88	0.919	0.009	0.93
Copper	12 Mo Fut	0.895	0.009	0.95	0.782	0.017	0.85	0.825	0.010	0.88
Precious Metals										
Gold	3 Mo Fut	0.999	0.004	1.00	1.003	0.003	1.00	1.002	0.002	1.00
Gold	6 Mo Fut	0.999	0.005	0.99	0.991	0.004	0.99	0.995	0.003	0.99
Gold	12 Mo Fut	0.979	0.007	0.98	0.978	0.007	0.98	0.978	0.005	0.98
Platinum	3 Mo Fut	0.982	0.012	0.97	0.924	0.017	0.94	0.950	0.010	0.95
Platinum	6 Mo Fut	0.951	0.015	0.95	0.947	0.014	0.96	0.948	0.010	0.95
Platinum	12 Mo Fut	0.900	0.041	0.91	0.903	0.018	0.93	0.903	0.017	0.93
Silver	3 Mo Fwd	0.992	0.002	0.99	0.996	0.003	0.99	0.994	0.002	0.99
Silver	6 Mo Fwd	0.974	0.004	0.98	0.978	0.004	0.98	0.976	0.003	0.98
Silver	12 Mo Fwd	0.943	0.004	0.97	0.958	0.005	0.97	0.953	0.003	0.97

[a] Regressions are estimated for all days (All), for days when the interest-adjusted basis is positive, and for days when the interest-adjusted basis is negative. Spot and three-month forward prices for aluminum, copper, lead, tin, and zinc, and spot, three-, six-, and twelve-month forward prices for silver are from the London Metals Exchange (LME). The LME spot and forward prices are not subject to limits on daily changes. Futures prices for copper and gold are from the New York Commodity Exchange (Comex), and futures prices for platinum are from the New York Mercantile Exchange (NYM). The sample period is 1972 to 1983 for all commodities except aluminum, which begins in 1979, and gold, which begins in 1975. To put all prices in the same units, LME spot and forward prices are translated into dollars using spot and forward dollar/pound exchange rates. Spot and three-month forward exchange rates are available for the 1972 to 1983 sample period. The six- and twelve-month forward rates needed to translate six- and twelve-month LME forward prices for silver into dollars are not available until June 1973. Sample sizes are in Table II.

average positive and average negative three-month interest-adjusted bases are all greater than 3.0 percent for the industrial metals. In contrast, average positive and negative three-month interest-adjusted bases for gold and silver differ by only 0.57 percent and 0.67 percent, and the difference for platinum is 1.99 percent. The standard deviation of daily changes in the three-month interest-adjusted basis for gold for all days is less than one sixth that of any industrial metal. The three-month interest-adjusted basis for silver is about half as variable as those for the industrial metals. Thus, at least for gold and silver, there is less variation in convenience yields to be explained than for the industrial metals.

The Table III regressions do provide some evidence that spot price changes for platinum and silver are not entirely permanent. If progressive production and consumption responses partly offset demand and supply shocks, the slopes in (3) should be smaller for longer maturity futures prices. The slopes for silver range from 1.00 at three months to about 0.95 (about ten standard errors from 1.0) at twelve months. The slopes for platinum drop from 0.95 at three months to 0.90 at twelve months. (All are at least 4.0 standard errors from 1.0.) Based on the point estimates, on average 95.0 percent and 90.0 percent of the changes in silver and platinum spot prices are permanent in the sense that they show up as changes in expected spot prices in twelve-month forward and futures prices.

E. Forward Prices and Forecast Power

The slopes in (3) for the industrial metals indicate that forward prices respond less than spot prices to demand and supply shocks when the interest-adjusted basis is negative. We interpret this as evidence that, when inventory is low, the market forecasts that only part of a current spot price change shows up in expected spot prices in forward prices. It is interesting to test whether these market forecasts of future spot prices, inferred from contemporaneous changes in spot and forward prices, are rational (unbiased).

Our attempts to test the rationality of market forecasts of spot prices have failed. The problem is familiar: variances of unexpected spot price changes are so large relative to variances of expected changes that we are unable reliably to extract expected changes from observed changes. (See Fama and French [3] for some details.) Thus, we are able to identify variation in forward prices due to market forecasts of spot prices, but we lack tests with power to infer whether the forecasts are rational.

IV. Price Inversions and the Business Cycle

Tables I to III are consistent with theory-of-storage predictions about (a) the variation of the interest-adjusted basis and (b) the relative variation of spot and forward prices as a function of the level of inventory. This section describes how the price behavior that produces these results relates to the business cycles of the 1973 to 1982 sample period.

A. The Behavior of Spot Prices

Table IV summarizes the behavior of spot prices around the business-cycle peaks, identified by the National Bureau of Economic Research as November

Table IV
Relative Spot Prices around 1973–1974 and 1979–1980 Business-Cycle Peaks[a]

Part A

	1/3/72	1/2/73	11/1/73	Maximum (Date)	7/1/74	1/2/75	6/2/75
Industrial Metals							
Copper	1.00	1.00	2.02	3.20 (4/1/74)	1.97	1.17	1.17
Lead	1.00	1.29	1.96	3.22 (5/6/74)	2.26	2.24	1.42
Tin	1.00	1.05	1.52	2.73 (5/6/74)	2.31	1.97	1.90
Zinc	1.00	1.01	3.47	5.67 (5/6/74)	2.84	1.89	1.96
Precious Metals							
Gold	1.00	1.48	2.20	4.06 (4/3/74)	3.23	3.94	3.66
Platinum	1.00	1.34	1.56	2.38 (4/3/74)	1.79	1.53	1.46
Silver	1.00	1.48	2.06	4.94 (2/26/74)	3.41	3.23	3.23

Part B

	1/3/78	1/2/79	9/4/79	Maximum (Date)	5/1/80	7/1/82	12/1/82
Industrial Metals							
Aluminum	1.00		1.25	1.76 (2/11/80)	1.49	0.74	0.77
Copper	1.00	1.22	1.66	2.46 (2/11/80)	1.57	1.03	1.16
Lead	1.00	1.35	1.86	2.03 (9/27/79)	1.20	0.79	0.67
Tin	1.00	1.17	1.27	1.55 (3/6/80)	1.45	0.98	0.98
Zinc	1.00	1.28	1.29	1.69 (2/15/80)	1.22	1.30	1.27
Precious Metals							
Gold	1.00	1.29	1.87	4.81 (1/21/80)	3.00	1.83	2.53
Platinum	1.00	1.79	3.29	4.77 (1/17/80)	3.64	1.38	2.12
Silver	1.00	1.25	2.25	10.17 (1/18/80)	2.47	1.18	2.08

[a] Spot prices for each metal in Part A are divided by the spot price on January 3, 1972. Except for aluminum, the spot prices in Part B are divided by the spot price on January 3, 1978. The prices for aluminum are divided by the spot price on January 2, 1979. The maximum relative price is the highest closing price between November 1, 1973, and April 4, 1974, in Part A and between September 4, 1979, and May 1, 1980, in Part B. Since platinum has only four maturing contracts each year, prices are reported for the following dates: 1/2/74, not 11/1/73; 10/1/79, not 9/4/79; 7/1/80, not 5/1/80; and 1/4/83, not 12/1/82. The spot prices for gold before 1975 are from Handy and Harmon.

Table V
Average Values of Daily Interest-Adjusted Bases (Percent for Periods around 1973–1974 and 1979–1980 Business-Cycle Peaks[a]

		1/72–12/72	1/73–10/73	11/73–6/74	Minimum (Mo.)	7/74–5/75	6/75–12/77
			Industrial Metals				
Copper	3 Mo Fwd	0.38	−3.93	−8.61	−14.80 (7312)	0.36	0.61
Lead	3 Mo Fwd	−0.69	−1.03	−1.99	−8.99 (7501)	−5.07	0.48
Tin	3 Mo Fwd	−1.11	−3.02	−5.06	−14.93 (7409)	−4.08	−1.35
Zinc	3 Mo Fwd	0.38	−2.93	−10.66	−14.95 (7402)	−4.22	0.27
Copper	3 Mo Fut	0.96	−11.56	−18.22	−18.22 (7312)	0.87	0.52
Copper	6 Mo Fut	1.31	−6.51	−15.51	−19.06 (7309)	0.96	1.46
Copper	12 Mo Fut	1.22	−16.30	−26.41	−32.73 (7312)	1.91	2.42
			Precious Metals				
Gold	3 Mo Fut						0.01
Gold	6 Mo Fut					0.87	0.19
Gold	12 Mo Fut					1.51	0.03
Platinum	3 Mo Fut	0.35	1.16	0.75	0.07 (7201)	1.45	0.62
Platinum	6 Mo Fut	0.38	1.85	1.12	0.31 (7201)	2.28	1.14
Silver	3 Mo Fwd	0.02	−0.05	−0.17	−0.50 (7402)	−0.04	0.02
Silver	6 Mo Fwd		−0.05	−0.68	−1.19 (7402)	−0.01	0.20
Silver	12 Mo Fwd		−0.53	−2.14	−3.07 (7402)	0.09	0.56

		1/78–12/78	1/79–8/79	9/79–4/80	Minimum (Mo.)	5/80–12/80	1/81–12/83
			Industrial Metals				
Aluminum	3 Mo Fwd		−3.05	−6.52	−9.52 (7911)	−2.69	0.69
Copper	3 Mo Fwd		−1.66	−2.49	−3.60 (7909)	−0.81	0.03
Lead	3 Mo Fwd		−8.52	−6.28	−12.13 (8003)	−0.16	0.62
Tin	3 Mo Fwd		−5.24	−5.00	−12.09 (8202)	−3.08	−2.06
Zinc	3 Mo Fwd		0.33	−0.76	−2.07 (8204)	0.13	−0.22
Copper	3 Mo Fut	0.44		−3.31	−5.41 (7912)	0.01	0.29
Copper	6 Mo Fut	1.10		−1.76	−3.83 (7907)	−0.80	0.53
Copper	12 Mo Fut	1.31		−8.26	−14.99 (7912)	−1.35	0.38
			Precious Metals				
Gold	3 Mo Fut	0.06	−0.15	0.14	−0.79 (8103)	0.27	−0.35
Gold	6 Mo Fut	0.24	−0.13	1.23	−1.09 (8108)	0.78	−0.29
Gold	12 Mo Fut	0.61	−0.08	2.43	−1.63 (8108)	2.08	−0.21
Platinum	3 Mo Fut	−0.06	−2.83	−1.10	−3.79 (7907)	0.25	−0.56
Platinum	6 Mo Fut	−0.52	−4.84	−2.34	−6.09 (7907)	0.70	−1.04
Platinum	12 Mo Fut		−8.94	−5.90	−10.45 (7904)	1.94	−1.68
Silver	3 Mo Fwd	−0.07	−0.21	−0.98	−2.51 (8002)	0.25	0.29
Silver	6 Mo Fwd	−0.17	−0.64	−2.48	−6.07 (8002)	0.51	0.45
Silver	12 Mo Fwd	−0.41	−2.13	−5.96	−13.46 (8002)	0.77	0.46

1973 and January 1980. There are large increases in the prices of all metals before the business-cycle peak of January 1980 and large declines thereafter. Gold and platinum prices grow to almost five times their January 1978 values and then fall by July 1982, gold to about forty percent and platinum to about thirty percent of peak values. Copper and lead prices double their January 1978 values and then fall to about forty percent of their peaks by July 1982. Silver has the largest price swing in the 1978–1982 period. The closing spot price on January 18, 1980 is more than ten times the price on January 3, 1978. From January 18, 1980 to July 1, 1982, the spot price falls almost to its January 1978 value.

There are similar price swings around the business-cycle peak of November 1973. All prices rise from January 1972 to November 1973, peak during the first half of 1974, and fall thereafter. The price of gold quadruples from January 3, 1972 to April 3, 1974 and then falls twenty percent from April to July. Silver peaks on February 26, 1974, at about five times its January 1972 price, before falling to seventy percent of its peak value on July 1, 1974. Copper, lead, and tin peak at about three times their January 1972 values in April and May 1974 and then fall between fifteen percent and forty percent by July 1974. Zinc has the biggest price swing, peaking on May 6, 1974, at almost six times its January 1972 value, and then falling about fifty percent by July 1, 1974.

B. *The Behavior of the Interest-Adjusted Basis*

The theory of storage and the pro-cyclical behavior of spot prices suggest that positive demand shocks near a business-cycle peak reduce inventories, raise convenience yields, and generate negative interest-adjusted bases. Table V shows that three-month interest-adjusted bases for the industrial metals, aluminum, copper, lead, tin, and zinc, are typically negative during both 1973–1974 and 1979–1980. The most extreme negative interest-adjusted bases tend to occur near the business-cycle peaks, November 1973 and January 1980.

The plot of the three-month interest-adjusted basis for copper in Figure 2 (plots for other industrial metals are similar) shows that, during the 1973–1974 and 1979–1980 periods when the interest-adjusted basis is negative, it is persistently negative. This suggests that production does not adjust quickly to positive demand shocks around business-cycle peaks. The large price swings for the metals (and the demand for forward and futures markets) also suggest industries in which production does not adjust quickly to shocks.

The periods around business-cycle peaks when interest-adjusted bases for the industrial metals are negative are the periods for which the regressions in Table III indicate that forward prices vary less than one for one with spot prices. Since spot price changes are on balance strongly positive during these periods, the market is apparently forecasting that the increases are in part temporary, to be reversed by future production and demand responses.

Except for tin, there are also periods, for example, June 1975 to January 1978 and January 1981 to December 1983, when interest-adjusted bases for the industrial metals are typically positive or close to 0.0, implying that inventories are relatively high. These are the periods for which the Table III regressions indicate that changes in spot prices are mostly permanent: changes in spot prices on average show up one for one in forward prices.

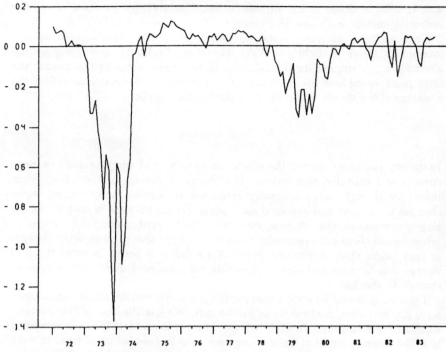

Figure 2. Interest-Adjusted Basis for Copper

C. A Squeeze in Silver?

Some claim that negative interest-adjusted bases (Table V) and the large spot price swing for silver in 1979 and 1980 (Table IV) are evidence of a squeeze. In a squeeze, colluding traders secretly take long nearby futures positions that exceed deliverable supply. As contract maturities approach and the market becomes aware of the squeeze, spot and nearby futures prices rise. Because the squeeze is temporary, there is an "inversion" of futures-spot relations; longer maturity futures prices are not sufficient to cover interest carrying costs. When the squeeze is over, the spot price falls and "normal" futures-spot relations return.

Although the price swing for silver in 1979 and 1980 is dramatic, it is not unique. Table IV shows that such swings are common for metals prices around both the November 1973 and January 1980 business-cycle peaks. The inversions of forward-spot relations in Table V are also not unique to silver or the 1979–1980 period. Inversions of forward-spot relations are similar for silver and platinum (both precious metals) and generally smaller for silver than for the industrial metals. During the September 1979 to April 1980 period, which includes the purported squeeze, the negative three-, six-, and 12-month interest-adjusted bases for silver are within 0.14 percent of those for platinum. The average value of the three-month interest-adjusted basis for silver from September 1979 to April 1980 is −0.98 percent. Among the industrial metals, only the average for zinc (−0.76) is closer to 0.0 for this period. The averages for three of the five industrial metals are below −5.0 percent.

Since we have no direct tests, we cannot infer that there was no squeeze attempt in silver in 1979 and 1980. However, Tables IV and V suggest an alternative explanation for the behavior of silver prices during this period; the large price swing and the inversion of forward-spot price relations reflect the workings of the theory of storage over the business cycle.

V. Conclusions

Inventory responses spread the effects of demand and supply shocks between current and expected spot prices. The theory of storage predicts that, when inventory is high, large inventory responses to shocks imply roughly equal changes in current and expected spot prices. Thus, changes in spot prices are largely permanent; they show up one for one in forward prices. When inventory is low, smaller inventory responses mean that current shocks cause larger changes in spot prices than in forward prices. Expected spot prices in forward prices change less because the market forecasts progressive demand and supply responses to shocks.

Tests on spot and forward prices for the industrial metals, aluminum, copper, lead, tin, and zinc, confirm these predictions. We use the sign of the interest-adjusted basis to proxy for high (+) and low (−) inventory. When inventory is low (the interest-adjusted basis is negative), the interest-adjusted basis is more variable (Table I), spot prices are more variable than forward prices (Table II), forward prices move less than one for one with changes in spot prices (Table III), and there is more independent variation in spot and forward prices (Table III). When inventory is high (the interest-adjusted basis is positive), the interest-adjusted basis is less variable, forward prices move roughly one for one with spot prices, and changes in forward and spot prices are almost perfectly correlated.

Results for gold, platinum, and silver are weaker. We suggest that low storage costs for the precious metals lead to inventories sufficient to keep convenience yields close to 0.0 and thus to ensure roughly one-for-one variation in spot and forward prices.

During our sample period, the variation of spot and forward prices for metals has a strong business-cycle component. There are sharp rises and declines in the prices of all metals around the business-cycle peaks of 1973–1974 and 1979–1980. We suggest that the price rises reflect near-term supply responses that are insufficient to absorb positive demand shocks around business-cycle peaks. The theory of storage then predicts that the demand shocks reduce inventories and generate positive convenience yields and negative interest-adjusted bases. The evidence is consistent with this prediction. Interest-adjusted bases are negative for all metals but gold around the peak of 1979–1980 and for all metals but zinc around the peak of 1973–1974. An interesting future project is to check whether the behavior of prices over the business cycle observed in our sample is characteristic of other periods.

REFERENCES

1. R. W. Anderson. "Some Determinants of the Volatility of Futures Prices." *Journal of Futures Markets* 5 (Fall 1985), 331–48.
2. M. J. Brennan. "The Supply of Storage." *American Economic Review* 48 (March 1958), 50–72.
3. E. F. Fama and K. R. French. "Commodity Futures Prices: Some Evidence on Forecast Power, Premiums and the Theory of Storage." *Journal of Business* 60 (January 1987), 55–74.
4. K. R. French. "Detecting Spot Price Forecasts in Futures Prices." *Journal of Business* 59 (April 1986, Part 2), S39-S54.
5. P. A. Samuelson. "Proof That Properly Anticipated Prices Fluctuate Randomly." *Industrial Management Review* 6 (Spring 1965), 41–49.
6. L. G. Telser. "Futures Trading and the Storage of Cotton and Wheat." *Journal of Political Economy* 66 (June 1958), 233–55.
7. H. Working. "The Theory of the Price of Storage." *American Economic Review* (December 1949), 1254–62.

[22]
Evidence for a Weather Persistence Effect on the Corn, Wheat, and Soybean Growing Season Price Dynamics

Stanley C. Stevens

INTRODUCTION

The growing season weather in the corn, wheat, and soybean production areas of the United States is an important determinant of the U.S. supply of these commodities. The weather and climatology literature strongly suggest that during the summer months there is a degree of persistence in the North American weather patterns. Given this nonrandom character of weather and given that the corn, wheat, and soybean belts are geographically concentrated enough to be dominated by a regional weather phenomenon, their futures markets are hypothesized to reflect this assimilation of nonrandom weather information as nonrandom price fluctuations. An empirical test of this question is the subject of this article.

THE GROWING SEASON

Most corn in the U.S. corn belt states is planted in May and harvested in October and November. Numerous studies point to midwestern weather conditions in the June through August period as being especially important determinants of national corn yields. See Teigen and Singer (1988), Ash and Lin (1987), Vroomen and Hanthorn (1986), Van Meir (1984), and Lin and Davenport (1982). A recent investigation of the subject by Westcott (1989) focuses on planting dates and June and July precipitation and temperature in the corn belt to explain national corn yields.

As noted by Westcott (1989, p. 18), typical daily water use rates for 110 growing day corn peaks at about the 60th day of growth; the largest water use occurs from about the 40th day to about the 80th day. Therefore, in the corn belt, corn planted in early- to mid-May experiences peak utilization of water in late-June and throughout July. Mid-June and early-August water use rates are also high for earlier and later planted corn, respectively. Westcott also notes that temperature plays an

---

I am indebted to Reynold Dahl, Earl Fuller, Robert King, Richard Levins, Mark Seeley, and Yacov Tsur for their helpful comments.

Stanley C. Stevens is an Assistant Professor in the Department of Agricultural and Applied Economics at the University of Minnesota.

important role in crop development, potentially stressing the corn plant at critical stages of crop formation and increasing the evaporation of moisture reserves from the soil.

Soybeans are known to be a more resilient crop, more capable of performing under stress. They have vulnerability in August when the soybeans are flowering and setting and filling pods. See Willimark and Teigen (1985, p. 28). But geographically, the corn and soybean belts are largely located in the same place. Therefore, adverse and/or favorable weather usually affects the national corn and soybean crops in a similar way from year to year.

The growing season for wheat is more difficult to define with precision at the national level. Winter wheat is planted in the fall. Spring wheat is planted in the spring. The harvest season ranges from June in Texas to August in North Dakota. The national wheat crop is more diversified against any persistent weather patterns.

This diversity is illustrated in an empirical study of regional wheat yields by Ash and Lin (1986). Six regions are studied: the Northern Plains, the Southern Plains, the Mountain, the Pacific and lake states, and the Corn Belt. Explanatory variables include March through July precipitation and temperature. Although both temperature and precipitation are frequently significant, the signs and level of significance varies substantially from region to region.

PERSISTENCE IN THE WEATHER

In the context of the subject of weather and climate, persistence refers to a regional stability in the weather pattern for a time period. While a thorough review of this literature is outside the scope of this article, some examples are given to support the view that regional weather patterns can often be persistent. Namias (1986) finds and summarizes extensive empirical evidence that North American weather, in terms of flow pattern, temperature and precipitation, is significantly persistent in the winter and summer months with a short period of nonpersistence around or just after the equinoxes. Trenberth, Branstator, and Arkin (1988, p. 1643) in an article focused on the origins of the 1988 North American drought state:

"The evidence suggests that persistent global-scale anomalies in the atmospheric circulation set the stage for the [1988] drought in the United States. Large-scale circulation anomalies have also been associated with earlier U.S. droughts. In summer droughts, there has always been upper-level anticyclonic conditions over the United States, usually associated in a wavelike pattern with a deeper than normal upper-level through along the west coast of North America and another anticyclonic region over the central North Pacific...

In general in summer, once anticyclonic conditions prevail over the United States, other more local factors probably help maintain the droughts and produce heat waves. In particular, land-surface processes involving the absence of soil moisture probably have a significant effect. Normally, heating from the sun is partitioned into evapotranspiration and sensible heating of the surface and atmosphere. But in drought conditions, evaporation and plant transpiration are greatly reduced so that nearly all heating is manifested as temperature increases. Moreover, the absence of moisture conspires against widespread precipitation. Heat waves result and a drought becomes, at least in part, self-perpetuating."

SEASONAL PRICE DYNAMICS

The importance of growing conditions in the late-June through early-July period, accompanied by some potential for the weather influence itself to persist in some fashion, raises an interesting question for corn price dynamics during this period. As stated by Anderson (1985, p. 333):

"For grains, total annual production is determined by acreage planted and yields. Yields in turn are heavily dependent upon weather conditions at certain times of the growth process. These crucial phases tend to occur at approximately the same times during the calendar year. Consequently, we would expect the resolution of production uncertainty to follow a strong seasonal pattern."

While Anderson's focus is on volatility, seasonal volatility and Samuelson's (1965, 1976) hypothesis that volatility increases as the maturity of a futures contract approaches, this study focuses on the seasonal randomness, or lack thereof, of these prices. Samuelson (1965) introduced the theoretical relationships between random walk and expected returns models in the theory of efficient markets. Previous and subsequent empirical investigation of the market efficiency literature, for the most part, concludes that the futures markets are in most cases efficient as measured by serial dependence in a time series. Fama (1965, p. 399), after an extensive review of the empirical literature, states:

"At this date the weight of the empirical evidence is such that economists would generally agree that whatever dependence exists in a series of historical returns cannot be used to make profitable predictions of the future. Indeed for returns that cover periods of a day or longer, there is little in the evidence that would cause rejection of the stronger random walk model, at least as a good first approximation."

On the other hand, there is significant research in the literature that finds exception. For example, Stevenson and Bear (1970, p. 80) in an investigation of corn and soybean serial correlations and analysis of runs, find evidence to "cast considerable doubt on the applicability of this hypothesis to the market for commodity futures." They note similar evidence against the random walk model in the work of Cootner (1964) and Larson (1960).

This study finds some evidence that during the growing season corn, wheat, and soybean prices do not vary as a random walk. It is hypothesized that persistent weather conditions in the growing season arrive with some degree of momentum as suggested by the weather and climate literature and induce similar momentum into commodity price dynamics.

To test the question a simple regression analysis is used:

$$P(t,k) = \text{Alpha} + \text{Beta}^*P(t-1,k) + E \tag{1}$$

where

$P(t,k)$ Change in futures price on day t during season k.
t Ranges from October 1, 1972 through September 30, 1989.
k Ranges across 48 time cells per year defined as the 1st through the 7th, 8th through the 15th, 16th through the 23rd, and 24th through the 31st of each calendar month.
E Randomly distributed error.

The null hypothesis, $B = 0$, is that during the growing season, the weather persistence does not, in fact, induce momentum into the price dynamics. That is, if $P(t - 1, k)$ contains some information about the current state of weather persistence, it does not significantly influence $P(t, k)$. The null hypothesis is rejected during those time periods when Beta is significantly positive.

THE DATA BASE

The study focuses on a 17-year period beginning October 1, 1972 and ending September 30, 1989. The study period includes major corn belt droughts during the years 1974, 1980, 1983, and 1988. Significant but more localized droughts in the western corn belt occurred in 1975, 1976, and 1977.

To achieve continuity across a 17-year time frame, the observed daily price change is drawn from the actively trading nearby futures contracts of Chicago corn, Chicago soybeans, and Chicago wheat according to the schedule in Table I.

EMPIRICAL RESULTS

Table II shows significantly positive values for Beta tending to cluster in the growing seasons for corn and soybeans. The season defined by May 24 through August 23 stands out with numerous positive t values at the 10 percent level of significance or better. Of the 24 corn and soybean time cells of this period, all but two are positive and 14 are significantly positive.

These results are in sharp contrast to the statistical character of the corn and soybean market during the rest of the year. Outside of this season 80 time cells are observed with only 13 containing significantly nonzero Beta values. Moreover, of these 13, eight are negative in sign. The nongrowing season statistical results are clearly more sporadic.

The lack of a cluster of significantly positive values of Beta for wheat suggests that either the wheat growing season has less weather persistence and/or that wheat, in its growing season, is less sensitive to weather than is corn or soybeans. On the

Table I
OBSERVED FUTURES CONTRACT SCHEDULE FOR CHICAGO BOARD OF TRADE CORN, SOYBEANS, AND WHEAT

Calendar Month	Chicago Board of Trade Futures Contract		
	Corn	Soybeans	Wheat
January	March	March	March
February	March	March	March
March	May	May	May
April	May	May	May
May	July	July	July
June	July	July	July
July	September	September	September
August	September	September	September
September	December	November	December
October	December	November	December
November	December	January	December
December	March	January	March

Table II
A SEASONALLY PARTITIONED STATISTICAL SUMMARY FOR THE PERIOD OCTOBER 1, 1972 THROUGH SEPTEMBER 30, 1989

Time Cell	Corn			Soybeans			Wheat		
	N	Beta	t	N	Beta	t	N	Beta	t
Jan 1– 7	69	–.19	–1.37	69	–.19	–1.51	69	.27	1.98*
Jan 8–15	96	–.11	–1.19	96	–.03	– .34	96	–.18	–2.03**
Jan 16–23	98	–.02	– .18	98	.09	.92	98	–.08	– .70
Jan 24–31	96	–.01	– .07	96	–.22	–2.22**	96	.00	.00
Feb 1– 7	85	–.02	– .15	85	.02	.15	85	–.13	–1.19
Feb 8–15	94	–.01	– .12	94	–.24	–2.44**	94	.19	1.75*
Feb 16–23	82	.33	2.87**	82	–.06	– .50	82	–.17	–1.54
Feb 24–29	64	.51	3.83**	64	.05	.39	64	.20	1.26
Mar 1– 7	85	–.14	–1.43	85	–.13	–1.30	85	.00	.02
Mar 8–15	97	.06	.59	97	–.11	–1.08	97	–.02	– .16
Mar 16–23	97	–.30	–2.93**	97	–.16	–1.53	97	–.05	– .45
Mar 24–31	93	–.10	–1.08	93	.15	1.48	93	.08	.71
Apr 1– 7	81	–.06	– .51	81	.02	.14	81	.04	.34
Apr 8–15	93	–.05	– .52	93	–.02	– .19	93	.13	1.19
Apr 16–23	92	–.07	– .64	92	–.01	– .09	92	.02	.18
Apr 24–30	85	.01	.09	85	.05	.38	85	.10	.87
May 1– 7	84	.08	.74	84	.25	2.69**	84	.06	.61
May 8–15	97	.05	.49	97	–.01	– .14	97	–.09	– .81
May 16–23	98	–.03	– .28	98	.01	.06	98	.11	1.21
May 24–31	80	.07	.55	80	.27	2.27**	80	.01	.05
Jun 1– 7	85	.44	4.01**	85	.74	6.87**	85	–.02	– .18
Jun 8–15	97	.22	2.30**	97	.04	.45	97	.14	1.31
Jun 16–23	97	.30	3.08**	96	.29	3.03**	97	.08	.79
Jun 24–30	85	–.19	–1.65	84	–.07	– .55	85	–.07	– .61
Jul 1– 7	68	.19	1.49	68	.34	3.59**	68	–.09	– .80
Jul 8–15	97	.13	1.30	97	.21	2.15**	97	–.17	–1.74*
Jul 16–23	97	.08	.76	97	.41	4.39**	97	–.09	– .89
Jul 24–31	97	.33	3.25**	97	.22	2.14**	97	–.09	– .88
Aug 1– 7	85	.19	1.81*	85	.27	2.69**	85	.14	1.23
Aug 8–15	98	.04	.41	98	.13	1.16	98	.24	2.37**
Aug 16–23	97	.14	1.46	97	.26	2.79**	97	–.05	– .55
Aug 24–31	97	–.04	– .41	97	–.14	–1.49	97	–.25	–2.48**
Sep 1– 7	68	.18	1.49	68	.03	.27	68	.00	– .01
Sep 8–15	97	–.09	– .96	97	.12	1.17	97	–.19	–1.86*
Sep 16–23	97	.04	.37	97	.04	36	97	–.17	–1.70*
Sep 24–30	84	.12	1.12	84	.17	1.58	85	.20	1.79*
Oct 1– 7	85	–.25	–2.35**	85	.06	.58	85	–.21	–1.97*
Oct 8–15	96	–.02	– .20	96	.20	1.94*	96	–.03	– .30
Oct 16–23	97	.01	.10	97	.13	1.29	97	.02	.24
Oct 24–31	98	.08	.72	98	–.21	–2.10**	98	.17	1.74*
Nov 1– 7	79	–.04	– .35	79	.12	1.12	79	–.04	– .37
Nov 8–15	97	.14	1.36	97	.01	.10	97	–.01	– .11
Nov 16–23	92	.13	1.34	92	.04	.39	92	–.12	–1.31

Table II—Continued

Time Cell	Corn			Soybeans			Wheat		
	N	Beta	t	N	Beta	t	N	Beta	t
Nov 24–30	73	.06	.50	73	−.07	−.58	73	.02	.13
Dec 1– 7	85	−.27	−2.51**	85	−.24	−2.21**	85	−.09	−.87
Dec 8–15	97	.08	.76	97	.20	1.95*	97	.10	.94
Dec 16–23	97	−.13	−1.35	97	−.19	−2.18**	97	−.17	−1.86*
Dec 24–31	73	−.05	−.47	73	.03	.19	74	.07	.55

*Significant at the 10% level, two tail test.
**Significant at the 5% level, two tail test.

former point, Namias (p. 1369) notes a lack of persistence in his data during both the spring and fall equinox period. On the latter point, it is hypothesized that this phenomenon may result in part from wheat generally being a hardier plant. Also, at the national level, wheat is more geographically diversified. There are five somewhat distinct regions: hard red winter, soft red winter, hard red spring, durham, and white wheat. Wheat growth and maturity is more diversified across time. (Wheat harvest begins in Texas in June and ends in N.D. in August.) Wheat, therefore, is probably more diversified against any persistence that may be present in weather patterns. Still, the fact that 10 of 12 coefficients are positive during the March 24 through June 23 period does suggest that there may be a weak weather influence underlying this period, a period that is a reasonable approximation of the wheat growing season.

Table III presents more aggregated statistical results that focus on the growing seasons of each of the three crops versus the rest of the year and the total sample. Price momentum is especially significant in corn and soybeans in the growing season, May 24 through August 23, with t values of 5.71 and 8.58, respectively. A split aggregation into two nongrowing season periods, January 1 through May 23 and August 24 through December 31, shows essentially random price motion during these periods. Note that the growing season influence is strong enough to demonstrate significant results at the total data level in corn and soybeans.

Table III
A SEASONALLY PARTITIONED STATISTICAL SUMMARY FOR THE PERIOD
OCTOBER 1, 1972 THROUGH SEPTEMBER 30, 1989

Time cell*	Corn			Soybeans			Wheat		
	N	Beta	t	N	Beta	t	N	Beta	t
Period 1	1686	.00	−.15	1686	.00	.11	1657	−.01	−.23
Growing	1083	.17	5.71**	1081	.25	8.58**	1082	.07	2.34**
Period 2	1512	.01	.23	1512	.02	.95	1544	−.04	−1.40
Total	4281	.08	5.11**	4279	.13	8.88**	4283	.00	−.06

*Period 1 is January 1 through May 23 for corn and soybeans and November 1 through March 23 for wheat. The growing season is May 24 through August 23 for corn and soybeans and March 24 through June 23 for wheat. Period 2 is August 24 through December 31 for corn and soybeans and June 24 through October 31 for wheat.
**Significant at the .05 level, two tail test.

In wheat, aggregation across the March 24 through June 23 period discussed above results in significantly positive results with a t value of 2.34. A lower value of Beta for wheat during its growing season, .07 versus .17 for corn and .25 for soybeans, reinforces the hypothesis that the weather is less persistent during this season and/or the national wheat crop is more spatially and temporally diversified against any persistent weather influence. Like corn and soybeans, the nongrowing season price dynamics appear to be essentially random. Contrary to the corn and soybean results, the growing season influence is not strong enough to create significant results at the total wheat data level.

CONCLUSION

Strong empirical evidence of nonrandom seasonal price dynamics is found in corn, wheat, and soybean futures prices during the period October 1972 through September 1989. The season of the nonrandom price motion aligns well with the growing season of all three commodities. The weather and climatology literature asserts that weather patterns are to some extent persistent in North America during the summer months. This study finds that these nonrandom weather events do transfer a nonrandom influence into corresponding commodity prices during their respective growing seasons.

These results suggest that producers, merchandisers, speculators, and others that own these commodities during their respective growing seasons may well benefit from strategies that take positions on the basis of a continuation of existing price trends.

Bibliography

Anderson, R.W. (1985): "Some Determinants of the Volatility of Futures Prices," *The Journal of Futures Markets,* 5:331–348.

Anderson, R.W., and Danthine, J. (1983): "The Time Pattern of Hedging and the Volatility of Futures Prices," *Review of Economic Studies,* 50:249–266.

Ash, M. S., and Lin, W. (1987): "Regional Crop Yield Response for U.S. Grains," USDA, ERS, AER-577, September.

Ash, M. S., and Lin, W. (1986): "Wheat Yield Response: Policy Implications on Projections," *Wheat Situation and Outlook Report,* USDA, ERS, WS-275, May:10:16.

Cootner, P. H. (1964): "Comments on the Variation in Certain Speculative Prices," *The Random Character of Stock Market Prices,* M.I.T. Press, Cambridge.

Fama, E. F. (1970): "Efficient Capital Markets: A Review of Theory and Empirical Work," *The Journal of Finance,* 25:383–417.

Larson, A. B. (1960): "Measurement of a Random Process in Futures Prices," *Food Research Institute Studies,* 3:313–324.

Lin, W., and Davenport, G. (1982): "Analysis of Factors Affecting Corn Yields: Projections to 1985," *Feed Outlook and Situation,* USDA, ERS, FdS-285, May:9–14

Namias, J. (1986): "Persistence of Flow Patterns Over North America and Adjacent Ocean Sectors," *Monthly Weather Review,* 114:1368–1383.

Samuelson, P. A. (1965): "Proof That Properly Anticipated Prices Fluctuate Randomly," *Industrial Management Review,* 6:41–49.

Samuelson, P. A. (1976): "Is Real-World Price a Tale Told by the Idiot of Chance," *Review of Economics and Statistics,* 58:120–123.

Stevenson, R. A., and Bear, R. M. (1970): "Commodity Futures: Trends or Random Walks?," *Journal of Finance,* 25:65–81.

Teigen, L. D., and Singer, F. (1989): "Weather in U.S. Agriculture: Monthly Temperature and Precipitation by State and Farm Production Region, 1950–88," USDA, ERS, SB789, November.

Trenberth, K. E., Branstator, G.W., and Arkin, P. A. (1988): "Origins of the 1988 North American Drought," *Science,* 242, December, 23:1640–1645.

Van Meir, L. (1984): *Feed Outlook and Situation Report,* USDA, ERS, FdS-294, September:4–5.

Vroomen, H., and Hanthorn, M. (1986): "1986–88 Corn Yield Projections for the 10 Major Producing States," *Feed Situation and Outlook Yearbook,* USDA, ERS, FdS-301, November:15–21.

Westcott, P. C. (1989): "An Analysis of Factors Influencing Corn Yields," *Feed Outlook and Situation Report,* USDA, ERS, FdS-310, May:16–22.

Willimack, D. K., and Teigen, L. D. (1985): "Regional Soybean Yields," *Oil Crops Outlook and Situation Report,* USDA, ERS, OCS-7, May:27–31.

THE EFFECT OF FUTURES TRADING ON SPOT PRICE VOLATILITY: EVIDENCE FOR BRENT CRUDE OIL USING GARCH

ANTONIOS ANTONIOU AND ANDREW J. FOSTER*

INTRODUCTION

There has been widespread interest in the effects of futures trading on prices in the underlying spot market. It has often been claimed that the onset of derivative trading will destabilize the associated spot market and so lead to an increase in spot price volatility there. Others have argued to the contrary, stating that the introduction of futures trading will stabilize prices and so lead to a decrease in price volatility. It has been suggested,[1] however, that the debate cannot be resolved wholly on a theoretical level and so should be analyzed by empirical investigation.

The purpose of this study is to empirically investigate the effects of the introduction of a futures contract for Brent Crude Oil in 1988 on the price volatility in the spot market for Brent Crude. This study differs from other studies of the effects of futures trading in two respects. First, we study a commodity which, to the best of our knowledge, has not been previously investigated for the above-mentioned effects. We also look at the UK market for oil whereas the majority of previous studies deal with the US market. Second, we use the GARCH family of statistical models which are a superior technique for modelling volatility. A dynamic linear regression model is also constructed in order to give insights into the possible effects of futures trading. Since this is a technique common to many previous studies it allows comparison of our regression results with those of other studies. In addition, it allows comparison of this study's GARCH results with those from the more traditional technique.

In the next section we present the opposing theoretical arguments as to the expected effects of futures trading on spot prices and explain why these effects are expected to occur. This is followed in the third section by a brief review of previous empirical studies which have investigated the question for a number of different markets. The fourth section outlines the methodologies used in this paper. The results from our tests are presented and discussed in this section. The final section provides a summary and conclusions.

* The authors are both from the Centre for Empirical Research in Finance, Department of Economics, Brunel University, Uxbridge. They gratefully acknowledge the comments of Charles Sutcliffe of the University of Southampton and Ian Garrett of Brunel University on earlier drafts of this paper. Thanks also go to the participants of the Finance and Market Based Accounting Research Conference, University of Manchester. This research was financed by the BRIEF award programme at Brunel University. The usual disclaimer applies.

THE THEORETICAL DEBATE

The introduction of futures trading enhances both the incentive and means for speculation. The speculative trade associated with futures trading has been accused, however, of destabilizing the underlying spot market inducing price volatility. Theoretical discussion of the influence of speculative activity in derivatives on primary markets does not, however, find a consensus of opinion. Harris (1989), suggests that the increase in well informed speculative trade brought to the market by the onset of derivative trading may have two opposite effects on volatility. The market may experience an increase in price volatility as futures trading enhances the price discovery mechanism and so new information concerning fundamentals is more rapidly impounded into prices.[2] Since futures markets face less friction than spot markets, particularly with respect to lower transaction costs, prices should respond more quickly to new information.[3] Through a process of arbitrage these price adjustments will be transmitted to the underlying spot market. In a similar vein Chassard and Halliwell (1986), comment that speculation can artificially distort price movements so as to exaggerate the normal response to fundamentals. This effect has been noted by a number of other commentators.[4]

Volatility could, however, perceivably decrease due to the liquidity which speculators provide the market. This added liquidity would allow spot traders to hedge their positions and so curb volatility attributable to order imbalances. The availability of the risk transference afforded by futures markets may also reduce spot price volatility by removing the need to incorporate a risk premium to compensate for possible adverse future price shifts.[5] Problems due to the lack of liquidity, and how this can induce volatility, are reviewed by Figlewski (1981).

A different view as to how speculation can reduce price volatility is furnished by Friedman (1953), who suggests that speculation can lead to a stabilization of prices as speculators buy when prices are low and sell when they are high. The result of these forces on prices will be to constantly check price swings and guide prices towards the mean. As previously stated, however, the question is unresolved on a theoretical level and so it is to empirical testing which we must turn in order to gain insights into this relationship.

PREVIOUS EMPIRICAL STUDIES

In this section we provide a brief review of past empirical work which has attempted to provide evidence as to the influence of derivative trading on spot price volatility. This review is in no way exhaustive but highlights the main techniques used in empirical investigations and assesses the weight of evidence for both sides of the debate.

Past studies have looked at the effects of futures trading in a number of

FUTURES TRADING AND SPOT PRICE VOLATILITY

different markets. Investigations have been carried out for a variety of physical commodities as well as for financial instruments, with analysis being mainly confined, as previously mentioned, to US markets. The empirical techniques used are varied but the general approach is to consider spot price variability in periods before and after the onset of futures trading and to test for significant changes. Less common is the use of cross-sectional analysis where spot volatility is compared for similar markets with and without futures trading.[6]

In general, past empirical studies have found that the establishment of futures trading has either reduced the price volatility of the underlying commodity/asset, or has had no discernable effect.[7] Technical assessment of the influence of futures trading has ranged from simple static regression, univariate Box-Jenkins analysis and causality tests to multivariate time series analysis, Box-Tiao intervention analysis, and more recently, ARCH models. In the following we review some examples of these investigations.

Simpson and Ireland (1982), investigated the effects of the introduction of futures trading on US Government National Mortgage Association (GNMA) certificates. The study used the first differences of both daily and average weekly prices. As a preliminary search into the effects of derivative trading the authors specified a static regression model with a proxy variable to remove extraneous influences, a dummy for the onset of futures trading, and an interaction term. The regression model was constructed for both pre-futures and post-futures sub-samples for daily and weekly volatility measures. Tests were carried out for significant changes in the model parameters for the two periods. As no significant changes were recorded the authors concluded that there had been no increase in spot price volatility since the advent of derivative trading.

Froewiss (1978), investigated the GNMA market using univariate Box-Jenkins analysis for weekly per cent changes in spot prices. Pre and post-futures sub-samples were modelled using Box-Jenkins techniques and significant parameter changes between the two periods were tested for. Results indicated that there had been no statistically significant parameter change, suggesting that spot volatility had not been influenced by the introduction of futures trading.

Bhattacharya et al. (1986), used the Figlewski[8] measure to calculate weekly volatility series for spot and futures prices for GNMAs. The authors hypothesised that the influence of futures volatility on spot volatility could be tested using causality tests. The study adopted a Granger definition and methodology for testing causality and results suggested no change in spot volatility since futures trading began. Whilst the Bhattacharya study improved on previous studies in its use of volatility measure, the use of causality tests have been criticized. Edwards (1988b), argues that causality tests cannot infer whether futures trading has stabilized or destabilized spot markets. He argues that the appearance of futures volatility leading spot volatility could be explained by futures markets reacting more quickly to information which will eventually reach the spot market where it will have a like effect on volatility.

Corgel and Gay (1984), investigated the effects of the onset of GNMA derivative trading on spot market prices using Box-Tiao intervention analysis. Intervention analysis has the advantages that it is specifically designed to model the impact of events on time series data, and that it can describe the nature of the impact. The study's results confirm the general finding that the onset of derivative trading did not have a destabilizing effect on spot market prices, but rather that a long-run stabilizing effect is found.

More recently, Baldauf and Santoni (1991), have used an ARCH analysis (see the next section) to test for increased volatility in the S&P 500 since the introduction of futures trading and the growth of program trading. Prices were modelled for periods before and after the onset of futures trading and the model specification tested for significant change. The study found no evidence of a shift in the model parameters suggesting no effect on volatility from derivative trading.

EMPIRICAL INVESTIGATIONS

Data and Preliminary Results

Weekly volatility series were constructed from daily spot closing prices for Brent Crude Oil as supplied by Datastream. The data set consisted of 240 weekly observations from January 1986 to July 1990. This represented 144 observations before futures trading and 96 observations afterwards.

The study considered six different measures of volatility in order to avoid test sensitivity to the measure of volatility used. The measures used were:

1. weekly price range,
2. absolute weekly average price change,
3. squared weekly average price change,
4. absolute log of weekly average price relative,
5. squared log of weekly average price relative,[9]
6. the Figlewski (1981) volatility measure (given below),

$$V_T = \sqrt{\frac{1}{N} \sum_{t=1}^{N} (P_t - P_{t-1})^2}$$

where V_T is volatility in week T
P_t is spot price on day t
N is the number of days per week.

For illustrative purposes the Figlewski volatility series is presented in Figure 1 below. Casual observation of Figure 1 does not, incidentally, reveal any obvious change in the level of spot price volatility.

Figure 1
Weekly Volatility of Brent Crude Spot Prices

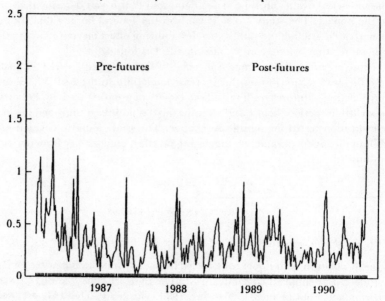

Regression Analysis

A general dynamic linear regression model was constructed to explain spot volatility. Preliminary model specifications included a dummy variable introduced to account for the onset of futures trading, proxy variables to account for general market volatility, and an interaction term.

The proxy variables nominated (for which there was no futures trading), were gold and a number of commodity indices.[10] The coefficients on the dummy for the onset of futures trading, on all proxy variables, and on the interaction term were found to be insignificant.[11] A well specified, parsimonious model was generated for each measure of volatility. All measures of volatility generated an AR(1) model except the Figlewski measure which (marginally) accepted an AR(2) process.

Chow tests were carried out on all models over the whole period to check for structural change in order to determine whether futures trading had had an effect on the dependent variable. In general the results were not sensitive to the measure of volatility used. The tests confirmed that there was no structural change after the introduction of futures trading, i.e. that each model's coefficients had not changed substantially between the pre-futures and post-futures periods, for all measures except the weekly price range (see Table 1).

ANTONIOU AND FOSTER

Table 1
Chow Tests for Structural Change

Volatility Measure	Computed Value	Critical Value
1	3.26*	3.04
2	2.39	3.04
3	2.65	3.04
4	2.66	3.04
5	2.32	3.04
6	0.42	2.65

* Indicates structural change between the two periods.

These results suggest that the onset of derivative trading had not influenced spot price volatility.

The insignificance of the proxy variables raises questions as to the reliability of inferences made about the impact of derivative trading on volatility, since changes could be due to a number of other factors.[12] Difficulties with filtering the effects of other determinants are, however, a common problem experienced by numerous other studies. The techniques for resolving this problem have also been questioned by Edwards (1988a and 1988b), who contends that the use of proxies implies an unacceptable assumption of market segregation. Thus, whilst it is important to realize that inferences made from empirical results must be evaluated with caution, it is recognized that no satisfactory alternative is apparent.

GARCH Analysis

Following Engle (1982), Diebold and Nerlove (1989), Schwert and Seguin (1990), *inter alia*, weekly returns for oil spot prices (S_t in equation (A) of Table 2) were used as the dependent variable in GARCH estimations. Returns were calculated from an arithmetic mean of daily closing prices. The resultant time series is shown in Figure 2. With GARCH analysis one aims to model directly the heteroscedasticity in the variance of a price series, hence the choice of dependent variable.

The investigation utilized the GARCH family of statistical models to investigate volatility in oil spot prices both before and after the onset of futures trading. Since GARCH models account specifically for systematic changes in the variance of a time series by modelling the conditional variance they are ideally suited to the study of volatility. A GARCH-M model was estimated for both pre-futures and post-futures mean equations which regressed returns on a constant and an error term.

The autoregressive conditional heteroscedastic (ARCH) model, first proposed by Engle (1982), differs from traditional regression techniques in that

Figure 2
Average Weekly Brent Crude Spot Returns

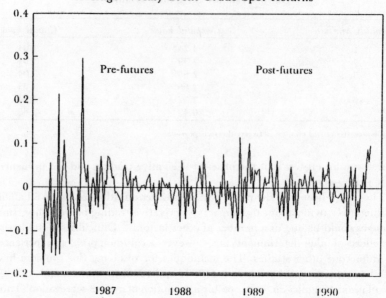

homoscedasticity of the error term is not assumed. Rather, the error variance is represented as a time series itself which evolves as a linear function of lagged squared errors. Thus, for example, an AR(1) process with errors that followed an ARCH(q) process has the following representation:

$$X_t = \alpha + \beta X_{t-1} \epsilon_t \qquad \epsilon_t \sim N(0,h_t) \qquad (1)$$

$$h_t = a_0 + \sum_{i=1}^{q} a_i \epsilon_{t-i}^2. \qquad (2)$$

Bollerslev (1986), extended Engle's ARCH to a generalized ARCH or GARCH process. With GARCH the conditional variance is modelled as a linear function of the lagged conditional variance in addition to the past error variances contained in ARCH representations. A GARCH(p,q) process is represented as:

$$h_t = a_0 + \sum_{i=1}^{q} a_i \epsilon_{t-i}^2 + \sum_{j=1}^{p} b_j h_{t-j}. \qquad (3)$$

In this study we model the oil returns directly as a GARCH process; the ARCH representation is not considered since it is implicit in the more general GARCH. Further extensions of GARCH include GARCH-in-mean (GARCH-

M)[13] and integrated GARCH (I-GARCH),[14] both of which are considered in the present paper.

GARCH-M differs from GARCH in that the conditional variance (h_t) is included as an explanatory variable in the mean equation. Thus where GARCH allows the conditional variance to be modelled, GARCH-M also allows the conditional variance to directly explain the dependent variable. Under GARCH-M, therefore, equation (1) could be rewritten:

$$X_t = \alpha + \beta X_{t-1} + \delta h_t + \epsilon_t \qquad (4)$$

where h_t is as in equation (3).

Engle and Bollerslev (1986), introduced a further extension to GARCH in which the model specification was characterised by nonstationary variances. In this situation any shock to the variance of a process is permanent. The model, referred to as I-GARCH may be thought of as the variance equivalent of a unit root in the conditional mean. For a process to be identified as I-GARCH the parameters a_i and b_i in (3) will sum to unity.

Results

Table 2 summarizes the test results obtained from this study. In order to select an adequate and parsimonious GARCH representation for the data we estimated a number of GARCH-M (p,q) equations for all combinations of $p = 1,2,3$ and $q = 1,2,3$. On the basis of log likelihood tests[15] the GARCH(1,1) was found to be the most appropriate representation for both pre-futures and post-futures samples. The same proxy variables as used in the OLS regression were introduced into the mean equation for GARCH. The proxies were found to be insignificant in all cases.

Table 2

GARCH-M Models For Oil Returns

$$S_t = \alpha + \delta h_t + \epsilon_t \qquad (A)$$
$$h_t = a_0 + a_1 \epsilon_{t-1}^2 + b_1 h_{t-1} \qquad (B)$$

	α	a_0	a_1	b_1	δ
Pre-futures	−0.764†	0.645‡	0.146	0.837	15.637
	(0.307)†	(0.162)‡	(0.022)	(0.019)	(3.507)
Post-futures	−0.026	0.269†	0.269	0.697	7.943
	(0.013)	(0.114)†	(0.117)	(0.098)	(3.417)

† = Coefficients multiplied by 10^2 for readability.
‡ = Coefficients multiplied by 10^4 for readability.
Figures in parentheses are standard errors.

Sample periods:
Pre-futures 06/01/86 to 26/09/88
Post-futures 03/10/88 to 30/07/90

FUTURES TRADING AND SPOT PRICE VOLATILITY

To test for significant change in the GARCH representations we tested the null hypothesis that the GARCH parameters were equal for the two periods. For all parameters the null of no change was strongly rejected.

The statistical adequacy of the model specification was tested using the Ljung-Box statistic for heteroscedasticity and serial correlation in the GARCH residuals. The tests are Chi-squared distributed and results attested to the adequacy of the specified models, see Table 3. In addition to these findings a number of important observations may be made from the results obtained.

First the pre-futures model and the post-futures model are candidates for an I-GARCH specification, with the parameters a_1 and b_1 in the pre-futures model summing to 0.98 and the post-futures parameters summing to 0.96. Dickey-Fuller tests were carried out on the two models to test for an I-GARCH specification. The tests revealed that whilst the pre-futures sample was integrated the post-futures model was stationary. This observation implies that the persistance of shocks has decreased since the onset of derivative trading.

Second, the coefficient on the conditional variance (δ) in the mean equation (4) has substantially reduced in the post-futures sample suggesting that spot returns volatility is less important in explaining spot returns after the advent of futures trading.

Finally, the parameters of the lagged square error (a_1) and the lagged conditional variance (b_1) of the GARCH representation experienced

Table 3
GARCH-M Test Statistics

	Pre-futures	Post-futures
Ljung-Box statistic (heteroscedasticity)		
Lag 4	1.16	2.47
8	4.24	7.2
12	6.03	8.03
16	9.25	21.84
Ljung-Box statistic (autocorrelation)		
Lag 4	5.94	6.16
8	8.26	9.96
12	14.54	10.39
16	25.23	13.19
Dickey-Fuller integration	−2.07	−26.52

Significance tests at the 5 per cent level.
Ljung-Box statistics are chi-square distributed.
Critical value for Dickey-Fuller: −2.86.

statistically significant changes since the onset of derivative trading, although interpretation of these changes is problematic. While a GARCH(1,1) process is maintained, the parameters of the GARCH process have undergone quite substantial changes. The values of a_0 and a_1 have increased which, in an ARCH representation, would suggest an increase in volatility.[16] The lagged conditional variance parameter has, however, decreased.

We interpret the increase in the ARCH parameters as showing an increase in informational efficiency in the spot market due to the information content of futures prices. This increased efficiency will lead to a greater reaction to news as suggested by the increase in the a_i 'news' coefficients. The decrease in the lagged conditional variance term (b_1) is taken as evidence that volatility is considered less important since the risk it implies can be hedged in the futures market.

SUMMARY AND CONCLUSIONS

In this paper we set out to examine the effects of the introduction of futures trading on the price volatility of the Brent Crude spot oil market, adopting the recently developed GARCH time series techniques. Weekly data from January 1986 to July 1990 was used.

Preliminary investigations utilized a dynamic linear regression model in order to provide results comparable to previous studies, and also to highlight the appropriateness of the GARCH process as a modelling technique in the study of volatility. Results from the regression analysis are consistent with the majority of previous studies in that they reveal no apparent change in volatility.

It has been documented, however, that time series of returns for speculative markets show a clustering of fluctuations i.e., large changes tend to be followed by large changes, and small by small of either sign. This appears to be the case for Brent Crude Oil. Such observations question the validity of linear regression models constructed under the assumption of homoscedasticity of the variance. It is for this reason that GARCH, which allows for time-varying variance in a process, is more appropriate to an analysis of volatility.

The results from the GARCH models reveal first, that while the pre-futures sample was integrated, suggesting that shocks have a permanent effect on prices, the post-futures sample was found to be stationary. This implies that the introduction of futures markets improves the quality of information flowing to spot markets, and spot prices accordingly reflect more promptly changes that occur in demand and supply conditions. The integratedness of the pre-futures market illustrates the lack of information and associated price inflexibility in the spot market. Such inflexibility prevents the immediate and continuing adjustment of prices in response to demand-supply conditions and necessitates eventual larger price and resource adjustments.

Second, the GARCH-M model indicates that the nature of spot market volatility has changed since the introduction of futures contracts. The increase in the 'news' coefficients of the GARCH process confirms the improvement in information regarding expected spot prices noted above. An indication of increase pricing efficiency in the spot market is the use by more and more companies of near-term futures prices to help set spot and forward prices.

Finally, the decrease in the coefficient on the lagged conditional variance attests to the view that with the introduction of futures contracts spot market volatility is not as important to spot market participants since price risk can now be hedged.

In conclusion we find no evidence to suggest that there has been a spillover of volatility from the futures to the spot market. Our results imply that futures markets serve their prescribed role of improving pricing efficiency and providing a hedging vehicle which lessens the importance of volatility.

The results generated by this study using GARCH provide insights into the effect of futures trading on spot prices. This study, however, covers only one commodity for the UK. Further investigations using the GARCH technique to examine the experience of other commodities would be interesting.

NOTES

1 See Baumol (1957 and 1959).
2 It is widely recognized that a major economic function of futures markets is their price discovery role. See Garbade and Silber (1983).
3 Cox (1976), presents a theoretical model in which spot price adjustments are quicker in the presence of derivative trading.
4 Kaldor (1939), argued that sophisticated speculators would exacerbate price changes by selling to less well informed agents at prices above that which a competitive equilibrium would dictate. Baumol (1957), proposed that speculators amplified price trends by buying or selling only after prices had changed thus increasing volatility. Edwards (1988a and 1988b), comments on the notion of investors searching for 'bandwagon' profits as a cause of increased volatility.
5 See Figlewski (1981).
6 Harris (1989) uses both forms of analysis to test for changes in stock index volatility since the onset of index futures trading.
7 For a guide to empirical studies into agricultural commodities see Turnovsky (1983). A brief review of studies into both storable and nonstorable commodities as well as for financial instrument is found in Corgel and Gay (1984).
8 See the following section headed Empirical Investigations, for an explanation of the Figlewski measure.
9 An explanation of these five measures is given, for daily data, in Board and Sutcliffe (1991). Weekly average prices were the arithmetic mean of daily closing prices.
10 The connection between gold and oil has been noted by Melvin and Sultan (1990). This study used London Gold Bullion prices. The index measures were Reuters Commodity Index and Moody's Commodity Index. The use of a product from oil as a proxy was considered but since crude oil and suitable products from oil are so closely related the proxy filters specific as well as general influences.
11 The failure to find a statistically significant proxy means that our analysis is necessarily crude since we cannot account for other determinants of volatility which may also have changed.
12 This point is discussed by Harris (1989).
13 See Bollerslev, Engle and Wooldridge (1989).
14 See Engle and Bollerslev (1986).

15 See Akgiray (1989).
16 See Baldauf and Santoni (1991).

REFERENCES

Akgiray, V. (1989), 'Conditional Heteroscedasticity in Time Series of Stock Returns: Evidence and Forecasts', *Journal of Business*, Vol. 62, No. 1 (1989), pp. 55–80.

Baldauf, B. and G.J. Santoni (1991), 'Stock Price Volatility: Some Evidence From an ARCH Model', *Journal of Futures Markets*, Vol. 11, No. 2 (1991), pp. 191–200.

Baumol, W.J. (1957), 'Speculation, Profitability, and Stability', *Review of Economics and Statistics* (August 1957), pp. 263–271.

_____ (1959), 'Reply', *Review of Economics and Statistics* (August 1959), pp. 301–302.

Bhattacharya, A.K., A. Ramjee and B. Ramjee (1986), 'The Conditional Relationship between Futures Price Volatility and the Cash Price Volatility of GNMA Securities, *Journal of Futures Markets*, Vol. 6, No. 1 (1986), pp. 29–39.

Board, J. and C. Sutcliffe (1991), 'Information, Volatility, Volume and Maturity: An Investigation of Stock Index Futures', *University of Southampton Discussion Paper*, No. 91–5 (1991), forthcoming in *Review of Futures Markets*.

Bollerslev, T. (1986), 'Generalized Autoregressive Conditional Heteroskedasticity', *Journal of Econometrics*, Vol. 33 (1986), pp. 307–327.

_____ R.G. Engle and J.M. Wooldridge (1988), 'A Capital Asset Pricing Model With Time Varying Covariances', *Journal of Political Economy*, Vol. 95 (1988), pp. 116–131.

Chassard, C. and M. Halliwell (1986), 'The NYMEX Crude Oil Futures Market: An Analysis of its Performance', *Oxford Institute for Energy Studies* (1986), Working Paper No. M9.

Corgel, J.B. and G.D. Gay (1984), 'The Impact of GNMA Futures Trading on Cash Market Volatility', *AREUEA Journal*, Vol. 12 (1984), pp. 176–190.

Cox, C.C. (1976), 'Futures Trading and Market Information', *Journal of Political Economy*, Vol. 84, No. 6 (1976), pp. 1215–1237.

Diebold, F.X. and M. Nerlove (1989), 'The Dynamics of Exchange Rate Volatility: A Multivariate Latent Factor ARCH Model', *Journal of Applied Econometrics*, Vol. 4, No. 1 (1989), pp. 1–21.

Edwards, F.R. (1988a), 'Does Future Trading Increase Stock Market Volatility?' *Financial Analysts Journal*, Vol. 44, No. 1 (1988), pp. 63–69.

_____ (1988b), 'Futures Trading and Cash Market Volatility: Stock Index and Interest Rate Futures', *Journal of Futures Markets*, Vol. 8, No. 4 (1988), pp. 421–440.

Engle, R.F. (1982), 'Autoregressive Conditional Heteroscedasticity With Estimates of the Variance of United Kingdom Inflation', *Econometrica*, Vol. 50, No. 4 (1982), pp. 987–1008.

_____ T. Bollerslev (1986), 'Modelling the Persistence of Conditional Variances', *Econometric Reviews*, Vol. 5, No. 1 (1986), pp. 1–50.

Figlewski, S. (1984), 'Futures Trading and Volatility in the GNMA Market', *Journal of Finance*, Vol. 36, No. 2 (1984), pp. 445–456.

Friedman, M. (1953), 'The Case for Flexible Exchange Rates', *Essays in Positive Economics* (UCP, 1953).

Froewiss, K.C. (1978), 'GNMA Futures: Stabilizing or Destabilizing?' *Federal Reserve Bank of San Francisco, Economic Review* (Spring 1978), pp. 20–29.

Garbade, K.D. and W.L. Silber, (1983), 'Price Movements and Price Discovery in Futures and Cash Markets', *Review of Economics and Statistics*, Vol. 65 (1983), pp. 289–297.

Harris, L. (1989), 'S&P 500 Cash Stock Price Volatilities', *Journal of Finance*, Vol. 44, No. 5 (1989), pp. 1155–1175.

Kaldor, N. (1939), 'Speculation and Economic Stability', *Review of Economic Studies* (Spring 1939), pp. 1–27.

Melvin, M. and J. Sultan (1990), 'South African Political Unrest, Oil Prices, and the Time Varying Risk Premium in the Gold Market', *Journal of Futures Markets*, Vol. 10, No. 2 (1990), pp. 103–111.

Schwert, W.G. and T.C. Ireland (1982), 'The Effects of Futures Trading on the Price Volatility of GNMA Securities', *Journal of Futures Markets*, Vol. 2, No. 4 (1982), pp. 357–366.

Turnovsky, S.J. (1983), 'The Determination of Spot and Futures Prices with Storable Commodities', *Econometrica*, Vol. 5, No. 5 (1983), pp. 1363–1387.

Name Index

Abraham, N. 230, 232
Adler, M. 279, 300
Akgiray, V. 211, 213, 216, 218
Akiake, H. 140–41, 146
Alexander, S. 96, 98, 196–7
Anderson, R. 201, 278, 301, 304, 311, 357, 378
Aradhyula, S. 234
Arkin, P. 377
Ash, M. 376
Ashley, R. 229

Bachelier, L. 173–5, 183, 190–91, 195, 197
Badrinath, S. 211
Baillie, R. 234
Baldauf, B. 387
Barnea, A. 199, 202
Barnett, W. 229
Bartlett, M.S. 149
Bartlett, M. 39
Baumol, W. 227, 233
Bear, R. 91–2, 96, 98, 229, 378
Bell, W. 140
Benhabib, J. 227, 233
Berndt, E. 283
Bessant, L. 68
Bhattacharya, A. 386
Bienaymé, J. 188
Black, F. 30, 307
Blank, S. 241
Blattberg, R. 202
Blume, M. 96
Bodie, Z. 69, 76
Bollerslev, T. 234, 279, 282, 284, 390–91
Bonninga, S. 278, 301, 311
Booth, G. 211, 218, 229
Booth, P. 82
Box, G. 142, 151, 159, 386–7, 392
Branstator, G. 377
Bray, M. 82
Breeden, D. 61, 296, 302, 308
Brennan, M. 61–2, 307, 357, 359
Brenner, M. 202
Brock, W. 227–8, 230–34
Brorsen, B. 201, 211
Brown, K. 156
Brown, M. 339, 352

Brown, S. 160
Bryant, A. 351

Candela, G. 227
Cargill, T. 91–2, 98
Carter, C. 69, 141
Cauchy, A.L. 175–6, 180, 188
Cecchetti, S. 278–9
Chamberlain, T. 222
Chassard, C. 385
Chatterjee, S. 211
Chen, P. 229
Cheung, Y. 234
Chow, G. 81–2
Clark, P. 200
Clinton, K. 82
Cootner, P. 61, 69, 91, 189, 378
Corgel, J. 387
Cornell, B. 59
Cornew, R. 199, 201, 211, 215, 229
Cox, C. 81
Cox, J. 29, 31–3, 46–9, 53–4, 58
Crowson, L. 211, 218
Cumby, R. 278–9

Danthine, J. 278, 301, 304, 311
Davenport, G. 376
Day, R. 227–8
De Canio, S. 82
De Groot, M. 85
DeBondt, W. 155
Dechert, W. 231, 233
DeGennaro, R. 234
DeLong, J. 156
Deneckere, R. 231
Detemple, J. 279, 300
Dickey, D. 140
Diebold, F. 389
Doukas, J. 140, 201, 219
Downes, D. 199, 202
Dusak, K. 30, 61, 69

Ederington, L. 257, 278
Edwards, F. 386, 389
Eldor, R. 278, 301, 311
Engle, R. 278, 282, 284, 389–91
Epps, M. 200

Epps, T. 200
Evans, E. 20

Fackler, P. 278
Fama, E. 69, 92, 96, 98, 156, 199–208, 211–15, 218, 368, 378
Fabozzi, F. 156
Feigenbaum, M. 230
Fielitz, B. 200, 202, 212, 215, 229
Figlewski, S. 278–9, 385–8
Forsythe, A. 339, 352
Frank, M. 228, 230–31, 240
French, K. 29, 31–2, 58, 66, 155–6, 340, 360, 368
Frenkel, J. 21
Friedman, M. 385
Froewiss, R. 386
Fuller, W. 140, 144

Garbade, K. 23
Garcia, P. 229
Gardini, A. 227
Gauss, F. 180
Gay, G. 387
Gibbons, M. 340
Gnedenko, B. 179, 185, 187
Godfrey, M. 92
Gonedes, N. 202
Goodwin, R. 227
Gordon, J.D. 199, 281
Granger, C. 92, 133, 142
Grassberger, P. 230–32
Grauer, F. 30
Gray, R. 80
Greene, M. 229

Hall, B. 283
Hall, J. 211–13, 215, 217–18
Hall, R. 283
Halliwell, M. 385
Hanthorn, M. 376
Hardy, C. 69
Harlow, C. 128
Harlow, W. 156
Harris, L. 200, 385
Hasza, D. 140, 144
Hausman, J. 283
Hayes, D. 80
Hazuka, T. 61, 69
Helms, B. 141, 229
Hess, P. 340
Hicks, J. 258
Hieronymus, T. 265
Higinbotham, H. 247

Hinich, M. 228–9
Ho, T. 296, 300, 311
Hoffman, G. 20, 21
Holt, M. 234
Houthakker, H. 21, 91, 96, 121, 188, 198
Hsieh, D. 234
Hudson, M. 199, 211–12, 281
Hull, J. 208

Ingersoll, J. 29, 31–3, 46–9, 53–4, 58
Ireland, T. 386
Irwin, S. 201, 211

Jarrow, R. 29
Jenkins, G. 142, 151, 159, 386
Jensen, R. 227
Johnson, H. 208
Johnson, L. 251
Just, R. 227

Kaen, F. 141
Kahl, K. 278, 281
Kahneman, D. 155
Kaldor, N. 61
Kamara, A. 127
Keim, D. 340
Kenyon, D. 201, 229
Keynes, J. 69, 258
Kolmogorov, A.N. 149
Koutrouvelis, I. 212–14, 216, 218–19

Lake, F. 20
Lamoureux, C. 213, 216, 234
Larson, A. 91, 378
Lastrapes, W. 234
Lau, A. 211, 214–16, 218–19
Lau, H. 211. 214–16, 218–19
LeBaron, B. 228, 230–31, 233–4, 236–7
Leitch, R. 202
Leuthold, R. 211, 281
Levich, R. 21
Lévy, P. 174, 176, 211
Lin, W. 376
Lindsley, D. 156
Litzenberger, R. 30
Ljung, G. 392
Longworth, D. 82
Lorenz, H. 227–8
Lyapunov, A.M. 230–32, 238–9, 242

Ma, C. 155–6
Makihija, A. 155
Mandelbrot, B. 200, 211, 215, 230
Margrabe, W. 29

Markov, A. 140–42, 146, 153
Markowitz, H. 316–17, 321, 329–30
Martell, T. 229
Mayers, D. 296
McCallum, B. 21
McCormick, F. 21
McKinnon, R. 264, 301
Melese, F. 227
Merton, R. 140, 279, 295–6, 299, 301–2, 308
Miller, R. 140
Mirowski, P. 227
Morgan, I. 200
Morgenstern, O. 34, 92
Muth, J.F. 82, 107
Myers, R. 278, 282

Nachtmann, R. 155
Namias, J. 377, 381
Neftci, S. 133
Nerlove, M. 8–14, 16, 389
Newbold, P. 133, 142
Ng, L. 234

Officer, R. 199
Ohlson, J. 222
Oldfield, G. 29

Pareto, V. 176–7, 179, 182–3, 185, 187, 211
Patterson, D. 228–9
Paulson, A. 202
Pearson, K. 176
Peck, A. 80, 277
Pelikan, S. 231
Perry, P. 200
Phaup, E. 21
Pitts, M. 200
Plumly, W. 257
Priestley, M. 146, 149, 229
Procaccia, I. 230–32

Radner, R. 82
Rahman, A. 140, 201, 219
Ramsey, J. 237
Rao, R. 155
Rausser, G. 69, 91–2, 98, 141, 227
Reinganum, M. 59
Richard, S. 29, 31, 58, 307
Rolfo, J. 301, 311
Roll, R. 155, 201–8, 212–15, 218
Rosansky, V. 69, 76
Rosenman, R. 141
Ross, S. 29, 31–3, 46–9, 53–4, 58
Rozelle, J. 200, 202, 212
Rubinstein, M. 280

Samuelson, P. 219, 222, 357, 360, 364, 378
Santoni, G. 387
Sarassoro, G. 211, 281
Savit, R. 227–8, 231
Sayers, C. 227–8, 230, 232–4
Scheinkman, J. 228, 230–31, 233–4, 236–7
Schmitz, A. 69, 80
Schwartz, E. 307
Schwert, W. 389
Sears, S. 155
Seguin, P.J. 389
Shanno, D. 208
Shiller, R. 155
Shleifer, A. 156
Shumway, R. 229
Silber, W. 20, 23
Simmons, W. 80
Simpson, T.D. 386
Singer, F. 376
So, J. 201, 211
Stein, J. 82, 85, 252, 311
Stengos, T. 228, 230–31, 240
Stevenson, R. 91–2, 96, 98, 229, 378
Stone, H. 128
Stulz, R. 279, 296, 300
Summers, L. 156
Sundaresen, M. 29, 31, 58, 307
Swift, J. 232
Swinney, H. 232

Takens, F. 232
Talpaz, H. 229
Tauchen, G. 200
Taussig, F. 189
Taylor, S. 199
Teichmoeller, J. 199
Teigen, L. 376–7
Telser, L. 61–2, 69, 104, 247, 357, 359
Teweles, R. 128
Thaler, R. 155
Thompson, S. 278, 282
Tiao, G. 387
Tinic, S. 156
Tobin, J. 316, 323
Tomek, W. 80
Town, D. 211, 215
Transue, W. 227
Trenberth, K. 377
Tversky, A. 155

van der Ploeg, F. 228–9, 231
Van Meir, L. 376
von Neumann, J. 34
Vrooman, H. 376

Waldman, R. 156
Warner, J. 160
Westcott, P. 376
Westerfield, R. 200
Weymar, F. 276
White, A. 208
Wiese, V. 20
Willimark, D. 377
Wingender, J. 211

Wolf, A. 231–2, 240
Wooldridge, J. 284
Working, H. 9, 20, 21, 61, 69, 91, 248–50, 259, 357

Yuan, H. 237

Zilcha, I. 278, 301, 311